P9-CEN-359

A CENTURY OF JUVENILE JUSTICE

EDITED BY

Margaret K. Rosenheim

Franklin E. Zimring

David S. Tanenhaus

and

Bernardine Dohrn

With a Foreword by

Adele Simmons

THE UNIVERSITY OF CHICAGO PRESS

CHICAGO AND LONDON

Margaret K. Rosenheim is the Helen Ross Professor Emerita in the School of Social Service Administration of the University of Chicago. **Franklin E. Zimring** is professor of law and director of the Earl Warren Legal Institute at the University of California, Berkeley. **David S. Tanenhaus** is assistant professor of history and law at the University of Nevada, Las Vegas. **Bernardine Dohrn** is director of the Children and Family Justice Center of Northwestern University Law School.

The University of Chicago Press, Chicago 60637
The University of Chicago Press, Ltd., London

Printed in the United States of America
11 10 09 08 07 06 05 04 03 02 5 4 3 2 1

ISBN (cloth): 0-226-72783-1

Library of Congress Cataloging-in-Publication Data

A century of juvenile justice / edited by Margaret K. Rosenheim . . . [et al.].
p. cm.
Includes bibliographical references and index.
ISBN 0-226-72783-1 (cloth : alk. paper)
1. Juvenile justice, Administration of—United States. 2. Child welfare—United States. 3. Juvenile corrections—United States. 4. Juvenile justice, Administration of—United States.—History. 5. Child welfare—United States—History. 6. Juvenile corrections—United States—History. I. Rosenheim, Margaret K. (Margaret Keeney), 1926–

KF9779 .C46 2002
345.73'08—dc21

2001043723

♾ The paper used in this publication meets the minimum requirements of the American National Standard for Information Sciences—Permanence of Paper for Printed Library Materials, ANSI Z39.48-1992.

A CENTURY OF JUVENILE JUSTICE

Contents

Foreword

Adele Simmons

It is not surprising that the first Juvenile Court in the United States was established in Chicago. At the turn of the last century, the Progressive Movement was flourishing across the country and Jane Addams had chosen Chicago as the place to focus her energies to "tear down these walls . . . between classes." A remarkable group of women joined Addams, including Ellen Starr, Julia Lathrop, and my great-grandmother, Lucy Flower, who was chairwoman of the Chicago Women's Club in the year Addams arrived in the city.

As a young girl growing up in Chicago in the 1950s, I never tired of the stories of these women and the courage and imagination they showed in overcoming civic ignorance and official disdain for both women and the poor. As a member of the Chicago Board of Education, Lucy Flower called for the introduction of kindergartens, supported the first manual training courses, and insisted schools install bathtubs, as there was no running water in tenements. She helped to found one of the first legal aid societies for children, and in her capacity as a board member of the Home for the Friendless, she once brought an abandoned baby to a hearing of the Board of County Commissioners, placed the baby on the desk of the chairman of the Board, and refused to leave until the Commission agreed to take responsibility for the child.

My childhood memories include visits to Hull House, to its summer camp, and to various residential programs for juvenile offenders. Each place was full of stories, the common theme of which was that Addams and her comrades had not been afraid to speak up, and their voices had made a considerable difference. The most significant place to me, however, was Juvenile Court, established by the state legislature in 1899, the culmination of a campaign, nearly a decade in duration, overseen in large part by Flower and Lathrop. The new court was grounded in the firm belief that young people who had made mistakes could be provided with the support they would need to one day become productive and law-abiding citizens.

Thirty years after those childhood visits I found myself, as president of the MacArthur Foundation, supporting research into the same questions that the founders of the court grappled with. What is the role of government in the lives of children and their families? How are children different from adults and from each other? How can society be protected from violent offenders? To what extent are violent offenders the product of their environment, and to what extent do their individual characteristics lead to their behavior? Do race and class matter in how young people who break the law are treated? To what extent are children responsible for their actions? Is the purpose of intervention to punish or to rehabilitate? Should young offenders be detained for minor offenses, or are there more effective and less costly interventions? These are some of the questions that researchers are addressing today.

In the past decade, the MacArthur Foundation alone has allocated many millions of dollars to support research teams to explore these and related questions. And in fact we have some answers. We know more about the cycle of violence: we know that children who grow up with violence are more likely to be violent themselves. We know that children who are tried and held as adults are more likely to end up back in prison. We know that investment in early childhood education reduces the chance of a child entering the jurisdiction of the court. We know that most juvenile crimes are committed between 3 P.M. and 6 P.M., so that "After School" matters. We know that most of the youth confined in training schools are not violent offenders, and we know that recidivism from training schools is uniformly high. We know that at least 20 percent of juvenile offenders suffer from a severe mental health disorder, and we know that the services extended to those juveniles are inadequate and uncoordinated.

We have also learned that context plays a major role. An astonishing number of young adults test the system in one way or another, but it is mainly those who are poor and minority that end up in detention, and, once in, find it hard to stay out. Black youths are seven times more likely to go to jail than their white counterparts who commit an identical crime. We also know that as people grow older, criminal behavior becomes less and less likely.

What is distressing is the extent to which all that we know about prevention and intervention does not shape public policy. If we do not want to spend more money on jails and prisons, why do we not invest more in early childhood education and after school programs? Why do we insist on imprisoning children with adults when we know that policy almost insures that the child will be imprisoned again and again as an adult? How can we explain why states fail to make investments that will help young offenders become effective members of their community?

This book will help the cause. The more we understand about the last century of juvenile justice, the better positioned all of us will be to take up the mantle of Julia Lathrop, Lucy Flower, and Jane Addams. If that trio were resurrected today, they'd berate us for our failure to move public policy. Then they'd roll up their sleeves and show us how much courage and commitment it takes to bring to bear all we know to make a difference.

Preface

The juvenile court is a remarkable legal and social institution that now plays an important role in the governments of most developed nations. Most modern legal institutions evolved over centuries, but the juvenile court was invented out of whole cloth in state legislation first passed in Illinois in 1899. Most legal systems are not based on revolutionary principles, but the juvenile court was intended to reverse long-standing legal traditions and place the child's interests first in areas of law ranging from dependency and neglect to disobedience and delinquency. Putting children first was a radical departure from common law tradition, but it was the most widely and immediately popular legal reform in American history. Within a generation, almost every state in the United States adopted some version of a child-centered juvenile or family court, and most major Western nations, including civil law countries not usually hospitable to Anglo-American reforms, had created juvenile courts inspired by the American example.

This volume was designed to meet two needs. The first was to create a volume to celebrate the centenary of a singular institution. The second was to assemble, for the first time, a standard reference work on juvenile courts and juvenile justice that would educate concerned citizens, legal scholars, and system professionals in the rich variety of topics and perspectives encountered in the modern juvenile courts of the developed world. Our ambitions were grandiose: to assemble a group of the top experts in the field, inspire them to write clear and accessible treatments of the important issues and objectives in juvenile justice, and provide illustrations from the first century of juvenile court practice to illuminate the practice of a second century. Could such a volume be assembled?

The venture was launched in 1998 with the support of the John D. and Catherine T. MacArthur Foundation and the participation of a superb group of experts on juvenile justice. The volume that resulted is the product of exemplary individual effort but also the collaboration of a large group of scholars working to produce an accessible, state-of-the-art summary for a wide readership.

We were aware of the variety and complexity of the subjects that needed to be addressed in such a book. A century after its beginning, a comprehensive analysis of juvenile justice must consider, first, the history of the ideas around which the system was organized and the institutions and practices that resulted; second, the ways in which this set of institutions and practices interacts with other aspects of government policy toward children in the United States and in other nations; and, third, the way in which changing social and legal meanings of childhood and youth have continued to influence the philosophy and operating reality of juvenile justice. The volume consists of sixteen chapters organized in five parts: (1) historical perspective; (2) legal theory; (3) social science; (4) child welfare; and (5) comparative law and practice.

Historical perspective is the first necessity for understanding the origins and evolution of juvenile courts. Part 1 presents three distinct but related histories. In chapter 1, Michael Grossberg provides an overview of changing conceptions of child welfare in the United States from 1820 to 1935. In chapter 2, David Tanenhaus details the early history and evolutionary development of the American juvenile court. In chapter 3, Paul Lerman examines the twentieth-century history of institutions for troubled and troublesome adolescents.

Part 2 covers legal theories of central importance to the operation of juvenile justice. Each of the three chapters in this section combines conceptual and historical analysis. Elizabeth Scott writes in chapter 4 on the criteria for and consequences of childhood as a special legal status. How are children treated differently in law than adults, and why? Franklin Zimring considers historical and modern theories dealing with the rationale for treating young criminals in juvenile rather than criminal courts in chapter 5. Lee Teitelbaum's chapter 6 describes the special category of juveniles who came to be known as "status offenders"—youths brought to court for behavior such as incorrigibility, truancy, or running away that would not be considered unlawful for adults. The contrast between original and modern notions of appropriate policy for such cases is more dramatic than for any other juvenile justice topic.

Part 3 is concerned with the relation of social science theory and research to juvenile justice policy. The juvenile court was established as a legal institution that would absorb and implement the lessons of social science to better serve the children within its jurisdiction. John Laub reports on a century of empirical research and criminological theories of delinquency in chapter 7. In chapter 8, David Farrington and Rolf Loeber focus on the serious and violent offenders who are the most serious cases to appear before the modern juvenile court. The last chapter in this section, chapter 9, extends one major branch of delinquency research, the ecological or area study, to show what Frank Furstenberg and Mark Testa call the ecology of child endangerment. They demonstrate that the same community conditions that produce high rates of delinquency also generate very high rates of child abuse and neglect in official counts.

Part 4 addresses the relationship between the institutions of juvenile justice and the other aspects of governance that affect the lives of children. The most important link between government and children is schooling, and Bernardine Dohrn discusses the manifold relationship between schools, children, and the institutions of juvenile justice in chapter 10. Peter Edelman analyzes youth policy as a political issue in national government in chapter 11.

Part 5, the longest section of the volume, provides a series of comparative studies of juvenile justice in the modern world. This neglected aspect of the study of legal-system responses to youth in trouble is important for two reasons. First, juvenile courts have been a worldwide phenomenon for almost the entire century of the court's existence. One cannot have a comprehensive knowledge of juvenile justice without some awareness of how different nations and cultures have adopted the juvenile court and its auxiliary institutions. The second use of comparative knowledge of juvenile justice is as a source of ideas and information about reforms that might work in the United States. This application of foreign experience is a great asset of comparative legal study—and has almost never in the past been used in juvenile justice.

Chapter 12 launches the comparative materials with an analysis of the structure, organization, and case flow of the American system by Margaret Rosenheim. In chapter 13, Akira Morita provides a history and functional description of the juvenile court and related institutions in Japan. In chapter 14, John Eekelaar recounts the history of legal approaches to neglected and abused children in twentieth-century England. Anthony Bottoms compares the modern development of delinquency policy in juvenile courts in England and Scotland over the past generation in chapter 15. Founded under the same organizing legislation in 1908, the two systems have taken sharply different paths since the 1960s. In chapter 16, the concluding chapter of the volume, Jaap Doek surveys legal policy toward juvenile offenders in Europe.

Our aim was to create a reference work that would guide readers through the major themes and institutions of juvenile justice at the present time and for many years to come. One of the pleasures of editing this effort has been the many new lessons we have learned, the fresh perspectives to which we have been exposed, in reading the chapters that have come together in this effort to commemorate and to comprehend the first century of a court established to serve the interests of troubled children.

PART 1

Juvenile Justice in Historical Perspective

The story of the origins and evolution of juvenile justice is the obvious starting point for a complete treatment of the topic, but the historical materials we assemble in this section must stop far short of being a comprehensive history. So many historical domains are implicated in the development of juvenile justice that each of the first eleven chapters in the volume has its own materials to consider. Even then, there are significant historical topics that are beyond the scope of this volume.

The materials presented in this first section cover three broad topics: general conceptions of child welfare, the juvenile court as an operating entity, and the custodial institutions that often become the temporary or long-term residences of troubled young people. In chapter 1, Michael Grossberg provides a general introduction to expert and public sentiments about child welfare in the United States between 1820 and 1935. Throughout the nineteenth and early twentieth centuries, Americans had mixed feelings about the disorderly and dependent children in their midst, a fear for children that was bound up with a fear of children. This mixture of sympathy and hostility informed governmental responses to troubled youth long before the official birth of juvenile courts.

David Tanenhaus, in chapter 2, shows that the juvenile court acquired its characteristic policies not immediately, as was often assumed, but through a process of evolutionary development in the first decades of its operation. Tanenhaus calls the notion that the juvenile court sprang from its legislative womb with all its procedures determined "the myth of immaculate construction," and he reveals instead a system that grows through experiential evolution.

Paul Lerman's chapter 3 profiles the variety of institutional systems that have confined young persons over the past century, including public and private detention and custodial facilities for delinquents, hospitals, and institutional residences for dependent children. Lerman demonstrates that rates of utilization of particular forms of institutions change with fashions and that trends in the *aggregate* use of institutions may tell us more than trends in the use of particular forms of institutional care and confinement.

1 Changing Conceptions of Child Welfare in the United States, 1820–1935

Michael Grossberg

"What the best and wisest parent wants for his own child," John Dewey declared in 1899, "that must the community want for all its children" (Dewey 1899, 3). The educational reformer's declaration echoed the sentiments of countless generations of Americans who have felt an innate responsibility for the nation's youth. Yet attempts to realize those enduring expressions of concern for children have revealed the complications of translating widely shared convictions into action. Most significantly, they have exposed a fundamental tension in American beliefs and policies toward the young. Americans have been torn between *a fear for children* and *a fear of children.* Historian Robert Bremner has laid bare this contradictory reality. He explains that, on the one hand, "Positively stated, the argument is that in a democracy, children, as future citizens, are the state's most valuable resource; for its own security the state must enforce the children's right to the nurture that will equip them for positive citizenship." Yet, he cautions, on the other hand, "Negatively stated, the argument is that the state must protect itself against the menace of hordes of young people allowed to grow up in ignorance and without discipline or respect for others" (Bremner 1983, 84). The basic tension between these two sentiments has pervaded American attitudes toward the young, though at particular moments in the past either hope or fear has been dominant. Nowhere is that tension more visible and consequential than in child welfare. United States welfare policies demonstrate that despite a consistent American rhetoric of child-centeredness, the reality has been a good deal more complex. And that reality is critical to understanding the construction and implementation of all American policies toward the young, including juvenile justice, the primary subject of this volume.

Since the founding of the republic, American child welfare policy has been a changing and yet a time-specific set of beliefs and practices. It has focused on children in need, primarily those deemed disorderly or dependent, but the nature of those needs and thus the children included in welfare policies have changed significantly over time. Indeed, the notion of children in need—or "dependent children" in the language of the nineteenth century, and "children at risk" in the words of the late twentieth—has itself been a changing and expansive set of ideas about the moral, physical, and social well-being of the young and how they should be reared. There has also been a changing cast of actors involved in child welfare. In addition to children, parents, and other caretakers, child welfare has involved a wide variety of individuals as well as public and private agencies.

Nevertheless, American debates over child welfare have been framed by a consistent set of concerns that emerge every time it becomes a subject of public debate. Prime among these are disagreements about the place of children in American society and the nature of legitimate parental, community, and state interests in children. These disagreements are fueled by the assumption that children are relatively powerless and have fundamentally different needs from adults, as well as the reality that the young are in many ways doubly dependent: on their parents and on the state. And, of course, children in need are always considered the most dependent of the young. At the same time, child welfare policies are the products of generational solutions to the persistent problem of determining the needs of the young. That is, particular policies have emerged at particular moments in time and produced time-bound welfare practices. These in turn have created a layered system of child welfare in which the past continues to influence the present in many critical ways. Consequently, the implications of changing forms of American child welfare for juvenile justice are best understood by examining their historical development.

Between 1820 and 1935, there were two distinct periods of American child welfare. Despite inevitable overlaps, the first era began early in the nineteenth century and lasted until the Civil War; the second started in the 1870s and ended in the 1930s. Reconstructing the periodized past of American child welfare is critical because, as historian Peter Stearns has argued, periodization is "the essential contribution of historians to the understanding of change" (Stearns 1982, 14). Providing examples of chronologically related changes demonstrates the power of the moment to influence policies and practices as well as the relative impact of change and continuity. Dividing the history of American child welfare into distinct periods reveals the centrality in each era of conceptions of children and of family and civic responsibility for them.

Equally important, the shifting periods of child welfare illuminate the development of American juvenile justice.

Historians trying to determine the place of children in American society have stressed the difference between childhood as a shifting set of ideas and the actual experiences of children at any particular time. Time-bound notions of childhood dominated American child welfare policies in each era. Ideas of innate child innocence or depravity were embedded in welfare policies, and these cultural constructions had very real consequences for children's lives. Nevertheless, the connections between public policies and the actual experiences of children reveal that the young have been more than simply the objects of policy. The age, gender, racial, and class diversity of American children, and the actions of individual parents and children, have consistently challenged the implementation of welfare policies. Though many past clashes over child welfare are difficult to document because children and most adults do not leave diaries, published declarations, and the other sources used to chronicle famous lives, enough evidence remains to demonstrate anew that all human relationships are in some way reciprocal and dynamic, and that no one, even in the most powerless position, lacks the ability to influence others. Thus any attempt to probe the history of changing conceptions of American child welfare must recognize the interactive relationship between ideas of childhood and the realities of children's lives.

At the same time, child welfare in these two eras was also linked to expressions of concern for the dependent young that sprang from changing relationships among children, parents, the state, and philanthropic organizations. Throughout the years under study, the family remained the primary welfare institution in the United States, as it does today. But the roles of American families as welfare institutions have changed considerably since the founding of the republic, and concern about the failure of some families made child welfare a continuous object of state policy and social action. Equally important, the state has been the major external source of assistance to children. Nevertheless, philanthropy has also been central to child welfare in the United States. Private voluntary associations have often taken the lead in the construction and application of policies for the young. Their actions reveal that at critical points in the past the public and private ordering of American child welfare has been linked to larger reconceptualizations of the relationship between strangers that expanded the boundaries of individual and collective moral responsibility and led to waves of American humanitarian reform that altered child welfare policies in each era.

Changing conceptions of children and changing notions of public and community responsibility for the young encouraged instrumental conceptions of child welfare policy. Welfare policies were not simply means to care for particular children in need, they were also tools to address larger policy objectives, from economic development to moral policing. As a result, each era produced dominant forms of child welfare policy that illuminate not only policies and attitudes toward disorderly and dependent children during a particular time but also broader social policies toward the young such as those examined in this volume.

CREATING AMERICAN CHILD WELFARE

A distinctive American approach to child welfare emerged in the first part of the nineteenth century. Although policies were constructed on an English and colonial foundation, change overwhelmed continuity during what might be called the formative era of American child welfare. The changes were rooted in new ideas of children, families, and public responsibility for the disorderly and dependent young. The result was the creation of an approach to child welfare that was in many ways tied to its time and yet also established practices that would dominate American policy into the twenty-first century.

English policies laid the basis for a colonial and then a post-revolutionary approach to child welfare. The Elizabethan Poor Law of 1601 was the most influential source. It established three fundamental features of Anglo-American welfare policy: local control; family responsibility; and a distinction between deserving and undeserving poor, tied to notions of work, gender, and age. The poor laws made parents legally liable for the support of their children and grandchildren, and children responsible for the care of their needy parents and grandparents. Embedded in the Elizabethan acts as well was a determination to limit demands on taxpayers' purses and to find alternative means of supporting the poor than public funding. These commitments expressed the continuing welfare reality that while parents might be willing to make financial sacrifices to give their own children an advantageous start in life, providing generously for children in need has never been a popular public policy. That reality was buttressed by a primal belief in parental responsibility, especially that fathers should support their children, and the collateral conviction that child poverty resulted from the moral failings of parents. As a result, English public welfare sought the best deal at the lowest price, which led to competition for public aid, in which children were consistently the least organized and had fewest advocates. The poor laws also promoted what legal scholar Jacobus Ten Broek has called a dual system of American family law. That system encouraged repressive policies for the lower classes and liberationist ones for the middle and upper classes (Ten Broek 1974). It is through this dual system that the question of class directly entered the discourse of child welfare. The result has been a class system in a society that thinks itself classless and a tendency to speak about what other Europeans call class with words like *depend-*

ent and *deviant*. Even so, the poor laws established a state responsibility to relieve want and suffering among those in need, including children. And it created a legal right to public assistance for helpless or needy people. Significantly, as historian Clarke Chambers has chronicled, the basic provisions of the Elizabethan poor laws "remained in place [in the United States] down to the federalization of assistance during the New Deal. Few legal arrangements in history have lasted over so many generations; that they did so in this instance indicates that they rested on social norms of unquestioned authority and on pragmatic realities of family behavior" (Chambers 1986, 421).

Colonial legislatures transferred the English system and its fundamental assumptions and policies to the new world with relatively few changes. Consequently, children also fell under the long-standing European doctrine of *parens patriae,* which established the state's responsibility for all dependents, especially the young. The doctrine made the state the ultimate parent. Central to those policies was the practice of lumping children with other dependents. Despite a few exceptions, the colonists did not create separate welfare policies for the young. Like the English, local poor-law officials continued to rely on apprenticeship and various forms of direct aid (outdoor relief) and institutions (indoor relief) to aid poor, neglected, and orphaned children, and they sanctioned placing children in almshouses and auctioning them off to the lowest bidder as it did other dependents. Slave children had the fewest protections against mistreatment of any American youngsters, and slave owners provided a minimal level of welfare in terms of food, shelter, and clothing. And, as Andrew Billingsley and Jeanne Giovannoni have argued, slavery had a powerful impact on the development of American child welfare: "The very existence of slavery meant that child welfare institutions could develop in this country without concern for the majority of Black children." At the same time, limited assistance to white children "could be rationalized by the notion that they were treated better than Black slaves" (Billingsley and Giovannoni 1972, 23–24).

Though the American Revolution had relatively little immediate impact on child welfare policies, significant changes began to occur in the early decades of the nineteenth century. New conceptions of childhood and new concerns about the disorderly and dependent young helped spur a reexamination of child welfare. As family historians have described in detail, new family beliefs and practices treated children more than ever before as distinct individuals with special needs and began to separate childhood out as a distinct phase of life. These beliefs also elevated the importance of the mother-child bond, made child nurture more directly a fundamental maternal responsibility, and enhanced the importance of the home as a nursery for future citizens and workers. An individualization of the household implicit in the new view of the family affected all aspects of children's lives from clothing to schooling, including welfare policies. In particular, the rise of a new set of ideas that have come to be called romanticism gave Americans an entirely new image of children's inner natures. Unlike many colonials, under the sway of romanticism more and more antebellum Americans came to regard children as innately good rather than depraved. Indeed, children were now thought to be morally superior to adults. This notion of youthful innocence coincided with a new sense of the importance of the environment in the development of individuals. The romantic view of children had important consequences for the growth and development of child welfare. It encouraged the development of particular policies for children and the need to arouse public opinion on their behalf. Even though many continued to fear poor children, particularly youths who lived by their wits as "street Arabs," as a threat to order and stability in the present and the future, hope not fear dominated this first era of American child welfare.

As a result of these new views of children and their place in society, policymakers struggled to find a way to talk about children as somehow distinct individuals and yet not adults in a system that tied power to individual autonomy. The result was to emphasize needs. This approach found its most revealing expression in a legal phrase that would dominant the welfare debates about children well into the twentieth century: *the best interests of the child.* Though the exact origins of the phrase are not clear, judges and other policymakers early in the nineteenth century translated the traditional power of *parens patriae* to include the newfound sense of children as having distinct interests in the new expression. As a Georgia superior court judge declared in an 1836 child custody case, "All legal rights, even those of personal security and liberty, may be forfeited by improper conduct, and so this legal right of the father to the possession of his child must be made subservient to the true interests and safety of the child, and the duty of the State to protect its citizens of whatever age" (*In the Matter of Mitchell,* 1 Charlton 489–95 [Georgia 1836]). The ambiguous phrase assumed separate children's needs yet expressed the conviction that others—most appropriately parents and, when they failed, judges or other suitable public or private officials, such as the overseers of the poor—must determine them. It sanctioned broad discretionary authority to determine the interests of children when family conflicts or failures made them disorderly or dependent, a power that would be central to the authority and jurisdiction of the juvenile court.

Concurrently, there also arose what historian Elizabeth Pleck has called "the Family Ideal": a set of ideological commitments that deified family privacy, made conjugal and parental rights sacrosanct, and promoted family preservation. The family ideal assumed a fundamental division between public and private realms of society, assigning the family to the private realm (Pleck 1987). This division proved critical because it helped ensure that children's problems would largely be considered private matters, not public ones. According to the family ideal, public and community intervention only became relevant when parents failed. And even in these circumstances such intervention remained suspect in the fundamentally anti-statist republic, that is, a polity in which citizens have been reluctant to entrust state bureaucracies with significant power and authority over their social and economic lives. A changing but resilient set of beliefs and practices, the family ideal has been a powerful influence on all attempts to devise children's policies, particularly child welfare. The "best interest of the child" rule and the "Family Ideal" institutionalized, without ever resolving, a fundamental tension in child welfare and juvenile justice between preserving the sanctity of the family and upholding the interventionist authority of the state.

New ideas about children, families, and the state were intertwined with the emergence of a massive humanitarian reform movement in the 1820s and 1830s that became a major source of child welfare innovation. Reformers tended to see social problems as dire threats to the larger society. They acted as well on the new belief that individual failings caused social ills and shared a new, optimistic faith in the possibilities of individual reformation. Unlike most colonials, who had assumed poverty and other human ills were natural and unchanging parts of human existence, antebellum Americans and particularly humanitarian reformers believed that individuals were largely responsible for their own fate. That idea encouraged the conviction that poverty and other human miseries were the results of individual failings that could be cured and thus spurred a greater sense of responsibility for the fate of strangers. Imbued with faith in the possibility of individual change, reformers relied on moral suasion as their primary tool of change and resisted direct state action whenever possible.

Humanitarian reform led to a vast expansion of civil society in the new republic. Civil society describes the social space between the family and state—a space of public discourse and action carried on by individuals who band together in nongovernmental or quasi-governmental organizations, institutions, and movements. Ideas and policies developed by these groups were broadcast through newspapers, magazines, journals, books, conferences, professional associations, and other mediums of the public sphere. The United States, with its relatively weak state and decentralized and underdeveloped bureaucracy, became a fertile host for an expansive and expanding civil society in the nineteenth century. In it, democratization, popular sovereignty, and individualism combined to promote the idea that individuals were responsible for themselves and their society; they had to act and not wait for government to act. The result was the rise to dominance of the voluntary association as a means of addressing the problems of the nation. As historian Kathleen McCarthy explains, "Voluntarism was the social currency which bound antebellum communities together, nurturing a sense of communal spirit and constantly renewing public commitment to community well-being" (McCarthy 1982, 4).

Children became significant objects of early-nineteenth-century reform, though they were not as central as they would be in the next era of humanitarian reform. Instead, disorderly and dependent children became one of many concerns as social reform found expression in a variety of mass movements from abolitionism and women's rights to campaigns against corporal punishment and alcoholism. Activism on behalf of children and others cannot be explained effectively, as most historians have attempted to do, by contending that it was the product of either benevolence or social control. The resulting debate about the motivations of reformers has produced useful ideas and information, but it has also created polar opposite arguments that unduly simplify reform movements. Altruism and self-interest clearly affected all humanitarian reforms, but in trying to understand their impact on policies like child welfare, it is more useful to examine the connections between reform and the time-bound creation of what anthropologists call "social knowledge" than to search for a single cause of social reform. By "social knowledge," anthropologists mean the ways in which people understand their world. In child welfare, it means determining how new conceptions of children, families, and individual reformation helped shape reformers' ideas and policies. New social knowledge in this era led to an expanded sense of individual and collective moral responsibility for disorderly and dependent children that propelled many women and men to act. They made philanthropy central to child welfare.

New social knowledge and the advent of social reform affected every aspect of antebellum child welfare. Their impact is evident in alterations of traditional poor-law practices and even more so in the creation of new child welfare measures. A few examples of both illustrate the emergence of a new and distinctive American child welfare system and suggest their implications for juvenile justice policies in the era.

Under the poor laws in England and colonial America, apprenticeship had been the preferred method of caring for poor and orphaned children. They were bound out to people who promised to maintain and educate them in exchange for whatever work the children could perform. Like other forms of bonded servitude in traditional society, indentures created a familylike relationship in which apprentices assumed the role of family members, and masters became surrogate parents. Colonial apprenticeships had been conceived of largely in terms of paternal responsibility, filial subordination, and hierarchal social arrangements. Within that scheme, they served a variety of functions for all classes from moral instruction and job training to the relief of poverty.

However, in the boom and bust antebellum economy, with its growing reliance on the self-regulating market and capitalist entrepreneurs, independent labor swept aside many older forms of workplace dependency. As a result, family-based apprenticeship became an increasingly anomalous economic relationship. At the same time, changing attitudes toward the family, particularly the importance accorded to mother-child bonds and the conception of the home as a nursery and refuge, undermined the attractions of indentures as a substitute household for the young. The creation of public schools also undercut the role of apprenticeship as a training system. The emergence of factory labor, especially its use of armies of untrained children and immigrants rather than artisans, and the general decline of the skilled trades reinforced these developments.

The effects of these changes were profound. The parental responsibilities of the master and the filial obligations of the apprentice withered as the relationship came to be considered primarily one of employer and employee. Equally important, preexisting class biases in apprenticeship law and practice emerged as a chasm opened between voluntary and involuntary apprenticeship. Private, voluntary indentures narrowed to a method of vocational training for young men seeking to be professionals, such as lawyers, or skilled artisans, such as blacksmiths. Involuntary indentures remained a primary form of poor-law relief for children of all ages and sexes.

Despite the new views of childhood, the welfare of the apprenticed children figured only secondarily in the calculations of poor-law officials, whose primary concern was to reduce the burden of poor relief for local taxpayers. Most state codes required that impoverished apprentices be taught the rudiments of an education, such as reading, writing, and (for males) arithmetic. Masters could also have their powers revoked for cruel treatment, failure to instruct the apprentice in a trade, and other violations of their parental office. The courts even insisted that a poor-law indenture did not convert the child into a servant and resisted attempts of masters to sell or assign their apprentices. These formal protections approximated those governing voluntary indentures and posed an ideal of apprenticeship as unbiased and classless. However, as in so many child welfare policies, the reality too often was otherwise. Protective laws were subject to widely fluctuating enforcement not only among the states but also among localities because of the broad discretionary powers granted community authorities. Moreover, poor apprentices, as children "of the public," in the words of a New Jersey judge in 1819, could not veto a particular indenture as could youths bound out voluntarily (*State v. Brearly,* 2 South. 556 [New Jersey 1819]). Statutory requirements mandating practical and moral training appear to have been ignored with impunity, as was evidence of physical and sexual abuse. In some communities, poor children even continued to be auctioned off to the lowest bidder along with other paupers. Freed black children endured the most drastic curtailment of rights. States like Kentucky, Missouri, and Indiana passed laws eliminating the educational requirements of their indentures. In other jurisdictions, masters received the right by statute to indenture black children regardless of parental finances. Poor-law indentures, especially for blacks, far too often resembled involuntary servitude.

The differing fates resulting from the two forms of indentures graphically illustrate the corrosive effect of dependency on children in antebellum America as well as the continuing impact of the dual system of family law on child welfare. Voluntary apprenticeship protected individual rights and limited state interference; involuntary apprenticeship used dependency to abridge individual rights and sanction broad public controls. As historian Maxwell Bloomfield concludes, by the 1840s apprenticeship had been robbed of much of its meaning; instead of "providing useful vocational training for the children of all classes, the apprenticeship system now functioned largely as a device for the recruitment and exploitation of young paupers" (Bloomfield 1976, 132). Consequently, while voluntary apprenticeship fell into desuetude and its legal provisions were incorporated into the labor law of a capitalist republic, involuntary apprenticeship remained embedded in the poor laws subject to the emerging welfare assumption that dependent poverty disqualified its victims from the full rights of citizenship. The dual system of apprenticeship thus reveals some of the emerging class boundaries of American child welfare.

The vagaries of antebellum child welfare are also evident in another traditional staple of the poor laws, bastardy. Bastards, as Anglo-American law had long classified children born out of wedlock, faced legal repression and discrimination. Statutes, doctrines, and customs used matrimony to separate legal from spurious issue. The latter suffered the legal status of *filius nullius,* the child and heir of no one. For centuries under English law, the bastard had no recognized legal relations with his or her parents, and no claims to inheritance, maintenance, or family membership. Nor did the illicit couple have any rights or duties toward the child. The English reluctance to help bastards was evident in the refusal to follow civil law and allow legitimation by the subsequent marriage of the parents. The only major reform in the law came with the inclusion of bastards in the Elizabethan Poor Law and the demand that parents aid in their upkeep. Bastardy law had two primary purposes: repelling challenges to established family arrangements, especially property distribution, and preventing the public from being saddled with the costs of rearing children born out of wedlock. Colonial Americans, beyond streamlining paternity hearings, made few alterations in the law.

After the Revolution, though, many Americans began to question the logic of bastardy law. Growing concern about the welfare of the illegitimate child, related to the new conceptions of children and a new determination to confer rights on its mother as the child's primary caretaker, helped transform the law. So did declining rates of illegitimacy and challenges to active state regulation of sexual behavior. State after state rewrote its bastardy laws after the Revolution to ease the burdens on these star-crossed children. Most changes reduced the chance of becoming a bastard. Statutes and judicial decisions declared the offspring of a couple who wed after its birth to be legitimate. They did the same for the children of annulled marriages. Reform did not stop there, though. Even if parents failed to wed, other legal innovations lessened the penalties of illegitimacy. Judges created a new legal household and bound it together with inheritance rights by turning the customary bonds between the bastard and its mother into a web of reciprocal rights and duties. The judiciary granted such women custody rights in a reinterpretation of the law that combined the new faith in maternal care with a postrevolutionary assertion of judicial authority over the allocation of domestic rights and responsibilities. Similarly, judges and legislators began to confer reciprocal inheritance rights on bastards and their mothers, and on other kin. Through these measures, judges tried to ease the perils of illegitimacy by distinguishing family membership rights from punishment for sexual immorality and property protection.

Yet innovations were only one part of the era; continuities existed as well. American bastardy law never jettisoned two traditional elements: fiscally conservative local officials anxious to control child support costs and a deeply ingrained prejudice against extramarital sexual relations. Most likely, the changes in the law aided only those who could support their offspring and thus further segregated impoverished mothers and couples who relied on poor relief. Protection of taxpayers' pocketbooks reinforced the era's conviction that proper child nurture required guardians capable of providing adequate material support. As the Vermont Supreme Court asserted, with no irony intended, the illegitimate child "has just the same rights as any pauper when its custody is shifted from one keeper to another" (*Adams v. Adams,* 59 Vermont 158–61 [1877]). In addition, postrevolutionary changes had little impact on paternity hearings. They continued to be dominated by fiscal fears and the trappings of criminal law. The proceedings were guided by gender biases as well, particularly the assumptions that nurture was a maternal responsibility, support a paternal one.

Modifications in traditional policies like apprenticeship and bastardy only partially reveal the changes wrought in antebellum child welfare. Even more significant are the innovations of the era. These were primarily institutional and focused on the creation of facilities and organizations devoted specifically to children. Prime among them was the public school. The ideal of universal education for all young Americans was the largest welfare measure of the era and one that most clearly expressed the period's faith in individual betterment. It also suggests the need to take a broad view of child welfare and not limit examination of the subject simply to public and private aid to impoverished or neglected youths.

During the first decades of the nineteenth century a new sense of the importance of the environment in human development and of childrearing combined with a postrevolutionary vision of the young as the perpetuators of political progress to confer great importance on the intergenerational transfer of skills, knowledge, and values. Popular ideology encouraged American families to define childrearing as preparation for, in historian Isaac Kramnick's telling phrase, the "race for life" (Kramnick 1990, 5). Believing in the possibility of generational advancement through education, mothers and fathers demanded that every restraint on their children be removed before they entered the race; doing so became part of their parental responsibilities. Schools became the repository of this new faith in education as the basic engine of individual mobility and the primary source of equal opportunity. They were invested with multiple, often clashing missions: producing an educated, disciplined workforce; attacking poverty and crime; and inculcating Christian morality. Education was thus envisioned as both a public responsibility and a public defense. As such it addressed both the hopes and fears aroused by children.

The public school, however, also represented a challenge to the power of families over childrearing and a transfer of family responsibilities that signaled new ideas of child welfare. According to Stanley Schultz, "The teacher could stand in place of the parent, examining the character, morals, and habits of each child, and exercising the moral authority that had once belonged exclusively to the family." Consequently, the public school was to be "a classroom, family room, a church house—all things to all children" (Schultz 1973, 55). Parents generally accepted the growing control of the schools over teaching skills and values and thus acquiesced in the diminution of their authority. However, they resisted a complete transfer of responsibilities, and many fathers and mothers fought over the creation of new boundary lines between the autonomy of the family and the authority of state agencies like the schools. Disputes erupted over the use of corporal punishment, mandatory Protestant religious instruction, and other practices that raised concerns about the allocation of power between families and the state, as well as the autonomy and authority of individual family members and public agents like teachers and school administrators. For example, California State Superintendent of Schools John Swett told the state legislature in 1864 that "the child must be taught to consider his instructor, in many ways, superior to the parent in terms of authority. . . . The vulgar impression that parents have a legal right to dictate to teachers is entirely erroneous. . . . Parents have no remedy as against the teacher" (Carlson 1998, 42). Such declarations document the emergence of a new authority over children that would be seized by a variety of public and private officials in the coming decades, including juvenile court judges. Always more than a place to learn rudimentary skills, the school became a critical arena for such conflicts. In this era, however, the voluntary school system made education a parental choice. Given the growing faith in schooling, such a policy expressed both the larger belief in family autonomy so dominant in these years as well as the period's optimistic faith that parents would do the right thing, which illustrates both the continuing power of the family ideal and how it was being modified.

And yet, of course, despite the conviction that all children should be educated and that education should be equal, distinctions appeared and became embedded in the system. Since attendance was voluntary, only those able and willing to attend consistently finished the curriculum. In addition, many children lacked the skills to compete successfully in the classroom. The great influx of immigrants in the 1850s exacerbated the problems in large cities. Other students suffered from the lack of sufficient schools. And still others were simply barred from attendance. The children of free blacks in many southern states lacked access to schools, while many in the north endured segregated schools. At the same time, the curriculum reproduced and reinforced gender divisions by focusing boys on the workplace and girls on the home.

Even so, the common school elicited strong support among antebellum Americans as an enlightened, necessary, and universal child welfare measure. For example, the Pennsylvania state representative and later radical Republican congressional leader Thaddeus Stevens defended school taxes in 1835 from charges that the state free school law took money from the successful to support the indigent. He argued that school levies benefited taxpayers because schooling for all children "perpetuates the government, and ensures . . . the due administration of the law under which they live, and by which their lives and property are protected" (cited in Bremner 1983, 85). As a result, the common school became a prime site for addressing social problems and thus an inspiration for a better future as well as an institution overloaded with expectations and responsibilities.

While the common school represented an inclusive ideal to benefit all children as well as the larger society, the other major child welfare innovation of the era did not. The House of Refuge was created specifically for the children of failed families (figure 1.1). These public institutions were the product of growing concerns about the plight of disorderly and dependent youths and about the consequences of consigning such children along with other paupers to almshouses where they were often mistreated and given little schooling. And they sprang as well from growing dissatisfaction with the tradition of outdoor relief and other established methods of support, such as auctioning off

Fig. 1.1 Philadelphia House of Refuge. Print Collection, Miriam and Ira D. Wallach Division of Art, Prints and Photographs, The New York Public Library, Astor, Lenox, and Tilden Foundations.

paupers. Though omnibus institutions like almshouses and workhouses had long been used to care for the needy, and orphanages flourished in the era as the primary institutional alternative to families, the House of Refuge illustrates the tenor of the era and the growing links between child welfare and juvenile justice. Antebellum institutional reformers argued that the new, specialized institutions would not be dumping grounds but rather reformatories that would provide the proper environment for individual reformation impossible in the traditional poor-law system. The new institutions also represented an expanding sense of civic responsibility toward the young as well as the now entrenched conviction that disorderly and dependent children needed specialized care and treatment. Thus their construction also expressed the hope and optimism of the era.

New York City established the first juvenile reformatory in 1824. Others soon followed. Believing that a structured environment could remold youthful characters, the founders of refuges stressed rigorous discipline, education, and work as the principal means of reformation. According to historian David Rothman, "At the core of the child-reformers' optimism was a faith completely shared by colleagues promoting other caretaker institutions that a daily routine of strict and steady discipline would transform [an] inmate's character" (Rothman 1971, 213). Thus the New York House of Refuge offered its inmates "such employment as will tend to encourage industry," basic education in "reading, writing, and arithmetic," and instruction in "the nature of their moral and religious obligations." Equally important, the institutions were granted broad jurisdiction over criminal, vagrant, neglected, or even unruly children to achieve their goals and thus lumped all disorderly and dependent children together and offered them basically the same treatment. Splitting disorderly and dependent children from adults and lumping them together as objects of similar policies would become a characteristic feature of American policies that increasingly combined child welfare and juvenile justice into a single set of practices and institutions. Typically, the Boston House of Refuge was authorized to take in "all such children who shall be convicted of criminal offences or taken up and committed under and by virtue of an act of this Commonwealth, 'for suppressing and punishing of rogues, vagabonds, common beggars, and other idle, disorderly and lewd persons.'" And the mayor, alderman, or overseers of the poor could recommend that "all children who live an idle or dissolute life, whose parents are dead, or if living, from drunkenness, or other vices, neglect to provide any suitable employment, or exercise salutary control over said children," be sentenced to the House of Refuge, where they were to "be kept governed and disposed of, as hereinafter provided, the males until they are the age of twenty-one years, and the females of eighteen years." Finally, the institutions conformed to gender and racial beliefs of the era by establishing separate departments for girls and blacks. In yet another recurrent reality of child welfare, directors of the New York institution stressed the prevention of sexual immorality as the primary reason for institutionalizing girls. It would serve young women who were "either too young to have acquired habits of fixed depravity, or whose lives have in general been virtuous, but who, having yielded to the seductive influence of corrupt associates, have suddenly to endure the bitterness of lost reputation, and are cast forlorn and destitute upon a cold and unfeeling public" (cited in Hawes 1991, 16, 15). These policies sprang from the conviction, shared with the proponents of other caretaker asylums such as prisons and mental institutions, that only a specialized, regimented environment would prevent their charges from falling victim to ignorance, vice, and crime. They thus suggest the depth of the segregationist impulse emerging in nineteenth-century America and its welfare system.

Houses of Refuge were expensive institutions, and their managers had to scurry to find funds for them. In their search for support, reformatory managers willingly relied on procedures that blurred the distinction between public and private authority. Some states, for instance, developed a subsidy system in which public monies were used to fund private institutions to care for the young. These public officials found such support was cheaper than building and maintaining state institutions. The result, though, was to grant private asylum managers extensive policy power and to create an environment in which those managers ran the institutions as profit-making enterprises. Other states authorized managers to contract with private businesses to provide work for refuge children. In these ways, antebellum refuge managers traversed the line between public and private spheres of action and responsibility, and in doing so they established yet another recurrent feature of American child welfare.

Concern about the jurisdiction and services offered by the reformatories led some parents to protest the incarceration of their children. The most influential challenge resulted in an 1838 decision by the Pennsylvania Supreme Court, *Ex Parte Crouse* (4 Wharton 9–12 [Pa. 1839]). The justices rejected a father's claim that his daughter had due process rights and thus her placement in a house of refuge at the request of her mother but without a trial was illegal. Tellingly, they argued that placement in the House of Refuge was treatment not punishment, and that the public had a right to act when parents failed. Upholding the constitutionality of the refuge, the court revealed the dominance of child welfare beliefs and practices over juvenile justice by ruling that the Philadelphia House of Refuge was not a prison but a school. They declared, "The infant has been snatched from a course which must have ended in confirmed depravity, and not only is the restraint of her person lawful, but it would be an act of extreme cruelty to release her from it" (12). The opinion gave legal expression to the underside of the family ideal being embedded in American child welfare policies and the class limitations of the 'family ideal': While the state must respect family sovereignty, failed families lost their rights. And children in failed families needed therapeutic treatment to integrate them back into society, not legal rights or adversarial proceedings. Ambiguous words in the Crouse case, such as treatment, welfare, and interests, would be repeated over and over again in the years to come and be given class, racial, and gendered meanings that also reveal the continuing impact of the dual system of family law. Even so, children, like other dependents in a society fundamentally divided by class, race, and gender, were determined to be special individuals, and the judiciary legitimated special institutions for them.

By the 1850s and 1860s, however, uncertain and limited support, overcrowding, and mismanagement had undermined the therapeutic goals of the Houses of Refuge. And little evidence emerged to demonstrate that their regimented routines had fulfilled the promised goal of individual reformation. Nevertheless, the institutional movement spread across the republic. The transfer of children from poorhouses to specialized institutions continued in various states for the rest of the century. Institutionalization had acquired its own appeal; if nothing else, it took children off the streets and out of failed families. The reformatories became a fundamental way of dealing with disorderly and other dependent youths. By 1861, when Ohio passed the first statute calling for the mandatory removal of all children from county almshouses, there were some seventy-five separate children's institutions in existence in the United States; there would be six hundred by 1890 (Trattner 1974, 100). Following similar logic and with similar faith in the curative powers of managed environments, religious denominations, ethnic groups, and fraternal and benevolent societies established orphanages so that children of deceased or disabled members could be raised in the faith and according to the traditions and values of their parents. Indeed, sectarian orphanages became the most prevalent form of specialized institution for the young. Many of these also elicited public support and served as way stations for impoverished or troubled families temporarily unable to care for children. Though they never dominated the assistance given disorderly and dependent children, institutions became permanent fixtures of American child welfare and were its most visible symbols until the advent of the juvenile court.

The final significant addition to antebellum child welfare represented both a critique of the era's assumptions and a portent of policy approaches that would dominate the next period. In 1853 the Reverend Charles Loring Brace founded the New York Children's Aid Society. Brace was driven to act out of fear of children, not simply fear for children: "There are no dangers to the value of property or the permanency of our institutions, so great as those from the existence of . . . a class of vagabond, ignorant, or ungoverned children" (cited in Bremner 1970, 1: 757). He coined the phrase "the dangerous classes" to describe the "outcasts, vicious, reckless multitude of New York boys, swarming . . . in every foul alley and low street." If these boys were neglected by society as they had been by their parents, Brace foresaw the possibility of "an explosion from this class which might leave the city in ashes and blood" (Brace 1872, 28–29). Alarmed over increasing juvenile delinquency and crime among the city's youths, and fearful of what might happen to property, morality, and political life if nothing were done to relieve New York of its homeless, vagrant, and delinquent children, he founded the Children's Aid Society to save the city. In the process, as Ashby contends, the "NYCAS politicized the concept of childhood, using it as a lever for social change. Brace wanted to disassemble slum families, and the NYCAS's rendering of the street urchin provided a reason for action. Ironically, such a rationale unquestionably reflected sympathy for children but typically displayed little regard for the misery and misfortune of their parents" (Ashby 1997, 46). Equally important, Brace served as a model for the child policy entrepreneurs who would play an increasingly prominent role in the formulation and implementation of child welfare and juvenile justice like juvenile court judge Ben Lindsey and the head of the Children's Bureau, Julia Lathrop.

The Children's Aid Society was yet another welfare hybrid. Though a private agency, it relied on both voluntary contributions and public subsidies. Indeed, its managers questioned the ability of state agents to address children's problems effectively and worried about patronage and corruption in public programs. The primary goal of the society was to get children off the streets.

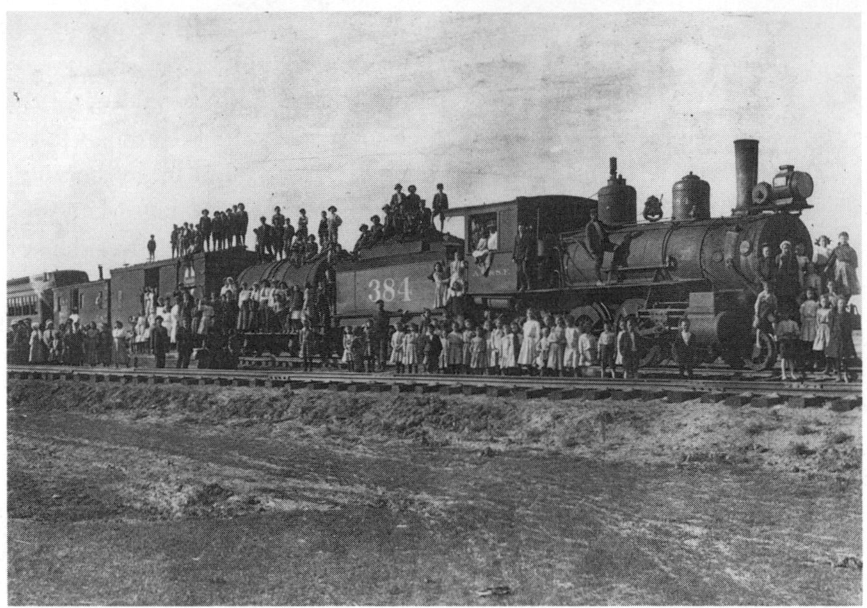

Fig. 1.2 "Orphan train" on the Atchison, Topeka & Santa Fe Railroad line. Courtesy of The Kansas State Historical Society, Topeka, Kansas.

It established an industrial school to provide vocational training and tried to find jobs for idle boys. It also opened a Newsboys Lodging House to get the paper hawkers off the streets.

However, Brace decided that these measures were insufficient and concluded that existing institutional alternatives, particularly the Houses of Refuge, were little better. Instead, Brace became a staunch opponent of institutionalization and championed placing urban children in rural families. The controversial policy sprang from his belief in the moral efficacy of family life, supplemented by public schools, and in the discipline inculcated in the young by doing farm work and home chores. He fervently believed that this environment would reclaim children from the vicious education of the streets; in some ways this was a resurrected version of the discarded apprentice ideal. Brace implemented his plan by sending children to farm families in the West beginning in 1854. Over the next twenty-five years orphan trains removed more than fifty thousand children from New York City (figure 1.2).

Brace's placement policy stirred intense opposition. Child reformers complained that the Children's Aid Society did little to ensure that girls and boys were placed well and treated well. They claimed that too often children were overworked, poorly fed and clothed, and rarely sent to school. Opposition also came from the poor, many of whom did not want their children sent so far from home. Even some western states opposed the policy, protesting that it turned them into dumping grounds for disorderly and delinquent urban youth, some of whom ran away from their new families. A few states banned the practice altogether, and others required the Children's Aid Society to post a bond for each child in the event that he or she became a public burden. Finally, the Catholic Church charged that the western placements represented yet another Protestant strategy to convert the Catholic children of the city. Thus Brace's program was a further incentive for the church to construct its own institutions for disorderly and needy Catholic children and helped spur the creation of a separate Catholic child welfare system.

Though the western placement policy remained controversial and little copied, more and more urban Americans founded Children's Aid Societies in the middle of the nineteenth century. The proliferation of the societies represented the growing conclusion that other policies had failed to resolve the problems of disorderly and dependent youth, particularly the specialized asylums, and a growing distrust (if not fear) of working-class families and their children. Their diffusion also demonstrated the increasing tendency of American social welfare policies to treat the young as distinct individuals with their own needs and interests separate from those of their families and thus in need of their own welfare programs. Finally, the Children's Aid Society movement represented the growing appeal of family care, indeed the advent of supervised foster families, rather than institutional treatment of the disorderly and dependent young. It thus initiated what would be a recurrent debate over the virtues and problems of institutionalization versus deinstitutionalization that would also be a permanent component of American child welfare.

Child welfare became a distinct set of policies and institutions for the first time in the United States during the first half of the nineteenth century. Larger social conceptions of the needs and problems of children in general and of disorderly and dependent children in particular led to the creation of child-focused welfare policies. Central to their development was the displacement of the family as the society's singular provider of child welfare and the construction of alternative child welfare institutions, particularly schools and reformatories. As a result of developments in this era, a distinct child welfare system arose on a base established by English and colonial poor-law policies. It produced a separate discourse of child welfare with endemic debates and contests over individual moral responsibility and the roles and duties of the young, their parents, others, and the state. These found expression in what would be persistent clashes over issues such as the legitimacy and efficacy of institutionalizing delinquent and dependent children, the line between public and private authority over children, and the desirability of segregating children from adults and from one another based on class, gender, race, and other distinctions. The new child welfare system established an infrastructure and set of beliefs and practices that would become permanent features of American social welfare and thus frame subsequent children's policies, particularly the creation of a separate system of juvenile justice around the turn of the twentieth century.

CHILD WELFARE IN INDUSTRIAL AMERICA

A new era in American child welfare began late in the nineteenth century. The basic system created earlier in the century remained largely in place, most notably the reliance on public support administered at the state and county level, and the use of hybrid public and private agencies to deal with particular groups of children in need. But the system underwent significant modifications as child welfare acquired a new focus and set of concerns in industrial America. Changes in the era represented both a growing disenchantment with particular policies and the emergence of new ideas and approaches to disorderly and dependent children that encouraged continued welfare innovation. Most directly, a second wave of American humanitarianism propelled further child welfare reform by creating new concerns about the children of strangers and a new sense of responsibility for them. However, unlike the first era, the new one was dominated by fear *of* children rather than *for* children. Typically, Boy's Club organizer J. F. Atkinson warned, "If we do not pull him up," the street waif "will pull us down" (cited in Ashby 1997, 80). Reformers in this period had much less faith in self-policing and individual and family autonomy; conversely, they had a much greater faith in public authority and the authority of experts. The shift is evident in the name ascribed to the new movement: child saving. As Michael Katz argues, "Child-saving not only shifted the focus of social welfare; even more, it rested on a new psychology, a series of major strategic innovations, an enhanced role for government, and a reordered set of relations between families and the state. For these reasons, child-saving heralded a new departure in welfare history" (Katz 1986, 123). And, as historian Hamilton Cravens argues, "probably the most prominent of such child-saving institutions was the juvenile court, first created by the Illinois legislature in 1899" (Cravens 1993, 7).

Child saving drew on interrelated sources that established the movement's goals and practices. Most important, it sprang from fears of disorder in the nation's families that stirred intense public debate about the fate of the nation's children. Beginning in the 1870s a flood of information seemed to document increasing household breakdown: rising divorce, increased participation of women in the workforce, low marriage rates among educated women, falling birth rates among the middle and upper classes coupled with rising birth rates among working-class and immigrant families, growing poverty, escalat-

histories!

II Acts/Legislation

III Offenses/off

III Statutes

irable. It is also understandable why

. However, both can be equally harmful to

downsides… depends on you. A well

r hurt them. What you decide to do with

ing juvenile delinquency, and on and on. Looking back, family problems and changes in the era were clearly the product of massive structural changes in the economy and society tied to industrial capitalism, urbanization, and immigration. At the time, though, the general diagnosis among much of the middle and upper classes that formed the recruiting grounds for child savers was less fundamental. Though points of emphasis shifted between heredity and environment, working-class and immigrant families and neighborhoods were labeled a contagion that threatened the rest of society. In short, a sense of family crisis led to a deepening understanding of the dire plight of many families and to fears that their troubles might undermine the society, and thus it sped efforts to save their children.

A redefinition of childhood throughout the European world also encouraged child saving. Extending the conceptions of the previous period, a new understanding of child development encouraged an ever more refined conception of children as separate and distinct individuals with their own needs and interests and a conception of childhood as a special time for study, growth, and play. These new ideas found numerous expressions in the era, most notably in what sociologist Viviana Zelizer has called the sacralization of childhood—the seemingly paradoxical notion of children gaining greater emotional value to their parents at the same time that their economic worth declined (Zelizer 1985).

As in the earlier era, such reconceptualizations of childhood led to new social knowledge that in turn altered welfare policies. In this period, they produced concerns about the particular vulnerability and needs of the young and kindled a determination to create more space in all children's lives by extending the years of youthful dependence and excluding the young as much as possible from the market and public life. The redefinition of childhood, in turn, made information about working-class and immigrant children even more alarming and thus undermined tolerance for family diversity. It encouraged the conclusion that a proper childhood must be imposed if it was not voluntarily embraced. The identification of children without a childhood as a problem in need of remediation was accompanied by and to some extent caused by a declining confidence in the abilities of families to rear their children properly by themselves. At the same time, the new ideas about the young also fed the opposition to institutions for dependent and disorderly children first voiced by Brace and his allies in the Children's Aid movement. Increasingly, institutions were deemed bad for children, who needed not the regimentation of the asylum but the individual nurture and training available only in a home. And thus, despite the family crisis, child savers also sought ways to preserve families by policing them more closely, or they sought to place disorderly and dependent children in foster homes.

An expansion of civil society also spurred child saving. By the end of the nineteenth century two critical elements combined to make children a growing concern of American civil society. First, women took an increasingly prominent role in it. The weak state that characterized the United States created greater room for women's political and civil activities than in most European countries. The gendered reality of American civil society thus provided a way for women to increase their sphere of influence. Among the results was a growing debate about issues of importance to women, particularly those involving children and families. Second, philanthropy and the professions also assumed a greater role in the public sphere. Philanthropists and the organizations that they created and staffed became ever more powerful actors in the discussion and implementation of vital public policies. And organized experts, particularly psychologists and social workers, donned the mantle of professionalism to carve out their own space in the public sphere based on claims of disinterested expertise. At times allies and at times adversaries, philanthropists and professionals became critical sources of information and action about children and the family.

Finally, child saving also sprang from a new willingness in the era to rethink the legitimate bounds of state authority. Social and economic change forced a reevaluation of the role of the state in all spheres of American life, including the home. The long-standing American embrace of anti-statism in general and the deference to household autonomy embedded in the family ideal in particular were reexamined. Seizing a critical metaphor of the era, activists and other political entrepreneurs demanded a new balance between public and private interests. They argued that the changes needed to save society required greater public action because only the state commanded the resources and legal tools to police families more vigorously. The new approach was evident in one of the major bureaucratic innovations of the era: the rise of State Boards of Charities. Beginning in Massachusetts in 1863, state legislators created these boards to supervise and coordinate welfare policies and institutions. As such a change suggests, unlike the reliance of the first humanitarian movement on moral suasion and non-statist solutions such as voluntary schools, the second discounted the possibility of individual self-reformation and turned to the coercive authority of the state to construct a just society. Such efforts were, in turn, part of larger struggles in the United States over the replacement of a night watchman state with a welfare state.

Child welfare was at the heart of this state construction. The scope and direction of child welfare change in the era was evident in the fact that in the United States, as in Britain, the phrase *the children of the state,* once used to refer exclusively to children in the direct care of public authorities, began to be used to refer to all children by advocates of a wider state role. "All children are the children of the state, or none are," declared Rev. Lloyd Jenkins Jones of Illinois in 1898 (cited in Tiffin 1982, 218). As a result, as political scientist

Matthew Crenson has argued in a recent study of orphanages, reformers of the era turned the asylum "inside out" as a way to move away from institutionalization while retaining the asylums' powers of surveillance. They did so by increasing the policing of children and parents by state authorities (Crenson 1998). Indeed, juvenile courts became one of the primary public policing agencies as they monitored parents and children by enforcing the new standards of family life and overseeing the removal and treatment of children from homes that failed.

These various developments combined to compel significant changes in American child welfare policies. Existing programs were modified; new ones were created as notions of the best interests of children were redefined. A few examples of child welfare modifications and innovations suggest the nature and consequences of this critical second chapter in the history of American child welfare (figure 1.3).

The creation of the Society for the Prevention of Cruelty to Children (SPCC) aptly illustrates the new tenor of child welfare policy. Spurred by stories of abused children, elite New York reformers founded the first anticruelty society in 1875. Chapters quickly spread through the republic, fueled by fears about the social consequences of family failure and a developing sense of children as holders of particular claims against the society, such as the right to a life free from physical violence in their homes as well as on the streets. Similarly, state legislators joined the campaign by creating new penalties for child abuse. As SPCC founder and child-policy entrepreneur Elbridge T. Gerry declared, "No matter how exalted the offender, the society has the right to confront him with its proofs; no matter how degraded the object of its mercy, the society is bound by its corporate duty to stretch out its hand and rescue from starvation, misery, cruelty, and perhaps death, the helpless little child who ought to have a protector, but for some reason, not its fault, has been deprived of that advantage" (cited in Pleck 1987, 76). In this way, the SPCC helped redefine and focus the concept of child abuse and made it a permanent part of American child welfare policy, even though direct concern would wax and wane. Critically, as Hawes emphasizes, "The SPCC was the first to articulate the idea of enforcing children's rights against their parents" (Hawes 1991, 22). Gerry, for instance, insisted that it was a fundamental "axiom that at the present day in this country, children have some rights which even parents are bound to respect" (Gerry 1882, 129). Thus the rise of anticruelty societies led to yet another modification of the family ideal by sanctioning greater policing of families.

Equally important, the anticruelty movement continued the institutional hybridization of American child welfare policy through the creation of quasi-public/quasi-private organizations. Statutes authorized private agents of the societies to work with police to arrest and prosecute abusive parents, and,

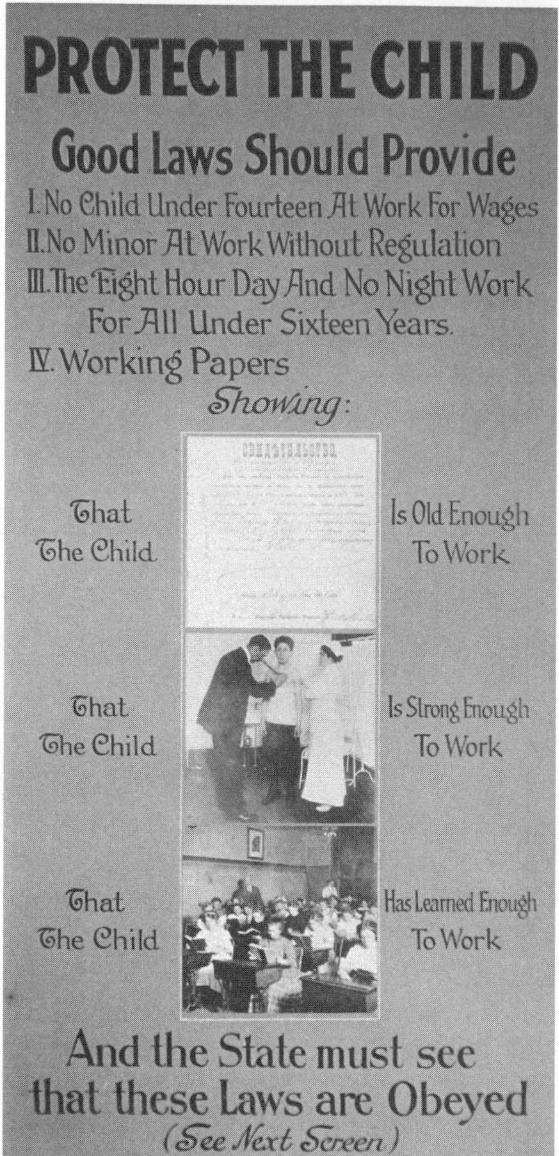

Fig. 1.3 *Protect the Child* by Lewis Hine. © Bass Museum of Art/CORBIS.

if necessary, remove children from their homes. Private agents like Gerry thus served as public officials determining which abuses would be prosecuted. The reliance on blurred public and private agencies, despite the era's fervent rhetoric about the importance of maintaining a rigid separation between public and private authority, continued the earlier policy of private agencies as creators and enforcers of children's policy. Its persistence suggests that the emerging American variant of the Western European welfare state retained a lingering uneasiness with public power, even though reformers championed greater state action. Instead of constructing new public bureaucracies, it relied on allocative strategies that used tax policy, subsidies, and dispersed responsibility to check the growth of the state by fostering a vibrant and powerful public sphere filled with private agencies authorized by state officials to tackle public problems like child abuse.

The societies adopted expansive definitions of cruelty that sanctioned extensive policing of working-class families aimed at imposing middle-class family norms on those households. Despite the child savers' rhetoric of family uniformity, there existed a wide, indeed a widening, variety of families with conflicting needs, interests, and internal differences. Logically, many working-class and immigrant families considered the societies, or "the Cruelty" as many called them, a direct threat to their household autonomy and an attack on their childrearing beliefs and practices. Thus, though child abuse clearly occurred, according to historian Linda Gordon, "Some cases of cruelty to children arose from disagreement about proper child raising," while others "arose from the inevitable cruelties of poverty." Those cruelties included "disease and malnutrition, children left unattended while their parents worked, children not warmly dressed, houses without heat, bedding crawling with vermin, unchanged diapers, injuries left without medical treatment" (Gordon 1987, 21–32). In this way, the anticruelty societies, like so many reforms of the era, dealt with symptoms, not causes, by trying to impose a single standard of child care while ignoring the larger context of the lives of the poor as well as the reality to be learned by a later generation of child savers that child abuse transcended class differences.

At the same time, the societies could not impose their policies on targeted families unilaterally. Parents and children were not just passive recipients of SPCC benevolence. As Gordon and others have shown, family members often turned the anticruelty laws to their own ends, just as they used orphanages and other child asylums as temporary shelters for their offspring during especially bad times. In particular, women and children filed cruelty complaints to renegotiate authority within their families. Parents would use "the Cruelty" to threaten or punish children they could not control; children would report parents. Thus, rather than simply chronicles of new levels of surveillance and the continued impact of the dual system of family policy, campaigns against child cruelty, like other child welfare reforms in the era, also helped renegotiate power and decision making between some families and the state and within some families. And they demonstrate how the impoverished and the dependent played critical roles in the operation of American welfare policy.

Equally emblematic of the new bureaucratic and statist approach to child welfare that dominated the era was the founding of the United States Children's Bureau in 1912. This fact-finding agency was a direct product of the

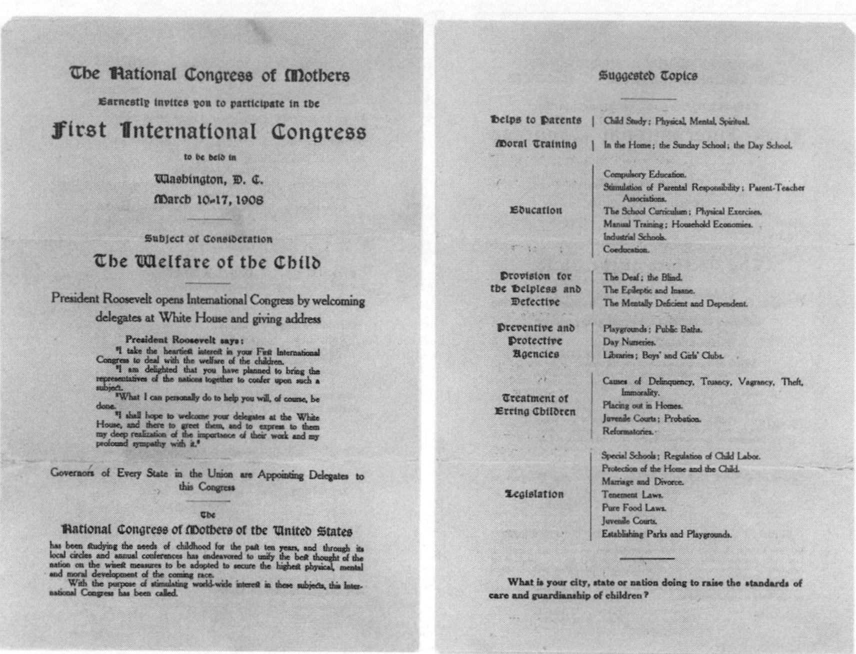

Fig. 1.4 National Congress of Mothers advertisement for the First International Congress on the Welfare of the Child. Courtesy of The Bancroft Library, University of California, Berkeley.

first White House Conference on the Care of Dependent Children (figure 1.4). Convened in 1909 to share information about needy children and to dramatize the need for action, the conference stressed the magnitude of the child welfare problem. In a message to the attendees, President Theodore Roosevelt referred to the thousands of children in institutions and foster homes to express the hopes and fears of the era: "Each of these children represents either a potential addition to the productive capacity and the enlightened citizenship of the Nation, or, if allowed to suffer from neglect, a potential addition to the destructive forces of the community. The ranks of criminals and other enemies of society are recruited in an altogether undue proportion from children bereft of their natural homes and left without sufficient care" (cited in Bremner 1983, 88). The president and others championed knowledge as a weapon to combat child delinquency and dependency; the conference endorsed the creation of a federal agency to gather information about the nation's young.

The Children's Bureau was authorized to investigate and report on "all matters pertaining to the welfare of children and child life among all classes of our people, and shall especially investigate the questions of infant mortality, the birth rate, orphanage, juvenile courts, desertion, dangerous occupations, accidents and diseases of children, employment, legislation affecting children in the several States and Territories" (cited in Hawes 1991, 47). Tellingly, however, fears for the autonomy and sanctity of the family led to a provision prohibiting Children's Bureau agents from entering a home without permission, which reveals the continuing power of the family ideal as a restriction on state policy. Like so many sunshine federal agencies created in the era, the bureau's primary charge was to gather information and use publicity to generate public support for changes in child welfare policies. Nevertheless, as historian Walter I. Trattner argues, "The Children's Bureau was extremely significant; it soon became the central, and in some cases, the sole, source of authoritative information about the welfare of children and their families throughout the United States. More important, its creation marked a significant departure in public policy. It was the first time the federal government recognized not merely the rights of children but also the actual need to create a permanent agency to at least study, if not yet protect them" (Trattner 1974, 183–84).

Some of the consequences of the era's new approaches to child welfare are evident in the intertwined attempts to reform two of the most fundamental aspects of the lives of the young: schooling and work. Compulsory attendance became a primary focus of child welfare reform. Though Massachusetts had instituted the first compulsory education law in 1852, the concept flourished in the new era with its fears about children, determination to prolong childhood, and distrust of immigrant and working-class families. Letting families decide when and how much schooling a child needed was no longer acceptable. Compulsory education laws further institutionalized the conviction that schooling would cure social problems from poverty to crime, train the young for successful futures, and extend childhood by ensuring that the young would be in classrooms for much of the first part of their lives. These attractions proved irresistible, and by 1930 most states required that children stay in school until they were at least fourteen and many decreed sixteen. Making schooling mandatory was justified along with other measures intended to separate out childhood as a distinct phase of life and to define children as individuals with special needs and interests. These included the creation of juvenile courts, higher marriage ages, and age-graded bans on access to substances such as alcohol and tobacco.

Despite limited enforcement, even with the advent of truant officers and juvenile court surveillance, the school laws succeeded in large part because so many parents shared the faith in schooling that they institutionalized. The laws reframed the debate and created a new balance between children, families, and state. The classroom became the fundamental shared experience of the nation's young, and regular attendance the norm. Indeed, the now entrenched American faith in schooling as the solution to all social problems ensured that the school would be the primary welfare site for children. With its now captive student body, the school became the place for pursuing social remediation of all sorts, from the Americanization of immigrant children to disease control.

Fig. 1.5 *Child Labor on the Farm,* 1930. Lewis Hine, American, 1874–1940. Gelatin silver print, 34 × 26.6 cm. Gift of David Vestal, 1965.353. Photograph by Christopher Gallagher. © 2001, The Art Institute of Chicago. All rights reserved.

Compulsory school laws also succeeded in getting more and more children out of the workforce. However, the direct assault on child labor was a more problematic quest, even though it sprang from sentiments quite like those propelling compulsory school laws, particularly the belief in a prolonged childhood of play and learning mandated by the state. As one reformer put it, "The term child labor is a paradox, for when labor begins . . . the child ceases to be" (cited in Cunningham 1995, 148). By labor, reformers did not mean the character-building activities they associated with work at home or even on family farms. Rather they meant employment for wages in factories, mines, tenement sweatshops, and city streets (figure 1.5). Saving children from such work became a crusade as reformers exposed the dangerous conditions in which many children labored. Child labor reform demonstrated the power of the new views of childhood in a country that had always prized work, even for the young. Now, with children designated as a valuable resource for the future, schooling, not labor, had become the mandatory method of learning to be an adult.

As with compulsory school laws, the American effort at child labor re-

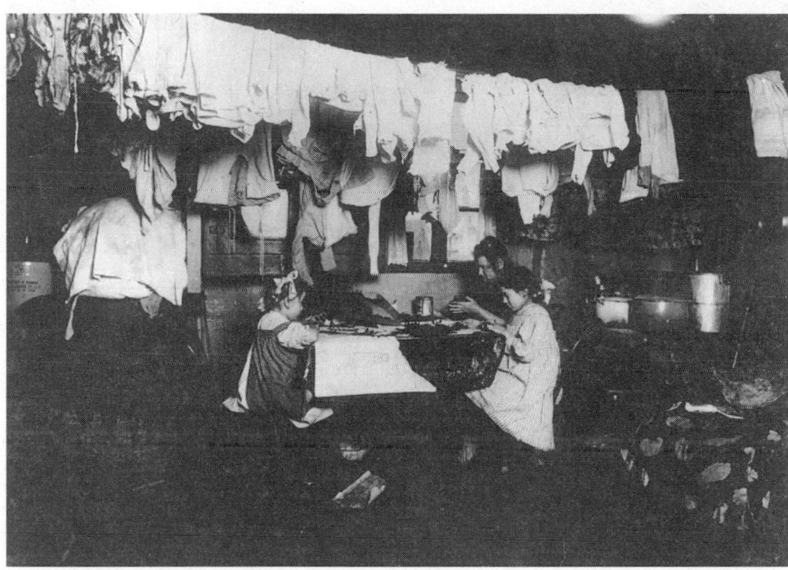

Fig. 1.6 Making artificial leaves in a tenement attic in New York City, 1912. Lewis Hine Collection. Courtesy of the National Library of Congress.

form began in New England at mid-century and soon spread through the north and west. Between 1885 and 1889, ten states passed minimum-age laws, and six prescribed maximum working hours for children. Seven more states passed curbs on child labor in the 1890s. Indeed, by the end of the century most industrialized nations had restricted child labor. Despite these state acts and the broader movement, however, the American child labor force continued to grow and the movement faltered.

Child labor reform was stymied in part because it generated intense opposition, particularly in the South, where textile mills relied on child workers. Opponents included not only factory owners who sought cheap workers, but also, as historian Hugh Cunningham reports, "Catholic priests who defended child labor on the grounds of the income that it brought to poor immigrant families, farmers who wanted the seasonal labor of children, and working people who resented intrusion by the government into their family work traditions" (Cunningham 1995, 178). Child labor reform thus exposed yet again the clashing interests and ideals of working-class families and child savers as well as the obstacles that federalism posed for uniform national welfare policies. For many working-class families, survival dictated shared contributions and the subordination of individual mobility to the family's collective welfare and advancement. Reformers, imbued with the ideal of the sacred child, responded to such practices by declaring that selfish parents exaggerated their dependence on their children's wages and overlooked the gruesome working conditions, stunted health, and abbreviated education that afflicted young workers (figure 1.6). Significantly, they did not combine "their early campaigns against child labor with an attempt to raise the real wages of adult workers, improve occupational health and safety, or otherwise remove the conditions that made children's wages a critical part of so many family economies" (Katz 1986, 132). In addition, loopholes in the initial laws and lack of effective enforcement undermined the campaign, as did the continued conviction that children should learn good work habits as early as practicable.

These obstacles led child labor reformers to initiate a national campaign. In 1904 they formed the National Child Labor Committee to direct the effort. The first national child welfare organization, the committee championed both state and federal legislation banning work by children twelve and under. Twice the committee succeeded in securing federal restrictions; yet both times the United States Supreme Court declared the acts unconstitutional, and a proposed constitutional amendment failed as well. Nevertheless, by 1920 every state had enacted some form of child labor regulation. Thus the committee only managed such piecemeal state reforms until the Great Depression and New Deal, when child labor restrictions were included in the Fair Labor Standards Act of 1938. The act prohibited employment of children under sixteen in industries engaged in interstate commerce and of those under eighteen in dangerous occupations. It passed constitutional muster in 1941. Even so, the number of child workers declined steadily through the first third of the twentieth century. New attitudes about children working combined with the compulsory school laws and changes in the workplace itself served to take more and more children out of productive labor and thus protect their welfare by extending their childhoods.

Changing sentiments about children and welfare led to an even more dramatic innovation with the rise of the mothers' pensions movement. The idea of preventing the breakup of homes by providing aid to worthy but poor mothers gained momentum in the first two decades of the twentieth century. A growing commitment to family preservation and equally powerful opposition to institutionalizing children fueled the effort. The report of the 1909 White House Conference on Dependent Children proclaimed, "Home life is the highest and finest product of civilization," and "children should not be deprived of it except for urgent and compelling reasons" (cited in Bremner 1971, 2: 358, 365). Unlike those in the previous era, reformers now argued that maternal poverty should never be considered such a reason. Yet, as the child savers' empirical studies documented, each year thousands of children were taken from their impoverished mothers and placed in institutions or foster families. Thousands of others were left unsupervised because of the long hours their mothers worked.

Mothers' pensions, direct stipends from the state, seemed the logical solution and became yet another child welfare reform. The pensions were justified as a means of keeping families together and as preventive measures that would cure juvenile delinquency and child dependency by keeping mothers home caring for their children. Supporters argued that changes in the family and the economic system necessitated this kind of direct government intervention. A family's survival required a steady income, yet unemployment, illness, and death of the family breadwinner meant that many mothers could not always support themselves and their offspring. They needed financial support to keep their children. Public funds would thus be used to reinforce women's maternal role. Proponents relied on the popular faith in mother-child bonds for success and support. They also argued that pensions would be less costly than institutionalizing children, though such promises meant that individual aid would be meager.

As opponents and supporters alike recognized, mothers' pensions represented another attempt at enlarging the role of the state in child welfare. The most vocal opposition came from charity organization officials and the leaders of eastern philanthropic organizations who feared pensions would be an entering wedge in the transformation of charity into public entitlements. They worried that the pensions would overturn the lingering nineteenth-century resistance to direct public aid to the poor, or outdoor relief. Instead they argued that public authorities should continue to maintain public institutions, or indoor relief, for the poor, while private agencies provided home or outdoor relief. But their arguments were to no avail. Missouri and Illinois passed the first mothers' pension legislation in 1911, and other states quickly followed. By the end of 1913, twenty states, mainly western and central, had authorized them; by 1919 the number had risen to thirty-nine along with the territories of Alaska and Hawaii. By 1931, two hundred thousand children in every state except Georgia and South Carolina lived in homes supported in part by the pensions.

All of the state pension programs were limited and restricted in ways that demonstrate continued popular uneasiness with outdoor relief as a form of child welfare, despite the new belief in family preservation. The stipends themselves were small and inadequate, and many of the laws included requirements that mothers work. Pensions were granted only to a fraction of the possible recipients—mostly to widows, who were deemed the worthiest of the worthy poor. Restrictions included strict behavioral standards, long residence, sometimes citizenship, and proof of utter destitution. The statutes also contained "suitable home" provisions; that is, they applied only to needy women who, in the opinion of the authorities, were fit or worthy parents, which generally meant widows or the wives of disabled or deserting men, though a few states included unmarried mothers (Goodwin 1997). They subjected women and children to new forms of surveillance and new levels of bureaucratic discretion and abuse. The pension plans also depended on the growing regulatory power of the juvenile court over indigent families because the courts were often given the power to administer the programs. Nevertheless, the pensions clearly helped some families stay together by providing a steady if meager income. Equally important, as Katz explains and opponents feared, "Mothers' pensions were a small, halting, but consequential step away from charity and toward entitlement. They were the precedent for the Aid to Dependent Children title of the 1935 Economic Security Act, which in turn, in a completely unanticipated way, became the foundation of the federal government's only mass program of public assistance, AFDC" (Katz 1986, 129).

Child welfare also expanded in the era through the establishment of new levels of public responsibility to children. Prime among the changes was a rising standard of public responsibility for children's health. More clearly than ever before, physical well-being became a claim American children and their parents could make on their society. And the notion of protecting children's health itself became an expansive idea that revealed both the breadth and some of the limits of industrial-era child welfare.

Infant mortality was the most galvanizing issue. Shocking stories and statistics propelled parents and child savers into action. At the turn of the century, the child death rate was approximately 135 per 1,000 in the poorest sections of larger cities. The young succumbed because of limited scientific knowledge about the causes of disease, malnourishment, polluted water, contaminated milk, and primitive sanitation. An international movement of infant welfare advocates argued that the good health of babies was a public concern. Accusations of ignorance and indifference were lodged against mothers. Education and assistance were championed as the remedies. The Children's Bureau took the lead in promoting breastfeeding and campaigns to teach mothers or potential mothers lessons in hygiene and in child care. A number of cities developed programs that sold pasteurized, Grade-A milk to mothers at below market price; taught mothers about hygiene, child care, and nutrition; referred sick children to the right medical services and poor parents to the appropriate charity or welfare agency; and sent municipal public health nurses to homes of expectant mothers before and after childbirth. These and kindred public health measures had dramatic results. The incidence of smallpox, diphtheria, and tuberculosis fell significantly, as did infant and early childhood mortality rates; children's life expectancy rates rose.

Buoyed by these achievements and the successful drive for mothers' pensions, child savers decided to change the way health care was delivered to children. Aided by the Children's Bureau, reformers pushed the Sheppard-Towner Act through Congress in 1921. The first use of federal funds to promote children's health, the act authorized matching grants to the states to fund information and instruction on nutrition and hygiene, prenatal and child-health clinics, and visiting nurses for pregnant women and new mothers. Prevention was its prime policy. Equally important, the Sheppard-Towner Act directly challenged the role and power of physicians, overwhelmingly male, in the nation's health care system.

The act proved very successful. Between 1921 and 1929, nearly three thousand child and maternal health centers were established in forty-five states, chiefly in rural areas. In addition, it strengthened state health departments and helped foster the development of county health units, which led to the better administration of local services. Most important, the nation's infant and maternal mortality rates dropped significantly during these years. However, success did not blunt the opposition. Opponents, led by the American Medical Association, attacked the clinics as socialized medicine and insinuated that they represented an inferior form of health care. Typical of the attacks was a pamphlet entitled *Shall the Children of America Become the Property of the State*, written and circulated by the Legislative Committee of the Illinois State Medical Society. Intense lobbying and President Herbert Hoover's opposition to the clinics succeeded. Congress repealed the act in 1929. As Katz concludes, the Sheppard-Towner Act had "tested the limits of reform in America. Unlike vaccination, better nutrition, pasteurized milk, or improved sanitation, its potential invasion of physicians' prerogatives and incomes had violated the fictive boundaries between public and private. Its defeat illustrates once again the barriers to the extension of public responsibility where economic decisions remain officially private" (Katz 1986, 144). Yet, like so many reforms of the period, the act had an important legacy. As the first statute to provide federal grants-in-aid to the states for welfare programs other than education, it became a model for many of the cooperative federal-state programs established under the 1935 Social Security Act, particularly Title V, which authorized the Children's Bureau to administer federal grants-in-aid to the states for work in maternal and child health.

The failure to renew the Sheppard-Towner act not only suggests some of the limits of the new idea of health as a child welfare measure, it underscores the power of continuity in American child welfare policy. Important and significant changes occurred in the industrial era, but, as in every era, they were conditioned by the persistent power of established policies and practices.

Illegitimacy is an apt example of continuity in child welfare. The industrial-era obsession with protecting the family reinforced the continued use of law to separate legitimate from illegitimate children, even though investigations of the squalid cities of industrial America by muckrakers and urban social reformers reignited the issue. The widespread diffusion of postrevolutionary innovations that limited the possibility of becoming illegitimate and the burdens of those that did had not solved the problem. Instead, reformers uncovered shocking evidence of mistreatment of bastards, higher rates of infant mortality among the illegitimate than among the lawfully born, and a thriving market offering bastard children for sale and barter. They called for further aid for these unfortunates. Radical reformers even demanded that bastards be accorded the same legal rights as legitimate children. Reformers were fired by the now orthodox child welfare belief that there "may be illegitimate parents but there can be no illegitimate children" (U.S. Children's Bureau 1921, 7). However, little support existed in the era for expanding the rights and claims of bastards any further, and there was almost none for the call to abolish the status of bastardy itself.

Instead, the only major changes that occurred in the plight of illegitimates came through statutes that increased state supervision of bastards and their putative parents. The new acts mainly tightened the procedures governing the most traditional aspects of the law—paternity and support. The most significant development for the fate of many illegitimates was the gradual exertion of control over bastardy by social workers and welfare bureaucrats. Yet, as in so many areas of child welfare, social workers grappled with the problem of trying to preserve families while also trying to aid children. Tension between the two goals arose in conflicts over whether or not further aid to bastards would undermine legitimately established families. In a nation now terrified of unsettled homes, further reform was not possible. Instead, illegitimacy demonstrated the continued power of the dual system of family policy.

Limits emerged in other areas of child welfare as well. For example, despite the dominant anti-institutional sentiments of the day, countless children continued to be placed in reformatories, orphanages, and other public and private asylums. As historian Timothy A. Hacsi discovered, "From the Civil War to the Great Depression, more of America's dependent children—children whose families, including extended families, were for a time unable to care for them—were helped in orphan asylums than any other means" (Hacsi 1997, 1). Another continuing source of contention was the fact that many child-saving institutions were run by religious or other private groups. The propriety of public support for such facilities, though generally affirmed by the courts, was a persistent matter of controversy. Some conflicts were defused, though, by the policy initiated in New York in 1875 requiring that children be placed in institutions of the same faith as their parents. And large institutions continued to have defenders, notably representatives of Catholic asylums, who pointed out that many parents sent children to them during times of family hardship and crisis. They argued that placing such children in foster families would be cruel to both parents and offspring. Still the most that supporters of institutions would claim was that they were unavoidable; all children could not be placed with foster families since they had living parents to whom they should return when family circumstances changed, and many were ill, handicapped, or incorrigible and thus unwanted. The placement of children in all institutions was increasingly supervised by the newly created juvenile courts as part of their expanding power over disorderly and dependent children.

Disagreements about the legitimate role of the state in child welfare persisted as well, even though by the early 1930s the public's role in the care and protection of delinquent and dependent children had increased dramatically. Though modified, anti-statism retained its hold on the American republic. As Cravens notes, "The United States was the only nation in the industrialized world to create a national welfare state without a national bureaucracy to administer it. As Americans used the State—meaning any level of government, but especially the states and the federal government—increasingly in modern times to address social problems, it was always with an eye to keeping state bureaucracy and machinery on as parsimonious a level of functioning as possible" (Cravens 1993, 4). At the same time, arguments raged over rival state welfare systems. New Yorkers, who supported their state's now long-established tradition of public subsidies to private institutions, questioned the dominance of public agencies in other states. They and others in the northeast doubted that public institutions could ever avoid political corruption and mismanagement. But in the West and Midwest there was less skepticism of public child welfare and thus greater reliance on governmental programs. And in most states, Boards of State Charities were empowered to supervise all children's institutions, even those not funded by public monies. States' rights arguments buttressed and legitimated these positions. Persistent anti-statism and differences about the role of the state in child welfare resulted in continued disagreements over the legitimacy and importance of public and private action, despite the increased power of public authorities to regulate relations between parents and their children. Consequently, diversity in child welfare policies and experiences continued as well.

Child welfare reform in the industrial era thus modified without transforming an inherited tradition of dealing with delinquent and dependent children. Each alteration was premised on the assumption that childhood was a distinctive and vulnerable stage of life and that public regulation of childrearing had to be expanded. Most of the changes in the era challenged an earlier faith in unregulated parental supervision of children by circumscribing youthful social and legal independence and by attempting to mandate cultural homogeneity in the nation's homes. The changes thus also challenged the existing allocation of rights among parents, children, and the state. And each expressed the central assumption of the age—that childhood must be prolonged through adolescence by keeping the young in their families to gain more extensive preparation for their inevitable adult roles. Proclaimed as supports for the private family, the intent, if not the full result, of these changes was to strengthen the dependence of children on adults and to remove the young from the adult spheres of the marketplace and the civic community in the name of child welfare. As Ashby concludes, reformers of the era "responded to child dependency, neglect, and abuse in ways that were innovative and traditional: They introduced the modern welfare state but at the same time encountered resistance and retained long-familiar judgments about poverty, the working class, and race" (Ashby 1997, 79–80).

CONCLUSION

By the mid-1930s a second era in American child welfare had ended, and a new one had begun. As in the past, the new period would be marked by continued change and innovation, most notably an expanded role of the federal government in child welfare. However, the past continued to guide the present, because by the 1930s the United States had an established system of child welfare. Its fundamental features had been put in place during the first part of the nineteenth century, and significant modifications had been made in the first decades of the twentieth. Prominent among those features were a persistent aversion to state authority that spawned hybrid public/private organizations; policy differences and variations spawned by federalism, regionalism, and localism; chronic funding and management problems that undermined innovations; and links between policy and sentiments toward children and their families generated by changing social knowledge about the young. These had in turn produced an instrumental approach to child welfare policy that resulted in generational solutions to the problems posed by disorderly and dependent children and thus the creation over time of layers of child welfare practices and beliefs.

The history of child welfare in the United States thus demonstrates both the rhetorical power of child-centered appeals and the difficulties of translating those appeals into policy as fears for children and fears of children waxed and waned. Most fundamentally, that past reveals, as Bremner concludes, that "although many people believe that the needs of dependent children should be a primary concern of the state, there is no consensus on method or priority. Some people think that the way to help children is to help their families. Others believe both families and children will remain in a bad way until the gross injustices and inequities in society are eliminated. Still others assign the interests of children lower priority than such matters as increased outlays for weapons, tax relief, balancing the budget, reducing deficits, and shifting the balance of power from the federal government to state and local communities" (Bremner 1983, 97). As a result of disagreements over the place of children in American society, child welfare practices and beliefs helped rearrange and redefine the relationship among children, parents, the state, and civil society. By making their fellow citizens hear what industrial-era child reformer

John Spargo called "the bitter cry of the children," child welfare activists of all stripes not only influenced their time but the future. They institutionalized their solutions in statutes, judicial decisions, administrative policies, agencies, and organizations that lingered on long after their initial reforming zeal had dissipated. Those institutionalized solutions became an integral part of an emerging American welfare state.

Despite its contradictions and incoherence by the 1930s, child welfare had become the changing but persistent way of addressing the needs of disorderly and dependent American children. The juvenile court arose out of this tradition of American child welfare. Child welfare supplied critical roles for the court as well as many of its most fundamental policies and practices.

REFERENCES

Ashby, Leroy. 1997. *Endangered Children: Dependency, Neglect, and Abuse in American History.* New York: Twyne Publishers.

Billingsley, Andrew, and Jeanne M. Giovannoni. 1972. *Children of the Storm: Black Children and American Child Welfare.* New York: Harcourt Brace Jovanovich.

Bloomfield, Maxwell. 1976. *American Lawyers in a Changing Society, 1776–1876.* Cambridge, MA: Harvard University Press.

Brace, Charles Loring. 1872. *The Dangerous Classes of New York and Twenty Years Work Among Them.* New York: Wynkoop and Hallenbeck.

Bremner, Robert H. 1970–74. *Children and Youth in America.* 3 vols. Cambridge, MA: Harvard University Press.

———. 1983. "Other People's Children." *Journal of Social History* 16: 83–103.

Carlson, Alan. 1998. "The State's Assault on the Family." In *The Family, Civil Society, and the State,* ed. Christopher Wolfe, 39–49. Lantham, MD: Rowman & Littlefield.

Chambers, Clarke A. 1986. "Toward a Redefinition of Welfare History." *Journal of American History* 73: 407–33.

Costin, Lela B.; Howard Jacob Karger; and David Stoesz. 1996. *The Politics of Child Abuse in America.* New York: Oxford University Press.

Cravens, Hamilton. 1993. "Child Saving in Modern America, 1870s–1990s." In *Children at Risk in America: History, Concepts, and Public Policy,* ed. Roberta Wollons, 3–31. Albany: State University of New York Press.

Crenson, Matthew A. 1998. *Building the Invisible Orphanage: A Prehistory of the American Welfare System.* Cambridge, MA: Harvard University Press.

Cunningham, Hugh. 1995. *Children and Childhood in Western Society Since 1500.* New York: Longman Press.

Dewey, John. 1899. *The School and Society.* Chicago: University of Chicago Press.

Felt, Jeremy. 1965. *Hostages of Fortune: Child Labor Reform in New York State.* Syracuse, NY: Syracuse University Press.

Gerry, Elbridge. 1882. "The Relation of Societies for the Prevention of Cruelty to Children to Child Saving Work." *Proceedings of the National Conference of Charities and Corrections* 9: 129.

Gittens, Joan. 1994. *Poor Relations: The Children of the State in Illinois, 1818–1990.* Urbana and Chicago: University of Illinois Press.

Goodwin, Joanne L. *Gender and the Politics of Welfare Reform: Mothers' Pensions in Chicago, 1911–1929.* Chicago: University of Chicago Press, 1997.

Gordon, Linda. 1987. "Family Violence in History and Politics." *Radical America* 5: 27–35.

———. 1988. *Heroes of Their Own Lives: The Politics and History of Family Violence in Boston, 1880–1960.* New York: Penguin Press.

Grossberg, Michael. 1985a. "Crossing Boundaries: Nineteenth-Century Domestic Relations Law and the Merger of Family and Legal History." *American Bar Foundation Research Journal* 799–847.

———. 1985b. *Governing the Hearth: Law and the Family in Nineteenth-Century America.* Chapel Hill: University of North Carolina Press.

———. 1993. "Children's Legal Rights? A Historical Look at a Legal Paradox." In *Children at Risk in America: History, Concepts, and Public Policy,* ed. Roberta Wollons, 11–40. Albany: State University of New York Press.

———. 1996. "Teaching the Republican Child: Three Antebellum Stories about Law, Schooling, and the Construction of American Families." *Utah Law Review* 429–60.

Hacsi, Timothy A. 1997. *Second Home: Orphan Asylums and Poor Families in America.* Cambridge, MA: Harvard University Press.

Halloran, Peter C. 1994. *Boston's Wayward Children: Social Services for Homeless Children, 1830–1930.* Boston: Northeastern University Press.

Hawes, Joseph M. 1991. *The Children's Rights Movement: A History of Advocacy and Protection.* Boston: Twayne Press.

Holt, Marilyn Irvin. 1992. *The Orphan Train: Placing Out in America.* Lincoln: University of Nebraska Press.

Katz, Michael B. 1986. *In the Shadow of the Poorhouse: A Social History of Welfare in America.* New York: Basic Books.

Koven, Seth, and Sonya Michel, eds. 1993. *Mothers of a New World: Maternalist Politics and the Origins of Welfare States.* New York: Routledge Press.

Kramnick, Isaac. 1990. *Republicanism and Bourgeois Radicalism: Political Ideology in Late-Eighteenth-Century England and America.* Ithaca, NY: Cornell University Press.

Ladd-Taylor, Molly. 1994. *Mother-Work: Women, Child Welfare, and the State, 1890–1930.* Urbana and Chicago: University of Illinois Press.

McCarthy, Kathleen D. 1982. *Noblesse Oblige: Charity and Cultural Philanthropy in Chicago, 1849–1929.* Chicago: University of Chicago Press.

Meckel, Richard A. 1990. *Save the Babies: American Public Health Reform and the Prevention of Infant Mortality, 1850–1929.* Baltimore: Johns Hopkins University Press.

Mink, Gwendolyn. 1995. *The Wages of Motherhood: Inequality in the Welfare State, 1917–1942.* Ithaca, NY: Cornell University Press, 1995.

Nasaw, David. 1985. *Children of the City at Work and at Play.* Garden City, NY: Anchor Press/Doubleday.

Odem, Mary E. 1995. *Delinquent Daughters: Protecting and Policing Adolescent Female Sexuality in the United States, 1885–1920.* Chapel Hill: University of North Carolina Press.

Pleck, Elizabeth. 1987. *Domestic Tyranny: The Making of Social Policy Against Family Violence from Colonial Times to the Present.* New York: Oxford University Press.

Polsky, Andrew. 1991. *The Rise of the Therapeutic State*. Princeton, NJ: Princeton University Press.

Rothman, David. 1971. *The Discovery of the Asylum: Social Order and Disorder in the New Republic*. Boston: Little, Brown.

Schultz, Stanley. 1973. *The Culture Factory: Boston Public Schools, 1789–1860*. New York: Oxford University Press.

Skocpol, Theda. 1992. *Protecting Soldiers and Mothers: The Political Origins of Social Policy in the United States*. Cambridge, MA: Harvard University Press.

Stearns, Peter. 1982. "History and Policy Analysis: Toward Maturity." *Public Historian* 4: 14.

Ten Broek, Jacobus. 1974. *Family Law and the Poor: Essays by Jacobus Ten Broek*. Ed. Joel Handler. Westport, CT: Greenwood Press.

Tiffin, Susan. 1982. *In Whose Best Interest? Child Welfare Reform in the Progressive Era*. Westport, CT: Greenwood Press.

Trattner, Walter I. 1970. *Crusade for Children: A History of the National Child Labor Committee and Child Labor Reform in America*. Chicago: University of Chicago Press.

———. 1974. *From Poor Law to Welfare State: A History of Social Welfare in America*. New York: Free Press.

U.S. Children's Bureau. 1921. *Standards of Legal Protection for Children Born Out of Wedlock*. Publication no. 77. Washington, DC: Government Printing Office.

Zelizer, Viviana A. 1985. *Pricing the Priceless Child: The Changing Social Value of Children*. New York: Basic Books.

2 The Evolution of Juvenile Courts in the Early Twentieth Century: Beyond the Myth of Immaculate Construction

David S. Tanenhaus

The world's first juvenile court law was enacted during a tense centennial moment. The Illinois General Assembly had waited until April 14, 1899, the last day of the last legislative session of the nineteenth century, to approve "An Act for the Treatment and Control of Dependent, Neglected and Delinquent Children." The law, when it went into effect on July 1, 1899, established the Cook County Juvenile Court (more generally known as the Chicago Juvenile Court). Led by the visionary philanthropist Lucy Flower and her friend Julia Lathrop, a child-welfare expert who later became the first Chief of the United States Children's Bureau in 1912, the moral crusaders for juvenile justice could now breathe a temporary sigh of relief. After a decade of concerted work, they had finally succeeded in writing their ideals about childhood innocence and public responsibility into law. In Chicago, the nation's second largest and fastest growing city, the cases of dependent and neglected children as well as ones accused of committing crimes could now be heard in a separate children's court. A sympathetic judge could now use his discretion to apply individualized treatments to rehabilitate children, instead of punishing them. Yet, as Flower and Lathrop understood perfectly well, especially after the long struggle to pass the legislation, their efforts to secure justice for the child had only begun.

Illinois's pioneering juvenile court act read like a rough blueprint. Most of the features that later became the hallmarks of progressive juvenile justice—private hearings, confidential records, the complaint system, detention homes, and probation officers—were either omitted entirely from the initial law or were included without any provisions for public funding (Bradwell

1899). As a result, the world's first juvenile court opened on July 3, 1899, with an open hearing, a public record, no means to control its calendar (i.e., no complaint system), and without public funds to pay either the salaries of probation officers or to maintain a detention home for children. It would, in fact, take more than eight years before the completion of the city's first juvenile court building, which would be located across from the famous social settlement, Hull House, on the city's Near West Side. Thus, the Chicago Juvenile Court had a rather inchoate beginning.

The juvenile court had such a tentative start partly because its invention raised fundamental questions about the role of legal institutions in the increasingly interdependent modern world of the early twentieth century. In Europe and America, progressive reformers had begun to question classical legal conceptions about the rule of law, free will, and the benefits of limited state intervention into social relations. The progressive efforts to extend the reach of the state into the everyday lives of predominantly working-class urban dwellers raised troubling questions about what the proper relationship of new institutions, such as the juvenile court, to "the public" should be. The inventors of the juvenile court designed this "new piece of social machinery" not only to remove children from the harsh criminal justice system, but also to shield them from stigmatizing publicity. In the juvenile court, its inventors envisioned, hearings would be closed to spectators and the press, a juvenile's record would remain confidential, and no private lawyers or juries would be part of the legal process. This vision of the juvenile court as a sheltered place to protect a child, especially during the storms of adolescence, would eventually become law in most states.

The process of making the juvenile court into a sheltered place, however, took many years (in some states, decades) to complete. The length of this construction process, which due to American federalism varied from state to state, is significant for two reasons. First, it challenges the common assumption that the history of juvenile justice has been a relatively simple story of decline, beginning with the juvenile court as a social welfare institution at the turn of the twentieth century and ending up as a quasi-criminal court by century's end. Instead, this chapter demonstrates that the juvenile court has been a work in progress and that many of the "defining features" of progressive juvenile justice—private hearings, confidential records, the complaint system, detention homes, and probation officers—were additions. Accordingly, scholars must be careful not to describe early juvenile courts in anachronistic terms that obscure how the actual process of state building played out in the early twentieth century. We need to know more about when and how in various states and in other nations these "defining features" became standard practices. Juvenile courts, including Chicago's model court, were not immaculate constructions; they were built over time.

Fig. 2.1 Juvenile Court in Session. From Cook County Charity Service Report, Fiscal Year 1905. Courtesy of The University of Chicago Libraries.

Second, the initial failure in Illinois to close juvenile hearings to spectators and members of the press allowed for the first juvenile courts to become much more public spaces than their progressive inventors would have liked (figure 2.1). The inaugural generation of juvenile court administrators struggled with the problem of how to shield the children in court from publicity while also desiring to publicize their plight in order to raise public consciousness and further the progressive crusade for social justice. Supporters of the court, including the presiding judges, adapted to the public nature of the early cases by using the free publicity to explain the rehabilitative mission of the court and helping to make the case for its benefits to the public. These efforts to educate the public about the court were critical to legitimizing the new institution. To help secure and sustain the legitimacy of the juvenile court, the early judges and staff delivered many public lectures, participated in child welfare exhibitions and, in the process, helped to spread the word about the benefits of the so-called new piece of social machinery.

This chapter posits that the "idea" of a juvenile court was a historical phenomenon that crystallized a number of nineteenth-century trends in child welfare and corrections, but it also contends that twentieth-century juvenile courts had diverse and dynamic histories worth knowing. The fact that juvenile courts have always been statutory creations, which state legislatures can alter at will, has contributed to many differences among these courts. The most fundamental difference has been whether courts used chancery proceedings, the Chicago model of informal hearings, or continued to remain part of the criminal justice system, retaining most of the features of criminal procedure, as New York courts did until the 1930s. In addition, the emphasis on informal procedures in courts using chancery proceedings also accounted for the adoption of very different procedures by individual courts. By 1925, however, every state except Maine and Wyoming at least had a juvenile court law, and juvenile courts were operating in all American cities with more than one hundred thousand people (Lenroot and Lundberg [1925] 1975, 1). Efforts to extend juvenile justice into the countryside began in the early twentieth century, but remained a troubling problem for most of the century. Since urban juvenile courts were built and then retrofitted over the course of the early twentieth century, these years offer especially promising sites for investigations into how earlier generations adjusted juvenile justice to meet pressing new conditions and concerns about the place of children and youth in American society.

The chapter focuses primarily on the Chicago experience for two reasons. First, the Chicago Juvenile Court since its creation has been closely studied by social scientists, and it is thus the most richly documented juvenile justice system from the early twentieth century. Second, the history of the Chicago court was typical of the development of these specialized courts based upon the chancery model in other large cities during this period. Thus, the Chicago experience is useful for making larger generalizations about the evolution of modern juvenile justice in its formative years.

By examining the roots of American juvenile justice, the first section of the chapter explains how the inventors of the juvenile court understood their own place in history. They believed that the removal of children from the criminal justice system would be one of their generation's major contributions to the ongoing historical process of improving the status of children in American society. The second section provides an overview of the early-twentieth-century process of retrofitting juvenile courts. This section also traces one child's path through the juvenile justice system and pays special attention to the attempts to make the juvenile court into a sanctuary for children. A brief analysis of juvenile courts' oversight of the nation's first welfare programs—state disbursements to single mothers to raise their dependent children at home—rounds out the analysis of the operations of juvenile justice in this formative era. The final section examines the rise of psychological and psychiatric approaches to the prevention of juvenile delinquency, which initially caused a crisis of confidence in juvenile courts by questioning their effectiveness but ultimately contributed (by the early 1920s) to a consensus among experts about procedural matters that served as the programmatic capstone for progressive juvenile justice.

TOWARD THE JUVENILE COURT

The inventors of the juvenile court considered themselves part of a humanitarian movement which, in the nineteenth century, had transformed the status of children from the sole property of their fathers into a dependent class in need of state protection. In the early 1880s, Florence Kelley, an undergraduate at Cornell University, explored in her senior thesis the causes and effects of this changing status of children. Kelley, like Julia Lathrop, later became one of the most distinguished graduates of the first generation of college-educated women in American history, a resident of Jane Addams's Hull House, and an internationally known child welfare expert. In her thesis, Kelley explained that the present century had witnessed "an ever-increasing recognition of the child's welfare as a direct object of legislation, apart from the family relation; and herein lies the cardinal distinction between the status of the child to-day and its status under Blackstone" (Kelley 1882, 84). The child, she declared, was becoming an individual in the eyes of the law, and every new piece of legislation aimed at protecting children without regard to their families made "the child more and more nearly the ward of the State" (Kelley 1882, 96). This development, she concluded, struck a blow at the entire concept of the legal family and its patriarchal foundations. Accordingly, Kelley and the reformers of her day believed that they had the legal opening as well as the social responsibility to carry this historical trend of improving child welfare forward.

By the early 1890s, reformers could point to two major advances in nineteenth-century corrections that complemented the changing legal status of the child: the reform school movement, which began with the building of Houses of Refuge in the mid-1820s; and the development of a juvenile probation system in Massachusetts during the Civil War. As scholars of juvenile justice have long noted, Jacksonian reformers through the construction of Houses of Refuge, which were often nothing more "than a mini-prison for children," introduced many of the legal innovations which progressive reformers would later draw upon to build the juvenile court (Schlossman 1995, 334; Schlossman 1977). These innovations, as the law professor Barry Feld has recently summarized, included "a formal age-based distinction between juvenile and adult offenders and their institutional separation, the use of indeterminate commitments, and a broadened legal authority that encompassed both criminal offenders and neglected and incorrigible children" (Feld 1999, 51). Progressive reformers, though often critical of the institutionalization of children, did credit these earlier reformers for at least firmly establishing the principle that the state had a responsibility toward its children (*parens patriae*) and its corollary that youthful offenders should be housed separately from adult criminals.

The Massachusetts juvenile probation system, which by 1891 required criminal courts to appoint probation officers in juvenile cases, turned out to be even more inspirational for the inventors of the juvenile court. The use of probation in juvenile cases in Massachusetts had begun unofficially during the Civil War, when the police court in Boston released delinquent boys to Rufus Cook, an agent of the Children's Aid Society and Suffolk County Jail chaplain, to place in suitable homes (Schneider 1992, 58). This system of probation and placement proved so successful that the state passed legislation in 1869 that enabled its Board of State Charities to place children in foster homes, and then in 1891 Massachusetts passed the law that required all criminal courts to employ probation officers (Abbott 1938, 2: 330).

In 1888, Lucy Flower, whom the social settlement leader Graham Taylor christened "the mother of the juvenile court," had first called for the creation of a "parental court" to hear the cases of dependent, neglected, and delinquent children under sixteen years of age (Taylor 1930, 450). Flower, a Bostonian by birth, had been orphaned and then adopted by a respectable eastern family in the 1830s. She later taught school in Wisconsin to support herself until she married a prominent Madison attorney, James Monroe Flower, and moved with him to Chicago in 1873, two years after the Great Fire. While her husband established himself in the legal community, she turned her attentions to philanthropy and served on the Board of Trustees of the Chicago Home for the Friendless and the Half-Orphan Asylum. Once enmeshed in the city's culture of Protestant charities, including serving as the president of the influential Chicago Women's Club in 1890–91, Flower learned about the dismal conditions for poor children in Chicago and forged important friendships, including one with Julia Lathrop (figures 2.2 and 2.3).

The friendship of Flower and Lathrop symbolized the converging of two important female reform traditions and set the stage for close ties between Chicago's philanthropists and the emerging juvenile justice system. Flower was a member of the generation of philanthropists that the historian Kathleen McCarthy has called the "Gilded Age patrons" (McCarthy 1982, 46). They were society women who generously supported the building of the city's charitable institutions like the orphan asylums on whose boards Flower served. Lathrop, on the other hand, was twenty years younger than Flower and, as a graduate of Vassar College, belonged to the first generation of college-educated women in American history. Although she was certainly comfortable rubbing shoulders with Chicago's elite, Lathrop made her home at Hull House. Lathrop opted for social work as a full-time career, not the more traditional combination of marriage, homemaking, and part-time benevolent work. This powerful union of a philanthropist and a child welfare expert not only made the crusade for a children's court viable, but it also established the

Fig. 2.2 Julia Clifford Lathrop (1858–1932) helped found the country's first juvenile court in 1899. © CORBIS.

close relationship between the city's elite and the juvenile justice system that would last well into the twentieth century. Without the support of the city's philanthropic community, the juvenile court, especially in its early years, would have had difficulties operating.

In 1890, the possibility of establishing a children's court in Chicago seemed remote, although a proposed bill introduced to the Illinois General Assembly the next year at least suggested that Catholic and Protestant child savers would be willing to work together. Timothy D. Hurley, the president of the (Catholic) Chicago Visitation and Aid Society, who would later serve as the first chief probation officer of the juvenile court, drafted the bill that would have given county courts the power to commit dependent children to any nonprofit, child welfare agency incorporated under Illinois law. Flower supported the bill because it would give judges more discretion in handling dependency cases; under the existing laws, they had few options in these cases and could only commit children to a limited number of training or industrial schools. Moreover, no public funds were available to support dependent children placed in noninstitutional settings, such as a relative's home. The proposed bill, however, did not become law. This failure taught Flower that she would have to build a broad coalition of organizations to sponsor future child welfare legislation.

The election of the reform-minded Democrat John P. Altgeld to the

Fig. 2.3 Lucy Flower. Courtesy of The Chicago Historical Society.

governorship the next year opened up new possibilities for building this coalition. In one of his first official acts, Governor Altgeld appointed Julia Lathrop to serve on the State Board of Charities. Lathrop, who was the first woman to serve on the board, visited all the jails and poorhouses in Illinois's 102 counties and worked to develop important political connections across the state. In the process, she established her national reputation as a child welfare expert. At the same time that Lathrop was making a name for herself as a state commissioner, Flower worked to ensure that women's organizations would sponsor future legislation for the establishment of a children's court. She helped to found the Every Day Club, whose membership comprised about forty civic-minded society and professional women. They met over lunch and invited specialists to join to them to discuss their work. Flower would use this club as forum with which to spread the idea of a children's court, and in January 1899 the draft of a proposed bill prepared by a Chicago Bar Association committee was presented to the city's judges for their consideration and comments at one of these luncheons.

Meanwhile, Flower and Lathrop worked to ensure that the proposed bill for a children's court would be a legislative priority in 1899. Their efforts paid off when "The Children of the State" was announced as the theme for the Third Annual Illinois Conference on Charities scheduled for November

1898. The two-day conference, held at the Eastern Hospital for the Insane in Kankakee, helped to galvanize support for the creation of a juvenile court. Frederick H. Wines, the aged secretary of the State Board of Charities, who had served on the board since its inception in 1870, laid out the vision for the court: "What we should have, in our system of criminal justice, is an entirely separate system of courts for children, in large cities, who commit offenses which could be criminal in adults. We ought to have a 'children's court' in Chicago, and we ought to have a 'children's judge,' who should attend to no other business" (Wines 1899, 336). Wines called for the adoption of special procedures for the court modeled after East Coast innovations, such as the separate detention of children and the Massachusetts system of juvenile probation (Wines 1899).

Flower's vision of a "parental court" for Chicago became an institutional reality on July 1, 1899, when the new law, the world's first juvenile court legislation, went into effect. She helped to raise the funds necessary for the new court to begin its pioneering work and proposed that the Chicago Woman's Club establish a separate organization to be known as the Juvenile Court Committee (JCC), which would run a detention home and pay the salaries of fifteen probation officers. Her friend Julia Lathrop became the JCC's first president in 1903. Flower stayed involved with the court's operations until 1902, when her husband fell ill and the Flowers moved to California. As her daughter later wrote, "There she cheerfully lived for the rest of her life far from the home she was used to, the friends that she loved, the life that stimulated her, and the interests that had so long been peculiarly her own" (Farwell 1924, 39). Flower's retirement from child saving symbolized the passing of her generation of Gilded Age patrons from the political scene. It would be up to Julia Lathrop and her fellow progressives to give form and substance to the idea of a juvenile court.

RETROFITTING THE JUVENILE COURT

As noted in the chapter's introduction, the Chicago Juvenile Court had a rather formless beginning. There was no public funding for probation officers, for a detention home for children, or for a physical structure to house the new court. To explain how the Chicago court actually operated in its formative era, this section explores the process by which the court's earliest distinguishing features—detention, probation, and the complaint system—were added on and suggests how widespread these practices had become in other urban courts by the mid-1920s. It then examines the controversial attempts to close juvenile hearings in an effort to make juvenile courts across the nation into sheltered spaces for children and their families. The section concludes with a brief analysis of the administration of mothers' pensions, the precursor to Aid to Dependent Children (later Aid to Families with Dependent Children). That juvenile courts administered welfare programs aimed at family preservation reminds us that juvenile justice was broadly conceived to handle the cases of both dependent and delinquent children and their families.

The Problem of Detention

Since no public monies were available to establish a detention home for the Chicago Juvenile Court, the JCC managed one located at 625 W. Adams Street, more than two miles from the County Building in downtown Chicago, where the court held its first sessions. Years later, Emily Washburn Dean, the secretary of the JCC, recalled how frustrating this early work could be (Dean 1931). Cook County had donated an old omnibus and two horses to the JCC to transport the children to the twice-weekly sessions of the court (the court would not hear cases five days a week until 1907). The bus, however, began to fall apart, and the driver grew concerned about the safety of the children. The county officials told Dean that this was a city matter and that she should see the chief of police. He, in turn, referred her to the city's construction department, which referred her to the mayor. The mayor then told her it was, after all, a county matter. After six weeks of going around in circles, the JCC finally decided to buy the new bus itself.

The bus, however, turned out to be too heavy for the association's small horse. The JCC was, after much effort, able to get a bigger horse from the city, which had belonged to the fire department and was now retired. "His legs," according to Dean, "were so long and he traveled so fast that he nearly dragged the small horse to an untimely end." Apparently, he would also gallop at the sound of the fire alarm to the nearest blaze. The JCC, once again, spent its own money to buy two new horses and convinced the city to donate a barn for their use. Fittingly, Dean noted, "The stalls proved to be so small that the horses could not lie down day or night, so finding that there was nothing else to do the Committee rented a barn and the feed!" (Dean 1931, 2).

Anecdotes like Dean's remind us how haphazard the administration of juvenile justice was during these early years and also reveal what a critical role the JCC played in keeping it going. But how did the JCC manage to raise the necessary funds to pay the salaries of probation officers, buy horses and omnibuses, and rent barns? In part, philanthropists like Mrs. Louise de Koven Bowen made large donations. Bowen was the granddaughter of Edward Hiram Hadduck, who had made his vast fortune through investing in the land that became the heart of Chicago's Loop. At the urging of Lathrop, the well-connected Bowen assumed the presidency of the JCC to help the association raise money.

Fig. 2.4 Juvenile court, built in 1907. Courtesy of The University of Illinois at Chicago: Jane Addams Memorial Collections.

Bowen would become the Lucy Flower of the twentieth century, a dedicated philanthropist who led the city's crusade for child welfare. Under Bowen's leadership, for example, the JCC sponsored cultural events to raise money, such as a Shakespeare Song Cycle performed at the Chicago Auditorium on February 3, 1904. The hosts of this gala read like a Who's Who of Chicago society, including Mrs. Marshall Field Jr., Mrs. Cyrus McCormick, Mrs. Potter Palmer, and Mrs. Julius Rosenwald. Such events not only raised revenue, but also helped to link the court in the public mind with the city's leading citizens.

A publicly funded detention home did eventually become part of the Chicago Juvenile Court and was located in the Juvenile Court Building that opened in August 1907, but other cities did not always follow Chicago's lead in retrofitting their courts (figure 2.4). In *Juvenile Courts at Work,* Katharine Lenroot and Emma Lundberg reported that in only six of the ten cities that they studied—Buffalo, Denver, Los Angeles, San Francisco, Seattle, and St. Louis—"a special detention home for children was maintained" (Lenroot and Lundberg [1925] 1975, 55). Boston, the District of Columbia, New Orleans, and Minneapolis did not have such facilities. They were also dismayed to discover that in eight of the ten cities that they investigated "detention of children in police stations or in jails was reported—in some as a rare occurrence and in others as a comparatively common practice" (Lenroot and Lundberg [1925] 1975, 55). The use of detention homes had become at least a fairly standard practice in urban courts by the Roaring Twenties, and, as chapter 3 demonstrates, juvenile courts used them in a host of ways over the course of the century.

The Problems of Probation

In Chicago, the JCC did not intend to fund the juvenile court indefinitely. It was a costly endeavor, and the association was having difficulty raising the necessary revenue. The members also believed that the court provided a vital public service and should be publicly financed. In addition, they imagined that public funding would help to make the court more attractive to gifted individuals who desired to embark upon long-term careers in juvenile justice. They realized that a professionally staffed and managed probation department was required to keep tabs on the behavior of the growing number of children in the system.

Influential members of the JCC like Julia Lathrop cautioned, however, that it would be risky to pay probation officers from public funds for fear these jobs might become objects of patronage. This tension between demanding public support for the juvenile court and yet desiring to retain control over its administration would lead to the creation of a hybrid system of juvenile justice, in which state power and private administration were often mixed together in a surprising fashion. The best example of this mixing of public responsibility with private administration was evident in the transformation of the probation department into a publicly supported branch of the court. The history of the development of the probation department would come to serve as a blueprint from which the progressives worked to retrofit the juvenile court.

Probation officers were the "right arm of the court" because they investigated homes; interviewed neighbors, teachers, and employers; made recommendations to the judge about what should be done with children; represented them during hearings; and supervised those on probation (Hurd 1905). The success of the juvenile court, its supporters argued, depended upon their training and effectiveness. In an often-quoted article, "Probation Work in Children's Courts," Judge Charles W. Heuisler of the Baltimore City court expressed why probation mattered: "No temporary veneer put upon the child by the most sympathetic judge, by reason of either counsel, suggestion, or threat, can be availing, if after the process the subject is sent back *alone,* and again into the same experiences because of which his trouble was occasioned." He added, "The voice of pity and compassion [i.e., the probation officer] must reach him in his home, and reach his parents also in his home" (Heuisler 1903, 400).

Scholars have described this entry by probation officers into the home as the beginning of a "therapeutic state," in which public officials work to "normalize" the social behavior of "deviants" (Polsky 1991). The child who got into trouble with the law, according to this interpretation, not only brought the state into his or her life, but also opened up the family home to state intervention and extended supervision. Thus, the entire family, not only the child, became the subject for extended case work, which could involve demands to change jobs, find a new residence, become a better housekeeper, prepare different meals, give up alcohol, and abstain from sex (Polsky 1991, 16). A refusal to follow these commands could result in a probation officer calling upon the power of the court to break up the disobedient family.

Yet as Julia Lathrop sadly noted, in Chicago heavy caseloads that averaged between 50 to 150 children per officer made it unrealistic to expect a probation officer "to exercise much more than the somewhat humorously designated 'official parenthood' over most members of such a brood" (Lathrop 1905, 346). In fact, due to heavy caseloads, some officers in Chicago and other large cities even met groups of children at settlement houses or libraries instead of visiting them in their homes.

In addition, juvenile courts in their use of probation explicitly drew the color line. Officers of one race as a general rule did not visit the homes of children of another race. From its inception, the Chicago Juvenile Court, for example, had assigned black children to the court's one black probation officer, and other courts followed this practice. The New Orleans Juvenile Court, for instance, placed all black children on "probation to volunteer officers of their own race, and their cases were rarely investigated" (Lenroot and Lundberg [1925] 1975, 162). Thus the state did not always show an interest in investigating all homes.

Although the limited number of probation officers certainly diluted the ability of the juvenile court to police the home, the authority to investigate homes did exist, and the progressives wanted to expand the probation department to take full advantage of this power. Lathrop, for example, proposed two solutions to the problem of inadequate probation. First, she called for Cook County to fund the officers. Second, to ensure that these positions did not become subject to patronage, she declared that the Civil Service Commission should administer a merit examination to all applicants. From the highest scores, the commission could then compile a list of the most qualified candidates, from which the juvenile court judge would pick his officers (Lathrop 1905). This approach to staffing promised to professionalize the court by hiring only those persons trained in the latest theories of social work.

The JCC drafted a bill to amend the Juvenile Court Act to allow for such a system to be put into place. In February 1905, Chester Church, a Republican representative from Chicago, introduced the JCC's bill, which was unanimously passed by both houses of the General Assembly and signed into law by Governor Charles S. Deneen, a staunch Republican who had made his reputation as the state's attorney for Cook County. According to the new law, the circuit court judges would inform the County Board of County Commissioners how many officers, including a chief probation officer, the juvenile court would require for the coming year. The commissioners would then determine whether the number was appropriate and what their salaries should be (*Laws of the State of Illinois* 1905).

Julian W. Mack, as the presiding judge of the juvenile court, was responsible for the implementation of this new law. Mack had graduated from Harvard Law School with honors and taught law at Northwestern University and the University of Chicago. Mack also wrote the classic law review article on the juvenile court, which laid out its theory and practice (Mack 1909–10). In addition, he taught courses on juvenile justice at the Chicago Institute of Social Science, an extension of the University of Chicago. These courses were intended to rear a crop of professionally trained probation officers to staff the court.

A citizens' committee developed the merit examination for probation officers, which tested spelling, arithmetic, and the applicant's understanding of the job, as well as his or her knowledge of the juvenile court Act. In addition, a series of sample cases forced the applicants to apply their knowledge to practical situations. Judge Mack ruled that all current probation officers would have to take the test, a decision that threatened to upset the delicate balance between Catholic and Protestant officers. Fortunately, all the officers scored highly enough on the examination for Mack to maintain the politically sensitive religious balance of the department.

Staffing the probation department, including determining who should direct it, also exposed ideological tensions among the founders about the court's mission. Although the founders all agreed that the court's primary purpose was to divert children from the harmful criminal justice system (what Franklin Zimring has labeled "the diversionary rationale"), they disagreed over the extent to which the juvenile court should intervene in the lives of children and their families (e.g., see chapter 5 in this volume for an analysis of the competing legal theories justifying a juvenile court). Judge Mack championed an interventionist approach, which envisioned that the juvenile court should be a social agency that could provide needed services and supervision to children and their families. This interventionist vision of the court worried Timothy Hurley, who was concerned that the female reformers of Hull House, such as Julia Lathrop and Jane Addams, who supported Mack, "had decided to capture the juvenile court in its entirety" (Hurley 1905b).

This tension between competing visions of juvenile justice was exposed when Henry Thurston, a professor of sociology at the Chicago Normal School, scored the highest mark on a separate examination given for the position of chief probation officer and was named to replace John McManaman, an Irish-Catholic lawyer who had been critical of the interventionist direction in which Judge Mack was taking the court. McManaman had raised concerns that "public officials [were] peeping into the home and attempting to establish a standard of living—a standard of conduct and morals—and then measuring all people by that standard" (McManaman 1905, 377). McManaman's replacement by Thurston, who had no legal training but had been working for the JCC, only confirmed growing suspicions among Catholic supporters of juvenile justice, including Timothy Hurley.

Although Hurley was critical of Mack, he sought only to discipline the juvenile court, not to destroy it. In 1905, for example, at the annual meeting of the National Conference of Charities and Corrections, Hurley had called for publicly appointed lawyers to represent children in juvenile courts and for the hearings to be more formal. Judge Mack also tried to appease the Catholic reformers. For instance, he appointed John McManaman to serve as an attorney for children brought before the juvenile court. Thus the growing mistrust in the Catholic reform community did not prevent reformers like Hurley from supporting additional amendments to the Juvenile Court Law passed in 1905 and 1907, which expanded its jurisdiction.

These amendments transformed *all* minors into potential wards of the court.[1] Now children found to be dependent, neglected, or delinquent would remain its wards until they reached the age of twenty-one or were discharged. This longer period of disciplinary control gave the court's probation officers an extended opportunity to work with children, including those who had been paroled from institutions.

Judge Mack and Chief Probation Officer Thurston were especially concerned about the behavior of children on parole and probation. Their concern grew out of the statistics kept by the court. Thurston discovered, for example, that close to 40 percent of the delinquent boys appearing before the juvenile court from 1904 to 1906 were recidivists (*Charity Service Reports* 1906, 115). Thurston believed that these children posed a threat to the legitimacy of the entire juvenile justice system because they openly flouted its authority, which diminished its power to persuade other young people to fly right. Thurston pointed out that every case of recidivism "tends to multiply itself many times among the associates of such delinquents." To prevent this from occurring, he urged that "boys and girls who persistently make no effort to improve under probation should quickly be put under such restraint that educational influences can get a chance at them" (*Charity Service Reports* 1906, 115). In other words, institutionalize them immediately.

The "persistent repeater," according to Thurston, also threatened to erode the support for the juvenile court among the public. He cautioned that "all right-minded people are willing to have boys and girls have chances to do the right thing, but after they persistently throw chances away, the same people have a right to insist that the young people be really controlled, even if it takes a criminal court process to do it" (*Charity Service Reports* 1907, 103). Thurston was well aware that the juvenile court at this juncture could not afford to lose public support. The court, he knew, was still an experiment and was not yet a permanent fixture of local governance. In an effort to convince Chicagoans of its worth, Thurston delivered seventy lectures in Cook County during 1905 about the virtues of the juvenile court.

The potential for the public to turn against the court for failing to solve "the boy problem" was a constant worry because the juvenile court had handled extremely difficult cases since its opening. In fact, nearly 40 percent of the children who appeared before the court during its first few months of operations in 1899 had already had encounters with the law. Many of these children had spent time in a training or industrial school and, in some instances, in the state reformatory at Pontiac. It would take more than a kindly touch on the arm by a friendly judge to help these children, whose delinquency was often indistinguishable from their dependency (Tanenhaus 1997, 1: 168).

A Boy in and out of Trouble

Edward Stark was a revealing example of a boy whose childhood experiences with the law began before the creation of the juvenile court and then continued into the twentieth century.[2] In 1897, when Edward was ten years old, a priest became worried about the boy's home, a site well known to the local authorities. The neighbors considered Edward's parents to be "habitual drunkards," and John Phelan, a district police officer, had arrested "some of the worst thieves Chicago ever knew out of their house." The father, an English Protestant, and the mother, an Irish Catholic, were having marital difficulties and paid little attention to Edward. In an attempt to save the neglected boy, the priest filed a dependent petition against him.

At a hearing in the Cook County Court, a six-member jury found Edward Stark to be a dependent child, and the judge committed him to St. Mary's Training School for Boys in Decatur, Illinois. Cook County then paid a monthly subsidy to the privately incorporated school, which Archbishop Patrick Feehan had founded in 1882. At "Feehanville," as the school was popularly known, Edward was slated to receive a good education and proper religious instruction. Edward, however, had different ideas about his upbringing and escaped. His freedom ended two years later when he was arrested in Chicago for stealing an expensive suit of clothes. On July 24, 1899, Edward, who was now thirteen years old, became the 108th child to appear before the juvenile court.

This snapshot from Edward Stark's life reveals that the connections between the boy's parents, priest, and police predated the creation of the juvenile court. The court, once established, relied upon these older social connections to conduct its business. John Phelan, for example, the police officer who had arrested "known thieves" in the Stark house in the mid-1890s, was now the probation officer for the Eleventh District. He no longer wore a uniform, carried a weapon, or wore a badge, and—much to the boy's chagrin—he became Edward's probation officer. Over the next few years, their lives would intersect on the many occasions when Edward would again get into trouble with the law.

Judge Tuthill committed Edward to Pontiac, where he spent eight months. While Edward was in the reformatory, his parents deserted him, and he was consequently paroled to live with a "reputable citizen" in his old neighborhood. It took the abandoned boy less than two months to end up in juvenile court again. This time he was arrested by a police officer for "keeping bad company." Edward had been in an alley at 3:30 A.M. with two other boys when the officer approached them. The boys all ran and only Edward was caught. This time Judge Tuthill committed him to the John Worthy School, where Edward would spend the next year of his life.

The cycle then began again. Edward was paroled to another foster family and four months later was again in court. This time he had been arrested for throwing stones at a man. Probation Officer Phelan in his report to Judge Tuthill noted that Edward "when arrested . . . gave the name of John Kain [and] also claimed that I did not known [*sic*] him." Familiarity made it nearly impossible for Edward, now fifteen years old, to use an alias to hide his checkered past.

The continuities revealed by Edward's case suggest that the significance of the juvenile court in its early years was its ability to centralize the preexisting system of policing children. Previously, a juvenile, just like an adult, could be brought before any one of the city's eleven police courts, but now when Edward was arrested, he entered a juvenile justice system that had a probation officer who knew him quite well. This made it more difficult for Edward to slip through the cracks, but this did not deter him from further mischief.

Edward did outgrow his delinquency. The turning point was his enrollment in the Junior Business Club. Over the next couple of years, the club found him employment in the navy and then helped him to get a job as a stockroom attendant for the Chicago Edison Company. What later became of Edward is not known, but he did, at least, survive a difficult adolescence and could be considered a success story for the new court.

Bureaucratizing Probation

After becoming chief probation officer in 1905, Henry Thurston applauded the efforts of the court's probation officers in handling cases like Edward's, especially their "missionary zeal," but after studying the department's administration, he announced that "the state of things was intolerable" (*Charity Service Reports* 1907, 115). The informal system, which had relied upon personal knowledge and cooperation among a small staff, no longer seemed adequate to keep track of the more than four thousand children on probation. A more sophisticated system, Thurston concluded, was required to prevent children from drifting through the system "without a record being made, except in the diaries of individual officers." Otherwise, it would be nearly impossible to determine how children "fared while they dwelt under the protection of the court and what happened to them afterwards" (*Charity Service Reports* 1907, 115).

Thurston wanted accurate records of each child's history in order to calculate the juvenile court's success rate. A standardized approach to record-keeping promised to yield the sociological data necessary to study the problem of juvenile delinquency more systematically, which would allow social scientists like himself to integrate the individual experiences of children like Edward Stark into a composite sketch of the delinquent child. This knowledge would, in turn, help to explain the causes of delinquency and ultimately produce a cure for waywardness.

Thurston's efforts to modernize the probation department were hampered by the Cook County commissioners, who would not provide him with the number of officers he requested, pay them a competitive salary, or even reimburse them for work-related expenses such as carfare. The result was heavy caseloads, an average of 120 children per officer, which discouraged talented individuals from becoming probation officers (*Charity Service Reports* 1907, 111). There maybe some truth to historian David Rothman's wry observation that "it is an odd but perhaps accurate conclusion to note that the dependent and deviant may owe what freedom they have more to the fiscal conservatism of elected officials than to the benevolent motives of reformers" (Rothman 1978, 81).

Chicago's overworked probation officers were not the exception to the national rule. Lenroot and Lundberg, for example, reported that "it is agreed that from fifty to seventy-five cases are all that one probation officer can handle effectively, but in only four of the [ten] courts studied was this standard generally observed. . . . In three courts it was more than one hundred" (Lenroot and Lunberg [1925] 1975, 171). Probation had certainly become a distinguishing feature of juvenile justice by the mid-1920s, but the majority of probation officers were generally underpaid and extremely overworked.

Installing the Complaint System

In addition to the problems associated with probation officers handling far too many cases, judges, such as Julian Mack, were also overwhelmed by their unwieldy calendars. In his first three years on the bench, Judge Mack had heard more than fourteen thousand cases and was convening semiweekly sessions, which often lasted late into the night. To gain control over his calendar, Mack needed to design a policy to prevent the cases that did not require his attention from coming to court. This change would not only free up his calendar for more serious cases, but it also would spare many children the unnecessary trauma and potential stigma of appearing before a judge.

The problem was that under the Juvenile Court Act the judge was required to hear *all* cases in which a petition had been filed. Mack had to find a method to limit petitioning, which was difficult because any "reputable person" who was a resident of Cook County could file a petition against any child within the county. The fact that family members, principals, neighbors, child welfare workers, and probation officers all filed petitions only complicated matters.

Mack devised an ingenious remedy: the complaint system. He requested that concerned individuals should make an informal complaint to the court's probation department instead of filing a formal petition against a child. This procedural change would allow the probation staff to investigate cases to determine whether they merited judicial attention. After an investigation, an officer could dismiss the complaint if it appeared groundless, attempt to resolve any minor problems independently, file a petition against the child if necessary, or charge the parents or guardians with contributing to the dependency or delinquency of a minor under a freshly minted state law. This policy gave the probation officers the discretion to determine which children should be brought to court. It also allowed these officers to use the threat of future legal action as a means to encourage cooperation with their commands.

The complaint system served as an effective technique for managing the court's caseload. In 1912, for example, the presiding Judge Merritt W. Pinckney estimated that only a quarter of the complaints received by the court led to petitions being filed (Breckinridge and Abbott 1912, 207). By the 1920s, the criminologists Clifford R. Shaw and Earl D. Myers discovered that police officers, assigned as probation officers for their precincts, were filing petitions in less than 10 percent of the cases that they handled (Shaw and Myers 1929). Thus only a small percentage of children who had contact with the juvenile justice system, including the police, actually ended up before a judge.

Other courts also adopted variations on the complaint system in the early twentieth century. Lenroot and Lundberg, for example, discovered that "the proportion of delinquency cases adjusted without formal court action varied from 43 percent to 86 percent in the four courts which utilized this method to any considerable extent and for which statistics were available" (Lenroot and Lundberg [1925] 1975, 114). Thus, by the mid-1920s, the complaint system, like detention and probation, had become a distinguishing feature of progressive juvenile justice.

Private Hearings and Public Concerns

Private hearings, the final distinguishing feature of progressive juvenile justice analyzed in this chapter, involved removing the general public from juvenile court hearings. The sponsors of the 1899 Illinois juvenile court legislation had wanted juvenile court hearings to be closed to spectators in order to protect the privacy of children and their families. The sponsors of the legislation believed that closed hearings would shield children from stigmatizing publicity and contribute to the court's mission of rehabilitation. Accordingly, the second provision of the juvenile court bill of 1899 had stated that "when a case is being heard, all persons not officers of the court or witnesses, and those having a direct interest in the case being heard, shall be excluded from the court room" (Hurley [1907] 1977, 28).

Critics of the city's private charity organizations, however, objected to the idea of closed hearings because they would envelop state action in secrecy. On the eve of the house hearings on the bill, the *Chicago Daily Inter-Ocean* ran a sensational front-page story with the lead "Child Slaves," which explained these concerns about secrecy ("Child Slaves" 1899). The article quoted anonymous sources, including "a prominent Representative," who declared that closed hearings in the juvenile court would only contribute to the enslaving of poor children by allowing charity organizations to remove them from their families and sell them as cheap laborers. The proposed juvenile court would allow charity associations to bring these poor children before the court, have them declared "dependent" by the court, and then sell the child to a downstate, out-of-state, or—worst of all—Canadian farmer.

As the "prominent Representative" cautioned, closed hearings would prevent the press from covering these cases and shield "the anguish of a mother whose child was being taken from her by the 'association'" from public scrutiny. Moreover, he warned, "Should this bill become law no child in the poorer sections of Chicago would be safe from the 'associations' interested in securing children. . . . The mother who permitted her little one to appear on the street not washed, curled, and combed to suit the critical inspection of an 'association' practicing philanthropy at $50 a head would be in danger of losing her child" ("Child Slaves" 1899).

The argument that private charity organizations stole poor children drew upon a reservoir of mistrust about private charity organizations dating to the mid-nineteenth century, which then was directed at the juvenile court. In New York, for example, similar accusations had been leveled at Charles Loring Brace's Children's Aid Society and its placing-out program of collecting street urchins and sending them to live in the Midwest. At the turn of the twentieth century, the charges of child slavery, or "traffic in children," reflected a new version of this older concern about separating children from their parents.

As a result of this campaign against closed hearings, the controversial provision was removed from the Illinois bill to secure its passage. Thus, juvenile court hearings in the Cook County Juvenile Court were open to the public. The local papers did, in fact, cover the new court's early cases and published stories about the children, including their names, addresses, and alleged offenses. Spectators also came to the court to see the most sensational cases.

In January of 1912, for example, the juvenile court was packed with spectators and reporters who came to witness a bizarre custody case involving twelve-year-old Billy Lindsay, the heir to his Pennsylvania family's fortune. Elizabeth Lindsay, Billy's mother, had become a follower of Dr. Otoman Zar-Adusht Hanish, a German émigré who was the leader of a society that sought to spread the word about Mazdaznan, an obscure religion. Elizabeth Lindsay had sent Billy to travel across the country with her new spiritual leader. The boy's relatives grew concerned that Hanish was in reality the leader of an immoral cult of sun worshippers and feared that he would corrupt Billy. After a coast-to-coast search for the boy, his uncle discovered that he was living in a temple on Lake Park Avenue in south Chicago. The uncle filed a dependent petition on Billy's behalf and he was taken into custody, but the mother and boy escaped before the hearing and set the stage for the case, which became front-page news.

During the juvenile court hearing on the dependency petition, the petitioner's attorney sought to prove that Billy had not only been neglected by his mother, but that the entire Mazdaznan religion was immoral. As evidence, the attorney read into the record a chapter on marital relations from Hanish's *Inner Studies,* a book of conduct for true believers. According to the *Chicago Daily News,* the reading prompted a number of women to leave the courtroom, and many of "those who remained held handkerchiefs to their faces and gazed at the floor." Apparently, even its author blushed at the recital of his own words ("Grill Hanish" 1912).

This very public hearing reveals that the idea of a private hearing, which would become one of the defining features of juvenile justice, had still not taken hold in Chicago by the early 1910s. Spectators flocked to the court to see the case unfold and also witnessed a melee, triggered by a photographer who took a picture of a true believer against her will. "The woman, who is not a small person," noted a reporter, "hurled herself at the photographer and only for the interference of several of the men followers of Hanish would have demolished his camera" ("Lindsay Boy Missing" 1912). This was not how the founders of the children's court had imagined it would operate.

Yet progressive supporters of the court, including the presiding judges, adapted to the public nature of these early cases by using the free publicity to explain the rehabilitative mission of the court and helped to make the case for its benefits to the public. These efforts to educate the public about the court were critical to establishing the legitimacy of the new institution. The stakes of this publicity campaign were high because the constitutionality of the juvenile court act itself was in question and would not be settled until the early 1910s. In fact it was the review of the Lindsay case by the Illinois Supreme Court in 1913 that produced the judicial declaration that the juvenile court act was constitutional (Tanenhaus 1997, 2: 267–75).

Publicizing the juvenile court, however, revealed a tension in progressive thought. Although the progressives wanted to protect the privacy of the individual child in court, they also sought to publicize the plight of poor children in general. Case histories, which included a great deal information about a child but not his or her actual name, served as one way of meeting the twin goals of educating the public about children through accounts of specific children who remained nameless. Case histories almost immediately became a standard feature of the studies of juvenile delinquency compiled in the early twentieth century.

In her introduction to Sophonisba Breckinridge and Edith Abbott's *The Delinquent Child and the Home* (1912), the first detailed study of the Cook County Juvenile Court, which contained numerous case histories, Julia Lathrop championed this faith in the education of the public. She declared that "the great primary service of the court is that it lifts up the truth and compels us to see that wastage of human life whose sign is the child in court." She fervently believed that the sad sight of the child in court, which she significantly called "the truth made public," would energize the public to ensure that the conditions facing children would be improved (Breckinridge and Abbott 1912, 8). The progressive faith that educating the public would rid society of corruption has often been described as naive. When, however, the public has forgotten about the juvenile court, as the United States Supreme Court later revealed, children were often treated more harshly than adults by the law (*In re Gault,* 387 U.S. 1 [1967]).

Although the progressive child savers learned how to use publicity to help legitimate the juvenile court, they still wanted to limit public access to juvenile court and give judges as much control of the courtroom as possible. It is significant, for example, that in 1910, when *The Annals of the Academy of Political and Social Science* published a special issue entitled *Administration of Justice in the United States,* it included an article, "Private Hearings—Their Advantages and Disadvantages," which addressed this question. Judge Harvey H. Baker, the presiding judge of the Boston Juvenile Court, wrote the article. In the introduction, he noted that "the limitations on publicity *now* being introduced in juvenile courts vary in strictness all the away from an understanding with the newspapers that the offenders' names shall not be published, to what may be called for convenience a private hearing" (Baker 1910; italics added). That these limitations on publicity were now—ten years after the invention of the juvenile court—being written into state laws was telling, but even more revealing was that Baker believed that it was necessary to explain what a private hearing was and why it was a potentially good thing.

Judge Baker used a series of analogies, comparing the role of the juvenile court judge to that of a parent, teacher, and physician, to support his argument in favor of private hearings, whose main feature was "the reduction of the number of persons present to minimum." Ideally, the judge, he believed, should talk with the child alone, unless she was a girl, who "of course, should never be talked with wholly alone." The major advantage of the private hearing was that it allowed the "judge the closest approach to the conditions under which the physician works." The danger of this analogy, Baker pointed out, was that a judge, unlike a doctor, had the power to deprive children of their liberty and parents of their natural authority, and the private hearing represented a "radical departure from the hard-won and long-established principle of full publicity in court proceedings." Potentially, as Baker acknowledged, a system of private hearings could shield not only the privacy of children and their families, but also shelter the "carelessness, eccentricities, or prejudices of an unfit judge" (Baker 1910).

Judge Baker concluded his article on a cautionary note. He recommended that "until the private hearing has been fully tested by experience, communities where the citizens are doubtful can proceed with caution, taking preliminary steps by suppressing newspaper reports of the names of the children and excluding all minors from the hearing except the offender and juvenile witnesses one at a time" (Baker 1910). Thus, even in 1910, one of the nation's leading proponents of private hearings did not think that they had been in existence long enough to be considered "fully tested by experience." Private hearings had not yet become a defining feature of progressive juvenile justice.

Private hearings had, however, become fairly standard practice by the time that many of the most influential studies of juvenile justice were published in the 1920s. Thus Lenroot and Lundberg's *Juvenile Courts at Work* (1925) and Herbert Lou's *Juvenile Courts in the United States* (1927) could declare that "the exclusion of the public from hearings of children's cases is generally recognized as a fundamental feature of juvenile-court procedure" (Lenroot and Lundberg [1925] 1975, 124; Lou 1927, 132). Later in the twentieth century, scholars relied upon these important studies from the 1920s, many of which were reprinted in the 1970s, to make generalizations about "the progressive juvenile court," including the assumption that private hearings had always been one of the distinguishing features of juvenile justice. Left out of these historical accounts, however, was the controversial and lengthy process of limiting public access to the juvenile court, echoes of which could still be heard in Herbert Lou's 1927 description of private hearings. He noted, for instance, that "it is to the advantage of the court to permit acquaintance with its work that will win the understanding and cooperation of the community and free the court from the suspicious criticism of holding 'star chamber sessions.' Undue privacy may be as injurious to the work of the court as undue publicity. Privacy should not appear to be secrecy" (Lou 1927, 132).

The Administration of Mothers' Pensions

That juvenile courts from the early 1910s to the mid-1930s administered mothers' pensions has, like the history of private hearings, often been ignored or simply forgotten. For many progressives, who saw the roots of delinquency in dependency, it made sense that mothers' pensions would become another addition to the juvenile court. In "Pensioning the Widow and the Fatherless," published in *Good Housekeeping,* the reformers Frederic Howe and Marie Jenney Howe made this argument about retrofitting matter-of-factly. They declared that the juvenile court already had "charge over child life" and "could be enlarged to take over one more department, and more appropriately so than any other agency, since the children who suffer from lack of home care are those brought to the juvenile court. When delinquency is due to this cause, it can be looked into and remedied by a Mothers' Pension" (Howe and Howe 1913).

In Chicago by 1920, the Aid-to-Mothers Division of the juvenile court, which had been first established less than a decade earlier in 1911, now handled a quarter of the court's caseload. Although in the 1920s a number of states began to put county social service agencies in charge of these welfare programs, in 1931 "seventeen out of the thirty-seven States with local administration" of mothers' pensions still relied upon the juvenile court to perform this function (United States Children's Bureau 1931, 6). The addition of mothers' pensions was simply another case of continuing to build the juvenile court in the early twentieth century, but the inclusion of these welfare programs in the court's jurisdiction also serves as a reminder that juvenile justice was broadly conceived. Juvenile courts often handled as many cases of dependent children as they did of delinquent ones, and the distinctions between dependency and delinquency were blurry at best.

As this section has demonstrated, most of the so-called distinguishing features of the progressive juvenile court were late additions, many of which were added on to juvenile courts across the nation after the Progressive Era itself had come to an end. These findings suggest not only that more historical research into early-twentieth-century juvenile justice is needed, but also that we should not assume that any period in the history of juvenile justice has been static. The history of the juvenile court has been a work in progress, not a mere story of declension.

CRISIS AND CONSOLIDATION

The last major addition to the juvenile court in the early twentieth century was the installation of psychiatric clinics, first the Juvenile Psychopathic Institute in Chicago in 1909 (later the Institute for Juvenile Research) and then clinics in a few other cities. Although the use of clinics in the juvenile justice system was extremely rare before the First World War, psychological and psychiatric approaches to the prevention of juvenile delinquency, including shifting the focus from adolescents to very young children, were the wave of the future (Horn 1989). Moreover, the psychiatric approach to delinquency prevention, which began as an addition to the court, shook its foundations by questioning the effectiveness of the court as a solution to the problem of juvenile delinquency. However, even though the social and psychological approaches to understanding and treating juvenile delinquency were often at odds, neither questioned the procedural innovations of the juvenile court. Proponents from both camps did work together in the early 1920s to declare what these standard practices ought to be.

William Healy, who had studied psychology with William James at Harvard in the 1890s and had then, after graduating from medical school, specialized in neurology, had served as the inaugural director of the Juvenile Psychopathic Clinic from 1909 to 1917. After moving to Boston, Healy began to wonder how the children whom he had examined in Chicago had turned out. He conducted a follow-up study, which revealed high rates of recidivism. These results, which Healy shared with child welfare experts at conferences in the early 1920s, contributed to the growing pessimism about the effectiveness of the juvenile justice system, reflected in professional discussions among social workers about "the passing of the juvenile court" (Baker 1921).

This loss of faith occurred at a critical moment, because members of the progressive generation of child savers, most notably Julia Lathrop, were trying to regain the earlier enthusiasm for the juvenile court by consolidating its gains through the creation of uniform standards and the preservation of its storied past. Yet at this moment, when the older reformers were striving to make the distinguishing features of juvenile justice into standard practices, a new generation turned away from the juvenile court and focused its attention on ways to work with young, more "normal" children, who had only minor behavioral problems (Cravens 1993).

This turning away from the delinquent child concerned Julia Lathrop, who was nearing the end of her long tenure as the chief of the United States Children's Bureau and was especially troubled by the findings presented by Evelina Belden in *Courts in the United States Hearing Children's Cases* (United States Children's Bureau 1920). Although forty-six out of the forty-eight states had passed juvenile court laws by 1920, Belden reported that the law in action did not even come close to matching the law on the books. She noted, for example, that "from at least one court in every State in the Union came reports of detaining children in jails" (United States Children's Bureau 1920, 13). In addition, less than half of the courts reported had probation service, which was supposed to be the cornerstone of modern juvenile justice (United States Children's Bureau 1920, 13). Moreover, psychiatric services were available in only 7 percent of the courts (United States Children's Bureau 1920, 14).

Belden calculated that approximately 50,000 out of the 175,000 juvenile cases heard during 1918 were conducted by courts "not adapted to the handling of children's cases" (United States Children's Bureau 1920, 15). Reflecting on this state of affairs, she concluded, "Statistics cannot adequately reveal the injury done these children through their association with adult offenders, their trial under the old criminal processes, and the absence of equipment for the study of their needs or for proper oversight and protection" (United States Children's Bureau 1920, 15). These troubling findings prompted Lathrop to take action.

In June 1921, the Children's Bureau along with the National Probation Association sponsored a three-day conference in Milwaukee to bring together child welfare experts to discuss "the fundamental problems of the juvenile court" exposed by Belden's report. The sessions would address questions about the jurisdiction of juvenile courts, the inherent tension between individual rights and socialized justice in chancery proceedings, the problem of extending juvenile justice into rural areas, and the best way to individualize treatment of cases. In attendance were many of the usual child welfare suspects who had spent the formative years of their careers in the Chicago court system before moving elsewhere and had remained personal friends of Lathrop, including Henry Thurston and William Healy.

Lathrop, who was now in her early sixties and about to retire from the Children's Bureau, delivered the introductory address. She used the example of the Chicago court, "whose development I know personally," to highlight the "continuous cooperation between public and private agencies" that had characterized the history of juvenile justice (United States Children's Bureau 1922, 7–8). She stressed that this cooperation, which had been so beneficial in the past, must continue into the future if the spirit of the juvenile court movement were to be kept alive. It was their mission, Lathrop declared, to reawaken public interest in the idea of the juvenile court. "If judges and laity could join in a committee to study practicable recommendations for juvenile-court standards," she asked, "would not much public interest be awakened in its work and a genuine advance be made in juvenile-court provision in those areas where it is now lacking?" (United States Children's Bureau 1922, 8).

At the conclusion of the conference, Lathrop appointed a committee whose mission would be "to carry on this work of standardization of juvenile court methods" (United States Children's Bureau 1922, 104). It took almost two years for this thirteen-member committee, chaired by Judge Charles W. Hoffman of Cincinnati, to produce its final report, whose recommendations reflected both the process of retrofitting the juvenile court as well as the more recent psychiatric turn made famous by Healy. Judge Hoffman had, in fact, visited Healy a few years earlier at the Juvenile Psychopathic Institute and had become a proponent of his methods.

Healy served on the committee while at the same time he was analyzing the preliminary results of his follow-up research on the Chicago cases. The findings convinced him that Chicago's reliance on institutionalization and failure to implement truly individualized treatment plans had contributed to its poor record. Healy used this evidence to argue for more extensive psychological and psychiatric work with young children to prevent them from developing into juvenile delinquents.

In addition, after the Milwaukee conference, Healy met with Barry Smith, the general director of the Commonwealth Fund, a new foundation established by the Harkness family, which had decided to put its resources into delinquency prevention and child health. Healy showed Smith his findings about Chicago, and their meeting foreshadowed the rejection of the juvenile court as the focus for child saving in the 1920s. Smith, for example, on the advice of psychiatrists like Healy, decided that the Commonwealth Fund would concentrate its efforts on young children, not older ones already in the juvenile justice system. He stated,

> The General Director is strongly of the opinion that the most effective program will not deal with delinquency beyond the stages of the Juvenile Court and Probation System. While undoubtedly there is a great need of more intelligent handling of crime and delinquency in our reformatories, jails, and prisons, the work with children in the earlier stages is far more hopeful, both as to the children served and as to general beneficial results to the country at large. (Horn 1989, 30–31)

As the historian Margo Horn has demonstrated, this focus on the young child anticipated a decision by the foundation to remove itself entirely from the field of juvenile delinquency (Horn 1989).

Thus, just at the moment when juvenile court standards were being completed, child welfare experts were turning their attention away from the delinquent child. In May 1923, the committee presented its final report to Grace Abbott, the new chief of the Children's Bureau. Abbott had been Lathrop's hand-picked heir and, like her mentor, had begun her career in Jane Addams's Hull House. In a foreword to the committee's recommendations, Abbott summarized the four principles underlying their report:

> (1) That the court dealing with children should be clothed with broad jurisdiction, embracing all classes of cases in which a child is in need of the protection of the State, whether the legal action is in the name of the child or an adult who fails in his obligations toward the child;
> (2) that the court should have a scientific understanding of each child;
> (3) that treatment should be adapted to individual needs;
> (4) that there should a presumption in favor of keeping the child in his own home and his own community, except when adequate investigation shows this not to be in the best interest of the child. (United States Children's Bureau 1923, vi)

The second and third principles revealed how influential Healy's ideas had become in the formulation of the relationship of the child to the state. The addition of a Juvenile Psychopathic Institute to the Chicago Juvenile Court, which fourteen years earlier had been hailed as a revolutionary addition, was now considered to be a necessary feature for future juvenile courts.

The completion of the *Juvenile-Court Standards* in 1923 established for the first time an official norm against which the actual operations of the nation's courts could be measured. However, Lathrop's prediction that it would reawaken interest in the idea of the juvenile court did not come to pass despite a barrage of press releases, radio promotions, and the printing of ten thousand copies of the standards that the bureau mailed to courts across the country (Rosenthal 1986). The juvenile court would fall into relative obscurity until a new generation of reformers rediscovered it after the Second World War (Manfredi 1998). Although the *Juvenile-Court Standards* failed to generate the public interest that Lathrop had hoped for, the report did become the programmatic capstone for progressive juvenile justice and would be reprinted and distributed by the Children's Bureau without any changes until 1954.

By 1923, as the juvenile court approached its second quarter century (figure 2.5), its inventors, supporters, and critics began to assess its successes and failures. Clearly, the "idea" of a juvenile court—that children should be removed from the criminal justice system—was firmly entrenched. The nation's experts now also agreed upon what practices—chancery proceedings, broad and exclusive jurisdiction until at least age eighteen, private hearings, the complaint system, detention, probation, confidential records, clinical ex-

New Cook County Juvenile Court and Detention Home

COOK COUNTY

Fig. 2.5 Cook County Juvenile Court and Detention Home, 1923. Courtesy of The University of Illinois at Chicago: Mary Bartelme Papers.

ams, and individualized treatment—should become standard (United States Children's Bureau 1923). However, more research into events of the 1930s and 1940s, the most understudied period in the first century of juvenile justice, must be done before we can know for certain how many of these distinguishing features actually developed into the standard operating procedures of American juvenile justice.

ACKNOWLEDGMENTS

I would like to thank Margaret Rosenheim, Mary Wammack, and Frank Zimring for their insightful comments on drafts of this chapter. I am honored to dedicate it to Jenifer L. Stenfors (1970–1999).

NOTES

1. The title of the law was even changed to reflect this new potential. It became "An Act relating to children who are now or may hereafter become dependent, neglected or delinquent, to define these terms, and to provide for the treatment, control, maintenance, adoption and guardianship of the person of such child." The act declared "that all persons under the age of twenty-one (21) years, shall, for the purpose of the Act only, be considered wards of this State, and their person shall be subject to the care, guardianship and control of the court as hereinafter provided" (*Laws of the State of Illinois* 1907, 71).

2. I have changed the boy's first and last names.

REFERENCES

Abbott, Grace. 1938. *The Child and the State.* 2 vols. Chicago: University of Chicago Press.

Baker, Harvey Humphrey. 1910. "Private Hearings: Their Advantages and Disadvantages." *Annals of the Academy of Political and Social Science* 36: 80–84.

Baker, Herbert M. 1921. "Passing of the Juvenile Court." *Survey* 45: 705.

Bradwell, James B., ed. 1899. *All the Laws.* Chicago: Chicago Legal News.

Breckinridge, Sophonisba P., and Edith Abbott. 1912. *The Delinquent Child and the Home.* New York: Survey Associates.

Charity Service Reports. 1906–1908. Prepared by the Board of Commissioners of Cook County, Illinois. Chicago: Henry O. Shepard.

"Child Slaves." 1899. *Chicago Daily Inter-Ocean*, February 28.

Cravens, Hamilton. 1993. "Child Saving in Modern America, 1870s–1890s. In *Children at Risk in America: History, Concepts, and Public Policy,* ed. Roberta Wollons, 3–31. Albany: State University of New York Press.

Dean, Emily Washburn. 1931. Dedication of Oakdale, the Women's Reformatory at Dwight, November 11. Dean Papers. Chicago Historical Society.

Farwell, Harriet S. 1924. *Lucy Louisa Flower, 1837–1920: Her Contribution to Education and Child Welfare in Chicago.* Chicago: Private printing.

Feld, Barry C. 1999. *Bad Kids: Race and the Transformation of the Juvenile Court.* New York: Oxford University Press.

"Grill Hanish in Trial." 1912. *Chicago Daily News* (January 6).

Hart, Hastings H., ed. 1910. *Juvenile Court Laws in the United States Summarized.* New York: Russell Sage Foundation.

Heuisler, Charles. 1903. "Probation Work in Children's Courts." *Charities: A Review of Local and General Philanthropy* 11 (November 7): 399–401.

Horn, Margo. 1989. *Before It's Too Late: The Child Guidance Movement in the United States, 1922–1945.* Philadelphia: Temple University Press.

Howe, Frederic C., and Marie Jenney Howe. 1913. "Pensioning the Widow and the Fatherless." In *Good Housekeeping* (September): 282–91.

Hurd, Harvey B. 1905. "Juvenile Court Law: Minimum Principles which Should Be Stood For." *Charities: A Review of Local and General Philanthropy* 13 (January 7): 327–28.

Hurley, Timothy D. 1905a. "Necessity for the Lawyer in the Juvenile Court." In *Proceedings of the National Conference of Charities and Correction,* ed. Alexander Johnson, 173–77. Portland, OR: Press of Fred J. Heer.

———. 1905b. Letter to Benjamin Barr Lindsey. May 29. Benjamin B. Lindsey Papers, Box 4. Library of Congress, Washington, DC.

———. [1907] 1977. *Origin of the Illinois Juvenile Court Law: Juvenile Courts and What They Have Accomplished.* 3d ed. Reprint, New York: AMS Press.

Jeter, Helen Rankin. 1922. *The Chicago Juvenile Court.* Washington, DC: Government Printing Office.

Kelley, Florence. 1882. "On Some Changes in the Legal Status of the Child since Blackstone." *International Review* 13 (August): 7–98.

Lathrop, Julia C. 1905. "The Development of the Probation System in a Large City." *Charities: A Review of Local and General Philanthropy* 13 (January 7): 344–49.

Laws of the State of Illinois. 1905. Springfield: Illinois State Journal.

Laws of the State of Illinois. 1907. Springfield: Illinois State Journal.

Lenroot, Katharine, and Emma O. Lundberg. [1925] 1975. *Juvenile Courts at Work: A Study of the Organization and Methods of Ten Courts*. Reprint, New York: AMS Press.

"Lindsay Boy Missing, Judge Raps Sun Cult." 1912. *Chicago Daily News* (January 4).

Lou, Henry H. 1927. *Juvenile Courts in the United States*. Chapel Hill: University of North Carolina Press.

McCarthy, Kathleen D. 1982. *Noblesse Oblige: Charity and Cultural Philanthropy in Chicago, 1849–1929*. Chicago: University of Chicago Press.

Mack, Julian W. 1909–1910. The Juvenile Court. *Harvard Law Review* 23: 104–22.

Manfredi, Christopher P. 1998. *The Supreme Court and Juvenile Justice*. Lawrence: University of Kansas Press.

McManaman, John. 1905. "The Juvenile Court." In *Eighteenth Biennial Report,* Board of Commissioners of Public Charities. Springfield, IL: State Journal Co., State Printers.

Polsky, Andrew J. 1991. *The Rise of the Therapeutic State*. Princeton, NJ: Princeton University Press.

Rosenthal, Marguerite G. 1986. "The Children's Bureau and the Juvenile Court: Delinquency Policy." *Social Service Review* 60: 303–18.

Rothman, David J. 1978. "The State as Parent: Social Policy in the Progressive Era." In *Doing Good: The Limits of Benevolence,* ed. Willard Gaylin et al., 67–96. New York: Pantheon Books.

Schlossman, Steven L. 1977. *Love and the American Delinquent: The Theory and Practice of "Progressive" Juvenile Justice*. Chicago: University of Chicago Press.

———. 1995. "Delinquent Children: The Juvenile Reform School." In *The Oxford History of the Prison,* ed. Norval Morris and David J. Rothman, 325–49. New York: Oxford University Press.

Schneider, Eric. 1992. *In the Web of Class: Delinquents and Reformers in Boston, 1810s–1930s*. New York: New York University Press.

Shaw, Clifford R., and Earl D. Myers. 1929. "The Juvenile Delinquent." In *The Illinois Crime Survey.* Springfield: Illinois Association for Criminal Justice.

Tanenhaus, David Spinoza. 1997. Policing the Child: Juvenile Justice in Chicago, 1870–1925. 2 vols. Ph.D. diss., University of Chicago.

Taylor, Graham. 1930. *Pioneering on Social Frontiers*. Chicago: University of Chicago Press.

United States Children's Bureau. 1920. *Courts in the United States Hearing Children's Cases: A Summary of Juvenile-court Legislation in the United States*. By Evelina Belden. Publication no. 65. Washington, DC: Government Printing Office.

———. 1922. *Proceedings of the Conference on Juvenile-court Standards Held under the Auspices of the U.S. Children's Bureau and the National Probation Association*. Publication no. 97. Washington, DC: Government Printing Office.

———. 1923. *Juvenile-court Standards: Report of the Committee Appointed by the Children's Bureau, August, 1921, to Formulate Juvenile-court Standards, Adopted by a Conference Held under the Auspices of the Children's Bureau and the National Probation Association, Wash-*

ington, D.C., May 18, 1923. Publication no. 121. Washington, DC: Government Printing Office.

———. 1931. *Mothers' Aid, 1931*. Publication no. 220. Washington, DC: Government Printing Office.

Wines, Frederick H. 1899. Address. In *Fifteenth Biennial Report*. Board of State Commissioners of Public Charities. Springfield, IL: Phillips Bros., State Printers.

3 Twentieth-Century Developments in America's Institutional Systems for Youth in Trouble

Paul Lerman

When the juvenile court was invented at the turn of the century, it inherited a broad mandate for engaging in public intervention in the lives of juveniles. At the same time that the court inherited a broad jurisdiction for addressing youth problems, it also relied on existing public and private institutions associated with three types of social arrangements or systems: adult corrections via local jails and state prisons; juvenile corrections via training schools and reformatories; and child welfare via orphan asylums and dependent/neglected facilities. While each system tended to specialize in dealing with specific problems and age groups, they each included youths who could just as easily be dealt with in one of the other systems.

The court's linkages to these three nineteenth-century systems have continued in varying ways over the century. Analyzing information about institutional trends across the three systems over the century can be quite useful for understanding the actual societal responses to youth in trouble, but the analysis would be incomplete without adding two other residential systems that have emerged during the last half of the twentieth century: the mental health and substance abuse systems. Conduct and adjustment "disorders" of children continue to be the leading official diagnosis for youths in the mental health system, and behaviors associated with alcohol and drug use constitute the leading problems for placing youths in juvenile detention facilities in recent years. Both new systems deal with many youths who could be subject to a juvenile court's jurisdiction but may have been placed in inpatient residences via different social/legal processes without the formal authorization of a juvenile court judge. If our concern is to find out how youth in trouble are actually being dealt with—and not formal judicial systems per se—then we cannot ignore the informal, nonlegal, utilization of these new types of facilities.

This chapter focuses primarily on the changes that have occurred in three of the five systems: the child welfare, juvenile corrections, and mental health systems. The substance abuse system is briefly discussed. Data on the adult correctional system is presented with that for the juvenile correctional system. Each of the three primary systems is viewed from a historical perspective by highlighting critical policies and beliefs, as well as utilization trends over time. Particular differences in utilization patterns by gender and race are examined, along with variability in funding and the size and length of stay associated with each system. The conclusion presents an overview of the utilization patterns of all of the systems in the mid-1990s in order to understand where we are and where we might be heading as a nation in our handling of youth in trouble.

THE CHILD WELFARE SYSTEM

By the time the juvenile courts had been accepted in a number of states, the child welfare system had already evolved to include the following major types of residential organizations: (1) institutions for dependent children; (2) institutions for dependent adults and children; (3) child-placing societies with temporary receiving homes; (4) day nurseries; and (5) homes for unwed mothers and their babies. Many of these organizations were developed or expanded in order to include children who were formerly housed in almshouses, jails, workhouses, or public hospitals during the nineteenth century.

Home Care: Ideal and de Facto Policies before 1935

The policy issue at the beginning of the twentieth century for the child welfare system, as well as for the juvenile court, was whether dependent children and youth could be aided in their own homes, rather than primarily in long-term, congregate institutions. In 1909, the leaders of the field reached a consensus on a children's policy at the first White House Conference on Dependent Children. The resolution on "home care," embodied in a letter to President Theodore Roosevelt, stated clearly that children could be financially assisted in their own homes only if their parents were of "worthy character," their mothers deemed "reasonably efficient and deserving," and they maintained a "suitable home." If mothers passed these assessment hurdles, then aid should be given preferably by "private charity." For youth "requiring special training," or those not readily placed in a foster home, "the use of institutions is necessary."

Despite the opposition of many leaders of private charities, publicly funded Mothers' Aid Laws were enacted in forty states by 1921 in order to help poor mothers to keep their children at home. However, until 1935 the laws were implemented with inadequate legislative assistance standards, skimpy appropriations, and meager assistance allowances. Therefore, poor parents continued to behave in a manner similar to those at the turn of the century. When burdened with poverty and too many mouths to feed, mothers voluntarily placed some or all of their children in Catholic, Protestant, or Jewish orphan asylums or in fraternal institutions in the 1920s, as they had done in the 1890s.

The 1933 census of children revealed that the major applicants for any type of out-of-home care continued to be parents. Out of all new referrals for substitute care reported to the census, 43 percent were from parents or relatives, followed by 34 percent from the courts. Besides being used by parents as a form of "indoor relief," child welfare institutions were also used as a placement for dealing with youth in conflict with parental authority or the law. In 1923 the authors of the national census of children's institutions wrote,

> The dividing line between dependency and delinquency is often so vague that in practice both types of children may be found in the care of organizations intended primarily for the care of a single class, and there is a growing tendency for organizations for dependents to accept pre-delinquents and the milder delinquents. . . . On the other hand, it is not uncommon to find dependent children in institutions for delinquents.

AFDC and de Facto Deinstitutionalization, 1935–62

Until passage of the Social Security Act of 1935, authorizing federal expenditures for Aid to Dependent Children (later called AFDC) and child welfare services, virtually no federal funds were available for the support of any of the children likely to come before the juvenile court. The federally sponsored AFDC program offered fiscal incentives to care for dependent children in their own homes, rather than in institutions, and ushered in de facto policies of deinstitutionalization of dependent/neglected children. State welfare dollars, formerly spent on institutional care, could now be used as the state's matching dollars for the new AFDC program.

By the end of World War II, a broad ideological consensus had developed that institutions were not necessary for the "garden variety" of "youth in trouble," since foster care could be used as an alternative. For youth with more serious behavioral problems, private residential facilities, staffed by expert professionals, could be used as an alternative to institutions for dependent/neglected children. By the early 1950s, residential treatment centers had become the new ideal models for residential child care. Many of these "new" institutions were actually "old" dependent/neglected youth facilities that had adapted to declining populations by becoming more progressive in their program offerings, providing "treatment" instead of just care and custody for youth in trouble—now redefined as "emotionally disturbed."

Changes in Federal Home Policy and Financing, 1960s–1990s

In 1960, an Advisory Council on federal child welfare services presented a report to the secretary of Health, Education, and Welfare that argued in favor of a new definition of child welfare services. The report was accepted by the secretary, and became incorporated as part of the amendments to the Social Security Act. The critical part of the proposal referred to a new federal responsibility for "care to be given in foster family homes, adoptive homes, and child-caring facilities or other facilities." The AFDC placement program explicitly required a judicial determination in order to legitimate the expenditure of federal funds on "foster care"—now defined as placement in a foster family home, shelter, group home, or institution.

Before the availability of federal funds, institutional placements were supported by a combination of state/local government and private funds (at about a 46 to 54 percent ratio, respectively, in 1933). The utilization of federal funds for foster care of AFDC children began slowly, so that by 1969 only about 5 percent of all youth residing in a foster care placement were supported by federal funds. By 1976, the states had learned how to master the new program and use matching funds from the state to make many more children eligible for federal reimbursement in out-of-home placements—including many status offenders and juvenile delinquents placed by the courts. However, some influential Congressmen were concerned that an open-ended funding stream was administered in a lax fashion by non-child-welfare officials and was costing the federal government too many dollars. The interest in reducing costs coincided with the growing belief among professionals that many children could be helped in smaller facilities like group homes.

The AFDC/Foster Care program was phased out after the implementation of a new title in the Social Security Act (Title IV-E) in the mid-1980s. This new title was explicitly administered by child welfare officials under tighter regulations and standards of payments. Federal funds could be used to pay for the following services: traditional and therapeutic foster care in family homes; shelters; group homes; child care institutions; adoption; and other services. Funds were to be spent in order to deal with problems associated with "preventing or remedying, or assisting in the solution of, problems that may result in the neglect, abuse, exploitation, or delinquency of children." Title IV-E was reauthorized in 1996 by the same Congress that ended AFDC as a federal entitlement program. It was continued as an open-ended entitlement for youth falling into one or more of the defined problem categories who also would have been deemed eligible for welfare assistance by a state as of July 16, 1996. Initial placements could be voluntary or via a court order, but continued placement had to be approved by a judicial determination. The total amount of federal funds budgeted for the foster care programs (i.e., foster homes, group homes, and institutions) has grown from $557 million in 1981 (via AFDC/Foster Care) to about $2.6 billion in 1993 and $5.6 billion in fiscal 2000 (via Title IV-E). A small amount of this increase is for adoption support.

States participate in the Title IV-E program by matching federal funds at their respective Medicaid rates, which varied between 50 and 78 percent in the mid-1990s. For the first time, for-profit organizations were eligible to receive funds subsidized by the federal government. All types of private facilities can receive the combined matching funds by including any of the covered youth problems, providing that not more than 50 percent of an institution's population can be classified as legal delinquents. In practice this meant that the same facilities could house youth placed by state or local child welfare or correctional agencies, using diverse funding streams.

Facility Types and Size over Time

In 1923, children could be found in almshouses and other institutions for adults, as well as facilities just for children and youth. The national average size for child welfare institutions was ninety-one, but in New York some facilities served one thousand youth.

By 1966, when a special national survey was conducted, the average size of child welfare facilities had been reduced to fifty-six. Besides the reduction in size, youth were no longer to be found mixed in with adults. These trends continued in a 1981 survey, with an average size of twenty-two for such facilities as shelters, homes for unwed mothers, dependent/neglected institutions, and group homes. Over the twentieth century, the total number of distinct youth facilities had increased, but the average size of each one had decreased significantly.

Overview of Child Welfare Placements, 1920s–1990s

In order to assess the overall impact of the infusion of federal funds, it is important to have a perspective over time. Since the 1923 census was the most comprehensive survey for the pre-federal period, this year was chosen for the comparison.

Figure 3.1 provides information about the number of children found to

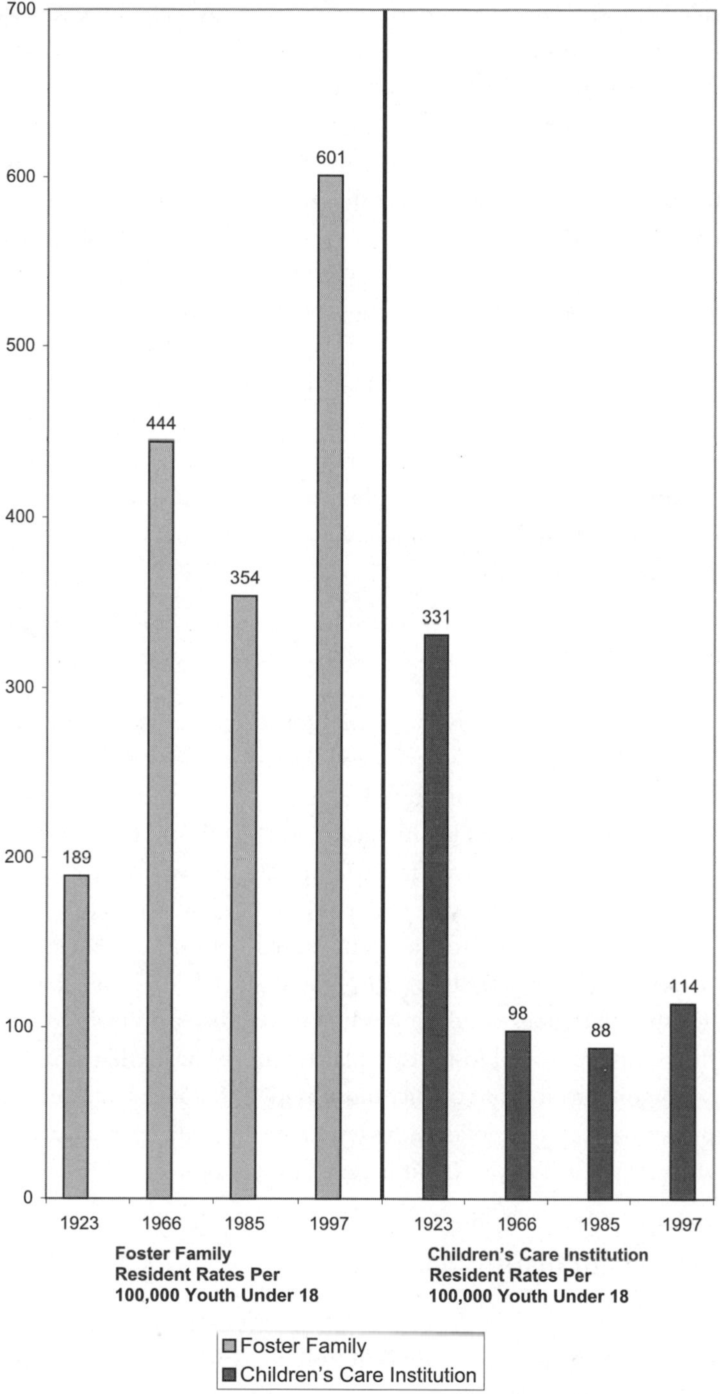

Fig. 3.1 Resident rates of foster care by type for selected years.

be placed in foster family homes on a census day, as well as the resident count of children living in child care facilities, controlling for the number of youth under eighteen living in the United States in the specific years. On the left side of figure 3.1 are the annual resident rates of foster family placements for the years 1923, 1966, 1985, and 1997. These years were chosen because the information is most reliable for those time periods. It is clear from the figure that the 1923 foster family care rate of 189 per 100,000 youths under eighteen is much higher in subsequent years, reaching a peak of 601 per 100,000 youths in 1997. The right side of figure 3.1 behaves in a far different fashion. The high institutional rate of 331, controlling for population, has not been surpassed; the rate fluctuates between 98 and 114. The primary impact of federal funding on the child welfare system has been in the direction of expanding the total number of youths residing in foster family homes. Controlling for population, many more youths under eighteen are indeed living away from their families in the 1990s, but the child welfare placements are less likely to be in group homes or institutions.

Estimates of Length of Stay

In 1933, about 50 percent of the youth under care in the average dependent/neglected institution had lived there for at least three years. In 1966, a special national survey estimated that about 67 percent of the youth left after staying about two years in similar types of facilities. By 1981, researchers estimated that no youth stayed in such facilities for two years. Instead, about 94 percent stayed less than a year in dependent/neglected facilities. In contrast, youth residing in facilities for the "emotionally disturbed" in 1981 stayed in institutions much longer; about 36 percent stayed for more than one year. Data for the 1990s does not distinguish between foster homes and institutional facilities; estimates for all foster care placements indicate that a median length of stay has gone from about twenty months in 1990 to eleven months in 1998–99. In summary, it appears that the length of stay has decreased substantially over the past sixty-five years, but it varies by the type of facility.

Variability in Rates of Institutionalization

Overall national trends are useful for understanding changes across time periods, but national averages tend to hide the variability among the states in their reliance on placement in institutions rather than with families or in foster homes. In 1923, for example, Massachusetts had only 28 percent of their "placed-out" children living in institutions, compared to 64 percent for the nation. Comparable states like Illinois, New York, Ohio, Pennsylvania, and California had proportions ranging from 82 to 66 percent. By 1997, the national proportion of placed-out children living in institutions had dropped to about 16 percent. Massachusetts, Illinois, and New York matched the national proportion, but California and Pennsylvania had proportions ranging from 25 to 28 percent. The gap between the states has become narrower over time, but variability remains among the states.

The age at which children are placed in institutions has also changed over time. When comparing the proportion of youth twelve years of age and above placed out and living in institutions in the 1933 U.S. Census with 1966 and 1981 national surveys, it is clear that older children are now the primary candidates for institutional living. The proportion of children twelve years of age and above living in institutions was 44 percent in 1933, 54 percent in 1961, and 77 percent in 1981. Another difference between foster care and institutions pertains to gender. Compared to the 1920s, boys are now much more likely to be found in institutions than girls.

There are also differences in using institutions by race. In 1933, about 4–5 percent of youth residing in boarding homes or in institutions were black. By 1997, the proportion of youth entering foster care (either foster homes or institutions) who were black was about 31 percent. It appears that blacks have gone from being underrepresented in child welfare to being overrepresented, since the proportion of all youth in the country under eighteen years of age who were black in 1997 was about 16 percent. By way of contrast, Hispanics made up about 14 percent of those entering child welfare in 1997, but they were only about 15 percent of the youth population.

Another source of variability in the use of group homes or institutions is associated with the types of presenting problems that counties and states choose to address via the child welfare system. In a 1994 study of one or more presenting problems of children receiving any type of child welfare services, the following proportions were noted for problems other than physical or sexual abuse and neglect: emotional problems, 35 percent; lack of or inadequate supervision, 34 percent; truancy, running away, or delinquency, 13 percent; and substance abuse, 5 percent. Each of these types of problems could have been dealt with in the juvenile corrections, mental health, or substance abuse systems, depending on the availability, ease of access, resources, and willingness to use these alternatives within local jurisdictions.

JUVENILE CORRECTIONS

The establishment of special institutions for the care and control of juvenile delinquents occurred about seventy-five years before the creation of the first juvenile courts. However, juveniles were still being admitted to the local jails and workhouses, as well as almshouses, state adult reformatories, and prisons.

Reformers set themselves the pragmatic goal of removing juveniles from the corrupting influences of these adult institutions. They also set a more idealistic goal of assisting the new juvenile courts in facilitating "progress in the understanding and scientific treatment of delinquency," so that juveniles could receive the "protective and educational" experience associated with probation or specialized juvenile institutions. Implementing these twin goals has continued to engage reformers of juvenile corrections throughout the twentieth century. The efforts to create alternatives to the use of adult institutions and to invent new "protective and educational experiences" have resulted in attempted solutions that differed before and after World War II.

Removing Youth from Jails and Prisons: Ideal and de Facto Policies, 1900s–1950s

A comparison of the U.S. Census data for traditional correctional facilities from 1910 and 1923 reveals that about the same number of juveniles entered all types of correctional facilities in both years—about 25,000–26,000. However, the distribution of the juveniles had shifted away from the use of adult facilities by 1923. About 72 percent of the total number of juveniles admitted to correctional facilities went to juvenile training schools or reformatories, instead of the 53 percent who entered such facilities in 1910. Jail admissions, as a proportion of admissions, had been reduced from 39 to 21 percent of all correctional admissions, but prison admissions remained quite stable. Lower utilization of short-term jails had, however, been offset by increased admissions to a new type of correctional institution—juvenile detention facilities (figure 3.2).

The first detention facilities designed exclusively for juveniles, as a local alternative to jails, police lockups, and workhouses, were in existence by the 1910 census in a few cities, but these were not counted by the U.S. Census until 1923. At that time, there were ninety detention homes providing information to the Census statisticians. Six were in cities of more than 500,000 population, nineteen were in cities of between 100,000 to 500,000, and sixty-five were in towns of 100,000 or less or in rural areas. It is clear that detention facilities were in use in a wide array of communities by 1923, not just in large cities.

During the census year of 1923, more than 33,000 juveniles were admitted to the new detention facilities—more than all of the juveniles admitted to all other correctional institutions (i.e., adult and juvenile combined). The one-day count of detention facilities, in contrast, was quite small—only 1,489 juveniles. For every juvenile resident on a census day, an average of 22.2 were admitted during the year. The larger the population size, the greater the

Fig. 3.2 The expanded facilities in the new (1907) juvenile detention home allowed many of the boys housed there to take workshop classes. Courtesy of The Chicago Historical Society.

ratio of admissions to residents, indicating that the turnover of detention beds was greatest in the largest towns (35.3 admissions to 1 resident), next highest in the medium-sized cities (25.0 to 1), and lowest in the smallest areas (12.2 to 1). The lower the ratio of admissions to residents, the longer the average lengths of stay. If an analysis had focused only on one-day counts, the inferences about the way detention was being used early in the court's history might have been quite misleading.

By 1925, one of the founders of the Chicago Juvenile Court, Louise Bowen, complained that the local detention home had every "appearance of being a jail, with its barred windows and locked doors," staffed by political patronage appointees. This description could be repeated across the country, except for a few isolated jurisdictions that attempted to use homelike boarding homes. From its earliest years, detention was used for a variety of social purposes other than for pretrial detention. Two respected mental health professionals, Healey and Bronner, who had worked in the early Chicago and Boston Juvenile Courts, complained that detention was used as a "dumping place" for the mixing of all types of youth in trouble—including dependent, neglected, truant, and incorrigible youth—and as a holding facility convenient for police, judges, and probation officers, regardless of the final disposition of cases. Healy and Bronner also discerned an early use of detention that was not part of the official rhetoric associated with the juvenile court, namely, as a "punishment of a milder sort, or as a measure of warning." They noted that "some police and probation officers hold strongly to the idea that a taste of segregation will turn a trick that no amount of talking to a boy or girl will effect." The removal of juveniles from adult institutions incurred the cost of having many more youth incarcerated in juvenile detention than were held under the traditional system. These early practices continued to develop and expand over the course of the twentieth century.

The Scientific Treatment of Delinquency: Ideal and de Facto Policies, 1900s–1950s

The belief in a scientific approach to and treatment of delinquents was associated with the hiring of psychiatrists, psychologists, and related professionals in mental hygiene clinics attached (or available) to the new courts in Chicago, Boston, St. Louis, and other cities. Unfortunately, these new professionals appear to have had little impact on the use of detention, the counseling activities of the new probation services, or the commitment of youth to correctional facilities.

Except for a few private institutions that were attempting to become residential treatment centers, the ideal training schools were developed with a different set of goals and personnel. The ideal training school attempted to provide schooling, vocational training, and individualized attention from sympathetic adults who supervised cottages with twenty-five juveniles in a disciplined environment. In actual practice, studies revealed that cottages were more than twice the ideal size, schooling was often minimal, and vocational training consisted of farming or performing maintenance tasks necessary for the institution. In addition, discipline tended to be harsh and often unusually punitive (figure 3.3). By the middle of the 1930s, staff of the U.S. Children's Bureau, the standard-setters of the nation, were no longer writing about training schools performing as sites of scientific understanding and treatment.

The Search for Alternatives to Training Schools: Ideal and de Facto Policies, 1950s–1970s

Beginning in 1950, spurred by a new generation of professionals, new correctional models were established within state and local correctional agencies. One model consisted of a small group home that relied on guided group interaction—a variant of group therapy—to talk about personal, relational, and behavioral problems. First used in New Jersey, these specialized group homes were emulated in Utah and other parts of the country. As the idea of guided group interaction spread, the practice was even incorporated into traditional training schools.

Probation departments also sought alternatives to commitments by

Fig. 3.3 The morning lineup at a juvenile delinquent training school. Boys stand outside their rooms awaiting inspection. © Hulton-Deutsch Collection/CORBIS.

working with child welfare departments to arrange family foster homes as well as group foster homes in local communities for youth who might have been committed to institutional placements. California probation departments began to experiment by placing youth in forestry camps and ranches, as a condition of probation, instead of committing them to state correctional facilities. Starting slowly in the 1940s and 1950s, probation-sponsored camps, ranches, and small schools expanded in California to fifty-three in 1970. Lengths of stays were often shorter than in state facilities.

While these alternatives were originally developed in lieu of a commitment to state training schools, local judges, assisted by probation recommendations, continued to fill correctional facility beds—often beyond their rated capacities. In order to deal with overcrowding, a number of state correctional authorities began using reception/diagnostic units as a means of selecting youth for short stays of 30–90 days and early parole to "community treatment," thereby creating short-term training-school stays.

The Emergence of a Federal Role: Ideal and de Facto Policies, 1970s–2000

All of these new initiatives became associated with the new, idealized model of "community-based corrections." This new ideal was promoted by several national commissions on crime and corrections in the mid-1960s and early 1970s. However, a federal role in direct funding for juvenile corrections was associated with the Juvenile Delinquency and Prevention Act of 1974. Funds were to be allocated to states on the condition that they remove status offenders and other nondelinquents from public detention and correctional facilities. For the first time since the creation of detention facilities, nondelinquent youth were no longer permitted to be mixed with delinquents in public facilities. However, the statute was silent on mixing in private facilities, unless they were "primarily" for delinquents. The movement to deinstitutionalize status offenders fit in quite well with the Gault decision and the federal expansion of child welfare boundaries and resources to support community-based alternatives for both systems.

The intermingling of funds and resources between the two federal lines of authority helped create a de facto policy that distinguished among three types of traditional "delinquents": status offenders, minor offenders, and serious offenders. The first two types became the primary recipients of community alternatives if efforts of diversion, probation, and nonresidential services failed. The traditional public sector was not to receive these types, but was to specialize in "hard core" offenders. An overview of recent trends of utilization, compared to past census data, confirms this assessment of the de facto division of labor between the public and private sectors.

An Overview of Correctional Trends: 1920s–1990s

Figure 3.4 presents data pertaining to one-day resident counts per 100,000 youth under eighteen years of age for all types of correctional facilities utilized by juveniles for two time periods separated by about seventy-five years. The rates control for the distinct youth population under age eighteen for each time period: 1923 and the mid-1990s. The rates for public facilities are virtually the same (66 and 64), but jails, prisons, and detention have grown appreciably (from 5 to 16 and 4 to 35, respectively). The largest growth in resident rates occurred in the expanded use of private juvenile correctional facilities (from 2 to 58).

Figure 3.5 presents admissions and resident data pertaining to the utilization of all types of correctional facilities, adult and juvenile, for two time periods separated by about seventy-five years. The rates are computed on the basis of combining information on the average daily residence in specific fa-

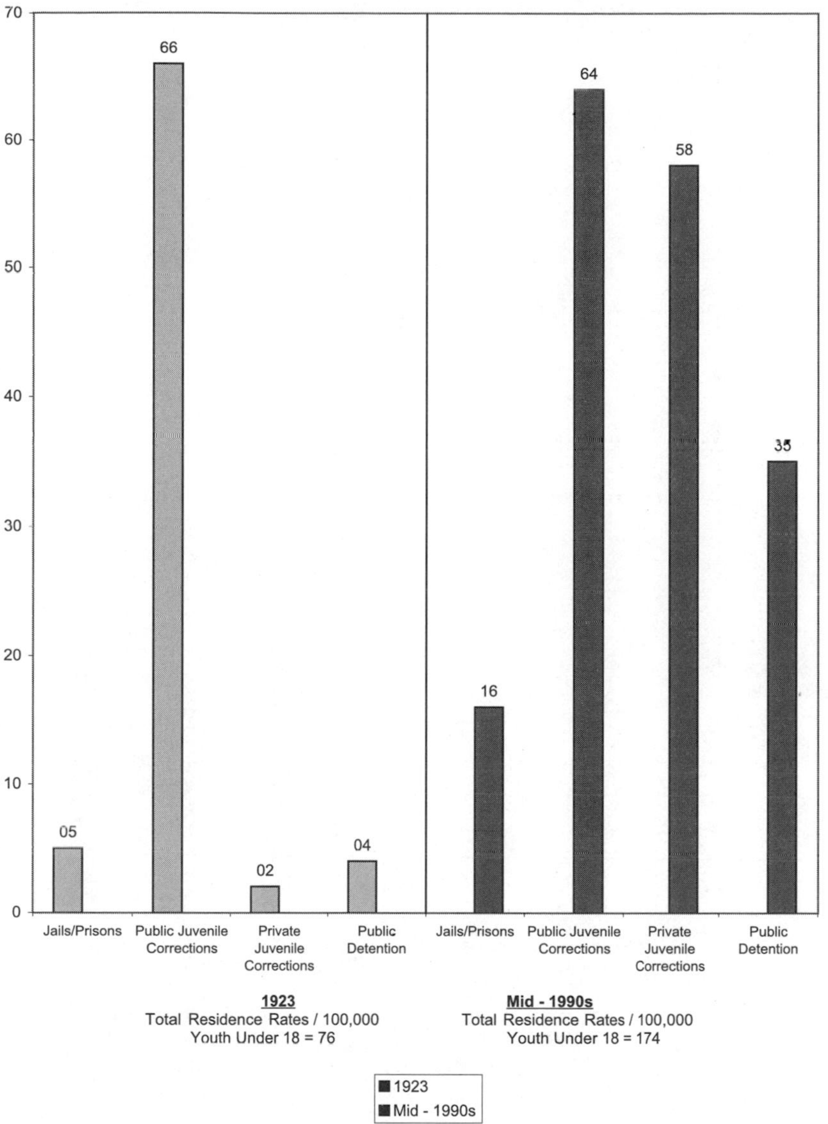

Fig. 3.4 Residence rates of correctional facilities per 100,000 youth under 18 years of age, by facility type in 1923 and 1990s.

cilities together with the annual admissions for those facilities. Combining these two counts provides the basis for calculating the rates of care, treatment, and custody episodes for each facility type for an entire year. Borrowing from the mental health field, we can conceive of the residents as living in the facility on any specific day of the year, and the admissions as persons who enter when the residents leave. We can then add the two rates together and consider the combined information as a total episode rate for each facility. For example, we can combine the number of detention residents and annual admissions in

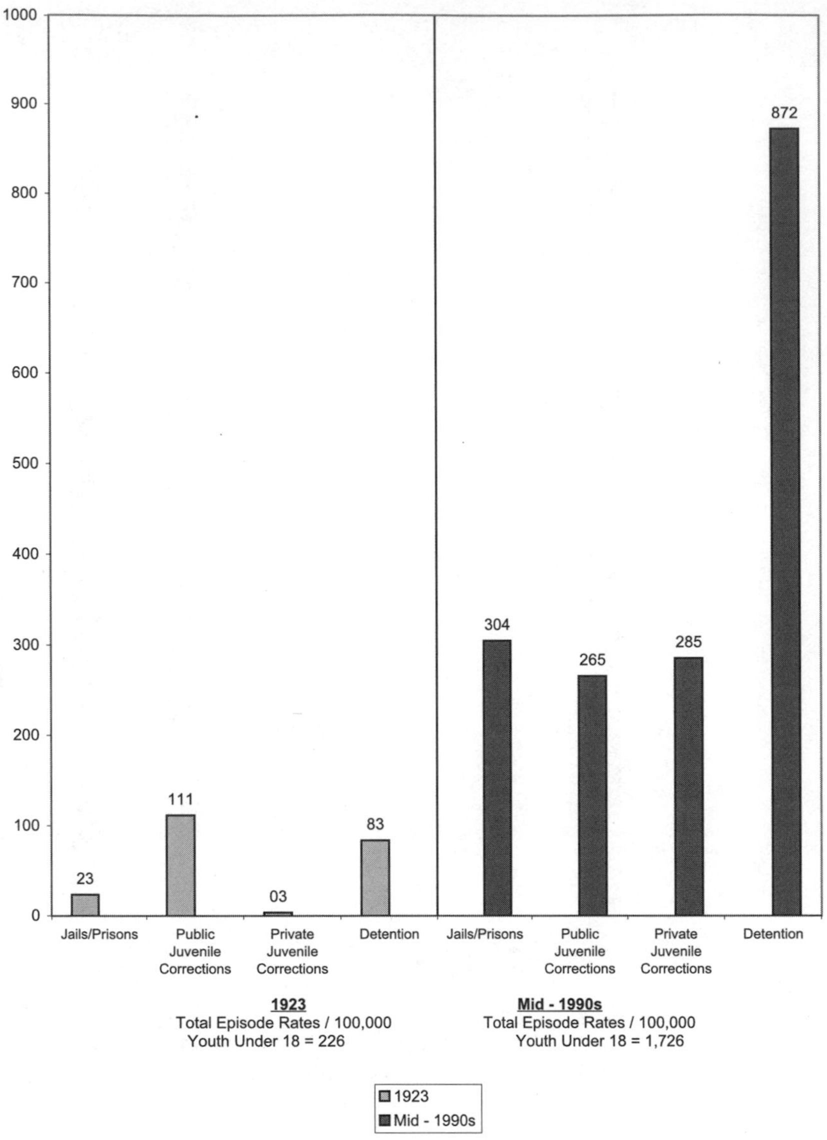

Fig. 3.5 Episode rates of correctional facilities per 100,000 youth under 18 years of age, by facility type in 1923 and 1990s.

1923, and refer to the utilization of this facility as an episode rate of 83 per 100,000 youth under age eighteen (see figure 3.5). In a similar manner, we can refer to the episode rate that public juvenile corrections had as 111 and the combined jail/prison episode rate as 23 (i.e., a rate of 14 for jails and 9 for prisons). Using episode rates, it is now possible to state that juvenile training schools in 1923 had the highest episode rate, followed by detention, jails/prisons, and then private facilities. The combined rate for all correctional facility types in 1923 was 220 per 100,000 youth under eighteen years of age.

Moving to the right side of figure 3.5, we can see that the episode rate for each comparable facility category has increased appreciably, controlling for youth population in the mid-1990s. At the end of the century, detention is clearly the most widely used correctional category, having increased by more than a factor of 10 from a rate of 83 to 872 per 100,000 youth under eighteen years of age. The combined use of jails (with a rate of 282) and prisons (with a rate of 22) has increased even more dramatically—13.2 times from an episode rate of 23 to 304 per 100,000 youth. The largest growth, however, is in the use of private correctional facilities, which has increased about 95 times from an episode rate of 3 to 285 per 100,000 youth.

Reviewing the data for the current time period provides strong evidence that detention episode rates are higher than all of the other rates combined—872 to 854. While officials, reformers, and policymakers may publicize probation or community-based alternatives as the ideal policies, local law enforcement and judicial officials operate as if short-term incarceration is the most favored response to youth in trouble. As a matter of historical fact, since the 1960s, any national annual comparison between detention admissions and new probation additions always yields a much higher rate of detention usage.

The increase in correctional episodes probably exceeds the increase in rates of juvenile arrests for serious crimes. National data is lacking for 1923, but is available for the 1960s. Using the FBI "crime index" offenses, the change in the juvenile arrest rate between the mid-1960s and the mid-1990s was about 43 percent. During the same time period, the episode rate for detention and jail combined increased by about 94 percent, or nearly twice the increase in arrests for serious offenses.

Division of Labor in Juvenile Corrections

The changes in child welfare definitions and funding of "foster child-care institutions," combined with federal funding to promote the removal of status offenders from detention and secure facilities, helped promote the growth of the private sector in corrections. Over time these sources of funding, as well as state and local interest in fostering "alternative placements," have also facilitated a striking division of labor between facilities categorized as public or private in the national custody surveys. In 1995 about 65 percent of all juvenile correctional facilities were private.

Here are some significant differences between public and private facilities, respectively, in 1995:

1. Detention: 89 percent public vs. 11 percent private
2. Shelters: 17 percent vs. 83 percent
3. Halfway houses/group homes: 14 percent vs. 86 percent

4. Probation/after-care custody: 25 percent vs. 75 percent
5. Voluntary admission: 7 percent vs. 93 percent
6. Maximum security: 83 percent vs. 17 percent
7. Least security: 20 percent vs. 80 percent
8. Mean number of staff per twenty-five juveniles: 35 vs. 45

It is evident that the private sector has developed into a "kinder and gentler" type of correctional facility in comparison to the public sector, partially because the private sector has control over its intake and, therefore, may have a diverse mix of youth residing in a facility. In 1989, for example, the reasons for a resident being in a private facility were as follows: 36 percent for a delinquent offense; 18 percent for a status offense; 29 percent for nonoffenders (i.e., dependency, neglect, abuse, emotional disturbance, or retardation); and 18 percent as "voluntary commitments." In contrast, we find the following reasons for a resident being in a public facility: 95 percent delinquent offenses; 4 percent status offenses; 1 percent nonoffenders; and less than 1 percent voluntary commitments.

Number of Facilities, Size, and Length of Stay

In 1995, there were 24,000 youths detained on a census day in 450 public detention facilities with an estimated size of about 53 youths per facility. The average length of stay was about 15 days. In 1995, there were about 43,963 youth living in 609 other types of public facilities on a census day, with an average size of about 227 per facility. The average length of stay in public facilities was about 228 days.

In the private sector there were about 39,671 youths living in 1,989 facilities in 1995 on a census day, with an estimated size of about 20 per facility. The average length of stay was about 163 days for committed youth in 1986, and about 32 days for voluntary placements.

In 1995, there were about 7,000 juveniles residing in a jail on a census day distributed in 3,304 jails with an estimated population size of about 2 youths per facility. The estimated length of stay in 1995 was about 15 days. In 1995, there were 3,600 youths in adult prisons distributed in 1,287 geographic locations, with an estimated population size of about 3 per facility. In 1993, the estimated length of stay was about 2 years.

Gender and Racial Disparities in Juvenile Corrections

The primary information about any discrepancies in institutional utilization is associated with single-day counts, rather than admissions. One of the major sources of gender and racial disparities is associated with the differences between public and private facilities. Since the first recent survey in 1975 located the number of private facilities that housed at least 10 percent delinquent youth, the private sector has displayed a persistent increase, particularly in facility types such as shelters for status offenders and nonoffenders, special training schools, and halfway houses/group homes. These three types make up about 88 percent of all of the census day residents and 84 percent of the admissions to private facilities.

In 1995, females were much more likely to be part of private facilities than public ones (about 29 to 11 percent, respectively). In 1995, blacks made up about 43 percent of public, nondetention facilities, and Hispanics made up about 21 percent. In contrast, in private facilities blacks made up about 32 percent and Hispanics about 9 percent of the resident population.

When private facilities are assessed by type, for 1991, clear racial and ethnic disparities are evident. Blacks were least likely to be in private halfway houses/group homes and shelters (the more open types of facilities) and most likely to be in such secure facilities as private detention and training schools. Hispanics were most likely to be in private detention centers. It is not possible to control for age, history, or current offense in making further assessments, but these disparities continue to warrant further study.

Available evidence also indicates that there are consistent ethnic/racial differences in the rates of detention for youth who are formally petitioned to appear before the court. If the type of current offense is controlled, as was done in an analysis of 1994 juvenile court data by the National Center of Juvenile Justice, then the following disparities in detention proportions appear for each type of offense:

1. Violent offenses: 21 percent white detained vs. 29 percent black
2. Property offenses: 14 percent white detained vs. 22 percent black
3. Drug offenses: 18 percent white detained vs. 43 percent black
4. Public order offenses: 21 percent white detained vs. 30 percent black

Disparities exist for all offenses, but they are particularly notable for the drug offenses.

Variability among the States

Focusing only on national data can obscure some rather significant differences that emerge when comparing data by states. A comparison of five states with a similar juvenile court jurisdiction of up to age eighteen and large urbanized populations reveals the disparity that can be found within America. We have chosen to examine California, Florida, New Jersey, Ohio, and Pennsylvania.

In 1974–75, the national admissions rate for public detention facilities alone was 872 per 100,000 youth under eighteen years of age. However, two states were substantially higher: California and Florida (2,771 and 1,455, respectively). One state, Ohio, was fairly close (944), and two states were appreciably lower, New Jersey and Pennsylvania (620 and 539, respectively). These findings indicate that public detention admission rates could vary by state between 2,771 and 539 in a single year, with a national average of 872.

In 1987, the total national admissions rate for all public and private facilities was 1,182 for the nation. California had a total admission rate of 2,279—about twice the national rate. Florida and Ohio also had rates above the national average (1,701 and 1,829, respectively). New Jersey and Pennsylvania remained below the national average (1,037 and 898, respectively). Again, we are confronted with marked admission-rate disparities between high-confinement and low-confinement states.

MENTAL HEALTH

The development and evolution of mental health institutions for youth in trouble is associated with two distinct historical paths: the residential treatment center and inpatient hospitals. The residential treatment center (RTC) evolved out of the application of child guidance clinic approaches and techniques to the institutions linked to the field of child welfare and the professions of social work and psychology. Beginning in 1965, the RTCs were perceived to be an integral part of the nation's "inpatient" mental health service delivery system, and have been included in the periodic surveys conducted by a unit of the National Institute of Mental Health (and after 1992 by the Center for Mental Health Services).

The second historical path associated with mental health hospitalization and the profession of child psychiatry began in the late 1950s and early 1960s and has continued to care for and treat an increasing number of youth in trouble. In order for the problems of youth to be dealt with in an inpatient hospital setting, however, there had to be changes in the belief systems of psychiatrists and a broader acceptance by referral and funding sources.

From Delinquent Acts to Mental Disorders

In the 1920s, institutionalization of youth for psychiatric reasons was a rare event. A major reason that so few of the residents of mental hospitals for "mental disease" were juveniles was the traditional belief about the "age of insanity." As the reporters of the 1923 census of mental hospitals wrote about the age of patients, "Mental disease occurs principally in adult life. Psychopathic disorders appear in children, but as a rule these are not serious enough to require commitment to a hospital for mental disease. . . . It will be noted that only 0.2 percent of the total patients were under 15 years of age, and only 1.5 percent were under 20 years."

The belief that few youth had a "mental disease" was based on the idea that only existing classifications of mental illness, pertaining only to adults, were within the boundaries of psychiatry. Beginning in 1951, five years after the founding of the National Institute of Mental Health (NIMH), the Group for the Advancement of Psychiatry (composed of William Menninger and other young psychiatrists) issued reports promoting the expansion of child mental health services in a variety of settings. These reports became the basis of the first nationally recognized classification of childhood disorders that were formally included in the *Diagnostic and Statistical Manual of Mental Disorders* (or *DSMR*). In 1968, *DSMR-II* described the disorders of "adjustment reactions to childhood and youth" and "behavior disorders of childhood and adolescence." Later editions of *DSM-III-R* and *DSM-IV* expanded on these early classifications.

In 1978, a prestigious President's Commission on Mental Health published the *Task Force Report on Children,* which communicated to the nation that "conduct disorders" are the "most serious childhood disorder." They asserted that "a large proportion of juvenile delinquents have conduct disorders." Unlike emotional disorders (e.g., fear, anxiety, depression, obsession, and hypochondriasis) and delays in development, which occur in the same frequency in boys and girls, conduct disorders are "significantly more common among boys." Conduct disorders were deemed by the commission to be difficult to treat, so that they might require lengthy stays in appropriately staffed mental health facilities.

In the 1978 report, the main indicators of conduct disorder were listed as theft and poor relationships. In 1994, the *Diagnostic and Statistical Manual IV,* published by the American Psychiatric Association, listed fifteen specific behaviors as the indicators of a "disorder": nine referring to behaviors that could be the basis of a delinquency charge (e.g., aggression towards people and animals, destruction of property, and theft), and three referring to violations of rules, or status offenses (e.g., running away, staying away overnight, and truancy). A youth under eighteen could qualify as having a conduct disorder by engaging in three or more of the behaviors within twelve months, with at least one behavior occurring in the last six months. In addition, "the disturbance in behavior causes clinically significant impairment in social, academic, or occupational functioning." An earlier version of the *Diagnostic Manual,* known as *DSM-III-R,* used thirteen behavior items and did not require evidence of an "impairment" in daily functioning.

The concept of childhood mental disorders has also been included in federal mental health legislation. In 1973, Medicaid legislation was amended to include mental health services for persons under twenty-two in public or private psychiatric institutions for "mental disease." In 1992, federal law required that in order for states to qualify for mental health block grants for outpatient and inpatient community services, they must identify and use the funds for children with a "serious emotional disturbance" (SED). The 1993 federal regulation defines children with an SED as those under eighteen who currently or during the past year have had a diagnosable mental, behavioral, or emotional disorder that meets *DSM-III-R* (and subsequent versions) criteria, and that resulted in one or more functional impairments in family, school, or community activities. Youth with substance abuse or developmental disorders do not qualify, unless they co-occur with another diagnosable SED.

The Utilization of State/County Mental Hospitals

From the mid-1950s until the mid-1970s, the admission rates of youth to state/county facilities increased quite rapidly. The deinstitutionalization of adults (beginning in 1955) had provided bed space and staff to care for the new occupants, since few states actually closed institutions in the early years of depopulating state/county mental hospitals. A 1966 study in Nebraska provides insight into what types of youth were using these facilities. A psychiatrist and a psychiatric social worker teamed up to conduct a study of 247 adolescents admitted to the Nebraska Psychiatric Institute (a state hospital) between 1961 and 1964. They found that most of the referrals were initiated by a local juvenile court, county attorney, social agency, doctors, or sheriffs rather than the patient or his family. The "real reasons" for the majority of referrals were socially deviant behaviors (about 71 percent), not classic mental health symptoms. Examples of deviant behaviors included "truancy, vandalism, robbery, sexual offenses, and other violations of law and social moral codes."

A separate analysis of the primary diagnosis of admissions to all state/county mental hospitals for 1975 revealed that about 72 percent of the admissions of youth under eighteen were for behaviors that were not associated with an adult type mental disorder. Instead, youth were admitted because of childhood disorders, personality disorders, drug disorders, and other undifferentiated problems. Evidently, Nebraska was not alone in discovering the multifunctional uses of state mental hospitals undergoing deinstitutionalization by adults.

The utilization of state/county hospitals by youth began to decline in the early 1970s after other types of mental health facilities became available (see figure 3.6). In 1994, it is estimated that about 6.8 percent of the state/county beds were utilized by youth under eighteen years of age, or about 5,570 beds distributed in 285 geographical locations. The average number of youth that could reside in a hospital on a census day was about twenty in 1994.

In the same year, it is estimated that the average length of stay for youth was about 151 days, or about 5 months. The total episode rate in 1994 was about 25 per 100,000 compared to a rate of 56 in 1971 (see figure 3.7).

Psychiatric Units of General Hospitals

Before World War II, only thirty-nine general hospitals in the country had a separate psychiatric service for all ages. By 1994, the nation had more than fifteen hundred locally based general hospitals with separate psychiatric

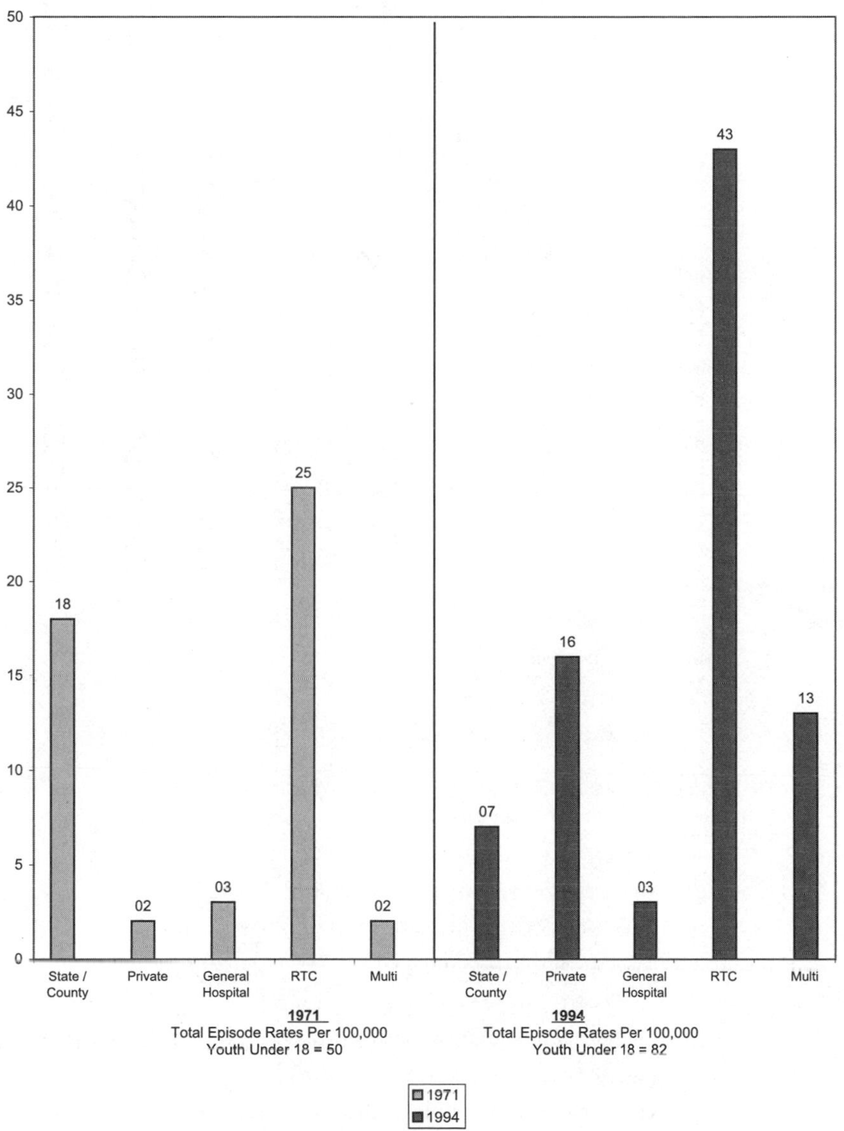

Fig. 3.6 Resident rates of mental health facilities per 100,000 youth under 18 years of age, by facility type in 1971 and 1994.

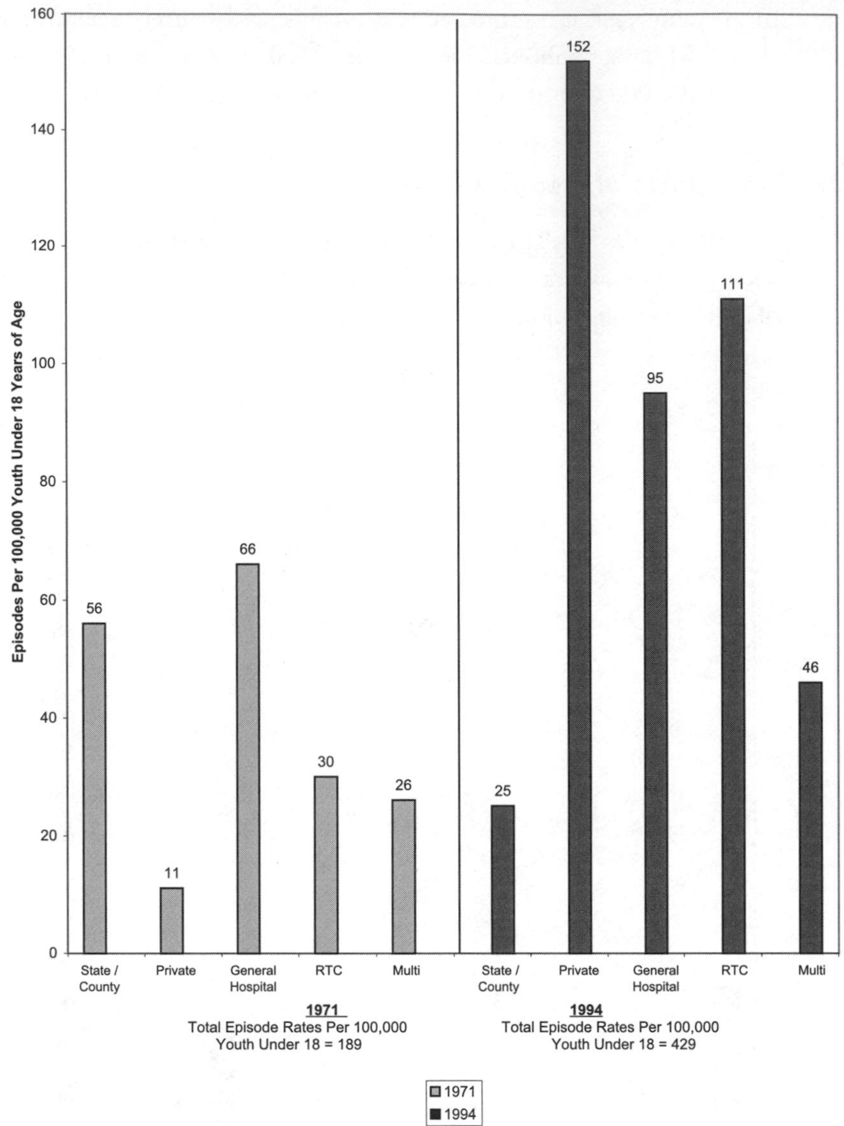

Fig. 3.7 Inpatient care episode rates of mental health facilities per 100,000 youth under 18 years of age, by facility type in 1971 and 1994.

inpatient units for juveniles and adults. The growth and further expansion was facilitated by the following factors:

1. The use of federal hospital construction funds for the creation of psychiatric beds
2. The increasing availability of psychoactive drugs that made it easier to deliver mental health services at a local level
3. The use of federal funding for the training of thousands of new psy-

chiatrists, psychologists, and social workers to staff inpatient and outpatient units

4. The gradual increase in less restrictive insurance payments by third-party payers
5. The passage of Medicare and Medicaid, permitting federal funding for psychiatric services for persons under twenty-two or over sixty-four

The resident rates for 1971 and 1994 are presented in figure 3.6.

The general hospitals were being used for youth under eighteen quite differently than was true for persons eighteen and older. In 1975, about 75 percent of the discharges of youth from the nation's general hospitals were for general/behavioral symptoms such as "transitional situational," childhood, personality, drugs, and undifferentiated problems. Adults had only 26 percent of the psychiatric unit discharges that could be categorized by such symptoms. In that same year, about 17 percent of the referrals came directly from a court, police, or correctional referral.

In 1994, it is estimated that about 5.8 percent of the general hospital psychiatric beds were utilized by youth under eighteen years of age, or about 3,100 beds distributed in 1,531 geographic locations. The average number of youth that could reside in a hospital on a census day was about two. However, the 1994 length of stay was only about twelve days. Because of the large number of admissions per available bed, the total episode rate in 1994 was about 95 per 100,000, compared to a rate of 66 in 1971 (see figure 3.7).

Private Psychiatric Hospitals

Private psychiatric hospitals were a very rare referral source for youth in trouble in the 1950s and the 1960s. By 1968, an NIMH survey identified 151 psychiatric hospitals nationwide: 69 nonprofit and 82 for-profit. During the 1970s, the number of proprietary hospitals increased sharply, while the nonprofit hospitals began to decline. The increase was in response to new sources of federal funding and the increasing availability of third-party insurance. Psychiatric hospitals had become a big business in America and were perceived as a growth industry by the *Wall Street Journal*. The resident rates for 1971 and 1994 are presented in figure 3.4.

For those under 18, inpatient episodes in private psychiatric facilities skyrocketed between 1971 and 1994—the last date for which we have good, reliable national data—from about 7,600 episodes in a year to more than 104,400 episodes. No other facility type has grown to this degree. More important, the episode rate per 100,000 youths under 18 is the largest rate of any psychiatric facility type, surpassing all types by a significant amount (see figure 3.7). In 1986, about 54 percent of the admissions to such facilities were diagnosed as having general/behavioral symptoms, with "pre-adult disorders" being the largest category.

In 1994, it is estimated that about 40 percent of the private psychiatric beds were utilized by youth under 18, or about 17,000 beds distributed in 430 geographic locations. The average number of youth that could reside in a hospital on a census day was about forty in 1994. In the same year, it is estimated that the average length of stay was about forty-two days. However, some private hospitals reported that they had reduced the length of stay to an average of about thirteen days for children under thirteen and eleven days for adolescents by using "improved medication management" (i.e., psychoactive drugs).

Residential Treatment Centers

As discussed in the child welfare section, many residential treatment centers (RTCs) had their origins as institutions for dependent/neglected children. Since the 1960s, they have become increasingly identified with the mental health system. Unlike other psychiatric facilities, RTCs were designed primarily for children with "emotional disorders" from their inception. For many years, RTCs did not need to make a certified, *DSM* type of diagnosis in order to receive reimbursement from a funding source. Instead, delinquent behaviors were judged to be signs of an underlying "emotional disorder" requiring residential treatment in a "structured environment." By the 1990s, many RTCs were using *DSM* classifications in order to receive third-party payments. The resident rates for 1971 and 1994 are presented in figure 3.6.

There is strong evidence that RTCs do have a population of youth with many problems. One of the most careful assessments of the residents of twenty-seven RTCs, located in six states, found that about 77 percent of youth could be classified as having a "conduct disorder." In addition, they found that other *DSM-III-R* problems existed for a number of youth, namely, the problems of attention deficit disorder, depression, and anxiety disorders. This study also found that residents of RTCs were likely to have been known to child welfare (62 percent), had experienced a stay in a detention facility (35 percent), had been on probation (39 percent), and had received psychotropic medication (53 percent). One of the surprising findings of this six-state study was that about one-half of the twenty-seven sites were locked facilities. In many correctional reports and master plans, such facilities are described as if all are open, but this can no longer be taken for granted.

In 1994, it is estimated that virtually all of the RTC beds were utilized by youth under 18, or about 32,100 beds distributed in 459 geographic locations. The average number of youth that could reside in an RTC on a census day was about seventy in 1994. In that year, it is estimated that the average length of stay was about 231 days, or about 7.6 months. However, a subgroup of 103 RTCs operated by proprietary psychiatric organizations reported that their length of stay had been reduced to about 77 days by using "improved medication management." In 1994, the total episode rate for all RTCs was 111, compared to a rate of 30 in 1971 (see figure 3.7).

Multiservice Organizations

In 1963, the federal government provided funds for the construction of community mental health centers. Funding was also supplied, to a limited extent, for the staffing of the new community centers over a twelve-year period, with the amount decreasing over the years. Centers would be supported if they provided inpatient beds as well as outpatient care, partial hospitalization, emergency care, and consultation and education. By 1976, there were more than six hundred facilities, and even after federal funding ceased, they continued to increase in number until there were more than fifteen hundred in the early 1990s. The resident rates for 1971 and 1994 are presented in figure 3.6. Like other inpatient admissions to mental health facilities, multiservice inpatient admissions tend to be for youth with symptoms that are general behavioral problems. In the most recent year for which data is available, 1984, about 62 percent of the admissions were for general behavioral reasons.

In 1994, it is estimated that about 16 percent of all multiservice beds were utilized by youth under 18, or about 9,700 beds distributed in 1,016 geographic locations. The average number of youth that could reside in a facility was about ten. In 1994, it is estimated that the average length of stay was about thirty-four days, and the inpatient episode rate was about 46 per 100,000 youths under 18, as compared to 26 in 1971 (see figure 3.7).

Variability in Sources of Financing Mental Health Facilities

The previous sections have noted that mental health facilities have relied on a variety of funding sources: state and local governments, the federal government, and third-party insurance/client fees. Each facility type relies on a distinct pattern of funding from these diverse sources. The funding pattern, in turn, influences the types of patients admitted, the lengths of stay, and the treatment services that are most likely to be reimbursed at a high rate. The private psychiatric sector, for example, has been quite interested in expanding the number of youth under their control. A 1998 annual report from the National Association of Psychiatric Health Systems noted how proprietary facilities are expanding by seeking out new sources of funding:

> Many of these programs have contracted with the public sector to provide a variety of services, including management of state hospitals, juvenile jus-

> tice programs, and programs for welfare recipients . . . Many of these populations, such as juvenile offenders have very complex and severe problems requiring a high intensity of services and relatively longer lengths of stay, which accounts for the growth in residential care as a proportion of total net revenue.

In 1997, the proprietary RTCs reported that an average daily rate was $215/day. At an average stay of 77 days, an episode in this type of ownership would cost an insurance company, a contracting organization, or Medicaid about $16,555. RTCs that kept youth for six months or 180 days would cost a third-party payer about $38,700. Unless nonprofit RTCs reduced their length of stay or lowered their daily rate, they would have a difficult time competing with the proprietary RTCs.

In 1994, the three facility types that were most likely to rely on federal funds were private psychiatric (43 percent), general hospital (38 percent), and multiservice (28 percent). The top three facility types relying on third-party insurance/client fees were private psychiatric (44 percent), general hospital (28 percent), and multiservice (8 percent). The top three facility types using state funds were state/county (70 percent), multiservice (39 percent), and RTCs (38 percent).

Variability in the Use of Mental Health Facilities

The most recent national data pertaining to gender and race are not broken down by age groups. Therefore, we must use data for all age groups in order to gain insight into the differential utilization of mental health facilities, using 1986 admissions. Nonwhites were most likely to be admitted to facilities in the following rank order: state/county (33 percent), general hospital (23 percent), multiservice (21 percent), and private psychiatric (17 percent). A special survey of RTCs, covering nineteen facilities in the mid-1990s, noted that about 59 percent of residents were "non-Caucasians."

Regarding the differential utilization of facilities by gender, using 1986 data for all ages, males were most likely to be admitted to state/county (63 percent), multiservice (58 percent), private psychiatric (52 percent), and general hospital (47 percent). The special survey of RTCs disclosed that 64 percent of residents were males.

Utilization of Psychoactive Drugs

The provision of various types of psychoactive drugs to youth admitted to inpatient facilities was first documented on a national scale in 1972. An NIMH survey found that 90–95 percent of inpatient hospital units reported offering tranquilizers and stimulants to youth as part of their "treatment services." RTCs reported offering comparable drugs at a rate of 56–63 percent in 1972. These practices have continued and have even begun to be widely used in outpatient mental health facilities, as well as in such correctional facilities as detention units and jails.

Surgeon General's Assessment of Mental Health Institutions

The increased utilization of residential and inpatient facilities is not associated with evidence of their effectiveness. The 1999 Surgeon General's report on mental health concluded that based on an assessment of research, it was "premature to endorse the effectiveness of residential treatment for adolescents." The report also concluded that inpatient hospitalization was "the clinical intervention with the weakest research support," since uncontrolled studies demonstrated that "community care was at least as effective as inpatient treatment." Because of these assessments and the estimate that these types of restrictive services consume about three-fourths of all dollars spent on child mental health services, the report recommends that greater attention be paid to "the development of community-based alternative services."

THE SUBSTANCE ABUSE SYSTEM

National-level data on admissions to federal substance abuse treatment programs was first mandated in 1972 as part of the Drug Abuse Office and Treatment Act, but reliable age data by inpatient treatment facility was not available until recently. The most recent reliable data is for 1996–97. However, because of the interest of child welfare and corrections in substance abuse, there is probably a degree of overlap for some of the facilities counted by these systems and the substance abuse reporting system. Mental health data are explicitly instructed not to count drug/alcohol units, but specific persons receiving drug treatment may also be counted in multiservice psychiatric facilities.

In 1996, 23,056 youths were admitted to one of the following inpatient substance abuse facilities: (1) detoxification in a hospital; (2) detoxification in a free-standing setting; (3) rehabilitation/residential in a hospital; and (4) rehabilitation/residential, free standing. More than 80 percent of the youth admissions were to free-standing rehabilitation/residential facilities. Of the 10,800 youths under eighteen in residence on a census day, about 90 percent were in a nonhospital residential facility. Controlling for population, the residence rate was about 16 per 100,000 under eighteen in 1996 (see figure 3.8).

If we add the number of admissions and youth in residence, we find that there were about 33,856 episodes in 1996–97. Controlling for population un-

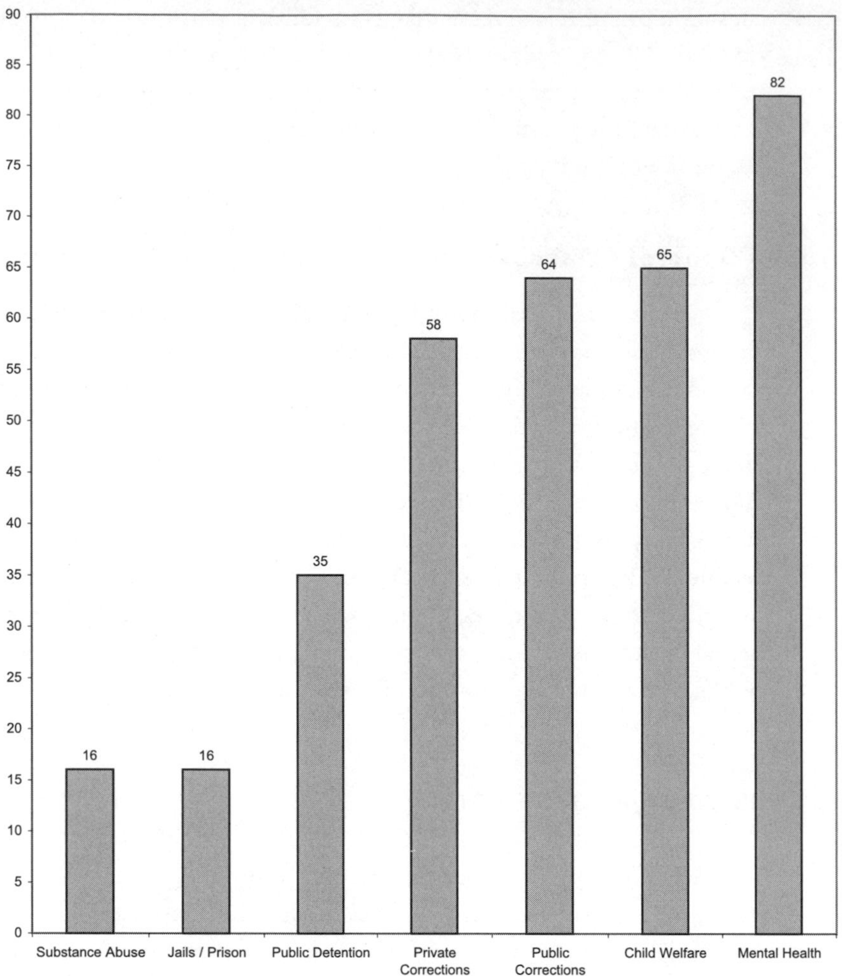

Fig. 3.8 Mid-1990s total resident rates for all systems per 100,000 youth under 18 years of age, by system type (N = 336).

der eighteen per 100,000, we find an episode rate of 49. If the high numbers of youth handled in juvenile court for drug offenses were handled in this system, rather than in the detention and correctional system, the episode rate would undoubtedly be much higher. In 1994–95, for example, more than 147,000 youths were formally arrested, and about 120,000 were formally processed in juvenile court for drugs. In that same year, more youth under eighteen were detained for drugs as part of their formal processing than were admitted to a drug treatment program in 1996 (about 33,600 to 23,000). The disparity would be even higher if we included detention admissions prior to formal processing.

A CURRENT OVERVIEW OF ALL THE SYSTEMS

In the mid-1990s, there were about 230,700 youths under eighteen counted as twenty-four-hour residents in institutions on a census day in all seven of the systems discussed in this chapter, for a resident rate of 336 per 100,000 (see figure 3.8). Far more important, there were more than six times as many youth admissions to all of these twenty-four-hour facilities. In the mid-1990s, it is estimated that about 1,560,000 episodes occurred for all of the systems combined. In order to control for population for the specific years for which data was available, the number of youth episodes per 100,000 for each facility type has been computed. If all of the episodes across systems are added, the relative importance of each system can be determined by calculating the proportion of episodes out of all of the combined episodes. For example, in the mid-1990s, detention had a rate of 872 per 100,000 youths under eighteen, while the rate for all systems combined was 2,300. This means that detention accounted for 37.9 percent of all episodes during 1994–95 (see figure 3.9).

There are a number of drawbacks to combining the episode rates for all of the systems. First, within each system, facilities vary in admitting the same youth more than one time, thereby possibly contributing to an overcount. Second, an overlap probably exists in surveys reported by child welfare and juvenile corrections referring to shelters, group homes, and halfway houses. Third, an overlap is likely between mental health and child welfare, referring to residential treatment centers. Unfortunately, given the way the nation collected information in the 1990s (compared to the 1923 census of children's institutions) it is not possible to control entirely for these problems. Some of the overlap can be compensated, to some degree, by counting all admissions to RTCs as mental health episodes and counting only child welfare episodes in group homes.

Figure 3.9 displays the episode-rate proportion that the major systems, or parts of systems, exhibit in the mid-1990s in a pie chart. The public detention episode rate, as noted, accounts for 37.9 percent of the total episode rate for all youth facilities in the mid-1990s. Such facilities process more juveniles in a year than any other system or facility type. Together with the other public juvenile correctional episode rates and the jail/prison rates (primarily jails), the most confining, secure facilities account for 62.6 percent of all the episodes (i.e., 37.9 percent for detention, 11.5 percent for all other public facilities, 12.2 percent for jails, and 1 percent for prisons).

The major alternatives to the secure facilities could be the mental health system (18.7 percent) and the private juvenile correctional facilities (12.4 percent). However, many adolescent units in hospitals were locked, as were many residential treatment centers in the mid-1990s. Child welfare and substance

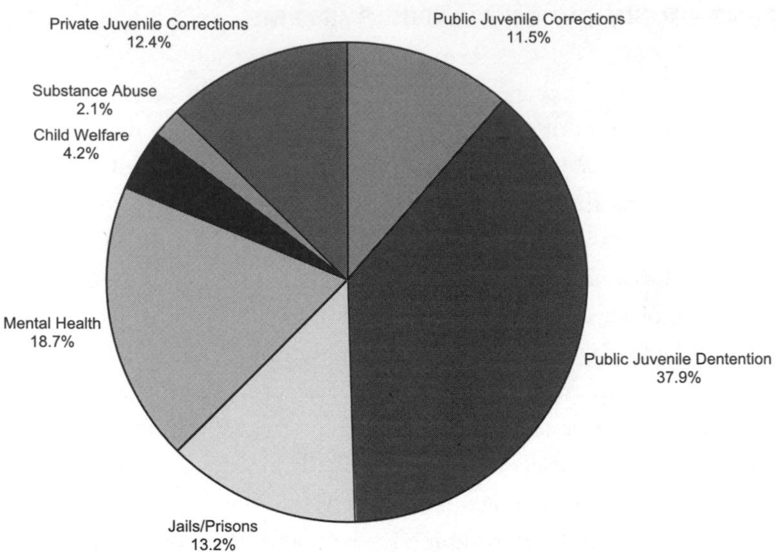

Fig. 3.9 Mid-1990s total episode rates for all systems per 100,000 youth under 18 years of age, by system type (in percent; N = 2,300).

abuse had the lowest episode rates (4.2 and 2.1 percent, respectively). Many substance abuse hospitals and residential facilities, however, were also locked.

In comparison to 1923, it is readily apparent that the child welfare sponsorship of institutional placements has diminished to an appreciable extent. In 1923, this system accounted for 64.3 percent of the total episode rates for the year, in contrast to the low episode-rate proportion in the mid-1990s. Of all the systems, this is the one that has been the most successful in deinstitutionalizing available resources and relying on "home care" in foster family homes. However, it is important to remember that child welfare dollars (via Title IV-E) are also funding a sizeable number of placements in private correctional facilities and RTCs.

For many years, the literature and statistical presentations associated with the juvenile court have perceived detention as a "predisposition" facility, designed to "hold" a juvenile pending informal or formal hearings. While more juveniles actually receive a stay in a detention center than are placed on probation during a calendar year, it is possible to focus only on facilities that are associated with a treatment or remediation program. Therefore, in order to appreciate the current balance in the nation's efforts to treat youth in trouble who could come before the court or actually appear in court, the episode rates used in figure 3.9 have been reanalyzed by excluding all episode rates for public detention and jail facilities. When this is done, as shown in figure 3.10, another perspective is offered for assessing the relative contributions of each residential treatment system's efforts to treat or remediate youth.

It is quite clear that mental health had emerged by the mid-1990s as the

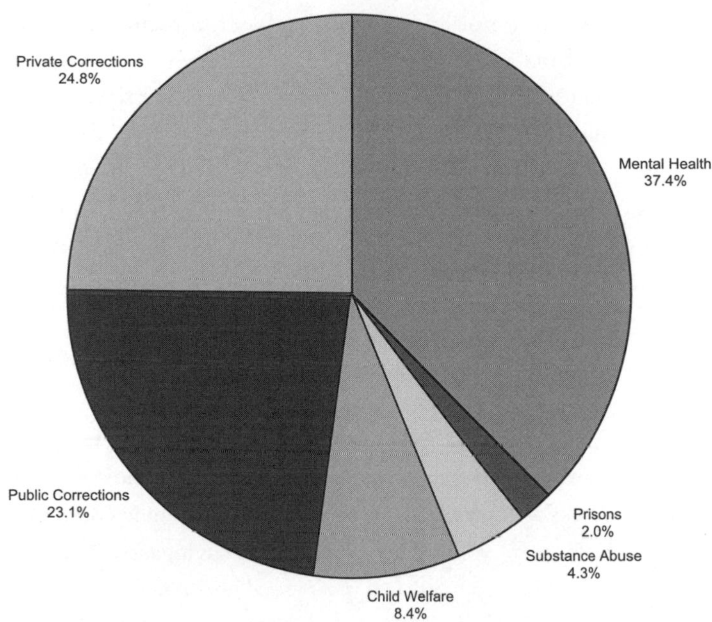

Fig. 3.10 Mid-1990s total episode rates for all treatment / remediation systems per 100,000 youth under 18 years of age, by system type (in percent; N = 1,146).

most likely system in which treatment episodes occur (37.4 percent). Private corrections had edged ahead of public corrections with the next highest episode rate (24.8 to 23.1 percent). Child welfare and substance abuse lagged far behind. Prisons were used quite sparingly, even though three states had age fifteen as an upper age of jurisdiction, eight states had age sixteen, and actually all states permit waivers to an adult court before age eighteen. The "child savers" who promoted the juvenile court would certainly have been pleased at the comparatively low utilization of prisons.

CONCLUSION

In comparison to the youth of the 1920s, many more youth in the 1990s experienced episodes in institutions, except in child welfare facilities. In addition, many more youth experienced episodes of confinement outside the correctional system in the 1990s, since many of the residential and inpatient mental health facilities were locked. However, the facilities of the 1990s tended to be smaller, and the lengths of stay were far shorter than in the 1920s. These trends occurred despite an absence of firm research evidence that the residential and inpatient mental health treatments were any more effective than the correctional approaches.

The current division of labor that has emerged between and within in stitutional systems is not due to planning based on scientific evidence, nor is it based on a rational allocation of resources. Rather, it is based on an accumulation of local and national ad hoc policies and practices, the growth in influence of professional interest groups, access to federal funds and third-party insurance, and the invention and dissemination of psychoactive medications as a means of controlling—as well as treating—youth in trouble. The interplay of these diverse influences can have diverse consequences for how institutions are utilized, depending on the variability of age, gender, race, type of problem, access to health insurance, and geographical location.

Available evidence indicates that the following outcomes occur:

- Youth under twelve are least likely to be admitted to any institution.
- Females are least likely to be admitted to a public correctional facility.
- Blacks are more likely to be admitted to a public correctional facility.
- Delinquent youth who are defined as having a conduct disorder are more likely to be treated in a mental health facility.
- Youth lacking health insurance or Medicaid are less likely to be treated in a mental health facility.
- Youth living in high-confinement states are more likely to experience a public correctional episode.

Looking ahead to the near future, it is likely that the redefinition of youth problems as signs of a "disorder" will continue to grow and that the use of mental health procedures—including psychoactive drugs—will spread to all of the institutional systems. Evidence already exists that detention facilities and local jails, the two most widely used correctional facilities, have begun to incorporate psychotropic medications as an integral part of their correctional mental health services. Whether the juvenile court will have a role in these and other institutional developments is not at all certain.

BIBLIOGRAPHIC NOTE

This chapter draws on my own work in understanding the utilization of multiple systems by youth in trouble: *Deinstitutionalization and the Welfare State* (New Brunswick, NJ: Rutgers University Press, 1982); "Child Welfare, the Private Sector, and Community-Based Corrections," in *Crime and Delinquency* 30, no. 1 (1984): 5–38; "Counting Youth in Trouble in Institutions: Bringing the United States Up to Date," in *Crime and Delinquency* 37, no. 4 (1991): 465–80; and *Community Treatment and Social Control* (Chicago: University of Chicago Press, 1975).

Important documentary readings on societal responses to youth problems are Grace Abbott, *The Child and the State,* 2 vols. (Chicago: University of Chicago Press, 1938); Robert H. Bremner, John Barnard, Tamara K. Haraven, and Robert M. Mennel, eds., *Children and Youth in America: A Documentary History,* 3 vols. (Cambridge, MA: Harvard

University Press, 1974); Edith Abbott, *Some American Pioneers in Social Welfare* (Chicago: Midway, 1974).

Useful background readings can be found in Jane Addams, *The Spirit of Youth and the City Streets* (New York: Macmillan, 1909); Sophonisba Breckenridge and Edith Abbott, *The Delinquent Child and the Home* (New York: Arno Press, 1912); Robert H. Bremner, *From the Depths: The Discovery of Poverty in the United States* (New York: New York University Press, 1956); Joseph M. Hawes, *Children in Urban Society* (New York: Oxford University Press, 1971); Michael B. Katz, *In the Shadow of the Poor House: A Social History of Welfare in America* (New York: Basic Books, 1986); Amos G. Warner, *American Charities* (New York: Russell and Russell, 1971. Revision of 1904 edition by M. R. Coolidge, re-issued in 1971 by Russell and Russell, a Division of Athenean Publishers); Homer Folks, *The Care of Destitute, Neglected, and Delinquent Children* (New York: Macmillan, 1902. Revised, Washington, DC: National Association of Social Workers, 1978); William Healy, *The Individual Delinquent* (Boston, 1915); William Healy and Augusta Bronner, "Juvenile Detention Homes," *Annals of the American Academy of Political and Social Sciences* 151 (September 1930): 180–93; Julia C. Lathrop, ed., *The Child, the Clinic, and the Court* (New York: New Republic, 1925); Theresa R. Richardson, *The Century of the Child: The Mental Hygiene Movement and Social Policy in the United States and Canada* (Albany: State University of New York Press, 1989); James Leiby, *A History of Social Welfare and Social Work in the United States* (New York: Columbia University Press, 1978); Steven L. Schlossman, *Love and the American Delinquent* (Chicago: University of Chicago Press, 1977); John R. Sutton, *Stubborn Children: Controlling Delinquency in the United States, 1640–1981* (Berkeley: University of California Press, 1988).

Since 1880, the U.S. Bureau of the Census has performed counts of persons residing in American institutions. The most useful ones to consult are *Benevolent Institutions, 1910* (Washington, DC: GPO, 1913); *Patients in Hospitals for Mental Disease, 1923* (Washington, DC: GPO, 1926); *Children under Institutional Care, 1923* (Washington, DC: GPO, 1927); *Children under Institutional Care and in Foster Homes, 1933* (Washington, DC: GPO, 1935); *Institutional Population, 1950,* vol. 4, *Special Reports, 1953* (Washington, DC: GPO, 1953); *Inmates of Institutions, 1960,* Final Report PC(2)-8A, 1963 (Washington, DC: GPO). For national and state population data, as well as other statistics, the U.S. Bureau of the Census also published *Historical Statistics of the United States: Colonial Times to 1970.* 2 parts (Washington, DC: GPO, 1975). National and state population data for the 1980s and 1990s can be found on the Internet at www.census.com.

Two special surveys conducted by researchers at the University of Chicago are invaluable for making up for some of the shortcomings of federal data in the 1960s and 1970s. See Donnell M. Pappenfort, Dee M. Kilpatrick, and A. Dinwoodie, *Population of Children's Residential Institutions in the United States, 1966,* 7 vols. Social Services Monographs, Series no. 4 (Chicago: Center for Urban Studies, 1970); Thomas Young, Donnell M. Pappenfort, and C. Marlow, *Residential Group Care, 1966 and 1981.* Mimeo (Chicago: University of Chicago, School of Social Service Administration, 1983).

Information used for analysis of child welfare relied on census data and on U.S. Children's Bureau, *Foster Care of Children: Major National Trends and Prospects* (Washington, DC: U.S. Department of Health, Education, and Welfare, 1966); U.S. General Accounting Office, *Children in Foster Care Institutions* (Washington, DC: General Accounting Office, 1977); U.S. Department of Health and Human Services, Office of Human Development Services, *Child Welfare Statistical Fact Book* (Washington, DC: Administration for Children, Youth, and Families, prepared by Maximus, Inc., 1988); U.S. Children's Bureau, *Adoption and Foster Care Analysis and Reporting System Reports* (Washington, DC: Administration for Children, Youth, and Families of the Department of Health and Human Services, 1997). Recent foster care and adoption statistics can be found on the Internet at www.acf.dhhs.gov.

Information used for analyses of trends in juvenile and adult corrections relied on census data and President's Commission on Law Enforcement and Administration of Justice, *Task Force Report: Corrections* and *Task Force Report: Juvenile Delinquency and Youth Crime* (Washington, DC: GPO, 1967); U.S. Law Enforcement Assistance Administration, *Children in Custody, 1971* and *Children in Custody, 1974* (Washington, DC: National Criminal Justice Information and Statistics Service, 1974 and 1977); U.S. Law Enforcement Assistance Administration, National Criminal Justice Information and Statistics Service, *Sourcebook of Criminal Justice Statistics, 1974* (Washington, DC: GPO, 1974); U.S. Department of Justice, *Children in Custody, 1975–1985* (Washington, DC: Bureau of Justice Statistics, 1989); National Council on Crime and Delinquency, *Juveniles Taken into Custody—Fiscal Year 1990 Report* (Washington, DC: Prepared for U.S. Department of Justice, Office of Juvenile Justice and Delinquency Prevention, 1991); National Council on Crime and Delinquency, *Juveniles Taken into Custody—Fiscal Year 1996 Annual Report* (Washington, DC: Prepared for U.S. Department of Justice, Office of Juvenile Justice and Delinquency Prevention, 1997); U.S. Department of Justice, *Prison and Jail Inmates at Mid-Year, 1997* (Washington, DC: Office of Justice Programs, NCJ 167247, 1998); U.S. Department of Justice, *Sourcebook of Criminal Justice Statistics, 1997* (Washington, DC: Office of Justice Programs, 1998).

Information used for analyses of trends in mental health relied on census data and National Institute of Mental Health, *Psychiatric Services and the Changing Institutional Scene, 1950–1980.* DHEW Publication no. (ADM) 77–433. (Washington, DC: GPO, 1977); National Institute of Mental Health, *Residential Psychiatric Services for Children and Adolescents: United States, 1971–72.* DHEW Publication no. (ADM) 74–78. (Washington, DC: GPO, 1972); National Institute of Mental Health, *Hospital Inpatient Units for Emotionally Disturbed Children: United States, 1971–1972.* DHEW Publication no. (ADM) 74–82. (Washington, DC: GPO, 1972); Center for Mental Health Services and National Institute of Mental Health, *Mental Health, United States, 1992.* DHHS Publication No. (SMA) 92–1942. (Washington, DC: GPO, 1992); Center for Mental Health Services, *Mental Health, United States, 1996* and *1998.* DHHS Publication no. (SMA) 96–3098, 1996 and DHHS Publication no. (SMA) 99–3285. (Washington, DC: GPO, 1996, 1998); National Association of Psychiatric Health Systems, *Trends in Behavioral Healthcare Systems: 1998 Annual Survey Report* (Washington, DC: National Association of Psychiatric Health Systems, 1999); Lois A. Weithorn, "Mental Hospitalization of Troublesome Youth: An Analysis of Skyrocketing Admission Rates," *Stanford Law Review* 40, no. 3: 773–838; President's Commission on Mental Health, *Task Panel Reports,* vols. 1–4 (Washington, DC: GPO, 1978); American Psychiatric Association, *Diagnostic and Statistical Manual of Mental Disorders,* 3rd and 4th rev. eds. (Washington, DC: American Psychiatric Association, 1987 and 1998); Starr E. Silver, Albert J. Duchnowski, Krista Kutash, Robert M. Friedman, Marvin Eisen, Mark E. Prang, Nancy A. Brandenburg, and Paul E. Greenbaum, *A Comparison of Children with Serious Emotional Disturbances Served in Residential and School Settings.* Mimeo (Tampa, FL: Research and Training Center for Children's Mental Health, University of South Florida, 1990); U.S. Surgeon General, *Mental Health: A Report of the Surgeon General.* (Rockville, MD: U.S. Public Health Service, 1999).

Information used for analyses of trends in substance abuse relied on census data and National Institute on Drug Abuse, *Data from the National Drug and Alcoholism Treatment Utilization Survey* and *Highlights from the 1987 National Drug and Alcoholism Treatment Unit Sur-*

vey (NDATUS). Mimeos (Washington, DC: Alcohol, Drug Abuse, and Mental Health Administration, 1980 and 1989); Substance Abuse and Mental Health Administration, *National Drug and Alcoholism Treatment Unit Survey (NDATUS), 1990–1993* (Washington, DC: Office of Applied Studies); Substance Abuse and Mental Health Administration, *National Admissions to Substance Abuse Treatment Services: The Treatment Episode Data Set (TEDS), 1992–1996* (Washington, DC: Office of Applied Studies, 1997). Recent information can be obtained from the Internet via www.samhsa.gov.

PART 2

Juvenile Justice and Legal Theory

The three essays in this section survey the legal theories of childhood most closely associated with the foundations of the juvenile court. Each essay also addresses a particular legal history. In chapter 4, "What Is a Child?," Elizabeth Scott shows that the consequences and boundaries of legal childhood have been linked to changing social conceptions of the character of children and the claims against public sympathy that these conceptions produce. Franklin Zimring's chapter 5 presents a revisionist history of the rationale for the juvenile court's delinquency jurisdiction, showing that diverting youth from the harms of criminal punishment was always an important element of the juvenile court, and that this diversionary rationale was the only major justification for the court to survive the reformulation of the jurisprudence of juvenile justice when *In re Gault* required procedural regularity in the juvenile courts of the United States.

If diversion from the harms of criminal punishment was the major success of the juvenile court in the United States, the coercive treatment of noncriminal misbehavior was the clearest failure to emerge from the first six decades of child saving. In chapter 6, Lee Teitelbaum describes the efforts to reform and rationalize the treatment of "status offenders" during the second half century of the juvenile court. This was the most significant substantive legal rethinking in the field and also an important example of the jurisprudence of the juvenile court adapting to changes in values and to the lessons of experience.

4 The Legal Construction of Childhood

Elizabeth S. Scott

For the most part, American lawmakers have had relatively clear images of childhood and adulthood, images that fit with our conventional notions. Children are innocent creatures, who are dependent, vulnerable, and incapable of making competent decisions. Several aspects of the legal regulation of childhood are based on this image. Children are not assumed to be accountable for their choices or for their behavior, an assumption that is reflected in legal policy toward their criminal conduct. They are also assumed to be unable to exercise the rights and privileges that adults enjoy, and thus are not permitted to vote, drive, or make their own medical decisions. Finally, children are assumed to need education, care, and support in order to develop into healthy productive adults. The obligation to provide these services critical to children's welfare rests first with parents and ultimately with the state. When children cross the line to legal adulthood, they are assumed to be autonomous persons who are responsible for their conduct, entitled as citizens to legal rights and privileges, and no longer entitled to support or special protections.

This picture is deceptively simple, of course. In fact, the law's account of childhood is extremely complex. Much of the complexity can be traced ultimately to a single source—defining the boundary between childhood and adulthood. Thus, the question, "What is a child?" is readily answered by policymakers, but the answer to the question, "When does childhood end?" varies in different policy contexts. This variation makes it extremely difficult to discern a coherent image of legal childhood. Youths in elementary school may be deemed adults for purposes of assigning criminal responsibility and punishment, while seniors in high school cannot vote, and college students are legally prohibited from drinking.

The picture is complicated further by the fact that policymakers have no clear image of adolescence. Generally, they ignore this developmental stage, classifying adolescents legally either as children or as adults, depending on the issue at hand. Thus, for many purposes, adolescents are described in legal rhetoric as though they were indistinguishable from young children and are subject to paternalistic policies based on assumptions of dependence, vulnerability, and incompetence that often seem more aptly applied to younger children. For other purposes, teenagers are treated as fully mature adults, competent to make decisions, accountable for their choices, and entitled to no special accommodation.

For many purposes, this dichotomous approach works well. Adolescents may well be mature enough to make some adult decisions or perform some adult functions, but not others, and policies that recognize these variations can be socially beneficial. For example, the gap between the minimum legal threshold for driving and drinking offers young persons independence and mobility, while protecting them (and us) from the costs of immature youthful judgment. Moreover, a rule that designates a particular age as the boundary between childhood and adulthood for multiple purposes (the "age of majority"), regardless of actual maturity, has the advantage of providing a clear signal of the attainment of adult legal status. It also protects parental authority and is administratively convenient. Even if such a crude classification distorts developmental reality, it generally may cause little harm. In some contexts, however, categorical assumptions that ignore developmental maturity can lead to policies that are harmful to youths as well as to society. For example, I will argue that juvenile justice policy provides ample evidence of the costs of using crude categories to define legal childhood and adulthood without regard to the underlying developmental realities.

This chapter begins with a description of legal images of childhood, sketching the traits that are assumed to distinguish children from adults and the policies based on these assumptions. In contrast to this clear account are the rather murky legal images of adolescence. I then turn to the the issue of how the boundary between childhood and adulthood is drawn for various legal purposes, focusing on three examples which suggest the complexity of the policy considerations that determine who counts as a child for legal purposes. The examples include the age of majority, voting rights, and medical decision making and abortion rights. The remainder of the chapter deals with juvenile justice policy; an area in which the boundary of childhood has changed radically over the past century. A perusal of legal rhetoric suggests that youthful offenders have been transformed from innocent children to hardened adult criminals over the course of the twentieth century. I will sketch how evolving policies have been linked to these changing conceptions of childhood. Both the traditional romantic vision and the modern account represent distortions that have been the basis of unsatisfactory policies. In the 1990s, the distortions have become extreme, as ever-younger children are treated as adults. I will argue that these policies are wrongheaded, both because they are harsh to immature offenders in a way that undermines core principles of criminal justice, and also because they are unlikely to provide the public safety and social welfare benefits that are promised.

LEGAL IMAGES OF CHILDHOOD AND ADOLESCENCE

Assumptions about Childhood and Legal Policy

Paternalistic legal regulation of children is based on powerful images of immature youths unable to look out for themselves and in need of adult supervision and guidance. Immaturity has several interrelated dimensions that shape legal policies that treat children differently from adults. First, children are dependent on others, initially for survival and then, as they grow, for the care that will enable them to mature to adulthood. This dependency requires that others provide for their basic needs—for food, shelter, health care, affection, and education, so that they may become healthy, productive participants in society. Children also lack the capacity to make sound decisions. Because of immaturity in cognitive development, they are unable to employ reasoning and understanding adequately to make choices on the basis of a rational decision making process. Children's decision making may also reflect immature judgment, which may lead them to make bad choices that are harmful to their interests and the interests of others. This decision-making immaturity warrants giving others authority over important decisions affecting children's lives. Children are also assumed to be vulnerable to both influence and harm from others. This vulnerability is due at least in part to children's dependence and immature decision making.

This image of childhood leads quite naturally to the conclusion that children must be subject to adult authority and that the deeply ingrained political values of autonomy, responsibility, and liberty simply do not apply to them. Under American law, primary responsibility for the welfare of children and authority over their lives is given to their parents. Justice Burger captured the conventional rationale for this allocation in *Parham v. J.R.*, a United States Supreme Court opinion dealing with parental admissions of their children to psychiatric hospitals:

> The law's concept of a family rests on a presumption that parents possess what children lack in maturity, experience, and capacity for judgment required to make life's difficult decisions. More importantly, historically it has recognized that natural bonds of affection lead parents to act in the best interests of their children. (442 U.S. 584, 602 [1979])

Parents are charged with the basic care of their children and the duty to protect them from harm. Parents also are authorized to make decisions on their children's behalf about matters ranging from nutrition, medical treatment, and residence to (in theory) choice of friends and reading material. Parental responsibility and authority go hand in hand. In some sense it is fair to view parental "rights" as legal compensation for the burden of responsibility which the law imposes on parents.

Of course, parents do not have total authority over their children's lives. Society has an important stake in the development of children into healthy and productive adults, and it will bear the costs when parents fail to fulfill their responsibilities. Moreover, under its historic *parens patriae* authority, the government has the responsibility to look out for the welfare of children and other helpless members of society. Thus, parental authority is subject to government supervision; if parents fail to provide adequate care, the state will intervene to protect children's welfare. The state also preempts parental authority more categorically on some issues. For example, under child labor and school attendance laws, parents cannot decide that their children should work instead of attending school. Traditionally, policy debates in this area have focused on the allocation of authority between parents and the state.

It may be useful to sketch briefly how assumptions about children's dependency, incapacity, immature judgment, and vulnerability are expressed in legal regulation. First, children's rights and privileges are far more restricted than are those of adults. Because they are assumed to lack the capacity for reasoning, understanding, and mature judgment, children cannot vote, make most medical decisions, drink, or drive. Their First Amendment right of free speech is more limited than is that of adults. Thus, the Supreme Court has held that the state can limit children's access to obscene material that would be protected speech for adults. Through curfew ordinances, the government can limit children's freedom to move about in society through restrictions that would clearly be unconstitutional for adults. The premise of these laws is that children roaming the streets at night may get in trouble (through the exercise of immature judgment) and that they will be vulnerable to harmful influences.

Children are also not held to an adult standard of legal accountability for their choices and behavior, because of assumptions about their immature judgment and their tendency to be subject to undue influence. Thus, under the infancy doctrine in contract law, minors are free to disaffirm most contracts. Most of the cases seem to involve motor vehicles or stereo equipment, which courts seem to believe that youths will be tempted to purchase without considering the obligation that they are undertaking. As one court put it, a minor "should be protected from his own bad judgments as well as from adults who would take advantage of him (Kiefer v. Fred Howe Motors, 158 N.W. 2d 288 [Wisc. 1968]).

Of broader importance is the traditional legal response to criminal conduct by juveniles. The founders of the juvenile court advocated against applying concepts of criminal responsibility and blameworthiness to the offenses of children. Children are not criminally responsible, under this view, because they lack the capacity for reasoning, moral understanding, and judgment on which attributions of blameworthiness must rest. The principle of retribution (and thus the integrity of the criminal law) is undermined if incompetent children are subject to criminal punishment. As Ben Lindsey, an early judge of the Denver Juvenile Court, put it, "Our laws against crimes are as inapplicable to children as they would be to idiots." The salience of the belief that children because of their immaturity are less blameworthy is suggested by the strategy of modern advocates of punitive justice policy reform. In arguing that young offenders should be held to adult standards of criminal responsibility, these reformers simply announce that young offenders *are* adults.

A third category of legal policies directed at children includes legal protections and entitlements that respond to children's dependency. The law requires parents and the state to provide children with the support, care, and educational services that they need to survive and develop and that they are unable to provide for themselves. Parental child support obligation, public welfare support, Medicaid, and Headstart provide a safety net that is designed to assure that children's basic needs are met. Public school education (including educational services to disabled children) is an entitlement in most states. It ensures that all children are given the opportunity to develop into citizens with basic capacities to participate in society. Moreover, because children are vulnerable and unable to assert their own interests, the state enforces parents' duty to provide adequate care through elaborate civil and criminal child abuse and neglect regulation. This system not only provides incentives for parents to identify their own interests with those of their children, but also offers the necessary substitute care when parents fail egregiously in carrying out their responsibilities.

Taken together, this complex network of legal regulation suggests that policymakers view children as a very special class of citizens, a group whose unique traits and circumstances warrant a different regulatory scheme from that which applies to the rest of us. In general these policies are grounded firmly in a consistent account of what it means to be a child.

Adolescence in Legal Rhetoric

No one thinks that adolescents are similar to toddlers in their reasoning and judgment, dependency, or vulnerability. The presumptions of developmental immaturity that shape the legal account of childhood do not fit comfortably with conventional images of adolescence. As compared with younger children, adolescents are close to adulthood. They are physically mature, and most have the cognitive capacities for reasoning and understanding that are necessary to make rational decisions. Yet, adolescents in many regards are not fully formed persons; they continue to be dependent on their parents, and their immature judgment may lead them to make poor choices which threaten harm to themselves or others. Conventional wisdom about adolescence probably tracks developmental knowledge: individuals in this group are proceeding through a developmental stage between childhood and adulthood—they are neither children or adults.

Although lawmakers have occasionally recognized the distinctive transitional character of adolescence, more typically this transitional stage is invisible, and adolescents are incorporated into the legal categories of childhood or adulthood. For many purposes—voting, military service, domicile, contracting, and entitlement to support—a clearly defined age of majority transforms adolescents from children subject to the authority of their parents and a paternalistic state into adults subject to the panoply of rights and duties of citizens. For other purposes, adult status is attained either before (driving) or after (drinking) the age of majority.

Where extending legal rights or responsibilities to minors is the subject of policy debate, the legal rhetoric employed casts adolescents as either children or as mature adults, depending upon the desired classification. For example, the Progressive reformers of the early twentieth century sought to protect youths from adult roles and responsibility. In advocating child labor laws, compulsory school attendance laws, and a separate court to respond to juvenile crimes, these reformers emphasized the immaturity of youth and the harms that would come to youngsters unless they were protected by a paternalistic state. In contrast, modern conservatives speak of "superpredators," and suggest that nothing distinguishes a fifteen-year-old offender from his adult counterpart (Bennett, DiIulio, and Walters 1996; Regnery 1985).

Abortion jurisprudence provides another good example of the elusiveness of adolescence as a legal category. When courts recognize parental authority and other constraints on pregnant minors' rights, they describe teens as children. Justice Powell, in *Bellotti v. Baird* for example, described the vulnerability of children, their lack of experience, perspective, and judgment, and the guiding role of parents in the upbringing of their children as the basis for limiting adolescent abortion rights (443 U.S. 622 [1979]). Legal arguments to confer adult abortion rights on teens present quite a different image of pregnant adolescents. In *H.L. v. Matheson,* for example, Justice Marshall argued (in dissent) that Utah's statutory restrictions amounted to a state-created obstacle to "the exercise of the minor woman's free choice" (450 U.S. 398 [1981]).

DRAWING THE LINE BETWEEN CHILDHOOD AND ADULTHOOD

As I have suggested, children cross the line to legal adulthood at different ages for different purposes. The baseline, of course, is the age of majority, which currently is eighteen. However, a complex regime of age grading defines childhood as a category with no clear boundaries. At age ten, youths charged with murder can be tried as adults in many states, and high school students have First Amendment rights of political expression. On the other hand, noncustodial parents may be obliged to contribute to their children's college expenses, and a young adult cannot consent to sterilization in many states. What explains this variation?

The logic of the legal regime that defines the boundaries of childhood is far from obvious. In part, age grading can be explained on the basis that different functions require different levels of developmental maturity. No one would challenge that the maturity demanded to fulfill the role of president (currently limited to citizens age thirty-five or older) is greater than that needed to drive a car or to vote. However, perusal of the scheme of regulations suggests that, although assumptions about maturity and concern about youth welfare usually play a policy role, age-grading policies are often shaped by considerations other than developmental maturity. Examination of specific policies suggests that lines are drawn on the basis of a number of diverse policy concerns. Ideology, protection of parental authority, and protection of society from the immature choices of young persons are all parts of the mix. This part of the essay will explore age grading in several contexts in the hope that some lessons can be extracted from the diverse responses that policymakers have offered to the question, "When does childhood end?"

The Logic of a Presumptive Age of Majority

The natural place to start is with the age of majority, the categorical designation of the point at which adult legal status is attained, and the restrictions, entitlements, and protections of childhood end. The common-law age of majority was twenty-one, apparently because in the Middle Ages it was the age at which most men were presumed capable of carrying armor. Currently adult status is attained at age eighteen. This milestone signals adult legal competence and freedom from parental authority. The financial support obligation of parents generally ends when the child attains the age of majority, as well as the parents' common-law right to the child's earnings. The state withdraws from its role as *parens patriae*. Adult citizens have the right to make decisions about domicile and about medical treatment. They also have the capacity to enter binding contracts, to sign leases, purchase real estate, and to make a will. Upon attaining the age of majority, individuals are accorded the rights and privileges of citizens, including the right to serve on juries and (perhaps of greatest symbolic importance) the right to vote.

The device of a categorical legal age of majority as the time at which individuals are given a package of adult rights and responsibilities can be understood as a crude determination that individuals at the designated age are mature enough to function in society as adults, and to make their own self-interested decisions. Before this threshold is crossed, most of these decisions are made by parents or by the state. Developmental psychology supports the view that by age eighteen, and certainly by age twenty-one, most individuals attain the presumed adult competency. In fact, one likely effect of such a categorical approach is that minors who are competent to make decisions and perform adult functions will continue to be treated as legal children. For this reason, this approach has been challenged, sometimes successfully, on the ground that it deprives competent youths of the ability to exercise rights that adult citizens enjoy (Melton 1983).

In general, the use of a rule to designate the end of childhood functions quite well, even though it ignores individual variations in developmental maturity as well as the varying maturity demands of the range of functions that may be included. For most purposes, no great harm results from postponing adult legal status until the designated age or from involving parents in their adolescent children's lives. Most adolescents have no pressing need to execute contracts, and if they do, parental involvement is probably usually desirable. Moreover, extending the presumptive dependency period offers benefits in the form of entitlement to support and other protections of childhood. Indeed, if maintaining parents' enthusiasm for their obligations toward their children is important, retention of parental authority may be worthwhile, as long as parents have no serious conflict of interest with their children. Moreover, a distinct age of majority is a clear signal, so that all who deal with a young person understand that he or she does—or does not—have legal capacity. A more tailored approach that attempted to confer adult status in different domains on the basis of a more targeted assessment of maturity would be likely to generate uncertainty and error, and it would be far more costly than the current system. Most cumbersome of all would be an approach that conferred adult legal rights or responsibilities on the basis of individualized assessments of maturity. Because such a strategy would be enormously expensive and administratively burdensome, predictably it is only employed when the stakes are high.

The upshot is that a categorical approach that treats individuals below a designated age as legal minors for most purposes works well, as long as that age corresponds roughly with some threshold of developmental readiness to assume the responsibilities and privileges of adulthood. Because of the advantages of this categorical approach, variations that depart from the presumptive age should attract our interest. These variations can be explained as serving some political or social goal that would be undermined by adherence to the conventional boundary of childhood.

The Right to Vote and the Passage of the Twenty-sixth Amendment

The right to vote has long been the defining marker of legal adulthood, and the age of majority has been linked with this important symbol of full-fledged citizenship. Until 1971, citizens could vote upon reaching their twenty-first birthday. In 1971, the Twenty-sixth Amendment to the United States Constitution was enacted, lowering the voting age to eighteen in both state and national elections (fig. 4.1). Predictably, the age of majority was lowered to age eighteen for many other purposes following the passage of the Twenty-sixth Amendment. The social and political forces that led to the passage of this constitutional amendment offer some interesting lessons about the way in which the boundaries of childhood are drawn. Moreover, the impact of

Fig. 4.1 President Nixon affixes his signature to signify that he witnessed the ratification of the 26th Amendment of the U.S. Constitution, July 15, 1971, Washington, D.C. © Bettmann/CORBIS

the downward shift of the age of majority on other areas of law, particularly on parental child support obligation, suggests the complexity of this boundary-definition process.

Like many other legal rights, the right to vote is withheld from minors because of crude assumptions about developmental immaturity. It is believed that political participation in a democracy should be based on an educated citizenry with an informed understanding of the issues, and that adults will be more likely to meet these criteria than children and adolescents. Although this is often untrue—many adolescents would be better informed voters than many adults—the withholding of the right to vote from minors has generated little controversy. This is probably because of a combination of two factors suggested above. The administrative cost of identifying mature minors "competent" to exercise their voting rights would be substantial, and the cost of postponing the opportunity to exercise voting rights does not seem to be a great deprivation.

How then can we explain the extensive effort undertaken to amend the United States Constitution to lower the age of enfranchisement to eighteen? The Twenty-sixth Amendment was enacted in the midst of the Vietnam War, when many legal minors between the ages of eighteen and twenty-one were drafted into military service. Moreover, across the country, college students involved in the civil rights and antiwar protest movements demonstrated an interest in political participation and a commitment to social change. The Senate committee that recommended the enactment of the Twenty-sixth Amendment emphasized these political facts. It also emphasized that the young adults who would be enfranchised under the new amendment were "mentally and emotionally capable of full participation in our democratic form of government."[1] Finally, the report noted that in all states, legal minors were treated as adults for the purposes of criminal responsibility and punishment, and that many were engaged in adult roles as employees and taxpayers. The common-law age of majority was dismissed as a matter of historical accident.

A couple of points about this political initiative are interesting. First, the reformers believed it was important that the common-law boundary between childhood and adulthood distorted the developmental reality. The argument for lowering the age of majority was based in part on an empirical claim that for most purposes psychological maturity was achieved by age eighteen, and that the common-law rule was based on a medieval criterion of no modern relevance. Another important theme was that a parity should exist between rights and responsibilities. On this view, fairness required the extension of voting rights to eighteen-year-olds because they were subject to the most onerous responsibility of citizenship (military service) and were often held legally accountable for their behavior under the criminal law. There is little question that the image of young persons dying for their country in Vietnam who were not deemed mature enough to participate in the electoral process carried much symbolic weight in the political process. It goes a long way toward explaining the timing of this constitutional reform. In general, this parity principle is one to which exceptions are often made, but it is powerful nonetheless.

The Limitations of the Categorical Approach: The Case of Child Support

The passage of the Twenty-sixth Amendment resulted in the lowering of the age of majority for many purposes, either automatically or through legislative or judicial action. Much of this reform was uncontroversial, and, for many purposes, age eighteen seemed a more suitable boundary between childhood and adulthood. In one area, however, the legal change was quite problematic. Many courts interpreted the legal reform to require that noncustodial parents' obligation to provide financial support for their minor children must end at age eighteen (because by definition, recipients were no longer minors).

The issue of when child support obligation should end continues to be the subject of debate. In many ways, modern eighteen-year-olds are ready to function as legal adults. However, college attendance has become the norm as preparation for a successful life, extending the period of financial dependency on parents for many young people. If the lowering of the age of majority to eighteen (when many children are still in high school) signifies the end of parents' legal obligation to provide financial support to their children, many children will obtain a college education only with great difficulty—if at all. In intact families, parents who have the financial means usually support their children's college education, implicitly acknowledging that in this domain a continuation of childhood status is in their children's best interest. Noncustodial parents may be less likely to identify their own interest with that of children with whom they no longer share a home. This may justify imposing a legal obligation on those parents to act toward their children as they would had the family remained intact, even though no such *legal* obligation is imposed on parents in intact families. In fact, noncustodial parents are often subject to formal legal mandates not applicable to parents in intact families—support for a minor child's private school education, for example. A legal directive is necessary because noncustodial parents cannot be counted on to act in their children's interest.

Some courts and legislatures have authorized the extension of parental child support obligation beyond the age of majority to provide financial support for college. The underlying premise is that children's financial dependency on their parents as they acquire a college education justifies extending the legal boundary of childhood beyond its presumptive limit for this purpose.

Legal recognition that in this domain older adolescents are not autonomous adults enhances social welfare as well as that of youths who receive the benefit of higher education.

Medical Decision Making

In general, the legal regulation of medical treatment of children and adolescents conforms to the categorical approach under which childhood ends at the age of majority. Most medical treatment of minors requires the consent of their parents. Thus, adolescents cannot obtain routine medical treatment on their own and, unlike adults, cannot refuse treatment that their physician and parents decide is necessary. The basis for parental authority in this area is relatively straightforward. Medical treatment must be based on informed consent—otherwise the treatment provider commits a battery on the patient. Because minors are presumed incompetent to give informed consent, parental consent is necessary. Developmental psychology evidence indicates that older minors are mature enough in their cognitive development to make competent medical decisions (Weithorn and Campbell 1982). Nonetheless, giving parents legal authority reduces uncertainty for medical service providers, who would otherwise need to assess the competence of their young patients. Beyond this, legal authority over health care decisions allows and encourages parents to fulfill their general responsibilities to provide for their children's welfare. For most medical treatments, parents can be counted on to have their children's interests at heart. Thus, in requiring parental consent for most medical treatments, lawmakers adopt the conventional categorical boundary of childhood for the conventional reasons.

The Mature-Minor Doctrine and Minors-Consent Statutes

There are many exceptions to this general rule, however. The requirement of parental consent is set aside under certain circumstances and for particular kinds of treatment, giving adolescents legal authority to make their own medical decisions. The most well-established of these exceptions historically is the mature-minor doctrine. Under this doctrine, legally valid consent can be obtained from an older competent minor for routine beneficial medical treatment or in an emergency situation. This exception facilitates necessary treatment when parental consent may be hard to get. It also protects medical providers from liability for what may be only technical violations of the informed consent requirement.

Aside from the general mature-minor rule, legislatures in many states have enacted more targeted minors-consent statutes that treat minors as adults for the purpose of consenting to particular kinds of treatments. These typically include treatment for sexually transmitted diseases, substance abuse, mental health problems, and birth control and pregnancy. The minors-consent statutes typically do not include a minimum age at which a minor is deemed an adult, but because of the nature of the specified conditions, only adolescents are likely to seek treatment. Implicitly, these laws assume that the young patients are competent to consent to the treatment, an assumption that is likely valid for mid-adolescents.

The policy behind these statutes is clear. The treatments targeted by the minors-consent statutes all involve situations in which the traditional assumption that parents can be counted on to respond to their children's medical needs in a way that promotes the child's interest simply might not hold. For example, some parents may become angry upon learning of their child's drug use or sexual activity. Moreover, even if most parents would act to promote their child's welfare, adolescents may be reluctant to get help if they are required to inform their parents about their condition, either because they fear their parents' reaction or because of a desire not to disclose private information. Removing this obstacle encourages them to seek treatment that may be critically important to their welfare. Of course, society also has an interest in reducing the incidence of sexually transmitted diseases, substance abuse, teenage pregnancy, and mental illness. Together these important social benefits largely explain why lawmakers shift the boundary of childhood for the purpose of encouraging treatment of these conditions.

The Battle over Adolescents' Access to Abortion

One kind of medical treatment for minors has been the subject of an intense legal and political controversy. In the generation since *Roe v. Wade,* legislatures and courts have struggled with the question of whether access to abortion by adolescent women can be regulated more restrictively than would be allowed for adult women. The larger ideological debate about abortion is expressed in this arena as a dispute about whether pregnant teens are autonomous adults with a presumed right of reproductive autonomy or children who should be subject to parental authority.

There are a number of reasons to distinguish abortion from other medical decisions that argue against adopting the traditional approach of requiring parental consent. First, as with the treatments that are covered by minors-consent statutes, the presumption that parents can be relied upon to make decisions in their children's interest seems problematic. Parents confronting a pregnant child may be learning for the first time that she is sexually active, and this information may be unwelcome evidence for some parents that their child has rejected their moral code. Moreover, some parents may strongly oppose abortion on moral or religious grounds and refuse to consent to a procedure that they find abhorrent. Abortion is quite different from most medical decisions in that parents' view of the right decision may be based on their personal moral values rather than on concern for their child's health per se. One focus of the debate has been whether parents should have the authority to impose their values on their adolescent child (whose own values may differ) on a matter of such critical importance to the child's welfare.

The challenge is strengthened by the fact that the decision about terminating pregnancy is a medical decision that is inherently an adult choice. A young woman's decision about whether to have an abortion or produce a child is one that will determine whether she herself will be a parent, with adult responsibilities and parental rights in the child. Under these circumstances, the traditional, paternalistic legal response seems less appropriate. Ironically, the option that is deemed superior by many who argue for parental authority on this matter is one that is more clearly associated with adult status—the experience of pregnancy, childbirth, and motherhood.

The right of a pregnant woman to make an autonomous decision about abortion is constitutionally protected, and this in itself distinguishes abortion from other medical decisions. However, this does not clarify whether minors should have the same authority as adult women. Many legal rights and privileges, as I have suggested, are not extended to minors. Is the right of privacy implicated in the abortion decision different from other important rights of citizens, such as the right to vote? There are some notable differences. One justification for deferring many legal rights until the age of majority is that postponement results in no great deprivation. In contrast, the decision about whether or not to have a child is both one that may have enormous consequences for the individual and one that cannot be postponed. Thus, a teen who is compelled to go through an unwanted pregnancy and to have a child may suffer substantial costs. As Justice Blackmun indicated in *Roe v. Wade,* an important justification for giving women control of this decision is that an unwanted pregnancy imposes a substantial burden on the individual. There is no reason to assume that this burden would be felt less acutely by an adolescent than by an adult woman.

Over the last generation, the constitutional parameters of minors' abortion rights have emerged in a series of United States Supreme Court decisions. The Court has examined state legislative efforts to restrict the freedom of minors to obtain abortions without involving their parents. Although some states give pregnant teens the same rights as adult women to make decisions about whether to terminate a pregnancy, the Supreme Court has made clear that adolescents can be subject to restrictions that would clearly be unacceptable for adults. In *Bellotti v. Baird,* Justice Powell suggested that an acceptable scheme of regulation must include a mechanism to protect the right of the *ma-*

ture minor to make her own decision about abortion (443 U.S. 584 [1979]). If a minor was found not to be mature (presumably through a judicial proceeding), then a determination should be made as to whether authorizing abortion without parental involvement was in her best interest.

Under Justice Powell's approach, which has been the model of legislation in several states, minors who demonstrate their maturity are deemed legal adults for the purpose of making abortion decisions. Immature pregnant teens are deemed children, and thus are subject to the paternalistic authority of the state or of their parents. The Supreme Court recognizes the unusual character of this particular medical decision, both in concluding that the constitution requires that the mature minor be deemed an adult and in providing for state supervision of the treatment decision when the minor lacks the maturity to make her own choice. For most treatment decisions, of course, parental authority would prevail.

It is not clear what capacities a minor must demonstrate to be deemed "mature" and thus to achieve adult legal status. The Supreme Court has never announced a standard to guide courts in making this determination, and (not surprisingly, perhaps) the judgment of where to draw the line between childhood and adulthood seems to depend on the attitude of the interpreter toward adolescent reproductive rights and toward abortion generally. Conservative courts raise the bar very high, evaluating petitioners under a standard for general maturity that most minors are unlikely to meet. For example, a Utah court rejected the petition of a seventeen-year-old who was described as a good student, concluding that she lacked the requisite "experience, perspective, and judgment." The court emphasized that she lived at home, engaged in sexual activity without contraceptives, sought counsel from friends rather than family members or church officials, and failed to recognize the long-term consequences of abortion (*H.B. v. Wilkinson,* 639 F. Supp. 952 [D. Utah 1986]). One is left to conclude that, in this court's view, a "mature" minor would have consulted with her parents (and thus have no need for the judicial bypass procedure) and probably would never have been foolish enough to become pregnant.

The legal framework endorsed by the Court represents an effort to find an acceptable resolution to a highly contested dispute about the boundary of childhood—a dispute that has more to do with conflicting attitudes about abortion itself than with views on parental authority or the maturity or autonomy interests of adolescents. In defining the constitutional restrictions on state authority to classify adolescents as children in this context, the Court allows states to limit abortion rights to mature adolescents. At the same time, it prohibits categorical classification of pregnant teens as children solely on the basis of age. In effect, this regulatory scheme creates a distinct legal category for adolescents and thus is a rare departure from the conventional binary classification of adolescents as either adults or children. On the one hand, even the mature pregnant teen is not quite an adult; the requirement that she demonstrate her maturity creates a substantive burden on her efforts to obtain abortion services that likely would be unacceptable for adult women. On the other hand, traditional parental authority to make medical decisions for their children is curtailed by the availability of the bypass hearing and by the right of mature minors to make their own decisions.

The endorsement of this unique regulatory scheme represents an effort by the Court to accommodate competing legal and political interests on a sharply contested moral issue. Under these circumstances, the Court may believe that the creation of an intermediate category is the only viable solution. The process is costly and cumbersome, however, and there is little evidence that it promotes the interests of pregnant teens or responds to their developmental needs. The requirement of a bypass hearing leads to costly delay and seems likely to result in later abortion in many cases—in part because it is viewed as an obstacle by many girls. Moreover, under the bypass model, judicial attitudes about abortion may color decisions about maturity and best interest, creating uncertainty and inconsistency. Setting aside the perceived need for constitutional compromise, this regulatory framework has little to recommend it.

Legislatures pursuing the conventional objectives that guide legal regulation of minors would focus on the health and welfare of the pregnant teen and on the social costs of teen pregnancy. From this perspective, the creation of an intermediate category of adolescence in this context holds no apparent advantage over the legislative line-drawing and binary classification of the minors-consent statutes. These statutes, which allow treatment without any inquiry into maturity, assume that the interests of young persons are promoted if barriers to treatment are lowered. Abortion could be understood in this way. One need not be an advocate for youthful autonomy to conclude that the predicament facing a pregnant teen threatens her welfare. Viewing the issue through a purely developmental lens (if this is possible), abortion may be in her best interest. Moreover, the more immature the teen, the greater the potential harm of pregnancy, childbirth, and parenthood. Thus we should probably not be surprised by the response of judges called upon to implement a Massachusetts statue enacted after *Bellotti v. Baird*. Robert Mnookin found that even on the rare occasions when courts concluded that a petitioner was not a "mature minor," the decision was almost always to order abortion without informing parents. The judges concluded that if a girl was too immature to make her own abortion decision, the alternative of having a baby was not a reasonable outcome (Mnookin 1985).

Summary

In spite of the struggle over abortion regulation, the law's approach to defining the boundaries of childhood is a success story for the most part. The categorical boundary—the age of majority—functions quite well, even though it may not mirror the developmental transition to adulthood of many adolescents, or even most adolescents for some purposes. That line is sometimes shifted downward to enable young persons to engage in useful adult activities, such as free expression and driving, or to meet adult challenges that arise before the presumptive age, such as dealing with sexually transmitted diseases. The line is shifted upward when extending childhood promotes individual and social welfare (e.g., parental college support and alcohol restrictions). The cumulative effect is to facilitate the gradual transition to adulthood through a series of rules that reflect society's collective interest in a young citizen's healthy development.

The rather simplistic scheme of binary categories, in which adolescents are classified as either children or adults, also works well generally to promote the interest of young persons and of society. In most contexts, the creation of a separate legal category for adolescents would add cost and complexity, with little payoff. A series of clear rules extends adult rights and responsibilities over an extended period of time into early adulthood without incurring the costs of establishing an intermediate category or of undertaking a case-by-case inquiry into maturity. Perhaps this is the lesson of abortion regulation.

JUVENILE CRIME AND THE DEFINITION OF CHILDHOOD

I turn now to juvenile justice regulation, a setting in which regulation has been less successful and in which, at least recently, the conventional goals of promoting youth welfare and the welfare of society have been treated as irreconcilable. Also, in this context, the standard strategies of binary classification have not worked well. The approach of treating young offenders as either children or as adults—and of ignoring the developmental reality of adolescence—has impeded the creation of effective policies for more than a century.

In the past one hundred years, legal policy toward youth crime has undergone three periods of reform. The first period began with the founding of the first juvenile court in Chicago in 1899. The goal of the Progressive reformers was to create a separate court and correctional system for juveniles that would focus on the welfare of young offenders, with a goal of rehabilitation rather than punishment. In the 1960s, a new wave of reform grew out of disillusion over the perceived failure of rehabilitation as the basis of juvenile justice policy. After the United States Supreme Court introduced due process into delinquency proceedings in *In re Gault* (387 U.S. 1 [1967]), legislatures and law reformers struggled to reform the juvenile justice system to introduce procedural protections and the principle of accountability without destroying its unique character (Zimring 1978; Juvenile Justice Standards 1980). In the 1990s, a new period of reform began, as policymakers responded to public fear of what was perceived to be a dramatic increase in youth crime. This reform movement aims to subject young offenders who commit serious crimes to the same standard of punishment as their adult counterparts.

One approach to understanding the evolution of the juvenile justice system over the course of the twentieth century is in terms of the empirical account of adolescence that is embedded in the reform rhetoric. Reformers of different periods have offered strikingly different images of young offenders and distinctive stories about their typical characteristics. The various descriptions of adolescence have been employed to shape and justify juvenile justice policy. Through this lens, the Progressive reformers in the early years of the juvenile court movement described young offenders as innocent and vulnerable children, to be molded through rehabilitative interventions into productive adults. The post-*Gault* reformers of the 1970s and 1980s offered a more realistic view of adolescence. In their view, young offenders were less culpable than adults because they lacked developmental experience and mature judgment, but they were not blameless children. In contrast, the descriptions of young "superpredators" by modern conservatives suggest that adolescent offenders are indistinguishable from adults.

Situating these accounts of childhood in the earlier discussion, one might describe the Progressive reformers as simply adopting the traditional approach of treating youths under the age of majority as legal children and thus ascribing to them the traits of innocence and vulnerability. The modern reformers, in contrast, advocate shifting the boundary of childhood radically, thereby defining adolescents as adults. As we have seen, these moves are not unusual among policymakers, although the contemporary "get tough" advocates would count youngsters as adults at age twelve or less, when they are deemed children for virtually every other legal purpose. For reasons that I will explore shortly, however, neither of these approaches works well as a basis for policy toward adolescent offenders. Simplistic dichotomous categories that ignore the developmental reality of adolescence fail as public policy because they undermine society's interest in public protection (the flaw of the traditional court) or because they harm young offenders and diminish their prospects for productive adulthood (deficiencies of contemporary policies). The legal response to juvenile crime presents what are perhaps unique challenges, in that successful policy must attend to adolescence as a distinct developmental stage between childhood and adulthood. Only the post-*Gault* reformers adopted this approach.

The Early Juvenile Court: Young Offenders as Innocent Children

The Progressive reformers at the turn of the century had an ambitious agenda for improving the lives of children and promoting their development into productive adults. Juvenile justice reform was only a part of a far-reaching program that included compulsory school attendance laws, restrictions on child labor, and the creation of a child welfare system. In an era in which mid-adolescents often assumed adult roles and burdens, an important component of the reform was to expand the boundaries of childhood, and to promote the idea that older youths, like younger children, should enjoy the protection and solicitude of the state. Miriam Van Waters described the underlying theory of the juvenile court in the following terms: "The child of the proper age to be under the jurisdiction of the juvenile court is encircled by the arm of the state, which, as a sheltering, wise parent, assumes guardianship and has power to shield the child from the rigors of the common law and from the neglect and depravity of adults" (Van Waters 1926, 3).

Several strategies were employed to accomplish this goal. First, as the statement by Van Waters suggests, reformers used romantic rhetoric that drew upon a shared understanding of the innocence, vulnerability, and dependency of childhood. Images of children working in factories under horrendous conditions were evoked to generate support for child labor and school attendance laws under which youths remained in school until age sixteen in many jurisdictions. Reinforcing this image of youthfulness was the metaphor of the state as the kind parent concerned only with the welfare of children.

The challenge of reshaping the image of young criminals was particularly daunting. At the dawn of the juvenile court movement, only children under the age of seven were immune from criminal prosecution on grounds of infancy. A primary goal of the Progressive reformers was the establishment of a separate court for the adjudication and correction of offenders up to the age of sixteen or eighteen, a court that would also respond to the needs of children who were subject to abuse and neglect by their parents. Central to the philosophy of the new juvenile court was the belief that very little distinguished delinquent youths from children who were neglected by their parents. *All* of the children who came within the jurisdiction of the court were innocent victims of inadequate parental care, and the state's role in delinquency cases was to intervene "in the spirit of a wise parent toward an erring child" (Van Waters 1926, 11). Indeed, parental neglect was understood to be the primary cause of delinquency. The political objective was to promote an image of young offenders as children whose parents had failed them rather than as criminals who threatened the community.

The reformers pursued this goal by emphasizing the similarity between young delinquents and neglected children. Judge Mack's famous challenge is representative: "Why is it not just and proper to treat these juvenile offenders, as we deal with the neglected children, as a wise and merciful father handles his own child?" (Mack 1909). Other juvenile court evangelists, such as Judge Ben Lindsey, offered heartwarming accounts of the wayward children who came before the court and were set on the right path with the guidance of the fatherly judge and other court personnel (Lindsay and O'Higgins 1909). These romanticized accounts described older youths as well as young boys and girls, and serious crimes as well as minor misdeeds. All of the young miscreants who came before the court were described sympathetically as innocent children gone astray who needed only the firm but kind parenting that the court could provide.

Although the Progressive reformers expanded the boundaries of childhood through child labor and school attendance reforms, their efforts in the juvenile justice context were somewhat less successful. The romanticized descriptions of adolescent offenders as innocent children played an important role in reinforcing the idealistic premise that no conflict of interest pitted the state against the young offender and that the purpose of state intervention in delinquency cases, as in child welfare cases, was solely to promote the welfare of youngsters who came before the court. This was always a shaky premise, which ignored the fact that young offenders, unlike children whose parents provide inadequate care, cause social harm through their criminal conduct. On reflection, it seems clear that the failure to recognize the state's inherent interest in protecting society in delinquency cases was a corrosive flaw in the rehabilitative model of juvenile justice. Moreover, acceptance of rehabilitation likely was always predicated on its effectiveness in reducing youth crime and protecting society. As the twentieth century progressed, the myth of the rehabilitative ideal was discredited, together with the image of the adolescent offender as an innocent child.

The Image of Childhood under Modern Punitive Reforms

In contrast to Progressive reformers who described young offenders as innocent children, conservative reformers today describe them as adults who should be held fully accountable for their crimes. Responding to an increase in violent juvenile crime (particularly homicide) in the 1980s and 1990s, reformers advocate policies under which juveniles (at least those who commit serious crimes) are tried in adult courts and sentenced in adult prisons. The goals of modern criminal justice reform are public protection and punishment, and in service of these goals, reform rhetoric has obliterated any distinctions between youthful offenders and adults. As one early supporter of "get tough" policies argued, "There is no reason to be more lenient with a sixteen-year-old offender than a thirty-year-old offender" (Regnery 1985, 68).

These contemporary reformers reject virtually every aspect of the Progressive image of young offenders as immature children or even as less mature or less culpable than their adult counterparts. In their view, the romanticized accounts of youngsters getting into scrapes with the law have no relevance in a world in which savvy young offenders commit serious crimes. Minors who inflict serious harm are engaging in adult criminal conduct, and they should be punished like adults, rather than slapped on the wrist—the typical response of the juvenile court. These reformers go further than simply rejecting the traditional account of adolescent offenders as children. They appear to assume that there are no psychological differences between adolescent and adult offenders that are relevant to criminal responsibility. Juvenile offenders are "criminals who happen to be young, not children who happen to be criminal" (Regnery 1985, 65).

Several legislative strategies have been employed in recent years to subject increasing numbers of juveniles charged with serious crimes to adjudication and punishment as adults. The age of judicial transfer has been lowered in many states, and a broader ranges of felonies can trigger a transfer hearing. Under legislative waiver statutes, young offenders charged with designated serious crimes are defined categorically as adults and excluded from juvenile court jurisdiction based on age and offense, without an inquiry into maturity. Under "direct charge" statutes, prosecutors decide whether to bring charges in adult or juvenile court for a range of serious offenses. Finally, blended sentencing statutes subject juveniles to stiff sentences that are begun in the juvenile system and completed through transfer to prison when the offender becomes an adult. The upshot is that the mantra of punitive reformers, "adult time for adult crime," is a reality for many juveniles, and in many states offenders who have not yet reached adolescence are tried and punished as adults.

The reformers who advocate treatment of juvenile offenders as adults do so primarily in pursuit of the utilitarian goal of reducing the social harm of youth crime. In this regard, the justice reforms bear some similarity to other laws that shift the boundary of childhood to define adolescent offenders as adults. The medical-consent statutes discussed previously also aimed to reduce the social cost of harmful behaviors by minors. An obvious difference, of course, is that punitive juvenile justice reform makes no serious claim that young offenders themselves will benefit. On this ground, the initiative to narrow the definition of childhood in the justice context is unique and seemingly inconsistent with the values and principles that generally shape the legal regulation of children. Holding immature offenders to adult standards of criminal responsibility also challenges important principles that define the boundaries of criminal punishment. Under these circumstances, it is fair at a minimum to require substantial evidence that the reforms will produce the promised social benefits. In fact, as I suggest shortly, even if the only goal of juvenile justice policy is to minimize the social cost of youth crime, punitive responses that treat young offenders as if they were adult criminals are unlikely to achieve that goal.

THE POST-*GAULT* REFORMERS: JUSTICE POLICIES IN A DEVELOPMENTAL FRAMEWORK

In re Gault exposed the flawed foundations of the rehabilitative model of juvenile justice and shattered the myth that delinquency interventions were aimed at promoting the welfare of wayward but innocent children. In the 1970s and 1980s, two major reform groups responded to the challenge of *Gault* by proposing juvenile justice policies based on a realistic account of adolescence. Both the Juvenile Justice Standards Project and a Twentieth-Century Fund task force on juvenile sentencing rejected the image of young offenders as innocent children that was so central to traditional policies. However, unlike modern conservative reformers, they did not view adolescents as fully responsible adults. In the view of the post-*Gault* reformers, young offenders possessed sufficient capacity for understanding, reasoning, and moral judgment to be held accountable for their offenses (and indeed needed lessons in accountability), but they were psychologically less mature and therefore less blameworthy than adult offenders.

Several traits of adolescence were thought to mitigate the criminal culpability of young offenders. As compared to adults, minors were assumed to have less life experience, to be more impulsive, and to have less capacity for self-discipline. They also were deemed susceptible to peer pressure and concerned about peer approval, more inclined to engage in risk taking, and more likely to focus on immediate rather than long-term consequences. These traits were not seen as deficiencies in the personalities of particular youths, rather, they were thought to characterize adolescence itself and therefore to justify a conclusion that young offenders should not be subject to adult standards of criminal responsibility. Moreover, these developmental traits contribute to a tendency to get involved in criminal activity during adolescence, and, predictably, many youths would mature out of this tendency.

The post-*Gault* law-reform groups struggled with the challenge of creating a modern juvenile justice system that recognized public safety and retribution as legitimate policy goals, but that also acknowledged the immaturity of young offenders (Zimring 1978; Juvenile Justice Standards 1980). Under this new justice model, juvenile dispositions were to be based on the seriousness of the offense rather than on the needs of the offender. However, because juveniles were less blameworthy than their adult counterparts, their dispositions should be categorically of shorter duration. Furthermore, separate dispositional programs were justified as a means to preserve the future life prospects of young offenders. This justification implicitly assumed that, given "room to reform," many juveniles would not become adult criminals.

These reform efforts influenced legislative change in the 1970s and 1980s. Many states enacted statutes that explicitly rejected the traditional notion that rehabilitation is the only purpose of juvenile justice intervention and recognized the importance of retribution and public protection. Modern statutory sentencing provisions focus on the seriousness of the offense and prior record of the offender as key considerations. Nevertheless, until recently, these statutory reforms also reflected the belief that was central to the post-*Gault* initiatives—that because of their developmental immaturity, most juveniles should be dealt with more leniently than adult offenders in separate courts and correctional facilities.

The Case for the Developmental Approach to Juvenile Justice

Although legal definitions of childhood for the most part ignore the transitional developmental stage of adolescence, the consequences of an approach that categorically defines adolescents charged with crimes as either children or adults are costly. Both the progressives who established the traditional juvenile court and modern conservatives are committed to fictional accounts about the clientele of the juvenile justice system because these accounts are essential to their policy agendas. The reality, as the post-*Gault* reformers recognized, is that young offenders are neither innocent children nor mature adults. Policies that fail to acknowledge this are unlikely to serve the public interest or that of young offenders.

The myth constructed by the architects of the traditional juvenile court was not persuasive when applied to older youths charged with serious crimes. Even assuming that the Progressive reformers had pure intentions (an assumption that some have challenged), the myth ultimately did more harm than good. It was rejected not only by those who thought the juvenile justice system was insufficiently concerned about public safety, but also by advocates for the interests of juveniles, who recognized that punishment and public protection were important but hidden influences shaping the disposition of young offenders. The juvenile court operated without the procedural constraints that protect adult criminal defendants, whose interest was always understood to be in conflict with that of the state. Further, because the ostensible purpose of intervention was to rehabilitate rather than punish the child, the court and correctional system had virtually unbridled discretion in fashioning dispositions, unconstrained by the principles limiting criminal punishment. As Justice Fortas pointed out in *Gault,* juveniles got the worst of both worlds. They were not accorded the procedural protections that adult criminal defendants received. At the same time, young offenders were sent to correctional institutions for long sentences where they received little rehabilitation.

Modern conservative reformers describe young offenders as adults because images of youth and immaturity are associated with legal protection and leniency. Policies that punish juveniles as adults are more palatable if youths are imagined as savvy criminals. The claim is that adolescents really *are* indistinguishable from adults in any way that is relevant to criminal responsibility. Elsewhere, I have called this the "competence assumption" (Scott and Grisso 1997). Moreover, modern punitive advocates argue that punishing young offenders as adults is essential to protecting society from the ravages of juvenile crime. This I call the "utilitarian assumption."

The empirical evidence from developmental psychology challenges both of these assumptions. First it supports the position that juveniles should be held to a standard of diminished criminal responsibility, because their decisions about involvement in criminal activity reflect immaturity of understanding and judgment. Second, the utilitarian assumption is challenged by research evidence about the role of antisocial behavior in adolescent development. This evidence suggests that many adolescents are inclined to engage in criminal activity but that they desist with maturity. Thus, policymakers focused on utilitarian goals must calculate not only the direct costs of the harm caused by young offenders, but also the long-term costs of punitive sanctions.

Criminal Responsibility in Adolescence

The criminal law assumes that most offenders make rational autonomous choices to commit crimes and that the legitimacy of punishment is undermined if the decision is coerced, irrational, or based on a lack of understanding of the meaning of the choice. The core criminal law principle of proportionality requires that punishment be proportionate to blameworthiness, which in turn is mitigated if the individual's decision-making capacity is deficient. Thus a defendant whose decision making is grossly distorted by mental illness may be fully excused from responsibility under the insanity defense.

The evidence from developmental psychology suggests that youthful choices to offend may be based on immature capacity to make decisions or shaped by transient developmental influences, although we must acknowledge that we have little direct research evidence about decision making "on the street." In general, youths are likely to have less knowledge and experience to draw on in making decisions than adults. Moreover, peer conformity is a powerful influence on adolescent behavior and may lead teens to become involved in criminal activity to win approval or avoid social rejection. It is not surprising that, in contrast to adult crime, most juvenile criminal activity takes place in groups. Adolescents also may perceive risks differently or less well than adults, and they are more inclined to engage in risky activities (smoking, drinking, unprotected sex, and delinquent behavior for example). Thus, a youth might be excited about the prospect of a convenience store holdup and not perceive risks that adults would recognize. In part, this may be due to a greater tendency of adolescents to discount the future and to focus on short-term consequences. Thus, in this situation, peer approval, the excitement of the situation, and the possibility of getting some money may all weigh more heavily in youthful decision making than the possibility of apprehension or the long-term consequences of a criminal conviction.

These influences on adolescent decision making—peer influence, risk perception and preference, and time perspective—together contribute to immature judgment, which may lead adolescents to make choices harmful to themselves or others (Scott, Reppucci, and Woolard 1995). It seems likely that these developmental factors distinguish adolescent decision making about involvement in crime from that of adults. However, at least by mid-adolescence, these differences are considerably more subtle than those that distinguish the insane defendant from the norm. Thus, adolescent immaturity should not excuse young offenders from criminal responsibility. Rather, the scientific evidence supports the argument of the post-*Gault* reformers that a presumptive diminished-responsibility standard be applied to juvenile offenders. Adolescents are not innocent children, and they should not be excused from responsibility. A diminished-responsibility standard holds young offenders accountable, but at the same time acknowledges that their choices are less blameworthy than are those of adults.

Adolescent Development and the Social Costs of Juvenile Crime

Many people who support punitive policies are unlikely to be persuaded by arguments that juveniles should be subject to a standard of diminished responsibility because they are less blameworthy than adults. The likely response, based on the utilitarian assumption, is that the differences between adults and adolescents (if they exist) are modest and should be ignored, because the top priority of justice policy must be to respond to the powerful threat to social welfare posed by juvenile crime. In short, to restate the utilitarian assumption, punitive policies are assumed to be the optimal means to achieve public protection and to minimize the social cost of youth crime. In this section, I challenge that claim—again on the basis of developmental knowledge—and suggest that utilitarian ends can be better served by policies that protect the future prospects of young offenders.

The argument for discounting youth as a mitigating factor in applying criminal sanctions has a superficial appeal, given the objective. After all, youths who are in prison cannot be on the street committing crimes. However, the utilitarian assumption is flawed because it ignores the long-term costs of punitive policies—costs that are likely to be substantial, given the developmental patterns of antisocial behavior in adolescence. Criminal behavior is rare in early adolescence; it increases through age sixteen and decreases sharply from age seventeen onward (Farrington 1983). Most teen age males participate in some criminal activity, leading one developmental criminologist to conclude that criminal conduct is "a normal part of teen life" (Moffitt 1993, 675). However, most youthful delinquent behavior is "adolescence-limited"; typical young offenders predictably mature into productive (or at least not criminal) citizens if they survive this stage without destroying their life chances. Only a small minority are what Terrie Moffitt has called "life-course persistent" offenders—youths who are at high risk for lives as career criminals (Moffitt 1993, 675). Whether and when individuals in the first group will assume conventional adult roles is likely to depend in part on the system's response to their adolescent criminal conduct. A policy of categorically imposing adult criminal penalties on young offenders may increase the probability that they will become career criminals, or it may delay desistence. At a minimum, criminal sentences undermine the future educational and employment prospects and general social productivity of those offenders whose criminal conduct is adolescent-limited.

Developmental analysis suggests that policy reformers who embrace utilitarian objectives have failed to include in their calculus some important social costs of punitive policies. Predictions about the effectiveness of these policies are based on one of two assumptions—perhaps on both. Either the reformers believe that most young offenders are simply young career criminals (and thus we need not concern ourselves about their future life prospects), or they believe that those offenders who predictably would otherwise outgrow their inclination to engage in criminal conduct will not be seriously harmed by adult criminal punishment. The psychological evidence indicates that the first assumption is simply inaccurate; the second seems implausible.

What would be the features of a juvenile justice policy based on a realistic account of adolescence and not on the myth that most young offenders were either innocent children or adults? First, such a policy would incorporate principles of accountability, through the adoption of a diminished responsibility standard. This is important for several reasons. First, accountability is important for purposes of public acceptance and moral legitimacy. Most young offenders are not innocent children, and the social harm they cause is not excused by the prediction that most will desist with maturity. Moreover, lessons in accountability are important; adolescents need to learn from their bad choices, so that they can successfully assume adult roles. Second, juvenile justice policy conceptualized in a developmental framework would seek to protect rather than damage adolescents' prospects for a productive future. Procedural protections that limit the stigma and lasting impact of delinquency status are worthwhile (for example, the right to a closed hearing). Also, dispositional programs that emphasize education and job skills are needed to prepare young offenders for adult roles. Finally, it seems important to maintain a separate system of adjudication and disposition for juveniles. Some observers have argued that a unified criminal justice system committed to procedural protections would better serve the interests of both young offenders and society (Feld 1997). I am skeptical, however, that the criminal justice system has either the ability or inclination to maintain a complex regime of policies tailored to respond to juvenile crime and to utilize the lessons of developmental psychology. In a volatile political environment, programs designed for young offenders and sentencing distinctions between juveniles and adults are more likely to be maintained in a separate juvenile justice system.

I am hopeful that reformers will begin to heed the lessons of developmental psychology. Even today, some courts insist on considering the immaturity of offenders in sentencing young criminals, despite statutory encouragement to impose "adult time for adult crime." Thus, a Michigan judge recently insisted on sentencing to a juvenile facility a thirteen-year-old boy who was convicted of committing homicide when he was eleven, despite a statutory provision authorizing adult penalties (Knott and Brand-Williams 2000). Some states have also undertaken statutory reform that incorporates the lessons of the developmental model, accommodating the interests of the young offender and that of society. For example, Pennsylvania has recently enacted a Juvenile Act adopting what it calls the "balanced approach." (Juv. Court Judges' Comm. 1997). This approach embraces three goals: community protection, accountability, and "competency development" (to enable young offenders to become productive community members when they return to society). As a long-term strategy to respond to juvenile crime without sacrificing the future prospects of offenders, this model is promising, and we may hope that it will represent the next generation of juvenile justice reform.

Adolescence in the Definition of Childhood

It could be said that adolescence and the juvenile court are of about the same age. Only in the latter part of the nineteenth century did psychologists recognize and name this transitional developmental stage between childhood and adulthood (Kett 1975). During the twentieth century, legal policy makers have tended to ignore adolescence and to classify and describe adolescents as either children or adults, shifting the boundary of childhood depending on the policy goal at issue. To describe the policy approach crudely, American law embodies an informal legal presumption that adolescents are children, subject to a fair number of exceptions. This generally works quite well, although it has resulted in what might be called the politicization of childhood on controversial issues such as abortion. It has not worked well in juvenile justice policy, where the simplistic categorization of young offenders as either children or adults has undermined our ability to achieve a viable, effective, and humane juvenile justice policy. In this sphere, good policy cannot ignore the empirical reality of adolescence as a developmental stage.

NOTE

1. Senate Committee on the Judiciary, *Report on Lowering the Voting Age to Eighteen,* 92d Congress, 1st sess. (1971), S. Rept. 26, 5.

REFERENCES

Bennett, W. J., Jr.; J. DiIulio; and J. P. Walters. 1996. *Body Count: Moral Poverty . . . and How to Win America's War against Crime and Drugs.* New York: Simon & Schuster.

Farrington, D. 1983. "Offending from Ten to Twenty-five Years of Age." In *Prospective Studies in Crime and Delinquency,* ed. K. Teilman and S. A. Mednick. Boston: Nijhoff.

Feld, B. 1997. "Abolish the Juvenile Court: Criminal Responsibility and Sentencing Policy." *Journal of Criminal Law and Criminology* 88: 68–136.

Institute of Judicial Administration–American Bar Association Joint Committee on Juvenile Justice Standards. 1980. *Standards Relating to Juvenile Delinquency and Sanctions.* Cambridge, MA: Ballinger.

Juvenile Court Judges' Commission. 1997. *Balanced and Restorative Justice in Pennsylvania: A New Mission and Changing Roles within the Juvenile Justice System.* Harrisburg, PA: Juvenile Court Judges' Commission.

Kett, J. F. 1975. *Rites of Passage: Adolescence in America, 1790 to the Present.* New York: Basic Books.

Knott, L., and O. Brand-Williams. 2000. "Young Killer Gets Juvenile Detention." *Detroit News,* 14 January, A1.

Lindsey, B., and H. O'Higgins. [1909] 1970. *The Beast.* Seattle: University of Washington Press.

Melton, G. B. 1983. "Toward 'Personhood' for Adolescence: Autonomy and Privacy as Values in Public Policy." *American Psychologist* 38: 99–103.

Mnookin, R. 1985. "*Bellotti v. Baird:* A Hard Case." In *In the Best Interest of Children,* ed. R. Mnookin, 149–264. New York: W. H. Freeman.

Moffitt, T. 1993. "Adolescent-Limited and Life-Course-Persistent Antisocial Behavior: A Developmental Taxonomy." *Psychological Bulletin* 100: 674–700.

Regnery, A. S. 1985. "Getting Away with Murder: Why the Juvenile Justice System Needs an Overhaul." *Policy Review* 34: 65–69.

Scott, E. S., and T. Grisso. 1997. "Adolescent Development and Juvenile Justice Reform." *Journal of Criminal Law and Criminology* 88: 137–89.

Scott, E.; N. D. Reppucci; and J. Woolard. 1995. "Evaluating Adolescent Decision Making in Legal Contexts." *Law and Human Behavior* 19: 221–44.

Stepp, L. 1994. "The Crackdown on Juvenile Crime: Do Stricter Laws Deter Youth?" *Washington Post,* 15 October, A1.

Van Waters, M. 1926. *Youth in Conflict.* New York: Republic. Reprint, New York: AMS Press.

Weithorn, L., and S. Campbell. 1982. "The Competency of Children and Adolescents to Make Informed Treatment Decisions." *Child Development* 63: 1589–98.

Wolfgang, M.; R. Figlio; and T. Sellin. 1972. *Delinquency in a Birth Cohort.* Chicago: University of Chicago Press.

Zimring, F. 1978. *Twentieth-Century Fund Task Force on Sentencing Policy toward Young Offenders: Confronting Youth Crime.* New York: Holmes and Merger.

———. 1982. *The Changing Legal World of Adolescence.* New York: Free Press.

5 The Common Thread: Diversion in the Jurisprudence of Juvenile Courts

Franklin E. Zimring

The first idea that should be grasped concerning the juvenile court is that it came into the world to prevent children from being treated as criminals.

Miriam Van Waters, 1925

The celebration of the Centennial of the Juvenile Court is not without its ironies. On the one hand, the institution has been a spectacular success in the United States and throughout much of the world. A juvenile court exists to deal with youthful law violators in all fifty states. No developed nation tries its youngest offenders in its regular criminal courts, and almost all the institutions that have been created in Europe, Japan, and the Commonwealth nations have been explicitly modeled in their language, procedures, and objectives on the American juvenile court. No legal institution in Anglo-American legal history has achieved such universal acceptance among the diverse legal systems of the industrial democracies.

On the other hand, the philosophy of state intervention that has been most prominently associated with the creation of the court had been effectively discredited for at least a generation before the centenary. Variously called "child saving," "the omnibus theory of delinquency," and, most memorably, "the rehabilitative ideal," the original justification we remember for the juvenile court was as an institution that would intervene forcefully in the lives of all children at risk to effect a rescue.[1] Informal proceedings were preferred to formal ones, so that the delinquent's needs could be determined. Broad and vague definitions of delinquency were favored, so that all children who needed help would fall within the new court's jurisdiction. Large powers could be exercised in all cases, so that help could be delivered to the deserving.

By the mid-1960s, the naive arrogance of the rehabilitative ideal had been exposed, never again to rule unchallenged in the juvenile courts.[2] Yet the court has thrived since the 1960s, just as it had before. Was this post–child saving juvenile court just an empty shell, an institution that had outlived its mission but continued to function on sheer momentum? Or is the juvenile court a chameleon, taking on new justifications and theories of function as old theories die? If so, why is this particular judicial weather vane so universally popular?

In my view, a substantial step toward understanding both the institutional status and justifying rationale of the modern juvenile court is to revise our view of the original justifications of the new court for delinquent children. I think that two justifications existed from the start for creating a juvenile court, and I shall call these two different policies the *interventionist* and *diversionary* justifications for a separate children's court. The diversionary justification for juvenile court was always the most important of the two rationales, and it remains so today.

In the foundational period of the juvenile court, when different groups formed coalitions for different reasons and when many reformers had multiple reasons to support a new court, the diversionary critique of criminal court processing of minors was always stronger and more widely accepted than the interventionist vision of the court. When it much later became apparent that the interventionist justification was in conflict with both the realities of court function and with the principles of legality and proportionality, the diversionary rationale for the court emerged as the central explanation for the court's separate operation. These diversionary principles of juvenile justice are well suited both to a modern theory of adolescent development and to principles of procedural fairness and proportionality in legal response to youth crime. My intention here is to show both the continuity and coherence of the diversionary rationale for juvenile courts through the first hundred years of their history.

The first section of this essay sets out the two discrete justifications for the creation of a juvenile court and documents the diversionary agenda of turn-of-the-century reformers. Section 2 shows the extent to which the major programmatic elements of early juvenile justice were consistent with diversionary justifications and methods. Much of the work of the juvenile court, in its early as well as later years, was aimed at allowing children to grow up in community settings. Section 3 addresses the modern concept of juvenile justice as reflected in two leading Supreme Court cases: *Gault* and *Winship*.[3] It was a diversionary theory of juvenile court that could accommodate due process rules without sacrifices of youth welfare. The fourth section concerns the contemporary understanding of juvenile justice as a passive judicial virtue. I show that the effectiveness of juvenile courts in protecting youth from full criminal punishment is the heart of the reason that the court has so many contemporary enemies.

TWO THEORIES OF CHANGE

Those who put their hopes in a new juvenile court that would assume responsibility over young offenders had two reasons to assume the new court would be an improvement on the criminal processing of children. The first belief was that a child-centered juvenile court could avoid the many harms that criminal punishment visited on the young. The reformers believed that penalties were unnecessarily harsh and places of confinement were schools for crime, where the innocent were corrupted and the redeemable were instead confirmed in the path of chronic criminality. From this perspective, the first great virtue of the juvenile court was that it would not continue the destructive impact of the criminal justice system on children. I call this theory of justification for juvenile court a *diversionary* rationale, an argument that the new court could do good by doing less harm than criminal processes. And those who believed the criminal courts to be destructive instruments that were best avoided included every one of the new court's prominent supporters.

The signal characteristic of a diversionary argument for juvenile justice

Fig. 5.1 Judge Stubbs talking to boys in an Indianapolis court, February 5, 1910.

is its attention to the harmful nature of criminal punishment for the young. A classic and nearly complete litany of the harms of the criminal law comes on the first page of Juvenile Court Judge Tuthill's 1904 account of the treatment of delinquents prior to reform:

> Prior to 1899 little was done in Illinois, and, so far as I know, in any other State in the Union, that was not wrongly done by the State toward caring for the delinquent children of the State. No matter how young, these children were indicted, prosecuted, and confined as criminals, in prisons, just the same as were adults pending and after a hearing, and thus were branded as criminals before they knew what crime was. The State kept these little ones in police cells and jails among the worst men and women to be found in the vilest parts of the city and town. *Under such treatment they developed rapidly, and the natural result was that they were thus educated in crime and when discharged were well fitted to become the expert criminals and outlaws who have crowded our penitentiaries and jails. The State had educated innocent children in crime, and the harvest was great. The condition in Chicago became so bad that all who were cognizant of this condition and were interested in correcting it sought a remedy* [emphasis added]. A bill was prepared and presented to the legislature of the State, which, in due time, and after overcoming much opposition, was enacted into a law known throughout the world as the "juvenile-court law of Illinois."[4]

A similar rhetoric is reflected in accounts of the criminal justice system issued before and after the founding of the court by every one of the major public figures in the movement. Among the more colorful examples was Judge Ben Lindsey's characterization of the criminal court as an "outrage against childhood."[5] William Stead speaks of a police station where "urchins of ten and twelve who have been run in for juvenile delinquency have found the police cell the nursery cradle of the jail."[6] The criminal court was the common enemy that launched juvenile courts in America.

The diversionary justification for juvenile court can easily be contrasted with what I will call the *interventionist* justification for the new court. While the diversionary approach promised the avoidance of the criminal court's harms, the interventionist argument emphasized the positive good that new programs administered by child welfare experts could achieve. A child-centered court was an opportunity to design positive programs that would simultaneously protect the community and cure the child. This was the notion of child saving that made the court's early justifications seem so extreme. While the diversionary and interventionist justifications are conceptually quite distinct, there seems to have been little awareness at the court's founding that these two approaches to justifying the new court might be in any conflict. The same people who believed in the diversionary virtues of a new court affirmed its interventionist potential as well.[7] Because there was no contemporary awareness of potential conflict, the court's supporters did not have to choose between these separate but attractive rationales for the new institution.

But the diversionary rationale had several obvious advantages over an interventionist theory as a justification for an untested reform. In the first place, the new court could be counted on to achieve social good whether or not its treatment interventions worked. Avoiding the harms of the criminalization of children was a near-term benefit, whatever the programmatic potential of the new court's interventions might prove to be. A second advantage of a diversionary perspective was the way that doing less harm fit the shape and orientation of the new court's major tool, probation. Community supervision is rarely a heroic intervention; it does not take extensive power over the lives of young offenders when compared to jails, prisons, and work camps. It is also, in addition to its high moral principle, a method of responding to official delinquency that is relatively cheap. At every level of discourse, then, from pro-child rhetoric to economic self-interest, the diversionary perspective was monumentally attractive to those who were organizing a new court. It was an argument for juvenile courts without any known opponents or identified disadvantages, a foundation for the new court that was too obvious to be remembered clearly as a distinctive justification for change.

If the diversion of youth from the rigors of criminal punishment was a dominant motive for the new court, why does this justification not play a larger role in the historical accounts of the creation of the court? While diversionary motives dominate the contemporary accounts of the court's early years, these efforts to reduce the gratuitous harms of the criminal court do not receive much notice in the historical critiques of the court that appeared in the 1960s and 1970s.[8] Part of the reason later scholars give more attention to the interventionist theory of juvenile justice is that such a claim was both novel and controversial, while child-protective sentiments are so widely shared as to be without any singular importance at any particular historical moment. The pro-child sentiments of 1899 do not set that era off from 1940 or 1980. The claims of interventionist prowess are considered, in contrast, a striking historical artifact by those writing in the 1960s and 1970s, if not before.

One other historical factor that produced more emphasis on interventionist dogma than was otherwise justified was that many accounts of the court's justifications were written by judges with a vested interest in expanding the powers and prestige of this new office. Avoiding harm for children is a modest objective, indeed, when compared to the therapeutic rescue of those about to fall to the lower depths. The rhetoric of Judge Mack, for instance, seems prone to such claims; even the writing of Judge Lindsey, a noninterventionist for his time, was full of accounts of judicial rescue.[9]

However understandable the failure of those who study court history to give sufficient attention to diversionary motives, this gap has led to a variety of unfortunate consequences. First, much late-twentieth-century work underestimates the capacities and misrepresents the motives of founding figures like Jane Addams and Julia Lathrop.[10] Second, the failure to give prominent attention to avoiding criminal stigma for children leaves these later histories with no explanation for the worldwide popularity of the juvenile court for delinquents. It was beyond doubt the avoidance of criminal justice damage that spread the juvenile court gospel across the world in the early years of the century, not an interventionist claim to judicial power. Such diversionary child saving generated nearly universal appeal. The third problem with ignoring the diversionary rationale for juvenile court is that it makes it impossible to understand much of the developing nature of juvenile justice in the first half of the twentieth century by referring to the court's justification.

The Aims and Means of the Early Juvenile Courts

The early years of the twentieth century were not a period when new forms of intensive behavioral therapies were applied to either adults or juveniles brought before the bar of justice. The most serious of the commitment options open to the juvenile court was the state reformatory or training school, an institution with a nineteenth-century program and a zero reputation for innovation or behavioral impact.[11] One searches the record in vain for major figures in creating the court who put their hopes in state schools of the industrial variety as an arena for child saving.[12] The sole virtue of the reform school was the fact that it was not a prison.

Where did the reformers rest their programmatic hopes in the first quarter of the twentieth century? On social and educational change generally and on community-based probationary supervision for the delinquent in his family setting. Compulsory education and child labor laws were the major objectives of progressive youth policy, not the operations of juvenile court. Within the juvenile court, the major programmatic advantage was probation.[13] The goal of the reformers, in the words of Jane Addams, was "a determination to understand the growing child and a sincere effort to find ways for securing his orderly development in normal society."[14] The dominant outcome of juvenile court process was probation as early as 1908, when probation was twice as likely in Milwaukee as all other court outcomes combined.[15]

The emphasis on probation and community-based supervision fits nicely with a diversionary justification for juvenile courts. The job of the court is first not to harm the youth and then to attempt help in community settings. This same programmatic emphasis does not mesh well with the romantic rhetoric of child saving. Probation is at its essence an incremental social control strategy, one that relies on the basic health and functionality of the subjects' community life.

Even the more ambitious plans of probation advocates to get involved with families and schools amounted to low-intensity social control, particularly given the tiny budgets and volunteer staffs characteristic of the early years of the juvenile court. The only new programs that fit the profile of child saving were the secure Chicago "parental schools" for truants, which hoped to marry coercive means to educational objectives and juvenile detention.[16] But this clearly interventionist institution was not emulated in the proliferation of juvenile courts. In this sense, the parental school may be the exception that proves the rule.

The other major increase in social control was the explicit extension of all juvenile court sanctions to noncriminal behavior, such as disobedience to adults, truancy, and violation of curfew. Clearly, the court was not extending jurisdiction in this direction in the name of diversion. But the same jurisprudence of childhood dependency that supported these powers for status offenders also were a foundation for keeping young offenders out of criminal courts.[17]

There is one final respect in which the role of the juvenile court was more modest in the reform imagination than in some of the court's interventionist rhetoric. If child labor regulation and public education are the important public-law enterprises of the new order for the young, both of these are centered in governmental operations that start apart from juvenile court, as does the settlement house created by Jane Addams. To do less harm than criminal courts, the new legal setting for delinquency did not need to be a superpower, and it was not.

THE JUVENILE COURT AND THE RULE OF LAW

It took two-thirds of the twentieth century before the United States Supreme Court considered the procedural protections that due process required when accused delinquents were in jeopardy of secure confinement in state institutions. One important issue in *In re Gault,* decided in 1967, was the need for informality if the court was to achieve its child saving mission.[18] Mr. Justice Harlan thought that rigid due process could disserve traditional juvenile justice. Dissenting from the *Gault* majority, which held that due process requires recognition of a privilege against self-incrimination, the right to confront witnesses, and the right to cross-examination, Harlan argued,

> First, quite unlike notice, counsel, and a record, these requirements might radically alter the character of juvenile court proceedings. The evidence

> from which the Court reasons that they would not is inconclusive, and other available evidence suggests that they very likely would. At the least, it is plain that these additional requirements would contribute materially to the creation in these proceedings of the atmosphere of an ordinary criminal trial, and would, even if they do no more, thereby largely frustrate a central purpose of these specialized courts [references deleted].[19]

His suggestion was that such procedures could jeopardize the substantive mission of the juvenile court. Yet, Justice Fortas, writing the majority opinion, argued that there was no serious tension between the therapeutic intentions of the juvenile court and procedural protections for the accused who come before the court. He argued,

> While due process requirements will, in some instances, introduce a degree of order and regularity to Juvenile Court proceedings to determine delinquency, and in contested cases will introduce some elements of the adversary system, nothing will require that the conception of the kindly juvenile judge be replaced by its opposite.[20]

Rather than take one side in this debate, I wish to argue that the contrast between interventionist and diversionary theories of the court will decide whether there is tension between the court's objective and due process standards. For an informal and interventionist juvenile court, standards of proof and defense lawyers are a major drawback to identifying children in need and providing them with help. If that is the mission of the juvenile court, then due process will be a major handicap to its achievement. But if saving kids from the gratuitous harms inflicted by the criminal process is the aim, there is no inherent conflict between due process and the court's main beneficial functions.

The best illustration of the tension between due process and an interventionist court is the issue raised by the case of *In re Winship* in 1970. The state of New York allowed a petition alleging delinquency to be sustained in juvenile court if the state proved such facts by a preponderance of the evidence, the usual standard of proof in civil trials.[21] The appellants, using *Gault* as authority, argued that delinquency could only be established by proof of its constituent facts beyond a reasonable doubt. The Supreme Court agreed with this conclusion.[22]

But what is the justification for requiring proof beyond a reasonable doubt in criminal cases? The usual law-day speech tells us that erroneous acquittals are less socially harmful than erroneous convictions: "It is better that ten guilty men go free than that one innocent man gets convicted!" But if the juvenile court is there to help delinquents, what is the sense in saying, "It is better that ten kids who need help do not get help than that one kid who does not need help is erroneously assisted!" If the dominant purpose of juvenile justice was forceful intervention for the child's own good, the rules in *Gault* and *Winship* were a decisive rejection of the juvenile court's jurisprudence.

But every aspect of due process protection can be consistent with a diversionary theory of juvenile justice. If the principal benefit of juvenile court is that it keeps children from the destructive impact of the criminal courts, this benefit may be provided whether or not the new court makes a formal sanctioning decision in a particular case. A high burden of proof or a children's lawyer will not cost the court its diversionary function. There is also no threat to the diversionary rationale of juvenile court from recognition that terms like *delinquent* carry stigma and that juvenile court sanctions may function as punishments. As long as the juvenile court can be seen as the lesser of evils, a diversionary view of the court can be quite worldly and need not deny that punitive motives might color sanctioning decisions in the children's court.

The interventionist view of court processes was always more fragile. A positive characterization of juvenile court interventions is necessary to justifying the venture. To call what the juvenile court does to delinquents a punishment is to deny the truth of a central premise of the interventionist theory. Viewed in this light, the majority opinion in *Gault* rejected one enduring rationale for a separate juvenile court and elevated a second theory to supremacy. The juvenile court that the United States Supreme Court approved protected children chiefly by keeping them out of prisons and jails.[23] Such an institution could be parsimonious with its own punishments—restricting them to cases with strong evidence and fair procedures—without threatening its own substantive mission. The arrogance of unqualified judicial power was not necessary to this version of the court's purposes. After *In re Gault* in 1967, diversion was the approved version of juvenile justice in the United States and probably in the rest of the developed world. Some juvenile court judges might have shed a tear at the way Abe Fortas deconstructed the interventionist facade of juvenile courts, but the *Gault* majority did not undo or completely reorient the court that Grace Abbott, Julia Lathrop, and Jane Addams supported. The diversionary institution they wished for had passed the tests of *In re Gault* and *In re Winship* with flying colors.

DIVERSION IN THE MODERN COURT

The twentieth century has seen many changes in the culture and institutions of the United States. The juvenile court, itself just an experiment at the beginning of the century, has witnessed changes to its clientele, its political and legal constituencies, and its operations.

Nevertheless, the core concern of the court "to prevent children from being treated as criminals" was just as clear in 1999 as in 1899. As the usual period of schooling and economic dependency in adolescence lengthened over the twentieth century, the maximum age for juvenile court delinquency first drifted upward to the eighteenth birthday in most states and then stayed at eighteen in most states, reflecting an age boundary close to the mode for high school graduation. The period of semiautonomy that now spans most of the teen years is spent for the most part in the delinquency jurisdiction of juvenile courts.[24] This section will show that a consistent diversion orientation of juvenile justice can be observed in recent policy developments.

Modern Reform: The Juvenile Justice and Delinquency Prevention Act of 1974

The due process requirements discussed in the previous section were closely followed by the first major federal legislation designed to influence the substantive content of state juvenile justice policy by providing financial rewards to state systems that met the federal standards.[25] The two major targets of the 1974 juvenile justice legislation fit quite comfortably under a traditional diversionary view of the court's objectives. The first push of the federal law was to remove minors from American jails and prisons.[26] The protective segregation of children had been at the heart of the diversion agenda in 1899. While the original reformers would have been disturbed to find that seventy-five years of American history had not yet achieved this primitive reform, the continuing struggle to attain separate housing for children in confinement was an essentialist diversionary reform in obvious accord with the original vision of the court.

So, too, was the second major objective of the 1974 legislation, the deinstitutionalization of status offenders.[27] The saga of the status offender was one of the great failings of the interventionist theory of juvenile courts. In the original legislation, the noncriminal behaviors later to be called status offenses were simply another behavior that could justify a finding of delinquency as well as any placement that the juvenile court was justified in ordering for a delinquent.[28] Kids who ran away from home or were disobedient or truant could be committed to the same institutions that were dispositional options for the juvenile burglar and auto thief. Two problems were associated with secure institutional confinement for noncriminal misbehavior: it was grossly unfair, and it was manifestly ineffectual. By 1974, the need to scale back on this branch of the rehabilitative ideal was a near consensus among the youth welfare profession.[29] The direct conflict between not allowing the juvenile courts to order secure institutions for truants and an interventionist theory of the court is obvious.

But there is no necessary conflict between limits on the coercive interventions allowed for noncriminal behaviors and a diversionary theory of juvenile justice. Simply because reformers wish to keep adolescent law violators out of prisons and jails does not mean that the same observers support serious punishment for noncriminal kids. Quite the opposite. While juvenile court treatments for young offenders are found in most developed nations, the strong interventionist claim that produced training schools for truants was nowhere near as widespread in popularity as the juvenile court itself. Foreign courts did not adopt such policies because diversionary theories did not require them. The federal legislation, like the constitutional cases that preceded it, can be seen as endorsing diversion as the theory of the modern court to the exclusion of interventionism.

Diversion and the Punitive Assault on Juvenile Justice

Perhaps the most dramatic evidence of the efficacy and importance of diversionary policies in modern juvenile justice is the sustained attack on the modern juvenile court by the political forces of law and order. At the federal level, Republican legislative majorities have been attempting to use federal financial incentives pioneered in the Juvenile Justice and Delinquency Prevention Act of 1974 to push a series of standards designed to create more punitive sanctions within the delinquency jurisdiction of the juvenile court and easier transfers of serious juvenile offenders to criminal courts.[30]

The rhetoric in support of this legislation uses new phrases to describe the juvenile court outcomes that are desired—terms like *accountability* and *graduated sanctions*.[31] But the common enemy of the transfer policies and the harsher juvenile court punishments proposed in the legislation is a juvenile court tradition that seeks to avoid permanent stigma and disfiguring punishments of delinquents. The terms of reprobation aimed at the court by its critics on the right are a tribute to the court's diversionary intent—"revolving door justice," "slap on the wrist," "Kiddie Court." To the extent that the attacks by its critics are based on empirical truth, those assaults pay tribute to the efficacy of a court that has been seeking to avoid the harshest outcomes for its caseload for the entire twentieth century.

Truth to the Rumor?

But is there any truth to the rumor that juvenile courts protect delinquents from destructive punishments? Looking behind the rhetoric of current debates about responses to youth crime, we find very little analysis that compares sanctions for similar offenses across the boundaries of juvenile and criminal courts, and ignorance of the impact of juvenile court processing on punishment outcomes for different types of crime is not a recent problem (see

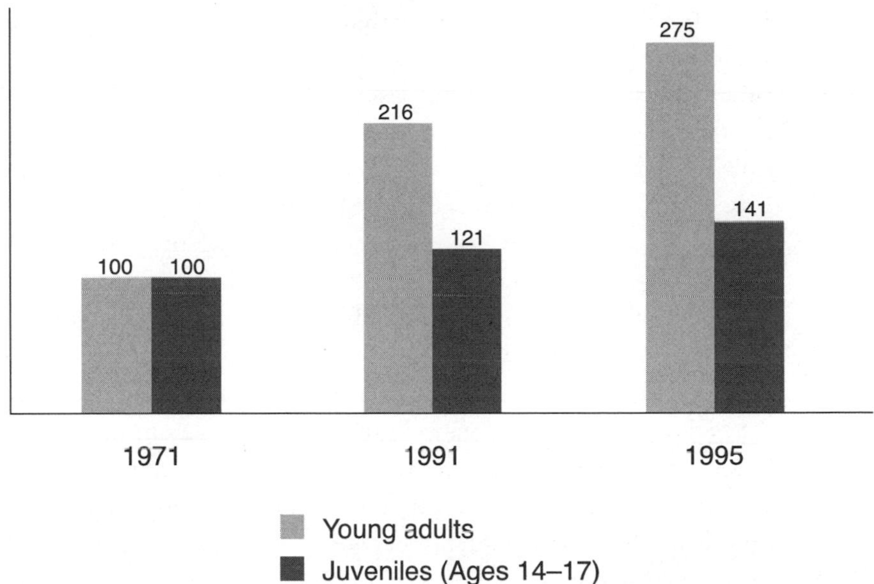

Fig. 5.2 Trends in incarceration for juveniles (age 14–17; 100 = 393 per 100,000) and young adults (age 18–24; 100 = 508 per 100,000). Data from U.S. Dept. of Justice, Bureau of Justice Statistics, in the following: *Correctional Populations in the United States* 21 (1995), *Bulletin,* Aug. 1996; *Special Report,* April 1998, and Feb. 2000; fax from Allen J. Beck to author, Oct. 26, 2000; from U.S. Dept. of Justice, Criminal Justice Resource Center, *Sourcebook of Criminal Justice Statistics* (1973, 353; 1976, 644–45; 1997, 607; 1999, 484, 503); from Darrel K. Gilliard and Allen J. Beck, *Prison and Jail Inmates, 1995;* Caroline Wolf Harlow, *Profile of Jail Inmates, 1996;* Kevin J. Strom, *Profile of State Prisoners under Age Eighteen, 1985–97;* from U.S. Dept. of Commerce, Bureau of the Census, fax to author, Oct. 24, 2000, and website <http://www.census.gov> (last visited Nov. 10, 2000). See also Joseph Moone, *Children in Custody 1991: Private Facilities,* in 2 and 5 *Office of Juvenile Justice and Delinquency Prevention Fact Sheet,* April and September, 1993; and Joseph Moone, *States at a Glance: Juveniles in Public Facilities,* 1995, 69 *Office of Juvenile Justice and Delinquency Prevention Fact Sheet,* Nov. 1997.

Greenwood, Petersilia, and Zimring 1980).[32] My own belief is that juvenile courts have always generated some diversionary benefits to many classes of young offenders, but that the size and distribution of diversionary benefits varies by period, by type of youth, and by type of offense. There is no excuse for the near-zero research base on this important issue, a situation that makes determining the aggregate impact of juvenile court case processing on punishments into a guessing game.

My best guess is that the protective impact of a diversionary juvenile court on sanctions for youth crime is largest when punitive policies are at their most dominant in criminal courts—that is, in ages like the American present. The larger the punitive bite of the criminal court system, the more likely it is that a separate court for the youngest offenders takes some of that bite out of the state sanctions that the youngest offenders receive.

Figure 5.2 provides fairly careful estimates of public-facility confinement for youth age 14–17 and young adults age 18–24 for 1971, 1991, and

1995. For the 14–17 group, I combine juvenile detention facilities, training schools, camps, and so on with the number of those age 14–17 in prisons and jails. Only the juvenile facilities are under the control of the juvenile court, but total secure incarceration is the best measure of total governmental control. The figure is formatted with each age group's rate in 1971 expressed as 100, so that the changes over time are emphasized.

As Figure 5.2 shows, the incarceration rates for the two groups were not greatly different in 1971: the 18-to-24-year-olds have a jail and prison rate that is 28 percent higher than the total public incarceration rate of 14-to-17-year-olds. Trends after 1971 for the two groups diverge. The period 1971–1991 was not a typical interlude in the history of American crime policy. It was, instead, the period of the most substantial growth in the scale of imprisonment in the history of the Republic.[33] Never was the pressure for confinement as consistent and substantial. Total confinement for the younger group increased by 21 percent, while the incarceration rate of young adults more than doubled. By 1991, the difference in incarceration rates for the two groups was more than 2 to 1, and this very substantial gap is one reason why those who had succeeded in radically altering punishments in criminal courts might have resented the stability in policy and outcome that occurred for younger offenders.

The pattern during the early 1990s is more complicated. The rate at which 14-to-17-year-olds were incarcerated rose almost as much in the four years after 1991 as in the two decades prior to 1991. For that reason, it may look like a significant shift toward toughness had finally taken hold. But the growth in young adult incarceration was much greater than in the younger age group, so that the gap between older juveniles and young adults actually widened in the early 1990s. The incarceration rate per 100,000 grew by about 80 for the 14–17 group, and more than three times that much for those 18–24.

Their consistent incarceration-limiting policy generated substantial political pressure on juvenile courts in the United States, while the criminal justice system experienced two decades of uninterrupted penal expansion. Indeed, the data in figure 5.2 suggest a new explanation for the flurry of legislative activity to create larger punishments for juvenile offenders. The usual account of juvenile crime legislation is based on the concern of politicians and citizens with juvenile crime and violence (Zimring 1998 at Chapter 1).[34] But what figure 5.2 shows is that the political forces that had produced extraordinary expansion through the rest of the penal system had been stymied in juvenile courts. In that sense, the under-eighteen population became the last significant battleground for a get-tough orientation that had permeated the rest of the peno-correctional system. The performance of American juvenile courts over the 1970s and 1980s had been exceptional, and this rendered the system vulnerable to the same attacks that had succeeded decades before in criminal justice.

From this perspective, the angry assaults on juvenile courts throughout the 1990s are a tribute to the efficacy of juvenile justice in protecting delinquents from the incarcerative explosion that had happened everywhere else. The largest irony of the 1990s from a diversionary standpoint is that the juvenile courts were under constant assault not because they had failed in their youth-serving mission, but because they had succeeded in protecting their clientele from the new orthodoxy in crime control.

There is a less comforting aspect to the statistics in figure 5.2 as a measure of juvenile court diversion. While the incarceration rate for 18-to-24-year-olds in 1995 was 2.5 times that of 14-to-17-year-olds, the juvenile rate had been only 28 percent below that of the older group in 1971. The optimistic spin on such data is that both the criminal and juvenile courts had been emphasizing diversion in 1971, resulting in the small difference in lock-up rates. The pessimistic interpretation is that an earlier and more confident era of juvenile justice was associated with levels of secure confinement uncomfortably close to those of criminal courts. In either case, the data from the last third of the twentieth century clearly show that the special policies of juvenile courts were much more significant in their impact on incarceration risks after the war on drugs and the sharp shift toward general incapacitation in the criminal courts.

CONCLUSION

For those who see adolescence as a stressful and experiment-laden transition to adulthood, growing up is the one sure cure for most juvenile crime. The policy objective that drew many adherents to the notion of a juvenile court was that it was to be a place where it would be possible "to understand the growing child—and to find ways for securing his orderly development in normal society."[35] A criminal law that removed youth from community settings and thrust them into lockups and jails was seen as a principal threat to adolescent development in normal society. For this reason, the juvenile court "came into the world to prevent children from being treated as criminals." This was and is "the first idea that should be grasped concerning the juvenile court."[36] It is a rationale of tremendous durability, more humble in its ambitions and closer to institutional reality than the rehabilitative ideal ever was. The diversionary theory of juvenile court jurisdiction was not an alternative to helping juvenile offenders, but it was a more particular and more limited kind of help than plenary child saving. It was a modest, focused way of helping young offenders survive both adolescent crime and the experience of social control with their life chances still intact.

The historical record suggests that the diversionary juvenile court was a reform more worldly and sophisticated than historical scholarship has yet acknowledged. There is in the early history of juvenile court the basis for a jurisprudence of patience and restraint, an institutional commitment to do less harm than the criminal courts did to young offenders. This was a very good idea in 1899. It still is.

NOTES

1. See Anthony Platt, *The Child Savers: The Invention of Delinquency* (Chicago: University of Chicago Press, 1969), chap. 1.

2. Francis Allen, "The Juvenile Court and the Limits of Juvenile Justice," in *The Borderland of Criminal Justice* (Chicago: University of Chicago Press, 1964), 42, 50–54.

3. *In re Gault,* 387 U.S. 1 (1967); *In re Winship,* 397 U.S. 358 (1970).

4. Richard S. Tuthill, "History of the Children's Court in Chicago," in *Children's Courts in the U.S.: Their Origin, Development, and Results,* ed. Jane Addams (1904; reprint Chicago: AMS Press, 1973).

5. Ben B. Lindsey, "Colorado's Contribution to the Juvenile Court," in *The Child, the Clinic, and the Court,* ed. Jane Addams, 274 (New York: New Republic, 1925).

6. William T. Stead, *If Christ Came to Chicago* (1894; reprint Chicago: Chicago Historical Bookworks, 1990).

7. See, for example, Julian Mack, "The Juvenile Court," *Harvard Law Review* 23 (1909): 104.

8. Compare Addams, ed., *The Child, the Clinic, and the Court* with Platt, *Child Savers* (note 1 above), and Steven Schlossman, *Love and the American Delinquent: The Theory and Practice of "Progressive Juvenile Justice"* (Chicago: University of Chicago Press, 1977).

9. Schlossman, *Love and the American Delinquent,* 55–57.

10. See, especially, Platt, *Child Savers.*

11. Julia Lathrop, "The Background of the Juvenile Court in Illinois," in *The Child, the Clinic, and the Court,* ed. Addams, 290.

12. Schlossman, *Love and the American Delinquent,* 64–66.

13. Lindsey, "Colorado's Contribution," 274.

14. Jane Addams, Introduction, in *The Child, the Clinic, and the Court,* ed. Addams, 1, 2.

15. Schlossman, *Love and the American Delinquent,* app. 2, table 2, 202.

16. Robert M. Mennel, *Thorn and Thistles: Juvenile Delinquents in the United States, 1825–1940* (Hanover: The University Press of New England, 1973), 106–7.

17. Franklin E. Zimring, *The Changing Legal World of Adolescence* (New York: Free Press, 1982), 35–40.

18. *Gault,* 387 U.S. at 25–26.

19. Ibid., 75 (Harlan, J., dissenting).

20. Ibid., 27.

21. *Winship,* 397 U.S. at 360.

22. Ibid., 368.

23. *Gault,* 387 U.S. at 22.

24. Zimring, *Changing Legal World,* chs. 3 and 7.

25. Juvenile Justice and Delinquency Prevention Act of 1974 §223(A), 42 U.S.C. §5633(a) (1994).

26. Ibid., §102, 42 U.S.C. §5602.

27. Ibid., §311, 42 U.S.C. §5711(a).

28. Zimring, *Changing Legal World,* 32–40.

29. Ibid., ch. 5.

30. See S.10, 105th Cong. (1997); H.R. 3, 105th Cong. (1997).

31. See, for example, S. Rep. No. 105–108 (1997); H.R. Rep. No. 105–86 (1997).

32. See Peter Greenwood, Joan Petersilia, and Franklin E. Zimring, *Age, Crime, and Sanctions: The Transition from Juvenile to Criminal Court* (Santa Monica, CA: Rand, 1980).

33. Franklin E. Zimring and Gordon Hawkins, *The Scale of Imprisonment* (Chicago: University of Chicago Press, 1991), chap. 5.

34. Franklin E. Zimring, *American Youth Violence* (New York: Oxford University Press, 1998), chap. 1.

35. Addams, Introduction, 2.

36. Miriam "The Juvenile Court from the Child's Viewpoint," in *The Child, the Clinic, and the Court,* ed. Addams, 217.

6 Status Offenses and Status Offenders

Lee Teitelbaum

> Why is it not just and proper to treat these juvenile offenders, as we deal with the neglected children, as a wise and merciful father handles his own child? Why is it not the duty of the state, instead of asking merely whether a boy or girl has committed a specific offense, to find out what he is, physically, mentally, morally, and then if it learns that he is treading the path that leads to criminality, to take him in charge, not so much to punish as to reform? It is this thought—the thought that the child who has begun to go wrong, who is incorrigible, who has broken a law or an ordinance, is to be taken in hand by the state, not as an enemy but as the ultimate guardian [which inspired the first juvenile court act].
>
> Julian Mack, "The Juvenile Court," 1909

Judge Mack's description of the unique goals of the juvenile court movement captures its essential innovation—the embracing of a wide variety of behaviors, not necessarily criminal in themselves but nonetheless suggesting a need for intervention. The scope of juvenile court jurisdiction was not merely a "reform" but revolutionary. It can be considered the outright substitution of an approach to judicial governance that departed radically from the formal method of Anglo-American criminal law.

One way of understanding the different approaches of the criminal and juvenile courts is to compare what have been called regimes of "legal" and "substantive" justice (Unger 1975). In a system of legal justice, which is the form found in the criminal law of 1899 or, for that matter, 1999, legal rules are stated as categorical formulas establishing the occasion for and amount of intervention. In theory, these formulas are announced in advance of their application and bind the rule-applier as well as the members of the general community governed by the rule. Accordingly, a court may act only when some person's conduct falls within previously and clearly stated categories of behavior. Discretion, while perhaps inevitable, is regarded as at best a necessary evil.

In contrast, the juvenile court, as Judge Mack makes clear, traditionally did not rely on specific behavioral categories. It sought to apply more general standards for intervention and focused on the actor rather than his or her conduct. Each decision was justified because it would best advance the accepted public objective embodied in the standard, such as prevention of future harm. Discretion and individualized decision making were accepted and, indeed, celebrated in this regime of substantive justice (Teitelbaum 1991). The juvenile court was, to be sure, remarkable in its abandonment of traditional theories of punishment for criminal misconduct by young people, but it was most remarkable in its readiness to embrace all forms of problematic conduct and circumstances suggesting that a child had "begun to go wrong." Thus it is in the scope of the juvenile court's authority over noncriminal misbehavior—that is, over status offenses—that the pure theory of the Chicago Juvenile Court and the American juvenile court movement is clearest.

THE MEANING OF STATUS OFFENSE

The term *status offense* in connection with juvenile court jurisdiction is a term of art. While the same phrase is used in connection with criminal proceedings, its meaning there is different. A status offense for criminal law purposes is a wrong defined by the existence of a condition, such as narcotics addiction. It has long been clear that criminal penalties cannot constitutionally be attached to a condition or status alone but must be directed to *acts* committed by the accused.

The status offense jurisdiction of the juvenile court, by contrast, often focuses on acts, but acts that are wrongful only because the actor is a minor. Minority is, of course, a status in the sense that it occurs without regard to choice or conduct by those who are minors. Thus children during their minority occupy a status and are subject to special restrictions because of that status. Conduct in violation of those special restrictions constitutes a status offense in the juvenile court sense.

The status offense jurisdiction of the juvenile court reaches violations of several classes of rules. One group includes proscriptive rules (of the "thou shalt not" variety) that apply only to young people, such as laws prohibiting those under some specified age from using alcohol or being on the streets past a certain hour. A second group includes prescriptive rules requiring their subjects to do something positive: for example, that children obey the commands of their parents or guardians. Disobedience to such a rule may result in a finding that a child is "incorrigible" or "unruly." The third group of rules reaches youths said to be "wayward" or "growing up in idleness or crime." These children may not have violated any specific ordinance applicable to children or disobeyed specific parental orders, but seem nonetheless to be in circumstances suggesting that they have committed or may commit some such wrong.

ORIGINS OF STATUS OFFENSE JURISDICTION

The justification for asserting jurisdiction over acts that are not, when committed by adults, sufficiently serious to warrant the exercise of public authority has both ancient and modern aspects. That part of status offense jurisdiction which enforces a child's duty to obey parental authority embodies a norm of untraceable antiquity and perhaps universal acceptance. The *Analects* of Confucius declare that "a young man's duty is to behave well to his parents at home and to his elders abroad." Pre-biblical custom, like Roman law much later, accorded the father sole authority over the life and death of his children. The Old Testament commanded filial obedience not only through the Fifth Commandment but in the Book of Deuteronomy (21: 18–21), which provides for the execution by stoning of any son found by the elders of the community to have been "disloyal and defiant" to his parents. This injunction was, of course, a liberalizing provision since it placed authority for capital punishment of a disobedient child with the community rather than with the father alone (Teitelbaum 1983).

American law has long reflected this same expectation. The earliest American statute concerning unruly children was adopted by the Massachusetts Bay Colony in 1646 and incorporated almost verbatim the language of Deuteronomy in declaring the death penalty for children above the age of sixteen who were "stubborn or rebellious." While it does not appear that any youth was actually put to death under this statute, the norm was well settled and, penalty aside, continues generally to be accepted.

However, the status offense jurisdiction of the American juvenile court also draws on more modern roots. Whereas Puritan theology attributed the willfulness of children to the original sinfulness of man, nineteenth- and twentieth-century views were essentially optimistic. Misconduct by children came to be understood as reflecting a wide variety of modern circumstances: parental failure (often specifically tied to waves of immigration), industrialization, and urbanization. This perception was strengthened by the appearance in the streets of large numbers of idle and sometimes homeless children who were thought to present the threat of widespread crime and perhaps the prospect of a permanently impoverished and embittered lower class that might rise to destroy the social fabric.

Fortunately, the same period saw not only the prospect of harm to and from these children but a method for addressing it. Late-nineteenth- and early-twentieth-century Americans were convinced that manipulation of the environment in which children were raised could positively influence their attitudes and behaviors. A number of programs seeking to remedy environmental factors arose, including Houses of Refuge and compulsory education. The most important expression of this optimism, however, was the American juvenile court, which provided a unified jurisdiction and common procedure for dealing with the various kinds of conducts evidencing a risk of maldevelopment and the various kinds of conditions leading to that risk.

STATUS OFFENSES IN THE TRADITIONAL JUVENILE COURT

The scope of the juvenile court's ambition is clearly reflected in the definition of juvenile delinquency that appears in the 1907 Illinois Juvenile Court Act:

> The words "delinquent child" shall mean any male child who while under the age of seventeen years or any female child who while under the age of eighteen years, violates any law of this State; or is incorrigible, or knowingly associates with thieves, vicious or immoral persons; or who without just cause and without [the] consent of its parents . . . absents itself from its home or place of abode, or is growing up in idleness or crime; or knowingly frequents a house of ill-repute; or knowingly frequents any policy shop or dram shop where intoxicating liquors are sold; or patronizes or visits any public pool room or bucket shop; or wanders about the streets in the night time without being on any lawful business or lawful occupation; or habitually wanders about any railroad yards or jumps or attempts to jump onto [any] moving train; or enters any car or engine without lawful authority; or uses vile, obscene, vulgar, profane or indecent language in [any] public place or about any school house; or is guilty of indecent or lascivious conduct.

The status offense aspect of this definition of juvenile delinquency includes everything after the first element (violation of any state law). This aspect of the court's authority reached not only acts defined with considerable specificity (such as begging and patronizing pool halls and bucket shops) but also far more generalized patterns of conduct, such as "growing up in idleness

Fig. 6.1 Newsboys smoke cigarettes outside a St. Louis pool hall while patrons watch. © CORBIS.

or crime." Status offense jurisdiction was justified both in terms of support for parental authority (through its extension to incorrigible and runaway youth) and by concern for the failure of parental authority (again, growing up in idleness or crime and, in many instances, curfew laws). The rationale of status offense jurisdiction, in common with the entirety of juvenile court jurisdiction, rested principally on two beliefs: the protocriminal nature of noncriminal misconduct and the capacity of public authority to educate or reeducate minors who seemed to be on the wrong path in the direction of "good, sound adult citizenship."

The undifferentiated treatment of criminal and noncriminal misconduct is also characteristic of traditional juvenile court theory. Proponents of the juvenile court viewed deviance as a developmental process, and the central premise of the juvenile court movement was the use of judicial authority to identify and rehabilitate, rather than punish, children whose acts or conditions bespoke the likelihood of future antisocial behavior. Accordingly, intervention did not depend on proof of specific conduct but considered all acts and circumstances indicating a lack of appropriate control or upbringing equally significant. Moreover, because intervention in all cases was regarded as therapeutic rather than punitive, no reason to differentiate between criminal and noncriminal behavior seemed to exist.

Given its breadth, it is not surprising that during the first part of this century, status offense jurisdiction made up a substantial part—at least a quarter and, by some accounts, as much as one-half—of the juvenile court docket. Because of its breadth and the variety of circumstances giving rise to juvenile court authority over noncriminal misbehavior, however, status offense jurisdiction never reflected a single phenomenon. In some localities, court authority was invoked by parents; more than 80 percent of all such complaints in one urban New York county arose in that way (Andrews and Cohen 1977, 55). The motivations for parental initiation of status offense complaints reflect varying circumstances. In some families, parents resort to a status offense petition when they have few other resources to enforce compliant behavior by their children; in others, it serves as a vehicle for removing unwanted children from home; in yet others, it is the only available means of securing social and mental health services for parents who, unlike their wealthier counterparts, cannot afford to purchase those services in the private sector (Mahoney 1977). In localities where parents have greater resources to secure compliance with their commands and to obtain services for their children, status offense jurisdiction is invoked more often by public officials; thus, almost one-half of all petitions in a suburban New York county came from schools and less than one-third from parents (Andrews and Cohen 1977, 64).

The ways in which status offense jurisdiction is used evidently had much to do with socioeconomic class. They also had much to do with adult, and especially parental, social perceptions. As with crime, the status offending population disproportionately included members of minority groups; unlike delinquents, however, status offenders were often young women. In the 1970s, young women accounted for almost two-thirds of youths accused of ungovernability, incorrigibility, or running away. Even after the disappearance of statutes that held young women subject to family or juvenile court status offense jurisdiction until a later age than young men, the vagueness of statutory definitions invited differential application. For cultural and biological reasons related to the risk of pregnancy, parents and police are more prone to disapprove of female than of male sexuality, and judges are more prone to be "protective" of young women than young men. Parental and public tolerance for behaviors that may lead to immorality or pregnancy, such as late hours or drinking, also differed by gender. Even views of the morality of behavior differed: noncoercive male sexual behavior was unlikely to come to public attention, whereas female sexual behavior met with strong disapproval (Sussman 1977).

As a result, young women—who rarely faced delinquency charges—made up a substantial portion of the juvenile court's status offense docket. Moreover, once in court, young women were less likely to receive informal dispositions, more likely to be detained, more likely to be committed to a secure facility, and more likely to spend longer times in training schools than were young men. Indeed, they were likelier to spend more time in institutions than were young men who had committed criminal acts because one of the central canons of traditional juvenile court theory held that dispositions were chosen on the ground of the child's need for treatment rather than his or her conduct. Accordingly, children found to be incorrigible or to have committed some other status offense, including young women who excited protective or moral concerns, were as likely to be placed in an industrial school as those who engaged in criminal misconduct (Sussman 1977; Chesney-Lind 1997; Office of Juvenile Justice 1996; Schaffner 1998).

THE CRITIQUE OF JUVENILE COURT STATUS OFFENSE JURISDICTION

It is possible to regard the original juvenile court as a great social experiment; indeed, its proponents often described it in that way. With few exceptions, this experiment was widely regarded as a great success for the first part of the century. During the second half of the century, however, a variety of questions emerged about that assumption.

To a considerable extent, these questions were part of a more general critique of public authority. The period of the 1960s and 1970s saw widespread distrust of governmental power and sharply diminished confidence in the effectiveness and benevolence of professionals and agencies engaged in the enterprise of social control. A line of United States Supreme Court decisions impeached the methods by which police secured confessions (*Miranda v. Arizona* 384 U.S. 436 [1966]) and seized evidence from adults prosecuted for crime (*Mapp v. Ohio* 367 U.S. 643 [1961]). Many commentators and some courts embraced a principle requiring agencies undertaking the treatment of mentally ill persons to employ, rather than institutionalization, the "least restrictive alternative" available under the circumstances. Dean Francis Allen in an elegant little book examined the risks associated with governmental claims to intervene in service of what he called "the rehabilitative ideal" (Allen 1964), while Aldous Huxley pilloried its practitioners. "Like Sir Galahad's," Huxley said, "their strength is the strength of ten because their heart is pure—and their heart is pure because they are scientists and have taken six thousand hours of social studies" (Huxley 1965, 26). This line of critique had special significance for juvenile courts. Judicial decisions and commentators doubted the virtues of the procedural informality characteristic of juvenile court proceedings, the claims that juvenile court intervention was benign rather than punitive, and the effectiveness of the court's remedial strategies.

Questions of these kinds appeared most visibly in connection with the juvenile court's response to criminal misconduct, but social and legal theory also challenged the desirability of treating status offenders in the same way as criminal offenders. On the social side, a newly popular theory of deviance suggested that labeling a delinquent as delinquent would promote rather than deter his becoming a criminal offender in the future. According to this labeling theory, once a person has been identified publicly as a deviant, a self-fulfilling prophecy is initiated. Members of the child's community perceive and respond to that youth as a delinquent, denying him opportunities that would otherwise be available; placement with a deviant group leads the child to identify himself with the delinquent group to which he has been formally assigned (Teitelbaum 1983, 987). The implications of labeling theory were supported as well by an increasing belief that attachment of a stigmatizing label to those whose behavior arose from their relations to their parents ignored the possibility that blame, if any there were, might better be assigned to parental choices and behavior, and by doubts about the effectiveness of intervention directed at children engaged in noncriminal misconduct.

The legalization of the juvenile court's delinquency jurisdiction no doubt also contributed to concern about the common treatment of criminal and noncriminal misconduct. In its seminal 1967 decision, *In re Gault* (387 U.S. 1), the Supreme Court largely rejected the traditional juvenile court emphasis on procedural informality. It found that the consequences of adjudication and commitment to an industrial school for delinquency were virtually indistinguishable from those associated with conviction for felony and imprisonment for crime. Consequently, the failure to provide written notice of specific charges, access to counsel, confrontation and cross-examination of witnesses, and the privilege against self-incrimination were held unconstitutional.

Although the Supreme Court did not address status offense proceedings in *Gault* and has not done so since, the Court's recognition of the severity of the consequences of treatment as a delinquent argued against the continued inclusion of children who had committed no criminal act. Moreover, the vagueness of some categories of status offense jurisdiction seemed inconsistent with the requirements of legal justice and with constitutional requirements of statutory definiteness. Legalization of delinquency matters also reflected doubts about the rehabilitative claims of juvenile court intervention.

These concerns resulted in proposals for substantial change in the legal response to noncriminal misconduct. The first stage was the separation of status from criminal offenders with respect to jurisdictional category and disposition. The former was expressed in a recommendation of the President's Commission on Law Enforcement and Criminal Justice, *Task Force Report: Juvenile Delinquency and Youth Crime* (1967, 226) that states follow the examples of Illinois (1966) and New York (1963) in defining delinquency in terms of conduct criminal for adults and adopting a new category, variously called "Minor in Need of Supervision" and "Person in Need of Supervision" (PINS), for minors engaged in noncriminal conduct. These changes responded specifically to general acceptance of the implications of labeling theory, and were widely adopted.

An even more dramatic proposal emerged in 1976 from the Institute for Judicial Administration–American Bar Association Juvenile Justice Standards Project (IJA–ABA 1976). That project's *Standards Relating to Non-Criminal Misbehavior* recommended the elimination of general juvenile court jurisdiction over status offenses in favor of a network of services based for the most part on voluntary participation, with judicial intervention available only in limited and special circumstances. Although the American Bar Association never adopted these standards, the approach they took was followed in a few states, most notably Maine (1977) and Washington (1982; see Feld 1999, 179).

Less generally adopted for some time was the differentiation of PINS from delinquents for correctional purposes. A number of states prohibited the pretrial detention and/or institutional confinement of noncriminal offenders with "delinquents." The enactment of the federal Juvenile Justice and Delinquency Prevention Act (JJDPA) in 1974, however, supplied a powerful impetus to remove noncriminal offenders from secure detention before trial and from correctional facilities after adjudication by conditioning federal grant awards on movement towards deinstitutionalization. And in fact, the number of status offenders in secure detention and training schools declined substantially during the following two decades. The decline was, to be sure, slow to develop. During the first five years after passage of the JJDPA, admissions of status offenders in custodial settings did not significantly decrease from the approximately 65,000 youths institutionalized in 1974 (Schwartz 1989). During the 1980s, however, the effect of the act was more evident. By 1989, about 9,000 status offenders—15 percent of the 1974 total—had been committed to a secure institution by state juvenile courts (Krisberg and Austin 1993, 74), and that figure had decreased to less than 7,000 in 1997 (Snyder and Sickmund 1999, 186–87). By 1992, thirty-seven states had complied fully or substantially with the act's requirements (Holden 1995, 22).

By the 1980s, accordingly, the unified approach of the traditional juvenile court had largely disappeared. Rather than treat all misconduct as important for its relevance to the likelihood of future misconduct, juvenile court law now took the approach of criminal law in focusing on the nature of the acts themselves. Rather than rely on a capacity for individualized treatment of youths in conflict with the law or with their parents, juvenile court statutes now categorically distinguished between criminal and noncriminal offenses. And rather than rely on the capacity of institutional programs to deal effectively with deviance of all kinds, juvenile court laws rejected the appropriateness of such programs for minors who had not engaged in criminal misconduct.

THE PRESENT AND THE FUTURE OF STATUS OFFENSE JURISDICTION

The reforms in status offense jurisdiction that occurred between the early 1960s and the 1980s can be considered social experiments in the same way that the original formulation of juvenile court jurisdiction and procedure can be so considered. It would be good to be able to evaluate the success of this experiment. However, relatively scant information is available to that purpose.

Some things are surely true. One is that status offense jurisdiction now makes up a much smaller part of the juvenile court's business than previously. While PINS and their counterparts accounted for one-quarter to one-half of the juvenile court's caseload at earlier times, the incidence of petitioned status offense cases was only about 15 percent of the incidence of petitioned delinquency matters between 1985 and 1995 (Sickmund et al. 1998). Another is that the institutionalization of children for status offenses is now far more uncommon than it was. These phenomena are, no doubt, related. The reduction in the number of jurisdictions retaining status offense jurisdiction is far too small to account for the reduction in status offense by itself. It seems likely that parents, police, and court intake offices have concluded that formal juvenile court response to juvenile misconduct is so unlikely that other community-based strategies are preferable, or that no institutional response is available. But what has happened to those children who, prior to the reforms of the last thirty years, would have been treated as status offenders and often committed to secure institutions?

Parental Responses

While status offense jurisdiction and residential placement of youths who had not committed criminal acts were sharply curtailed, the social circumstances giving rise to such jurisdiction remained in place. Many of these cases were experienced as crises, especially for parents whose children were disobedient, had run away, had poor school attendance or performance, spent time with undesirable companions, stayed out past curfew, engaged in sexual relations, or used drugs or alcohol. If the juvenile court would not respond, those parents would predictably seek other avenues of relief.

The Mental Health System

One alternate vehicle for parents was the mental health system. Mental health treatment for "emotionally disturbed" or chemically dependent children does not present the same procedural barriers or the same limits on institutionalization that parents now encounter in juvenile courts. Most states allow parents to commit their minor children "voluntarily" for residential mental health treatment without any judicial process. The United States Supreme Court has held that an informal commitment process by parents is constitutionally valid as long as a staff mental health professional evaluates the child and approves the admission (*Parham v. JR,* 442 U.S. 609 [1979]).

In fact, parents would not need to look far for information about the availability of sources of help outside the juvenile justice system. The kinds of conduct that the juvenile court labeled status offenses could equally well be considered signs of emotional disturbance, personality disorders, or adjustment reactions to adolescence. And although mental health policy analysts, like juvenile court commentators, urged reduction in the inpatient care of children and youths during the 1980s, the number of hospital commitments in fact rose dramatically (approximately 400 percent) during the decade when juvenile courts withdrew from the institutionalization of status offenders (Weithorn 1988).

The inference that the mental health system served as an alternative to juvenile court jurisdiction is suggested not only by the dramatic increase in admissions itself but by the conditions surrounding the increase in admissions. As we have just noted, there was no general call by mental health policymakers for increased hospital treatment of minors; rather, the contrary was true. Nor was there an increase in serious mental health problems among children. Although between one-half and two-thirds of adults admitted to mental hospitals suffered from serious disorders, less than one-third of juvenile admittees did so (Weithorn 1988, 788–89). Rather, their characteristics resembled those of status offenders more than those of severely disturbed children; they were young people who had experimented with drugs or alcohol, suffered from eating disorders, ran away, had school problems, or were generally in conflict with their parents or other authorities (Binder and Binder 1994).

If the juvenile court had become too legalistic to deal with these children, private mental health providers were ready to do so; in fact, they mounted an aggressive campaign to reach just those parents who might earlier have gone to juvenile court. The percentage of mental hospitals advertising in newspapers increased from 43 percent in 1982 to 75 percent in 1988, and many marketed their services to schools, juvenile probation officers, and social services agencies as well (Binder and Binder 1994, 359–60).

The relationship between the conduct of status offenders and that of the children addressed by private mental health providers is evident in their newspaper and television advertisements. One example must serve for many. An ad by a private mental health hospital begins with a bold heading that says "Busted" in large block capitals and then continues, "Don't wait until you get a call from the police to get help for your teenager. If your child's behavior is pushing the limits and you are losing control call. . . . We treat adolescents who have trouble with drugs and alcohol, illegal behavior, runaway, school failure, and emotional problems" (Binder and Binder 1994, 359). And despite the relative infrequency of serious disturbances, juveniles on average remained in hospitals twice as long as did adults.

Exclusion

Another response to the reduction in the availability of status offense jurisdiction and of residential treatment for children in conflict with their parents that has not been much studied is exclusion. Children who run away may simply stay away, and parents who cannot control their children may exclude them from the home by telling them to leave or by refusing to allow their return after some violation of parental rules. The popularity of "toughlove" approaches has given legitimacy to these exclusions. While the proponents of de-judicialization of status offense problems vigorously urged the creation of alternative, community-based residential and counseling programs that might have served these children, legislatures have proven generally unwilling to invest funds in creating and staffing such resources.

As of 1988, the National Incidence Study: Missing, Abducted, Runaway, and Thrownaway Children in America (NISMART) reported that almost 500,000 children were "runaways" and another 127,000 minors were "thrownaways"—that is, abandoned or exiled by their parents. These categories are, of course, hard to distinguish causally and, for that matter, demographically. Some part of this population has found its way into the foster care system, but plainly not all have done so. As of the 1990 census, more than 5 million children were living in households headed by neither of their parents—often with relatives and otherwise with friends or in institutions. Thrownaway children may be at disproportionate risk of dangerous circumstances; the NISMART survey found that of the 127,000 minor children it identified as excluded from the home, almost 60,000 had no "familiar and secure" place to live away from home. Moreover, the trend to nonfamilial residence seems to be increasing; the number of children living in non-parent-headed households increased by 400,000 from 1980 to 1990, although the population in that age group decreased slightly (Loken 1995).

Law Enforcement Responses

It is to be expected that parents, faced with a crisis, would find alternate ways of responding to juvenile misconduct within the home. The conduct involved also was of substantial concern for police and law enforcement, and that concern has grown with the increase in gang activity and public concern about juvenile crime.

Even during the highest point of enthusiasm for de-institutionalization of status offenders, some children who would previously have been treated in that way now found their way into the delinquency jurisdiction of the juvenile court. To the extent that status offense jurisdiction is used by police as a residual category for proceedings that involve delinquency as well, some of these children may now be brought to juvenile court on delinquency charges alone. An evaluation of the effects of eliminating status offense jurisdiction in Washington state indicates some such effect, although it clearly appeared that status offense behavior had been eliminated as a formal judicial category.

A far more pervasive response from law enforcement has emerged in recent years, however. After an early decline, the use of the juvenile court's status offense jurisdiction began to rise again from the mid-1980s to the mid-1990s. The number of formally petitioned status offense cases rose from less than 83,000 in 1986 to more than 146,000 in 1995: an increase of 77 percent during that period. Case rates (per 1,000 minors) grew slowly and steadily during the 1980s, from 3.2 in 1986 to 3.4 in 1991, and then more significantly, from 3.4 in 1991 to 5.2 in 1995.

Much of this recent increase is found in one status offense category, "miscellaneous offenses," which grew from a case rate of 0.3 in 1991 to 1.0 in 1995. The increase in miscellaneous offenses, in turn, seems attributable almost entirely to the proliferation of curfew ordinances. Approximately a thousand localities have adopted local curfew ordinances since 1990, as well as several states. A study of the two hundred largest United States cities indicates that while only 47 percent had curfew ordinances in 1990, by 1995 almost three-quarters had such laws on their books (Office of Juvenile Justice 1996, 1). Less dramatic increases were also found in truancy and liquor offenses, with no substantial change in the rates of petitions for runaways and ungovernability.

The current tendency to use status offense jurisdiction as a vehicle for law enforcement control of threatening behavior is also found in the adoption of ordinances and statutes addressed to gang affiliation. California, which is home to well over a hundred thousand gang members (Truman 1995, 683), adopted the Street Terrorism Enforcement and Prevention Act (1988), which, among a variety of provisions, makes it a crime to "actively participate in any criminal street gang with knowledge that its members engage in or have engaged in a pattern of criminal gang activity and assist in any felonious criminal conduct by that gang" (Cal. Penal Code §§ 186.20–28 [WEJT Supp. 1994]). The same statute defines every building used by members of a gang to be a public nuisance, and has also created what may be secondary status offense liability by declaring the responsibility of parents for the reasonable care and control of their children—a provision clearly intended to enlist parents in the effort to eradicate gangs. Chicago, which has its own substantial gang problems, adopted a city ordinance in 1992 allowing police to order an individual to move along if that individual was reasonably believe[d] to be a criminal street gang member loitering in a public place with at least one other person (*City of Chicago v. Morales,* 527 U.S. 41 [1999]).

With the widespread adoption of curfew laws and statutes directed to gang affiliations has come widespread challenge to their use. A number of cases have addressed claims of statutory vagueness, interference with parental rights, denial of equal protection, and unconstitutional interference with minors' freedom of movement, with mixed results. Curfew laws have met various fates, depending in part on the specificity of their language and in part on the extent to which courts attach importance to freedom of movement by minors (Chudy 2000). The Chicago gang ordinance was declared unconstitutional by the United States Supreme Court on the ground that several of its terms, including "remaining in any one place with no apparent purpose," were vague on their faces and that the breadth of the ordinance failed to provide minimal guidelines to govern law enforcement (*City of Chicago v. Morales,* 527 U.S. 41 [1999]). On the other hand, the parental liability statute, narrowly interpreted, was upheld by the California Supreme Court. The California court also upheld issuance of an injunction under state nuisance law against individual members of a "criminal street gang" prohibiting gang members from associating with any other known gang member and gathering in any form in public view within a gang-dominated area of the city (*People v. Acura,* 929 P.2d 596 [1997]).

Evaluation of status offense jurisdiction in its current form—as an adjunct to police control of minors more than as a vehicle for parental support—must await the results of these legal challenges to its use as well as information about the meaning and effects of these laws in the various communities where they are invoked. But it does seem clear that the social and political function of status offense jurisdiction has changed dramatically.

As we saw earlier, status offense jurisdiction had given parents access to public power and resources for assistance in dealing with problems with children. That avenue is now far less available than before and has been replaced by other social systems, such as the mental health system, or by informal responses, such as exclusion from home. However, police and public concerns, after a period of decline, have reemerged. The adoption of curfew and gang affiliation laws clearly responds to public safety concerns and violations of these ordinances usually initiated by public authorities. Law enforcement accounted for 54 percent of "miscellaneous" referrals in 1986, for 56 percent of such referrals in 1991, and for 77 percent of miscellaneous petitions in 1995. Police have always been heavily responsible for petitions alleging liquor violations; in 1995, 93 percent of all such petitions were initiated by law enforcement (Sickmund 1998).

The shift in the function of status offense petitions is also clear from an examination of the origin of status offense charges. Prior to reform, parents and schools were the primary and, in many communities, the only substantial sources of status offense referrals. In 1996, however, law enforcement officials nationally referred fully half of all status offense cases to juvenile court. The status offense jurisdiction of the court has accordingly become a device for public control rather than public assistance.

OLD AND NEW QUESTIONS ABOUT JUVENILE COURT STATUS OFFENSES

In her 1976 essay entitled "Notes on Helping Juvenile Nuisances" (Rosenheim 1976), Margaret Rosenheim suggested several ways of thinking about social response to noncriminal misconduct by children. The judicial approach of the juvenile court was, of course, one response, but it had fallen under sharp criticism by that time. A second model was that of social service agencies of the kind recommended by the IJA-ABA *Standards on Non-Criminal Misbehavior.* This approach promised voluntary rather than coercive involvement in the lives of troubled youths. However, the performance of youth service bureaus and similar social service programs was unimpressive, and their activities carried the risk that the benefits they provided would widen rather than constrain the net of control over young people. A third response resembled the welfare model of helping services: services based on an individualistic, social-pathological perspective employing individual treatment to restore healthy functioning. This, however, entailed an expense that was unlikely to be borne by public authorities. Finally, Professor Rosenheim proposes a model that had not yet been employed: one that accepted much juvenile misconduct as normal, rejected classification and labeling of that misconduct, and relied on multipurpose, community-based resources to provide counseling and other services when requested by clients.

This summary reviews a variety of possible responses to misconduct defined as wrongful only for minors and raises, directly or by implication, many of the questions presented by status offense jurisdiction that have troubled and still trouble public policy. I will only suggest some of those questions here. One is the set of questions arising from one traditional use of juvenile status offense jurisdiction that concerns the appropriate relation between law and social policy on the one hand and parent-child relations on the other. Is it an appropriate goal for public authority to support efforts by parents to control their children? Does such an enterprise suppose the acceptability of parental commands and enforce parental dominance during a time when we also expect children to develop a capacity for autonomous decision-making? And if the goal is to support parental authority, can that successfully be done through judicial intervention, which declares the authority of courts at the moment it purports to enforce the authority of parents (Katz and Teitelbaum 1977–78)? Finally, to what extent is it appropriate under modern doctrine to enforce parental authority in general, when core decisions having to do with morality—procreative decisions—are for minors to make if they are mature and for courts to make if they are immature?

A second set of questions arises from efforts at reform. If judicial authority over misbehaving children is to be curtailed, what will follow? Are legislatures willing to supply on a voluntary basis the services juvenile courts made available coercively, or is the legislative interest directed solely to secure institutions demonstrating "serious" concern about juvenile misconduct? If not—and the experience in most states justifies great pessimism—where will children and families go for services? Will providers of those services recreate the problems associated with juvenile court intervention in a child's liberty without any of the process associated with even traditional juvenile court practice? Equally important, how will parents respond to the decreased availability of public authority? The incidence of runaway and exiled youth—particularly those without a familiar and safe place to stay—suggests reasons for grave concern.

Questions also arise concerning the use of generally stated laws for control of behavior that is not criminal but is thought to create some degree of risk that criminal misconduct will occur or has occurred. These laws, whether phrased in terms of "growing up in idleness or crime" or as curfew and gang affiliation ordinances, raise all of the customary concerns of vague statutes. They lend themselves to enforcement against individuals and groups who create concern because of their appearance or racial or ethnic identity rather than because their conduct is itself obviously dangerous. They provide bases for interrogation and investigation when ordinary standards for those activities could not be justified. And they declare the impermissibility of associations that may be centrally important to members of those associations.

The problem is, of course, that we do not know what to do about the conflict that comes with the strains between parent and teenage child and the fact that some misbehavior is a normal aspect of adolescent life. Indeed, we do not know what we *want* to do about these phenomena. We do know, however, that if we treat them as problems, they will be just that, and that we have found little that effectively persuades adolescents to conform to commands or even to good advice. And we know that most adolescents who misbehave when they are young do not become adult deviants and ultimately get exactly what they deserve—their own children. Perhaps we might start with the few things we know, and then consider what we are willing to do about that.

REFERENCES

Allen, F. A. 1964. *The Borderland of Criminal Justice.* Chicago: University of Chicago Press.

Andrews, R. H., and A. H. Cohen. 1977. "PINS Processing in New York: An Evaluation." In *Beyond Control: Status Offenders in the Juvenile Court,* ed. L. E. Teitelbaum and A. R. Gough, 45–113. Cambridge, MA: Ballinger.

Binder, A., and V. L. Binder. 1994. "The Incarceration of Juveniles: From the Era of Crouse to that of Freud and Skinner." *Legal Studies Forum* 18: 349–66.

Chesney-Lind, M. 1997. *The Female Offender.* Thousand Oaks, CA: Sage.

Chudy, P. J. 2000. "Doctrinal Reconstruction: Reconciling Conflicting Standards in Adjudicating Juvenile Curfew Challenges." *Cornell Law Review* 85: 518–85.

Confucius. *The Analects of Confucius.* Tr. Arthur Waley. New York: Macmillan, 1939.

Feld, B. J. 1999. *Bad Kids: Race and the Transformation of the Juvenile Court.* New York: Oxford University Press.

Holden, G. 1995. *Unlocking the Doors for Status Offenders: The State of the States.* Washington, DC: GPO.

Huxley, Aldous. 1965. *Brave New World Revisited.* New York: Harper & Row.

Institute for Judicial Administration–American Bar Association. 1976. *Juvenile Justice Standards Project, Standards Relating to Non-Criminal Misbehavior.* Tentative Draft. Cambridge, MA: Ballinger.

Katz, A., and L. E. Teitelbaum. 1977–78. "PINS Jurisdiction, the Vagueness Doctrine, and the Rule of Law." *Indiana Law Journal* 53: 1–34.

Krisberg, B., and J. Austin. 1993. *Reinventing Juvenile Justice.* Thousand Oaks, CA: Sage.

Loken, G. A. 1995. "'Thrownaway' Children and Throwaway Parenthood." *Temple Law Review* 68: 1715–62.

Mahoney, A. R. 1977. "PINS and Parents." In *Beyond Control,* ed. Teitelbaum and Gough, 161–77.

Office of Juvenile Justice and Delinquency Prevention. 1996. *Juvenile Justice Bulletin* 1 (April). Washington, D.C.

The President's Commission on Law Enforcement and Administration of Justice. 1967. *TASK Force Report: Juvenile Delinquency and Youth Crime.* Washington, DC: GPO.

Rosenheim, M. K. 1976. "Notes on Helping Juvenile Nuisances." In *Pursuing Justice for the Child,* ed. M. K. Rosenheim, 43–66. Chicago: University of Chicago Press.

Schaffner, L. 1998. "Female Juvenile Delinquency: Sexual Solutions, Gender Bias, and Juvenile Justice." *Hastings Women's Law Journal* 9: 1–25.

Schwartz, I. M. 1989. *(In)Justice for Juveniles: Rethinking the Best Interests of the Child.* Lexington, MA: Lexington Books.

Sickmund, M., et al. 1998. *Juvenile Justice Statistics, 1995.* Pittsburgh, PA: Office of Juvenile Justice and Delinquency Prevention.

Snyder, H. N., and M. Sickmund. 1999. *Juvenile Offenders and Victims: 1999 National Report.* Washington, DC: Office of Juvenile Justice and Delinquency Prevention.

Sussman, A. 1977. "Sex-Based Discrimination and PINS Jurisdiction." In *Beyond Control,* ed. Teitelbaum and Gough, 179–99.

Teitelbaum, L. E., 1991. "Youth Crime and the Choice between Rules and Standards." *Brigham Young University Law Review* 1991: 351–402.

———. 1983. "Juvenile Status Offenders." In *Encyclopedia of Crime and Justice,* ed. Sanford H. Kadish 3: 983–91. New York: Free Press.

Truman, D. R. 1995. "The Jets and Sharks are Dead: State Statutory Responses to Criminal Street Gangs." *Washington University Law Quarterly* 73: 683–735.

Unger, R. 1975. *Knowledge and Politics*. New York: Free Press.

Weithorn, L. A. 1988. "Mental Hospitalization of Troublesome Youth: Skyrocketing Admission Rates." *Stanford Law Review* 40: 773–838.

PART 3

Juvenile Justice and Social Science

The progressive reformers who founded the juvenile court were optimistic in their belief that social and behavioral scientific progress could be translated into effective classifications and treatments of troubled young persons, whether delinquent, neglected, or dependent. This legal embrace of empirical human science coincided with a sharp expansion in social and psychological investigations of juvenile delinquency. The close relationship between social scientists and juvenile court practitioners has continued, with a variety of results documented by the chapters in this section. In chapter 7, John Laub surveys one hundred years of scholarly investigations of the causes and prevention of juvenile delinquency. There have been a substantial number of investigations into the roots of delinquent behavior, exactly the kind of study that those who founded the court had hoped for. But were these scientific findings useful for policymakers? And were the lessons of social studies actually integrated into the jurisprudence of the courts?

Chapters 8 and 9 consider the lessons of social science on two more specific problem populations that are within the jurisdiction of the modern juvenile court. David Farrington and Rolf Loeber focus in chapter 8 on the research profile of serious and violent offenders, the most troubling population of adolescents within the jurisdictional boundaries of the modern juvenile court. In chapter 9, Mark Testa and Frank Furstenberg extend the area-study perspective that was created by Clifford Shaw and Henry McKay to study delinquency in the 1920s. Testa and Furstenberg show that disorganized community areas also display extraordinary levels of child endangerment. Thus, the chapters in this section both describe and extend the rich social science tradition of research in delinquency and (more recently) child endangerment.

7 A Century of Delinquency Research and Delinquency Theory

John H. Laub

At first glance, ideas about juvenile delinquency in the United States have changed remarkably over the last hundred years. For a moment, consider the evolution of conceptions of juvenile delinquents as "defective" in the early 1900s, to conceptions of "wayward youth" in the 1930s, "delinquent boys" in the 1950s, "chronic offenders" in the 1970s, and "superpredators" in the 1990s. As Hirschi and Rudisill (1976) have observed, biology, psychology, and sociology have successively dominated American criminological thought at various points throughout the past century. Not surprisingly, with the rise and dominance of different disciplines, explanatory frameworks have shifted as well. For example, as sociology became more dominant in criminology, Hirschi and Rudisill have argued that "explanatory attention moved away from the offender toward social processes creating him" (1976, 21). Likewise, the focus in delinquency research has shifted from individual characteristics (like intelligence) and the family to the gang, community, and social structural characteristics (like social class). Eventually, attention was directed to systems of social control and the larger political economy. In light of these changes in thinking about the sources and causes of delinquency, it is not surprising that thinking about delinquency prevention and control has changed as well. For example, as the field focused less and less attention on the distinguishable differences between offenders and nonoffenders, policies have directed less attention to child guidance clinics and individual training for delinquent youth and their parents.

In this essay, I trace the intellectual history of juvenile delinquency and delinquent youth over the last hundred years. For my purposes, I am defining delinquency broadly to include violations of criminal law as well as so-called status offenses (violations of law for those under the age of majority). My focus is on the natural history of American delinquency theory and research. Special emphasis is devoted to classic research studies and prominent theories of delinquency in the United States, and to assessing their influence on popular perception and societal response to juvenile offending. For example, I review the classic research studies of William Healy, Sheldon and Eleanor Glueck, Clifford Shaw and Henry McKay, and Marvin Wolfgang and his colleagues. I also review the prominent theories of juvenile delinquency, including the work of Edwin Sutherland, Robert Merton, Albert Cohen, Walter Miller, Richard Cloward and Lloyd Ohlin, David Matza, Edwin Schur, and Travis Hirschi.

Despite the appearance of significant change over the last hundred years, specific issues of concern appear time and time again. At all times throughout the twentieth century, concerns regarding race/ethnicity, biology, poverty and inequality, cultural values and norms, the claims of academic disciplines, the role of the state, and the hopes and dreams of the juvenile court movement have been commonplace. How these enduring issues are resolved in each generation influences what are regarded as the important sources of juvenile delinquency. Unraveling this process of social construction is essential to understanding the varying interpretations of data on delinquency and juvenile offenders over time, the different explanations of the causes of delinquency, and the accompanying remedies for its control.

CLASSIC RESEARCH STUDIES AND THEORIES OF DELINQUENCY

Over the last hundred years, thousands of research studies of delinquent youth and a multitude of theories have been offered to explain delinquent behavior. My goal here is to highlight what are considered to be the classic research studies and the more prominent theories of juvenile delinquency. During this period, the study of delinquency consisted of two dominant strands. One is a focus on the correlates of crime. This perspective emerged from what was called the "multiple-factor" framework, which was the dominant criminological paradigm in the first part of this century. The multiple-factor approach (now referred to as the crime-correlate approach) examines a series of biological, psychological, and sociological factors that might distinguish offenders from nonoffenders. This approach recognizes that there is no single cause or risk factor for crime and violence; rather, multiple pathways lead to crime and violence. The range of risk factors considered is typically quite broad and largely influenced by disciplinary preferences and available data. The second dominant strand has been theorizing about crime and delinquency. Generally speaking, theories in criminology have been dominated by sociological theories of crime; thus, the central idea is that crime is the result of social forces that are external to the individual. When one speaks of traditional criminology, one thinks of theories like social disorganization theory, differential association theory, strain theory, cultural deviance theory, social control theory, and labeling theory.

Despite a rich tradition of research and theory, it is surprising to see that much research was conducted independently of theory, and most theories were offered absent sound research. In rare moments, research and theory were integrated. The key theme that emerges from this review is that shifts in theoretical emphasis have been largely independent of the results of research, and research has been largely conducted without a strong theoretical base. Thus, what is emphasized in particular periods has more to do with social construction than with the truthfulness of research and soundness of theoretical ideas. Such a state of affairs does not portend well for developing effective policies for youth in trouble with the law.

The Research Enterprise

A variety of techniques have been used to study crime and delinquency, ranging from single case studies (e.g., *The Jack Roller,* by Clifford Shaw [1930]) to analysis of case records for very large groups of offenders (e.g., *One Thousand Juvenile Delinquents,* by Sheldon and Eleanor Glueck [1934b]). Studies of delinquency and delinquent offenders tend to rely on official data such as police reports and arrest rates. For an incident to be recorded as a crime, it must be known to the police and regarded as a criminal incident. These two conditions may vary due either to victims' reports of crime or police practices of arrest and crime recording or both. Fortunately, during the latter part of the century, alternative sources of crime data have been made available, namely, self-reports of offenses drawn directly from juveniles and victimization surveys designed to measure the extent of personal and household victimization in the United States. Recently, investigators have become quite sophisticated in collecting data on delinquent behavior using multiple methods across different sites (e.g., the Office of Juvenile Justice and Delinquency Prevention's Causes and Correlates of Juvenile Delinquency Research Program).

Multiple Factors and Individual Characteristics

In the first part of the century the intellectual interest centered on the biological, psychological, and sociological characteristics of the juvenile offender. This approach sought to identify as many characteristics as possible that might distinguish juvenile delinquents from nondelinquents. Because in quiries were not tied to any one academic discipline or set of a priori assumptions about delinquency, no stone was left unturned in the search for its causes. The research strategy was straightforward: collect data to examine which characteristics were associated with the delinquent groups in comparison to the general population or some control group of nondelinquents. The basic idea was that there were immediate causes of delinquency and that these causal agents were reflected in the differences between delinquents and nondelinquents. The goal of research then was to discover the correlates of delinquent behavior. This scientific view coupled with the notion that nondelinquency was preferable to delinquency ushered in a golden age of research on the causes of delinquency (Hirschi 1979). Moreover, the connection between social science research and social policy could not have been stronger. Once the correlates were identified, the solution to the problem of delinquency would emerge from the data. Pragmatism rather than abstract theorizing ruled the day.

Initially, criminologists were interested solely in the biology of the juvenile offender, especially constitutional defects. Soon attention shifted away from the body to the mental ability of the offender. Feeblemindedness was soon deemed the primary cause of delinquency. Social factors were also considered in the search for the causes of delinquency. Important research by Sophonisba Breckinridge and Edith Abbott (1912) on the wards of the juvenile court in Chicago revealed that childrearing and family life were most important in preventing delinquency. These authors also emphasized the negative effects of poverty and deprivation as well as the culture of the immigrant ghetto, revealing the wide array of factors that might be implicated in the study of delinquency using a multiple-factor approach.

Embracing a multiple-factor approach, William Healy concluded that the case study of the offender would preclude "the acceptance of general social or biological theories of crime" (1915, 32). Through his research at the Chicago Juvenile Court, Healy identified a wide array of factors associated with delinquency, but he highlighted hereditary and mental abnormalities as more important than family relations and community factors such as bad companions.

Perhaps the best illustration of the multiple-factor approach can be found in the study by Sheldon and Eleanor Gluecks, *Unraveling Juvenile Delinquency* (1950). The title of the book says it all: What are the facts surrounding the origins and development of delinquent behavior? In the first chapter, the Gluecks pointed out the inadequacy of existing knowledge and theory of crime causation and called for an eclectic approach that embraced a multidisciplinary, multiple-factor research strategy. The Gluecks believed that all "promising leads to crime causation" had to be systematically examined. The research design for the *Unraveling* study was instructive. The study entailed a systematic comparison of five hundred "persistently delinquent boys" with five hundred "truly nondelinquent boys." Both groups were matched with respect to "ethnic derivation, age, intelligence quotient, and residence in underprivileged areas." The thousand boys were classified anthropologically according to body types and were given medical and psychiatric examinations, intelligence and achievement tests, and the Rorschach Test. The family, school, and community background of each boy was investigated by skilled social workers. "In the interest of objectivity, each line of investigation was pursued independently; no investigator had access to another's findings. As a result of this intensive multi-disciplinary approach, the authors arrive at a synthesis of the dynamic factors involved in juvenile delinquency." In the end, the Gluecks examined some twenty-five hundred factors relating to the causes of juvenile delinquency.

The Gluecks are well known for their longitudinal studies of offenders over time (see Glueck and Glueck, 1930, 1934a, 1934b, 1937, 1940, 1943). In the *Unraveling Juvenile Delinquency* study, the Gluecks followed both the delinquents and nondelinquents into young adulthood. A wide range of data was collected on family life, employment, education, and military service, as well as criminal and deviant behavior in adulthood. The Gluecks were especially interested in changes in crime as individuals aged. The Gluecks ended their twenty-five-year study, which followed the boys from adolescence through age thirty-two, with the following statement: "The major theme of the account, borne in upon us by the facts, is the original and persisting difference between those persons who, over the years, pursued stumblingly an antisocial career and those who managed to abide by the 'rules of the game' of conventional, relatively law-abiding society" (Glueck and Glueck 1968, 197).

The dream of the Gluecks was to identify the factors distinguishing delinquents from nondelinquents that could be used to develop prediction tables whereby one could differentiate potential juvenile offenders and nonoffenders at early ages. Thus this line of research, especially in the first half of the twentieth century, was characterized by a sense of optimism that policies could change criminogenic influences once they were identified.

Similar longitudinal inquiries into the multiple causes of delinquency with an eye to affecting social policy can be found in William and Joan McCord's classic study of youth in Cambridge-Somerville, Massachusetts, *Origins of Crime* (1959; see also McCord, 1979); Lee Robins's seminal study, *Deviant Children Grown Up* (1966); and the current, ongoing, longitudinal studies of the causes and correlates of delinquency in Denver, Pittsburgh, and Rochester, funded by the Office of Juvenile Justice and Delinquency Prevention. These latter studies are particularly noteworthy because they involve a set of common measures in each site. For more details regarding findings from these three sites, see Huizinga, Loeber, and Thornberry (1994) and Loeber et al. (1999).

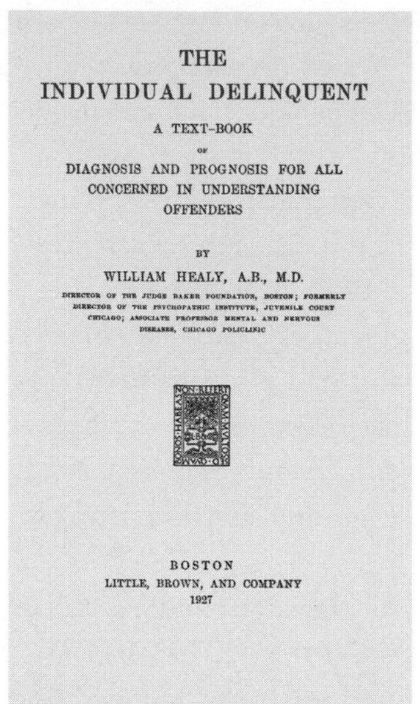

THE
INDIVIDUAL DELINQUENT
A TEXT-BOOK
OF
DIAGNOSIS AND PROGNOSIS FOR ALL
CONCERNED IN UNDERSTANDING
OFFENDERS

BY

WILLIAM HEALY, A.B., M.D.
DIRECTOR OF THE JUDGE BAKER FOUNDATION, BOSTON; FORMERLY
DIRECTOR OF THE PSYCHOPATHIC INSTITUTE, JUVENILE COURT
CHICAGO; ASSOCIATE PROFESSOR MENTAL AND NERVOUS
DISEASES, CHICAGO POLICLINIC

BOSTON
LITTLE, BROWN, AND COMPANY
1927

Fig. 7.1 Title page from *The Individual Delinquent* by William Healy.

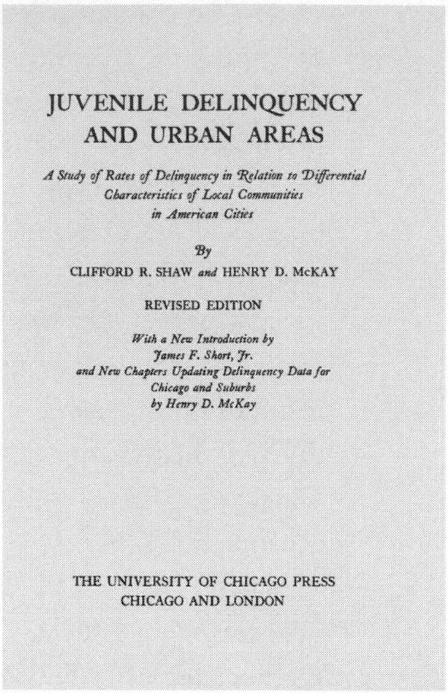

JUVENILE DELINQUENCY
AND URBAN AREAS

A Study of Rates of Delinquency in Relation to Differential Characteristics of Local Communities in American Cities

By

CLIFFORD R. SHAW *and* HENRY D. McKAY

REVISED EDITION

*With a New Introduction by James F. Short, Jr.
and New Chapters Updating Delinquency Data for Chicago and Suburbs
by Henry D. McKay*

THE UNIVERSITY OF CHICAGO PRESS
CHICAGO AND LONDON

Fig. 7.2 Title page from *Juvenile Delinquency and Urban Areas* by Clifford R. Shaw and Henry D. McKay.

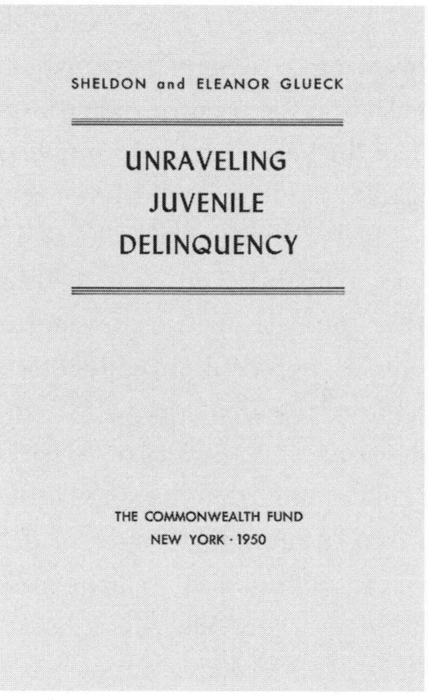

SHELDON and ELEANOR GLUECK

UNRAVELING
JUVENILE
DELINQUENCY

THE COMMONWEALTH FUND
NEW YORK · 1950

Fig. 7.3 Title page from *Unraveling Juvenile Delinquency* by Sheldon and Eleanor Glueck.

DELINQUENCY
IN A
BIRTH COHORT

Marvin E. Wolfgang
Robert M. Figlio
Thorsten Sellin

The University of Chicago Press
Chicago and London

Fig. 7.4 Title page from *Delinquency in a Birth Cohort* by Marvin E. Wolfgang, Robert M. Figlio, and Thorsten Sellin.

What Have We Learned?

Many factors have been found to be precursors of juvenile delinquency and antisocial behavior, including individual, family, school, and peer factors. For example, children who in the preschool years tend to be fearless, restless, or difficult to manage are more likely to have antisocial behavioral problems in later childhood and adolescence. There is also empirical evidence that hyperactivity, impulsivity, and attention deficit are related to early-onset of offending, particularly among boys (see Loeber and LeBlanc 1990). Family characteristics, especially poor family functioning and childrearing practices, are significantly associated with juvenile and adolescent conduct problems (Loeber and Stouthamer-Loeber 1986). Researchers also report that poor school achievement and failure in school are consistently related to adolescent offending (Maguin and Loeber 1996). Extensive research has also shown that peers play a key role in the development of offending (Thornberry et al. 1994).

Recidivists, Chronic Delinquents, Serious, Violent Offenders, and Superpredators

More than fifty years ago, Sheldon and Eleanor Glueck found that virtually all of the 510 reformatory inmates in their study of criminal careers "had experience in serious antisocial conduct" (1930, 142). Their data also confirmed "the early genesis of antisocial careers" (143). This finding was confirmed in several studies; indeed, one of the most consistent findings in the research literature is that those offenders with the highest rate of offending tend to begin their involvement in crime at earlier ages than offenders with shorter careers and fewer offenses.

A second significant finding was that a small proportion of "chronic" offenders were responsible for the majority of crime incidents (Wolfgang, Figlio, and Sellin 1972). In an analysis of the famous Philadelphia Birth Cohort data, Wolfgang and associates reported that 6 percent of the subjects (or 18 percent of the delinquents) accounted for nearly 52 percent of the crimes committed by this cohort. They also found that chronic offenders were more likely than nonchronic offenders to be nonwhite; come from a lower socioeconomic background; experience more family moves; have lower IQs; have fewer school grades completed; exhibit more school discipline problems; commit more serious offenses; and begin criminal careers early in the life course as measured by age of first arrest. Similar results were soon reported elsewhere in the United States and abroad.

Soon after the pioneering birth cohort study was published, research began to focus on a subset of chronic offenders known as serious, violent offenders. In fact, research and policy attention have been directed toward this group of offenders over the last two decades, culminating in the publication of a report by the Study Group on Serious and Violent Juvenile Offenders (Loeber and Farrington 1998). Funded by the Office of Juvenile Justice and Delinquency Prevention, this study group integrated the literature on risk and protective factors and information on prevention and intervention strategies. One of the key findings is that serious and violent juvenile offenders start displaying behavior problems and delinquency at an early age. Thus it is never too early to intervene with at-risk children and their parents.

Recently, John DiIulio has referred to the new generation of juvenile criminals as "superpredators" and has argued that "today's bad boys are far worse than yesteryear's, and tomorrow's will be even worse than today's" (Bennett, DiIulio, and Walters 1996, 26–27). Extending these ideas even further, DiIulio argues the result is that "America is now home to thickening ranks of juvenile 'superpredators'—radically impulsive, brutally remorseless youngsters, including ever more preteenage boys, who murder, assault, rob, burglarize, deal deadly drugs, join gun-toting gangs, and create serious communal disorders. They do not fear the stigma of arrest, the pains of imprisonment, or the pangs of conscience" (27).

The underlying cause of the superpredator phenomenon is "moral poverty"—children growing up without love, care, and guidance from responsible adults (Bennett, DiIulio, and Walters 1996, 59). In other words, these authors contend that there has been a substantial change in the nature of kids as a consequence of nonexistent or inadequate socialization. However, it is not immediately apparent whether "superpredators" are any different from the "serious, violent juvenile offenders" of the 1970s and 1980s and the "chronic offenders" of the 1960s and 1970s. Are these really distinct entities, or are they all one and the same? For that matter, it is not clear whether so-called "chronic delinquents" are different from "nonchronic delinquents" other than by the breadth and frequency of their involvement in offending.

The Theoretical Enterprise

Most theories of juvenile delinquency come from sociology. A wide range of factors was considered to be important in explaining delinquency, including community organization, peer group associations, opportunity structures, social class and poverty, cultural values, and the juvenile justice system itself. Ignoring good research, theories of delinquency for the most part downplayed the role of the family and individual differences in generating delinquent behavior. Moreover, despite a long tradition of research indicating that multiple factors were implicated in delinquency, theorists often focused on single variables such as poverty as the key explanation of delinquency. This suggests that theories of delinquency and research on delinquent youth were often out of step.

Initially, explanations of delinquency were closely tied to solutions. As explanations of delinquency became more complex, there was a breakdown in the nexus of cause and cure. As Travis Hirschi points out, "In principle, a theory of delinquency does two things: it tells us what delinquency is, and it tells us the antecedents or causes of delinquency. In principle, then, a theory of delinquency should tell us how to predict delinquency and how to prevent or control its occurrence" (1979, 183–84). Despite good intentions, there has been a disconnect between theory, research, and juvenile court practices.

Social Disorganization Theory: The Role of Community

The research of Clifford Shaw and Henry McKay in Chicago, which began in the 1920s, has been among the most influential in the development of delinquency theory. The most important reason is that their work drew attention to the ecological aspects of crime and delinquency. Specifically, Shaw and McKay studied the distribution of *delinquent areas* in Chicago over time (1931, 1942). They found that rates of delinquency were highest in areas that exhibited the most "social disorganization"—high rates of poverty, ethnic heterogeneity, and residential mobility. Moreover, the rates of delinquency were highest in neighborhoods that were socially disorganized, regardless of which racial or ethnic group inhabited the community at a given time.

Thus Shaw and McKay were drawn to the ecological, cultural, and group-processes that generated delinquency. In sharp contrast to earlier approaches, their approach assessed broader social processes, such as immigration, industrialization, and urbanization, and linked their effects to the breakdown of traditional institutions, such as family, church, peer groups, and the neighborhood at large. One result of their analysis was the idea of *cultural transmission:*

> The heavy concentration of delinquents in certain areas means . . . that boys living in these areas are in contact not only with individuals who engage in proscribed activity but also with groups which sanction such be havior and exert pressure upon their members to conform to group standards. . . . This means that delinquent boys in these areas have contact not only with other delinquents who are their contemporaries but also with older offenders, who in turn had contact with delinquents preceding them, and so on, back to the earliest history of the neighborhood. This contact means that the traditions of delinquency can be and are transmitted down through successive generations of boys, in much the same way

> that language and other social forms are transmitted. (Shaw and McKay 1942, 174)

The work of Shaw and McKay, then, shifted attention from individual characteristics of delinquents and nondelinquents to group traditions in delinquency and to the influence of the larger community.

Not surprisingly, Shaw and McKay centered on the community as a source of crime and delinquency prevention. The Chicago Area Project, community-based organizations designed by indigenous community members, emerged from this interest. Solomon Kobrin has summarized the theory behind the Chicago Area Project:

> Taken at its most general aspect, delinquency . . . in the modern metropolis is principally a product of the breakdown of the machinery of spontaneous social control. The breakdown is precipitated by the cataclysmic pace of social change to which migrants from a peasant or rural background are subjected when they enter the city. In its more specific aspects, delinquency was seen as adaptive behavior on the part of male children of rural migrants acting as members of adolescent peer groups in their efforts to find their way to meaningful and respected adult roles essentially unaided by the older generation and under the influence of criminal models for whom the inner city areas furnish a haven. (Kobrin 1959, 22)

The role of Shaw and his colleagues was to help local leaders to organize their communities more effectively for delinquency prevention and the rehabilitation of offenders. At the heart of the Chicago Area Project was an optimism and faith in the ability of communities to solve their own problems (see Short 1969).

Culture Conflict Theory: The Role of Cultural Values

In 1938, Thorsten Sellin wrote a classic monograph entitled *Culture Conflict and Crime*. Although Sellin did not provide a specific theory of delinquency, he did reorient the field by offering a guiding principle on which future research and theory would develop. Sellin argued that since law varies over time and across cultures, legal definitions of crime were not universal categories and hence could not be used to formulate a basis for a study of criminal behavior (Sellin 1938, 23). As a substitute for the legal definition of crime, Sellin suggested that criminologists study conduct norms and the violation of these norms:

> For every person there is from the point of view of a given group of which he is a member, a normal (right) and abnormal (wrong) way of reacting,

> the norm depending upon the social values of the group which formulated it. *Conduct norms are, therefore, found wherever social groups are found, i.e., universally. They are not the creation of any one normative group; they are not confined within political boundaries; they are not necessarily embodied in law.* These facts lead to the inescapable conclusion that the study of conduct norms would afford a sounder basis for the development of scientific categories than a study of crime as defined in the criminal law. (1938, 30; emphasis in original)

Thus, for Sellin, culture conflict was the conflict of conduct norms. Furthermore, as culture became more complex, the number of divergent conduct norms increased, which in turn led to greater conflict in society. Writing in the 1930s, Sellin's views were undoubtedly influenced by immigration, urbanization, and industrialization. Given this context, Sellin's perspective on crime appeared valid, and the idea that the diversity of values causes crime still holds appeal today. Some theorists have moved beyond culture conflict to the idea of separate value systems within the American society. In the 1950s and 1960s, Walter Miller, for example, developed a theory of delinquency in which he maintained that delinquency was the result of socialization to a set of values that condoned or permitted violations of law. Thus delinquency is conforming not violative behavior. For Miller, "The dominant component of the motivation of 'delinquent' behavior engaged in by members of lower class corner groups involves a positive effort to achieve states, conditions, or qualities valued within the actor's most significant cultural milieu" (1958, 18). Miller further stated that illegal acts are either "explicitly supported by, implicitly demanded by, or materially inhibited by factors relating to the focal concerns of lower class culture" (18). The focal concerns of the lower-class culture include trouble, toughness, smartness, excitement, fate, and autonomy. Miller saw the lower-class culture as a "generating milieu" for delinquency (5).

Another classic theory of delinquency that focused on values and norms was put forth in David Matza's *Delinquency and Drift,* published in 1964. Matza contended that delinquent values were not oppositional to the dominant culture, but were the result of several streams of subterranean value systems within the dominant value system. The subculture of delinquency allowed individuals to excuse their delinquent behavior in terms of conventional values. In other words, justifications—what Sykes and Matza (1957) called "techniques of neutralization"—are used to avoid norms or rules without rejecting them. Rules or norms were deemed inapplicable in certain situations. Techniques of neutralization include denial of responsibility, denial of injury, denial of a victim, condemnation of the condemners, and appeal to higher loyalties.

In short, the role of cultural values and norms in explaining crime and delinquency is an enduring issue in the field. Contemporary works that focus on values as important in understanding urban delinquency include Elijah Anderson's work, *Code of the Street* (1999). Anderson contends that there are two value orientations or cultures—decent and street—in poor, inner-city, black neighborhoods. These value orientations "organize the community socially, and the way they coexist and interact has important consequences for residents, particularly for children growing up in the inner city" (23). The decent culture embraces mainstream values, including the importance of hard work, self-reliance, and sacrifice for one's children. In contrast, the street culture entails "a code of the street, which amounts to a set of informal rules governing interpersonal public behavior, particularly violence" (23). In the context of persistent poverty, joblessness, and widespread alienation from key institutions, especially the criminal justice system, the street code "emerges where the influence of the police ends and where personal responsibility for one's safety is felt to begin" (34).

Differential Association Theory: The Role of Peers

Edwin Sutherland constructed one of the dominant theories of crime and delinquency in existence today: differential association theory. Sutherland provided a sociological interpretation of crime and delinquency that sharply contrasted with psychological and biological theories popular during the early part of the century (see Sutherland and Cressey 1955, 77–79). According to Sutherland, criminal behavior, like noncriminal behavior, is learned in interaction with other people: "A person becomes delinquent because of an excess of definitions favorable to violation of law over definitions unfavorable to violation of law" (78). This statement is the essence of the differential association theory. Sutherland also emphasized culture in his theory of crime; in his view, society consisted of a number of diverse groups with varied cultures. Underlying the phenomenon of criminal behavior was the principle of culture conflict, which leads to differential association, which in turn leads to criminal behavior.

Differential association, perhaps because of its implicit simplicity, became one of the most popular criminological theories in existence today. Broadening the theoretical focus of differential association theory, over the last twenty-five years Ronald Akers (1998) has developed a social learning theory to explain delinquency, crime, and other forms of deviant behavior. Nevertheless, the core of social learning theory is the idea of differential association and the role of peer influence as originally developed by Edwin Sutherland more than fifty years ago.

Structural and Subcultural Theory: The Role of Poverty and Social Class

In 1938 Robert Merton published an influential paper entitled "Social Structure and Anomie." The paper laid the foundation for a perspective on crime and delinquency that contrasted with the cultural explanations offered by Thorsten Sellin and Edwin Sutherland. Referred to as anomie theory, social structural theory, or strain theory, Merton's model distinguished between cultural goals, that is, the aspirations of men and women in society, and institutionalized means—the processes or opportunities to achieve cultural goals. For Merton, the major concern was the apparent lack of integration between aspirations and opportunities for achievement in the American society. He argued that success goals in American society are overemphasized, and that lack of opportunity to achieve such goals creates "strain," particularly among those of the lower class, and this leads to a condition of anomie—a state of normlessness. One consequence of this anomic condition is a high rate of deviant and criminal behavior among lower-class individuals whose access to the institutionalized means of achievement is severely restricted.

Merton's work was used and expanded both by Albert Cohen and by Lloyd Ohlin in collaboration with Richard Cloward in the design of their particular versions of delinquency theory. Larger societal forces evident after the Depression and World War II were also a concern to scholars in this period; namely, an apparently rigid class structure, widespread poverty, large-scale urbanization of black Americans, the low social status of youth, and the overall inconsistencies and contradictions of American society. Thus, according to Finestone (1976), the focus of the 1940s and 1950s was on "social status" and "social structure" rather than on "social change," as was the case in the 1920s and 1930s.

Albert Cohen's book, *Delinquent Boys: The Culture of the Gang,* published in 1955, was considered a "breakthrough" (Cohen's term). In a review of delinquency theory, Finestone stated,

> Cohen's theory was a contribution of the greatest importance to the development of criminology. . . . It gave form and substance to the burgeoning interest in gangs characteristic of the 1940s and 1950s. By linking up in such clear-cut fashion the relation between social class and delinquency, it offered many suggestive guides to social policy in dealing with gang problems. Perhaps its greatest contribution lay in the intellectual excitement and stimulation it produced. (1976, 173)

Cohen was the first to use the term "delinquent subculture" to refer to the delinquent traditions that Shaw and McKay had identified (Empey 1978, 308).

He was also the first theorist to explicitly link lower-class status and delinquent subcultures.

Like Merton, Cohen believed that all Americans share the same success ethic. Problems ensue because the socialization process of lower-class children is such that they cannot effectively compete for these success goals with middle-class children in middle-class institutions like schools. This condition produces "strain," and lower-class children turn to the delinquent subculture as a mechanism for reducing strain (Cohen 1955, 24–32, 121–37). According to Cohen, the delinquent subculture is characterized by nonutilitarian, malicious, and negativistic behavior. Short-run hedonism and group autonomy are also emphasized within the delinquent subculture. "The hallmark of the delinquent subculture is the explicit and wholesale repudiation of middle-class standards and the adoption of their very antithesis" (129). The delinquent subculture thus offers an alternative mechanism by which lower-class males can achieve status and thus remove the strain resulting from trying to compete in the middle-class world, in which they are not adequately equipped to compete.

Another influential work drawing on structural strain, social class, and subcultures was written by Richard Cloward and Lloyd Ohlin, *Delinquency and Opportunity: A Theory of Delinquent Gangs* (1960). These authors were the first to argue that different types of delinquent subcultures can be linked to different types of communities. Thus not only can one examine the pressures toward deviance and crime from a structural perspective, but one can also assess the form of the subcultural response on the basis of the local social structure in each community. Moreover, Cloward and Ohlin contended that there are not only legitimate opportunity structures but also illegitimate opportunity structures. Finestone has alluded to the importance of their effort:

> The culminating statement of the subcultural approach was presented in Cloward and Ohlin's *Delinquency and Opportunity* (1960), an ambitious effort of synthesis. It incorporated within a single formulation a typology of types of slum communities and a typology of gangs based upon variations in subcultural patterns of law-violative behavior. The most important theoretical contribution was Cloward's concept of the illegitimate opportunity structure. This is most appropriately viewed as a bridging concept between the larger social structure and the milieu. (1976, 175)

Cloward and Ohlin, liked Cohen, focused on delinquent gangs that "are typically found among adolescent males in lower-class areas of large urban centers" (1960, 1). They also believed that all Americans share the same success ethic. However, those in the lower class often find opportunities for success blocked, and these individuals suffer strain. This strain leads to the formation of delinquent subcultures that eventually lead to delinquent behavior.

Labeling Theory: The Role of Juvenile Justice

Labeling theory, or societal reaction theory, focuses on behaviors that are labeled as deviant, criminal, or delinquent, on what groups are selected for labeling, and on the consequences of the labeling process. Rudimentary elements of labeling theory can be found in Frank Tannenbaum's book, *Crime and the Community* (1938). For example, the idea of the dramatization of evil captures some of the basic notions of current labeling theory:

> The process of making the criminal, therefore, is a process of tagging, defining, identifying, segregating, describing, emphasizing, making conscious and self-conscious; it becomes a way of stimulating, suggesting, emphasizing, and evoking the very traits that are complained of. . . . The person becomes the thing he is described as being. Nor does it seem to matter whether the valuation is made by those who would punish or by those who would reform. . . . The harder they work to reform the evil, the greater the evil grows under their hands. The persistent suggestion, with whatever good intentions, works mischief, because it leads to bringing out the bad behavior that it would suppress. The way out is through a refusal to dramatize the evil. The less said about it the better. (Tannenbaum 1938, 19–20)

Not until the 1950s was labeling theory developed in more detail by Edwin Lemert. Like Tannenbaum, Lemert was concerned with the social processes through which definitions of deviance and conformity arise. He focused on the interaction between social control agents and rule-violators, and how certain behaviors come to be labeled "criminal," "delinquent," or "deviant" (Lemert 1951, 1972). Lemert, like other theorists, was struck by the diversity of values in American society; however, unlike other theorists, he linked this idea of value pluralism not only to deviance but to conformity and social control as well. By arguing that there are, in fact, few if any distinctions between lawbreakers and law abiders, Lemert offered one of the first alternatives to positivist theories of crime. He also allowed the notion of "contingency" to enter his theoretical model (Laub 1983).

Lemert developed the basic ideas of the societal reaction approach in *Social Pathology* (1951, 22–23). His critical contribution lay in the distinction between societal reaction, primary deviance, and secondary deviance (75–76). Societal reaction is "a very general term summarizing both the expressive reactions of others (moral indignation) toward deviation and action directed to its control" (Finestone 1976, 201). Primary deviance can be characterized as the initial norm violation that is not responded to by agents of social control and thus is of little consequence to the rule-violator. In contrast, secondary deviance is the deviation that occurs in response to societal reaction and is in accordance with the view of self as deviant. Lemert further noted, "When a person begins to employ his deviant behavior or a role based upon it as a means of defense, attack, or adjustment to the overt and covert problems created by the consequent societal reactions to him, his deviation is secondary" (1951, 76). Therefore, for Lemert, social control was treated as another variable in understanding criminal and deviant behavior.

During the 1960s and 1970s, labeling theorists focused almost exclusive attention on the criminogenic effects of the juvenile justice system. Perhaps Edwin Schur's plea, "Leave Kids Alone Whenever Possible," best symbolizes the spirit of labeling theory in action (Schur 1973). This effort, referred to as a policy of "radical nonintervention," involved diverting delinquent youth from the juvenile justice system, redefining delinquency to "accommodate society to the widest possible diversity of behavior and attitudes" (154) in an attempt to restrict the scope of juvenile justice intervention, and offering treatment to delinquent youth on a voluntary basis rather than making it compulsory. Ultimately, labeling theorists like Schur concluded that the only way to significantly reduce delinquency was through large-scale "sociocultural change" (155).

Social Control Theory: The Role of Family

In contrast to theories that focus on motivations for delinquency, social control theories focus on the restraints and circumstances that prevent delinquency. Social control theory rose to prominence as a major theory of delinquency in 1969 with the publication of *Causes of Delinquency* by Travis Hirschi. In this version of social control theory, the delinquent is viewed as "relatively free of the intimate attachments, the aspirations, and the moral beliefs that bind most people to a life within the law" (Hirschi 1969, preface). The theoretical focus is on the socialization processes that constrain antisocial and delinquent behavior, which comes to all individuals naturally. The key question is, "Why do men obey the rules of society?" (10).

For Hirschi, delinquency occurs when an individual's bond to society is weak or broken. Because of the emphasis on social bonds, Hirschi's social control theory is often referred to as a social bonding theory. There are four separate but interrelated elements of an individual's social bond to society. These are attachment (e.g., affection for and sensitivity to others), commitment (e.g., investment in conventional society), involvement (e.g., the amount of time spent on conventional activities), and belief (e.g., the extent to which people believe they should obey the rules). To illustrate, the more strongly a juvenile is attached to his or her parents or teachers, the less likely he or she is to engage in delinquent behavior. Along similar lines, a juvenile who has invested time and effort in conventional activities in school has a "stake in conformity" and is less likely to jeopardize this investment by engaging in delinquent behavior.

Hirschi was unusual in that he developed his theory of delinquency and then tested his theory and other popular theories by using empirical data derived from self-reports of adolescents about their attitudes and behavior, the dominant research technique during the 1960s. This "testing" approach to assessing theories of crime and delinquency became the standard in the field. As Akers has noted, Hirschi's "combination of theory construction, conceptualization, operationalization, and empirically testing was virtually unique in criminology at that time and stands as a model today" (1994, 116). Perhaps more than any other delinquency theorist, Hirschi also brought the family, especially family relations, back into the picture. Thus, for a variety of reasons, "social bonding theory has been the dominant theory of criminal and delinquent behavior for the past twenty-five years. It is the most frequently discussed and tested of all theories in criminology" (Akers 1994, 115).

CHANGING CONCEPTIONS OF JUVENILE DELINQUENTS OVER TIME

One of the enduring findings from delinquency research over the last hundred years is that multiple factors are associated with juvenile delinquency. Delinquents, and chronic delinquents in particular, have multiple risk factors in their backgrounds, including *individual* factors such as hyperactivity, impulsivity, and attention deficit; *family* characteristics, especially poor family functioning and childrearing practices; *school* factors such as poor school achievement and low commitment to school; and *peer* factors, especially association with delinquent peers and gang membership. In addition, *community* influences, such as poverty and inequality, and *cultural* factors, such as norms that encourage the use of violence to resolve disputes, are important risk factors for juvenile delinquency, especially violence. These factors tend to be cumulative and interact with one another over time.

Research demonstrating that multiple factors lead to delinquency first appeared in the early part of the twentieth century in the works of Breckinridge and Abbott (1912) and Healy (1915), and these same findings are repeated anew at the end of the twentieth century in the work of Loeber and Farrington (1998). Moreover, Healy noted that "practically all confirmed criminals begin their careers in childhood or early youth" (1915, 10). He also pointed out that "repeated offenders (recidivists)," because of the frequency of their offending and the seriousness of their offenses, "have the greatest significance for society" (10). Finally, Healy called attention to the "advantage of beginning treatment early" (172). More than eighty years later, Loeber and Farrington write, "In general, violent behavior results from the interaction of individual, contextual (family, school, peers), situational, and community factors" (1998, xxii). Loeber and Farrington note that serious and violent juvenile offenders "tend to start displaying behavior problems and delinquency early in life, warranting early intervention" (xx). They contend that because this group of offenders is responsible for a disproportionate amount of all crime, they "pose a great challenge to juvenile justice policy" for society as a whole (1).

Tracing the history of thinking and research on delinquency and delinquent youth reveals a pattern. Typically, old studies are discarded as outdated and inadequate; the emphasis is on new data because of the belief that crime and delinquency are different in every era. This idea is rarely examined in any systematic manner. Moreover, much evidence suggests that delinquency has remained the same. Delinquent behavior primarily consists of property crimes, not violence. Delinquent behavior is exhibited primarily by males. Such behavior tends to begin in childhood and peaks in adolescence. It is concentrated primarily among the poor and ethnic/racial minorities, and in certain neighborhoods within cities. While many youths engage in delinquency, relatively few commit serious crimes frequently. Those who do are responsible for a large share of the crime problem. In short, the traditional correlates of delinquency have not changed over time (see Hirschi and Rudisill 1976). Yet the same risk factors are discovered and rediscovered by each generation of scholars. The rediscovery of known facts leads in turn to a reinterpretation of old data/findings. Over the last hundred years, we have held a variety of conceptions of delinquent youth, but the reality is that everyone is talking about the same group of kids, but in different ways.

It is clear that conceptions of juvenile delinquents have changed over time. I maintain that these changing conceptions are social constructions and do not reflect changes in the nature and extent of delinquent behavior. In fact, to the contrary, there is little evidence to suggest that the underlying causes of juvenile delinquency have changed over the last hundred years. The causes of delinquency appear largely rooted in structural disadvantage and weakened informal bonds to family, school, peers, and community. What has changed is how researchers and theorists interpret various data on delinquent behavior and delinquent youth.

Interpretations and reinterpretations of data occur again and again. Recently, James Q. Wilson, writing about the legacy of Marvin Wolfgang in the *New York Times Magazine* (1999), contended that Wolfgang's classic study, *Delinquency in a Birth Cohort* (Wolfgang, Figlio, and Sellin 1972) showed that the most serious offenders had lower IQ scores than the nonoffenders. Wilson concluded that this finding set the stage for a search for constitutional factors in the study of crime. Wilson writes, "Because IQ is largely inherited, something in addition to social factors was obviously at work" (1999, 31). The finding that Wilson highlighted does appear in the Wolfgang study. In fact, according to the book's index, material on IQ can be found on 11 pages out of 318. In contrast, material on socioeconomic status (SES) is found on 66 pages out of 318. Furthermore, material on race can be found on 86 pages of 318. In the summary chapter, Wolfgang and his colleagues wrote,

> After examining the relationship between the various background variables of race, SES, types of school attended, residential and school moves, highest grade completed, I.Q., achievement level, and the state of being delinquent or not, we concluded that the variables of race and SES (of somewhat lesser importance) were the most strongly related to the offender-nonoffender classification. The remaining variables in the school records had little or no relationship to delinquency status. (245)

On the next page of the chapter, Wolfgang and his colleagues find that "a nexus of factors related to race and delinquency" reflects a "disadvantaged position." More precisely, they find that "the nonwhite delinquent boy is likely to belong to the lower socioeconomic group, experience a greater number of school and residential moves (that is, be subject to the disrupting forces of intracity mobility more than the nondelinquent) and have the lowest average grade completed, the lowest achievement level, and the lowest IQ score" (246). They conclude that factors such as IQ are "indirectly" related to delinquency because they are strongly correlated with race, which in turn is related to being an offender, especially a chronic, violent offender.

It may be that Wilson's interpretation of Wolfgang's data is the correct one. However, it is also possible (indeed, likely) that Wilson's interpretation is influenced more by ideological concerns than science. James Q. Wilson and Richard Herrnstein are the authors of *Crime and Human Nature* (1985), which presents an explanation of crime and delinquency focusing on constitutional differences like impulsiveness and temperament in interaction with familial factors. They write that there "appears to be a clear and consistent link between criminality and low intelligence" (148). For Wilson and Herrnstein, intelligence is strongly linked to a short time horizon—a present-orientation—which is in turn associated with how one assesses the rewards (and penalties) for crime and noncrime (166–72). Wolfgang's data on IQ are more consistent with Wilson's thesis regarding the prominence of individual differences in explanations of crime and delinquency than are his data on race and social class.

Crime and Criminality

Let me be clear. I am not arguing that juvenile delinquency has not changed over the last one hundred years. For example, one of the major changes has involved the use of guns by juvenile offenders (e.g., Cook and

Laub 1998). However, a change in weaponry may reflect changes in opportunities to offend or in the means to offend that are independent of changes in the propensity to offend. What appears to be lacking is a framework within which to understand constancy and change in the evolution of thinking about delinquency over time. In order to understand the natural history of juvenile delinquency, one needs to distinguish crime and criminality. According to Gottfredson and Hirschi (1990), crime is defined by short-term, circumscribed events that presuppose a particular set of necessary conditions. In contrast, criminality is defined as the propensity to commit crime. These authors argue that criminality is due to stable differences (e.g., self-control) across individuals.

Crime is the result of the confluence of three factors: motivated offenders, suitable targets, and the absence of capable guardians (Cohen and Felson 1978). Thus crime occurs because of a variety of factors that are independent of traditional risk factors: for example, opportunities, situations, events, victims, goods, routine activities, and adversaries. Cohen and Felson have argued that "the convergence in time and space of suitable targets and the absence of capable guardians can lead to large increases in crime rates without any increase or change in the structural conditions that motivate individuals to engage in crime" (604).

Some factors are related to the propensity of offending (e.g., poor family functioning), and other factors are related to the occurrence of crime events (e.g., gun-carrying). Some factors (e.g., peer groups, structural conditions) can affect both propensities to offend and opportunities for crime. Like propensities to offend, opportunities for crime are also concentrated in time and space. Thus, the distribution of criminality and the distribution of crime is highly concentrated.

Criminal acts reflect crime and criminality. Criminality is one factor accounting for variation in crime. Manifestations of criminality may appear different in varying historical eras—more violent, for example—but the causes of criminality may not change. As pointed out by Hirschi and Gottfredson (1986), because the same indicator is used to measure both crime and criminality—a count of criminal acts—crime and criminality are often used interchangeably and are indistinguishable. What varies is our interpretation of the meaning of the indicator and related accompanying variables. Changes in crime may not indicate changes in criminality. In fact, I would argue in most cases they do not. Crime can fluctuate dramatically and remain independent of the pool of motivated offenders.

One other point is worth mentioning. Recent research by William Julius Wilson and his colleagues (Wilson, 1987, 1991, 1996; Sampson and Wilson 1995) suggests that the social milieu of urban life has changed significantly in the past few decades (see also Massey and Denton 1993; Massey

1996). Specifically, social transformations have resulted in a disproportionate concentration of the "truly disadvantaged" segments of the U.S. population within inner cities—especially poor, female-headed, black families with children. Urban minorities have been especially vulnerable to structural economic changes related to the de-industrialization of central cities (e.g., the shift from goods-producing to service-producing industries; increasing polarization of the labor market into low-wage and high-wage sectors; and relocation of manufacturing out of the inner city). This set of circumstances has contributed to increased income inequality along racial lines.

Perhaps it is not surprising that as structural conditions in urban centers worsened with respect to concentrated poverty, attention was focused on the unique aspects of the relationship between race, delinquency, and juvenile justice policy (see Feld 1999). However, I would argue that we need to place race in a broader context when thinking about the causes of crime and delinquency. Research has shown that the sources of violence—whether committed by juveniles or adults—appear to be similar across race and rooted in the structural differences across communities and cities (see Sampson 1987; Sampson and Lauritsen 1994, 1997). Racial differences in levels of neighborhood poverty and family disruption have been shown to be particularly pronounced. Whereas the majority of poor blacks live in communities characterized by high rates of family disruption, poor whites live in areas of relative family stability. According to Sampson and Wilson (1995), racial differences in poverty and family disruption are so large that the most deprived urban areas in which whites reside are considerably better off than the average context of black communities.

In sum, it is clear that race is a salient issue in delinquency research and juvenile justice policy circles. However, this is not a new phenomenon. As Feld has noted, "From the juvenile court's inception, the social control of ethnic and racial minority offenders has constituted one of its most important functions" (1999, 5). In spite of this long-standing concern, considerable evidence supports the conclusion that the causes of delinquency are rooted not in race and ethnicity, and not simply in drugs, gangs, and guns—today's policy obsessions—but in structural disadvantage; weakened informal social bonds to family, school, and work; and the disruption of social relations between individuals and institutions that provide social capital (Sampson and Laub 1993, 255).

CONCLUSION

In assessing the last hundred years of delinquency theory and research, a number of significant patterns emerge. First, a great deal of change has occurred in

Fig. 7.5 New York's juvenile delinquents can sometimes be brought together in friendly groups through the efforts of a youth club. Here, in the shadow of the 81st precinct station, former enemies become friends, February 24, 1958. © Bettmann/CORBIS.

our popular conceptions of delinquency and in our images of delinquent youth. In the 1920s, the popular image was a boy stealing apples from a street peddler. In the 1950s, it was a "hood" hanging out in front of a candy store. In the 1990s, it was a gun-carrying, drug-dealing "gangbanger." However, these conceptions appear to be derived independently of empirical research on delinquency and delinquent youth. In fact, these popular conceptions often drive research agendas rather than the reverse. Second, a great deal of change has occurred in our ideas about the sources and causes of delinquency. On the one hand, individual differences such as IQ have been promoted as the most important cause of delinquency. At the other extreme, the juvenile justice system has been implicated as the main cause of serious youth crime. Theories of delinquency have also been constructed and promoted as valid regardless of research results. Third, the worlds of delinquency research and theory have been largely disconnected from the world of juvenile court practice and law. Indeed, few theories of delinquency have embraced the philosophy of the juvenile court. Moreover, recent changes in juvenile court practice (e.g., expanding waiver to adult court) have occurred without any solid theoretical or research support.

It is apparent then that theory, research, and popular conceptions each have had a separate and cyclical development over the last hundred years. For example, popular conceptions of delinquent youth, such as "bad boys," "chronic offenders," and "superpredators," imply that delinquents are distinct and different from nondelinquents and can be identified as such. Other conceptions, like "wayward youth," "disaffiliated youth," and "alienated youth," suggest that delinquents have strayed off the path but can be saved from a life of crime by the appropriate intervention.

There is also a cyclical pattern of research results. Throughout the twentieth century, juvenile delinquency has been linked to minority race and ethnicity; to poverty and inequality; and to disadvantaged families, schools, and neighborhoods. What varies, however, is how much emphasis is placed on single factors like poverty compared with multiple factors which emphasize a wide range of variables, often cutting across disciplinary boundaries.

A cyclical pattern of theoretical concerns is also evident throughout the last hundred years. For instance, the multiple-factor approach, including a role for biology, dominated theories of delinquency in the early part of the twentieth century. This approach was relegated to the background during the middle of the century when sociological perspectives reigned supreme as explanations of delinquent behavior. Finally, multiple-factor approaches, including a role for biology, have reemerged as important in the latter part of the century.

What is most striking about these cyclical patterns is their independence from each other. For example, although empirical research has consistently found that family variables are strongly associated with delinquent behavior, the role of the family in theories of delinquency, especially in many sociological theories, has been totally ignored (see, e.g., Cloward and Ohlin's differential opportunity theory). This neglect has also generated a marked divergence between both empirical findings and the conventional wisdom of the general public—especially parents—and the views of social scientists who study criminal behavior (see Hirschi 1983). A theoretical focus on families did finally emerge in the late 1960s with Travis Hirschi's social control theory of delinquency. However, family-centered theories could easily have emerged during the 1920s and 1930s or, for that matter, at any time in the twentieth century.

Another example is that while much delinquency research indicates that antisocial behavior occurs in childhood, virtually all theories of delinquency focus on adolescence and ignore childhood characteristics. Even more important is the fact that most theories of delinquency have ignored the linkage between early childhood behaviors and later adolescent and adult outcomes. Finally, while most empirical research has demonstrated a weak relationship between social class and crime, theories of delinquency are often built on the assumption of a strong class-crime relationship. Despite this weak foundation and the apparent disregard of the heterogeneity of experiences of individuals and groups living in poor communities, the "poverty causes crime" paradigm dominates both theoretical and popular conceptions (see Sampson 2000).

All of these cyclical patterns—almost always operating independently of each other—suggest that the sources of ideas about delinquency are socially constructed and cannot be understood by simple reference to the truth and salience of research findings. Critical questions abound—What leads to changes in the conception of delinquency and delinquent youth over time? Changes in the concerns of the various disciplines vying to dominant the field of criminology? Changes in the nature of delinquency? Changes in the images of delinquent youth? Changing calls for social action? We need to understand the processes by which knowledge is socially constructed. Robert Jones has written, "For surely it is curious that, at the same time that modern sociologists struggle to expand their imaginations and thus to develop new ideas to account for the complexities of human behavior, there is nothing of which we are more ignorant than the nature of the process by which such ideas emerge, are received, grow, change, and are eventually surpassed" (1977, 311). More attention ought to be devoted to understanding the underlying contexts in which ideas about delinquency and delinquent youth are socially constructed. Otherwise "new" developments will be constantly offered in an environment characterized by a collective amnesia about the past (Laub and Sampson 1991).

ACKNOWLEDGMENTS

I thank Travis Hirschi, Ray Paternoster, Rob Sampson, and Frank Zimring for their comments on an earlier draft of this chapter.

REFERENCES

Akers, Ronald L. 1994. *Criminological Theories: Introduction and Evaluation.* Los Angeles: Roxbury.

———. 1998. *Social Learning and Social Structure: A General Theory of Crime and Deviance.* Boston: Northeastern University Press.

Anderson, Elijah. 1999. *Code of the Street: Decency, Violence, and the Moral Life of the Inner City.* New York: W.W. Norton.

Bennett, William J.; John J. DiIulio; and John P. Walters. 1996. *Body Count: Moral Poverty and How to Win America's War against Crime and Drugs*. New York: Simon and Schuster.

Breckinridge, Sophonisba P., and Edith Abbott. 1912. *The Delinquent Child and the Home*. New York: Russell Sage Foundation.

Cloward, Richard A., and Lloyd E. Ohlin. 1960. *Delinquency and Opportunity: A Theory of Delinquent Gangs*. New York: Free Press.

Cohen, Albert K. 1955. *Delinquent Boys: The Culture of the Gang*. Glencoe, IL: Free Press.

Cohen, Lawrence E., and Marcus Felson. 1978. "Social Change and Crime Rate Trends: A Routine Activity Approach." *American Sociological Review* 44: 588–608.

Cook, Philip J., and John H. Laub. 1998. "The Unprecedented Epidemic in Youth Violence." In *Youth Violence,* ed. Michael Tonry and Mark H. Moore, 27–64. Chicago: University of Chicago Press.

Empey, LaMar T. 1978. *American Delinquency.* Homewood, IL: Dorsey Press.

Feld, Barry C. 1999. *Bad Kids: Race and the Transformation of the Juvenile Court*. New York: Oxford University Press.

Finestone, Harold. 1976. *Victims of Change: Juvenile Delinquents in American Society.* Westport, CT: Greenwood Press.

Glueck, Sheldon, and Eleanor Glueck. 1930. *500 Criminal Careers*. New York: Alfred A. Knopf.

———. 1934a. *Five Hundred Delinquent Women*. New York: Alfred A. Knopf.

———. 1934b. *One Thousand Juvenile Delinquents*. Cambridge, MA: Harvard University Press.

———. 1937. *Later Criminal Careers*. New York: Commonwealth Fund.

———. 1940. *Juvenile Delinquents Grown Up*. New York: Commonwealth Fund.

———. 1943. *Criminal Careers in Retrospect*. New York: Commonwealth Fund.

———. 1950. *Unraveling Juvenile Delinquency.* New York: Commonwealth Fund.

———. 1968. *Delinquents and Nondelinquents in Perspective*. Cambridge, MA: Harvard University Press.

Gottfredson, Michael R., and Travis Hirschi. 1990. *A General Theory of Crime*. Stanford, CA: Stanford University Press.

Healy, William. 1915. *The Individual Delinquent*. Boston: Little, Brown.

Hirschi, Travis. 1969. *Causes of Delinquency.* Berkeley, CA: University of California Press.

———. 1979. "Reconstructing Delinquency: Evolution and Implications of Twentieth-Century Theory." In *Juvenile Justice: The Progressive Legacy and Current Reforms,* ed. LaMar T. Empey, 183–212. Charlottesville: University of Virginia Press.

———. 1983. "Crime and the Family." In *Crime and Public Policy,* ed. James Q. Wilson, 53–68. San Francisco: Institute for Contemporary Studies.

Hirschi, Travis, and Michael Gottfredson. 1986. "The Distinction between Crime and Criminality." In *Critique and Explanation: Essays in Honor of Gwynne Nettler,* ed. Timothy F. Hartnagel and Robert A. Silverman, 55–69. New Brunswick, NJ: Transaction Books.

Hirschi, Travis, and David Rudisill. 1976. "The Great American Search: Causes of Crime, 1876–1976." *Annals of the American Academy of Political and Social Science* 423: 14–22.

Huizinga, David; Rolf Loeber; and Terence P. Thornberry. 1994. *Urban Delinquency and*

Substance Abuse: Initial Findings. Washington, DC: Office of Juvenile Justice and Delinquency Prevention.

Jones, Robert Alun. 1977. "On Understanding a Sociological Classic." *American Journal of Sociology* 83: 279–319.

Kobrin, Solomon. 1959. "The Chicago Area Project: A Twenty-Five Year Assessment." *Annals of the American Academy of Political and Social Science* 322: 20–29.

Laub, John H. 1983. *Criminology in the Making: An Oral History.* Boston: Northeastern University Press.

Laub, John H., and Robert J. Sampson. 1991. "The Sutherland-Glueck Debate: On the Sociology of Criminological Knowledge." *American Journal of Sociology* 96: 1402–40.

Lemert, Edwin M. 1951. *Social Pathology.* New York: McGraw-Hill.

———. 1972. *Human Deviance, Social Problems, and Social Control.* 2d ed. Englewood Cliffs, NJ: Prentice-Hall.

Loeber, Rolf, and David P. Farrington, eds. 1998. *Serious and Violent Juvenile Offenders: Risk Factors and Successful Interventions.* Thousand Oaks, CA: Sage.

Loeber, Rolf, and Marc LeBlanc. 1990. "Toward a Developmental Criminology." In *Crime and Justice, An Annual Review of Research,* vol. 12, ed. Michael Tonry and Norval Morris, 375–437. Chicago: University of Chicago Press.

Loeber, Rolf, and Magda Stouthamer-Loeber. 1986. "Family Factors as Correlates and Predictors of Juvenile Conduct Problems and Delinquency." In *Crime and Justice,* vol. 7, ed. Tonry and Morris, 29–150.

Loeber, Rolf; Evelyn Wei; Magda Stouthamer-Loeber; David Huizinga; and Terence P. Thornberry. 1999. "Behavioral Antecedents to Serious and Violent Offending: Joint Analyses from the Denver Youth Survey, Pittsburgh Youth Study, and the Rochester Youth Development Study." *Studies on Crime and Crime Prevention* 8: 245–63.

Maguin, Eugene, and Rolf Loeber. 1996. "Academic Performance and Delinquency." In *Crime and Justice,* vol. 20, ed. Tonry, 145–264.

Massey, Douglas. 1996. "The Age of Extremes: Concentrated Affluence and Poverty in the Twenty-First Century." *Demography* 33: 395–412.

Massey, Douglas, and Nancy Denton. 1993. *American Apartheid: Segregation and the Making of the Underclass.* Cambridge, MA: Harvard University Press.

Matza, David. 1964. *Delinquency and Drift.* New York: John Wiley.

McCord, Joan. 1979. "Some Childrearing Antecedents of Criminal Behavior in Adult Men." *Journal of Personality and Social Psychology* 37: 1477–86.

McCord, William, and Joan McCord. 1959. *Origins of Crime.* New York: Columbia University Press.

Merton, Robert K. 1938. "Social Structure and Anomie." *American Sociological Review* 3: 672–82.

Miller, Walter B. 1958. "Lower Class Culture as a Generating Milieu of Gang Delinquency." *Journal of Social Issues* 14: 5–19.

Robins, Lee N. 1966. *Deviant Children Grown Up.* Baltimore, MD: Williams and Wilkins.

Sampson, Robert J. 1987. "Urban Black Violence: The Effect of Male Joblessness and Family Disruption." *American Journal of Sociology* 93: 348–82.

———. 2000. "Whither Sociological Criminology?" *Annual Review of Sociology.*

Sampson, Robert J., and John H. Laub. 1993. *Crime in the Making: Pathways and Turning Points Through Life*. Cambridge, MA: Harvard University Press.

Sampson, Robert J., and Janet Lauritsen. 1994. "Violent Victimization and Offending: Individual, Situational, and Community-Level Risk Factors." In *Understanding and Preventing Violence: Social Influences,* vol. 3, ed. Albert J. Reiss and Jeffrey Roth, 1–115. Washington, DC: National Academy Press.

Sampson, Robert J., and Janet Lauritsen. 1997. "Racial and Ethnic Disparities in Crime and Criminal Justice in the United States." In *Crime and Justice,* vol. 21, ed. Tonry, 311–74.

Sampson, Robert J., and William Julius Wilson. 1995. "Toward a Theory of Race, Crime, and Urban Inequality." In *Crime and Inequality,* ed. John Hagan and Ruth Peterson, 37–54. Stanford, CA: Stanford University Press.

Schur, Edwin M. 1973. *Radical Non-Intervention: Rethinking the Delinquency Problem*. Englewood Cliffs, NJ: Prentice-Hall.

Sellin, Thorsten. 1938. *Culture Conflict and Crime*. New York: Social Science Research Council.

Shaw, Clifford R. 1930. *The Jack-Roller.* Chicago: University of Chicago Press.

Shaw, Clifford R., and Henry D. McKay. 1931. "Social Factors in Juvenile Delinquency." In *Report on the Causes of Crime,* vol. 2. National Commission on Law Observance and Enforcement. Washington, DC: GPO.

———. 1942. *Juvenile Delinquency and Urban Areas*. Chicago: University of Chicago Press.

Short, James F. 1969. "Introduction to the Revised Edition." In *Juvenile Delinquency and Urban Areas,* by Clifford Shaw and Henry McKay, xxv–liv. Chicago: University of Chicago Press.

Sutherland, Edwin H., and Donald R. Cressey. 1955. *Principles of Criminology.* 5th ed. Philadelphia: J. B. Lippincott.

Sykes, Gresham, and David Matza. 1957. "Techniques of Neutralization: A Theory of Delinquency." *American Sociological Review* 22: 664–70.

Tannenbaum, Frank. 1938. *Crime and the Community.* Boston: Ginn.

Thornberry, Terence P.; Alan J. Lizotte; Marvin D. Krohn; Margaret Farnworth; and Sung Joon Jang. 1994. "Delinquent Peers, Beliefs, and Delinquent Behavior: A Longitudinal Test of Interactional Theory." *Criminology* 32: 47–84.

Wilson, James Q. 1999. "Marvin E. Wolfgang: Charting the Devious Mind." *New York Times Magazine,* January 3, 1999, 30.

Wilson, James Q., and Richard Herrnstein. 1985. *Crime and Human Nature*. New York: Simon and Schuster.

Wilson, William Julius. 1987. *The Truly Disadvantaged: The Inner City, the Underclass, and Public Policy.* Chicago: University of Chicago Press.

———. 1991. "Studying Inner-City Social Dislocations: The Challenge of Public Agenda Research." *American Sociological Review* 56: 1–22.

———. 1996. *When Work Disappears: The World of the New Urban Poor.* New York: Alfred A. Knopf.

Wolfgang, Marvin E.; Robert M. Figlio; and Thorsten Sellin. 1972. *Delinquency in a Birth Cohort*. Chicago: University of Chicago Press.

8 Serious and Violent Juvenile Offenders

David P. Farrington and Rolf Loeber

Between 1987 and 1994, the national U.S. rate of arrests of juveniles for serious violence (homicide, rape, robbery, aggravated assault) increased by a staggering 70 percent (Snyder and Sickmund 1999). The juvenile murder rate doubled. Robbery increased by 68 percent, and aggravated assault increased by 79 percent. These were remarkably large increases over a very short time period. In contrast, forcible rape stayed constant, as did arrests of juveniles for serious property crimes. Also, 1994 proved to be the peak year, and arrests of juveniles for serious violence then decreased by 22 percent up to 1997.

The remarkable increases in juvenile violence presented a challenge to criminologists to explain them. Alfred Blumstein (1995) of Carnegie-Mellon University suggested that they were linked to increases in gun carrying, gangs, and battles over the selling of crack cocaine. Others blamed the reluctance of juvenile courts to incarcerate youths and the ineffective socializing efforts of families, schools, and neighborhoods (Bennett, DiIulio, and Walters 1996). The Office of Juvenile Justice and Delinquency Prevention set up the Study Group on Serious and Violent Juvenile Offenders, chaired by ourselves, to review knowledge about these juveniles and about the most effective techniques for reducing their numbers. This study group, which met from 1995 to 1997, produced the book *Serious and Violent Juvenile Offenders: Risk Factors and Successful Interventions* (Loeber and Farrington 1998). Some of the key conclusions are highlighted in this chapter.

Some researchers and policymakers advocated a tougher, "zero-tolerance" reaction to juvenile violent offenders: "America is now home to thickening ranks of juvenile "super-predators"—radically impulsive, brutally remorseless youngsters, including ever more preteenage boys, who murder, assault, rape, rob, burglarize, deal deadly drugs, join gun-toting gangs, and create serious communal disorders. They do not fear the stigma of arrest, the pains of imprisonment, or the pangs of conscience" (Bennett, DiIulio, and Walters 1996, 27). In response, most states modified their statutes in the early 1990s to make it easier to prosecute juveniles in adult court, and there was an increase in targeted prosecution programs for serious and violent juvenile offenders. The study group on the other hand, advocated *risk-focused prevention:* that key risk factors for offending should be identified and prevention methods targeted on them should be implemented.

This chapter presents current empirical knowledge on serious and violent juvenile (SVJ) offenders, largely drawn from national surveys and from longitudinal (follow-up) studies. Contrary to what many lay people and professionals outside the court often think, the majority of offenses dealt with in the juvenile court are neither serious nor violent (Snyder 1998). Knowledge about the characteristics of SVJ offenders and their offenses is necessary for juvenile courts to deal with these offenders effectively.

The first section defines SVJ offending and summarizes information about its prevalence and incidence. The second section reviews knowledge about the careers of SVJ offenders, including early behavioral precursors and key risk and protective factors. The third section examines the most effective prevention programs, focusing on children, families, schools, and communities. The fourth section reviews key juvenile justice issues, including the best screening and risk-assessment techniques to identify potential SVJ offenders at their first court referral, the effectiveness of graduated and intermediate sanctions, and whether SVJ offenders should be dealt with in juvenile or adult courts. In conclusion, after summarizing key research findings about SVJ offending, we offer research and policy recommendations for the second century of American juvenile justice.

DEFINITION, PREVALENCE, AND FREQUENCY

Definition

The study group defined serious offenders as those juveniles who have committed one or more of the following offenses: violent offenses (defined in more detail below), felony larceny/theft, auto theft, burglary, carjacking, extortion, forgery and counterfeiting, fraud, dealing in stolen property, embezzlement, drug trafficking, and arson (other than of an occupied dwelling). Not included in this definition were status offenses, violations of ordinances, vandalism, drunkenness, malicious mischief, disorderly conduct, and traffic and motor vehicle law violations. Violent offenses are a subset of serious offenses, and include homicide, aggravated assault (including weapons offenses and attempted murder), robbery (including armed robbery), kidnapping, voluntary manslaughter, rape or attempted rape, and arson of an occupied dwelling. Considerable judgement, however, is necessary to distinguish violence from other forms of aggression of a less serious nature. For example, at what point should a physical fight between two adolescents be considered as a violent incident?

Prevalence

The prevalence of SVJ offending varies greatly according to the method of measurement, geographic location, demographic factors (age, gender, race), and time period. The most common method of measurement is to use official records of arrests or court referrals. For example, out of 30 million juveniles in the United States aged 10–17 in 1996, 2,400 were charged with homicide, 6,900 with forcible rape, 37,300 with robbery, 89,900 with aggravated assault, 141,100 with burglary, 51,600 with motor vehicle theft, and 8,900 with arson (Snyder and Sickmund 1999). About a quarter of all juvenile court referrals are for SVJ offenses, and about a third of juveniles referred to court commit an SVJ offense during their juvenile court career (Snyder 1998). In analyses of complete populations of juveniles in Phoenix, Arizona, about 45 percent of boys and 20 percent of girls in each birth cohort were referred to the juvenile court, and about 19 percent of boys and 3 percent of girls were SVJ offenders (Snyder and Sickmund 1999, 81).

It is well known, however, that the percentage of juveniles with an arrest for SVJ offending is much smaller than the true population of SVJ offenders in the community. The best estimates of the true prevalence and frequency of SVJ offending are obtained from confidential surveys in which juveniles are asked to admit their offending. For example, Franklin Dunford and Delbert Elliott (1984) of the University of Colorado compared self-reported and officially recorded offending in the U.S. National Youth Survey (of 1,725 youth originally aged 11–17) and found that 86 percent of juvenile career offenders (defined in terms of high frequency, severity, and persistence of self-reported delinquency) did not have a record of arrest. Many self-reported SVJ offenders are arrested for less serious offenses (Huizinga, Esbensen, and Weiher 1996), so that their official record is misleading.

The comparison between self-reported delinquency and official records gives some indication of the probability of an SVJ offender being caught and convicted. In the Cambridge Study in Delinquent Development, which is a longitudinal survey of 411 London boys from age eight, 45 percent admitted

Fig. 8.1 Los Angeles gang members. © Daniel Lainé/CORBIS.

starting a physical fight or using a weapon in a fight between ages fifteen and eighteen, but only 3 percent of the cohort were convicted of assault between these ages (Farrington 1989). Therefore, only 7 percent of self-reported violent offenders between ages fifteen and eighteen were convicted. Self-reported violence had predictive validity: 10 percent of these who admitted assault up to age eighteen were subsequently convicted of assault, compared with 5 percent of the remainder.

The prevalence of SVJ offenders is higher in certain states and in inner metropolitan areas in the United States than in suburbs or rural areas. Restricting the analysis to states with reasonably complete reporting, juvenile violent arrest rates in 1997 were highest in the states of Maryland, New Jersey, California, Massachusetts, and Louisiana (Snyder and Sickmund 1999). Taking juvenile homicide as an extreme indicator of juvenile offending, 88 percent of the 3,139 counties in the United States reported no juvenile murders in 1997, while 6 percent of the counties reported a single homicide offender. Homicides were significantly clustered in urban areas, with more than a quarter of all known juvenile murderers in just 8 counties, representing the cities of Chicago, Los Angeles, Houston, New York, Baltimore, Detroit, Philadelphia, and Dallas. We can safely assume, similarly, that SVJ offending other than homicide is also concentrated in major inner cities.

In 1997, the arrest rate for index violence (murder, robbery, rape, and aggravated assault) increased to a peak at age sixteen and then decreased (Snyder and Sickmund 1999). Self-report studies also show that the prevalence of offending increases with age up to age 15–17, but this varies according to the severity of the offense. The less serious forms of delinquency increase with age first, followed by an increase in moderately serious forms of delinquency, while serious delinquency tends to increase last (Loeber et al. 1993).

Boys are more likely than girls to commit SVJ offenses. For example, in the United States, girls committed only 16 percent of index violent crimes and 28 percent of all index property crimes (burglary, theft, auto theft, arson) in 1997 (Snyder and Sickmund 1999). The peak age of offending is earlier for girls than for boys (Elliott 1994).

The prevalence of offending also varies according to race in the United States. In particular, African American youth have a higher prevalence of violent offending than their Caucasian counterparts. For example, official data show that African American youth are 6.5 times more likely than Caucasian youth to commit murder (194 versus 30 murderers per million youth in 1997; Snyder and Sickmund 1999). The racial differential is larger when based on arrest records instead of self-reports (Elliott 1994; Wolfgang, Figlio, and Sellin 1972). However, race differences frequently disappear or become smaller when other factors are taken into account, such as where individuals live or degree of juveniles' exposure to known criminogenic risk factors (Farrington and Loeber in press; Peeples and Loeber 1994).

Frequency and Co-Occurring Problems

The frequency of offending is an important marker, because it distinguishes those juveniles who only rarely commit delinquent acts (sometimes called occasional offenders or experimenters) from those who frequently commit delinquent acts (the persisters or chronic offenders), who are few in number but account for a substantial fraction of all SVJ offenses. In a study of juvenile offenders in Phoenix, Arizona, Rolf Loeber and Howard Snyder (1990) found that the frequency of offending increased up to age seventeen. Specific subgroups of offenders vary in their rate of offending. For example, juveniles who commit both property and violent offenses have a higher rate of offending than those who commit property offenses only (Capaldi and Patterson 1996; Farrington 1991).

SVJ offenders have many other co-occurring problems and tend to be multiple-problem youth. In particular, they disproportionally show problematic alcohol and drug use (Huizinga and Jakob-Chien 1998). Also, 91 percent of male and 81 percent of female violent offenders in the Denver Youth Survey (of 1,500 youth originally aged 7–13) had school problems, such as truancy, suspension, and dropping out, compared with 40–42 percent of nondelinquents in this deprived sample. About half of male violent offenders and 22 percent of female violent offenders had been victims of violent offenses.

Similarly, in the Rochester Youth Development Study (of 987 youth originally aged 13–14), the SVJ offenders disproportionally used alcohol and marijuana, sold drugs, dropped out of school, and were gang members and teenage parents (Thornberry, Huizinga, and Loeber 1995).

CRIMINAL CAREERS

Criminal Career Concepts

Criminal careers have a beginning (onset), a time course, and an end (desistance). Youth differ greatly in the features of their delinquency careers. It is important to differentiate at an early stage between those whose offending will be minor and temporary and those whose offending will be serious and persistent. The field of "developmental criminology" (LeBlanc and Loeber 1998; Loeber and LeBlanc 1990) aims to describe the development of offending patterns over time, to identify risk and protective factors that help explain individual differences in delinquency careers, and to identify interventions that can prevent juveniles from escalating to SVJ offending or reduce SVJ offending once it has begun to occur.

Generally, the earlier the age of onset of offending, the longer the delinquency career, the higher the frequency of offending during the career, and the more serious the later offending (Farrington et al. 1990; Loeber 1982). These findings have encouraged researchers and practitioners to pay special attention to offending up to age twelve (Loeber and Farrington 2001). For example, Howard Snyder (2001) of the U.S. National Center for Juvenile Justice found that in 1997 arrests up to age twelve constituted 9 percent of all juvenile arrests. The offense profiles of child delinquents differed from those of older juvenile offenders: the most characteristic offenses by very young offenders were arson (35 percent), vandalism (19 percent), and sex offenses (18 percent).

Several researchers have suggested that there are qualitative differences between early-onset and late-onset offenders. For example, Terrie Moffitt (1993) of London University proposed that the early childhood onset of antisocial behavior led to "life-course-persistent" offending, or long criminal careers, whereas later adolescent onset led to "adolescence-limited" offending, or short criminal careers. SVJ offenders tend to be early-onset, life-course-persistent offenders.

Early Behavioral Precursors of SVJ Offending

Research on developmental pathways to SVJ offending shows that, as a rule, the great majority of juveniles who progress to serious offenses usually first develop nondelinquent problem behavior, then engage in less serious forms of delinquency, and finally advance to serious delinquent acts. Rolf Loeber and his colleagues at the University of Pittsburgh (Loeber et al. 1993; Loeber, Keenan, and Zhang 1997; Loeber et al. 1998) proposed three developmental pathways to offending:

1. An overt pathway, starting with minor aggression, followed by physical fighting, then by violence
2. A covert pathway, recently qualified as prior to age fifteen, consisting of a sequence of minor covert behaviors (e.g., frequent lying or shoplifting), followed by property damage (firesetting or vandalism), and then moderate to serious forms of nonviolent delinquency
3. An authority-conflict pathway prior to age twelve, consisting of stubborn behavior, then defiance, and then authority avoidance (truancy, running away, staying out late at night).

Boys can progress along each of the pathways at the same time. Evidence for the three pathways has been obtained in different studies in the United States and for African American and Hispanic populations of males (Loeber et al. 1999; Tolan and Gorman-Smith 1998).

Risk Factors for SVJ Offending

Risk factors predict a high probability of offending, while protective factors predict a low probability of offending. Bear in mind that neither risk nor protective factors are necessarily causes of offending (Kraemer et al. 1997). At a minimum they are markers indicating the future course of development. The last three decades have seen a large accumulation of findings on risk factors, which we will briefly summarize (see Loeber and Farrington 1998, for more details). Less is known about protective factors.

SVJ offending is never associated with a single risk factor; it is best predicted by multiple risk factors. These risk factors rarely occur in a single domain, such as child behavior or family interactions; typically, risk factors from multiple domains predict later SVJ offending. The major domains identified so far are child characteristics (e.g., low intelligence, impulsivity, attention problems); family characteristics (e.g., poor supervision, harsh physical punishment, marital discord); peer factors (e.g., association with deviant peers, peer rejection, gang membership); and neighborhood context (e.g., a socially disorganized neighborhood, low socioeconomic level of the neighborhood). In addition, certain biological factors (e.g., a low heart rate) are associated with SVJ offending, but we will not review them here because they have fewer implications for prevention or intervention.

Fig. 8.2 Teen gang members in Los Angeles, January 14, 1955. Some of the eighteen youngsters rounded up by Los Angeles police last night just in time to avert a murderous teen gang fight are shown behind a table on which are displayed some of the weapons police say comprised their arsenal. © Bettmann/CORBIS.

As an example of research on risk factors for SVJ offending, we investigated how far, in a survey of 508 Pittsburgh boys, risk factors measured at age ten predicted later petitions to the juvenile court for serious violent offenses between ages ten and sixteen (Farrington and Loeber in press). The most important risk factors were lack of guilt, low school achievement, low parental approval, a low social class family, a broken family, a young mother, large family size, and coming from a bad neighborhood. (For extensive reviews of risk factors for SVJ offending, see Farrington 1998; Hawkins et al. 1998; Lipsey and Derzon 1998.)

Gang membership is an important risk factor for SVJ offending in the United States. In the Rochester Youth Development Study, about 30 percent of the sample were gang members, but they accounted for 70–80 percent of the SVJ offenses (Thornberry 1998). Gang members have relatively high rates of violence before they join a gang. Nevertheless, their violence increases and remains high during periods of gang membership, and then decreases after leaving a gang. About half of gang members had used a gun in a crime (Snyder and Sickmund 1999).

In general, the larger the number of risk factors, the greater the likelihood that a youth will engage in SVJ offending. For example, in the Cambridge study, a "vulnerability" score was developed on the basis of five risk factors measured at age 8–10: low family income, large family size, a convicted parent, low intelligence, and poor parental childrearing behavior (poor supervision and harsh and erratic discipline). The percentage of boys convicted for violence between ages ten and twenty increased significantly, from 3 percent of those with none of these risk factors to 31 percent of those with four or all five risk factors (Farrington 1997). The "false positive" rate (see later) was high in this analysis because the overall prevalence of convicted violent offenders was only 10 percent. Remarkably, many of the same risk factors that predict SVJ offending also predict substance abuse, dropping out of school, early sexual involvement, teen pregnancy, and other social problems. Therefore, a prevention program that succeeds in reducing a risk factor for SVJ offending is likely to have wide-ranging benefits in reducing other types of social problems as well.

Not all risk factors are in place during development toward SVJ offending, but they become apparent as juveniles grow older. For example, whereas many child characteristics are present from an early age onwards (e.g., attention problems, impulsivity), other risk factors, such as those in the peer and neighborhood domains, usually start to have an impact at later ages. Some of this expansion of risk factors with age is a consequence of earlier risk factors. For example, an impulsive child is more likely to elicit negative reactions from parents and siblings, whose aggressive reactions may contribute to the child's development of aggressive modes of interacting with others. Thus, some risk factors may have effects on other risk factors, cumulatively increasing the risk of SVJ offending.

Protective Factors and Later Criminal Careers

With regard to protective factors, many of the points made about risk factors also apply, but in the reverse direction. For example, the larger the number of protective factors, the lower the probability of SVJ offending. Protective factors may also be drawn from one or more domains (e.g., individual, family, peer group, or neighborhood). Research shows that many factors can have both a risk and a protective effect. For instance, poor supervision by parents is a risk factor for SVJ offending, while good supervision is associated with a low probability of SVJ offending. Research findings indicate that most risk factors also have a protective counterpart; only a minority of risk factors have no opposite protective effect (Stouthamer-Loeber et al. 1993).

Overall, SVJ offenders have a much higher likelihood of continuing to offend into adulthood than less serious juvenile offenders. However, this likelihood is not the same for all juvenile populations. For example, in the U.S. National Youth Survey, Delbert Elliott (1994), using self-reports, found that almost twice as many African American as Caucasian adolescent males continued violent offending as adults. Much needs to be learned about factors that predict those juveniles who continue to offend into adulthood compared with those who do not.

PREVENTING SVJ OFFENDING

Risk-Focused Prevention

Recent years have seen an enormous increase in the influence of risk-focused prevention in criminology (Farrington 2000). The basic idea of this approach is very simple: identify the key risk factors for offending and implement prevention methods designed to counteract them. There is often a related attempt to identify key protective factors against offending and to implement prevention methods designed to enhance them. Typically, longitudinal follow-up studies provide knowledge about risk and protective factors, and experiments are used to evaluate the impact of prevention and intervention programs. Thus, risk-focused prevention links explanation and prevention; links fundamental and applied research; and links scholars, policymakers, and practitioners. For a detailed exposition of this approach as applied to SVJ offenders, see *Serious and Violent Juvenile Offenders: Risk Factors and Successful Interventions* (Loeber and Farrington 1998).

Risk-focused prevention was imported into criminology from medicine and public health by pioneers such as David Hawkins and Richard Catalano of the University of Washington (Hawkins and Catalano 1992). This approach has been used successfully for many years to tackle illnesses such as cancer and heart disease. For example, the identified risk factors for heart disease include smoking, a fatty diet, and lack of exercise. These can be reduced by encouraging people to stop smoking, to have a more healthy low-fat diet, and to take more exercise. Typically, the effectiveness of risk-focused prevention in the medical field is evaluated using the "gold standard" of randomized controlled trials, and there has been increasing emphasis in medicine on cost-benefit analysis of interventions. Not surprisingly, therefore, criminology in the 1990s placed a similar emphasis on high-quality evaluations and on cost-benefit analysis.

Cost-Benefit Analysis

Arguments such as "for every dollar spent on the program, seven dollars are saved in the long term" (Schweinhart, Barnes, and Weikart 1993) have proved particularly convincing to policymakers. The monetary costs of crime are enormous; for example, Ted Miller and his colleagues (1996) estimated that they totaled $450 billion in the United States in 1993. There are tangible costs to victims, such as replacing stolen goods and repairing damage, and intangible costs that are harder to quantify, such as pain, suffering, and reduced quality of life. There are costs to the government or taxpayer for police, courts, prisons, crime prevention activities, and so on. There are also costs to offenders—for example, those associated with being in prison or losing a job.

To the extent that crime prevention programs are successful in reducing crime, they will have benefits. These benefits can be quantified in monetary terms according to the reduction in the monetary costs of crime. Other benefits may accrue from reducing the costs of associated social problems such as unemployment, divorce, educational failure, drug addiction, welfare dependency, and so on. The monetary benefits of a program can be compared with its monetary costs to determine the benefit:cost ratio. The adequacy of an economic analysis of the monetary benefits and costs of a crime prevention program depends crucially on the methodological adequacy of the underlying evaluation design.

Surprisingly few cost-benefit analyses of crime prevention programs have ever been carried out (Welsh and Farrington 2000). Existing analyses are difficult to compare, because researchers have included different types of program costs and program effects, and have used different methods for calculating monetary costs and benefits. There is a great need for a standard manual to be developed and followed that specifies a list of costs and benefits to be measured in all studies and their monetary values. More cost-benefit analyses of crime prevention programs are needed.

Individual and Family Prevention Programs

Four types of programs have been particularly successful in reducing childhood antisocial behavior and juvenile delinquency: parent education (in the context of home visiting), parent management training, child skills training, and preschool intellectual enrichment programs (Farrington and Welsh 1999). Generally, the programs focus on the risk factors of poor parental child-rearing, supervision, or discipline (parent education or parent management training); high impulsivity, low empathy, and self-centeredness (child skills training); and low intelligence and attainment (preschool programs).

In the most famous intensive home visiting program, David Olds and his colleagues (1986) in Elmira, New York, randomly allocated four hundred mothers either to receive home visits from nurses during pregnancy, or to receive visits both during pregnancy and during the infancy of the child, or to receive no visits (control group). Each visit lasted about one and a quarter hours, and the mothers were visited on average every two weeks. The home visitors gave advice about prenatal and postnatal care of the child, about infant development, and about the importance of proper nutrition and the avoidance of smoking and drinking during pregnancy.

The results of this experiment showed that the postnatal home visits caused a decrease in recorded child physical abuse and neglect during the first two years of life, especially by poor, unmarried teenage mothers; only 4 percent of visited versus 19 percent of nonvisited mothers of this type were guilty of child abuse or neglect. This last result is important because children who are physically abused or neglected tend to become violent offenders later in life (Widom 1989). In a fifteen-year follow-up, the main focus was on lower-class, unmarried mothers. Those who received both prenatal and postnatal home visits had fewer arrests than those who received prenatal visits or no visits (Olds et al. 1997). Also, the children of mothers who received prenatal and/or postnatal home visits had less than half as many arrests as the children of mothers who received no visits (Olds et al. 1998).

Several economic analyses show that the benefits of this program outweighed its costs for the lower-class, unmarried mothers. The most important are by Lynn Karoly and colleagues of the Rand Corporation (1998), and Steve Aos and colleagues of the Washington State Institute for Public Policy (1999). However, both measured only a limited range of benefits. The Rand researchers measured only benefits to the government or taxpayer (welfare, education, employment, and criminal justice), not benefits to crime victims consequent upon reduced crimes. The Washington researchers measured only benefits to crime victims (tangible, not intangible) and criminal justice savings, excluding other types of benefits (e.g., welfare, education, and employment). Nevertheless, both reported a benefit:cost ratio greater than 1 for this program: 4.1 according to Karoly and 1.5 according to Aos. The benefit:cost ratio was less than 1 for the low-risk part of the sample.

The most famous preschool intellectual enrichment program is the Perry project carried out in Ypsilanti, Michigan, by Lawrence Schweinhart and David Weikart (1980). This was essentially a Head Start program targeted on disadvantaged African American children, who were allocated (approximately at random) to experimental and control groups. The experimental children attended a daily preschool program, backed up by weekly home visits, usually lasting two years (covering ages 3–4). The aim of the "plan-do-review" program was to provide intellectual stimulation, to increase thinking and reasoning abilities, and to increase later school achievement.

This program had long-term benefits. At age nineteen, the experimental group was more likely to be employed, more likely to have graduated from high school, more likely to have received college or vocational training, and less likely to have been arrested (Berrueta-Clement et al. 1984). By age twenty-seven, the experimental group had accumulated only half as many arrests on average as the controls (Schweinhart, Barnes, and Weikart 1993). They also had significantly higher earnings and were more likely to be homeowners. More of the experimental women were married, and fewer of their children were born out of wedlock.

Several economic analyses show that the benefits of this program outweighed its costs. The benefit:cost ratio was 2.1 according to Karoly and 1.5 according to Aos. For reasons explained above, both of these figures are underestimates. The Perry project's own calculation (Barnett 1993) was more comprehensive, including crime and noncrime benefits, intangible costs to victims, and even projected benefits beyond age twenty-seven. This generated the famous benefit:cost ratio of 7.2. Most of the benefits (65 percent) were derived from savings to crime victims.

The Montreal longitudinal-experimental study was based on child skills training and parent management training. Richard Tremblay and his colleagues (1995) identified disruptive (aggressive/hyperactive) boys at age six, and randomly allocated 319 of these to experimental or control conditions. Between ages seven and nine, the experimental group received training designed to foster social skills and self-control. Coaching, peer modeling, role-playing, and reinforcement contingencies were used in small-group sessions on such topics as "how to help," "what to do when you are angry," and "how to react to teasing." Also, their parents were trained using the parent management training techniques developed by Gerald Patterson (1982) in Oregon, which focus on promoting the use of consistent and contingent rewards and penalties.

The Montreal prevention program was quite successful. By age twelve, the experimental boys committed less burglary and theft, were less likely to get drunk, and were less likely to be involved in fights than the controls (according to self-reports). Also, the experimental boys had higher school achievement. At every age from ten to fifteen, the experimental boys had lower self-reported delinquency scores than the control boys. Interestingly, the differences in antisocial behavior between experimental and control boys increased as the follow-up progressed. No cost-benefit analysis of this program has yet been carried out.

Peer, School, and Community Prevention Programs

Peer, school, and community risk factors are less well established than individual and family risk factors. For example, while it is clear that having delinquent friends, attending a high-delinquency-rate school, and living in a high-crime-rate area all predict SVJ offending, the precise causal processes are not well understood.

The most important intervention program whose success seems to be based mainly on reducing peer risk factors is the Children at Risk program (Harrell et al. 1997), which targeted high-risk youths (average age twelve) in poor neighborhoods of five cities across the United States. Eligible youths were identified in schools and randomly assigned to experimental or control groups. The program was a comprehensive, community-based prevention strategy targeting risk factors for delinquency, including case management and family counseling, family skills training, tutoring, mentoring, after-school activities, and community policing. The program was different in each neighborhood.

The initial results were disappointing, but a one-year follow-up showed that (according to self-reports) experimental youths were less likely to have committed violent crimes and to have used or sold drugs (Harrell et al. 1999). The process evaluation showed that the greatest change was in peer factors. Experimental youths associated less often with delinquent peers, felt less peer pressure to engage in delinquency, and had more positive peer support. In contrast, there were few changes in individual, family, or community risk factors, possibly linked to the low participation of parents in parent training and of youths in mentoring and tutoring (Harrell et al. 1997, 87). In other words, there were problems in implementing the program linked to the serious and multiple needs and problems of the families. No cost-benefit analysis of this program has yet been carried out, but its relatively low cost ($9,000 per youth) and its targeting of high-risk youths suggest that its benefits would probably outweigh its costs.

One of the most important school-based prevention experiments was carried out in Seattle by David Hawkins and his colleagues (Hawkins, von Cleve, and Catalano 1991). The program combined parent management training, teacher training, and child skills training. About five hundred first-grade children (age six) in twenty-one classes in eight schools were randomly assigned to be in experimental or control classes. The children in the experimental classes received special treatment at home and school which was designed to increase their attachment to their parents and their bonding to the school. Also, they were trained in interpersonal, cognitive problem-solving. Their parents were trained to notice and reinforce socially desirable behavior in a program called "Catch them being good." Their teachers were trained in classroom management—for example, to provide clear instructions and expectations to children, to reward them for participation in desired behavior, and to teach them prosocial (socially desirable) methods of solving problems.

This program had long-term benefits. One evaluation by Julie O'Donnell and her colleagues (1995) focused on children in low-income families and reported that, in the sixth grade (age twelve), experimental boys were less likely to have initiated delinquency, while experimental girls were less likely to have initiated drug use. In the latest follow-up, David Hawkins and his colleagues (1999) found that at age eighteen the full intervention group (those who received the intervention from grades 1 to 6) reported less violence, less alcohol abuse, and fewer sexual partners than the late intervention group (grades 5–6 only) or the controls. The benefit:cost ratio of this program according to Aos was 1.8.

Programs targeting community risk factors such as community disorganization have not been notably effective (Hope 1995). However, community-based programs have been effective. For example, Marshall Jones and Dan Offord (1989) implemented a skills training program in an experimental public housing complex in Ottawa, Canada, and compared it with a control complex. The program centered on nonschool skills, both athletic (e.g., swimming and hockey) and nonathletic (e.g., guitar and ballet). The aim of developing skills was to increase self-esteem, to encourage children to use time constructively, and to provide desirable role models. Participation rates were high; about three-quarters of age-eligible children in the experimental complex took at least one course in the first year. The program was successful; delinquency rates decreased significantly in the experimental complex compared to the control complex. The benefit:cost ratio (focusing on taxpayer savings, excluding costs to crime victims) was 2.5.

One of the most important community-based treatment programs is multisystemic therapy (MST), which is a multiple-component program pioneered by Scott Henggeler and his colleagues (1998). The type of treatment is chosen according to the particular needs of the youth; therefore, the nature of the treatment is different for each person. The treatment may include individual, family, peer, school, and community interventions, including parent training and child skills training.

Typically, MST has been used with SVJ offenders. For example, in Missouri, Charles Borduin and his colleagues (1995) randomly assigned 176 juvenile offenders (average age fourteen) either to MST or to individual therapy focusing on personal, family, and academic issues. Four years later, only 29 percent of the MST offenders had been rearrested, compared with 74 percent of the individual therapy group. According to Aos, the benefit:cost ratio for MST is very high (13.5), largely because of the potential crime and criminal justice savings from targeting chronic SVJ offenders.

Community-based policing programs can also be effective in reducing SVJ offending. The most impressive of these programs target "hot spots," or places where large numbers of crimes occur. For example, Lawrence Sherman and David Weisburd (1995) carried out an experiment in Minneapolis in which more than one hundred high-crime places were randomly assigned either to receive increased police patrolling (a target of three hours per day) or not, on the assumption that increased police presence would deter offending. Calls for police service for crime were monitored in the year before and the year of the experiment. Crime and disorder were also measured in the second year using systematic observation in all places. The experiment showed that the increased patrolling led to decreased crime in the experimental places. No benefit:cost analysis has yet been carried out.

Universal or Selective Programs?

High-quality evaluation research shows that many programs are effective in preventing offending and that the financial benefits of these programs often outweigh their financial costs. However, a key issue is whether prevention programs should be universal (applied to all children) or selective (applied to high-risk children). In favor of selectivity, programs that are narrowly targeted on potential and actual SVJ offenders offer the greatest potential for financial benefits, since these individuals are a burden on society in many different ways (not just in offending and drug use but also in mental health problems, unemployment problems, educational problems, relationship problems, welfare dependency, and so on) and because there is continuity from one generation to the next in multiple-problem families. Mark Cohen (1998) of Vanderbilt University estimated that the monetary cost to society of a high-risk youth was about $2 million, taking account of tangible and intangible costs over the lifetime. He pointed out, therefore, that a program serving one hundred high-risk youth and costing $5,000 per youth would have an impressive benefit:cost ratio of 4 even if it "saved" only one high-risk youth from dropping out of school and embarking on a career of drug abuse and crime.

Against selectivity, identifying individual children as potential delinquents might have stigmatizing and labeling effects, and it is unpopular. Any such program would be difficult to implement and would inevitably be dogged by controversy. Another problem is that an accumulation of evidence now shows that putting groups of delinquents together in programs can have delinquency-amplifying effects because of delinquent peer influence (Dishion, McCord, and Poulin 1999). The best way to achieve the benefits of selectivity while avoiding its problems is to implement programs in high-risk areas (e.g., high-crime, deprived areas of public housing) and to offer the programs to everyone living in those areas. This achieves the benefits of maximizing the yield of high-risk individuals and families while avoiding the problems of labeling individuals and problems caused when everyone served by a program comes from a multiple-problem family or is antisocial. Therefore, community-based programs are needed.

Communities That Care

In order to maximize effectiveness, what is needed is a multiple-component, community-based program, including several of the successful interventions listed above. Many of the programs reviewed above are of this type. One of them, Communities That Care (CTC), has many attractions. Perhaps more than any other program, it is evidence-based and systematic: the choice of interventions depends on empirical evidence that identifies the important risk and protective factors in a particular community and on empirical evidence about "what works." This program is being implemented widely in the United States; the Rowntree Foundation is sponsoring it at several sites in England; and it will be implemented at several sites in Scotland and the Netherlands, and perhaps also in Australia. While the effectiveness of the overall CTC strategy has not yet been proved, the effectiveness of its individual components is clear.

CTC was developed as a risk-focused prevention strategy by David Hawkins and Richard Catalano (1992), and it is a core component of the U.S. Office of Juvenile Justice and Delinquency Prevention's (OJJDP's) Comprehensive Strategy for Serious, Violent, and Chronic Juvenile Offenders (Wilson and Howell 1993). CTC is based on a theory (the social development model) of how risk and protective factors interact to influence offending. The intervention techniques are tailored to the needs of each community. The "community" could be a city, a county, a small town, or even a neighborhood or a public housing area. This program aims to reduce delinquency and drug use by implementing prevention strategies that have demonstrated effectiveness in reducing risk factors or enhancing protective factors. It is modeled on large-scale, community-wide public health programs designed to reduce illnesses such as coronary heart disease by tackling key risk factors (e.g., Farquhar 1985; Perry, Klepp, and Sillers 1989). CTC strives to enhance protective factors and build on strengths, because this is more attractive to communities than tackling risk factors; it is more attractive to communities to promote health than to prevent delinquency.

CTC programs begin with community mobilization. Key community leaders (e.g., the mayor, school superintendent, police chief, business leaders) are brought together, with the aim of getting them to agree on the goals of the prevention program and to implement CTC. The key leaders then set up a community board that is accountable to them, consisting of neighborhood residents and representatives from various agencies (e.g., school, police, social services, probation, health, parents, youth groups, business, church, media). The community board takes charge of prevention on behalf of the community.

The community board then carries out a risk and protective factor assessment, identifying key risk factors in that particular community that need to be tackled and key protective factors that need enhancing. This risk assessment might involve the use of police, school, social, or census records, or local neighborhood or school surveys. After identifying key risk and protective factors, the community board assesses existing resources and develops a plan of intervention strategies. With specialists providing technical assistance and guidance, they choose programs from a menu of strategies that have been shown to be effective in well-designed evaluation research.

The menu of strategies listed by David Hawkins and Richard Catalano (1992) includes prenatal/postnatal home visiting programs, preschool intellectual enrichment programs, parent training, school organization and curriculum development, teacher training, and media campaigns. Other strategies include child skills training, anti-bullying programs in schools, situational prevention, and policing strategies. The choice of prevention strategies is based on empirical evidence about effective methods of tackling each particular risk factor, but it also depends on what are identified as the biggest problems in the community.

OJJDP's Comprehensive Strategy also emphasizes that communities should take the lead in developing comprehensive prevention approaches that address known risk factors using CTC and also target youth at risk of delinquency. However, the Comprehensive Strategy is more wide-ranging than this; it includes strengthening the family, supporting schools and other core social institutions, and implementing graduated sanctions in the juvenile justice system. A guide has been developed to assist communities in large-scale implementations of the Comprehensive Strategy (Howell 1995).

SVJ OFFENDERS AND THE JUVENILE JUSTICE SYSTEM

Screening and Risk Assessment

Many screening and risk assessment instruments have been devised to classify juvenile offenders (often at first court referral) for intervention programs in the juvenile justice system (Wiebush et al. 1995). The aim of these instruments is to predict a juvenile's probability of subsequent escalation into SVJ offending and to use this risk in allocating juveniles to appropriate programs. Typically, these instruments include a variety of risk factors that are known to predict both offending and reoffending. The most widely used juvenile offender classification system in the United States is the Wisconsin system (Baird 1981), which includes risk and needs assessment. Its predictive validity has been established at a number of sites (Bonta 1996).

The Eight Percent Early Intervention Program in Orange County, California, is one of the most interesting programs that aim to identify, among first-time referrals to the juvenile court, juveniles who are at risk of becoming SVJ offenders (Krisberg and Howell 1998). This program is based on an analysis of court referrals showing that 8 percent of juveniles accounted for more than half of all repeat offenses (Kurz and Moore 1994). The risk assessment instrument was derived empirically from an analysis of more than six thousand court referrals. Family problems (abuse/neglect, criminal parents, poor supervision), school problems (truancy, suspension, expulsion), individual problems (drug and/or alcohol abuse), and predelinquent behavior (gang activities or running away) predicted later SVJ offending and were included in the risk assessment instrument. The program includes a broad range of sanctions (from day reporting to community confinement), together with family preservation and support services, individualized treatment for mental health problems and substance abuse, and a range of community service opportunities. A preliminary evaluation of the program suggested that it reduced reoffending by half (Krisberg and Howell 1998).

The Early Assessment Risk List for Boys (EARL-20B) is one of the most promising recently developed instruments (Augimeri et al. 1999). It is derived from the scientific literature, from previous risk assessment instruments designed to predict violence and sexual offending in adults (Kropp et al. 1995; Webster et al. 1997), and from clinical experience gained in the Under Twelve Outreach project of the Earlscourt Child and Family Center in Toronto, Canada. Based on twenty risk items, it is simple for clinicians to use and is designed to promote multidisciplinary team assessment of the risk of SVJ offending. The items fall into three broad categories: child, family, and amenability (responsiveness and treatability). Each item has multiple indicators; for example, indicators of family stressors include divorced parents, unemployed parents, imprisoned parents, and so on. The EARL-20B is currently being validated, and a version for girls (the EARL-20G) is currently being developed.

An ambitious risk assessment instrument is currently being implemented statewide in Washington by the Washington State Institute for Public Policy (Howell 2001). The Washington Association of Juvenile Court Administrators Risk Assessment (WAJCA-RA) instrument consists of three components: criminal history, social skills, and protective factors. Training in the use and administration of the instrument is managed by computerized software (Allvest Information Services 1999). This instrument is being used in conjunction with juvenile court probation functions to match juvenile offenders with effective programs (Aos et al. 1999). A validation study is under way.

Risk assessment is expanding rapidly, but a number of key research issues must be tackled. First, how should the risk factors included in the risk score be chosen? (According to the strength of the relationship with SVJ offending?) Second, how should the risk factors be combined into a score? Simple point scores are easy to use but do not take into account the degree to which risk factors are independently related to SVJ offending, nor the interactions between risk factors. Third, how much predictive efficiency is gained by combining protective factors with risk factors? Fourth, what cut-off point or criterion score should be used in identifying juveniles for interventions? This depends on issues such as the tolerable level and social costs of false positives and false negatives and on the number of juveniles who can be served by a program. A "false positive" is a person who is predicted to become an offender but does not, while a "false negative" is a person who is predicted to become a nonoffender but who in fact becomes an offender. Risk scores should be validated prospectively by investigating to what extent they are predictive in a new sample (different from that used in the construction of the risk assessment device). For example, to what extent can risk assessment devices designed for use with clinical samples be used with community samples? It is important to establish the applicability of risk assessment instruments in different times and places.

Graduated and Intermediate Sanctions

OJJDP's Comprehensive Strategy aims to improve the juvenile justice system's response to SVJ offenders through a system of graduated sanctions and a continuum of treatment alternatives that include immediate intervention (e.g., as in the Orange County program); intermediate sanctions (e.g., home detention); community-based sanctions, including restitution and community service; and secure corrections, including community confinement and incarceration in training schools, camps, and ranches. The appropriate placement depends on risk and needs assessments, as well as on state juvenile codes that prescribe specific sanctions for specific offenses. As SVJ offenders progress through the continuum of treatment options, treatments become more structured and intensive to deal with the more intractable problems of the more serious and dangerous juvenile offenders (Krisberg and Howell 1998).

Intermediate sanctions (intermediate between probation and institutionalization) include electronic monitoring, house arrest, home detention, intensive supervision, day treatment/reporting centers, community service, and restitution (Altschuler 1998). An important aim of intermediate sanctions is to provide a credible alternative to institutional treatment and hence to reduce institutional populations. There are strong suggestions in the existing research on intermediate sanctions that, to the extent that treatment is available and implemented, they can be effective in reducing recidivism. However, many studies found that offenders received little or no treatment, and intermediate sanctions in practice mainly consisted of surveillance and control.

Despite the influence of the Comprehensive Strategy, many juvenile courts have only three main choices for adjudicated delinquents: residential placement, probation, or release. Alex Holsinger and Edward Latessa (1999) studied the juvenile justice system in a medium-size county in a Midwestern state that was "quite progressive in terms of the number and variety of programs and sanctions" (156). The county had developed graduated sanctions in an effort to meet the specific needs and risk levels of a wide variety of juvenile offenders. These sanctions included diversion programs; probation; a specialized probation group-facilitation program designed to address the individual needs of each offender (including skills training and parent education groups); a secure juvenile rehabilitation center providing many services, from the most basic (e.g., education and vocational training) to the most complex (e.g., individualized emotional and psychiatric counseling); residential placement for treatment (usually for sex or drug offenders); and a secure facility under the Department of Youth Services. The researchers showed that the sanctions were being used as a graded continuum, according to the persistence of juvenile offending careers.

Juveniles in Adult Court

Traditionally, the juvenile court has emphasized rehabilitation and the best interests of the child in choosing dispositions. However, as mentioned previously, the massive increase in serious violent offenses by juveniles in 1987–94 led many policymakers to argue that tougher penalties were needed to deter and incapacitate SVJ offenders. This in turn led to a great increase in the number of juveniles sentenced in adult criminal courts. It also coincided with targeted prosecution programs such as SHOCAP (Serious Habitual Offender Comprehensive Action Program) and HSVJOP (Habitual Serious and Violent Juvenile Offender Program), which aimed to increase arrest, prosecution, and sentencing severity for SVJ offenders. However, research on these programs (e.g., Cronin et al. 1988) did not find that they deterred juveniles from continued criminal behavior.

Between 1992 and 1995, all except ten states modified their statutes to make it easier to prosecute juveniles in adult court (Torbet et al. 1996). There are five main ways in which juveniles get to adult court (Torbet and Szymanski 1998):

1. Discretionary judicial waiver (in 1997, all except five states allowed this)
2. Mandatory judicial waiver (fourteen states)
3. Presumptive judicial waiver, where the burden of proof is on the juvenile to show that the juvenile court is more appropriate (fifteen states)
4. Prosecutorial discretion to file charges in the adult court (fifteen states)
5. Statutory exclusion provisions, which automatically exclude certain juvenile offenders, including provisions for an upper age of juvenile court jurisdiction below age seventeen (twenty-eight states).

In 1997, thirty-one states had "once an adult, always an adult" exclusion provisions, which required that once a juvenile was prosecuted in adult court, all subsequent cases involving that juvenile should be under criminal court jurisdiction (Griffin, Torbet, and Szymanski 1998).

Between 1987 and 1994, the number of delinquency cases judicially waived to the adult court increased by 73 percent from 6,800 to 11,700 (Snyder and Sickmund 1999). This number decreased by 15 percent up to 1996, partly because more SVJ offenders were sent to the adult court by statutory exclusion and prosecutorial discretion. In 1996, according to the National Juvenile Court Data Archive, 43 percent of waived cases involved violent offenses, 37 percent involved property offenses, 14 percent involved drug offenses, and 6 percent involved public order offenses. Of the waived offenders, 95 percent were male, 88 percent were aged sixteen or seventeen, and 46 percent were African American.

According to the Bureau of Justice Statistics, there were about 11,800 felony convictions of juveniles transferred to adult courts in 1994, while another 9,200 persons under eighteen were convicted in adult courts because of state laws defining them as adults (Snyder and Sickmund 1999). The transferred juveniles were more serious cases than the under-eighteen adults (e.g., 53 percent as opposed to 28 percent committed serious violence). Four-fifths of the transferred juveniles were sent to prison or jail, compared with two-thirds of under-eighteen adults. The average maximum sentence length was 9 years and 3 months for transferred juveniles, 7 years and 3 months for under-eighteen adults, and 5 years and 9 months for older adults convicted of felonies in state courts. Transferred juveniles tended to be violent or repeat offenders.

Many states (seventeen in 1995; Torbet and Szymanski 1998) have introduced "blended sentencing," which is a combination of juvenile and adult sanctions for SVJ offenders who have been adjudicated in a juvenile court or convicted in a criminal court. For example, Elizabeth Clarke (1996) reported that, in Connecticut, Kansas, and Minnesota, youth charged with serious felonies could receive both a juvenile and an adult sentence. If they violated the juvenile sentence, the adult sentence would take effect. The effectiveness of these kinds of measures is unknown. Richard Redding and James Howell (2000) have provided a useful review of blended sentencing.

Comparing Juvenile and Adult Court

Two key questions are (1) Do juveniles in adult courts receive more severe sentences than equivalent juveniles in juvenile courts? (2) Are juveniles sentenced in adult courts less likely to reoffend than equivalent juveniles sentenced in juvenile courts? In addressing these issues, the problem is to obtain comparable samples of juveniles. From the viewpoint of answering these questions accurately, it would be ideal to assign SVJ offenders randomly either to juvenile or adult court, but this has not yet been done, no doubt because of the ethical, legal, and practical problems of such a study.

Three particularly important recent projects have addressed these key questions. Jeffrey Fagan (1995) of Columbia University compared youths aged 15–16 in New York (where they were dealt with as adults because of statutes) with youths aged 15–16 in four matched counties of New Jersey, who were dealt with as juveniles. All eight hundred youths had committed felony robbery or burglary offenses. He found that robbery cases were more likely to result in a finding of guilt in the adult court, but this was not true for burglary cases. Both robbery and burglary cases were more likely to be given sentences of incarceration in the adult court than in the juvenile court. However, average sentence lengths were very similar in both courts. For robbery, rearrests were significantly higher after adult court sentencing (76 percent versus 67 percent) but the percentage of burglars rearrested was the same after both juvenile and adult court sentencing (81 percent). The main problem of interpretation in this study is that it is not clear that the juveniles in New Jersey were very comparable to the adults in New York.

In Minneapolis, Marcy Podkopacz and Barry Feld (1996) investigated 330 juveniles who had transfer motions filed, of whom about two-thirds were transferred (judicially waived) to adult court. The best predictors of the decision to transfer were age (especially seventeen), prior record (especially four or more prior out-of-home placements), and present offense (especially a violent offense involving a weapon). Race was not a significant predictor. Juveniles dealt with in adult court were more likely to be incarcerated (85 percent versus 63 percent), received longer sentences, and were more likely to reoffend after release (58 percent versus 42 percent).

In Florida, Donna Bishop and her colleagues (1996) compared more than 2,700 juvenile offenders who were transferred to the adult court with more than 2,700 matched delinquents dealt with by the juvenile court. Both samples were matched case by case on the seriousness of the offense, the number of prior offenses, age, gender, and race. The matching on race was least exact. More than 80 percent of the transferred cases were transferred through prosecutorial filing, while the remainder involved judicial waivers. The transferred youth received more severe sentences, serving much longer periods of incarceration. Nevertheless, they had significantly higher rearrest rates (0.54 offenses per year at risk, compared with 0.32 for those dealt with by the juvenile court). However, a longer-term follow-up showed that the lower arrest rates of the juvenile court cases disappeared for felonies after about 3.5 years (Winner et al. 1997). Surprisingly, transferred property offenders had lower rearrest rates, but other types of transferred offenders had higher rearrest rates.

Other effects of adult court processing need to be considered. For example, Martin Forst and his colleagues (Forst, Fagan, and Vivona 1989) interviewed transferred juveniles incarcerated in adult prisons and compared them with matched youths in juvenile training schools. The juveniles in adult prisons were more likely to be physically and sexually assaulted and less likely to receive basic education and job training services. After reviewing the literature on juvenile versus adult court processing, Barry Krisberg and James Howell (1998) concluded that "there is remarkably little empirical evidence that transferring juveniles to the criminal justice system produces any positive benefits" (356). Recent evaluations, therefore, are concordant with the earlier conclusions of Simon Singer and David McDowall (1988) that dealing with juveniles as adults in New York State did not reduce the juvenile crime rate.

SUMMARY OF KEY RESULTS

Despite the recent decreases in their prevalence, serious and violent juvenile offenders remain a troubling social problem. Existing empirical evidence suggests that it is not effective to transfer such offenders to adult courts. Risk-focused prevention is a more effective and cost-effective method of reducing their numbers.

Research suggests that about 20 percent of boys and 3 percent of girls in large urban areas have a juvenile court referral for an SVJ offense, but the prevalence of SVJ offenders is higher in self-reports. African American juveniles have a higher rate of SVJ offending than Caucasian juveniles, but this difference may be attributable to differences in residence in underclass neighborhoods. SVJ offending increases to a peak at age 15–17 and then decreases with age.

SVJ offenders tend to be multiple-problem youth. Minor aggression leads to juvenile violence in a developmental pathway. An early onset of offending predicts a relatively high likelihood of becoming an SVJ offender. The main risk factors for SVJ offending include high impulsivity, low intelligence, harsh physical punishment by parents, poor parental supervision, gang membership, and living in a high-crime neighborhood. The probability of SVJ offending increases with the number of risk factors, and SVJ offending tends to be followed by an adult criminal career.

Several programs are effective in preventing SVJ offending, including home visiting/parent education programs, preschool intellectual enrichment programs, child skills training, parent management training, multisystemic therapy, and increased police patrolling of "hot spots" of crime. Cost-benefit analyses show that the monetary benefits of these programs outweigh their monetary costs. Programs offered to everyone living in high-crime areas, such as Communities That Care, are likely to be most effective.

Many screening and risk assessment instruments have been devised to classify first-time juvenile offenders according to their risk of later SVJ offending, but few have been validated. OJJDP's Comprehensive Strategy recommends a combination of early prevention and graduated sanctions; as we have argued (Loeber and Farrington 1998), it is "never too early, never too late" to reduce SVJ offending. In recent years, there has been a great increase in the transfer of juveniles to the adult criminal court. Studies suggest that juveniles in adult court receive more severe sanctions but have higher recidivism rates. Also, juveniles are more likely to be victimized in adult correctional facilities than in juvenile facilities.

Research Recommendations

Longitudinal follow-up studies are needed that focus specifically on the development of SVJ offenders. More research is needed on the developmental pathways leading to SVJ offending and on protective factors, especially in high-risk neighborhoods. It is particularly important to compare self-reported offending and court referrals, to quantify the probability of a court referral given an SVJ offense, and to make estimates of "true" offending on the basis of court referrals. Large-scale, repeated self-report studies are needed to investigate changes over time in SVJ offending, especially studies that measure changes over time in risk and protective factors.

Experimental studies are needed that focus specifically on the effectiveness of prevention and intervention techniques with SVJ offenders. Communities That Care and other multiple-component, community-based programs need to be evaluated. It is important to investigate what works best, with whom, in what contexts. More efforts should be made to link risk factors and intervention research; risk factors should inform the choice of interventions, and intervention experiments should be designed to throw light on which risk factors have causal effects. More cost-benefit analyses of prevention and intervention techniques are needed.

More research is needed on the development and validation of screening and risk/needs assessment instruments. It is especially important to investigate to what extent, and when, future SVJ offenders can be predicted and distinguished from minor and temporary delinquents, who constitute the majority of those referred to the juvenile court. Validation studies need to be carried out on existing instruments. More research is also needed on the effectiveness of adult court compared with juvenile court processing and on the effectiveness of blended sentencing.

Policy Recommendations

More resources should be devoted to the prevention of SVJ offending, and special local agencies with a mandate for prevention should be created. Since many SVJ offenders begin offending at an early age (up to age twelve), better methods of dealing with child delinquents by juvenile court, child welfare, and mental health agencies are needed. More efforts should be made to integrate these different services for child delinquents.

Risk and needs assessment instruments should be used more widely to distinguish potential SVJ offenders from others at the time of their first juvenile court referral. Screening should be followed by effective interventions designed to reduce the probability of later escalation. Risk-focused prevention should be implemented widely. Both early prevention and later intervention programs should be expanded. Fewer juveniles should be dealt with in adult criminal courts or held in adult correctional facilities.

REFERENCES

Allvest Information Services. 1999. *Helping Manage Youth on Community Supervision: Focusing on Risk and Increasing Protective Factors.* Seattle, WA: Allvest Information Services.

Altschuler, D. M. 1998. "Intermediate Sanctions and Community Treatment for Serious and Violent Juvenile Offenders." In Loeber and Farrington 1998.

Aos, S., P. Phipps, R. Barnoski, and R. Lieb. 1999. *The Comparative Costs and Benefits of Programs to Reduce Crime (Version 3.0).* Olympia, WA: Washington State Institute for Public Policy.

Augimeri, L. K., C. D. Webster, C. J. Koegl, and K. S. Levene. 1998. *Early Assessment Risk List for Boys (EARL-20B, Version 1).* Toronto, Ontario: Earlscourt Child and Family Center.

Baird, S. C. 1981. "Probation and Parole Classification: The Wisconsin Model." *Corrections Today* 43: 36–41.

Barnett, W. S. 1993. "Cost-Benefit Analysis." In Schweinhart, Barnes, and Weikart 1993.

Bennett, W. J., J. J. DiIulio, and J. P. Walters. 1996. *Body Count: Moral Poverty . . . and How to Win America's War against Crime and Drugs.* New York: Simon and Schuster.

Berrueta-Clement, J. R., L. J. Schweinhart, W. S. Barnett, A. S. Epstein, and D. P. Weikart. 1984. *Changed Lives: The Effects of the Perry Preschool Program on Youths through Age Nineteen.* Ypsilanti, MI: High/Scope Press.

Bishop, D. M., C. E. Frazier, L. Lanza-Kaduce, and L. Winner. 1996. "The Transfer of Juveniles to Criminal Court: Does It Make a Difference?" *Crime and Delinquency* 42: 171–191.

Blumstein, A. 1995. "Youth Violence, Guns, and the Illicit-drug Industry." *Journal of Criminal Law and Criminology* 86: 10–36.

Bonta, J. 1996. "Risk-Needs Assessment and Treatment." In *Choosing Correctional Options That Work,* ed. A. T. Harland. Thousand Oaks, CA: Sage.

Borduin, C. M., B. J. Mann, L. T. Cone, S. W. Henggeler, B. R. Fucci, D. M. Blaske, and R. A. Williams. 1995. "Multisystemic Treatment of Serious Juvenile Offenders: Long-term Prevention of Criminality and Violence." *Journal of Consulting and Clinical Psychology* 63: 569–87.

Capaldi, D. M., and G. R. Patterson. 1996. "Can Violent Offenders Be Distinguished from Frequent Offenders?: Prediction from Childhood to Adolescence." *Journal of Research in Crime and Delinquency* 33: 206–31.

Clarke, E. E. 1996. "A Case for Reinventing Juvenile Transfer: The Record of Transfer of Juvenile Offenders to Criminal Court in Cook County, Illinois." *Juvenile and Family Court Journal* 47: 3–21.

Cohen, M. A. 1998. "The Monetary Value of Saving a High-risk Youth." *Journal of Quantitative Criminology* 14: 5–33.

Cronin, R., B. Bourque, F. Cragg, J. Mell, and A. McGrady. 1988. *Evaluation of the Habitual Serious and Violent Juvenile Offender Program*. Washington, DC: American Institutes of Research.

Dishion, T. J., J. McCord, and F. Poulin. 1999. "When Interventions Harm: Peer Groups and Problem Behavior." *American Psychologist* 54: 755–64.

Dunford, F. W., and D. S. Elliott. 1984. "Identifying Career Offenders Using Self-reported Data." *Journal of Research in Crime and Delinquency* 21: 57–86.

Elliott, D. S. 1994. "Serious Violent Juvenile Offenders: Onset, Developmental Course, and Termination." *Criminology* 32: 1–21.

Fagan, J. 1995. "Separating the Men from the Boys: The Comparative Advantage of Juvenile versus Criminal Court Sanctions on Recidivism among Adolescent Felony Offenders." In *Sourcebook of Serious, Violent, and Chronic Juvenile Offenders,* ed. J. C. Howell, B. Krisberg, J. D. Hawkins and J. J. Wilson. Thousand Oaks, CA: Sage.

Farquhar, J. W. 1985. "The Stanford Five-city Project: Design and Methods." *American Journal of Epidemiology* 122: 323–34.

Farrington, D. P. 1989. "Self-reported and Official Offending from Adolescence to Adulthood." In *Cross-national Research in Self-reported Crime and Delinquency,* ed. M. W. Klein. Dordrecht, Netherlands: Kluwer.

———. 1991. "Childhood Aggression and Adult Violence: Early Precursors and Later Life Outcomes." In *The Development and Treatment of Childhood Aggression,* ed. D. J. Pepler and K. H. Rubin. Hillsdale, NJ: Lawrence Erlbaum.

———. 1997. "Early Prediction of Violent and Non-violent Youthful Offending." *European Journal on Criminal Policy and Research* 5, no. 2: 51–66.

———. 1998. "Predictors, Causes and Correlates of Male Youth Violence." In *Youth Violence,* ed. M. Tonry and M. H. Moore. Chicago: University of Chicago Press.

———. 2000. "Explaining and Preventing Crime: The Globalization of Knowledge: The American Society of Criminology 1999 Presidential Address." *Criminology* 38: 1–24.

Farrington, D. P., and R. Loeber. In press. "How Can the Relationship between Race and Violence Be Explained?" In *Violent Crimes: The Nexus of Ethnicity, Race and Class,* ed. D. F. Hawkins. New York: Cambridge University Press.

Farrington, D. P., R. Loeber, D. S. Elliott, J. D. Hawkins, D. B. Kandel, M. W. Klein, J. McCord, D. C. Rowe, and R. E. Tremblay. 1990. "Advancing Knowledge about the Onset of Delinquency and Crime." In *Advances in Clinical Child Psychology,* ed. B. B. Lahey and A. E. Kazdin, vol. 13. New York: Plenum.

Farrington, D. P., and B. C. Welsh. 1999. "Delinquency Prevention Using Family-based Interventions." *Children and Society* 13: 287–303.

Forst, M., J. Fagan, and T. S. Vivona. 1989. "Youth in Prisons and Training Schools." *Juvenile and Family Court Journal* 40, no. 1: 1–14.

Griffin, P., P. Torbet, and L. Szymanski. 1998. *Trying Juveniles as Adults in Criminal Court:*

An Analysis of State Transfer Provisions. Washington, DC: Office of Juvenile Justice and Delinquency Prevention.

Harrell, A. V., S. E. Cavanagh, M. A. Harmon, C. S. Koper, and S. Sridharan. 1997. *Impact of the Children at Risk Program: Comprehensive Final Report.* Vol. 2. Washington, DC: Urban Institute.

Harrell, A. V., S. E. Cavanagh, and S. Sridharan. 1999. *Evaluation of the Children at Risk Program: Results One Year after the Program.* Washington, DC: National Institute of Justice.

Hawkins, J. D., and R. F. Catalano. 1992. *Communities That Care.* San Francisco: Jossey-Bass.

Hawkins, J. D., R. F. Catalano, R. Kosterman, R. Abbott, and K. G. Hill. 1999. "Preventing Adolescent Health Risk Behaviors by Strengthening Protection during Childhood." *Archives of Pediatrics and Adolescent Medicine* 153: 226–34.

Hawkins, J. D., E. von Cleve, and R. F. Catalano. 1991. "Reducing Early Childhood Aggression: Results of a Primary Prevention Program." *Journal of the American Academy of Child and Adolescent Psychiatry* 30: 208–17.

Hawkins, J. D., T. Herrenkohl, D. P. Farrington, D. Brewer, R. R. Catalano, and T. W. Harachi. 1998. "A Review of Predictors of Youth Violence." In Loeber and Farrington 1998.

Henggeler, S. W., S. K. Schoenwald, C. M. Borduin, M. D. Rowland, and P. B. Cunningham. 1998. *Multisystemic Treatment of Antisocial Behavior in Children and Adolescents.* New York: Guilford.

Holsinger, A. M., and E. J. Latessa. 1999. "An Empirical Examination of a Sanction Continuum: Pathways through the Juvenile Justice System." *Journal of Criminal Justice* 27: 155–72.

Hope, T. 1995. "Community Crime Prevention." In *Building a Safer Society: Strategic Approaches to Crime Prevention,* ed. M. Tonry and D. P. Farrington. Chicago: University of Chicago Press.

Howell, J. C. 2001. "Risk Assessment and Screening Instruments." In Loeber and Farrington 2001.

———, ed. 1995. *Guide for Implementing the Comprehensive Strategy for Serious, Violent, and Chronic Juvenile Offenders.* Washington, DC: Office of Juvenile Justice and Delinquency Prevention.

Huizinga, D., F.-A. Esbensen, and A. Weiher. 1996. "The Impact of Arrest on Subsequent Delinquent Behavior." In *Program of Research on the Causes and Correlates of Delinquency: Annual Report 1995–1996,* ed. R. Loeber, D. Huizinga, and T. Thornberry. Washington, DC: Office of Juvenile Justice and Delinquency Prevention.

Huizinga, D., and C. Jakob-Chien. 1998. "The Contemporaneous Co-occurrence of Serious and Violent Juvenile Offending and Other Problem Behaviors." In Loeber and Farrington 1998.

Jones, M. B., and D. R. Offord. 1989. "Reduction of Antisocial Behavior in Poor Children by Non-school Skill-development." *Journal of Child Psychology and Psychiatry* 30: 737–50.

Karoly, L. A., P. W. Greenwood, S. S. Everingham, J. Hoube, M. R. Kilburn, C. P. Rydell, M. Sanders, and J. Chiesa. 1998. *Investing in Our Children: What We Know and Don't*

Know about the Costs and Benefits of Early Childhood Interventions. Santa Monica, CA: Rand Corporation.

Kraemer, H. C., A. E. Kazdin, D. R. Offord, R. C. Kessler, P. S. Jensen, and D. J. Kupfer. 1997. "Coming to Terms with the Terms of Risk." *Archives of General Psychiatry* 54: 337–43.

Krisberg, B., and J. C. Howell. 1998. "The Impact of the Juvenile Justice System and Prospects for Graduated Sanctions in a Comprehensive Strategy." In Loeber and Farrington 1998.

Kropp, P. R., S. D. Hart, C. D. Webster, and D. Eaves. 1995. *Manual for the Spousal Assault Risk Assessment Guidance*. 2d ed. Vancouver, BC: British Columbia Institute on Family Violence.

Kurz, G. A., and L. E. Moore. 1994. *The '8% problem': Chronic Juvenile Offender Recidivism*. Santa Ana, CA: Orange County Probation Department.

LeBlanc, M., and R. Loeber. 1998. "Developmental Criminology Updated." In *Crime and Justice,* vol. 23, ed. M. Tonry, 115–98. Chicago: University of Chicago Press.

Lipsey, M. W., and J. H. Derzon. 1998. "Predictors of Violent or Serious Delinquency in Adolescence and Early Adulthood: A Synthesis of Longitudinal Research." In Loeber and Farrington 1998.

Loeber, R. 1982. "The Stability of Antisocial and Delinquent Behavior." *Child Development* 53: 1431–46.

Loeber, R., M. DeLamatre, K. Keenan, and Q. Zhang. 1998. "A Prospective Replication of Developmental Pathways in Disruptive and Delinquent Behavior." In *Methods and Models for Studying the Individual,* ed. R. Cairns, L. Bergman, and J. Kagan. Thousand Oaks, CA: Sage.

Loeber, R., and D. P. Farrington, eds. 1998. *Serious and Violent Juvenile Offenders: Risk Factors and Successful Interventions*. Thousand Oaks, CA: Sage.

Loeber, R., and D. P. Farrington, eds. 2001. *Child Delinquents: Development, Intervention, and Service Needs*. Thousand Oaks, CA: Sage.

Loeber, R., K. Keenan, and Q. Zhang. 1997. "Boys' Experimentation and Persistence in Developmental Pathways toward Serious Delinquency." *Journal of Child and Family Studies* 6: 321–57.

Loeber, R., and M. Le Blanc. 1990. "Toward a Developmental Criminology." In *Crime and Justice,* vol. 12, ed. M. Tonry and N. Morris, 375–473. Chicago: University of Chicago Press.

Loeber, R., and H. N. Snyder. 1990. "Rate of Offending in Juvenile Careers: Findings of Constancy and Change in Lambda." *Criminology* 28: 97–109.

Loeber, R., E. Wei, M. Stouthamer-Loeber, D. Huizinga, and T. Thornberry. 1999. "Behavioral Antecedents to Serious and Violent Juvenile Offending: Joint Analyses from the Denver Youth Survey, Pittsburgh Youth Study, and the Rochester Youth Development Study." *Studies in Crime and Crime Prevention* 8: 245–63.

Loeber, R., P. Wung, K. Keenan, B. Giroux, M. Stouthamer-Loeber, W. B. van Kammen, and B. Maughan. 1993. "Developmental Pathways in Disruptive Child Behavior." *Development and Psychopathology* 5: 101–32.

Miller, T. R., M. A. Cohen, and B. Wiersema. 1996. *Victim Costs and Consequences: A New Look*. Washington, DC: National Institute of Justice.

Moffitt, T. E. 1993. "Adolescence-limited and Life-course-persistent Antisocial Behavior: A Developmental Taxonomy." *Psychological Review* 100: 674–701.

O'Donnell, J., J. D. Hawkins, R. F. Catalano, R. D. Abbott, and L. E. Day. 1995. "Preventing School Failure, Drug Use, and Delinquency among Low-income Children: Long-term Intervention in Elementary Schools." *American Journal of Orthopsychiatry* 65: 87–100.

Olds, D. L., J. Eckenrode, C. R. Henderson, H. Kitzman, J. Powers, R. Cole, K. Sidora, P. Morris, L. M. Pettitt, and D. Luckey. 1997. "Long-term Effects of Home Visitation on Maternal Life Course and Child Abuse and Neglect: Fifteen-year Follow-up of a Randomized Trial." *Journal of the American Medical Association* 278: 637–43.

Olds, D. L., C. R. Henderson, R. Chamberlin, and R. Tatelbaum. 1986. "Preventing Child Abuse and Neglect: A Randomized Trial of Nurse Home Visitation." *Pediatrics* 78: 65–78.

Olds, D. L., C. R. Henderson, R. Cole, J. Eckenrode, H. Kitzman, D. Luckey, L. Pettitt, K. Sidora, P. Morris, and J. Powers. 1998. "Long-term Effects of Nurse Home Visitation on Children's Criminal and Antisocial Behavior: 15-year Follow-up of a Randomized Controlled Trial." *Journal of the American Medical Association* 280: 1238–44.

Patterson, G. R. 1982. *Coercive Family Process*. Eugene, OR: Castalia.

Peeples, F., and R. Loeber. 1994. "Do Individual Factors and Neighborhood Context Explain Ethnic Differences in Juvenile Delinquency?" *Journal of Quantitative Criminology* 10: 141–57.

Perry, C. L., K.-I. Klepp, and C. Sillers. 1989. "Community-wide Strategies for Cardiovascular Health: The Minnesota Heart Health Program Youth Program." *Health Education and Research* 4: 87–101.

Podkopacz, M. R., and B. C. Feld. 1996. "The End of the Line: An Empirical Study of Judicial Waiver." *Journal of Criminal Law and Criminology* 86: 449–92.

Redding, R. E., and J. C. Howell. 2000. "Blended Sentencing in American Juvenile Courts." In *The Changing Borders of Juvenile Justice: Transfer of Adolescents to the Criminal Court,* ed. J. Fagan and F. E. Zimring. Chicago: University of Chicago Press.

Schweinhart, L. J., H. V. Barnes, and D. P. Weikart. 1993. *Significant Benefits: The High/Scope Perry Preschool Study through Age Twenty-seven*. Ypsilanti, MI: High/Scope Press.

Schweinhart, L. J., and D. P. Weikart. 1980. *Young Children Grow Up: The Effects of the Perry Preschool Program on Youths through Age Fifteen*. Ypsilanti, MI: High/Scope Press.

Sherman, L. W., and D. Weisburd. 1995. "General Deterrent Effects of Police Patrol in Crime 'Hot Spots': A Randomized Controlled Trial." *Justice Quarterly* 12: 625–48.

Singer, S., and D. McDowall. 1988. "Criminalizing Delinquency: The Deterrent Effects of the New York Juvenile Offender Law." *Law and Society Review* 22: 521–35.

Snyder, H. N. 1998. "Serious, Violent, and Chronic Juvenile Offenders: An Assessment of the Extent of and Trends in Officially Recognized Serious Criminal Behavior in a Delinquent Population." In Loeber and Farrington 1998.

———. 2001. "Epidemiology of Official Offending by the Youngest Delinquents." In Loeber and Farrington 2001.

Snyder, H. N., and M. Sickmund. 1999. *Juvenile Offenders and Victims: 1999 National Report*. Washington, DC: Office of Juvenile Justice and Delinquency Prevention.

Stouthamer-Loeber, M., R. Loeber, D. P. Farrington, Q. Zhang, W. B. van Kammen, and E. Maguin. 1993. "The Double Edge of Protective and Risk Factors for Delinquency: Interrelations and Developmental Patterns." *Development and Psychopathology* 5: 683–701.

Thornberry, T. P. 1998. "Membership in Youth Gangs and Involvement in Serious and Violent Juvenile Offending." In Loeber and Farrington 1998.

Thornberry, T. P., D. Huizinga, and R. Loeber. 1995. "The Prevention of Serious Delinquency and Violence: Implications from the Program of Research on the Causes and Correlates of Delinquency." In *Sourcebook on Serious, Violent, and Chronic Juvenile Offenders,* ed. J. C. Howell, B. Krisberg, J. D. Hawkins and J. J. Wilson. Thousand Oaks, CA: Sage.

Tolan, P. H., and D. Gorman-Smith. 1998. "Development of Serious and Violent Juvenile Offending Careers." In Loeber and Farrington 1998.

Torbet, P., R. Gable, H. Hurst, I. Montgomery, L. Szymanski, and D. Thomas. 1996. *State Responses to Serious and Violent Juvenile Crime.* Washington, DC: Office of Juvenile Justice and Delinquency Prevention.

Torbet, P., and L. Szymanski. 1998. *State Legislative Responses to Violent Juvenile Crime: 1996–97 Update.* Washington, DC: Office of Juvenile Justice and Delinquency Prevention.

Tremblay, R. E., L. Pagani-Kurtz, L. C. Masse, F. Vitaro, and R. O. Pihl. 1995. "A Bimodal Preventive Intervention for Disruptive Kindergarten Boys: Its Impact through Mid-adolescence." *Journal of Consulting and Clinical Psychology* 63: 560–68.

Webster, C. D., K. S. Douglas, D. Eaves, and S. D. Hart. 1997. *HCR-20: Assessing Risk for Violence (Version 2).* Vancouver, BC: Mental Health Law and Policy Institute, Simon Fraser University.

Welsh, B. C., and D. P. Farrington. 2000. "Monetary Costs and Benefits of Crime Prevention Programs." In *Crime and Justice,* vol. 27, ed. M. Tonry. Chicago: University of Chicago Press.

Widom, C. S. 1989. "The Cycle of Violence." *Science* 244: 160–66.

Wiebush, R. G., C. Baird, B. Krisberg, and C. Onek. 1995. "Risk Assessment and Classification for Serious, Violent, and Chronic Juvenile Offenders." In *Sourcebook on Serious, Violent, and Chronic Juvenile Offenders,* ed. J. C. Howell, B. Krisberg, J. D. Hawkins and J. J. Wilson. Thousand Oaks, CA: Sage.

Wilson, J. J., and J. C. Howell. 1993. *A Comprehensive Strategy for Serious, Violent, and Chronic Juvenile Offenders.* Washington, DC: Office of Juvenile Justice and Delinquency Prevention.

Winner, L., L. Lanza-Kaduce, D. M. Bishop, and C. E. Frazier. 1997. "The Transfer of Juveniles to Criminal Court: Re-examining Recidivism over the Long Term." *Crime and Delinquency* 43: 548–63.

Wolfgang, M. E., R. M. Figlio, and T. Sellin. 1972. *Delinquency in a Birth Cohort.* Chicago: University of Chicago Press.

9 The Social Ecology of Child Endangerment

Mark F. Testa and Frank F. Furstenberg

For over a century, the city of Chicago has provided a natural laboratory for research on juvenile delinquency and child neglect and abuse. In an era of increasing globalization, it is easy to overlook the importance of local community context as a major focus of social reform and scientific investigation. A century ago, it was the city rather than the nation-state that was the key site of social agitation, political mobilization, and governmental action (Rodgers 1998). Chicago, in particular, became a symbol of the destiny of modern society. It was at "ground zero" when the forces of industrialization and immigration first hit the great cities, uprooting traditional rural communities and accelerating the spread of a highly complex and differentiated pattern of urban settlement. The social dislocations stimulated by these transformations made Chicago a leading focus of social reform during the Progressive Era and an important object of sociological investigation after World War I (Ward 1989).

Two influential traditions developed out of the efforts to understand the problems and processes of modern urban society: the Chicago settlement house movement and the Chicago School of urban sociology. Not only do the studies that emanate from these traditions serve as important milestones in the development of urban social science, but they also gave rise to a powerful new perspective—social ecology—for understanding the problems of child protection and juvenile justice, and their interconnections.

When the Cook County Juvenile Court was established in 1899, prevailing opinion located the problems of juvenile delinquency, child neglect, and dependency squarely within the person or the family. The delinquent child was thought to be innately inferior, psychologically abnormal, or both. The neglectful family was perceived as morally corrupt. Little regard was given to the larger community, institutional, or cultural contexts. The ecological perspective, in contrast, sought to understand human behavior within the contexts in which it naturally occurs—family, school, neighborhood, and the society at large. By applying this perspective to the problems of juvenile delinquency and child neglect, settlement workers and urban sociologists were able to uncover powerful new facts about the interconnections among early childhood development, adolescent problem behavior, and community context.

One fact, in particular, has been repeatedly documented: the tendency for delinquent and neglected children to concentrate geographically in a common set of Chicago neighborhoods. Sophonisba Breckinridge and Edith Abbott (1912) identified this spatial pattern for delinquent youth as far back as the early 1900s. Clifford Shaw and Henry McKay (1942) replicated their findings for the decades that followed. More recently, James Garbarino and Kathleen Kostelny (1992) found a similar distribution for reports of neglected and abused children who were likely to come under the jurisdiction of the Cook County Juvenile Court. The issue that this pattern raised back then and that its persistence raises today is the extent to which the production of delinquency, neglect, and abuse is not simply an attribute of the individuals and families who reside in these neighborhoods but also a systemic property of the neighborhoods in which these families reside.

Our chapter begins with a review of the pioneering work of the Chicago settlement house movement. It then examines the evolution of the ecological perspective within the Chicago School of urban sociology and follows its generalization to the interdisciplinary study of child and youth development as formulated by Urie Bronfenbrenner (1979) and others. It brings together these different literatures and looks at the interrelation between child maltreatment and juvenile delinquency. Finally, it considers the role that purposive community organization may play in the reduction of juvenile delinquency and child neglect and abuse, and in the prevention of formal child protective intervention by the state.

What is nearly as intriguing as the consistency of the empirical findings on the spatial clustering of juvenile and family problems in Chicago are the periodic breaks in the continuity of this knowledge. Although Shaw and McKay were aware of the work of Breckinridge and Abbott, they included only a single citation in their study, and this was to fault their predecessors for failing to compute population-based delinquency rates. Likewise James Garbarino and his associates were familiar with the work of Shaw and McKay, but their studies built on the ecological framework of developmental psychologist Urie Bronfenbrenner rather than upon the ecological perspective of the Chicago School of urban sociology.

To some extent, these breaks in cumulative knowledge reflect differences in academic orientations. Breckinridge and Abbott were faculty at a school of social work, Shaw and McKay were trained as sociologists, and Bronfenbrenner and Garbarino were educated as developmental psychologists. But another reason for them is the deficiencies that each succeeding generation of researchers found in the programmatic and policy prescriptions of their predecessors. The men of the Chicago School dismissed the educational and cultural programs of the women of the Chicago settlement movement as largely ineffectual against the natural social processes of urban growth and community disorganization that they saw as influencing juvenile and family deviance (Deegan 1988). Likewise, developmental psychologists perceived the indigenous experiments in community participation favored by urban sociologists as too scattershot to have much of an impact on the early childhood conditions that they linked to the development of adolescent problem behaviors.

Also working against meaningful collaboration was the incomplete institutionalization of the ecological perspective in program and policy. In spite of the well-known successes of Hull House (Addams 1910) and the Chicago Area Project (Schlossman et al. 1984), reformers and policymakers had difficulty translating the insights of ecologically informed research into the person-focused operations of juvenile courts, child protective services, and child welfare agencies. The juvenile court may have been created so that judges, probation officers, and social workers could exercise compassion and discretion by taking into account the social contexts in which juvenile and family deviance occurred. But the courts were largely incapable of affecting those contexts, lacking both the power and means for doing very much about neighborhood instability, family fragmentation, and concentrated poverty. In the absence of a broader institutionalized response, community-based experiments floundered, and promising research trails turned into dead-ends.

There are some encouraging signs that the cycle of rediscovery of the same old ecological facts may be coming to an end. Large-scale local studies, such as the Project on Human Development in Chicago Neighborhoods (Sampson, Morenoff, and Earls 1999) and the Illinois Subsidized Guardianship Waiver Experiment (Illinois Department of Children and Family Services 2000), are advancing the interdisciplinary study of the impacts of neighborhood context and government policy on juvenile delinquency and child protection. Under the dual influence of a thriving economy and the unforeseen successes of welfare reform, state and local human services organizations are finally attaining the capacity to combat the underlying conditions of neighborhood disadvantage that threaten community and family well-being. Since the early 1990s, child poverty, welfare receipt, juvenile crime, teenage pregnancy, foster care, and child neglect and abuse have all fallen. Whether the institutionalization of the new "ecologically aware" policies, such as work-related child care, generous earning-disregards in welfare, subsidized guardianship for kinship care, and family support centers, can survive the next economic downturn remains to be seen. In the meantime, it is important to take stock of the new lessons being learned, so that the last century's cycle of rediscovery of the social ecology of child protection won't have to be repeated in the current century.

ORIGINS OF THE ECOLOGICAL PERSPECTIVE

The reformers and social workers who spearheaded the settlement house movement in Chicago were among the earliest to champion the ecological point of view. Hull House founder Jane Addams rejected the person-focused accounts of deviant behavior. Instead, she argued that many of the city's child and family problems arose from the lack of fit between the Old World ways of newly arriving immigrant groups and the New World ways of modern city life (Addams 1910). Although her primary prescription was to Americanize the foreign-born, she sought to accomplish this goal by fostering a reciprocal exchange of sympathy and understanding between immigrant and American-born groups through a new form of social organization: the settlement house.

The settlement house concept was rooted in Protestant "social gospel" teachings in England and the United States. It was inspired by the belief that all people were united in an organic "human brotherhood of Christ" (Carson 1990, 10). By bearing witness to the plight of the disadvantaged and acquainting Hull House's mostly middle-class residents with their less fortunate neighbors, Addams hoped to stimulate public empathy for the poor and promote first-hand knowledge of their conditions. A critical piece of this endeavor was the insistence that every new philanthropic undertaking be preceded by carefully ascertained facts.

These basic tenets of the settlement house movement found expression in one of the first systematic studies of delinquency in Chicago, *The Delinquent Child and the Home,* by Sophonisba Breckinridge and Edith Abbott (1912). Their inquiry relied on careful case-record transcription and tabulation of a decade's worth of delinquency cases handled by the Cook County Juvenile Court. From these records, they were able to obtain information on the number, nationality, and age of the children, and the disposition made of their cases. They supplemented these data with additional information collected from home visits with the parents and interviews with the probation officers of children brought to the court. Their descriptions frequently blurred the distinctions among delinquent, dependent, and neglected children. They noted that while the court dealt under the statutes with three classes of children—

Plates

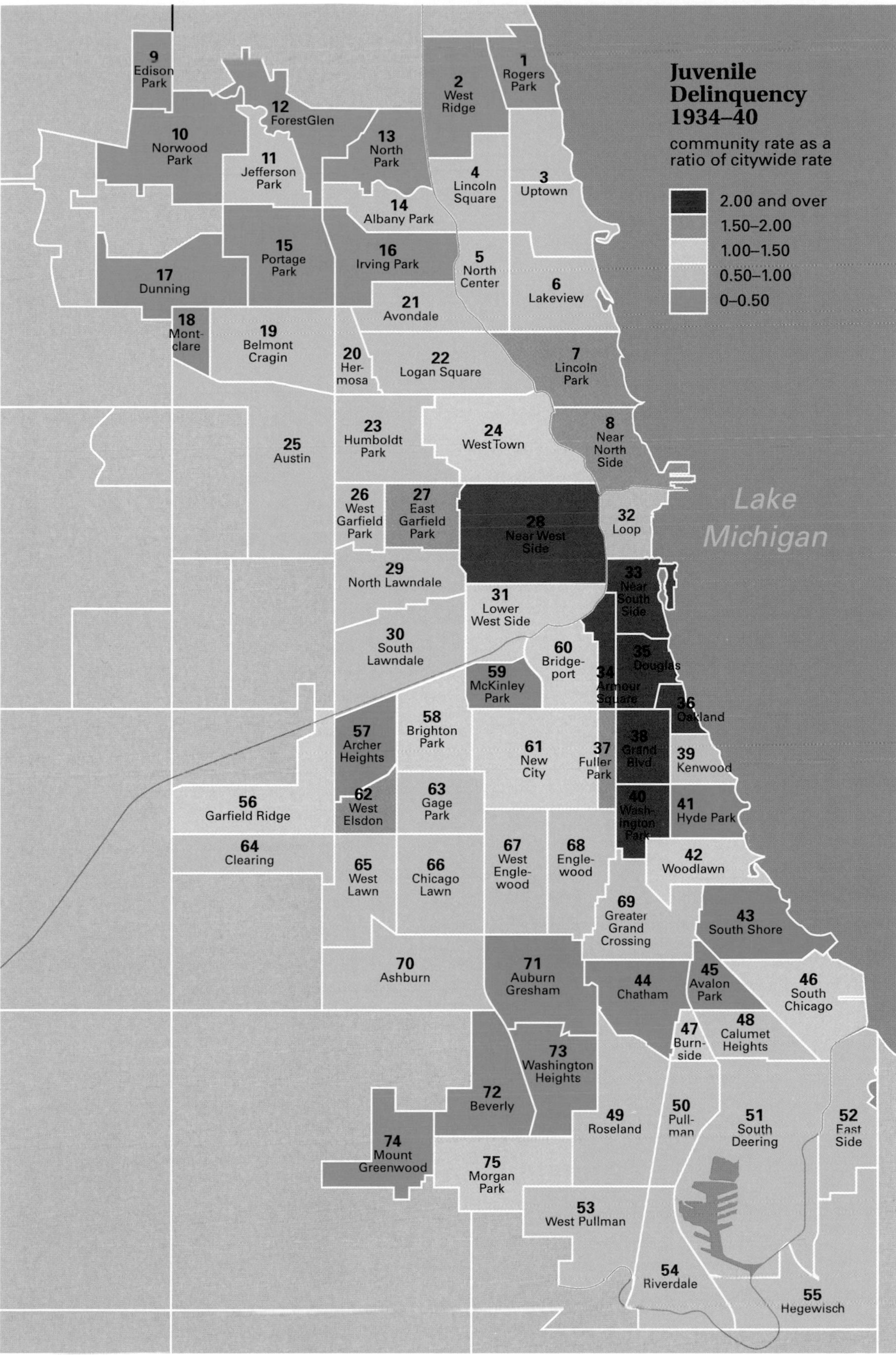
Juvenile Delinquency 1934–40
community rate as a ratio of citywide rate
2.00 and over
1.50–2.00
1.00–1.50
0.50–1.00
0–0.50
Lake Michigan
1 Rogers Park
2 West Ridge
3 Uptown
4 Lincoln Square
5 North Center
6 Lakeview
7 Lincoln Park
8 Near North Side
9 Edison Park
10 Norwood Park
11 Jefferson Park
12 ForestGlen
13 North Park
14 Albany Park
15 Portage Park
16 Irving Park
17 Dunning
18 Mont-clare
19 Belmont Cragin
20 Her-mosa
21 Avondale
22 Logan Square
23 Humboldt Park
24 West Town
25 Austin
26 West Garfield Park
27 East Garfield Park
28 Near West Side
29 North Lawndale
30 South Lawndale
31 Lower West Side
32 Loop
33 Near South Side
34 Armour Square
35 Douglas
36 Oakland
37 Fuller Park
38 Grand Blvd
39 Kenwood
40 Wash-ington Park
41 Hyde Park
42 Woodlawn
43 South Shore
44 Chatham
45 Avalon Park
46 South Chicago
47 Burn-side
48 Calumet Heights
49 Roseland
50 Pull-man
51 South Deering
52 East Side
53 West Pullman
54 Riverdale
55 Hegewisch
56 Garfield Ridge
57 Archer Heights
58 Brighton Park
59 McKinley Park
60 Bridge-port
61 New City
62 West Elsdon
63 Gage Park
64 Clearing
65 West Lawn
66 Chicago Lawn
67 West Engle-wood
68 Engle-wood
69 Greater Grand Crossing
70 Ashburn
71 Auburn Gresham
72 Beverly
73 Washington Heights
74 Mount Greenwood
75 Morgan Park

Plate 9.1

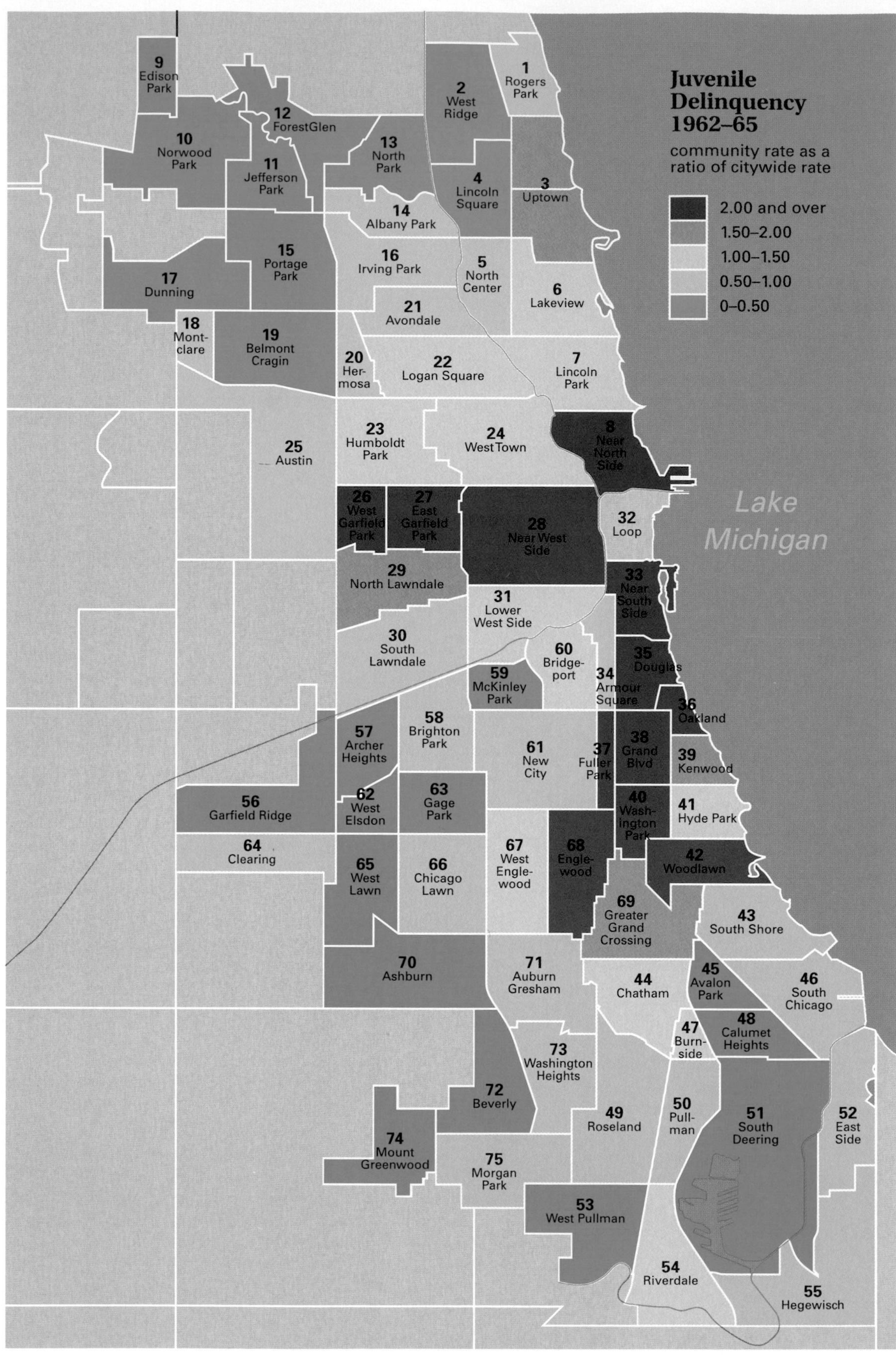

Juvenile Delinquency 1962–65
community rate as a ratio of citywide rate
2.00 and over
1.50–2.00
1.00–1.50
0.50–1.00
0–0.50
Lake Michigan
1 Rogers Park
2 West Ridge
3 Uptown
4 Lincoln Square
5 North Center
6 Lakeview
7 Lincoln Park
8 Near North Side
9 Edison Park
10 Norwood Park
11 Jefferson Park
12 ForestGlen
13 North Park
14 Albany Park
15 Portage Park
16 Irving Park
17 Dunning
18 Mont-clare
19 Belmont Cragin
20 Her-mosa
21 Avondale
22 Logan Square
23 Humboldt Park
24 West Town
25 Austin
26 West Garfield Park
27 East Garfield Park
28 Near West Side
29 North Lawndale
30 South Lawndale
31 Lower West Side
32 Loop
33 Near South Side
34 Armour Square
35 Douglas
36 Oakland
37 Fuller Park
38 Grand Blvd
39 Kenwood
40 Wash-ington Park
41 Hyde Park
42 Woodlawn
43 South Shore
44 Chatham
45 Avalon Park
46 South Chicago
47 Burn-side
48 Calumet Heights
49 Roseland
50 Pull-man
51 South Deering
52 East Side
53 West Pullman
54 Riverdale
55 Hegewisch
56 Garfield Ridge
57 Archer Heights
58 Brighton Park
59 McKinley Park
60 Bridge-port
61 New City
62 West Elsdon
63 Gage Park
64 Clearing
65 West Lawn
66 Chicago Lawn
67 West Engle-wood
68 Engle-wood
69 Greater Grand Crossing
70 Ashburn
71 Auburn Gresham
72 Beverly
73 Washington Heights
74 Mount Greenwood
75 Morgan Park

Plate 9.2

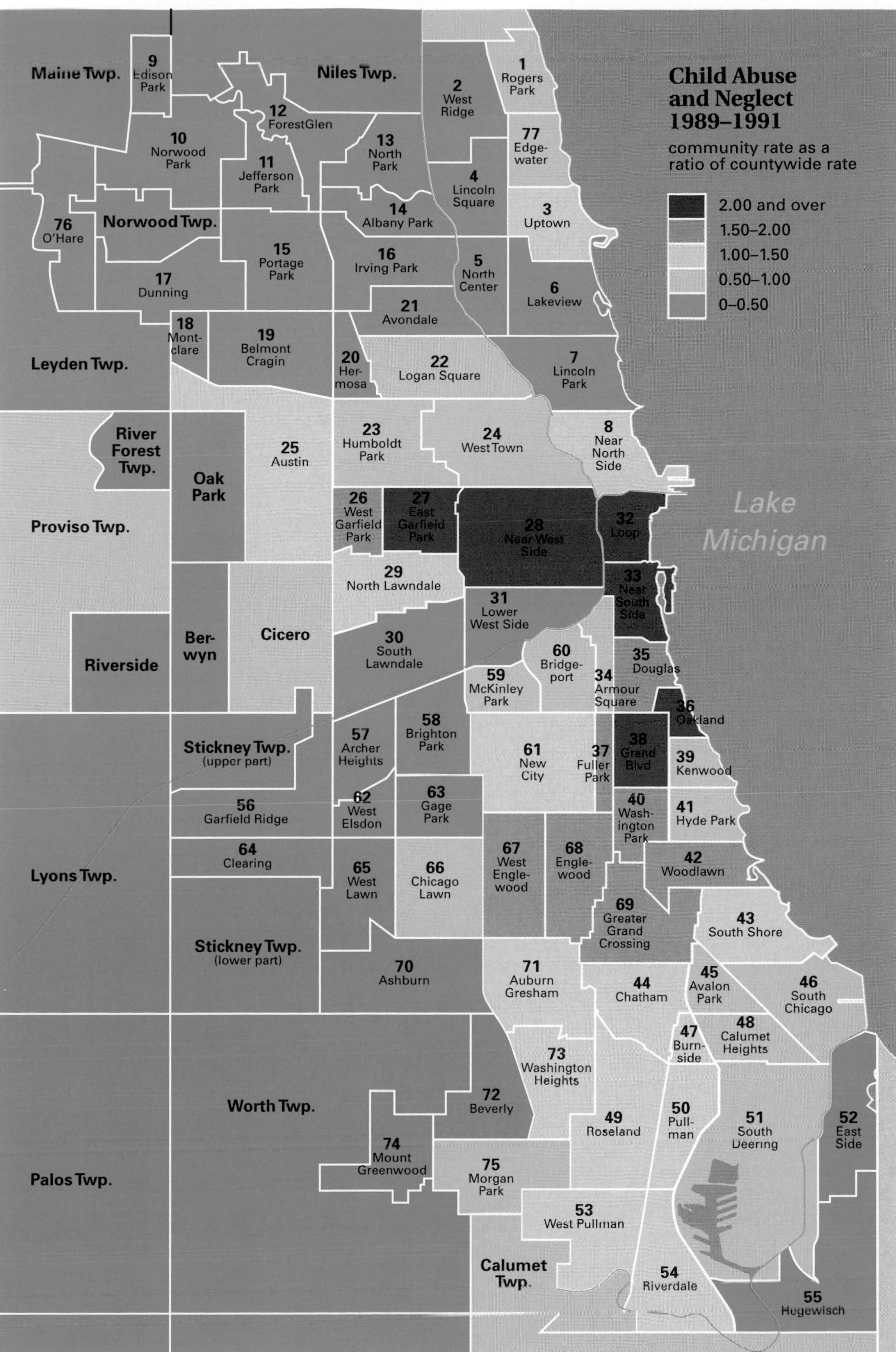
Child Abuse and Neglect 1989–1991
community rate as a ratio of countywide rate
2.00 and over
1.50–2.00
1.00–1.50
0.50–1.00
0–0.50
Lake Michigan
Maine Twp.
Niles Twp.
Norwood Twp.
Leyden Twp.
River Forest Twp.
Oak Park
Proviso Twp.
Ber-wyn
Cicero
Riverside
Stickney Twp. (upper part)
Lyons Twp.
Stickney Twp. (lower part)
Worth Twp.
Palos Twp.
Calumet Twp.
1 Rogers Park
2 West Ridge
3 Uptown
4 Lincoln Square
5 North Center
6 Lakeview
7 Lincoln Park
8 Near North Side
9 Edison Park
10 Norwood Park
11 Jefferson Park
12 ForestGlen
13 North Park
14 Albany Park
15 Portage Park
16 Irving Park
17 Dunning
18 Mont-clare
19 Belmont Cragin
20 Her-mosa
21 Avondale
22 Logan Square
23 Humboldt Park
24 West Town
25 Austin
26 West Garfield Park
27 East Garfield Park
28 Near West Side
29 North Lawndale
30 South Lawndale
31 Lower West Side
32 Loop
33 Near South Side
34 Armour Square
35 Douglas
36 Oakland
37 Fuller Park
38 Grand Blvd
39 Kenwood
40 Wash-ington Park
41 Hyde Park
42 Woodlawn
43 South Shore
44 Chatham
45 Avalon Park
46 South Chicago
47 Burn-side
48 Calumet Heights
49 Roseland
50 Pull-man
51 South Deering
52 East Side
53 West Pullman
54 Riverdale
55 Hegewisch
56 Garfield Ridge
57 Archer Heights
58 Brighton Park
59 McKinley Park
60 Bridge-port
61 New City
62 West Elsdon
63 Gage Park
64 Clearing
65 West Lawn
66 Chicago Lawn
67 West Engle-wood
68 Engle-wood
69 Greater Grand Crossing
70 Ashburn
71 Auburn Gresham
72 Beverly
73 Washington Heights
74 Mount Greenwood
75 Morgan Park
76 O'Hare
77 Edge-water

Plate 9.3

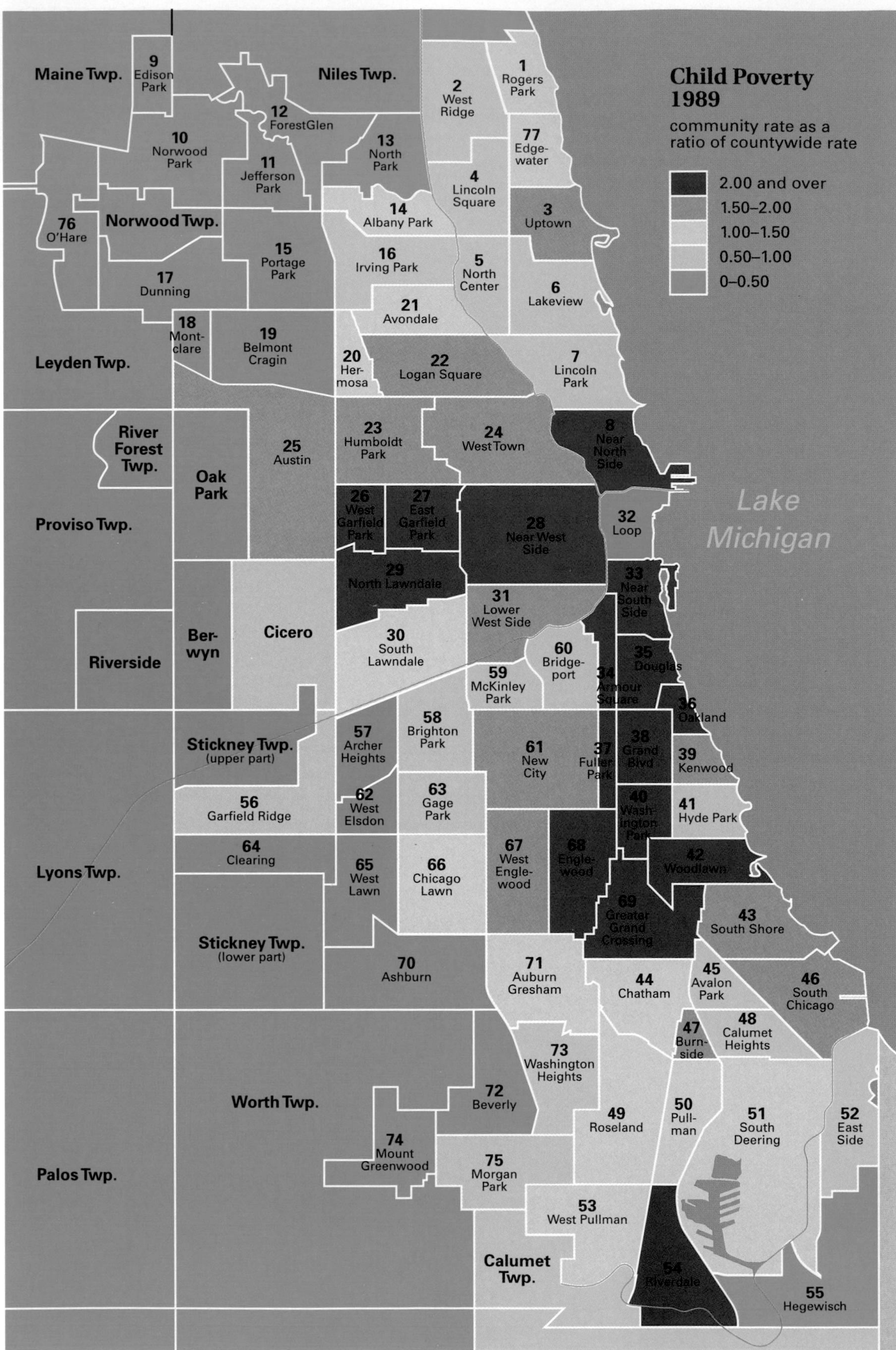

Child Poverty 1989
community rate as a ratio of countywide rate
2.00 and over
1.50–2.00
1.00–1.50
0.50–1.00
0–0.50
Lake Michigan
Maine Twp.
Niles Twp.
Norwood Twp.
Leyden Twp.
River Forest Twp.
Oak Park
Proviso Twp.
Cicero
Ber-wyn
Riverside
Stickney Twp. (upper part)
Lyons Twp.
Stickney Twp. (lower part)
Worth Twp.
Palos Twp.
Calumet Twp.
1 Rogers Park
2 West Ridge
3 Uptown
4 Lincoln Square
5 North Center
6 Lakeview
7 Lincoln Park
8 Near North Side
9 Edison Park
10 Norwood Park
11 Jefferson Park
12 ForestGlen
13 North Park
14 Albany Park
15 Portage Park
16 Irving Park
17 Dunning
18 Mont-clare
19 Belmont Cragin
20 Her-mosa
21 Avondale
22 Logan Square
23 Humboldt Park
24 West Town
25 Austin
26 West Garfield Park
27 East Garfield Park
28 Near West Side
29 North Lawndale
30 South Lawndale
31 Lower West Side
32 Loop
33 Near South Side
34 Armour Square
35 Douglas
36 Oakland
37 Fuller Park
38 Grand Blvd
39 Kenwood
40 Wash-ington Park
41 Hyde Park
42 Woodlawn
43 South Shore
44 Chatham
45 Avalon Park
46 South Chicago
47 Burn-side
48 Calumet Heights
49 Roseland
50 Pull-man
51 South Deering
52 East Side
53 West Pullman
54 Riverdale
55 Hegewisch
56 Garfield Ridge
57 Archer Heights
58 Brighton Park
59 McKinley Park
60 Bridge-port
61 New City
62 West Elsdon
63 Gage Park
64 Clearing
65 West Lawn
66 Chicago Lawn
67 West Engle-wood
68 Engle-wood
69 Greater Grand Crossing
70 Ashburn
71 Auburn Gresham
72 Beverly
73 Washington Heights
74 Mount Greenwood
75 Morgan Park
76 O'Hare
77 Edge-water

Plate 9.4

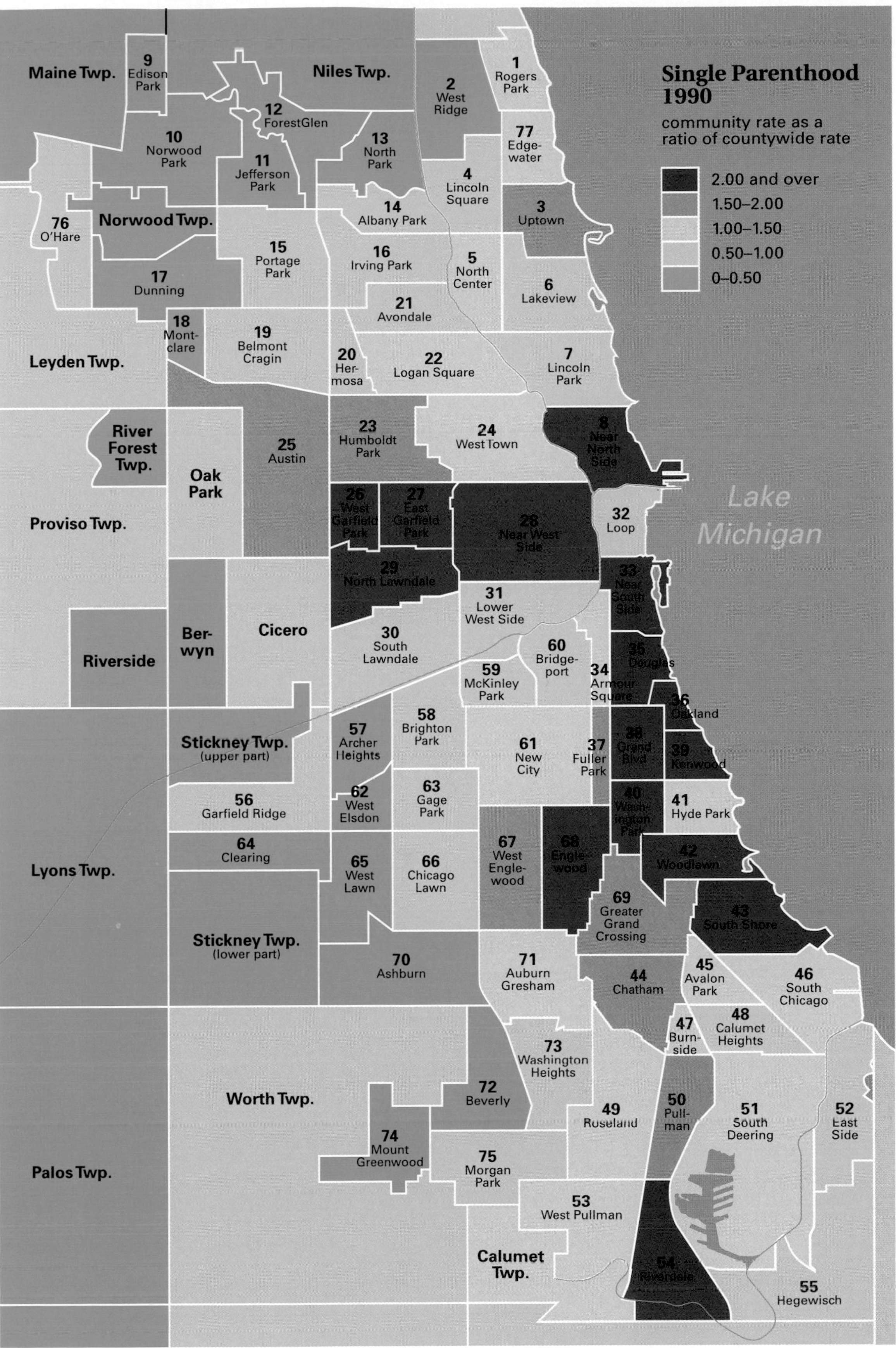

Single Parenthood 1990
community rate as a ratio of countywide rate
2.00 and over
1.50–2.00
1.00–1.50
0.50–1.00
0–0.50
Lake Michigan
Maine Twp.
Niles Twp.
Norwood Twp.
Leyden Twp.
River Forest Twp.
Oak Park
Proviso Twp.
Riverside
Berwyn
Cicero
Stickney Twp. (upper part)
Lyons Twp.
Stickney Twp. (lower part)
Worth Twp.
Palos Twp.
Calumet Twp.
1 Rogers Park
2 West Ridge
3 Uptown
4 Lincoln Square
5 North Center
6 Lakeview
7 Lincoln Park
8 Near North Side
9 Edison Park
10 Norwood Park
11 Jefferson Park
12 ForestGlen
13 North Park
14 Albany Park
15 Portage Park
16 Irving Park
17 Dunning
18 Mont-clare
19 Belmont Cragin
20 Her-mosa
21 Avondale
22 Logan Square
23 Humboldt Park
24 West Town
25 Austin
26 West Garfield Park
27 East Garfield Park
28 Near West Side
29 North Lawndale
30 South Lawndale
31 Lower West Side
32 Loop
33 Near South Side
34 Armour Square
35 Douglas
36 Oakland
37 Fuller Park
38 Grand Blvd
39 Kenwood
40 Wash-ington Park
41 Hyde Park
42 Woodlawn
43 South Shore
44 Chatham
45 Avalon Park
46 South Chicago
47 Burn-side
48 Calumet Heights
49 Roseland
50 Pull-man
51 South Deering
52 East Side
53 West Pullman
54 Riverdale
55 Hegewisch
56 Garfield Ridge
57 Archer Heights
58 Brighton Park
59 McKinley Park
60 Bridge-port
61 New City
62 West Elsdon
63 Gage Park
64 Clearing
65 West Lawn
66 Chicago Lawn
67 West Engle-wood
68 Engle-wood
69 Greater Grand Crossing
70 Ashburn
71 Auburn Gresham
72 Beverly
73 Washington Heights
74 Mount Greenwood
75 Morgan Park
76 O'Hare
77 Edge-water

Plate 9.5

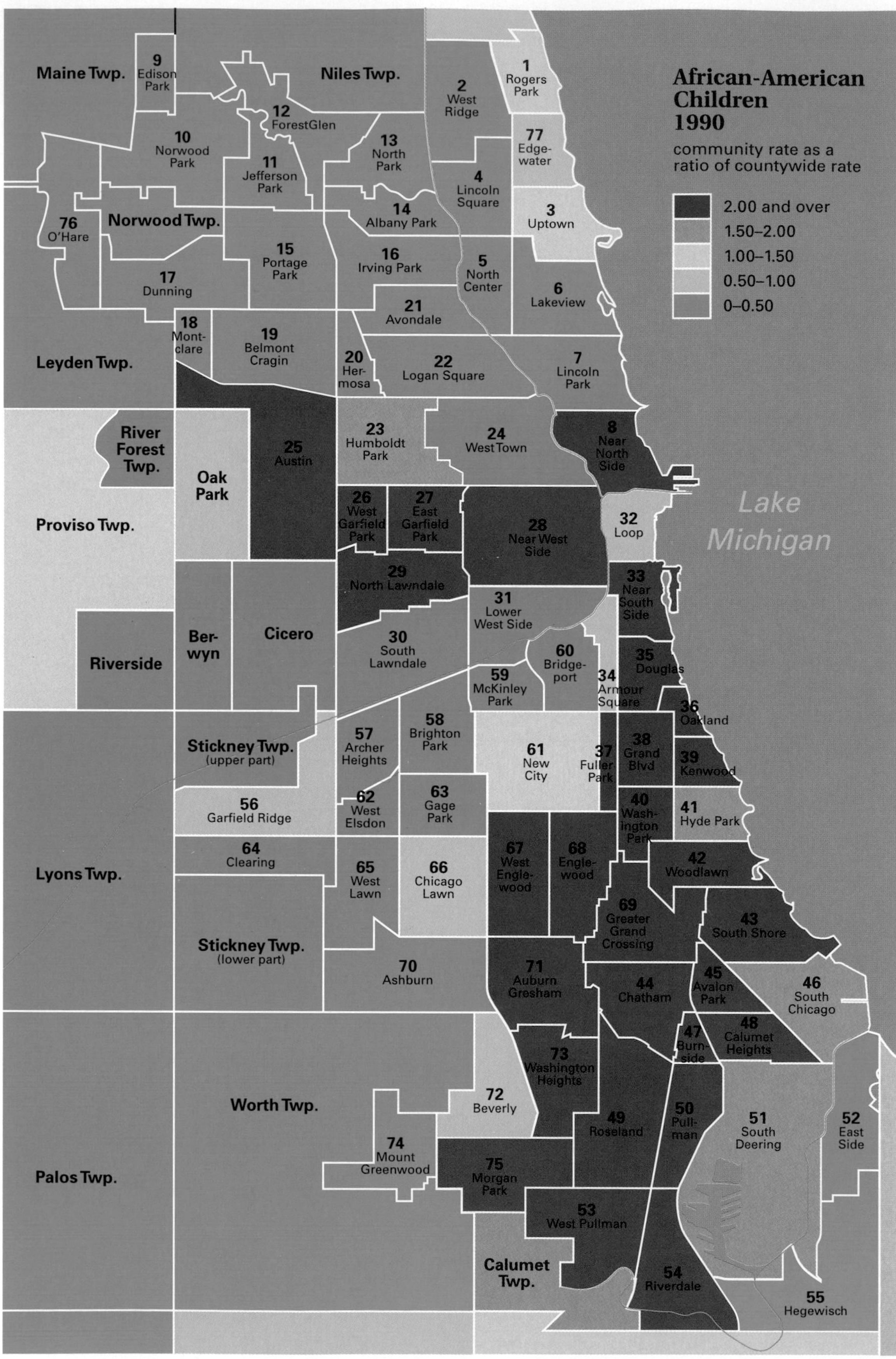
African-American Children 1990
community rate as a ratio of countywide rate
2.00 and over
1.50–2.00
1.00–1.50
0.50–1.00
0–0.50
Maine Twp.
Niles Twp.
Norwood Twp.
Leyden Twp.
River Forest Twp.
Oak Park
Proviso Twp.
Riverside
Berwyn
Cicero
Stickney Twp. (upper part)
Lyons Twp.
Stickney Twp. (lower part)
Worth Twp.
Palos Twp.
Calumet Twp.
Lake Michigan
1 Rogers Park
2 West Ridge
3 Uptown
4 Lincoln Square
5 North Center
6 Lakeview
7 Lincoln Park
8 Near North Side
9 Edison Park
10 Norwood Park
11 Jefferson Park
12 ForestGlen
13 North Park
14 Albany Park
15 Portage Park
16 Irving Park
17 Dunning
18 Montclare
19 Belmont Cragin
20 Hermosa
21 Avondale
22 Logan Square
23 Humboldt Park
24 West Town
25 Austin
26 West Garfield Park
27 East Garfield Park
28 Near West Side
29 North Lawndale
30 South Lawndale
31 Lower West Side
32 Loop
33 Near South Side
34 Armour Square
35 Douglas
36 Oakland
37 Fuller Park
38 Grand Blvd
39 Kenwood
40 Washington Park
41 Hyde Park
42 Woodlawn
43 South Shore
44 Chatham
45 Avalon Park
46 South Chicago
47 Burnside
48 Calumet Heights
49 Roseland
50 Pullman
51 South Deering
52 East Side
53 West Pullman
54 Riverdale
55 Hegewisch
56 Garfield Ridge
57 Archer Heights
58 Brighton Park
59 McKinley Park
60 Bridgeport
61 New City
62 West Elsdon
63 Gage Park
64 Clearing
65 West Lawn
66 Chicago Lawn
67 West Englewood
68 Englewood
69 Greater Grand Crossing
70 Ashburn
71 Auburn Gresham
72 Beverly
73 Washington Heights
74 Mount Greenwood
75 Morgan Park
76 O'Hare
77 Edgewater

Plate 9.6

dependent or neglected, truant, and delinquent—it was often difficult to draw such hard and fast distinctions in practice.

In their chapter on neighborhoods, Breckinridge and Abbott made an important observation that would become a staple of all future ecological studies of juvenile delinquency. Borrowing a method of investigation that Chicago settlement workers had used two decades earlier in *Hull House Maps and Papers* (1895), Breckinridge and Abbott located, by block, the home addresses of all delinquent children in the city. The resulting map revealed that the densely populated Near West Side of the city, the segregated vice district and "black belt" of the South Side, and the Italian quarter on the North Side were the most conspicuous centers of delinquency. Because they plotted only addresses and did not compute rates of delinquent cases per child population, it took another couple of decades of data collection and mapping for the famous "concentric circle" pattern to take shape and capture the imagination of urban ecologists.

After World War I, descriptive surveys of urban problems in Chicago gradually gave way to systematic analyses of the ecological processes that contributed to delinquency, neglect, and dependency. A key figure in this development, which came to be called the Chicago school of urban sociology, was Robert Park. His seminal contribution was to view juvenile delinquency and other forms of personal and social disorganization as "socially constructed." According to Park (Park and Burgess 1925), it is at the level of the organizational community, which originates with the local neighborhood and extends outward to encompass the city, state, and nation, rather than within the person or the family, that we have juvenile delinquency and child neglect. This is not to deny the everyday reality of harms committed by and against children outside and within the home. But it is only when such behaviors are observed, reported, investigated, and processed by the formal organizations of the school, police, hospital, child welfare department, and the juvenile court that they become the official facts of juvenile delinquency and child neglect.

Clifford R. Shaw and Henry D. McKay (1942) were among the first urban sociologists to apply Park's insight to the systematic study of the spatial distribution of juvenile delinquency in the city. Their work established two powerful facts. The first was that rates of official delinquency formed a consistent spatial pattern. Like their predecessors, Shaw and McKay had laboriously gathered information on all official delinquents in Chicago from police records, juvenile court hearings, and correctional commitments for various periods between 1900 and 1940. In addition to plotting the home addresses of each juvenile on a city map, they computed incidence rates based on the ratio of delinquent cases to the number of youth in a census area. In this way, they uncovered a pattern of "concentric circles" that Ernest W. Burgess (Park and Burgess 1925) had first popularized as characteristic of the growth of most industrial cities. Official delinquency rates were highest in the inner-city areas adjacent to the central business district, and they declined progressively the farther away one traveled from this core. Second, they found that this spatial pattern correlated with several social conditions of the neighborhoods in which these juveniles resided. The highest delinquency areas were characterized by physical deterioration, population decline, concentrated poverty, and racial and social isolation.

Plates 1 and 2 reproduce the famous data from *Juvenile Delinquency and Urban Areas* on male delinquents brought before the Cook County Court during the years 1934–40 and 1962–65. We follow the measurement conventions used by Shaw and McKay (1942). Delinquency rates are first formed by dividing the number of official delinquents in a community area by the total population of males aged 10–16. An index ratio is then computed by dividing the community rate by the grand mean rate for the entire city. An index ratio of 1.0 means that a community area has the same delinquency rate as the average for all community areas. An index ratio of 0.5 means that the community rate is one-half of the average rate, and an index of 2.0 means the community rate is twice the average rate. The color shadings correspond to grouped indexes of community delinquency rates ranked from highest (red) to dark green (lowest). The fanning-out of hues from the red around the city's Loop area to orange and light green at mid-distance from the Loop to the dark greens of the surrounding city suburbs vividly illustrates Shaw and McKay's central finding.

Today this pattern is regarded as commonplace. But what was remarkable for the time was that Shaw and McKay were able to show that this spatial pattern and accompanying statistical correlations persisted decade after decade even though the ethnic and racial makeup of these residential areas had changed from the European immigrants of German, Irish, Italian, and Polish decent in the early twentieth century to the southern blacks and Latinos at mid-century. Plates 1 and 2 illustrate the first of two key points. First, the top seven areas that had twice or greater the average delinquency rate for the years 1934–40 reappear in the top twelve list for the years 1962–65. Three of the five next highest delinquency areas for 1934–40 move into the top twelve for 1962–65. Second, the five areas in the second tier of highest delinquency rates for 1934–40 were inhabited entirely by whites. Two decades later, African-Americans were in the majority.

If innate inferiority or moral depravity were at the root of the problem, Shaw and McKay reasoned, then suburban delinquency rates should have risen proportionately as the children of the foreign-born made their way outward from the tenement slums. But they did not; rather, the relative ordering of community delinquency rates remained unchanged. Instead of reinforcing conventional thinking that personal traits or family abnormality were at fault,

Shaw and McKay's findings suggested the spatial concentration and social isolation of people in economically disadvantaged neighborhoods were somehow implicated in the production of delinquency.

THE SOCIAL ECOLOGY OF CHILD ENDANGERMENT

Shaw and McKay, like Breckinridge, Abbott, and others before them, recognized that delinquency was not an isolated phenomenon. They observed that communities characterized by high rates of delinquency were also areas of high rates of infant mortality, low birth weight, tuberculosis, and other social problems. Other scholars educated in the Chicago tradition documented similar patterns for suicide (Cavan 1928) and mental illness (Faris and Dunham 1939). Not until laws about reporting child abuse and neglect went into effect in the late 1960s, however, were researchers able to add child abuse and neglect to the list.

In their 1912 study, Breckinridge and Abbott had noted that the juvenile court faced a major obstacle in finding children from what they called the degraded home: "the home where there are brutality, drunkenness, immorality, or crime" (105). They were convinced that many of the court's delinquent children were victims of neglectful and abusive surroundings, but lamented the lack of any sure method of reaching these children until it was too late. Although the home conditions might be shockingly bad, as long as the parents maintained outward appearances, they despaired, there would be no occasion for an outside agent to enter the home.

This changed in the 1960s. A Denver pediatrician, C. Henry Kempe, and his colleagues published an article entitled "The Battered Child Syndrome" (Kempe et al. 1962). Based on 302 emergency room cases of physical abuse of small children, they concluded what Breckinridge, Abbott, and others could only allege, that these injuries were inflicted by the parents. In the storm of publicity that ensued, the U.S. Children's Bureau promulgated model legislation for the states that would require physicians to report suspected cases of child maltreatment. Between 1963 and 1967, all fifty states passed some version of reporting legislation (Nelson 1984).

With regard to the development of child abuse and neglect reporting laws, Robert Park's concept of social problems as properties of the organizational community becomes especially useful. Just as the meaning of delinquency cannot be taken for granted, the kinds of behaviors that are recognized as child abuse and neglect also change. As Robert Dingwall (1989, 28) notes, during the past several decades the problem of child abuse has undergone considerable "diagnostic inflation." C. Henry Kempe and his associates originally framed the problem narrowly in terms of the battered child syndrome: "a clinical condition in young children who received serious physical abuse, generally from a parent or foster parent" (Kempe et al. 1962). This definition was later incorporated into the child abuse reporting laws that most states passed. Since that time, state and federal lawmakers have enlarged the definition of child abuse and neglect beyond physical abuse to encompass malnutrition, sexual abuse, emotional abuse, risk of injury, excessive corporal punishment, lack of supervision, and, most recently, fetal drug exposure. Occasionally, the label has also been narrowed, for example, to exclude spiritual healing or parental abandonment of children to the care of relatives.

A substantiated finding of child maltreatment means that an allegation of abuse and neglect has been reported and investigated, and that sufficient reason was found to suspect child maltreatment. According to the latest government figures, physical abuse of children now accounts for only one-fifth (21 percent) of all substantiated findings of child abuse and neglect in the United States (U.S. Department of Health and Human Services 2001). The majority of substantiated reports are for neglect (58 percent), which includes depriving a child of the physical, medical, or educational necessities of life. Sexual abuse accounts for another 11 percent, emotional abuse for 8 percent, and the remaining percentages cover miscellaneous harms, such as abandonment, fetal drug exposure, and failure to thrive.

The creation of state child abuse and neglect registries that named victims and perpetrators in all substantiated cases of child maltreatment created the opportunity to study the social ecology of child maltreatment just as juvenile court records had done for juvenile delinquency decades earlier. One of the first Chicago-based studies was by James Garbarino and Kathleen Kostelny (1992). Focusing on the same Chicago community areas that figured in Shaw and McKay's work, they found a strong relationship between per-capita reports of child abuse and neglect and socioeconomic and demographic indicators of community context.

Plate 3 updates Garbarino and Kostelny's analysis with 1989–91 data on substantiated reports of child abuse and neglect supplied by the Office of the Research Director of the Illinois Department of Children and Family Services. Comparing plates 1 and 2 with plate 3 illustrates the remarkable continuity in the set of communities at highest risk of delinquency in the 1960s and child abuse and neglect in the 1990s. The indexes of child abuse and neglect rates are mapped for Chicago community areas and townships of Cook County. Restricting attention to the seventy-five Chicago community areas that Shaw and McKay studied shows that all twelve of the highest delinquency areas for 1962–65 appear in the first or second tier of highest child abuse and neglect areas for 1989–91. The simple ecological correlation between 1962–65 community delinquency rates and 1989–91 abuse and neglect rates yields a Pearson's *r* of 0.79. This means that *almost two-thirds of the variation in 1989–*

91 community abuse and neglect rates from their grand mean is explained statistically by the community's 1962–65 delinquency rate.

This is an important finding that has not been previously reported. The high correlation between 1989–91 child maltreatment and 1962–65 juvenile delinquency illustrates a continuity and linkage between community-level maltreatment and delinquency rates that earlier research was not able to demonstrate because of the lack of geographically coded child abuse and neglect data. The fact that child neglect and abuse tends to concentrate in neighborhoods of historically high delinquency yields a similar set of correlations with neighborhood conditions that Shaw and McKay were able to establish for delinquency and Garbarino and Kostelny were later able to establish for child abuse and neglect reports.

For measures of community poverty, Shaw and McKay had to rely on public assistance statistics, median rental costs, and home ownership rates. Beginning in 1970, the U.S. Census Bureau began publishing community-level statistics based on Mollie Orshansky's poverty index. This statistic, which takes into account family size, more broadly measures the prevalence of child and family poverty separate from welfare receipt. Plate 4 shows the familiar spatial pattern for the plot of indexes of 1989 child poverty rates in Cook County. Other measures of community conditions, such as rates of single parenthood, are highly correlated with family poverty. In order to replicate the statistical associations that Garbarino and Kostelny found for community abuse and neglect, we performed an ecological regression analysis of community-level counts of child abuse and neglect on child poverty and single parenthood (plate 5). To ascertain the extent to which racial composition matters, we also include the counts of black children in the community (plate 6).

Our procedure is as follows. First, we adjust for the number of children at risk of abuse and neglect by computing the differences between the logarithm of the count of abused and neglected children for 1989–91 and the expected count based on the best-fitting line for the regression of the former on the logarithm of the 1990 census count of children in the community. This divides communities into higher-than-expected and lower-than-expected counts of child abuse and neglect based on child population size only. We do the same for counts of child poverty, single parenthood, and African-American children. Second, we correlate these adjusted counts with the same for abused and neglected children.

The partial *R*-squares displayed in column 1 of table 9.1 show that counts of children living with single parents and counts of children living in poor homes are both highly correlated with community levels of indicated child abuse and neglect reports of all types. The count of African-American children adjusted for child population size is only moderately correlated. The remaining columns in table 9.1 disaggregate the overall child abuse rate by al-

Table 9.1

Community-level predictors of the 1989–91 community rates of substantiated reports of child neglect and abuse by type of maltreatment, Cook County

Community predictors	(1) All Child Abuse and Neglect	(2) Physical Abuse	(3) Sexual Abuse	(4) Substance-Exposed Infants	(5) Lack of Supervision
	Partial R^2	Partial R^2	Partial R^2	Partial R^2	Partial R^2
Child poverty	0.8079	0.6163	0.6352	0.8078	0.7520
Single parenthood	0.8536	0.6512	0.6578	0.8555	0.8058
African American	0.5292	0.3884	0.3219	0.5518	0.5468

Source: Office of the Research Director, Illinois Department of Children and Family Services, 2000.

legation type into physical abuse, sexual abuse, infant substance exposure, and lack of (parental) supervision. These four allegation types account for over half of all indicated findings of child abuse and neglect. The partial *R*-squares show much weaker ecological correlations with physical and sexual abuse as compared with the neglect allegations of substance exposure and lack of supervision. Thus most of the association between community variables and child abuse and neglect is attributable to the underlying correlation with neglect findings rather than with abuse findings. This is important because it suggests that physical and sexual abuse are more evenly distributed among neighborhoods, while child neglect, lack of supervision, and drug addiction tend to cluster in areas of high neighborhood poverty and family fragmentation.

THEORIES OF THE SOCIAL ECOLOGY OF DELINQUENCY, NEGLECT, AND ABUSE

A century of investigation into the social ecology of juvenile delinquency and child neglect and abuse in Cook County reveals that rates of official reports and findings vary systematically and consistently across community areas. In the past, these rates correlated strongly with immigrant populations, residential mobility, and public relief. As socioeconomic census data became available, community poverty and single parenthood emerged as prominent predictors. Although the ethnic composition of neighborhoods also matters, its relative importance is clearly secondary to economic and family indicators of high-risk neighborhoods. What theories have researchers drawn upon to explain these facts?

The theoretical framework that Breckinridge and Abbott proposed in *The Delinquent Child and the Home* would now be recognized as a variant of culture conflict theory (see chapter 7, by John Laub, in this volume). Their analysis echoed themes that Jane Addams had earlier advanced in her 1909 monograph, *The Spirit of Youth and the City Streets.* Nearly three-fourths of delinquent children brought before the Cook County Juvenile Court during its early years had parents who were foreign-born. Although these statistics reinforced prevailing stereotypes, Addams and Breckinridge and Abbott were quick to point out that the disproportionate representation of the children of foreign-born parentage did not mean that they were any "worse" than children of native-born parentage. Rather they framed the problem in terms of a conflict of cultures: the Old World's emphasis on child obedience and wage contributions to the family economy versus the New World's emphasis on personal autonomy and investments in secondary education. When immigrant families were slow to become assimilated to New World ways, Breckinridge and Abbott argued, truancy ran high, children became alienated from parental authority, and the lure of the streets brought juveniles within the reach of the court.

Shaw and McKay also located the source of delinquent behavior in a conflict of values. But it was not just the disarticulation between Old World and New World values that Breckinridge and Abbott had identified. Shaw and McKay argued that there also existed within areas of high "social disorganization" a competing cultural system that condoned delinquent acts in direct opposition to the mainstream values symbolized by the family, the church, and other conventional institutions (see chapter 7 in this volume). To account for the persistence of these delinquent subcultures in community areas, they turned to the theory of urban growth that Park and Burgess (1925) had developed.

According to the ecological theory of urban growth, impersonal market and technological forces tend to bring about a typical geographical sorting of the city's population. These geographical groupings develop over time a local organization and neighborhood identity of their own. Once formed, the neighborhood imposes itself as an external structure that defines the quality of life and opportunities of its residents. In this way, a neighborhood takes on an organized existence of its own that is more or less independent of the individual persons and families who temporarily inhabit it.

Shaw and McKay adapted this general theory to their explanation of juvenile delinquency. First, they distinguished between neighborhoods with high and low degrees of social organization. Neighborhoods with low degrees of organization comprised diverse immigrant and racial groups whose cultural standards conflicted with each other and with the larger society. In addition, these neighborhoods were constantly besieged by the destabilizing forces of high mobility, chronic unemployment, family breakdown, and a host of additional urban ills. Under these disorganizing conditions, immigrant and poor families lost control of their children to the competing influences of local street gangs. Local gangs then became the primary transmitters of criminal traditions and delinquent values to each successive generation of children that inhabited the streets of these disorganized areas.

In many respects, Shaw and McKay's social disorganization theory complements Breckinridge and Abbott's culture conflict theory. Despite the enduring relevance of their respective works, however, later theorists have found both theories lacking because of the missing element of the ontogenic development of the child. Not all children from immigrant homes became delinquent; not all children in disadvantaged neighborhoods were abused or neglected. What accounts for the difference?

LINKAGES BETWEEN CHILD MALTREATMENT AND JUVENILE DELINQUENCY

Later researchers such as Sutherland (1939), Glueck and Glueck (1968), and Tannenbaum (1938) began to appreciate that delinquency was a manifestation of an unfolding sequence of underlying problems that often was initiated long before birth and that could be located as well in community conditions. They located children's developmental trajectories in the cultural and community conditions that shaped both the structure and process of family life. Instead of looking for single causes resulting in distinctive outcomes, later students of the ecological approach to child and youth development examined more broadly the ways that community processes shaped the socialization of children. The focus on socialization provided a way of exposing how community conditions insinuated themselves in the development of the child, both inside the family early in life and later on as the child moved into school, formed peer relationships, and engaged in the life of the surrounding community. This process of movement through progressively larger contexts was a way of understanding the formation of problem behaviors over the early part of the life course. It also showed how syndromes of behavior could be traced back to very early childhood: neglect, illness, accidents, poor mental health, low cognitive skills, and physical disabilities early in life; truancy, aggressiveness, and school failure in primary school; and delinquency, dropout, sexual promiscuity, drug use, and suicide in the teen years.

In the middle decades of the last century, sociologists and psychologists began to study the origins of aggressive behavior in children and its link to later forms of delinquency and low achievement. Discoveries by Sheldon and Eleanor Glueck (1968) and later by Lee Robins (1974) traced the origins of delinquency to early behaviors in the family that often gave rise to social responses by parents, teachers, and neighbors that reinforced rather than extinguished acting out. (For more recent versions of this argument, see Dodge 1986). The interplay between children's actions and the responses of adults and the larger community traces the development of delinquent careers in what Edwin Lemert (1951) referred to as the process of "secondary deviance," the response of significant others to the initial acts of misbehavior (see also chapter 7 in this volume).

Other social scientists began to devise more systematic ways of understanding the social ecology of deviant and conforming behaviors. Notable among these is Urie Bronfenbrenner (1979), who mapped a broad conceptual scheme for studying the worlds of children. Bronfenbrenner viewed the ecological system as a set of Russian dolls, providing a set of ever-widening contexts in which children grow up—each successively embedded in a larger one. The smallest system is the *microsystem* of immediate family, friends, and neighbors. The circle then widens to encompass the *mesosystems* of schools, playgrounds, clubs, and peer groups. These systems in turn are embedded in the larger *exosystems* of parental workplace, neighborhood, local government, and other aspects of what Park called the organizational community. Finally, there is the *macrosystem* of culture, nationhood, and globalization. When the contexts are integrated and coherent to children, as they are in some societies, successful incorporation into adult society is very likely. When they are not, children often lack the necessary skills and competencies that are required in adulthood, and they may acquire traits that are ill suited to moving from one context to another (for example, from the family to the school or the school to the labor force).

In many respects, Bronfenbrenner's ecological theory has much in common with the ideas of Émile Durkheim (1951), which were later imported into the sociology of deviance by Robert Merton (1968) in his well-known essay, "Social Structure and Anomie." Like Durkheim, Merton argued that lack of social integration creates the conditions under which deviance arises because it fails to instill common or achievable objectives that can be realized with the social means available to participants in that system. The result is that individuals will devise means to realize the goals or opt out altogether.

Many researchers have pursued these two closely related avenues of understanding the development of problem behavior. Both theories focus attention on how the social system generates and forms problems that it condemns. In the following decades, researchers from both sociology and psychology began to document these theories. (See, for example, Richard and Shirley Jessor 1977; Robert Cairns and Beverly Cairns 1994; and K. Hurrelmann and S. F. Hamilton 1996). As the scope of this research has broadened, it has become more explicitly comparative, going beyond communities to examine the nations across time (Furstenberg et al. 1999).

EXPLAINING THE LINKAGES BETWEEN MALTREATMENT AND DELINQUENCY

The co-occurrence of high rates of child maltreatment in the same community areas with high rates of juvenile delinquency raises a question about the nature of the linkages between these two phenomena. As with other social problems, there are several possible explanations for the correlation. One is that the co-occurrence simply reflects the tendency of families and persons with a proneness toward child neglect, domestic violence, and juvenile delinquency to concentrate in the same neighborhoods. Differences in community child maltreatment and juvenile delinquency rates may simply mirror differences in the population composition of the neighborhoods. This is a restatement of the longstanding hypothesis of child abnormality and family pathology that social ecologists have historically found wanting.

An alternative is the ecological proposition that it is the context of the neighborhood that matters. Concentrated poverty, single parenthood, social isolation, and residential mobility strain the individual and collective child-rearing capacities of families, resulting in neglect and abuse when children are young and in juvenile delinquency, teenage pregnancy, and other problem behaviors when children are older. This formulation makes no assumption about the neglected child growing up to become the delinquent juvenile. Rather it could just be that a common set of social factors independently weaken family capacity at crucial stages of the child's development in the absence of an ontogenic link between early experiences and later behavior. Neglected infants can grow up to be well-adjusted adolescents, and delinquent youth can come from upstanding homes.

But the possibility of an ontogenic link between child maltreatment and juvenile delinquency offers still another explanation for the co-occurrence. Child maltreatment may reinforce certain psychological adaptations and behavioral tendencies early in life that fix the child on a future trajectory that is likely to culminate in juvenile delinquency, regardless of changes in community context. Clinical studies and retrospective surveys have shown that juvenile delinquents and adult criminals have a much higher rate of reported abuse than the general population (Lewis et al. 1989; Vissing et al. 1991). Catherine Widom's prospective studies (1989, 1996) demonstrate that child maltreatment is associated with a moderate but significant difference in future arrests (26 percent among the maltreated sample versus 17 percent among the matched controls). Because children tend to stay in the same (or similar) neighborhood in which they were raised, communities with high rates of child maltreatment will show up as areas with high rates of juvenile delinquency.

Several lines of research have attempted to sort out these alternatives. One line has maintained a problem-specific focus, seeking to understand the etiology of particular social ills in the structural, cultural, or individual circumstances. Research on substance abuse, suicide, and mental illness often look for special (often biologically based) explanations for the onset and maintenance of problem behavior. Alternatively, some researchers have argued that such behaviors arise developmentally as part of a careerlike sequence of behaviors or a syndrome of related actions. Jessor's research on early precursors of serious problem behavior has led to a lively debate over the clustering and ordering of problem behaviors. Other researchers have sought to understand not the etiology of problem behavior but its persistence. Robert Sampson and John Laub (1993) in their longitudinal follow-up of the Gluecks' sample are able to show how and why certain criminals desist when they become engaged in conventional activities and find it difficult, inconvenient, or costly to continue their criminal careers.

A different line of research has focused on the contexts that give rise to problem behaviors. Again, much of this research examines one context at a time, giving special emphasis to the role of the family, peers, school, or neighborhood either in promoting problems or in protecting individuals from problem behavior. This context-specific research has often acknowledged that some settings can be "risky" and others "supportive" to the development of conventional behaviors; however, only rarely has research considered the impact of multiple contexts.

Much of the research on contextual influences, moreover, assumes that individuals are influenced by contexts, not taking full account of the way that individuals react differently to contextual influences depending on their perceptions of the context and their personal skills in addressing risks and opportunities. Sociologists have sometimes too readily assumed a position that is very nearly deterministic. Surely, poverty in the family, schools, and neighborhoods significantly structures opportunities in later life, but individuals who endure the same conditions do respond quite differently.

THE MACARTHUR NETWORK ON SUCCESSFUL ADOLESCENCE

In 1988, the MacArthur Foundation set up an interdisciplinary Research Network on Successful Adolescence in Disadvantaged Communities to explore the developmental paths to success during adolescence among youth living in difficult or less than privileged circumstances. The network, headed by Richard Jessor, included other psychologists (Albert Bandura, Jacques Eccles, Norman Garmazy, and Arnold Samaroff), physicians (Beatrix Hamburg, James Comer, and Robert Haggarty), and sociologists (Tom Cook, Glen Elder, Delbert Eliot, Frank Furstenberg, Marta Tienda, and William Julius Wilson). (For a description of the origins of the network, see Jessor 1993).

Drawing heavily upon the Chicago School tradition, the ecological theories and research of Urie Bronfenbrenner and his students, and the ideas and work of William Julius Wilson on the consequences of growing up in high-poverty neighborhoods, the network set out to build a series of related studies (using a common conceptual framework and related approaches to data collection) that would identify some common principles of successful development during the adolescent years. Wilson's own ideas are indebted to the Chicago School, especially in the way that he draws links between the composition of neighborhoods and the development of adolescents.

Wilson (1987) argues that a central fact of urban neighborhoods is the growing spatial concentration of poverty. The withdrawal of the middle class and the decline of employment opportunities in the inner city created in the 1970s and 1980s a sharp increase in joblessness. This, in turn, Wilson reasons, results in a shrinking pool of marriageable males and an increase of female-headed families. These families, to a growing extent, become segregated in distinct urban neighborhoods that create a "ghetto-specific" culture that affects the aspirations and opportunities of children.

Wilson's theory suggests that children living in certain neighborhoods will be exposed to distinctively different styles of socialization via the family, peers, and neighbors that affect their likelihood of gaining the values, motives, and skills necessary for incorporation into mainstream society. Specifically, Wilson argues that in areas of concentrated poverty, young people are exposed to a limited range of mentors and models who demonstrate how to succeed. They also lack the social ties and networks that help them gain opportunities and the institutional support to equip them with the human capital needed to function in the marketplace. Finally, Wilson suggests that family life itself is corrupted by the absence of work and civic roles that are conspicuously absent in high-poverty neighborhoods.

Many scholars in the 1990s began to examine the influence of neighborhoods on the developmental trajectories of children and youth. However, as Christopher Jencks and Susan Mayer (1989) note in an important synthesis of the literature on neighborhood effects, the evidence of direct neighborhood influences was, at best, only suggestive. Indeed, the most compelling data came from qualitative data of fieldworkers who observed that children in highly disadvantaged neighborhoods did indeed appear to be drawn to the life of the streets and had great difficulty during the transition to adulthood. However, the ethnographic data is not typically comparative and as such is not well designed to speak to the issue of whether neighborhood influences help to shape life-course trajectories of youth.

The MacArthur Network on Successful Adolescence took up the challenge of investigating this question but recast it to allow for the possibility that youth in poverty neighborhoods are exposed, in fact, to multiple and differing contexts. As indicated earlier, the assumption that residents of a high-poverty community are homogeneous in their response to local conditions is highly questionable. Therefore, the network began to develop a series of studies in different communities involving a fieldwork component that looked in depth at how parents and adolescents navigated within communities with different levels of poverty and social disorganization. The fieldwork was accompanied by surveys of families that permitted systematic comparison of intra- and inter-neighborhood variation.

Over the past ten years, a series of studies have been produced from the work of the MacArthur Network that point to several interesting conclusions. First, differences across neighborhoods can be detected, but they are rarely sizable and never uniform. These differences are typically greater in the demographic and social features of neighborhoods or the level of resources available to families than in the values and behaviors of family members. Put differently, there is much more variation within than between neighborhoods in both the values of parents, styles of parenting, expectations for children, and the behavior of young people. Poor families are no more alike in their practices than are wealthy families. This was especially evident in parenting practices, such as warmth or discipline effectiveness, which showed very little neighborhood-level variation. On the other hand, parents in highly disadvantaged communities did adopt different family management strategies for monitoring their children and were far less likely to avail themselves of local social programs aimed at cultivating skills, in part because such programs were less available to them. By contrast, in the better organized (largely white) neighborhoods the availability of resources gave parents an opportunity to cosocialize with local institutions such as churches, schools, or preschool and after-school programs. While some problem behaviors may be concentrated at the neighborhood level, many are not. Several of the network studies show that delinquency in early adolescence is not strongly linked to neighborhood. However, adolescent problem behavior may be handled differently in different communities and hence may have more serious and lasting consequences in poverty communities than in working or middle-class areas. Thus, neighborhood differences exist and they can be quite important, but their specific impact may be contingent and related to a host of other conditions. This set of findings led the network to postulate that understanding developmental trajectories involves examining multiple contexts over time. It is insufficient to consider family *or* peer *or* school *or* neighborhood influences—taken one at a time—to understand a child's developmental pathway. Instead, we must consider multiple and overlapping influences through time if we are going to chart the pattern of successful development during the adolescent years.

It turns out that the relationship of "quality" contexts, however we measure the attributes of an environment for any particular child, is only moderate.

If children grow up in well-functioning families, they do not necessarily attend well-functioning schools, or live in well-functioning neighborhoods. Cook and his colleagues (1999) were able to demonstrate that the correlation from context to context is not nearly as high as might have been expected by most observers. This finding helps to explain the high amount of variation among children that occurs within particular settings (siblings within the family, or peers in school, or youth within the same neighborhood). These contextual differences generate specialized or distinctive clusters of experience among individuals within what appear from a distance to be similar environments.

In part, these differences are accounted for by sorting processes that take place by actors (parents and children) over time. Parents look for good neighborhoods when they can afford them or move when they are able to find better opportunities for their children. If they are unable to move, they look for the best schools that they can find and hence maneuver within neighborhoods to promote their children's chances of succeeding. Of course, better organized parents with greater material, social, and psychological resources are more adept at managing their children's course of development, but parents are by no means the only actors that sponsor their children. Teachers, coaches, and neighbors help children to navigate difficult environments, and children themselves show different abilities to locate such mentors and make use of their assistance. This element of agency on the part of parents and children has been greatly underappreciated and its importance has been underestimated in explaining successful development. When parents possessed high amounts of it, we referred to it as "successful family management," an aspect of socialization that has been largely overlooked because it pertains to oversight of the external world rather than to face-to-face interaction. Children's own managerial skills have received more attention in the psychological literature in the form of "self-efficacy" or cognitive skills related to mastery of tasks, but even the study of these qualities has not explored the full range of children's abilities to organize and navigate their own course of development.

Despite these individual-level characteristics, there can be no question that some environments are more difficult to manage because they are more chaotic, lack institutional resources, and provide sparse social networks or mentors who can provide access to opportunities for development. The Network on Successful Adolescence carried out several studies of youth in rural and suburban communities that reveal vast differences in the quality of contexts for youth in different parts of the United States. Indeed, it is interesting to speculate whether this uneven distribution of opportunities is more characteristic of the United States than other nations in the developed world. It is equally important to explore whether the quality of contexts changed over the course of the twentieth century, especially in the latter decades when economic inequality was increasing.

COMMUNITY ORGANIZATION AND SOCIAL POLICY

The development of the ecological perspective over the last century from the early investigations of the settlement house movement to the theoretically oriented studies of the Chicago School and recently to the interdisciplinary endeavors of the MacArthur Network has been propelled as much by a set of policy interests as by scientific concerns. The leaders of the Chicago settlement movement were explicit about their desires to apply scientific findings to practical solutions. The Chicago sociologists, while openly skeptical of the efforts of settlement workers to establish nonindigenous, philanthropic outposts in disorganized communities (Thomas and Znaniecki 1918–20), did recognize the necessity of understanding the values and culture of immigrant populations and the importance of strengthening the institutions of self-help and community organization as a means of linkage to the wider society (Janowitz 1978).

While the Cook County Juvenile Court looked favorably upon community-based experimentation in delinquency prevention and family support, there was very little it could do in the form of service provision or funding. Legislative action was required, and it wasn't until the expansion of juvenile justice, child protective, and child welfare services at the county and state level in the 1960s that much attention could be focused on the community conditions of juvenile and family deviance. With the creation of the Illinois Department of Children and Family Services in 1964, a floor of child protective and child welfare services was created in every county in the state. This facilitated the establishment of a system of community planning and organization that is now woven into the formal operations of the Cook County Juvenile Court and Illinois Department of Children and Family Services. Through the structure of Local Area Networks (LANs), the court and the Department of Children and Family Services plan and organize service delivery using the same Chicago community areas that the Chicago sociologists identified as the natural ecological areas of urban growth. Still the establishment of genuine reciprocal channels of influence between the indigenous leadership of the local community and the bureaucratic and market institutions of the wider society remains an ongoing challenge.

Several issues resurface time and again as reformers, activists, government officials, and sometimes researchers themselves attempted to translate the ecological outlook into practical action. The first concerns the extent to which successful community organization depends upon using locally based leadership and indigenous workers as opposed to importing professional staff from the outside. The settlement movement faced this quandary early on. On the one hand, their ideology accepted and sometimes celebrated the ethnic heritages of the people they were attempting to acculturate. On the other, their unswerving belief in the superiority of American, middle-class values caused them to recruit professionally educated, nonindigenous workers for the task. Even though settlement workers may have believed in the organic unity of the different classes, the obvious disparities in language, dress, tastes, and education were not lost on local residents. It was precisely this tension between indigenous leadership and external staffing that led to an open split between the sociologists of the Chicago school and the social workers of the settlement movement. Chicago sociologist W. I. Thomas was among the first to question the effectiveness of externally sponsored experiments in community organization. In *The Polish Peasant* (Thomas and Znaniecki 1918–20), he argued that it was a mistake to suppose that a "community center" established by an outside agency could have much influence in reversing the effects of social disorganization. Such a purpose could only be fulfilled by organizing local self-help and encouraging indigenous leadership. His views later found expression in the organizing efforts that flowed out of the Chicago Area Project (CAP), which Shaw and McKay started in 1932. Taking their cue from Thomas, they proceeded from the proposition that community organization could be effective only to the extent that it drew from the local resources of the neighborhood in which the programs were situated. Consequently, they focused on the recruitment of indigenous leaders and workers to represent CAP and establish local affiliates in cooperation with other influential residents and groups. Part of this process involved the assignment of "detached workers," preferably from the neighborhood, whose job it was to establish informal relationships with the youth and gang members in the area.

Shortly after the CAP started, it became the target of strident counterattacks. Settlement and social workers charged CAP leadership with encouraging anti-professionalism, relying on uneducated and untrained staff, and placing former criminals on the public payroll. It took years for the animosity between the social work establishment and CAP to cool down (Sorrentino 1959), but in the end many of the CAP precepts were absorbed into social work training and voluntary service efforts, such as community drop-in centers, peer-support groups, and family support programs (Weissbourd 1987).

The infusion of community concepts into bureaucratic operations through identifying and involving "community stakeholders" in the planning, implementation, and running of government juvenile justice and child welfare programs is now routine. Several major federal, state, and voluntary collaborations, such as federally funded family preservation and support services, and state and privately funded "Healthy Family America" initiatives, draw on many of the key concepts of community organization, family support, and local self-help.

While beneficial in many respects, the infusion of community concepts into bureaucratic operations touches upon a sensitive organizational nerve.

The community approach emphasizes particularistic needs and flexible responses, while the bureaucratic approach stresses universalistic definitions and uniform solutions. Although states and some county governments have the discretion to decide what constitutes child abuse and neglect, few communities can tolerate a definition of behavior as maltreatment in one section of town and as acceptable childrearing in another part. Sometimes a particular social group can mobilize political resources to carve out an exception, such as spiritual healing, but in most cases majority opinion prevails, as with the recent inclusion of ritual genital mutilation as abuse in many states. The consequence is that many community-based initiatives that are sponsored by government agencies tend to draw from a narrower range of cultural opinion and political leadership than might be optimal for effective organization and pop ular acceptance at the local level.

Although bureaucracy restricts the diversity of policy options at the level of goals, most government-sponsored, community-based initiatives encourage flexibility in the selection of means. For this reason, it is often difficult to evaluate the impact of multisite, community-based initiatives. For example, the decentralized structure of the CAP program permitted communities to tailor crime and delinquency prevention programs to local conditions. This made it difficult to identify common parameters of the intervention across sites for purposes of evaluation (Schlossman et al. 1984). The same holds true for more recent federal and state efforts, such as the 1993 Family Preservation and Support Services of Title IV-B of the Social Security Act.

Another complicating factor is that many of the problem behaviors, such as juvenile delinquency, child abuse, and neglect, that are the objects of community-based prevention programs are relatively rare even in the highest-risk communities. For example, the annual incidence of substantiated child abuse and neglect in Illinois LANs averages about 1.3 victims per 100 children with the highest showing 4.5 victims per 100 children in one of the most impoverished LANs. Delinquency rates average only slightly higher when the population base is restricted to adolescents. The rare incidence of these problems means that many more children than are likely ever to come to the attention of child protective authorities are rolled into the target population of community-wide prevention efforts. By diluting the dose of the intervention in this way, it becomes very difficult to detect a significant change, let alone link an improvement to a particular intervention.

In the absence of large-scale governmental involvement, the extent to which purposive community organization can realistically contribute to the overall quality of community life remains an open issue. The surviving remnants of the settlement movement and the Chicago School, such as Hull House and the Chicago Area Project, have taken on the person-focused attributes of the juvenile court and the traditional social service agencies for which they were originally alternatives. Even with a large infusion of public dollars, skepticism remains. Most of the sociologists affiliated with the Chicago School were inclined to view political decisions as impotent to affect "social processes" (Shils 1961). Macrosystem economic and technological forces were assumed to be far more influential. Indeed, the significant fall in crime, child abuse and neglect, teenage pregnancy, and drug addiction that paralleled the uninterrupted expansion of the American economy in the last half-decade of the twentieth century makes a fairly compelling case for the power of economic and technological change over community organization. But while economic growth and declining unemployment may be necessary for community revitalization, without "ecologically aware" policies, such as publicly subsidized child care, earnings-disregards for welfare participation, and subsidized guardianship for kinship care, many of the societal-level advantages would not be efficiently channeled to local areas of greatest need.

Recent findings from the Project on Human Development in Chicago Neighborhoods (Sampson, Morenoff, and Earls 1999) suggest that concentrated neighborhood affluence exerts a greater influence on supportive environments for children than concentrated disadvantage. For example, more affluent neighborhoods, as measured by the percentage of well-paid and highly educated residents with professional or managerial jobs, enjoy higher levels of adult supervision and child socialization by neighbors than less affluent neighborhoods, over and above the amount of private resources parents possess. Likewise, more affluent neighborhoods experience a greater degree of neighborly exchange and reciprocal help than less affluent neighborhoods. In addition, neighborhoods located near communities of concentrated affluence reap additional advantages simply from their ecological proximity, regardless of their own standing on measures of adult-child interaction and reciprocal neighborly exchange. In contrast, the usual measures of "underclass neighborhoods," such as the percentage of single-parent families, families below the poverty line, and unemployment rate, exhibited little systematic association with the above two indicators of supportive environments for children.

Without government involvement, the unequal advantages that accrue to communities of concentrated affluence are not likely to be successfully dispersed under existing conditions of economic differentiation and racial segregation in Chicago. It is more likely that some of the surplus affluence can be redirected through tax transfers and government policy to less advantaged communities by subsidizing local networks of adult-child interaction and mutual aid. Successful experimentation in promoting supportive environments for children at the microsystems and mesosystems of kinship, neighborhood, and schools are pointing to new ways of incorporating the ecological outlook into juvenile justice and child welfare policies. Instead of cutting off family, friends, neighbors, and teachers from involvement in the problems of parents and children, the trend is to engage their active participation through family group conferences, conflict mediation, and publicly subsidized mutual aid. The purpose is not to substitute informal processes for formal ones, but to open up new channels of reciprocal influence so that bureaucratic goals can be achieved through flexible means that are fashioned in collaboration with the child's and parent's informal network of social support. The key to success is subsidizing a range of functionally equivalent solutions to a particular problem, such as work-related child care and subsidized adoption or guardianship by kin, so that local officials and citizens can exercise some choice over what solution works best in their particular circumstances.

The flexibility that the federal government has given states under Temporary Assistance to Needy Families (TANF) and child welfare waivers to spend federal dollars are examples of this new direction (Cornerstone Consulting Group, Inc. 1999). After Congress converted the AFDC entitlement program into a block grant in 1996, many states used the flexibility to fund generous earnings-disregards so that welfare recipients could supplement beginning wages with welfare benefits. In Illinois, it is now policy to keep a TANF case for a family of three open until that family's income has reached 99 percent of the poverty level. This is a welcome change from AFDC, under which inadequate grant levels kept family incomes well below the poverty line. In addition, many states have reinvested TANF savings into work-related subsidies so that working families, both on and off TANF, can receive help in paying for child care. Since 1997, TANF caseloads have fallen 50 percent in Illinois and the nation as a whole with no adverse impact on child poverty or foster care.

Another way that states are using financial flexibility to promote "ecologically aware" policies is to subsidize the permanent care of children by relatives who become the adoptive parents or legal guardians of children who cannot live with their parents. In 1993, Congress gave the U.S. Department of Health and Human Services the authority to permit states to spend federal foster care dollars on new approaches to the delivery of child welfare services. In 1996, Illinois obtained waiver authority to offer the option of subsidized guardianship to relatives and foster parents who were hesitant about adopting but were willing to raise their foster children to adulthood. An evaluation of the subsidized guardianship experiment, which included random assignment to control and demonstration groups, showed that offering caregivers a choice produced a 15 percent boost in the rate of moving children to legally permanent homes as compared to the control group (Illinois Department of Children and Family Services 2000).

The common denominator in both TANF and the child welfare waivers is the greater flexibility that states have in establishing federal-state partnerships to address the social ecology of child endangerment. Greater attention to the needs of children, families, and communities at multiple system levels is also a trend in the voluntary sector, such as the Neighbor-to-Neighbor program of the Hull House Association in Chicago and the Family-to-Family program of the national Casey Foundation. These efforts all recognize that improved coordination between informal and formal systems of prevention, support, and care is essential for preserving the vitality of community-based social capital as well as for legitimating the ongoing dependence of vulnerable populations on the financial capital of the welfare state.

CONCLUSION

Over the last hundred years, the urban environment of the Cook County Juvenile Court has shown a remarkable continuity. Despite significant demographic and economic changes, a common set of inner-city neighborhoods has produced a disproportionate share of delinquency, dependency, neglect, and (most recently) abuse cases. Three generations of researchers—social workers, sociologists, and developmental psychologists—have observed and carefully documented this pattern. In spite of differences in interpretation and policy recommendations, they reached similar conclusions.

Considered together, they found little evidence to buttress the "kinds of people" argument that innate inferiority, psychological abnormality, or deviant values of ghetto inhabitants accounted for the much higher rates of community delinquency, abuse, and neglect. In statistical terms, the within-community variance was larger than the between-community variance. Inhabitants of high-risk neighborhoods differed as much in natural proclivities, mental states, and value orientations as inhabitants of low-risk neighborhoods.

Shaw and McKay did the most thorough job in establishing that it was certain "kinds of neighborhoods" that consistently produced the highest delinquency rates, even though the demographic composition of the areas had repeatedly changed as successive waves of ethnic and racial groups moved through them. Economic competition and later racial segregation consigned the least advantaged of each newly arriving group to those sections of the city with the fewest available resources and highest density of need. This imbalance overburdens systems of informal control and support, and eventually leads to their collapse. Formal systems are then invoked to restore some semblance of order. At the early phases of child development, the imbalance depletes social networks of sharing and nurturing resources, and overwhelms individual parenting capacities, which leads to higher rates of child maltreatment and formal child protective intervention (Garbarino and Eckenrode 1997). At later phases, the imbalance inhibits the formation of effective, informal networks of supervision and control, which leads to higher rates of juvenile delinquency and formal juvenile justice intervention (Sampson 1997). Furthermore, there is some evidence of a direct carryover at the ontogenic level from child maltreatment to juvenile delinquency (Widom 1996).

These fundamental facts of the social ecology of child endangerment will probably remain valid well into the twenty-first century. The dilemma that policymakers will continue to confront is whether to buttress the coping capacities of disadvantaged communities to withstand the concentrated effects of poverty, family breakdown, and community disorganization, or to disperse these effects more widely through housing, transportation, and educational policies that put an end to the spatial isolation of the poor. The essential facts have been rediscovered time and again over the last hundred years. How a twenty-first-century democracy acts upon these facts remains an open issue.

REFERENCES

Addams, Jane. 1909. *The Spirit of Youth and the City Streets.* New York: Macmillan.

———. 1910. *Twenty Years at Hull House.* New York: Macmillan.

Breckinridge, Sophonisba P., and Edith Abbott. 1912. *The Delinquent Child and the Home.* New York: Charities Publication Committee.

Bronfenbrenner, Urie. 1979. *The Ecology of Human Development: Experiments by Nature and Design.* Cambridge, MA: Harvard University Press.

Cairns, Robert B., and Beverly D. Cairns. 1994. *Lifelines and Risks: Pathways of Youth in Our Time.* New York: Cambridge University Press.

Carson, Mina. 1990. *Settlement Folk.* Chicago: University of Chicago Press.

Cavan, Ruth. 1928. *Suicide.* Chicago: University of Chicago Press.

Cook, T.; M. R. Herman; M. Phillips; and R. A. Settersten. Forthcoming. *How Neighborhoods, Families, Peer Groups, and Schools Jointly Affect Changes in Early Adolescent Development.* Manuscript.

Cornerstone Consulting Group, Inc. 1999. *Child Welfare Waivers: Promising Directions, Missed Opportunities.* Houston: Cornerstone Consulting Group.

Deegan, Mary Jo. 1988. *Jane Addams and the Men of the Chicago School, 1892–1918.* New Brunswick, NJ: Transaction Books.

Dingwall, Robert. 1989. "Some Problems about Predicting Child Abuse and Neglect." In *Child Abuse: Public Policy and Professional Practice,* ed. Olive Stevenson, 28–53. Hemel Hempstead, U.K.: Harvester Wheatsheaf.

Dodge, Kenneth A. 1986. *Social Competence in Children.* Chicago: University of Chicago Press.

Durkheim, Émile. 1951. *Suicide.* Glencoe, IL: Free Press.

Faris, Robert E. L., and H. Warren Dunham. 1939. *Mental Disorders in Urban Areas.* Chicago: University of Chicago Press.

Furstenberg, Frank F; Thomas Cook; Jacqueline Eccles; Glen H. Elder Jr.; and Arnold Sameroff. 1999. *Managing to Make It: Urban Families in High-Risk Neighborhoods.* Chicago: University of Chicago Press.

Garbarino, James, and Kathleen Kostelny. 1992. "Child Maltreatment as a Community Problem." *International Journal of Child Abuse and Neglect* 16: 455–64.

Garbarino, James, and John Eckenrode. 1997. *Understanding Abusive Families.* San Francisco: Jossey-Bass.

Glueck, Sheldon, and Eleanor Glueck. 1968. *Delinquents and Nondelinquents in Perspective.* Cambridge, MA: Harvard University Press.

Hull House Maps and Papers, by Residents of Hull House, A Social Settlement. 1895. *A Presentation of Nationalities and Wages in a Congested District of Chicago, Together with Comments and Essays on Problems Growing Out of Social Conditions.* New York: Crowell.

Hurrelmann, Klaus, and Stephen F. Hamilton, eds. 1996. *Social Problems and Social Contexts in Adolescence.* New York: Aldine de Gruyter.

Illinois Department of Children and Family Services. 2000. *Interim Evaluation Report: Illinois Subsidized Guardianship Waiver Demonstration.* Springfield, IL: Department of Children and Family Services.

Janowitz, Morris. 1978. *The Last-Half Century.* Chicago: University of Chicago Press.

Jencks, Christopher, and Susan E. Mayer. 1989. *The Social Consequences of Growing Up in a Poor Neighborhood: A Review.* Evanston, IL: Center for Urban Affairs and Policy Research Working Paper, Northwestern University.

Jessor, Richard. 1993. "Successful Adolescent Development among Youth in High-Risk Settings." *American Psychologist* 48: 117–26.

Jessor, Richard, and Shirley L. Jessor. 1977. *Problem Behavior and Psychological Development: A Longitudinal Study of Youth.* San Diego: Academic Press.

Kempe, C. Henry; Frederic N. Silverman; Brandt F. Steele; William Droegemueller; and Henry K. Silver. 1962. "The Battered-Child Syndrome." *Journal of the American Medical Association* 181: 105–12.

Lemert, Edwin M. 1951. *Social Pathology: A Systematic Approach to the Theory of Sociopathic Behavior.* New York: McGraw-Hill.

Lewis, Dorothy Otnow; Catherine Mallouh; and Victoria Webb. 1989. "Child Abuse, Delinquency, and Violent Criminality. In *Child Maltreatment: Theory and Research on the Causes and Consequences of Child Abuse and Neglect,* ed. Dante Cicchetti and Vicki Carlson, 707–21. Cambridge: Cambridge University Press.

Merton, Robert K. 1968. "Social Structure and Anomie." In *Social Theory and Social Structure,* ed. R. K. Merton, 185–214. Enlarged edition. New York: Free Press.

Nelson. Barbara. 1984. *Making an Issue of Child Abuse: Political Agenda Setting for Social Problems.* Chicago: University of Chicago Press.

Park, Robert E., and Ernest W. Burgess. 1925. *The City.* Chicago: University of Chicago Press.

Patterson, Gerald R. 1982. *Coercive Family Process.* Eugene, OR: Castalia.

Robins, Lee. 1974. *Deviant Children Grown Up: A Sociological and Psychiatric Study of Sociopathic Personality.* Huntington, NY: R. E. Krieger.

Rodgers, Daniel T. 1998. *Atlantic Crossings: Social Politics in a Progressive Age.* Cambridge, MA: Belknap Press of Harvard University Press.

Sampson, Robert. 1997. "The Embeddedness of Child and Adolescent Development: A Community-Level Perspective on Urban Violence." In *Violence and Childhood in the Inner City,* ed. Joan McCord, 31–77. Cambridge: Cambridge University Press.

Sampson, Robert J., and John H. Laub. 1993. *Crime in the Making: Pathways and Turning Points through Life*. Cambridge, MA: Harvard University Press.

Sampson, Robert J.; Jeffrey D. Morenoff; and Felton Earls. 1999. "Beyond Social Capital: Spatial Dynamics of Collective Efficacy for Children." *American Sociological Review* 64: 633–60.

Schlossman, Steven; Gail Zellman; and Richard Skavelson; with Michael Sedlak and Jan Cobb. 1984. *Delinquency Prevention in South Chicago: A Fifty-Year Assessment of the Chicago Area Project*. Santa Monica, CA: Rand Corporation.

Shaw, Clifford, and Henry McKay. 1942. *Juvenile Delinquency and Urban Areas*. Chicago: University of Chicago Press.

Shils, Edward. 1961. "The Calling of Sociology." In *Theories of Society,* ed. Talcott Parsons, Edward Shils, Kaspar D. Naegele, and Jesse R. Pitts, 1405–48. New York: Free Press.

Sorrentino, Anthony. 1959. "The Chicago Area Project after Twenty-Five Years." *Federal Probation* 23: 40–45.

Sutherland, Edwin H. 1939. *Principles of Criminology*. New York: Lippincott.

Tannenbaum, Frank. 1938. *Crime and the Community*. Boston: Ginn.

Thomas, William I., and Florian Znaniecki. 1918–20. *The Polish Peasant in Europe and America*. 5 vols. Boston: Richard G. Badger.

U.S. Department of Health and Human Services. Administration on Children, Youth, and Families. 2001. *Child Maltreatment 1999*. Washington, DC: GPO.

Vissing, Yvonne M.; Murray A. Strauss; Richard J. Gelles; and John W. Harrop. 1991. "Verbal Aggression by Parents and Psychological Problems of Children." *Child Abuse and Neglect* 15: 223–38.

Ward, David. 1989. *Poverty, Ethnicity, and the American City, 1840–1925*. Cambridge: Cambridge University Press.

Weissbourd, Bernice. 1987. "A Brief History of Family Support Programs." In *America's Family Support Programs: Perspectives and Prospects,* ed. S. L. Kagan, D. R. Powell, B. Weissbourd, and E. F. Zigler, 38–56. New Haven, CT: Yale University Press.

Widom, Cathy S. 1989. "The Cycle of Violence." *Science* 244: 160–66.

———. 1996. "Psychopathology and Violent Behaviors in Abused and Neglected Young Adults." *Criminal Behavior and Mental Health* 6: 253–71.

Wilson, William J. 1987. *The Truly Disadvantaged: The Inner City, the Underclass, and Public Policy*. Chicago: University of Chicago Press.

PART 4

Juvenile Justice and Child Welfare

The juvenile court was not designed as a stand-alone governmental incursion into the lives of children and has never operated in isolation from other institutions designed to treat and control young people. The two chapters in this section trace the development of governmental efforts to influence and protect youth over the twentieth century. In chapter 10, Bernardine Dohrn traces the manifold relationships between juvenile courts and public schools during a century when educational performance became the defining element for personal, social, and economic advancement in the United States. No governmental institution is anywhere near as important to young people as the public school. Dohrn describes the two-way traffic between court and school, with the school system referring kids to courts and the court system trying to make schools work for kids at risk as part of community-based probation. The chapter documents the unmet need to use detention and institutional placements to educate, a continuing failure of local governments to bring education and juvenile justice into positive alliance.

Peter Edelman's chapter 11 outlines the struggle for a coherent youth policy at the national level of government in the United States. What Edelman calls the politics of youth has never been static or uncontested throughout the twentieth century, and very hard choices of strategy and tactics confront the youth advocate at the turn of the twenty-first century. As the chapter suggests, juvenile justice policy has always been closely linked to the politics of youth and will almost certainly remain so.

10 The School, the Child, and the Court

Bernardine Dohrn

THE HISTORIC DYNAMIC OF SCHOOL AND COURT

The schools and the court were intertwined from the beginning. Theoretically and in practice, the court and the school were part of a social and legal effort to transform the lives of children and their families. The historical development of the juvenile court coincided with social movements for compulsory public education, for the abolition of child labor, and for public playgrounds—a comprehensive program for the development of children. Indeed, justice for children emerged as part of the philosophical mosaic during Reconstruction, linking the freedom and status of African Americans with lively legal and conceptual debates on the nature of children; for if slaves are human, if women are people, then what kind of persons are children? This reframing of the purposes of childhood underlay the effort to create a separate court for children, and was part of the larger effort to expand public education at the turn of the century. When children attend school every day, they will no longer be in the sweatshops and the mines, nor incarcerated with adults in poorhouses and jails. Child well-being, the extension of childhood, and the lawful behavior of children can—in large measure—be understood by the expansion and quality of public education.

The women of Hull House, Jane Addams, Lucy Flower, Julia Lathrop, Florence Kelley, and Alzina Stevens, identified a series of projects regarding the improvement in the lives of predominantly immigrant children on the Near West Side of Chicago at the end of the nineteenth century. Appointed by Governor John R. Tanner to report on institutions in the state as a member of the State Board of Charities, Julia Lathrop inspected jails, prisons, and poorhouses, discovering that children were a substantial part of the populations of these adult institutions. Her efforts galvanized Lucy Flower's ongoing interest in creating a separate court for children in Chicago, a court premised on differences between children and adults and the greater amenability of children to recovery and rehabilitation.

Simultaneously, the founders of the juvenile court were engaged in a massive campaign to remove children from lengthy and hazardous labor—to abolish or restrict child labor through legislation establishing a minimum age and regulating the occupations and hours of child labor. The families at the edge of subsistence living in the neighborhood of Hull House frequently removed a bright daughter or son from school to place them in a factory (Addams 1912, 41–47). Orphaned and dependent children in poorhouses in southern Illinois were apprenticed to notoriously hazardous glass factories (Kelley 1905, 45–56). Children, who turned over their wages to their pauperized parents, remained illiterate, since they were consumed by the daily task of contributing food and rent. Child labor lowered wages for all workers. And working children did not have school time secured to them and a chance for literacy, citizenship, or manual training. For the first two decades of the twentieth century, the founders of the juvenile court investigated, analyzed, and reported upon the presence or absence of children in school, as the singular apt bellwether of progress toward the elimination of child labor and child delinquency.

John Dewey, the preeminent educational philosopher of the twentieth century, frequently lectured at Hull House, where he was a resident and board member during the invention of the juvenile court. His dynamic engagement with both the reformers and the people of the surrounding tenements was a crucible for his thinking and theory on the relationship between life experience and education. His first book, *The Curriculum and the Child,* written while living at Hull House, concludes, "The case is the Child. It is his present powers which are to assert themselves; his present capacities which are to be exercised; his present attitudes which are to be realized" (Dewey 1902). Dewey contributed to a consequential vision of the court as a pedagogic instrument alongside the common school. Both would be public institutions with a mission to create an educated and critical future citizenry capable of adapting to rapidly changing circumstances.

The juvenile court itself was conceived by its founders to be a pedagogy for wayward children, a locus for education, and an instrument of social instruction in the path to citizenship. The court as a "kind and just parent" had guidance and rehabilitation, as well as control or punishment, at its conceptual core. Thus, the divergence between aspiration and reality was fundamental to the juvenile court from its inception. The educative mission of the state, through the person of the judge, was sometimes kind, sometimes harsh, reflecting the inherent tension in a relaxed and individualized court proceeding, but in either event the petitioning of a child or parent to the court was, in good part, perceived as instructive.

Throughout its first century, the court was in dynamic interplay with the public common school. In part, crime and education are understood to be in perpetual tension and interaction; as schools fail immigrant children or exclude children of color, for example, the enticements of life on the streets gain allure and strength. Youngsters fleeing or excluded from school are turned over to the court for truancy adjudication. Schools are asked to adapt to new flocks of children with the challenges of diverse languages, the mobility of rural migrants, physical and mental disabilities, and fragmented families. Various movements to expand or contract resources and support for the public enterprise of education resulted in immediate consequences for the numbers and nature of youthful offenders arriving at the court.

The court and the school are engaged in a complex and flowing dance, sometimes converging in a restless embrace, on occasion moving indifferently back-to-back, often contentiously adhered or calmly linked. The ebbing is both simultaneous and sequential. The liaison runs deep. The orchestration of the public life of childhood insists on dissonance. From time to time, new instruments join in: due process, mandatory reporting, disability education, and zero tolerance. The school and court are bound in an intricate public mission: to teach, to care for, to sanction the young.

Three forces influence this intimate relationship of school and court. First, the historical currents which affect children (for example, the economy, war, racial segregation) impact both school and court. Second, the foundational concepts of the juvenile court—its inherent contradictions, flaws, and limitations—presage recurrent backtracking and swings between rehabilitative and punitive priorities. Third, eras of punishment and control have direct consequences for both school and court. This chapter analyzes these forces in four fundamental aspects of the interplay between school and court: (1) from school to court: the referral of school children to juvenile court; (2) from court to school: probation and parole in schools; (3) the school of the court: schooling in and after correctional, residential custody; and (4) the court as a school: a public pedagogy on the child.

FROM SCHOOL TO COURT: THE REFERRAL OF CHILDREN FROM SCHOOL TO JUVENILE COURT

Schools have been and remain a principal referral source for the juvenile court. Initially, the state used the juvenile court to extend its regulatory thrust to enforce compulsory school attendance by referring habitually absent pupils to court, but the use of the juvenile court to police children greatly expanded over the course of the century. In addition to handling truancy cases, the juvenile court's role expanded as school officials began to refer a wider range of cases involving the regulation of girls and status offenses, school-based offending and violence, and abuse and neglect.

After examining the court's role in policing truants, including the establishment of parental schools in the early twentieth century, this section analyzes the social regulation of girls as truants, runaways, or status offenders for errant behavior such as being "vicious, incorrigible, or immoral in conduct" (Lindsey 1925, 275). This section also examines court referrals of school miscreants as well as student offenders, and the erosion of school-based discipline with the proliferating zero-tolerance policies of the 1990s and the heightened policing of schools. In addition, it focuses on the school as a principal public site where child maltreatment is frequently identified; as mandatory reporters, teachers and school personnel have been permitted for a century, and required for twenty years, to refer children and report parents for suspected child abuse or neglect. Without the wellspring of these abundant school referrals, juvenile court dockets might be more spare.

Policing School Attendance: Truancy and the Parental Schools

Traditional Conceptions of Childhood, School, and Court

The critical philosophical role of school attendance for the founders of the juvenile court cannot be overstated. "The belief that childhood is the period for education and should be spent neither in idleness nor in labor was haltingly expressing itself in our child-labor laws and school laws," wrote Julia Lathrop, reflecting twenty-five years after the establishment of the first juvenile court (Lathrop 1925, 290). The economic pressure on immigrant families to remove their bright sons and daughters from public school and put them to work in factories was documented and lamented (Addams 1916, 40–41). Decades of efforts led to legislative restrictions on the occupations in which children were allowed to work, regulations of their hours of labor, and the minimum age at which children could be employed.

The public common (elementary) school served not only as the educator of the immigrant child, but provided a bridge to the laboring immigrant family. The English language, customs, and social life were—and are—often first acquired by the immigrant child in school. Children become the connectors between parents and society, serving as interpreters, buffers, and facilitators of adult family needs.

School attendance was also perceived as a child protector from the vices, temptations, and distractions of the street. The seductions of urban life, gambling, entertainment, and corruption were to be avoided by compulsory school attendance. "If a boy is once thoroughly caught in these excitements, nothing can save him from over-stimulation and consequent debility and worthlessness; he arrives at maturity with no habits of regular work and with a distaste for its dulness" (Addams 1916, 188). The African American population of Chicago lamented the concentration of vice enterprises in the segregated neighborhoods of the South Side and their influence on African American youth hanging out on the streets. Prominent leaders such as Ida B. Wells Barnett and Irene McCoy-Gaines were early juvenile court probation officers and well versed in concerns about the relationship between lack of education and juvenile delinquency (Canaan 1999, 42).

Schooling was expected only through the primary grades. The child of twelve or thirteen became a wage-earner or wife. The social recognition of childhood as a distinct phase of human development, the extended definitions of childhood, and the emergence of a transitional period of adolescence all clashed on the terrain of the public common school and mandatory school attendance. Compulsory education laws eventually extended to secondary school attendance, but while some form of public school education was typical, less than 7 percent of all seventeen-year-olds graduated from high school at the end of the nineteenth century. By 1940, 51 percent of youth completed high school (Zimring 1982, 26); at the end of the twentieth century, 88 percent of youth graduated from high school (this percentage includes those who completed a high school diploma or an equivalent credential, including a GED; National Center for Education Statistics 1999, 15). Lengthened school attendance reshaped the role and meaning of adolescence, resulted in protracted economic dependence, and spilled over into the social and legal purposes, expectations, and significance of the court (see Edelman, chapter 11 in this volume).

The extended childhood of compulsory education legislation was never synonymous with definitions of legal adulthood. The original age of jurisdiction for both the Denver Juvenile Court and the Chicago Juvenile Court was less than the age of sixteen for any child. Within five years, Illinois extended the age of jurisdiction upward, to include boys under the age of seventeen and any female child under the age of eighteen. Prior to the creation of the juvenile court, the age of criminal responsibility in Illinois was advanced from seven (the English common law age) to ten (Gittens 1994, 91). The shifting legal ages of adulthood today remain in a state of anarchy: states establish different ages for compulsory education, juvenile court jurisdiction, voting, driving, drinking, marriage, consenting to medical procedures, enlisting in the military, execution, termination from foster care, emancipation, and contracting. The perplexing questions of independence and dependency, autonomy and control, and competence and development continue to characterize discourse on the nature of childhood.

Truancy

The regulatory thrust of the juvenile court expanded to sanction truancy and then mushroomed to include punishment and control of status offenders and the control of young females. The significance of schooling for citizenship provided the rationale for jurisdictional interference to compel the education of children. Whether criminal or civil, incarcerating or encouraging, threatening or therapeutic, the court and the school combined forces to identify, regulate, and sanction school absence—and then court jurisdiction ballooned to include punishing the consequent behavior of status offenders such as incorrigibles, runaways, and recalcitrants (see Teitelbaum, chapter 6 in this volume) and the social control of young women.

Truancy predated the juvenile court as a form of delinquency offense. Of the children jailed at the Bridewell (Chicago House of Correction) in 1898, a full 25 percent were incarcerated for truancy. These children were vividly described in the 1889 Annual Report of the Chicago Board of Education: "We should rightfully have the power to arrest all these little beggars, loafers, and vagabonds that infest our city, take them from the streets and place them in schools where they are compelled to receive an education and learn moral principles." This school edict pithily summarizes the simple idea and impossible task of linking arrests with learning.

Truancy loomed so large among youthful offenders that the Colorado juvenile court, under the pioneering vigor of Judge Ben B. Lindsey, established jurisdiction under a truancy law passed just before the Illinois Juvenile Court Act. The statute, which was part of the school law of Colorado, provided for truant officers or teachers in the form of probation officers. It applied to children who were habitually truant, vicious, incorrigible, or immoral in conduct and deemed to be disorderly persons. The Colorado law was "a connecting link between school and court whereby the school helped the court and the court helped the school" (Lindsey 1925, 276).

In Colorado, court jurisdiction and practice extended to parents. Contributory laws of 1903 established chancery jurisdiction for parents and other adults who contributed to the troubles of children, with resort to criminal court only in severe cases. Judge Lindsey repeatedly proposed legislation for compulsory education of parents, mandating attendance at lectures under the direction of the school board on discipline, hygiene, and diet.

Parental coercion necessarily accompanied parental education about compulsory education, for mandatory schooling ran directly against the immediate economic interests of the family. To convince a destitute immigrant family that their child could not be sent into a factory or perform street labor, or a farm family to forgo the morning toil of growing sons, was not simple. Additional parental concerns about religious convictions, cultural practices, and ethnic integrity contributed to resistance. In Illinois, the ties between school and court, truancy and delinquency, while less theoretically explicit than those of Colorado, were similar. In attendance at the Chicago Bar Association committee meeting in Judge Harvey B. Hurd's office on December 10, 1898 was A. G. Lane, superintendent of the public schools. The first certified chief of probation after passage of the Illinois Juvenile Court Act was the president of the Chicago Normal School and an educator of note, Henry W. Thurston.

Intensive studies of school attendance, undertaken by Gertrude Howe Britton of Hull House with the Chicago School Board and visiting nurses, found that the illness of the child or family member and the poverty or ignorance of a parent were the major causes of truancy, while indifferent parents or willful truancy constituted a small minority. In fact, only 2 of the 178 children tracked for school absence were found to be truly incorrigible (Britton 1906, 10). Their report concluded with a series of remedies for problems arising from *without* the school (such as health care and the effects of home environment) and from *within* the school (such as overcrowding, methods of registration and transfer, and suspensions). The report suggested that children no longer be suspended for incorrigibility.

In the succeeding decades, the link between school attendance, truancy, and the abolition of child labor led to continued active monitoring of school truancy by Hull House social activists and scholars Edith Abbott and Sophonisba Breckinridge (Abbott and Breckinridge 1917). Court sanctions for school absence were a consequence of the reformers' drive to regulate hazardous labor and restrict the temptations of idleness for children. These lofty goals, however, repeatedly resulted in reliance on the incarceration of children in the name of education.

Parental Schools

The parental school was conceived of by the reformers as an institution where truants would be committed to be educated. Lucy Flower and the Chicago Women's Club campaigned to establish the John Worthy School for boys incarcerated in the Bridewell, and they supported efforts for compulsory education laws. Male truants were committed to the Parental School established in Chicago in 1902; a similar institution for girls was finally established in 1917. The Parental School Law provided that any truant officer, any agent of the Board of Education, or any reputable citizen could petition the juvenile court to inquire into the conditions of children aged seven to fourteen who were not attending school, were habitually truant, or were in persistent violation of school rules.

The Parental School, located on a 110-acre farm in the northwest corner of Chicago known as Bowmanville, provided the first seven grades of schooling and offered manual and agricultural training until the age of fourteen (Gittens 1994, 116). At the time of the passage of the law, compulsory schooling was mandated until age fourteen. Although schooling was made compulsory until the age of sixteen in 1907, the Parental School Law was not duly extended. By June 1915, 4,198 boys had been sentenced to the Parental School. While the majority of the children were twelve and thirteen years old, youngsters as young as eight were also committed. Most children came from homes of great poverty; one-third were from homes where one parent had died. Boys could be discharged to home from the Parental School if their conduct was appropriate during their first four weeks after commitment, subject for one year to the control of the school. Reports from the home school principal confirmed attendance and behavior. If returned to the Parental School, a boy had to stay for at least three months to be eligible for parole.

By 1899 there was a strong theoretical commitment to keep children at home with their families, utilizing the probation system as the cornerstone of education and community support for both children and their families. However, during the first ten years of the Chicago Juvenile Court, 21 percent of delinquent boys and 51 percent of delinquent girls were committed to institutions such as the Parental School (Breckinridge and Abbott 1912, 9). These institutional "schools" fully embodied the contradictions of *parens patriae* which animated reformers who, before the Civil War, established the initial antecedents to the Parental School: the Chicago Reform School and schools for handicapped children. The strengths and limitations of those earlier schools for children in crisis were to shadow efforts into the present. (See the section entitled "Schooling in and after Residential Juvenile Justice," below.)

With the establishment of the Parental Schools, in tandem with the new Illinois Juvenile Court Act, the regulatory authority of the state over truants was extended and secured, although battles over liberty and state intervention, education and punishment, prevention and imprisonment, protection and parental authority would rage into the present.

Midcentury and Contemporary Shifts in Truancy and Status Offenses

Not until the due process transformations of the 1960s was there a theoretical and substantive change in the role of truancy in juvenile court adjudication. The 1965 Illinois Juvenile Court Act explicitly separated status offenders, including truants, from delinquents, in effect decriminalizing a new category called Minors in Need of Supervision (MINS; see Gittens 1994, 152). Because such truant status offenders were regularly back-doored into detention or correctional facilities by being held in contempt for violation of court orders to attend school, for example, Illinois amended the law to prohibit confinement in secure detention or corrections for MINS defiance of a court order.

Illinois's mid-century experiment of distinguishing status offenders from delinquents failed to result in effective predelinquency intervention. A 1981 study found that less than half of MINS cases received any services, almost 75 percent returned to court, and less than 5 percent of parents received services (Reed et al. 1981, 186). Subsequent legislation, which renamed the status offense category to Minor Requiring Authoritative Intervention (MRAI), sought to rely on voluntary intervention, active youth agencies, and the court as a last resort. With few vigorous youth services thriving for the most vulnerable and impoverished children and virtually no MRAI cases brought to court over the next twenty years, critics suggested that truants, runaways, liquor law and curfew violators, and recalcitrant children were again recriminalized in practice, under simple and growing numbers of delinquency charges.

The Juvenile Justice and Delinquency Prevention Act (JJDPA) of 1974 prohibited the secure detention of status offenders and established federal policy mandating deinstitutionalization of status offenders from juvenile detention and correctional facilities. Truancy allegations dominated those status offender cases brought to juvenile court; some 80 percent of arrests for status offending are diverted at the police station, yet hundreds of thousands of children were arrested each year for truancy. By 1993, as a result of JJDPA, 33,900 children were petitioned to court for truancy, and some 1,099 truants were incarcerated in public or private facilities on a given day, a 33 percent decline from the same measurement taken in 1985 (Steinhart 1996, 88–89). Overall, status offender detention in the fifty states dropped 95 percent by 1988.

Categories such as "stubborn children" or "unruly children" became more frequently used for children who were truant or had special needs. Public order offenses, such as disorderly conduct, liquor law violation, or the ubiquitous delinquency category of "other" increasingly resulted in formal court processing during the 1990s. Part of this backlash against adolescents included legislative efforts to recriminalize and incarcerate truants and runaways in the name of accountability and services. As economic coercion, new provisions in the 1996 welfare reform law (Personal Responsibility and Work Opportunity Reconciliation Act of 1996) mandated school attendance as a condition of eligibility for TANF benefits.

Currently, some jurisdictions petition parents to appear at truancy hearings, with fines or mandatory parenting classes as the remedy. Some states apprehend and evaluate truants during school hours; some penalize truant youth with driver's license revocation or delayed eligibility. Truancy courts are held within lower and middle schools in some jurisdictions, in an effort to identify family problems that are interfering with regular school attendance. In Louisville, Kentucky, the juvenile court initiated the Truancy Court Diversion Project, where court is held in public schools early in the morning. In New Mexico, the Grade Court provides reading and study time during weekend detention, monthly court reviews, and a public (probation)/private partnership with the local college, the public library, parent support in the evenings, and a scholarship fund to attack truancy head-on and to support school attendance.

Public fear of adolescents, concern over youth access to handguns, escalating homicides, and high-profile school shootings have resulted in political shifts and harsher youth control agendas. These forces challenge the quarter-century commitment to decriminalize and deinstitutionalize truants and all status offenders.

Schooling and the Vexing Social Control of Girls

Animating the zeal of early reformers was the condition of girls. Transgressions by girls, in school and in the family, have historically been treated differently than male misbehavior. The combined double standard of paternalism/harshness against young females results in increasing loss of freedom for girls and inequitable responses in juvenile justice programming.

For a century, the impulse to protect children from vice, violence, and corruption has resulted in the disproportionate social control and incarceration of girls. By means of status offense categories which included truants, runaways, incorrigibles, recalcitrants, immoral conduct, unruly children, and involvement in sexual acts or associations, the paternalistic and parental authority of the state moved to protect female children in ways which resulted in their lengthy confinement under brutal conditions—from the Industrial School for Girls to residential placements today. Girls were potentially infectious with venereal diseases as well as moral contamination. In addition, girls were subject to pregnancies, still-births, and abortions.

Girls, Schools, and the Early Reformers

Before the invention of the juvenile court, Lucy Flower and the Chicago Women's Club helped to establish the Protective Agency for Women and Children in Chicago in 1887, providing legal assistance, housing, and employment to women and girls who had been swindled, violently beaten by fathers or guardians, or sexually assaulted. This pioneering work of social justice, spearheaded by Charlotte Holt, was in contrast to the predominant notion of girls and women as carriers of disease, temptation, and immorality. Rape reform included efforts to raise the age of consent for statutory rape from ten to sixteen. This meant that intercourse with a girl under the age of sixteen constituted the crime of sexual assault and was an official acknowledgment of the sexual violence and abuse hidden by families, institutions, and male guardians (Odem 1995).

Similar social purity movements against prostitution and alcohol, spearheaded by the Women's Christian Temperance Union and the Juvenile Protective Association (JPA), worked to monitor places of licentious behavior, such as movie theaters, dance halls, gambling dens, and steamboats, and to establish a morals court. For two decades, the JPA issued investigative pamphlets on the conditions of children, such as exposure of a girl raped by her family's boarder, or the large numbers of girls living in disreputable houses. In 1920, the JPA published *Fighting to Make Chicago Safe for Children,* arguing for supervised social centers, parks, and beaches. The JPA reports, however, which portrayed the black community as a place of debauchery, lewd and indecent dancing, vice, and "free intermingling of the races," were harshly denounced as racist and provocative by the Chicago Urban League. This exchange took place in the aftermath of the 1919 "Race Riot," in which tensions over residential segregation, joblessness, and racism exploded in lethal assaults by whites against African American residents.

The Industrial School for Girls in Evanston was established before the juvenile court for those girls, ages 10–16, who were begging on streets, wandering through streets or alleys, consorting with thieves, loitering in houses of ill fame, or living in poorhouses. The "School" removed girls from incarceration in the Bridewell jail and instead committed them to an institution where, it was hoped, they would be taught and uplifted. Delinquent girls were committed to the Geneva Reformatory for Girls (1895), but their situations were similar to those of girls in the Industrial School (and, indeed, to those of girls throughout the century) convicted of sexual activity (Schaffner 1998, 3–4). The exploitation of girls, confirmed by nineteen cases of venereal disease among the eighty-nine children in Geneva, did not lead to adequate funding or support, and the prevailing Victorian attitude toward "fallen" females penalized children. The Chicago Women's Club also hired a matron to watch over women and girls confined in police stations and jails.

By 1907, delinquent girls confined in the Detention Home were segregated on the third floor, to isolate the "moral contamination" (Knupfer 1999, 52–53). Girls were subject to mandatory pelvic examinations and vaginal cultures, not only to gather evidence about cases of venereal disease, pregnancy, rape, or incest, but also to know whether they had engaged in sexual activity. Parents brought their daughters to the Home to be committed because of immorality, to be disciplined, to alleviate family conflict or economic distress, or to receive medical attention. African American girls were held longer in detention and disproportionately represented.

In the first eight years of the court, 45 percent of girls on probation were returned to court, in contrast to 20 percent of boys. Even the female activists like Breckenridge and Abbott, who acknowledged that the girl herself should be held blameless, wrote, "Yet if she has had intimate knowledge of vice or vicious persons and of vicious conditions, she is not a safe companion for the child who is still ignorant and innocent." In 1910, 81 percent of the girls were brought to court "because their virtue was in peril if it has not already been lost." For girls already involved in prostitution, "there must be recognized the possibility of spiritual contagion and physical infection" (Gittens 1994, 117). Morals offenses committed in and around the school were viewed as particularly dire.

By 1913, the first woman assistant judge, Mary Bartelme, convened a Girls' Court to hear cases of dependent and delinquent girls brought to juvenile court. The closed court was held in a separate room where all personnel—clerk, bailiff, and probation officers—were female. Bartelme recruited the women's clubs to provide suitcases containing clothing, undergarments, and toiletries for each girl appearing before the court. She established Mary Clubs for those girls unable to return to their parents' homes as a way of resisting commitment to a state institution. The first two Mary Clubs, opened in 1914 and 1916, accepted white girls only. By 1921, the board of the Mary Clubs joined with the Friendly Big Sister's League, an organization of African American women reformers, to open a third Mary Club for girls of color. In ten years, more than 2,600 girls passed through the group homes (Gittens 1994, 65–67).

Throughout the 1920s, Bartelme asserted that the social neglect of girls was dramatic, that poverty was the principal cause of delinquency, and that parents must speak frankly with their daughters about sex and spend time understanding their children. Based on her rehabilitative approach, Mary Bartelme ran for elected judge in 1920, after the passage of the Nineteenth Amendment which recognized the citizenship of women; with the support of the National Association of Colored Women's Clubs, the juvenile court judge, and women's clubs, she served for another decade as a Chicago, a national, and an international champion for children who relied on probation and volunteer services to keep most children from institutional incarceration.

Contemporary Girls, Truancy, and Gender-Related Offenses

Girls, historically and still today, constitute an invisible but substantial proportion of less serious delinquent behavior, such as larceny (shoplifting) and status offenses (behavior which would not be criminal for adults). Girls constitute 47 percent of truants, 63 percent of runaways, 44 percent of incorrigibles, 35 percent of alcohol violators, and 28 percent of those arrested for curfew violations (Snyder and Sickmund 1999, 198–200). Girls' offenses commonly involve sexually related and gender-specific behavior such as school truancy related to pregnancy or family problems, having an older boyfriend, running away to escape sexual abuse, or participation in prostitution. Evidence of delinquent girls' extreme victimization in the form of sexual and physical abuse is well documented (Chesney-Lind and Shelden 1998; Schaffner 1998).

In 1995, 23.4 percent of girls' arrests involved status offenses (compared to less than 10 percent for boys); another 25 percent of girls who are arrested are charged with larceny theft (shoplifting). Girls in foster care or group home placements who run away can be classified as delinquent and incarcerated, for example, rather than identified as foster children who could be supported with special programming, or status offenders who cannot be incarcerated. Girls are perceived as defiant and oppositional by courts and police; curfew arrests of girls mushroomed 155.2 percent between 1987 and 1996 (Chesney-Lind 1999).

Constitutional challenges to status offense statutes, such as "danger of leading an idle, dissolute, lewd or immoral life" (*Gonzalez v. Maillard,* Civil No. 50424, N.C. Cal. [1972]) or "danger of becoming morally depraved" (*Gesicki v. Oswald,* 336 F. Supp. 371, S.D.N.Y. [1971]), have sometimes led to court rulings that they are impermissibly vague. Concurrently, statutes which disproportionately affect girls by permitting "voluntary" commitment to a mental institution of youths by their parents have been sustained (*Parham v. J.R.,* 442 U.S. 584 [1979]). The constitutional protection of the right to counsel for children in trouble with the law does not extend to status offenders.

Females constituted 47 percent of the youthful status offenders confined in residential placement in 1997, although they were only 11 percent of youth confined in residential placement as delinquents (Snyder and Sickmund 1999, 109). Girls were increasingly incarcerated in private facilities (62 percent) for violations of court orders or status offenses (85 percent of those in private institutions), while the population in public detention facilities remained steady. The contemporary two-track system of juvenile justice, based on race and economic status, results in white girls being referred for "treatment," while African American and Latina girls are detained; more than half the population in private facilities for girls are white females. The juvenile court, for a century, has received referrals from schools for both truancy and gender-related offenses, which disproportionately affect young females.

School-Based Offending and the Court

Most school-based offenses are addressed within the schoolhouse. Traditional school discipline policies, including classroom reprimands ("time-out," dunce cap, standing in a corner or hallway, writing on the blackboard, special assignments), referral to the vice principal's office (calling parents, after-school detention, written apologies), corporal punishment, and suspension or expulsion, have sufficed to maintain decorum, order, and an appropriate code of conduct within the school. At critical junctures—and increasingly—law enforcement, constitutional standards, and court jurisdiction have extended into school life.

Traditional School Disciplinary Policies

By 1905, the court founders had broadened the scope of delinquency jurisdiction and the terrain on which youth misbehavior could occasion court intervention. The sweeping statutory revision raised the age of childhood to seventeen for boys and eighteen for girls, and encompassed any child who "wanders about the streets in the night time without being on any lawful business or occupation; . . . or habitually uses any vile, obscene, vulgar, profane, or indecent language; or who is *guilty of any immoral conduct in any public place or about any school house*" (Laws of the State of Illinois 1905, 152). Confidence in the restorative and broad discretionary powers of the juvenile court judge led to sweeping expansion of the mission.

Yet the stakes of school discipline remained mild, if unsettlingly varied and inequitable. Most school sanctioning was swift and carried the approval or acquiescence of parents or guardians. Battles fought within the schools over prayer, religion, flags, appropriate reading material, and school holidays raged on through the legal system and control of school boards, but was not centered on discipline. The pervasiveness of corporal punishment in schools gradually shifted as mores, practices, and liability changed, although statutes permitting corporal punishment of children in schools persisted through the twentieth century. Significant racial differences are documented in the application of corporal punishment (and other forms of discipline) in schools (Gregory 1996).

Little rulemaking was undertaken by schools. Since schools were traditionally and fiercely a local undertaking, a wide range of regional and cultural practices and procedures developed. Until the rights upheaval of the late 1960s, schools conducted the bulk of their punishment within the building, and called on police and the courts only for extreme or protracted criminal activity by students.

By 1975, the due process revolution reached schools on the issue of student suspensions. In *Goss v. Lopez,* a closely divided Supreme Court held that notice and the opportunity for "some kind of hearing" were required before a school could suspend a student. The due process clause of the Constitution would not, in a school setting, require the full-fledged formal hearing, with the accompanying right to counsel, and the evidentiary burden of proof beyond a reasonable doubt. Balancing fairness with the realities of school life and authority, the slim majority held that the student must be provided with an opportunity to be heard in an informal exchange with school administrators. Four dissenting justices felt that even this requirement would undermine school discipline (*Goss v. Lopez,* 419 U.S. 565 [1975]). Subsequent court decisions upheld a range of law enforcement penetration into the traditional domain of school governance: locker searches, drug testing, and speech and dress code restrictions to maintain school order and lawful behavior were constitutionally approved (Raskin 2000).

Disabled Children and Special Education

For three quarters of a century, children with disabilities were segregated at home, placed in special schools, institutionalized, or petitioned to the court as delinquents for "acting out" in disruptive school misbehavior. Parents, juvenile court judges, probation officers, and correctional superintendents struggled to alert the public to the injustices to which disabled children were subject. Upset and disorderly youngsters who learn differently were—and continue to be—shipped from school to court to training school.

In 1975, the Individuals with Disabilities Education Act (IDEA) assured that all children with disabilities have available to them a free, appropriate, public education regardless of the handicap, which includes special education and related services designed for their unique needs. This watershed extension of educational rights remains one of the few entitlements for children, and extends to age twenty-one. The law requires children to be identified, evaluated, and provided with individualized educational programs. IDEA applies to all disabled children in detention, in correctional facilities, and upon release from custody. Furthermore, a child cannot be excluded from school for conduct related to his or her disability (*Honig v. Doe,* 484 U.S. 305 [1988]). Although a school is permitted to suspend or expel a disabled or special-education child for conduct unrelated to his or her disability, the school district remains obligated to provide appropriate education.

Two additional vehicles for the social control of children in schools are risk assessment instruments and pharmacology. Increasingly, children are profiled, identified, and medicated (sometimes without assessment, evaluation, or consent; see FBI 2000). The need for order in school behavior can become the rationale for medicating difficult, disruptive, or just different children for a condition or syndrome. Each decade produces emerging labels for nonconforming children: from unruly and incorrigible to disadvantaged and deprived; from autistic or dyslexic to bipolar or low-functioning; from at-risk and vulnerable to attention deficit disorder (ADD), attention deficit hyperactivity disorder (ADHD), post–traumatic stress disorder (PTSD), behavior disorder (BD), and learning-disabled (LD). Certain behavior labels carry pharmacological remedies, administered in schools as a condition of school attendance. In many ways, the contemporary medication of children in schools, detention, and correctional facilities is the echo of the early progressives' optimism about science, experts, and psychology.

Though far from fully implemented, IDEA was a culmination of efforts by parents and professionals to obtain a decent education for their children—not unlike the two centuries of struggle by parents and teachers to insist on the teaching of African American children. Broad and varying strategies were employed—integration and mainstreaming, separation and private academies or boarding schools to promote excellence—to marshal the social will and the resources to teach those children, who were too often isolated, marginalized, and excluded.

Yet disabled and mentally ill children continue to be referred from school to court to corrections. At the end of the century, human rights reports document pervasive abuses in the Georgia juvenile correctional system and at the Jena and Tullulah, Louisiana, private, for-profit juvenile facilities where mentally retarded and disabled children are brutalized by untrained staff, left naked on concrete cell floors, and confined without sufficient food or medical treatment (Human Rights Watch 1996; Butterfield 1998, 2000).

Violence, Policing Schools, and Zero Tolerance

In the 1990s, public fear of adolescents mounted. A tangled interplay of factors accounted for this concern, including increased youth access to lethal handguns, the syndicalization of territorial youth gangs into illegal drug cartels, racist stereotyping of urban youth, academic and political pandering, media frenzy, and a spate of high-profile school shootings of students by their fellow students (Zimring 1998). These elements reinforced and strengthened each other, leading to practices which criminalize more youth behavior and sanction the expulsion of substantially greater numbers of children from school. In fact, the fear of youth violence led, quite innocently, to a series of laws and practices which transformed school environments and punished children by depriving them of an education.

The subsequent increased policing of schools resulted in a significant increase in school-based arrests. The presence of police and school personnel dedicated to security is only a piece of the transformation of the school landscape in the 1990s. Many schools became more prisonlike: locked doors, closed campuses, metal detectors, classroom lock-downs and simultaneous locker searches, heavily armed tactical police patrols, dogs, camera surveillance, uniforms, expansive disciplinary codes, interrogations, and informers—these are some elements that contributed to the criminalization of school life. Policies, funding streams, and hardware for militarizing schools increased. Public fear resulting from a handful of high-profile school shootings and a decade of vilifying adolescents led to the abdication by educators of the pedagogic responsibility of discipline—the "teachable moment" (Brooks, Schiraldi, and Ziedenberg 2000). Teachers and principals ceded their authority to law enforcement personnel, particularly police and prosecutors, and willingly participated in excluding troublemakers, difficult kids, and children in trouble from the very education that is their primary hope (Dohrn 2000a; Dohrn, forthcoming).

Schools became more direct feeders of children into juvenile and adult criminal courts. Although victim self-reports indicate that school crime numbers have not significantly changed in twenty years, there were increased arrests and court referrals: some 350,000 school arrests in 1997—just prior to the major escalation in school policing and surveillance. Most school crime is theft (about 62 percent). Fighting, vandalism, and theft, traditionally handled within school disciplinary systems, were transformed into delinquency offenses. The primary offenses resulting in school arrests at a major Chicago high school in 1996–97 were pager possession, disorderly conduct, and mob action. For most of the twentieth century, it would have been difficult to imagine police being called, arrests and handcuffs employed, and court filings and incarceration being options for incidents where no serious injury resulted.

Punishment by exclusion from school exploded as a national trend in the 1990s. Fueled initially by federal legislation (i.e., Gun-Free Schools Act [1994]) aimed at excluding guns from schools, which mandated a one-year exclusion for possession of a firearm on school property, state legislatures rushed to comply to maintain federal funding eligibility. Within a year, the federal prohibition was revised to "dangerous weapon" rather than firearm, and the school exclusion stampede was launched. As states added drug possession, drug paraphernalia, or assaults on school personnel as a basis for suspension or expulsion, school exclusion skyrocketed.

Disproportionate discipline of students of color, particularly African American boys, has been documented for twenty-five years. Corporal punishment, humiliation, isolation, and referrals to the vice principal historically, and suspensions or expulsions today, are imposed disproportionately on African American youth, providing evidence of pervasive and systemic bias in school discipline (Skiba et al. 2000; Gordon, Piana, and Keleher 2000). Many states and localities have no requirement or provision for alternative education for excluded students. Since school attendance is widely accepted as a major protective factor against arrest and delinquency, school expulsion can lead to a greater likelihood of arrest, detention, and prison. School expulsion becomes a harsh life sentence, narrowing future options for literacy, employment, and family life, and increasing the likelihood of prison.

By the end of the twentieth century, changes in confidentiality provisions permit greater interpenetration of school and court. The school is informed of the arrest, detention, or conviction of a youth, whether related to or distant from school activity. Police, probation, and law enforcement have immediate access to the school records of a child. The widespread police presence within schools as well as laws requiring the exclusion of certain youth restricts access to public education for misbehaving children. Pupils or gangsters—the polarized choices about who children are and where children belong, and the resulting allocation of social resources to engage them, continue to reflect the contested aspects of childhood.

The synergistic relationship of schools and law enforcement goes further in jurisdictions like Chicago, which permit schools to suspend or expel students who have been charged with or convicted of violating the law even when the alleged delinquent or criminal behavior did not occur on school property or during school hours. A series of federal and state laws facilitate an even greater exchange of previously confidential records among schools, juvenile courts, and police. This increased relaxation of confidentiality protections for youth may further increase the incidence of school suspensions or expulsions and school-based arrests. School notification of a student's arrest, probation, and detention may be a factor in greater classroom scrutiny or in being identified as a "bad kid."

At the end of the twentieth century, the administration of school discipline has been transferred, in part, directly to the court and its agencies. The nature of the punishment for school offending or disruption is more likely to be school arrest or school expulsion.

School Referrals to Court for Child Abuse and Neglect

When parents can no longer care for their children, it is a catastrophe. Without caretakers, fortunate children may rely on relatives or friends, but many are left with the ultimate backup of the broader society and public care. The maltreated, the orphan, the abused child is a trope of literature and popular culture, yet the children are generally isolated, without a constituency, and largely invisible. School is one of the few places where a child's suffering is visible outside the home, and schooling is potentially an institution of safety and protection. Thus, the schoolhouse became a primary location and referral source for state child welfare intervention. State interference in the family and efforts to raise the minimum standard of protection for children have encountered public indifference and, at times, the concentrated opposition of existing private and religious child welfare agencies, since caretakers of dependent children were political appointees from the post–Civil War days of the Illinois Soldiers' Orphans' Home (Gittens 1994, 24–25). Furthermore, dependent children were costly to the state.

Traditional Orphanages and Poorhouses

Poor and dependent children were apprenticed under conditions of hard labor and obedience, often by poor laws which provided no legislative assurance of an education. Orphanages and poorhouses were crowded with youngsters. By 1870, the Illinois Humane Society worked to find homes and create institutions for rescued children such as foundlings' homes (abandoned infants), the homeless children "waif's mission," and the Evanston Industrial School for Girls.

The industrial schools acts of 1879 and 1883 provided state subsidies to create institutions that were a mixture of orphanages and reform schools; actual schooling included a common school education, domestic skills for girls, and vocational (primarily farming) skills for boys. The industrial schools survived legal challenges based on unconstitutional incarceration when the Illinois Supreme Court found them to be schools, not prisons (*In re Ferrier,* 103 Ill. 367 [1882]). Yet as juvenile court founders later noted, children who were found dependent by county or probate judges would automatically be committed to an industrial school for their minority. The schools, as guardians, could discharge, place out, or institutionalize at their discretion (Lathrop 1925, 292).

The removal of children from homes of "absolutely nothing hopeful," from families who were debauched, drunken, or utterly wretched, was perceived as delinquency prevention. And many abandoned and impoverished children were found begging and stealing in order to survive. The links between dependent, abused, and delinquent children were flexible, permeable, and constant.

Despite decades of efforts, the almshouses and poorhouses remained crowded with women and children, who shared space with the chronically sick, the insane, the mentally and physically handicapped, and the desperately poor. Julia Lathrop reported on the Cook County poorhouse as a member of the State Board of Charities in 1894: "There are usually from fifty to seventy-five children, of whom a large proportion are young children with their mothers, a very few of whom are for adoption. The remainder, perhaps a third, are the residuum of all the orphan asylums and hospitals, children whom no one cares to adopt because they are unattractive or scarred or sickly. These children are sent to the public school across the street from the poor-farm. Of course they wear hideous clothes, and of course the outside children sometimes jeer at them" (Lathrop 1970, 144).

A movement by private agencies to remove children from the poorhouses into private child care institutions met with the fierce opposition of parents, for the agencies required the termination of parental rights before they would take the children. In desperation, most mothers found interim placements for their children, rather than relinquish their parental rights. By 1870, the county agent refused to enforce the rule prohibiting access to the Cook County Poorhouse to all parents who refused to give consent to the adoption of their children as a precondition to admission (Gittens 1994, 94–95).

The Early Court and Children Harmed

The juvenile court founders broke ground for state intervention on behalf of children on the issue of compulsory education. The vital and public interest in a child's schooling could override the common law right of a father to control and determine his children's education. The changing conditions of industrial society, urbanization, and immigration required that children be prepared for life by being literate, skilled, and protected during childhood. New conditions required preparation, flexibility, and an individualized response for each child. These elements and the corresponding need for state intervention into the private family domain were ingredients for the new juvenile court jurisdiction as well as for compulsory education laws. These developments also provided arguments against placing children in institutions as a substitute for families: regimentation, obedience, and dependence were the opposite qualities of the healthy, schooled, and independent citizens needed by society.

The early juvenile court's jurisdiction over dependent and abused children was more limited than the court's delinquency power. Only children brought to the court's attention by parents, police, or interested citizens were covered. Children could be placed in private agencies without becoming wards or being subject to the court's scrutiny and review. The Industrial Schools, which predated the juvenile court, resisted the court's assertion of guardianship and decision making. Outside of Chicago, the rural counties rarely employed probation officers or had social service agencies at all. Even by 1940, just over one-third of the counties in Illinois employed a probation officer.

Boarding homes and foster homes which received payments for keeping a neglected child became the preferred choice of child welfare advocates, in large part because the academic education of the child, not the child's labor contribution, could become the first priority.

But the flaws and limitations in the court's early foundational concepts resulted in a significant gap between theory and practice. The Children's Bureau study of the juvenile court in 1922 reported that 40.7 percent of dependent children in Chicago's court from 1915 to 1917 were sent to institutions, primarily the state subsidized industrial schools. Girls who had been severely abused or harmed but considered contaminated were sent to reformatories for delinquent girls to keep them away from more innocent dependent children. A study of the Geneva Reformatory found thirty-two girls placed for dependency, one girl for "rape, venereal disease, St. Vitus dance, and tuberculosis," and three more for rape (Gittens 1994, 42).

The Colored Women's Clubs of Chicago established homes for dependent children, such as the Phyllis Wheatley Home, the Giles Charity Club, and the Children's Aid Society, and worked tirelessly to make social services available to black Chicago residents. Settlement houses, such as the Frederick Douglass Center and the Wendell Phillips Settlement, were founded to deal directly with youth activity, education, and delinquency prevention, as were neighborhood branches of the YMCA and the Urban League.

Black dependent children, despite these efforts, were more likely to be placed in delinquent facilities or jails. In 1913, the Juvenile Protective Association reported that one-third of the young girls and women in Cook County jail were African American, and in 1923, 16 percent of the girls at Geneva Reformatory were black, although they constituted only 2 percent of the population of Illinois. This inequality and disproportion accelerated as the century progressed.

The five white agencies, which had a policy of accepting children of color in the first two decades of the court, generally segregated black children. The sudden closing of two major institutions for African American dependent children, the Amanda Smith Home for Girls (where two children were killed in a fire), and the Louise Manual Training School for Colored Boys in 1919–20, created a precipitous crisis. African American leaders were outspoken about the conditions of inequality and poverty; Ida B. Wells Barnett, antilynching crusader and a former juvenile court probation officer, and Irene McCoy Gaines were among those who identified unemployment and inequality as the foundations for delinquency. Louise deKoven Bowen produced a major report in 1913 on "The Colored People of Chicago," directly attacking the conditions of race prejudice and discrimination which exacerbated the difficult conditions of poor housing, unemployment, and police arrests (Bowen 1913). Abbott and Breckinridge studied and publicized the impact of racial discrimination on colored children and the continuing struggle faced by their parents.

By the 1930s, the scandals from orphanage brutality, staff turnover, and the high cost of institutional care were factors leading to the Depression-era formalization and later federalization of mothers' pensions. Welfare payments to single parents became a cost-effective way of subsidizing home care for needy children, where possible.

Midcentury Child Abuse and the Battered Child

Not until the 1960s were the terms *dependent, neglected,* and *abused* children made distinct with a new medical awareness of child abuse made possible by pediatric radiology, which revealed patterns of repeated physical injuries. In 1961, the American Academy of Pediatrics introduced the phrase *battered child syndrome* at a symposium on child abuse. Most states passed legislation regarding medically confirmed abuse and mandated professional reporting. New laws granted reporters immunity from retaliatory lawsuits, in order to overcome the reluctance to interfere in family privacy. By 1975, Illinois had expanded its jurisdiction with the Abused and Neglected Child Reporting Law, requiring mandatory reporting of neglect, a more elusive concept, as well as physical abuse, sexual abuse, and mental injury.

Contending Rights and Federal Legislative Child Welfare Standards

Legal challenges to the court-sanctioned removal of children led to a series of court opinions reshaping parental rights and the role of state interference. In two cases, the residual rights of parents were affirmed by the U.S. Supreme Court. *Santosky v. Kramer* held that parental rights could not be terminated unless unfitness was proven by clear and convincing evidence; *Stanley v. Illinois* affirmed the right of unmarried fathers to participate in hearings on the care and custody of their children (*Santoskey v. Kramer,* 455 U.S. 745 [1982]; *Stanley v. Illinois,* 405 U.S. 645 [1971]). And in *Smith v. Organization of Foster Families for Equality and Reform,* long-term foster parents sought and lost the right to a court hearing before their foster child was removed because, despite the bonds created by their role as psychological parents, they did not have the same due process rights as biological parents because they were a creation of the state (*Smith v. Organization of Foster Families for Equality and Reform (OFFER)),* 431 U.S. 816 (1977).

By 1980, the Illinois legislature had further expanded the universe of mandated reporters and initiated a twenty-four-hour hotline for anonymous reports of child abuse or neglect. Abusers could be teachers, child-care workers, or foster parents, as well as parents and family members. Reports skyrocketed and child welfare agencies, ordered to investigate within twenty-four hours or immediately in an emergency, ballooned in staff.

In 1980, major child welfare legislation unintentionally resulted in substantially more children becoming state wards or foster children; they endured longer stays in foster care and suffered multiple placements, or "foster care drift," with the attendant school disruption and school failure. The Adoption Assistance and Child Welfare Act (AACWA), an amendment to Title IV-B of the Social Security Act, was the result of a consensus that because the state was a poor parent, its child protection intervention should be restricted. The law provided 75 percent federal matching funds for state foster care, mandated permanency planning hearings, and required reasonable efforts to prevent removal of children from their families and reasonable efforts to return them before termination of parental rights. AACWA set timetables to restrict the lengthy delays in court proceedings and subsequent foster care drift, and required a case plan and periodic court reviews.

Due to a combination of complex factors, including recession, welfare restrictions, and an epidemic of cocaine and crack addiction among poor women of childbearing age, child welfare systems by the late 1980s found themselves swamped with increasing cases of extreme poverty as well as physical and sexual abuse, despite the legislative intent to limit state interference with families. Agency inability to implement the spirit, let alone the letter, of the act was challenged. Children who were not quickly returned home were moved from foster care home to foster care or institutional placement; their school placements multiplied and their educational lives suffered. Legal advocates challenged the practices of state child welfare agencies in class action litigation and exposed *official* abuse and neglect. Class action cases confronted agencies about their failure to educate state wards, their classification of all wards as special education students, and their practice of bouncing children from school to school. Growing up in foster care became synonymous with hardship, separation, and scandal.

One consequence of late-century circumstances was the increasing placement of foster children with relatives. The urban explosion of kinship care had proponents and opponents, but one consequence was the greater likelihood that a neglected or dependent child would remain in a familiar neighborhood with known family as foster parents and would therefore be more likely to sustain a stable school placement.

In the 1990s, federal legislation attempted to repair some of the official abuses of child welfare through the Adoption and Safe Families Act (AFSA). AFSA shortened the length of wardship, mandated and eased termination of parental rights, and provided dollar incentives for adoption. Reformers in Chicago seized the opportunity to reduce unconscionable case backlogs, and more than twenty thousand terminations of parental rights and subsequent adoptions were adjudicated within three years (Dohrn 2000b). Screening and gatekeeping were instituted to assure that cases which did not require court adjudication were handled directly by the child welfare agency.

Thus a century of efforts failed to prevent the state removal of destitute children from families who wanted to care for them: mothers' pensions, welfare, and federal legislation mandating state efforts to prevent removal all failed in fundamental ways to build a sustained consensus to alleviate poverty. Public concern for the most sympathetic children, those who were harmed or without a caring family, led primarily to strategies which promoted permanency planning, particularly adoption. The stark choices of strengthening families, removing children into institutions, or placing them with substitute families remained the same, but the implementation was frighteningly complex. The life-altering role of schools and schooling for children who were harmed remained a pivotal way-station. But punishing children for their misfortune recurred in different decades and across the nation.

Thus in a myriad of ways across the twentieth century, schools referred children to the juvenile court: for truancy; to control girls; to punish school disciplinary offenses; and to respond to child abuse or neglect. As education was weakened or failed specific children, crime and delinquency flourished. Both school and court were founded with dual purposes of guidance or education, and control or punishment, which furthered their profound interdependence as various economic and social currents affected children. The school consistently emerged as a principal referral source for juvenile court cases.

FROM COURT BACK TO SCHOOL: JUVENILE COURT PROGRAMS FOCUSED ON SCHOOLS

The juvenile court referred children under its jurisdiction back to school. Most court orders, whether for dependent, neglected, or delinquent children, included an order to attend school, and part of the court's authority was to enforce its sentencing order through monitoring and sanctions. Social control "in the best interest of the child" included schooling as its centerpiece—for the same reasons that made truancy a court offense in the first instance. In the legal transition from court to school, educational continuity loomed large. Probation became the new tool for extending the reach of the court into the child's community, and school was the primary institution for probationary supervision. (See the discussion of probation in Tanenhaus, chapter 2 in this volume.) Conditions of school attendance became a routine part of court sentencing. Some courts themselves developed schools, which delinquent children were ordered to attend as part of an alternative sentencing scheme.

The School, Probation, and Court Enforcement of Educational Continuity

A unique invention of the juvenile court was the system of community implementation and monitoring through the person of a skilled, committed probation officer responsible for overseeing the home situation of dependent, neglected, and delinquent children. The probation officer's assignments were to supervise, control, support, and *educate* the child and the family; enforce school attendance; and report back to the court. Through probation, the court became a direct social welfare agency, as well as a monitoring unit. Probation was the linchpin which allowed the court to keep children at home and attending school wherever possible, and therefore out of reform schools, training schools, correctional facilities, and institutional custody.

Probation, Schools, and the Early Years

The original Illinois Juvenile Court Act provided for the essential role of a probation officer, but made no salary provision. Lucy Flower created the Juvenile Court Committee (JCC), led the first year by Julia Lathrop and thereafter by Louise deKoven Bowen. The JCC provided volunteers to assist and sit next to the judge during juvenile court sessions and raised private funds to support first one and then four probation officers. Alzina Stevens, a Hull House activist, factory inspector with Florence Kelley, and investigator of tenants, was appointed as the court's first probation officer. Timothy Hurley, president of the Catholic Visitation and Aid Society, was appointed chief probation officer as great care was given to balance and support among religious interests. Court founders agitated to have probation officers hired by the county but selected by civil service examinations. Judicial appointment of probation officers was resisted as an opportunity for corruption and patronage. In 1905, a legislative amendment provided funding for probation officers' salaries and made their appointment subject to a civil service exam. Henry Thurston of the Chicago Normal School became chief probation officer after a career as an educator, replacing Hurley. The careful effort to provide multireligious unity was challenged, and then reachieved.

Almost from the beginning, black as well as white probation officers were hired. Activists from the Chicago YWCA and outspoken Colored Women's Club members attacked the causes of African American juvenile delinquency, high discriminatory unemployment, low wages, and the scarcity of parks, playgrounds, and recreational facilities for youth. By the time of the great migration of African Americans from the South and the formation of the Black Metropolis, black youth accounted for 21.2 percent of the delinquency arrests in Chicago (Drake and Cayton [1970] 1993; Canaan 1999, 41).

Initially, probation officers reported to the police, and Chicago's mayor assigned one police officer from each district to patrol the streets in civilian clothes conducting probation work. By 1900, however, the officers reported to the chief of probation (McNamee 1999, 19–20). Probation's relationship to police and law enforcement, and the issue of their primary allegiance, foreshadowed a century of tension and inherent conflict, which accelerated as the court became more adversarial after the due process transformations of the 1960s.

Probation officers investigated cases petitioned to juvenile court, conducted home visits to understand the conditions of children, and offered advice to parents. In the winter of 1900, probation officers went with police to a home where sixteen African American children, ages eleven and younger, were found cold and starving. Brought to juvenile court and placed out by Judge Tuthill, the children made headlines and were cared for, and charges were dismissed against the woman who ran the home.

As remembered by Mrs. Bowen, probation officers initially met frequently with the Juvenile Court Committee about their duties. Since there was no literature and no model, they developed their own best understanding. "They must be men and women of many sides, endowed with the strength of a Samson and the delicacy of an Ariel. They must be tactful, skillful, firm, and patient. They must know how to proceed with wisdom and intelligence and must be endowed with that rare virtue—common sense" (Bowen 1925, 300). In short, probation officers conducted most of the court's day-to-day business.

In contrast to Chicago probation officers' ties to police, Colorado probation officers were truant officers or teachers, since the initial statute was part of the school law in Colorado. Judge Ben B. Lindsey was himself chief probation officer. Twenty-five years later, Judge Lindsey noted that their statute foreshadowed what child welfare advocates were fostering: a plan to make juvenile court part of the school system. All children were either school children or working children.

In 1911, juvenile probation became the center of a firestorm when the Cook County Board of Supervisors accused it of incompetence, corruption, and child-snatching. Seized upon by the Hearst papers, the issue rocked the juvenile court and became the topic of hearings by the board-appointed Hotchkiss Commission. Their report suggested improvements but reaffirmed the value of the juvenile court (Tanenhaus 1999).

A chronic shortage of probation officers in rural settings led to an inflated use of correctional sentences. A 1931 Illinois child welfare study reported the story of a boy with no previous record who stole twelve dollars' worth of merchandise from a filling station. Although the state's attorney noted that the lad's father was dead and that the court believed he could be reformed, he was given a one-year-to-life sentence at Pontiac prison (Report of the Committee 1931, 200–207).

At its heart, the mechanism of probation allowed children to be brought under the net of social control and monitoring enforced by the juvenile court without removing them from their families, communities, and schools. Educational continuity could not only be preserved but assured with confidence by regular visits and the scrutiny of a probation officer. The wayward child would be under the watchful eye of the legal system, but—theoretically at least—committed to reformatories and training schools only as a last resort. Confidentiality of juvenile court records and a strong probation staff permitted delinquency to become a minor event in the life of the child and family and preserved the offender's opportunities for education, career, and normal family life.

Middle Years: Professionalizing Probation, Social Work, and the Court Clinic

By the court's third decade, notions of the scientific, psychological, and sociological complexity of delinquency eclipsed the fervor for public-spirited justice of the founders. Probation officers were expected to be specialists—not simply kind-hearted persons with common sense. One such "objective" and authoritative school of Freudian thought posited internal childhood conflict between aspects of the psyche and the maladjustment of the individual to surroundings. In certain ways, this perspective challenged the reformers' perspective on the developmental nature of childhood and the underlying corruption of brutal social conditions. Yet the psychological framework was to influence generations of court officials, youth workers, and the emerging profession of social workers.

By the late 1930s, social circumstances included the Depression, labor strikes and organizing drives, impending world war, and fear of the unemployed; together, these conditions affected both the children and the resources of the juvenile justice system. Illinois Senate hearings on conditions at St. Charles Reformatory in 1939 revealed that 56 percent of the boys' families were dependent, 25 percent were marginal, and only 20 percent were self-supporting. No mention was made in the commission's hearings of the Depression or its consequences for children (A History 1939, 129).

An alternate view came from the Institute for Juvenile Research and its affiliated sociology faculty from the University of Chicago. To them, delinquency and related gang activity was a reasonable, not maladjusted, response to circumstances and social options. Clifford Shaw and his team initiated the Chicago Area Project to promote positive opportunities for youth within four specific communities based on each community's identification of values and appropriate measures. Community action staff was a mixture of neighborhood residents, university students, and older youth released from reformatories. The strategy, reminiscent of 1960s community organizing projects such as those of Saul Alinsky and the federally funded War on Poverty, was to keep neighborhood youth away from police and juvenile court with informal settlements and community solutions.

School as a Condition of Court Sentencing

During the ensuing decades, probation officers coerced and reinforced school attendance for children under their jurisdiction as a condition of probation. Violation of that condition was a violation of a court order, and could result in detention or a sentence to corrections. Compelling the school attendance of youth on probation is difficult because of the lure of the street, gang life, illiteracy, or the discomfort of having fallen behind, combined with the frequent desire of the school *not* to have the youth enrolled.

There are sound reasons for a school's reluctance to reenroll a delinquent or disruptive youth. Teachers and principals may well have exhausted their internal remedies for sanctioning a misbehaving youth. In contemporary times, a delinquent youth may bring down the schools' test scores. The delinquent may be a continuing disruptive force in class or a temptation to younger students. Confidentiality provisions long prohibited probation officers from discussing the specific underlying offense with school officials. Probation officers might pay a home visit, remind parents and the youth of their obligation under the court order, and work to solve problems with both families and school.

Within school settings today, youthful drug offenders may be monitored and tested for drug use by probation officers. Delinquents may be in violation of probation for fighting in school, for substance abuse, for school vandalism or theft, as well as for truancy. Violation of probation results in a return to court, frequently leads to automatic detention, and may lead to a sentence to a correctional facility. The discretion of the probation officer has remained vast: to place in violation and send to detention or corrections, or to nudge, encourage, command, and facilitate.

School-based probation officers offer one form of direct partnership with schools. Teams composed of both school personnel and probation can provide the control, supervision, and incentives that both delinquent youth and the schools they attend require. Probation officers located at schools can intervene in crises, monitor attendance, and assist with disruptive behavior. Ideally, this would be one way to alert schools to the need for individualized or special educational needs, to conduct home visits, to coordinate other intervention services, and to prepare for school reentry for youth released from juvenile corrections.

The economic benefits of neighborhood probation closely linked with individualized schooling are a dramatic incentive, although jockeying between county and state costs obscures the reality to taxpayers. It costs, at the end of the twentieth century, approximately $35,000 to $60,000 per year to imprison a child (Wilson and Howell 1999, 193). The same funding can support a highly skilled, experienced probation officer, a year in a public school, and a plethora of youth services for twenty youngsters (Snyder and Wirt 1998, 58).

Court Schools: Alternative Sentencing

In some jurisdictions, court community schools become alternative schools for children on probation or parole. In rural areas, such schools may also include pregnant teens, expelled students, and disruptive children. In court community schools, teachers and probation officers work closely together to keep kids in school and de-institutionalized (Malcolm Terence, private conversation, July 2000).

In the closing decades of the twentieth century, court programming expanded to include court schools as an alternative form of sentencing. A juvenile court judge might order youngsters charged with auto theft or drug possession, for example, to attend Saturday court classes for ten weeks and dismiss charges if the order was successfully implemented. Youth drug courts became an example of a court school, where delinquent youth were supervised closely by probation and counselors and mandated to attend classes on abstinence.

Courts return the child to school with sentencing conditions, and the enforcement mechanisms of a term of probation and a court order. The person of the probation officer or truant officer may enforce the court-ordered sentencing terms. In addition, courts have devised a school-like court sanction as an alternative to delinquency adjudication and sentencing. Through a variety of mechanisms, the court relies on the school as a primary location for its sanctions and enforcement.

SCHOOLING IN AND AFTER RESIDENTIAL JUVENILE JUSTICE

Juvenile justice is replete with oxymorons, perhaps including juvenile justice itself. None, however, are more ironic than the reform school or the training school—those dismal places where children are incarcerated under the promise of education, learning, schooling. Children in detention custody who are awaiting trial, those adjudicated delinquent or convicted as criminals, and youth sentenced to residential placement—all are entitled to a free public education. There is virtually total verbal agreement that schooling is a key element, perhaps second only to strong families, in preventing juvenile crime and developing future productive citizens. Yet the gap between goals and practice, rhetoric and reality, mandates and options is enormous. Detention combined with correctional education is nonexistent or woefully inadequate. The transition of youngsters from correctional systems and residential custody back into community environments and school enrollment is fraught with failure. "The training school," as Frank Zimring notes, "neither trains much nor schools effectively" (Zimring 1982, 72).

Worse yet, juveniles released from serving a sentence in a correctional facility—whether it is called a training school, a youth center, a boot camp, or a juvenile prison—find themselves back in the peer or family environment which led them into trouble, without a source of income, and without access to schools willing and eager to enroll them, or organized to teach them. These are indeed, to use the Justice Department's quaint euphemism, "youth out of the educational mainstream or 'YOEM'" (Stephens and Arnette 2000, 2). Efforts to breathe life into schooling for kids in trouble with the law have been ongoing and occasionally successful.

Detention and Education

Early reformers sought to take advantage of the conglomerate of young people in detention by providing excellent and useful schooling as part of separate detention of the young. The Chicago Women's Club established the John Worthy School in 1893 by proposing to replace a male guard with a female teacher at a much lower salary ($50 per month) to educate children detained at the jail. A teacher at the school reported that his students were distraught after an execution at the jail: "Conversation for two weeks had been chiefly of its harrowing details, and the boys suffered either from nervousness and horror or were brutalized according to their age or temperament" (Lathrop 1925, 292). Some two thousand of these children who were incarcerated in the Bridewell in 1897 and 1898 were held because of their inability to pay fines, for offenses such as petty theft, disorderly conduct, killing birds, stealing rides on the railroad, and "flipping" street cars (Hurley 1925, 321).

The women established the Detention Home at 625 West Adams Street to confine children until their hearing with the city of Chicago. They paid eleven cents a day for food for each child, and the county provided the services of a physician and transportation to court. A teacher from the Board of Education kept the boys occupied and charted their progress (see figure 10.1). By 1911, Florence Scully had been hired as the teacher who taught arithmetic, pottery, and basket weaving. Overcrowding was immediate and persistent. In 1905, almost three thousand children passed through the Detention Home in Chicago.

Plans for a new building to house both the juvenile court and the De-

Fig. 10.1 School room in the detention home of the Chicago Juvenile Court.

tention Home were to include a "children's block" and a compulsory education center adjacent to Hull House and across from the Dante Public School. When the new Detention Home was built in 1907, however, it was without the educational center and child study department.

Education for girls in detention consisted of character building and moral education, as well as academic schooling. Girls were awakened at 5 A.M. to scrub the unit, clear and clean from breakfast, and prepare vegetables for dinner. Sewing, crocheting, and needle work were part of domestic science, as well as table manners, cooking classes, and habits of neatness and housekeeping. Literacy included letters of remorse for the judge and letters home, which were monitored. Although corporal punishment was not used at the home, isolation cells and bread and milk diets were utilized.

On the occasion of the twenty-fifth anniversary of the court, Bowen mourned conditions at the Detention Home, which had "every appearance of being a jail, with its barred windows and locked doors. Its attendants do not understand the psychology of childhood; they know very little about dependents and delinquents; their idea seems to be that every child is in the institution for punishment" (Bowen 1925, 309).

By 1937, there were riots and a letter-writing campaign by children in detention in Cook County, spurred by severe overcrowding and lengthy delays in transfers to corrections, without time served in detention counting as time served on their sentence. Decades later, a report in 1963 referred to conditions in the detention center as Dickensian; there were isolation cells; no exercise yard; a mixture of dependent, neglected, and delinquent children; and patronage-appointed staff lacking in high school education and without training (National Council on Crime and Delinquency 1963, 23–32).

Detention remained a perennial source of scandal and overcrowding throughout the century. Rare were the institutions—such as the Nancy B. Jefferson Chicago Public School, which serves five hundred children each day at the Cook County Juvenile Temporary Detention Center—which included a full-time school, operated by a board of education. More typical were "letter of the law" arrangements where an instructor spent two hours per day with incarcerated children, with only magazines and newspapers available for reading.

Detention centers and short-term facilities became legally obligated to implement the right to a free public education for all children, including appropriate educational obligations for disabled, special-education-eligible kids in the mid-1970s. These requirements include the federal legislative "child-find" obligations to identify, locate, and evaluate children who have a disability, and to obtain parental consent for special education evaluations. Neither probation officers nor employees of correctional facilities may serve as surrogate parents (Educational Claims for Students 1995–96, 1–5).

Overcrowding and the ability to provide appropriate education for youth in detention are closely linked, but reduced populations are no assurance of decent education in confinement. Efforts to provide objective screening instruments for admissions to detention, to improve court processing times, and to improve placement have shown success at reducing both detention overcrowding and lengths of stays (Burrell 2000). The education of detained children requires that schooling become a central goal of custody and that alternatives to detention focus on keeping children enrolled in and attending appropriate and effective schools.

Training Schools and Juvenile Correctional Facilities: Where Is the School?

The contradictions between the aspirations of the new juvenile court and the entrenched industrial schools and reformatories were reflected in the original founding legislation. Existing law gave guardianship of the child, exclusive wardship, to the institution's superintendent. The court relinquished future control when a child was placed, and it was within the sole discretion of the reformatory whether the inmate would be released, schooled, placed elsewhere, or confined until majority. The new legislation provided that it did not supersede any existing legislation, but in a conflicting section stated that the juvenile court reserved ultimate guardianship of the child, including the right to return a child to his or her home.

This inherent conflict—the power of the court vis-à-vis the authority and clout of agencies and institutions—continued in different forms throughout the first century. The compromises and philosophical conflicts, like those between the juvenile court and the adult criminal court over original jurisdiction of serious juvenile offenders, loomed large or receded from visibility in different eras over the decades.

Early Antecedents: Education and Reform Schools

The Chicago Reform School, established in 1855 and modeled on similar facilities in New York, Boston, and Philadelphia, was a school governed by "parental discipline," without bars, without corporal punishment, and administered on the honor system. All four cities with early reform schools, significantly, chose progressive educators as their first superintendents (Gittens 1994, 93). Children carried keys to the gates, were given passes for visiting and leaves, and attended school four hours a day and workshops for six hours. Yet they were confined until age twenty-one or "until they became good boys," whichever came first.

Children who were in need of proper parental care were confined to the Chicago Reform School. These included youngsters in trouble with the police for street rioting and mail robbery, but also non-adjudicated homeless children, and youth lacking proper supervision—vulnerable children in need of care and guidance, in the view of reformers, police, and magistrates. In fact, parental and family visiting were restricted and discouraged. The only recourse for parents whose children were removed was legal; some thirty boys each year were released on writs of *habeas corpus*. The religious and ethnic conflict embodied in that decidedly Christian and Protestant institution and its immigrant (and frequently Catholic) charges added to parental and community opposition and resistance. The experience of the Chicago Reform School was a lesson learned by the Hull House activists forty-five years later, who actively sought and received the support and endorsement of Timothy Hurley, then president of the Catholic Visitation and Aid Society and first chief probation officer of the new juvenile court.

Steady pressure by parents and religious forces who thought their children had been pirated by the authorities and shipped to the Chicago Reform School resulted in a landmark Illinois Supreme Court case based on the placement of fourteen-year-old Daniel O'Connell in the Chicago Reform School for instruction, employment, and reformation. His father petitioned for his release. The Court agreed, holding that nonconvicted children could not be incarcerated without due process and ordering Daniel's immediate release. "If, without crime, without the conviction of any offense, the children of the State are to be thus confined 'for the good of society,' then society had better be reduced to its original elements and free government acknowledged a failure," the court declared. Furthermore, parental rights could not be set aside unless "gross misconduct or almost total unfitness on the part of the parent should be clearly proved" (*People ex. rel. O'Connell v. Turner,* 55 Ill. 280 [1870]).

To the supporters of the Chicago Reform School, the court decision was a philosophical as well as practical blow. Their intention was education, not punishment. Their net was cast to intervene with predelinquent, troubled children before the experience of jail or trial. A year later, the Great Chicago Fire of 1871 destroyed the school, and it was not rebuilt. Boys were transferred to the new state reformatory at Pontiac, where they served fixed sentences in overcrowded conditions or were dismissed by judges reluctant to sentence boys 10–18 to prison.

Homeless, abandoned, and exploited children continued to multiply among crowded urban tenements, and within a decade, the legislature authorized the establishment of an industrial school for girls. Mindful of *O'Connell,* the new law provided for a six-man jury to assess the girl's dependency before her commitment. The industrial school was a mixture of reform school and orphanage, and both Catholic and Protestant industrial schools were established, undercutting some of the parental opposition to the Chicago Reform School. By 1882, the Illinois Supreme Court, in response to another legal challenge to the incarceration of unfortunate children, held that the industrial school act established that the nature of the institution was a school, not a prison. "We perceive hardly any more restraint of liberty than is to be found in any well-regulated school" (*In the matter of the petition of Alexander Ferrier,* 103 Ill. 367 [1882]). The legislature followed by providing for industrial schools for boys.

Midcentury Training Schools and the Failure to Educate

St. Charles Reformatory for Boys began operations in 1904. By 1920, the Children's Committee report cited the repressed and joyless atmosphere, the rule of silence during meals, and an exhausted staff who worked twenty-four hours per day. Most significantly, the report noted the failure of the Illinois training schools to provide retraining of their young inmates. The 1931 legislative report was harsh: the institutions were not rehabilitative but overcrowded, repressed, and only devoted one-half of each day to education. Staff was overworked, unqualified, and untrained to work with children. In addition, even the staff at St. Charles thought that one-quarter of the boys there should not have been committed to corrections. The downstate counties without probation services continued to send dependent, truant, and misbehaving children to state corrections, rather than providing local, non-institutional services on the county payroll (*Report of the Committee* 1931, 200–207).

The incarceration of children worsened during the Depression as unemployment, impoverished public schools, and shrinking mothers' pensions made life desperate for families. In 1937, St. Charles held 783 boys, despite the official legal capacity of 677. By 1939, the situation had deteriorated into a crisis of escapes and runaways from St. Charles, resulting in legislative hearings which reflected the public's harsher view of tougher boys, including children who were sentenced by the adult criminal court but were serving their sentences at St. Charles. Furthermore, young inmates in corrections were segregated in cottages by race, and African American youth were kept out of occupational training classes; although one-quarter to one-third of the children were African American, there was not a single African American housefather. African American staff, charged the Urban League, were treated poorly and assigned demeaning tasks, and no African American ministers were hired to serve the youth (A History 1939, 44–45, 55–58).

In 1941, a boy at St. Charles was beaten to death by two housefathers, forcing another blue ribbon committee investigation. Brutality was found to permeate the institution's environment; the report cited harsh punishments such as "swabbing": a basement was half-filled with water, and the boys were ordered to soak it up with only burlap and buckets and no food or respite. This committee ordered the institution to combine educational and vocational services, add more recreational programs, and provide staff training, and underscored the critical need for education in an institution for children (*Study and Reorganization* 1941, 139). The war created further shortages of staff and resources, but a legislative child welfare commission continued oversight and reported on the needs of probation as well as those of the St. Charles and Geneva training schools. African American youth continued to be confined in disproportionate numbers, and girls were incarcerated for pregnancy and venereal diseases.

A 1949 report documented the impossible mixture of feeble-minded, psychotic, dependent, and aggressive delinquents in the same facility. By the fiftieth anniversary of the juvenile court, the perspective was dismal: "In the overall picture, we must face the tragic facts of neglect of suffering, and of the waste of opportunities and money which could be prevented. . . . Conditions exist which reflect grave discredit on a state which had the vision, the progressive motivation, to enact the first Juvenile Court Law in our country" (Child Welfare Commission 1949, 9, 15).

Late-Century Efforts to Provide Education in Juvenile Corrections

The state created an Illinois Youth Commission in 1953 to operate the state youth reformatories, create a central intake and diagnostic center, and develop a series of forestry camps for boys. The effort was to coordinate delinquency prevention, including institutionalizing the Chicago Area Project. Yet the juvenile prison at Sheridan (Illinois Industrial School for Boys), with cell block structure, harsh discipline, sexual and physical abuse, and sixteen hours each night without food erupted finally with revelations that the boys were beaten and confined naked in dark cells; prison administrators *and* the school principal were fired. In the other juvenile institutions, school was available only to children under sixteen, because of severe overcrowding.

By 1974, the new mandates of the Juvenile Justice and Delinquency Prevention Act focused on removing status offenders from correctional facilities and delinquent children from adult jails. However, President Reagan appointed a National Advisory Committee, which found that the OJJDP was concentrating on the wrong problem and redefined the issue as that of the serious, chronic juvenile offender. Instead of prevention or rehabilitation, the executive report called for enhanced ability to "identify, apprehend, prosecute, and treat or incarcerate these juveniles."

The emphasis on getting tough with "vicious" youngsters signaled a return to emphasizing retribution and accountability rather than childhood and poverty. The closing decades reflected a declining national emphasis on children's social needs and further trial of children in adult criminal courts (Fagan and Zimring 2000). In the context of swelling incarceration rates, greater disproportional institutionalization of African American children, and longer sentences, the educational needs of youth in correctional facilities took a back seat (Poe-Yamagata and Jones 2000).

Although state constitutions guarantee a free public education to all children, educational resources and schooling in state juvenile correctional facilities (or adult prisons where children are incarcerated) generally fail to teach, educate, provide credit, or prepare young inmates at even a minimally acceptable level. Budgets are constrained, institutions are located in rural areas where the pool of qualified teachers is limited, facility culture regularly interrupts normal school hours, and priorities differ. Access to each youth's prior school records is bureaucratically complicated. Testing, assessments, and special education IEPs (Individualized Educational Plans) are replicated and waste time. Lock-downs, punishment, infirmary calls, visits, transfers, and staff absences and turnovers characterize correctional life and become impediments to schooling. Rare indeed are the institutions which overcome these hurdles and place education at the center of facility management.

Despite research that indicates that inmates who participate in educational programs are more likely to be employed upon release and less likely to return to prison, the overall performance of juvenile correctional facilities in achieving educational goals is dismal (Barton and Coley 1996). Students cannot receive academic credit toward diplomas or transfer, their programs are not approved by state educational departments, and their education does not meet the individualized needs of regular or disabled students. It is estimated that 50–80 percent of all children confined are eligible for disability services (Portner 1996).

For example, of the approximately 8,300 youths incarcerated in the California Youth Authority, some 70 percent qualify for special education which is unavailable to most in the juvenile halls or ranches of the state. Students entering or exiting the correctional system rarely have cumulative educational files available, funding is not equitable, students are reluctant to self-identify, and there are no unified advocacy groups to support the educational needs of confined youth (Advisory Commission 1996). The report firmly concluded that the existing educational options of a resource specialist program, a special day class, and designated instruction services were not adequate. As New York City juvenile court Judge Jeffrey Gallet says, "If you cannot read, there are only two ways to make a living—the welfare system or crime—and crime has more status."

A federal initiative to assist juvenile corrections administrators in improving education for detained and incarcerated young offenders in 1992 produced a training and technical assistance manual and three state-operated pilot sites to establish model learning environments. Effective educational programs were those which concentrated on basic academic skills and high school completion, pre-employment training (workplace competencies), and life skills (*Effective Practices* 1994; Gemignani 1994).

Back to School: Release from Residential Custody to Public School

Across the political spectrum, it is widely accepted that youngsters must reenter school immediately after their release from corrections, yet everything conspires against success. It is difficult enough for students to enter classes in the middle of a semester and to succeed academically without being involved in the curriculum. For youth coming out of a correctional facility, generally without credit for school work done while in custody, or with poor academic performance prior to incarceration, even a fierce desire for schooling and success may meet with closed schoolhouse doors. Funding for juvenile parole officers who might assist youth in the endeavor of enrolling in public school has been drastically cut back in the 1990s.

Schools may reject applicants coming from corrections or refer them to a form of alternative education. Transitional support from the facility or juvenile parole officers is often intended and rarely executed. Special education and special needs make the task more complicated and require systems' coordination. In New Jersey, for example, the Gateway Academy opened in 1999 as a twelve-month program to provide a single place for all students returning from incarceration to the Newark public schools. The project includes assessment, planning, placement, after-school, community service, and weekend activities for twelve months until students can return to their regular school.

The simple truth is that efforts to place the obvious priority of education at the center of youth rehabilitation and corrections have been a grim failure. Incarcerated children are invisible. They are isolated from family, community, and power. They almost never continue to have legal counsel. The staff at juvenile correctional facilities, with rare and notable exceptions, constantly turn over, without training or preparation in adolescent development or teaching. Dollars for educating "bad kids" are never flowing. The real subtext of incarceration for children is a different kind of learning: how to survive amidst gangs and violence, anonymity, and bureaucracy. The few who discover books as a pathway to the intellect and possibility are rare indeed.

THE COURT AS A SCHOOL

The juvenile court was conceived, in good part, as a school for the children, youth, and parents who appeared there. The content of the school was the proper management and care of children. The court "procedure contemplated care, attention, and formation, rather than reformation" (Hurley 1925, 328). The court, through its judges, probation officers, child clinics, and volunteers, was an instrument of social instruction to parents and youth. The court had an educative mission.

The lengthy decades during which the court functioned informally were, in part, characterized by the court's developing a classroom quality. Judges lectured to wayward parents and youth, instructing them on proper behavior. Class, cultural, gender, and racial superiority had full sway. Whether well-intentioned or supremacist, judicial attitudes toward the population making court appearances before them reflected the sense that parents and children must be corrected, lectured to, and directed to reform their ways. Confidentiality provisions shielded judges from public scrutiny and excesses. Parents and youth who did not conform, express remorse, or remain servile were subject to severe sanctions from their judicial taskmaster.

The court has also been a cauldron for the study of the child. The Juvenile Psychopathic Institute, later the Institute for Juvenile Research, conducted examinations of the child and the parent, provided the court with diagnostic information, and recommended treatment for each individual. William Healy, the institute's first psychiatrist, undertook the pioneering studies of delinquents which overthrew existing conceptions of biological theories of criminality. In *The Individual Delinquent,* Healy developed theory through the close study of individual cases, based on the child's "own story" (Healy 1915). His work revolutionized the perception of delinquent children, inserted psychiatric perspectives into the judicial process, and created an institutional mechanism for diagnosis, research, and study. The establishment of the nation's first child guidance clinics at the juvenile court in Chicago and then at the Judge Baker Foundation in Boston, is evidence of the court's generative role in developing new pedagogy.

Similarly, the engagement of the University of Chicago sociologists with the court produced a series of landmark reports. Clifford Shaw's *The Jack-Roller: A Delinquent Boy's Own Story* continued this intellectual tradition of plumbing individual narratives (Shaw 1930). Shaw was hired by the Institute for Juvenile Research to direct its sociological research. Decades later, work on the "best interest of the child" was forged by a multidisciplinary team of psychiatrists, lawyers, and educators with direct experiences in the juvenile court in Connecticut (Goldstein, Freud, and Solnit 1973; 1980; 1986).

The emerging fields of social work, probation, and applied research on human behavior had wellsprings in the court. Intellectuals and activists who changed American life and knowledge were early participants in the court: Roger Baldwin, founder of the American Civil Liberties Union, for example, worked as a probation officer in the St. Louis juvenile court as a young man; Ida B. Wells Barnett, leader of the national antilynching crusade, worked as a Chicago juvenile probation officer.

The court itself was therefore a school for the public or a public school: an educator of the public about the child, a school for the parents and youth who appeared in delinquency and child protection cases, and a pedagogic cauldron for intellectual inquiry, research, and investigation into the nature of the child and society. Its work compels the conclusion that if the first century of juvenile court teaches anything, it is that children, to thrive, require an intricate linkage and convergence where school is the more important institution than the court.

REFERENCES

Abbott, Edith, and Sophonisba P. Breckinridge. 1917. *Truancy and Non-Attendance in the Chicago Schools: A Study of the Social Aspects of the Compulsory Education and Child Labor Legislation of Illinois*. Chicago: University of Chicago Press.

Addams, Jane. 1912. *Democracy and Social Ethics*. New York: Macmillan.

———. 1916. *Democracy and Social Ethics*. New York: Macmillan.

———. 1925. Introduction. In *The Child, the Clinic, and the Court,* ed. Jane Addams. New York: New Republic.

Advisory Commission on Special Education. 1996. "California Incarcerated Youth Task Force Report." *LDA Newsbriefs* 31, no. 1, supplement (January/February): 21.

Ayers, William. 1996. *A Kind and Just Parent: The Children of Juvenile Court*. Boston: Beacon Press.

Barton, Paul E., and Richard J. Coley. 1996. *Captive Students: Education and Training in America's Prisons*. Princeton, NJ: Educational Testing Service.

Bowen, Louise deKoven. 1913. "The Colored People of Chicago: An Investigation Made for the Juvenile Protective Association." *Survey,* November 1.

———. 1927. "The Early Days of the Juvenile Court." In *The Child, the Clinic, and the Court,* ed. Jane Addams. New York: New Republic.

Breckinridge, Sophonisba P., and Edith Abbott. 1912. *The Delinquent Child in the Home: A Study of the Delinquent Wards of the Juvenile Courts of Chicago*. New York: Charities Publication Committee.

Britton, Gertrude Howe. 1906. "An Intensive Study of the Causes of Truancy in Eight Chicago Public Schools, including a Home Investigation of Eight Hundred Truant Children. Report presented to the Conference on Truancy—Its Causes and Prevention." Chicago: Chicago Board of Education.

Brooks, Kim; Vincent Schiraldi; and Jason Ziedenberg. 2000. *Schoolhouse Hype: Two Years Later.* Washington, DC: Justice Policy Institute, Children's Law Center.

Burrell, Sue. 2000. *Improving Conditions of Confinement in Secure Juvenile Detention Centers.* Pathways to Juvenile Detention Reform, no. 6. Baltimore: Annie E. Casey Foundation.

Butterfield, Fox. 1998. "Profits at Juvenile Prisons Earned at a Chilling Cost." *New York Times,* July 15, A1.

———. 2000. "Privately Run Juvenile Prison in Louisiana Is Attacked for Abuses of Six Inmates." *New York Times,* March 16, A14.

Canaan, Gareth. 1999. "The Economic and Class Dimensions of Juvenile Delinquency in Black Chicago During the 1920s." In *A Noble Social Experiment? The First Hundred Years of the Cook County Juvenile Court, 1899–1999,* ed. Gwen Hoerr McNamee. Chicago: Chicago Bar Association.

Chesney-Lind, Meda. 1999. "Challenging Girls' Invisibility in Juvenile Court." *Annals of the American Academy* 564 (July).

Chesney-Lind, Meda, and Randall G. Shelden. 1998. *Girls, Delinquency, and Juvenile Justice.* 2d ed. Belmont, CA: West/Wadsworth.

Child Welfare Commission. 1949. Cited in Gittens 1994.

Dewey, John. 1902. *The Child and the Curriculum*. Chicago: University of Chicago Press.

Dohrn, Bernardine. 2000a. "'Look Out Kid: It's Something You Did': The Criminalization of Youth." In *The Public Assault on America's Children: Poverty, Violence, and Juvenile Injustice,* ed. Valerie Polakow. New York: Teachers College Press, Columbia University.

———. 2000b. "Child Protection Division Matures Under Its First Chief." *Chicago Daily Law Bulletin,* January 11, 22.

———. Forthcoming. "'Look Out Kid, It's Something You Did': Zero Tolerance for Children." In *Zero Tolerance: A Handbook for Parents, Teachers, and the Community,* ed. William Ayers and Bernardine Dohrn. New York: New Press.

Drake, St. Clair, and Horace R. Cayton. [1970] 1993. *Black Metropolis: A Study of Negro Life in a Northern City.* Chicago: University of Chicago Press.

"Educational Claims for Students with Disabilities in Juvenile and Adult Correctional Facilities." 1995–96. *Children's Rights Chronicle* 14 (November).

Edwards, Leonard P. 1996. "The Future of the Juvenile Court: Promising New Directions." *Future of Children* 6, no. 3 (winter): 131–39.

Effective Practices in Juvenile Correctional Education: A Study of the Literature and Research, 1980–1992. 1994. National Criminal Justice 150066. Washington, DC: U.S. Department of Justice.

Fagan, Jeffrey, and Franklin E. Zimring, eds. 2000. *The Changing Borders of Juvenile Justice: Transfer of Adolescents to the Criminal Court.* Chicago: University of Chicago Press.

Federal Bureau of Investigation (FBI). 2000. *The School Shooter: A Threat Assessment Perspective.* Quantico, VA: Critical Incident Response Group, National Center for the Analysis of Crime, FBI Academy.

Gemignani, Robert J. 1994. *Juvenile Correctional Education: Time for Change.* OJJDP Update on Research. Washington, DC: U.S. Department of Justice, Office of Justice Programs, Office of Juvenile Justice, and Delinquency Prevention.

Gittens, Joan. 1994. *Poor Relations: The Children of the State in Illinois, 1818–1990.* Urbana: University of Illinois Press.

Goldstein, Joseph; Anna Freud; and Albert J. Solnit. 1973. *Beyond the Best Interest of the Child.* New York: Free Press.

———. 1980. *Before the Best Interest of the Child.* New York: Free Press.

———. 1986. *In the Best Interests of the Child: Professional Boundaries.* New York: Free Press.

Gordon, R.; L. Della Piana; and T. Keleher. 2000. *Facing the Consequences: An Examination of Racial Discrimination in U.S. Public Schools.* Oakland, CA: Applied Research Center.

Gregory, J. F. 1996. "The Crime of Punishment: Racial and Gender Disparities in the Use of Corporal Punishment in the U.S. Public Schools." *Journal of Negro Education* 64: 454–62.

Healy, William. [1915] 1929. *The Individual Delinquent: A Text-Book of Diagnosis and Prognosis for all Concerned in Understanding Offenders.* Boston: Little, Brown.

A History, *Report and Recommendations Submitted by the Committee Appointed by the Legislature to Study the Illinois St. Charles School for Boys and the Whole Subject of Juvenile Delinquency.* 1939. Cited in Gittens 1994. (Referred to as the Gunning Commission Hearings.)

Human Rights Watch. 1996. *Modern Capital of Human Rights? Abuses in the State of Georgia.* New York: Human Rights Watch.

Hurley, Timothy D. 1925. "The Origin of the Illinois Juvenile Court Act." In *The Child, the Clinic, and the Court,* ed. Jane Addams. New York: New Republic.

Kelley, Florence. 1905. *Some Ethical Gains through Legislation.* New York: Macmillan.

Knupfer, Anne Meis. 1999. "The Chicago Detention Home." In *A Noble Social Experiment? The First Hundred Years of the Cook County Juvenile Court, 1899–1999,* ed. by Gwen Hoerr McNamee. Chicago: Chicago Bar Association.

Lathrop, Julia C. 1925. "The Background of the Juvenile Court in Illinois." In *The Child, the Clinic, and the Court,* ed. Jane Addams. New York: New Republic.

———. [1895] 1970. "The Cook County Charities." In *Hull House Maps and Papers: A Presentation of Nationalities and Wages in a Congested District of Chicago.* New York: Arno Press.

Laws of the State of Illinois. 1905. Springfield: Illinois State Journal.

Lindsey, Benjamin B. 1925. "Colorado's Contribution to the Juvenile Court." In *The Child, the Clinic, and the Court,* ed. Jane Addams. New York: New Republic.

Mack, Julian W. 1925. "The Chancery Procedure in the Juvenile Court." In *The Child, the Clinic, and the Court,* ed. Jane Addams. New York: New Republic.

McNamee, Gwen Hoerr. 1999. "The Origin of the Cook County Juvenile Court." In *A Noble Social Experiment? The First Hundred Years of the Cook County Juvenile Court, 1899–1999,* ed. Gwen Hoerr McNamee. Chicago: Chicago Bar Association.

Miller, Jerome G. 1998. *Last One Over the Wall: The Massachusetts Experiment in Closing Reform Schools.* 2d ed. Columbus: Ohio State University Press.

National Center for Education Statistics. 1999. "Fast Facts: Educational Attainment." Washington, DC: National Center for Education Statistics, U.S. Department of Education.

National Council on Crime and Delinquency. 1963. *The Cook County Family (Juvenile) Court and Arthur J. Audy Home: An Appraisal and Recommendations.* Washington, DC: National Council on Crime and Delinquency.

Odem, Mary E. 1995. *Delinquent Daughters: Protecting and Policing Adolescent Female Sexuality in the United States, 1885–1920.* Chapel Hill: University of North Carolina Press.

Poe-Yamagata, Eileen, and Michael A. Jones. 2000. *And Justice for Some: Differential Treatment of Minority Youth in the Justice System.* Washington, DC: Building Blocks for Youth.

Portner, Jessica. 1996. "Jailed Youth Get Shortchanged on Education." *Education Week,* October 2.

Raskin, Jamin B., ed. 2000. *We the Students: Supreme Court Cases for and about America's Students.* Washington, DC: Congressional Quarterly.

Reed, David; Harris Meyer; Kim Zalent; and Janice Linn. 1981. *Promises, Promises . . . : Does the Juvenile Court Deliver for Status Offenders? The Record in Cook County, Illinois.* Chicago: Chicago Law Enforcement Study Group.

Report of the Committee on Child Welfare Legislation, 1931. Cited in Gittens 1994.

Schaffner, Laurie. 1998. "Female Juvenile Delinquency: Sexual Solutions, Gender Bias, and Juvenile Justice." *Hastings Women's Law Journal,* 9: 1.

Second Chances: Giving Kids a Chance to Make Better Choices. 1999. Washington, DC: Justice Policy Institute and Children and Family Justice Center.

Shaw, Clifford Robe. 1930. *The Jack-Roller: A Delinquent Boy's Own Story.* Chicago: University of Chicago Press.

Skiba, Russell J.; Robert S. Michael; Abra Carroll Nardo; and Reece Peterson. 2000. *The Color of Discipline: Sources of Racial and Gender Disproportionality in School Punishment.* Bloomington: Indiana Education Policy Center, Indiana University.

Snyder, Howard N., and Melissa Sickmund. 1999. *Juvenile Offenders and Victims: 1999 National Report.* Washington, DC: Office of Juvenile Justice and Delinquency Prevention, National Center for Juvenile Justice.

Snyder, Thomas, and John Wirt. 1998. *The Condition of Education, 1998.* Washington, DC: U.S. Department of Education, National Center for Educational Statistics.

Steinhart, David J. 1996. "Status Offenses." *Future of Children: The Juvenile Court* 6, no. 3 (winter): 86–99.

Stephens, Ronald D., and June Lane Arnette. 2000. *From the Courthouse to the Schoolhouse:*

Making Successful Transitions. Washington, DC: U.S. Department of Justice, Office of Justice Programs, Office of Juvenile Justice and Delinquency Prevention.

Study and Reorganization of Illinois State Training School for Boys. 1941. Cited in Gittens 1994.

Tanenhaus, David S. 1999. "'Rotten to the Core': The Juvenile Court and the Problem of Legitimacy in the Progressive Era." In *A Noble Social Experiment? The First Hundred Years of the Cook County Juvenile Court, 1899–1999,* ed. Gwen Hoerr McNamee. Chicago: Chicago Bar Association.

Wilson, John J., and James C. Howell. 1999. *Comprehensive Strategy for Serious, Violent, and Chronic Juvenile Offenders.* Research Report. Washington, DC: U.S. Department of Justice, Office of Justice Programs, Office of Juvenile Justice and Delinquency Prevention.

Zimring, Franklin E. 1982. *The Changing Legal World of Adolescence.* New York: Free Press.

———. 1998. *American Youth Violence.* New York: Oxford University Press.

11 American Government and the Politics of Youth

Peter Edelman

A volume about the first hundred years of the juvenile court would be incomplete without examining how policy and attitudes toward its clientele—American youth—have evolved, especially regarding the segment of young people most likely to show up in court. The juvenile court was not founded in isolation and was not intended to be an isolated institution. It was a product of its time, created at a moment when the concept of childhood was changing dramatically due to economic trends and new theories of child development. Its establishment was one aspect of a project to protect children and prolong childhood, the most salient features of which were a push to have more young people go to and finish high school and a companion effort to have fewer young people in the workplace.

That project, however, did not result in a unitary or coherent national youth policy. National policy efforts were undertaken—by progressives in particular—concerning specific issues, but even as to those, large segments of children and youth were ignored or consciously excluded, with differences as to race, class, and gender. The lack of any overarching policy continued through the century, although the individual policy foci developed and changed, and the ranks of the excluded shrank somewhat.

This chapter begins by examining the changing role of youth in the early twentieth century, including the beginnings of the modern concept of a transition to adulthood—a period of delay between physical maturity and the assumption of the responsibilities and status of adulthood. It traces the origins of this concept to economic changes at the time, aided by the efforts of child savers to pursue policies that would have the effect of prolonging childhood.

It then explores youth policy during the New Deal, the post–World War II era, the sixties, and the last third of the century. The chapter concludes that as the United States enters the twenty-first century it still does not have a unified youth policy, but instead one that is fragmented along class and racial lines.

YOUTH IN THE EARLY TWENTIETH CENTURY

The first third of the twentieth century produced the first stirrings of the prolongation of childhood that then continued to develop over the course of the century. The child savers of the time invented a series of institutions and policies that focused more public policy attention on children and responded to economic changes that reduced the demand for work by children. The Children's Bureau, established within the federal government in 1912, focused primarily on younger children but did important, although less visible, work on child labor. High school, an institution of interest to only a small minority in 1900, became an important training ground between 1900 and 1930. Child labor law and economic changes removed large numbers of young people from the labor market during that time.

Youth and adolescence were not terms in common usage in 1900. When, in 1904, G. Stanley Hall authored a two-volume study entitled *Adolescence: Its Psychology and Its Relations to Physiology, Anthropology, Sociology, Sex, Crime, Religion, and Education,* the work elicited lively public discussion and further scholarly publications (Lindenmeyer 1997, 12). Hall argued that childhood had come to include a period of "Sturm und Drang" during which young people struggled to define their own personal identities. Margaret Mead's famed study, *Coming of Age in Samoa,* was written partially to refute Hall by arguing that the existence of such a period is culturally determined and not inevitable (Demos 1986, 94).

Young people in 1900 assumed adult responsibilities at younger ages than they do now. Except for the relative few who finished high school, and the even smaller number who attended university, most young people (young men in particular)—especially on farms and among immigrant families—went to work at a time that we would today consider adolescence. Eleven percent of the nation's 14–17 year olds were attending high school in 1900, a figure that would double by 1920 and nearly double again by 1930 (Bremner 1971, 1392). Most jobs did not require a high school education. People married young.

The situation in 1900, on the other hand, was not the same as in 1800. Then—except for orphans and apprentices and poor children bonded out—children learned about adulthood and took on adult responsibilities while still living at home. Those who went away to learn or work elsewhere went not by choice but because they were sent.

As the nineteenth century passed, boys in particular began spending periods of time in the outside world. Economic choices began to appear that had been unavailable to parents. Sometimes these were positive and sometimes they were a matter of necessity. Marriage became increasingly a matter of choice rather than arrangement. The growing cities around the country were an attraction to migration, to the point where there was much worry about the dangers posed by unattached youth living in cities. Immigration produced a new category of youth whose parents, unused to America, were unable to orient them to the American economy or to social custom. They had no choice but to acquire socialization to America outside of their families (Demos 1986, 97–107).

For young women, the changes of the nineteenth century had been somewhat different from what happened to men. Until late in the century upper-class women experienced something like today's gap between childhood and adulthood, waiting at home until marriage came along. As the twentieth century approached, more young women of all classes were working outside the home. The social fallout from this occasioned great concern—that young women engaging in public social behavior we would now consider typically adolescent were on the verge of prostitution. Many states took a protective stance and raised their age of adult sexual consent, most often to sixteen. Bills were repeatedly introduced in Congress to impose a national age of eighteen as the threshold for adult sexual consent (Nathanson 1991, 78–91, 119–23).

Communities began assuming a greater responsibility for socializing youth to the adult world through new organizations like the Boy Scouts, the Campfire Girls, the YMCA and the YWCA, and the 4-H Clubs, although some, like the Boy Scouts, were more successful with children fourteen and under than with the population we might call youth (Macleod 1987, 403–7). They were responding both to the increased number of unattached youth in cities and to the surge in immigration, as well as to a general perception that more moral guidance was needed regardless. By the early twentieth century, "youth" was a much more meaningful idea than it had been in 1800.

As the twentieth century went on, physical maturity began to occur earlier, and the labor market—to ration available jobs—welcomed entrants later. The period of hiatus between childhood and adulthood came into being as an economic fact in the Depression, although it did not become what the historian Joseph Kett somewhat misleadingly calls "the mixture of leisure, affluence, and education that now distinguishes" it for the majority of young people until after World War II (Kett 1977, 4). The forced economic hiatus seemed to have disappeared in the late forties, when the hot postwar economy drew young people—white young people, anyway—into plentifully available after-school jobs, and industrial jobs were still available to people with less than a high school education. For a while the transition seemed sufficiently seamless that in 1958 the sociologist Edgar Z. Friedenberg could write a well-received book entitled *The Vanishing Adolescent.* But the hiatus reappeared in the early seventies and has been with us since, along with the age-segregation of the group that had been developing steadily for decades.

Public policy in 1900 did concern itself with issues covering a portion of what we now see as the adolescent years—child labor, compulsory education, and the juvenile court itself—but these issues, important as they were, were overshadowed by issues concerning young children. Criticism mounted of orphanages and other congregate residential institutions for children, and advocates pressed the use of family foster care and other small-group settings. Mothers' pensions swept from state to state across the country, as policymakers decided that enabling children to stay with their own mothers would for the most part be a better solution than placing them outside of their own homes (Ashby 1997, 88–98). The new federal Children's Bureau focused on infant and maternal mortality and pressed the states to enact birth registration laws (Muncy 1991, 55–60). Even those areas of activity relating to youth started with a focus on the early and mid-teen years and only gradually came to cover older youth.

Massachusetts had passed the first compulsory education law in 1852, and by 1900, thirty-two states had such laws; Mississippi was the last state to adopt a compulsory education law, doing so in 1918 (Katz 1986, 130–31). But the initial laws typically required children to stay in school only until age twelve, and the laws were filled with loopholes, mainly to accommodate working children. Pennsylvania's revised and ostensibly improved law, enacted in 1897, allowed 13–16-year-old children to drop out of school and go to work if they could demonstrate that they could read at about a third-grade level, and for twenty-five cents they could get a certificate that obviated any examination of their reading capacity (Troen 1976, 240–41). These loopholes were gradually closed in the early years of the twentieth century, at the same time as child labor regulations were being tightened (Bremner 1971, 1422–29). In a parallel trend, ungraded classrooms were replaced in the late nineteenth century by grades, with a separation created between elementary schools and high schools, thus beginning one element of the age segregation that has become a characteristic of adolescence (Demos 1986, 105).

Child labor regulation began with gaps both as to age and type of job. The first laws applied to children twelve or fourteen and under, depending on the occupation, and even these laws were not stringently enforced (figure 11.1). Florence Kelley, who first gained national prominence as inspector of factories and workshops in Illinois, said that her work was impeded by the fact that she had only twelve staff people to inspect thousands of workplaces around the state (Troen 1976, 241). Nonetheless, in 1900, twenty-eight states had laws that both limited child labor and required school attendance (Feld 1999, 43). Over the first four decades of the twentieth century, the laws were

Fig. 11.1 Child cotton pickers in South Carolina, ca. 1930. © Hulton-Deutsch Collection/CORBIS.

applied more broadly and to older youth. Employment of 10–13-year-olds dropped from 12.3 percent in 1910 to 2.4 percent in 1930, and employment of 14- and 15-year-olds dropped from 30.7 percent to 9.2 percent over the same period. Employment of 16- and 17-year-olds decreased less, from 44.7 percent to 31.7 percent. Regional figures are even more striking. In the East South Central region, employment of 10–13-year-olds went from 32.9 percent to 9.7 percent, of 14–15-year-olds from 40.9 percent to 13.8 percent, and of 16–17-year-olds from 42.6 percent to 37.8 percent. In New England, by contrast, only 1 percent of 10–13-year-olds were working in 1910, while 57 percent of 16–17-year-olds were working, a figure that dropped to 36.9 percent by 1930 (Lindenmeyer 1997, 115).

Of course these trends reflected changes in the economy as well as changes in regulatory patterns. For example, in 1900 department stores were the largest employers of youth between twelve and sixteen in Chicago. They served as cash boys and cash girls, running back and forth between merchandise counters and back offices to complete transactions. The invention of the pneumatic tube in 1902 destroyed these jobs. Similarly, the widespread construction of telephone wires in cities greatly reduced the need for telegram delivery boys. Schools began to see the need to offer manual training and vocational education to prepare youth for the more complicated emerging economy of the day and, for that matter, keep them in school. This became important enough that Congress in 1917 enacted the Smith-Hughes Act to provide federal funds for vocational training (Troen 1976, 241–43, 247).

Joseph Kett says "the era of the adolescent dawned" between 1900 and 1920 (Kett 1977, 215). The expansion of high school attendance and the increasing role of vocational education over that period had the effect of extending the age span covered by adolescence to eighteen or nineteen. Until then the age span encompassed by the term was more typically from twelve to sixteen. This had been the time frame concentrated on by child labor reformers and so-called "boys-workers"—the Boy Scouts, YMCAs, and others who had decided that moral development and the need for supervised recreation were important responsibilities to be undertaken by people in the community beyond the parents (Kett 1977, 221–28, 238). All of this occurred in the context of massive demographic changes. Between 1860 and 1920, the country's population more than tripled due to immigration, and the population of cities, where the immigrants largely settled, grew from 6.2 million to 54 million, or from about 20 percent of the population to over 50 percent (Trotter 1993, 58).

By the end of the twenties, changes in the economy and schooling, coupled with the large-scale demographic changes and added to by a growing community concern for the moral development of young people, had produced a clear if tacit agreement that adolescence was a separable stage in life existed and required particular attention. Compulsory education and child labor regulation, along with various morally based strictures, had taken hold to accelerate, enforce, and respond to changes occurring in the larger society. It took the Depression, though, to add an enforced economic delay to the time of arrival at adulthood.

THE DEPRESSION

The Depression had a powerful effect on youth employment patterns and consequently drew more attention to a public policy that would respond to the new situation. In 1937, for example, unemployment among 16–24 year olds was about 30 percent of those counted as wanting to work. Another 14 percent were working part-time, most of whom were thought to desire full-time employment. The unemployed among the age group constituted about a third of all the unemployed people in the nation. Funding for jobs for 18–25-year-olds had been provided through the Civilian Conservation Corps earlier in the decade, and some additional young people had found work or participated in work-study activities through other federal agencies. In 1935 President Franklin Roosevelt by Executive Order carved $50 million out of the $4.9 billion budget for work relief and created the National Youth Administration (Lindley and Lindley 1972, 6–8, 13). World War I, like all military conflicts, had represented a form of national youth policy, but the first time a major focus on youth appeared in federal policy was with the creation of the National Youth Administration (Reiman 1992, 3–10).

Nearly five hundred thousand young people, mainly 18–24 year olds, were participating in various NYA activities by early 1938. The bulk were in work activities geared to out-of-school youth, which included construction, work in machine and maintenance shops, and various community service positions, including libraries and health and hospital settings. Because program decisions were decentralized to federal offices located in individual states, a variety of other activities were encompassed as well, with different initiatives in different places. Youth community centers—enrichments of local Boys Clubs or YMCAs—were funded in a number of places, as were college and high school work-study programs. "Resident" programs, in effect precursors of today's Job Corps, were opened in some localities. Activities that introduced and oriented high school students to the world of work were on the menu, too (Lindley and Lindley 1972, 17–67, 86–121).

Physical examinations revealed widespread health problems among the clientele of the NYA, and testing showed huge gaps in literacy and other skills. Participants complained bitterly about unresponsive and incompetent teaching in the schools they had attended. Much of the mission of the NYA was devoted, one way or another, to providing education and training that young people had not received during their years of formal schooling (Lindley and Lindley 1972, 156–201).

Two firsts in the NYA were the attention paid to Negroes and the attention paid to girls (in both cases I use the terminology of the time). The famed educator and Roosevelt confidant Mary McLeod Bethune was the Director of Negro Affairs of the NYA (while maintaining her position as president of Bethune-Cookman College), and the result was a number of programs (segregated, to be sure) for African American youth. Special efforts were made to create programs for young women as well (Lindley and Lindley 1972, 18, 48, 61–62, 219).

The NYA attracted critics from a variety of perspectives, including school people worried about a possibly hidden agenda of supplanting local control of educational policy and politicians opposed to its work with Negro youth. Nonetheless, it grew and changed with the times, adding attention to refugees as they began to appear in the wake of Hitler's increasing depredations, and also training geared to youth who would then take jobs in the wartime production effort. By 1941 its budget was $119 million, and it was the only work-related New Deal agency not experiencing budget cuts (Reiman 1992, 176).

The Depression had brought a national youth policy into existence, although the war ultimately replaced it with the massive youth policy of military mobilization. The experience of the NYA had exposed (at least to a cadre of activists and reformers) the inadequacy of American education and the inhospitable nature of the job market for a large cohort of young people, but the insight was lost in the postwar euphoria. Until Michael Harrington's pathbreaking book *The Other America* appeared in the early sixties, and the Kennedy administration began focusing on large numbers still being left behind even though the Depression was over, the postwar assumption was that the new prosperity was reaching everyone and that schooling was broadly competent and caring, with any failure attributable not to the system but to the deficiencies of the individual child.

THE POST-WORLD WAR II ERA: THE ROOTS OF THE MODERN BIFURCATION

Prosperity returned after World War II, but the gap between childhood and adulthood, while temporarily masked in the red-hot postwar economy, did not go away. The economic facts of the Depression had created the extended transition from childhood to adulthood that is now a staple of American life.

The increasing complexity of the economy and the gradually growing demand for greater equality began to bring about two changes in the status of youth—one theoretically positive, and the other negative—neither much noticed until the sixties. The first was the commitment, at least in concept, to see that every American child finishes high school. With all the growth in high school attendance prior to the war, there had never been any shared aspiration that every child should graduate from high school. The second, more negative, development was the precipitous shrinkage in the number of jobs for which a high school diploma was not required. The failure in practice of the commitment to the former coupled with the power of the movement toward the latter framed the subsequent fate of a large number of American young people.

Also a factor, especially for people of color, was the country's move from a predominantly rural base to one centered in cities and suburbs. Most African Americans lived in cities by 1960, with particular growth in the largest cities (Sugrue 1996, 7). The African American population of Chicago, for example, more than tripled from 1940 to 1960, from 278,000 to 813,000 (Lemann 1991, 70). Some 5 million African Americans moved north between 1940 and 1970, following on the nearly 2 million who had come during the twenty-five years prior to World War II (Katz 1993, 451). African-American migrants found themselves confined to the inner city, and discriminated against in hiring, all of which had a particular impact on young people.

The number of good jobs available to urban residents began to diminish. Shortly after the war ended, plants began to relocate to the suburbs and away from urban settings altogether, followed later by a larger process of deindustrialization, increasing technological sophistication, and globalization that intensified the difficulties of the non-college-bound young in getting a foothold in the job market. Detroit, for example, lost nearly 130,000 manufacturing jobs between 1948 and 1967 (Sugrue 1996, 143). New York City lost more than 600,000 manufacturing jobs between 1953 and 1985 (Kantor and Brenzel 1993, 394). In the major cities stretching east from Chicago to New York, the decade of the seventies saw a decline of over 40 percent in the number of jobs held by people with less than a high school education (Kantor and Brenzel 1993, 395). The earnings of people with less education plummeted, too. Men with a high school education were earning 7–10 percent less in 1986 than in 1959, and those who had dropped out were earning 20–30 percent less (Ford Foundation 1989, 33).

The decline in manufacturing jobs hit African American migrants hard, and was especially tough on young people looking for their first jobs. African Americans found themselves underrepresented in better-paid, safer, and higher-status jobs. Their jobs tended to be in unskilled occupations, particularly vulnerable to replacement by automation (Sugrue 1996, 100). The proportion of employed 20–29-year-old black men working in manufacturing fell from three in eight to one in five between 1973 and 1987 (Wilson 1996, 31). Whites were able to follow the jobs when they moved to the suburbs. Blacks could not, which exacerbated their vulnerability. In addition, as whites left, cities became "poorer and blacker" (Sugrue 1996, 149). The income gap between the suburbs and cities continued to widen even in the nineties. Suburban median household income was 58 percent higher than central-city income in 1989 and 67 percent higher in 1996 (Katz 2000, 8).

By the end of the fifties the duality of youth experience was sufficiently ensconced—although not recognized in the mainstream culture—that *The Vanishing Adolescent* and *The Other America* could appear only a few years apart and both be correct as to a part of the population. Each, like the blind man, had touched a part of the elephant and found truth (although Harrington was clearly aware that there was another part to the elephant). The fragmenting trends attracted broader notice in the sixties, and ultimately produced the current bifurcated structure of class- and race-based public attitudes and policy that governs "youth."

YOUTH AND AMERICAN LIBERALISM, 1960–1973

The sixties were a watershed decade by anyone's estimation, producing both progressive change and the seeds of what became a continuing backlash against some of the young, a backlash that took economic root with the Arab

Fig. 11.2 President Kennedy at juvenile delinquency bill signing. © Bettmann/CORBIS.

oil shock of 1973. In terms of both political participation by young people and policy focus on them, the sixties surpassed any previous period in our history. Young people were at the heart of the civil rights movement, and were equally central to the urban violence and "black power" periods that ensued. In part because their age group was asked to do the fighting and dying in Vietnam, they were also front and center in the intense controversy over that conflict. "Delinquency prevention" was the terminology that captioned the initial planning for what became the war on poverty (figure 11.2), and the war on poverty itself featured a significant focus on young people. The Supreme Court, unprecedentedly responsive under Chief Justice Warren to the more vulnerable in the society, began paying attention to the special situation of children and youth. And perhaps because young people were fighting and dying in Vietnam, the vote was extended to eighteen-year-olds by way of the Twenty-sixth Amendment to the Constitution.

Youth and the Civil Rights Movement

The best aspect of the sixties was the progress made on race, and young people were vital participants in the accomplishments. The context included the simmering rejection of Jim Crow by black veterans of World War II, and intertwined litigation and organizing strategies pursued by NAACP lawyers and activists. By the time the sit-ins began at the end of the fifties, *Brown v. Board of Education* (347 U.S. 483 [1954]) was on the books, and Rosa Parks had already ignited the Montgomery bus boycott (Branch 1988, 143). Nonetheless, young people were the force behind the wave of nonviolent protest when it finally occurred. Dr. King was the nationally visible proponent of the Gandhian ethic (Branch 1988, 400), but hundreds of young people were the organizers on the ground, and thousands more made the effort into a movement (Kluger 1976, 755).

Thurgood Marshall and the lawyers created the legal framework, but the young people of the Student Nonviolent Coordinating Committee (SNCC) created the movement. SNCC, predominantly young and African-American, coordinated projects that ranged from sit-ins to extensive voter-registration efforts. The organization also coordinated several historical, cultural, and political education programs (Greenberg 1998, 8). While SNCC was the smallest of the civil rights groups, it had a tremendous impact on the civil rights movement (Marable and Mullings 2000, 395). SNCC maintained that it was focused on "direct action," which consisted of confrontational yet peaceful demonstrations against segregation (Greenberg 1998, 39).

The height of the civil rights revolution—the dismantling of the legal structure of apartheid in America—was reached with the Civil Rights Act of 1964, the Twenty-fourth Amendment outlawing the poll tax, and the Voting Rights Act of 1965, and young people made a major difference in bringing those historic laws to enactment (Kluger 1976, 757–59). SNCC's voter-registration efforts included Freedom Vote in 1963 and Freedom Summer in 1964. Freedom Summer sought to mobilize African American southerners in an effort to highlight the issue of black voting rights. The summer project sought to create "parallel institutionalism" by encouraging African American voters to participate in a mock election. In the years following the adoption of the Civil Rights Act, the Justice Department filed suit against more than five hundred school districts and took on more than four hundred antidiscrimination cases against establishments catering to the public (Kluger 1976, 759). Additionally, in 1964, the Supreme Court, in *Heart of Atlanta Motel v. United States* (379 U.S. 241 [1964]), ruled that the Civil Rights Act was constitutional (Kluger 1976, 759). The Voting Rights Act closed the remaining loopholes in the 1964 Civil Rights Act and restricted the use of "tests and devices" used to discourage and prevent African Americans from voting. (Kluger 1976, 759).

Youth were central to the unraveling of the movement as well. "Black and white together" and "We shall overcome" were replaced by clenched fists and cries of black power (Greenberg 1998, 11). African American youth in cities outside the South rebelled, reacting to the fact that the changes in the legal framework had not brought commensurate change in their daily lives. The violence—along with the diversion of focus and of resources to the war in Vietnam—provoked a diminution of domestic commitment and a backlash against low-income, African American youth (Kluger, 1976, 762) that is still with us, especially in crime and welfare policy.

"Delinquency Prevention" and the War on Poverty

When President Kennedy took office, his brother, the attorney general, established a small group based in his office to study ways to reduce juvenile delinquency (Katz 1986, 272). Robert Kennedy saw a connection between problems of youth crime, especially among African American youth, and the differential availability of jobs. This was before the civil rights movement had produced any serious pressure for comprehensive legislation to assure legal rights, and before any widespread perception that civil rights were not of full value without an accompanying strategy for economic opportunity. Over the nearly three years of JFK's presidency, RFK's group gradually came to see their assignment as a broader one—to deal with poverty (Katz 1986, 257).

When Lyndon Johnson acceded to the presidency, Robert Kennedy handed over the planning to Johnson's people. President Johnson declared war on poverty in his first State of the Union address, bringing the economic and social gap into the national spotlight. The resulting Economic Opportunity Act retained a significant emphasis on children and youth: Head Start for small children; the Job Corps, to help seriously disadvantaged youth prepare for work; VISTA, to provide opportunities for young people to be of service to others (this had been a favorite idea of Robert Kennedy); Upward Bound, to help low-income youth get to college; and the Neighborhood Youth Corps, to provide work opportunities for disadvantaged young people in their own neighborhoods (Lemann 1991, 112, 272).

The overall policy reality never matched the rhetoric. Attention to assuring enough jobs for all who needed them and to making sure that people had enough income to get out of poverty would have been necessary for a full-scale onslaught. Instead, the emphasis of the War on Poverty and of the Great Society generally was on education and training—necessary but not sufficient (Danziger and Gottschalk 1995, 18–19). The Department of Labor advocated job creation and a focus on the labor market, but the policy chosen focused on promoting the capacity of people, especially young people, to pursue the job opportunities that a healthy economy was assumed to offer—a supply-side view of poverty reduction (Katz 1993, 14). There were initiatives for children and youth, but there was no direct assault on issues of jobs and income (Grubb and Lazerson 1982, 48).

The theory of President Johnson's Great Society was to follow the establishment of legal rights with policies to change the economic realities, but the war and the change in attitudes at home choked off continuing pursuit of serious policy to close the gaps. Nonetheless, poverty was reduced in the sixties, through a combination of the general health of the economy and the results of the opportunity strategy, including antidiscrimination efforts (Stern 1993, 238). But the sixties turned out to be a high-water mark for movement toward a national commitment to economic justice and inclusive policies for young people.

Youth and the Courts

The sixties as high-water mark characterized the attitude of the courts toward young people, too. This was the time of *In re Gault* (387 U.S. 1 [1967]), in which the Supreme Court recognized in strong language that the kind, paternalistic intent of the juvenile court's creators had mutated into an institution that, lacking due process and a guarantee of legal representation, was as likely to punish the innocent or overreact to minor offenders as it was to pursue a rehabilitative path. *Gault* was not an isolated phenomenon, though. The continuing pressure from the Court toward remedies that would effectively desegregate public schools reflected judicial concern for children, and in *Tinker v. Des Moines School District* (393 U.S. 503 [1969]) the Court held that children in school had free-speech rights that did not necessarily have to give way to the authority of school officials.

As with civil rights and antipoverty policies, the judicial activism of the period gave way in the seventies to a much more conservative stance. In the area of criminal justice, the backlash meant a wave of pressure to handle increasing numbers of youth in the adult criminal justice system and a simultaneous push to incarcerate more youth in prisons, jails, and other locked environments. The arrest rate for young African American males rose by nearly 50 percent between 1966 and 1974 (Lemann 1991, 283). The Supreme Court turned more conservative in a number of areas. *San Antonio Independent School District v. Rodriguez* (411 U.S. 1 [1973]) was a particularly important instance of the transformation, especially concerning children. The plaintiffs claimed that inequalities caused by Texas's method of school finance were of unconstitutional dimension. The Court held that education is not a fundamental right, and rejected the challenge.

Youth and the Constitution

Even the Constitution proved briefly amenable to change for the benefit of young people. Congress tried in 1970 to legislate the vote for eighteen-year-olds, but the Supreme Court held that the Constitution would have to be amended to do that for elections other than federal elections (*Oregon v. Mitchell,* 400 U.S. 112 [1970]). Congress responded by promulgating the Twenty-sixth Amendment, and the states quickly ratified it ("Developments in the Law" 1982, 1430, 1439). It was as though an exclamation point had been added to the positive attention of the time toward youth.

As President Nixon's time in office continued, the developing bifurcation of our national attitudes toward large numbers of young people was fertilized by the sudden acceleration in the pace of structural economic change (Kluger 1976, 763). The steady economic improvement that African American youth had experienced from the end of World War II until the end of the sixties took a sharp turn in the other direction. Despite the manifest impatience of urban African American youth, their rate of labor market participation had been going up quite steadily and their rate of unemployment had been going down. Inner-city youth had not shared fully in the changes, but the trend had been encouraging. That was about to change.

LATE-TWENTIETH-CENTURY TRENDS

The deterioration in the nation's economy for half or more of its population—a multidecade process of deindustrialization, automation, and globalization that was accelerated and accentuated by the Arab oil shock of 1973—was a vital element in forming the political economy of youth that was still in place as the twentieth century ended. MIT professor Frank Levy labeled the decade from 1973 to 1982 the "quiet depression," because median family income dropped and poverty rates rose substantially (Danziger and Gottschalk 1995, 7–9). Things turned bad for lower-income workers of all races, but worse for people of color and worse yet for people of color who had dropped out of high school. Youth unemployment rates shot up, and labor force participation rates plummeted, with young people of color who had less schooling hurt the most. The economic changes caused a large group of people at the lower end to become surplus workers, and young people of color felt the impact the most.

A common denominator in the new duality was race. The loss of good jobs for which little education was required hurt young people of all races, but its impact was greater on young people of color. Young people in the inner city, disproportionately Latino as well as African American as time went on, attended schools of ever-deteriorating quality, dropped out in large numbers, and lagged substantially in gaining a fair share of the diminishing number of good jobs. Inner-city schools got worse and worse as talented people whose predecessors had chosen teaching careers pursued other professions now open to them. The schools became more segregated than ever, now all-poor as well as all African American or otherwise all minority.

The politicized violence of the sixties evolved into street crime that often reflected a personal anger which inflicted gratuitous injury on its victims. The victims were disproportionately people of color, but people of all races were victims. A public demand for tougher law enforcement ensued. In the wake of the inner-city violence of the late sixties, attitudes hardened. Four out of five respondents in a 1969 poll said law and order had broken down, blaming "Negroes who start riots" and "communists" (Mauer 1999, 53). The juvenile court and the juvenile justice system have been under continuous attack since. Again, the irony is that the skyrocketing rates of incarceration of young people of color came after we professed a new commitment to equality. By the early nineties it was a constant fact that African Americans were overrepresented throughout the criminal justice system, from arrest through incarceration (Hacker 1992, 180). By the end of the nineties, seven out of ten youth held in secure confinement were African American, Latino, or other minorities (Children's Defense Fund 1999, 119).

As the century ended, the picture of American youth had evolved further since 1973, accentuating the duality of America's approach to its young. Families had changed, neighborhoods had changed, workplaces had changed, and demographics had changed. The ladder to adulthood had acquired more rungs and therefore more places to fall off along the way. Silicon Valley and the world of dot-coms were an insurmountable distance away for a significant portion of American young people.

The schools attended by low-income youth, and especially low-income youth of color who lived in neighborhoods and areas of concentrated poverty, had gotten worse as the educational attainment required for success in the labor market had become more rigorous. As the rest of the country reached high school graduation rates of well over 90 percent, inner-city drop-out rates persisted at well over 50 percent (Jargowsky 1996, 111). Prestigious study panels concluded that dropout prevention and other add-on programs would not succeed on a large scale unless schools themselves were improved (National Research Council and Institute of Medicine 1999, 22) The vocational education system put in place during the first half of the century offered little to inner-city youth, and, while community colleges offered a second chance to some, no structure existed to help low-income young people surmount the barriers to entry into a job market that for the most part didn't need them.

Twice as many youth in 1990 as in 1970 lived in neighborhoods where over 40 percent of the people were poor, and these were overwhelmingly neighborhoods isolated by both race (or ethnicity) and poverty (Jargowsky 1996, 30). Poverty among the young as a whole was higher in 1998 than it had been throughout the entire decade of the 1970s. It remained at nearly one in five children, with over 36 percent of African American children and 34 percent of Hispanic American children living in poverty (Rawlings 2000, 23). In addition, the face of youth had changed to include many more immigrants and children of immigrants. Urban poverty rates were twice as high as suburban poverty rates (Katz and Bradley 1999, 2).

The flight of much of the middle class from inner-city African American and Latino neighborhoods severely damaged the sense of community in those places, and a variety of social problems worsened. Many more youth had been born to mothers who were not married, and more grew up in single-parent households. Beginning in 1960, there was a decline cutting across lines of race and income in the number of children living in two-parent households, but it was much greater among African American families than among white families—a drop of 46 percent compared to 18 percent (Child Trends 2000, 3). Among African Americans, female-headed households accounted for 80 percent of all poor families (Rawlings 2000, 16).

The trend to more unmarried births, including higher rates of unmarried teen births, existed across lines of income and race but was most pronounced in places where race and poverty intersected. Teens from families in poverty are at greater risk of becoming pregnant. Because African American and Hispanic American youth are poorer than their white counterparts, poor teens of color are at particular risk. A majority of black and Hispanic teen mothers live in poverty, while a quarter of white teenage mothers are in poverty (Institute of Medicine 1995, 28, 56).

There was an across-the-board decline in the teen birth rate in the nineties, but rates remained higher for African American and Hispanic youth between ages fifteen and nineteen. In 1998 there were 94 births per 1,000 Hispanic teenagers, 85 per 1,000 African American teenagers and 35 per 1,000 non-Hispanic/white teenagers (Child Trends 1999, 2). A mother's age at the time her first child is born is related to whether she and her family will be poor later on. She will be more likely to drop out of school and have a larger family, and less likely to get married, have steady work, and earn enough to escape poverty (Institute of Medicine 1995, 56–57). Teen births thus transmit disproportionate racial poverty to the next generation.

Drug and alcohol abuse—again, problems throughout society—reached much higher levels in inner cities. In the mid-1980s, "crack cocaine"—a mixture of cocaine powder, water, and baking soda—invaded inner-city neighborhoods in Los Angeles, Miami, and New York. "Crack" was sold in small quantities and was marketed at lower prices than powder cocaine (Mauer 1999, 62). In 1999, about 1.5 million people were current cocaine users, and about 200,000 were current heroin users, with inner-city neighborhoods disproportionately represented, especially among those whose use was habitual (SAMHSA 2000, 14).

The nature of violence changed—fights that previously ended in bruises now ended in the cemetery or the emergency room. Between 1989 and 1993, intentional and unintentional firearm injuries were the leading cause of death for youth ages 10–24 (Policy Council on Violence Prevention 1995, 33–36).

The changes in the economy made it harder and harder for young people to get back on track once they had dropped out of school or had gotten in trouble, both because good jobs required more qualifications and because there was a shortage of good jobs. During the 1970s and 1980s, there was a further decline in the proportion of manufacturing jobs in the overall economy. The percentage of young African Americans in manufacturing jobs was cut almost in half (National Research Council 1993, 28). Between 1979 and 1998 the earnings gap between male college and high school graduates went from 29 percent to 68 percent. For women, the weekly wage gap between college and high school graduates increased from 43 percent to 79 percent (Danziger and Reed 1999, 16). The education gap between African Americans and whites meant that the increased earnings gap had a disproportionate racial impact.

All of these issues made the transition to adulthood far more difficult for youth growing up in poverty or a little above the poverty line, especially for those growing up at the intersection of race and poverty. The factors shaping the political economy of youth in the United States since 1945 have sorted heavily although not exclusively by race, ethnicity, and national origin. On the other hand, opportunities appeared for large numbers who were previously excluded, both young people of color and women of all races and ethnicities. Glass ceilings still existed, but elite universities, the professions, and the business world all looked quite different. The military was a vital avenue to upward mobility. These changes affected millions. They were enormously important. By the end of the century, America had, de facto, two youth policies, one for those well enough off not to need much assistance by way of public policy and one for everyone else.

For young people growing up in reasonably healthy and fairly secure families and attending good public or private schools, the policy was the human version of market economics: leave things to the invisible hand, and they will turn out all right. That policy was successful for most of the people for whom it fit. The problem came when the market failed, as it did for too large a segment of American youth, including disproportionate numbers of African American, Latino, and immigrant youth. Then our policy was inadequate schools, nonexistent or inadequate attention to off-school hours, weak efforts to help young people get into the job market, an increasingly punitive juvenile and criminal justice system, and, as of 1996, withholding cash welfare assistance to induce changes in the behavior of young women and men who have children without being married.

There are thousands, probably millions, of Americans, and hundreds, probably thousands, of organizations of one kind or another who have a different policy—who work full-time or contribute money or volunteer time so individual youth can transcend the circumstances that conspire to keep them from success. A central question of American life in the new century is why the clearly extensive commitment of so many to improve the life chances of those who need something extra does not result across the board in better schools, better communities, better job opportunities, and a more humane justice system.

The private commitment of a substantial number of Americans to help on an individual basis is clear. But so many who act privately lack conviction about the efficacy of public policy to help or their efficacy to contribute to changing public policy. So the political economy of the position of youth in the American polity does not change substantially, and in some ways—for example, the punitive trends in the worlds of criminal justice and welfare—gets worse.

RETHINKING AMERICA'S YOUTH POLICY

There are four concentric circles of policy to examine in considering directions the nation might take concerning those youth holding the short end of the stick. All involve a role for government, with differing responsibilities among the federal, state, and local levels, and all involve a role for private action. Even as to those where the governmental responsibility is primarily state and local, or where a significant portion of the responsibility is civic and private, there is a substantial role for national leadership, especially presidential leadership, in pointing the way.

One circle, the widest, involves looking at the issues from the perspective of the economic structure and associated public policies that cause so many young people to grow up in lower-income families (both poor and near-poor) in this wealthy nation. In this circle the policies to be considered are not specific to children and youth. A second, narrower circle relates specifically to children and youth, and concerns the education we provide and what we offer in the out-of-school hours. Of special concern are those who live in high-risk neighborhoods, who need help to make it through to adulthood. Here, though, our particular focus is on children on the basis of where they live or whether they live in low-income families, not on children who have made themselves a matter of concern because of their own behavior. How well we do here will reduce the number who get into trouble. A third circle, narrower yet, concerns our response to those youth (and children) who show by their behavior that unless we pay extra attention to them (and maybe even if we do) they are going to be clients of the juvenile court, or the mental health system, or a drug or alcohol treatment facility, or some other place or system that is supposed to serve those who fall out of the mainstream. The last circle, the smallest, is the way we handle youth accused of crimes—mentioned above and discussed earlier in this volume. Suffice it to say we have chosen a course that is among the more punitive among the possible paths for this group, and we need to get back to solutions and approaches that deal with young people as individuals with a measure of promise, at the same time as we make sure that we do what is necessary to protect the community. All four circles bear analysis, although, as indicated, the last has been the subject of much of this book and needs no further elaboration here.

All four have a flip side—young people who grow up in economically comfortable families. Youth of all backgrounds can have problems, of course. But people of means can buy their way out, by way of military schools, private psychiatrists, and expensive residential facilities for the emotionally disturbed. Parents with higher incomes can purchase music and ballet lessons and pay for soccer leagues, computer camps, and all of the other out-of-school enrichments that contribute to child and youth development. Poverty and the juvenile court go hand in hand. Behavior of upper-income youth that would be tolerated or only mildly sanctioned (or result in therapy or alternative schooling) results in a trip to juvenile court when the child is from a lower-income family. Race and ethnicity compound the gap.

The Relevance of Family Economics and Income

The widest circle of policy transcends youth and has to do with policies and attitudes not specifically directed at education and youth development. It is obvious, but too often not part of the advocacy agendas of people who really do care deeply about improving life chances for those facing long odds. The issues here relate to the poverty of the families in which young people grow up, and along with it the particular consequences of the race or ethnicity of some lower-income young people in relation to their chances of making it out of poverty.

Family strength matters, of course. So do school quality, programs during off-school hours, and neighborhood safety. Economic security, though, not only matters intrinsically, but also is likely to afford families the possibility of affecting the other forces that impinge on the life chances of their children. Yet too often people who work with or advocate for youth adopt a narrow view that is confined to the funding and the effect of a specific program, instead of thinking in broader strategic terms about what young people and the families of which they are a part need in order to succeed. If we are going to change the political economy of youth, then, we have to change the political economy of poverty, and not just poverty in a narrow sense, but the larger equation that has left millions in a position where they cannot support their families even though they are not poor by the narrow official definition of poverty that we have adopted.

The policy choices here are not simple, of course. How do we succeed in maximizing the number of people for whom earnings from work are the primary way they support their families? What is the right mix between wages and public supplements to wages, including health coverage, child care assistance, and help with the costs of housing and college attendance? What is the line between the expectation that parents will work and the provision of a safety net to make sure that children of parents not in a position to work will be protected from injury? What is the correct definition of disability? How can we improve our systems to seek child support from absent parents and promote greater involvement of noncustodial parents, especially fathers, with their children? How much of all of this should involve national policy, and how much should be left to local decision-making, with or without federal fiscal involvement?

Education and Out-of-School Hours

The challenge to improve the education of all children is a pressing issue. Debates on the issue tend to focus on particular solutions that cannot possibly help all children, like charter schools and vouchers. The use of so-called "high-stakes" tests relates to all children but is too often not accompanied by the extensive and complex strategies necessary to see that all children are taught so as to have the maximum chance of performing up to their capacity on the tests. The promise of educating all children has been present in theory for over half a century. While fulfilling the promise is still too distant a prospect, it is probably fair to say it is receiving increased attention with the passage of time.

We also hear much more than we used to about the importance of the off-school hours. Estimates are that 40 percent of young people's time is unstructured and unsupervised (National Research Council and Institute of Medicine 1999, 12). Experts and advocates have talked for years about the need to provide constructive alternatives for young people after school, in the evening, on weekends, and during the summer, especially as more and more mothers are working. Interest in such programs has accelerated as concern about the performance of urban schools has finally become more widespread, with the idea that academic reinforcement during off-school times could make a difference for struggling students.

The need here is for both public funding and citizen involvement. Young people need sympathetic and supportive adults in their lives. They need opportunities to serve and help others. They need support for their academic work, and they need recreation and a variety of other enrichments. They need help as they get older in understanding and penetrating the complexities of the job market. The nineties saw a marked expansion of programs in the off-school hours. New York City's Mayor David Dinkins began an initiative which resulted in the use of school buildings as sites for programs run by nonprofit community organizations. The program, called Beacon Schools, was continued by Mayor Rudolph Giuliani, and was in place in more than eighty schools by 2000. Other localities began new programs, too, some funded by foundations both national and local, and some by state and local government or a combination.

As the federal deficit was replaced by a surplus in the late nineties, a new federal after-school program was initiated with bipartisan support in the otherwise highly partisan atmosphere of the time, and by 2000 had nearly half a billion dollars in annual federal funding. This infusion of funds dwarfed what had gone on up until that time. Experts debated the merits of the new federal program, which was called Twenty-first Century Community Learning Centers, with the Beacon Schools and other recent local initiatives being pointed to by some as better models. The federal program made grants to school systems, and the local programs funded by it put heavy emphasis on academic enrichment. The critics stressed the importance of a number of characteristics of Beacon Schools and similar programs that are typically not present in the efforts being funded under the new federal thrust: activities that go beyond academics, especially including opportunities to help other people; for older youth, help in gaining access to the job market; involvement of nonprofit, youth-serving organizations in running the programs; hours that include evenings, weekends, and summers; and a community-building perspective, where there is a sense not just of one-on-one help but of the community taking responsibility for its young people and everyone contributing to making the neighborhood a safer and nicer place to live.

The phrase "after-school program" is immediately understandable to parents and voters generally. But it is in fact not descriptive of the responsibility that communities need to take for their young people. What happens during off-school hours will of course never have maximum impact unless attention is paid to what happens in school at the same time, and the two should be connected. In addition, however, foundation-sponsored and other initiatives of the nineties have demonstrated more clearly than ever that community-based programs for young people—be they relatively new efforts like the Beacon Schools or outposts of traditional organizations like the Boys and Girls Clubs and the YMCA and YWCA—need to connect themselves to their surroundings as closely as they can. This means connecting not only to schools, but to families, churches, and employers, and, insofar as older youth are concerned, to the juvenile and criminal justice systems, and to the community generally.

To build and maintain these connections as well as function successfully on a day-to-day basis, community youth centers need paid staff—people who are well trained and paid enough so they can support a family and do the work as a career. They are a perfect place for volunteers, as well, but mentors and tutors and other volunteers cannot even begin to function without the presence of paid staff to organize things. A particular role for community youth centers is in relation to the juvenile and criminal justice systems, beyond the obvious point that the availability of positive and constructive things to do will reduce the number of young people who get into trouble. Such places can be settings to which young people who have gotten into trouble can be referred for activities that are more tightly supervised than those for the usual clientele. And they can be the organizing points for reaching out with specialized staff to young people whom the community and the schools identify as particularly at risk of getting into trouble.

From the time when settlement houses first came into being more than a century ago, the out-of-school hours have been seen as important foci for attention. When the problems of the inner city were allowed to fester without a satisfactory response, attention to the off-school hours languished along with everything else. That was changing for the better as the new century began.

Responding to Youth with Problems

Schools have never wanted to cope with children and youth who are disruptive for one reason or another. This is not wholly surprising, with unduly large classes compounding the problem in so many places. In one area, relating to disabled children, there has in fact been great improvement, although more in suburban than urban systems. Beginning with landmark federal legislation in the mid-seventies, large numbers of children who would previously have been institutionalized, sent to a special school, or pushed out of school altogether are in mainstream classrooms and are doing well. The Education for All Handicapped Children Act (PL 94-142), enacted in 1974, gave all handicapped children the right to an appropriate public education. School teachers and administrators are the key decision makers in creating individualized educational plans for disabled children, with the required participation of parents. Now, many for whom expensive residential placement or special schooling is appropriate are receiving it when they would not have gotten it in the past, or it would have been a backbreaking financial burden for their families. Teachers and school officials complain, and lower-income children of color are still disproportionately labeled as children with special needs, but there has on the whole been major positive change (Handler 1988, 1009–10).

But where disability overlaps with behavioral disruption, and even more so when behavioral problems exist in the absence of legally cognizable disability, the trend is in the other direction. The guns and other dangerous weapons and the consequent violence that have appeared in schools have rightly engendered intense efforts to assure safety in schools. But "zero tolerance" has gone much further. Students are being suspended and expelled in considerable numbers, without provision for alternative education, based on behavior that in the past would not have drawn anything more than an in-school suspension for a few days, if that. This expansion of "zero tolerance" came after serious and violent youth crime had declined by 11 percent in the mid-nineties (Levick 1999). The widespread current utilization of suspensions and expulsions is troubling. In 1998, 3.1 million students were suspended and another 87,000 were expelled (Civil Rights Project 2000).

The sanctions are being applied in the same racially disproportionate fashion that has long characterized school suspensions and expulsions. African American youth are more likely to be classified early as behavior problems and forced out of the classroom or otherwise discouraged from succeeding in school (Krisberg and Austin 1993, 132). According to Department of Education data, while black students account for only 17 percent of public school enrollment, they represent 32 percent of out-of-school suspensions. However, white students, constituting 63 percent of students enrolled in public schools, represent only 50 percent of suspensions and 50 percent of expulsions (Civil Rights Project 2000). These issues were brought to public attention in the seventies, and school systems across the country changed their policies to handle disruptive young people more fairly, both procedurally and substantively. The youth violence of the eighties and early nineties brought back the tendency to suspend and expel on a broader basis.

Perhaps even more serious in terms of the numbers of youth who may be pushed out of the schools is the current fad of "high-stakes" testing. The ostensibly well-motivated determination to end social promotion means students are being subjected to tests that will result in their being held back if they fail, but few school districts place enough emphasis on the good teaching and remediation necessary to give students the tools they need to succeed. This is deeply distressing. Some jurisdictions are backing off from their tests, now that they see how many students do not pass. Others are moving ahead, with the consequence that students, especially from lower-income families, and even more especially lower-income students of color, are being pushed out of school. It should be possible to have appropriate standards and good teaching and remediation so students who make the effort can succeed. That is not the reality in most urban school districts at the present time. All of this increases the workload of the juvenile court, and of the criminal justice system beyond. The racially disproportionate operation of the juvenile and criminal justice systems begins in our schools.

Those who end up in court are the tip of an iceberg. Almost no inner-city school has available to it in-house or by referral the psychological, counseling, or other mental health services that many children and youth need. Most of these young people will never be customers of the juvenile court—their problems will show up in other ways. But looking at it from a juvenile justice perspective, we lack a system that articulates between the court and the schools. Part of it is the gaping hole in support services for the schools but, bad as that is, it is not the whole picture. Another part is attitudes within the schools that lean toward pushing young people out instead of figuring out how to help them. There is a counterpart gap at the court where the choice is often limited to sending a youth home or processing and labeling him, because there are no alternatives available. If he is placed on probation, his former school will typically not want him back, and his probation officer is generally too busy and otherwise not disposed to push the school on his behalf. If he is coming back after being in a residential facility, the school is often unwelcoming, and the juvenile aftercare people too often make no effort to advocate for him. There has been little attention to innovative policies focusing on aftercare and reentry of offenders into their communities. Planning for a youth's return to his community, if it occurs at all, typically does not begin until almost the eve of his release (Krisberg and Austin 1993, 176).

The result is that when young people slip a little, they may slip a long way, because services that ought to catch them are not there. This is an underexamined problem that deserves attention everywhere. Too few discussions of the juvenile court widen their lens and look at the community context. So many youth who get in trouble started years earlier down a path that eventuated in their coming to court. They started acting out in school and met only repeated suspensions instead of efforts to understand their problems and deal with them. Once they appeared in court, few entities existed to work with them and help them get on a different path. In virtually any juvenile corrections facility there are disproportionate numbers of learning-disabled youth and disproportionate numbers of youth who were abused by a parent or other adult at an earlier age. The earlier lack of remediation or lack of response to the problems caused by the abuse caused frustration and anger to develop that could well have been alleviated—not in all cases, but in many.

And, as Krisberg and Austin write, "A public health approach to delinquency inevitably would point us to the exploration of environmental factors in the promotion of delinquency" (1993, 182). There should be (although there almost never is where poor and minority youth are concerned) a continuum of services, with up-front investment in a developmental, preventive approach that minimizes the number who will fall by the wayside. This means schools that teach all children. It means maximum mainstreaming of children and minimum use of separate classes, of separate schools within a school system, and of separate schools outside the system, although all of those alternatives should be available for those who need them because of disability or behavioral problems.

Learning disabilities should be identified early and remediated immediately. Behavior problems and what is causing them should be noticed and responded to promptly, with help for the youth and the family, as needed, utilizing in-school suspensions and other constructive policies that carry the maximum chance of ending the bad behavior and holding the child in school. A full strategy would include community schools, community centers, settlement houses, and afterschool programs to engage youth and their families constructively with activities, recreation, and academic supplementation.

The perspective should be one of community-building. Some entity or group of entities in a neighborhood should know all of the young people in the neighborhood, and when one of them gets in trouble, they should step forward and claim him or her and, if at all possible, take responsibility for seeing that it doesn't happen again.

When the behavior gets bad enough that the justice system gets involved, it is harder to create the right response, but we should still think in terms of a continuum rather than a bright-line departure into a realm of residential institutions. But there has to be a response. Young people need structure. They need to know that unacceptable behavior has consequences. Slaps on the hand, or even less, for early offenses invite more offending. The response doesn't have to mean formal processing, let alone taking the matter to adjudication and use of actual probation. It depends on the offense, of course. But if what has occurred is a property offense where no one was physically hurt or endangered, we can do much more with ideas of restorative justice and community service than we have done. Youth can pay back for what they have done, either literally with cash that they earn or through serving the community.

We need a new structure in communities to respond when the problem has moved from one of generalized prevention to one of preventing a specific youth from offending again. The police, the schools, the nonprofit youth-serving community, and the faith community need to work together to create active responses to young people who are no longer merely at risk but have crossed the line into some kind of offending. The police, the prosecution, and the courts need specific options in the community to involve youths who are not at a point where they need to be deprived of their liberty or subjected to a formal sanction. If there has been a serious undertaking to build a set of youth-involving community institutions in a neighborhood, including a community police presence, a partnership will be naturally present to take responsibility when a youth offends. To do nothing until we lose patience and throw the book is counterproductive and wrong.

Strategic Implications of the Four Circles

If youth advocates want to make progress on all of this, what should their strategic stance be? The issues are fraught with dilemmas and difficulties. If they want to be precise about the target population, they run the risk of focusing the discussion on providing help to a group that elicits little sympathy from the broader population. If they want to focus on a broader definition of those who need attention, they run the risk that those who need help the most won't get it at all or at least won't get the extra help they need.

For example, "youth" itself is not the most attractive idea. Small children are cute and have all of life's potential ahead of them. Their innocence is unassailable. Adolescents are, well, adolescents. Even our own try our patience. It is tempting to hold them more responsible for their behavior. For those who already have problems, interventions will be successful with a lower percentage. But if youth advocates fold their advocacy into a broader concept of policy for children, they may be more successful in general and less successful in getting help to the youth who need it the most.

Youth advocates might ask how other nations approach these dilemmas. Do any have a good national youth policy, and what was their strategic approach to getting it adopted? What we find generally is that the nations of western Europe, plus Canada, Australia, and New Zealand, have more comprehensive social services and safety nets generally, and narrower disparities between top and bottom. The issue turns out to be how they care for members of their population generally. Some of them have policies that are describable as positive youth policies, but the reason they do is that their social policies in general are informed by a perspective more generous than what our approach in the United States continues to be.

There are some strategic points that youth advocates can make, though. One is that they have never made clear that the problems of family economic success—the returns from work plus the social policies adopted to add up to a total "social" wage—cut across a much bigger part of the population in the United States than we see discussed politically. These problems affect children growing up and the life possibilities of the young people in those families as they go through high school and consider what to make of their coming adult lives. There is a potential politics in emphasizing that a broader unfairness exists in the American distribution of income and opportunity. The "social" wage would consist of income from work (and everything that would maximize it), income supplementation, health coverage, child care, housing assistance, and help with postsecondary education. All of this would affect young people significantly. Focusing on this broader definition of the target population does run the risk of an inadequate response to those actually in poverty, but it is politically more promising, and is a framework within which arguments can be inserted for those at the bottom—perhaps with more success if they are not the headline.

A second strategic (and substantive) point is the value of emphasizing education. Youth advocates must explain that fulfilling our theoretical commitment to offer a good education to every American child means reforming public school systems to the end that every school is a good school. Vouchers and charters may or may not be good ideas, but neither is sufficient in the face of what our aim should be—to educate every child. "Education" is always a concern that is on or potentially on the front burner. Subsuming the educational needs of low-income youth into a broader educational agenda is again risky, but also offers a framework for insertion of arguments on behalf of low-income youth.

Nonetheless, there is no getting around the need for youth advocates to focus explicitly on the adolescent years. School reform too easily stops at the water's edge of the high school, let alone at the water's edge of low-income youth. Extra effort must be made to focus on the quality of the high school—it is too easy to decide, implicitly if not explicitly, that reforming high schools is too hard and we're just not going to do it, or we'll only give it lip service. The same goes for after-school programs. It is much easier to serve younger children. The path of least resistance is to forget those of high school age. Extra effort is needed to include those of high school age in off-school hours programming.

And if it is true that there is no avoiding a focus on youth in school-reform strategies and off-school hours strategies, it is even more true that there is no broader framework—of income, family, race, community, education, after-school, disability, mental health, or anything else—within which to frame attention to those young people who have already begun to get into trouble. Youth advocates must also focus on the juvenile justice system itself, and on its relation to the community around it.

So, while there are broader frameworks that will help gain better policies for young people, there is no alternative to building a broader base of interest in young people directly. If this is not done, the United States will continue its bifurcated approach to youth.

REFERENCES

Ashby, Leroy. 1997. *Endangered Children: Dependency, Neglect, and Abuse in American History.* New York: Twayne Publishing.

Branch, Taylor. 1988. *Parting the Waters: America in the King Years, 1954–63.* New York: Simon & Schuster.

Bremner, Robert H., ed. 1971. *Children and Youth in America: A Documentary History.* Cambridge, MA: Harvard University Press.

Child Trends. 2000. *A Century of Children's Health and Well-Being.* Washington, DC: Child Trends.

———. 1999. *CTS Facts at a Glance.* Washington, DC: Child Trends (December).

Children's Defense Fund. 1999. *The State of America's Children Yearbook.* Washington, DC: Children's Defense Fund.

Civil Rights Project. 2000. *Opportunities Suspended: The Devastating Consequences of Zero Tolerance and School Disciplinary Policies*. Cambridge, MA: Harvard University Press.

Danziger, Sheldon, and Peter Gottschalk. 1995. *America Unequal*. Cambridge, MA: Harvard University Press.

Danziger, Sheldon, and Deborah Reed. 1999. "Winners and Losers: The Era of Inequality Continues." *Brookings Review* (fall 1999): 14–17.

Demos, John. 1986. *Past, Present and Personal: The Family and the Life Course in American History*. New York: Oxford University Press.

"Developments in the Law: The Interpretation of State Constitutional Rights, Privacy and Education: The Two Faces of Fundamental Rights." 1982. *Harvard Law Review* 95, no. 6: 1324–1502.

Feld, Barry. 1999. *Bad Kids: Race and the Transformation of the Juvenile Court*. New York: Oxford University Press.

Ford Foundation. 1989. *The Common Good: Social Welfare and the American Future*. New York: Ford Foundation.

Greenberg, Cheryl Lynn, ed. 1998. *A Circle of Trust: Remember the SNCC*. New Brunswick, NJ: Rutgers University Press.

Grubb, W. Norton, and Marvin Lazerson. 1982. *Broken Promises: How Americans Fail Their Children*. New York: Basic Books.

Hacker, Andrew. 1992. *Two Nations: Black and White, Separate, Hostile, Unequal*. New York: Charles Scribner's Sons.

Handler, Joel. 1988. "Dependent People, the State, and the Modern/Postmodern Search for the Dialogic Community." *UCLA Law Review* 35, no. 6.

Institute of Medicine. 1995. *The Best Intentions: Unintended Pregnancy and the Well-Being of Children and Families*. Washington, DC: National Academy Press.

Jargowsky, Paul. 1996. *Poverty and Place: Ghettos, Barrios, and the American City*. New York: Russell Sage Foundation.

Kantor, Harvey, and Barbara Brenzel. 1993. "Urban Education and the 'Truly Disadvantaged': The Historical Roots of the Contemporary Crisis." In Michael Katz, ed., *The "Underclass" Debate: Views from History*. Princeton, NJ: Princeton University Press.

Katz, Bruce. 2000. "Enough of the Small Stuff! Toward a New Urban Agenda." *Brookings Review* (summer): 6–11.

Katz, Bruce, and Jennifer Bradley. 1999. "Divided We Sprang!" *Atlantic Monthly* (December) <http://www.theatlantic.com/issues/aadec/9912Katz.htm>

Katz, Michael B. 1986. *In the Shadow of the Poorhouse: A Social History of Welfare in America*. New York: Basic Books.

———. 1993. "Reframing the Underclass Debate." In Michael Katz, ed., *The "Underclass" Debate: Views from History*. Princeton, NJ: Princeton University Press.

Kett, Joseph F. 1977. *Rites of Passage: Adolescence in America, 1790 to the Present*. New York: Basic Books.

Kluger, Richard. 1976. *Simple Justice*. New York: Alfred A. Knopf.

Krisberg, Barry, and James F. Austin. 1993. *Reinventing Juvenile Justice*. Newbury Park, CA: Sage Publications.

Lemann, Nicholas. 1991. *The Promised Land: The Great Migration and How It Changed America*. New York: Alfred A. Knopf.

Levick, Marsha. 1999. "Zero Tolerance." *Oxygen* <http://www.oxygen.com>.

Lindenmeyer, Kriste. 1997. *"A Right to Childhood": The U.S. Children's Bureau and Child Welfare, 1912–46.* Urbana and Chicago: University of Illinois Press.

Lindley, Betty, and Ernest K. Lindley. [1938] 1972. *A New Deal for Youth: The Story of the National Youth Administration.* New York: Da Capo Press.

Macleod, David I. 1987. "Act Your Age: Boyhood, Adolescence, and the Rise of the Boy Scouts of America." In Harvey Graff, ed., *Growing Up in America: Historical Experiences.* Detroit: Wayne State University Press.

Marable, Manning, and Leith Mullings, eds. 2000. *Let Nobody Turn Us Around: Voices of Resistance, Reform, and Renewal—An African-American Anthology.* Oxford: Rowman & Littlefield.

Mauer, Marc. 1999. *Race to Incarcerate: The Sentencing Project.* New York: New Press.

Muncy, Robyn. 1991. *Creating a Female Dominion in American Reform, 1890–1935.* New York: Oxford University Press.

National Research Council. 1993. *Losing Generations: Adolescents in High-Risk Settings.* Washington, DC: National Academy Press.

National Research Council and Institute of Medicine. 1999. *Risks and Opportunities: Synthesis of Studies on Adolescence.* Washington, DC: National Academy Press.

Nathanson, Constance A. 1991. *Dangerous Passage: The Social Control of Sexuality in Women's Adolescence.* Philadelphia: Temple University Press.

Policy Council on Violence Prevention. 1995. *Violence Prevention: A Vision of Hope.* Sacramento, CA: Crime and Violence Prevention Center (August).

Rawlings, Lynette. 2000. *Poverty and Income Trends: 1998.* Washington, DC: Center on Budget and Policy Priorities.

Reiman, Richard A. 1992. *The New Deal and American Youth: Ideas and Ideals in a Depression Decade.* Athens: University of Georgia Press.

Stern, Mark. 1993. "Poverty and Family Composition Since 1940." In Michael Katz, ed., *The "Underclass" Debate: Views from History.* Princeton, NJ: Princeton University Press.

Substance Abuse and Mental Health Services Administration (SAMHSA). 2000. *Summary of Findings from the 1999 National Household Survey on Drug Abuse.* Washington, DC: Department of Health and Human Services.

Sugrue, Thomas. 1996. *The Origins of the Urban Crisis: Race and Inequality in Postwar Detroit.* Princeton, NJ: Princeton University Press.

Troen, Selwyn K. 1976. "The Discovery of the Adolescent by American Educational Reformers, 1900–1920: An Economic Perspective." In Lawrence Stone, ed., *Schooling and Society: Studies in the History of Education.* Baltimore: Johns Hopkins Press.

Trotter, Joe William, Jr. 1993. "Blacks in the Urban North: The 'Underclass Question' in Historical Perspective." In Michael Katz, ed., *The "Underclass" Debate: Views from History.* Princeton, NJ: Princeton University Press.

Wilson, William Julius. 1996. *When Work Disappears: The World of the New Urban Poor.* New York: Alfred A. Knopf.

PART 5

Juvenile Justice in Comparative Perspective

The last and largest section of this volume documents the variety of different systems of juvenile justice that now function in many developed nations and the particular histories that account for current conditions. With so many juvenile justice systems in operation, comparisons of law and practice are an essential part of serious scholarship. Margaret Rosenheim describes the current components and functions of the American juvenile court system in chapter 12. Akira Morita's chapter 13 is a history and description of juvenile justice in Japan. In chapter 14, John Eekelaar provides a history of the laws and institutions regarding child endangerment and child protection in England and Wales. In chapter 15, Anthony Bottoms compares the divergent evolution of delinquency policy in England and Scotland from the late 1960s, when the two systems were quite similar, to the turn of the twenty-first century, when they had different orientations and practices. Chapter 16, the final chapter in the collection, is Jaap Doek's survey of juvenile justice systems in Europe and his analysis of the current issues confronting juvenile justice policy.

Collectively, these contributions are an encouraging start to a comparative enterprise that should be a major part of the scholarly work that informs a second century of juvenile justice.

12 The Modern American Juvenile Court

Margaret K. Rosenheim

Juvenile justice is an umbrella term, variously used to refer to a novel jurisprudential approach to young miscreants; to the juvenile court, the institutional linchpin of this innovation; and to a stream of affiliated institutions that carry responsibilities for control and rehabilitation of the young, including the police, the juvenile court itself, its auxiliary staff, prosecuting and defense attorneys, juvenile detention centers, and juvenile correctional facilities. From the day of the juvenile court's creation in 1899, the institutions of juvenile justice have spread; in some form, they are now found in all the jurisdictions of the United States, in the industrialized nations of the world, and in many developing countries. The rapid implementation of the ideas behind the juvenile court attests to the power of modern views about the needs of children and the accompanying demand for a special response to children at risk, a response significantly different from that afforded by the criminal justice system or by the public and voluntary agencies and education.

From its beginning, the juvenile court had a broad child-saving mission. Delinquency, or acts that would be crimes if committed by an adult; "incorrigibility" and neglect, which rendered the child vulnerable because of an absent or incompetent caretaker; and dependency were all to fall within the court's purview. The basic categories of juvenile court jurisdiction have included lawbreakers, children in need of state intervention to curb potentially self-destructive behavior, and children in need of protection. The founders of the court assumed that the case for state intervention was self-evident. They sought the creation of a forum and a set of procedures through which children could be dealt with in ways that were sensitive to and would have a positive impact upon those brought before the bench.

The juvenile court is the symbol and focus of juvenile justice. In the courtroom, and in the activities surrounding it, a new legal approach to handling children was instituted. The idea of a juvenile court proceeding was modeled on an informal conference rather than on a trial, which has adversary overtones. Not only the judge but the gatekeepers of the court—those who sat at the reception desk or staffed the detention center—were to be chosen from people sympathetic and sensitive to children. The early rhetoric of juvenile justice emphasizes the difference in the atmosphere to be created in juvenile court as contrasted to the criminal court.

The effort to chart a child-saving mission for the juvenile court led to a separation of the juvenile court from the mainstream of legal institutions; a salient feature of the juvenile court through much of its history has been its isolation from the bar and the larger court system. As recently as the 1950s, there was little general awareness displayed among attorneys or judges of the purpose or procedures of juvenile court or other juvenile justice agencies. That situation began to change in the 1960s, and not only in the United States. The juvenile court and its related institutions presently attract the attention of members of the legal profession and have achieved a visibility advanced materially by the landmark decisions of the United States Supreme Court in such juvenile court cases as *Kent v. United States,* 383 U.S. 541 (1966); *In re Gault,* 387 U.S. 1 (1967); *In re Winship,* 397 U.S. 358 (1970); and *McKeiver v. Pennsylvania,* 403 U.S. 528 (1971). In essence, these decisions concern the applicability to juvenile delinquency proceedings of due process requirements imposed in criminal law. It is clear from these Supreme Court decisions that there are important limitations on the informality of process in juvenile court, which was highly prized by the founders of the court. The Supreme Court has, however, demonstrated its appreciation of the special character of juvenile justice by refusing to grant jury trials to accused delinquents.

Since the late 1970s, however, there has been a growing trend to recriminalize American juvenile justice and also to transfer more cases of juvenile offenders into criminal court. This dual trend accelerated in the early 1990s as a response to public concerns about the ability of the juvenile justice system to address the problem of youth violence. Despite these late-twentieth-century changes that made juvenile courts more like adult courts and also allowed more youths to be tried as adults, one hundred years after its creation, "the juvenile justice system remains unique, guided by its own philosophy and legislation and implemented by its own set of agencies" (Snyder and Sickmund 1999).

ORGANIZATION AND PROCESS OF JUVENILE JUSTICE

The organization and process of juvenile justice are often referred to as the juvenile justice system. The term *system* is loosely used here, for it refers to a set of institutions that make serial and interrelated decisions regarding state intervention into children's lives; it does not describe a series of coherently connected institutions that reach decisions against the backdrop of a shared set of goals.

The *juvenile justice system* refers to the police, the juvenile courts, their intake and probation staffs, the attorneys for the state and for the child (and sometimes his or her parents), juvenile detention centers, juvenile correctional facilities, and social agencies that take children in placement on order of the juvenile court. Each group has a particular set of responsibilities, expectations, and reference points. The groups do not always work in harmony or with reference to shared values. The volume of their work varies, as do their professional perspectives and qualifications, and these factors influence the way the agencies work together. Moreover, the institutions of juvenile justice do not exist in a vacuum. They operate in an environment in which other child-serving agencies, such as the schools, claim an important share of public attention and public resources, and in a political environment in which the views of citizens and the special attention of the mass media are factors not to be ignored, factors that impinge somewhat differently on each constituent organization within the system.

It has been said that the only one who experiences the juvenile justice system is the person who is processed by it, meaning the child and his parents, not the staff of the several agencies with which they may have contact. Nonetheless, the emerging interest in exploring systemic connections has augmented understanding of the ties between the various organizations, and this may produce fruitful insights for future improvements in the process of juvenile justice.

The Character of the Juvenile Justice Caseload

Notwithstanding the rhetoric of juvenile justice, which supports an expansive state mandate to protect and redirect "vulnerable" and "bad" children, the major task of juvenile justice is, as it has always been, the correction and control of delinquents. Delinquency dominates the caseload of juvenile courts.

Referrals of delinquency account nationally for more than three-fourths of the caseloads of the juvenile courts, and delinquency combined with status offense cases amount to more than four-fifths of the court referrals. Among delinquency cases, males are three times as numerous as females; arrest statis-

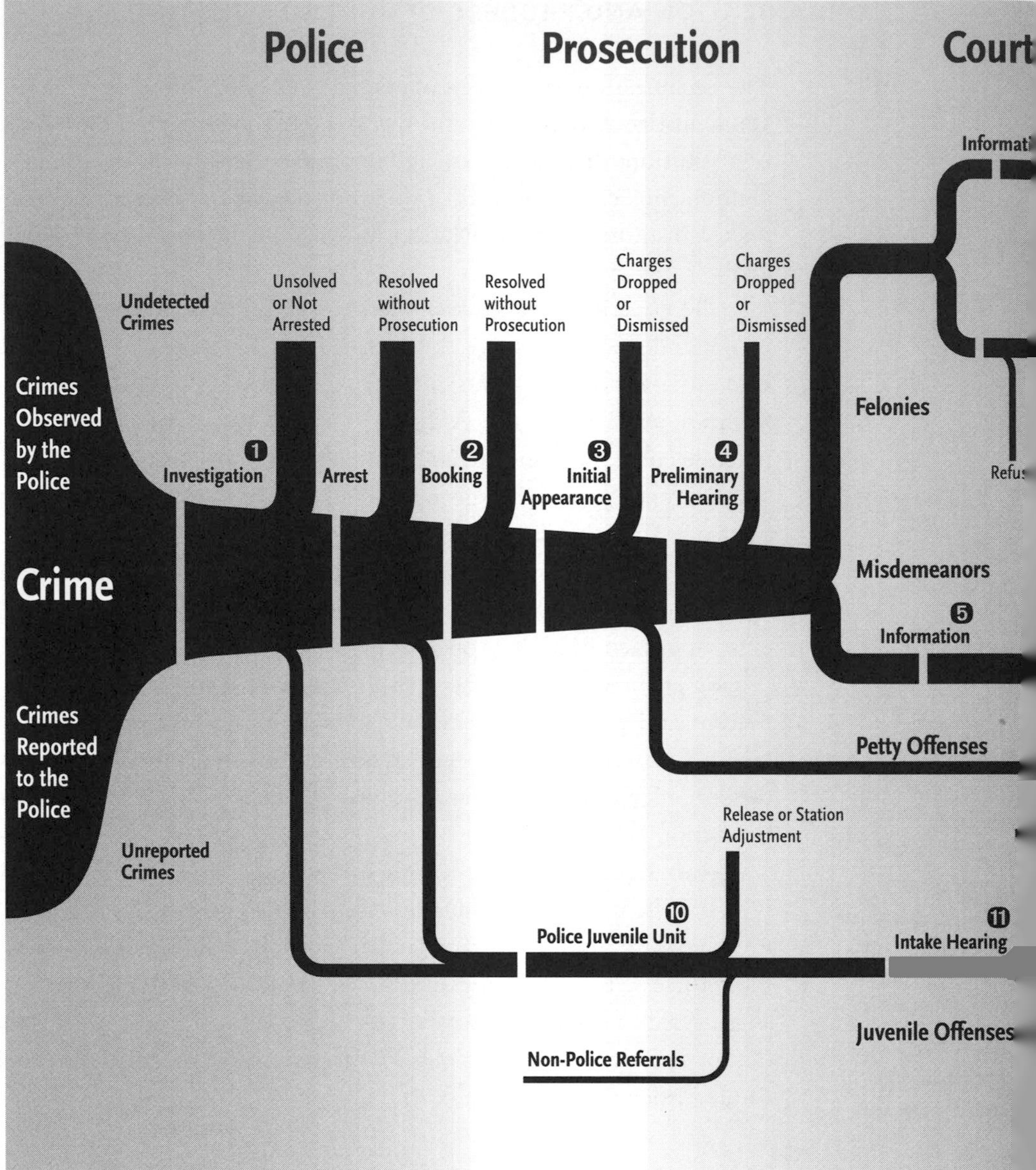

Fig. 12.1 General view of the criminal justice system. Taken from The President's Commission on Law Enforcement and Administration of Justice, *The Challenge of Crime in a Free Society,* Washington, D.C.: The Commission, 1967, pp. 7–8.

tics reveal an even greater numerical disparity between the sexes with respect to violent crimes. The wide gender gap for arrests for property crimes, however, has been decreasing. In 1981, for example, females accounted for less than 20 percent of arrests, but in 1998 they accounted for nearly 30 percent.

There is a very rough relationship between the size of the youth population at risk and the volume of juvenile court referrals, so that observers at-

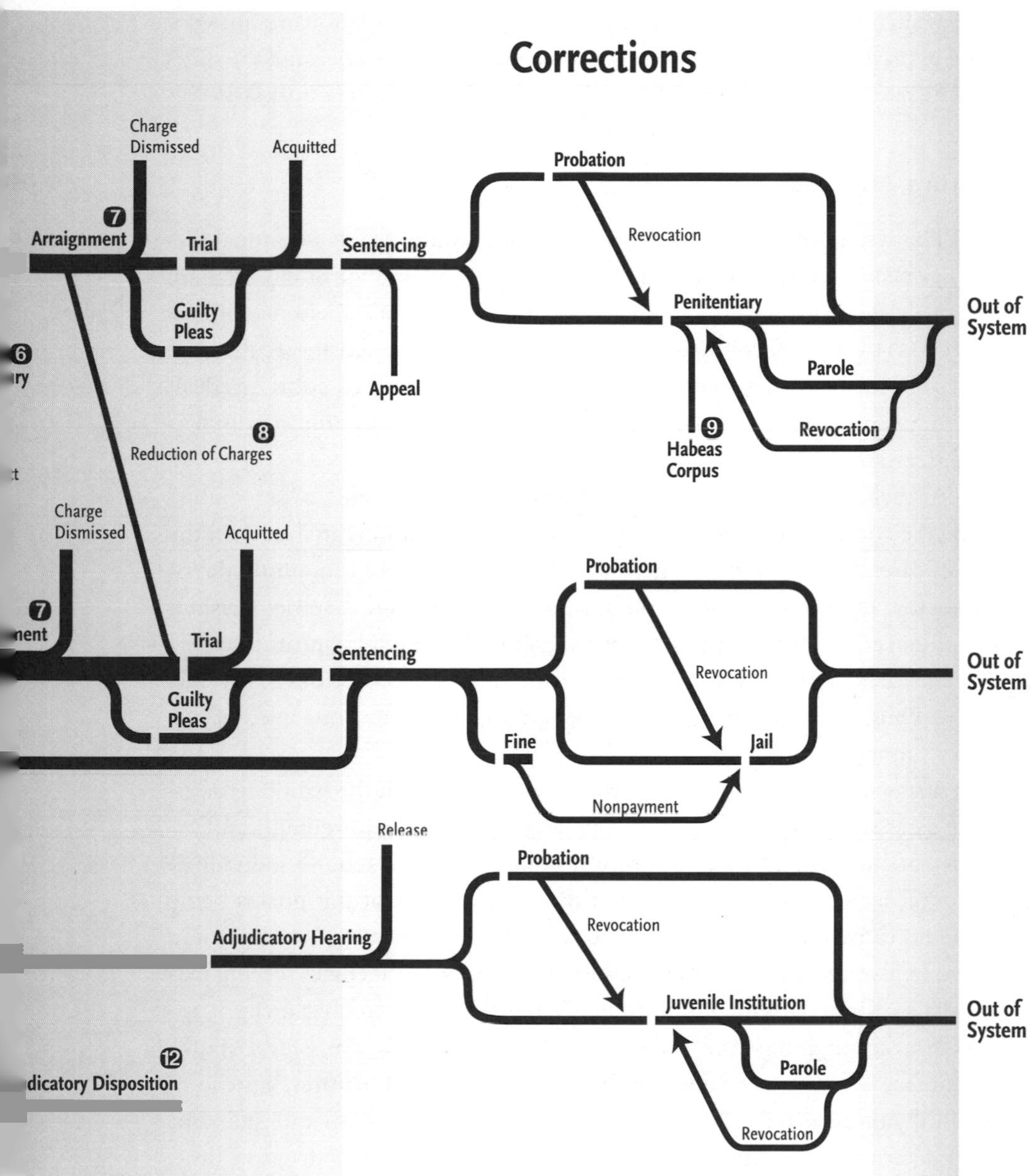

tempt to make midrange predictions about the burden on the courts from demographic projections of the youth population. The margin of error in such exercises is considerable. Most recently some commentators have projected a substantial increase in youth crime and court referrals between 1995 and 2010 because of a 15 percent increase in the teen population. But just as the predictions were being publicized, rates of youth arrest began to drop substantially, again proving that modest fluctuations in youth population are not very useful in predicting rates of serious cases in the juvenile court because the shifts in crime rate are more substantial than the shifts in population (Zimring 1998).

The Screening Process

The system of juvenile justice, like its adult counterpart of criminal justice, has been compared to a funnel. A much larger number of children are potentially subject to juvenile court jurisdiction than ever experience official contact. Of those who come to police attention, the vast majority are diverted away from further official notice. Those who are referred to court are dealt with in a variety of ways, referral out of the court being a common dispositional decision.

At each stage of institutional contact with children's cases, a "screening" or "intake" decision occurs. However, not all these decisions are based on the kind of careful, youth-focused, investigative procedure and thoughtful deliberation that the funnel simile implies. Instead, it appears that some decisions are influenced more by workload or the vagaries of a particular institution's organizational goals than by a generally shared vision of the priorities of juvenile justice. Thus, the funnel image would be more exact if one conceived of it as a leaky funnel.

A stated objective of juvenile justice has always been the handling of juvenile cases in a manner sensitive to the developmental requirements and capacities of children. The execution of this goal is seen to require individualization of decisions at every stage, but the assumption that this goal is being reached is thrown into question by the facts. "Mass processing" is a common feature of juvenile justice agencies, especially apparent in agencies serving major urban areas beset with a multitude of cases. In these circumstances, it appears that the screening process focuses on aberrant cases at every level of official contact. Cases are screened with regard for unusual features, instead of being fully investigated and recorded as a basis for deliberation and individualized determination. Minutes, not hours, frame the official's decision time, and the routines of each institution place a premium on quick decisions.

It has been estimated, for example, that of every one hundred street stops by the police, about twenty children are taken into custody; of these, approximately 70 percent are referred to the juvenile court, where the intake staff, usually with advice from the prosecuting attorney, returns roughly one-half of these juveniles to the community without filing a formal petition. Of the remaining cases, a substantial fraction result in dismissal in court. The remainder, in which a finding of delinquency is entered either on plea by the alleged delinquent or by court action after an adjudicatory hearing, are largely disposed of in one of the following ways: by continuance and eventual dismissal without the entry of a formal disposition or order, by an order of commitment to a juvenile correctional institution, or by an order of placement. The predominant court dispositions are probation, or continuance and eventual dismissal. Relatively few delinquents are placed or committed, and a very small proportion of cases reaching the juvenile court is transferred to criminal court; in 1997 they amounted to 1.0 percent of all referred cases for which formal petitions were filed.

"Case mortality" in the screening process is high. A certain amount is to be expected. The alleged delinquent is, like his [or her] adult criminal counterpart, entitled to a presumption of innocence and is, in the aftermath of the Supreme Court rulings in such cases as *Kent, Gault,* and *Winship,* entitled to many of the constitutional protections afforded by the criminal law, with the notable exception of the right to trial by jury *(McKeiver).* As a result, a significant number of cases will fail to meet the legal requirements of proof and will therefore be screened out (or "dismissed") for insufficiency in some element of a legal case.

Other, and possibly more important, factors also influence the screening-out of cases at every stage of the process. Some are similar to those that influence the administration of criminal law: the felt severity of overbreadth of the criminal law as applied to particular delinquents, and the sheer volume of the workload, which requires choice in the allocation of scarce resources. In addition, a primary consideration in juvenile justice is its rehabilitative goal. Children are thought to merit "room to reform" (Zimring 1978); this view influences decisions down the line, from the police through the correctional authorities, who decide upon dates of return to the community. Clearly, discretion pervades the administration of juvenile justice, as in criminal law, and its exercise generates community debate on the broad goals of juvenile justice, as well as on the application of discretion to particular cases.

THE AGENCIES OF JUVENILE JUSTICE

The Police

Large police departments in metropolitan areas have specialized units or divisions to handle juveniles. These units keep records on juvenile contacts, perform limited investigative functions, frame the guidelines for referral of juveniles to the court, and act as liaison between the entire police force and the juvenile court. The police carry responsibility for initiating court referrals of delinquents and such other juveniles as abused children or runaways, and they are empowered to place certain juveniles in secure facilities and to remove children found in hazardous surroundings to places of temporary safekeeping.

The existence of specialized youth divisions in police departments should not, however, be equated with a judgment on the importance of their function. Although specialized units play useful roles, it is the police on patrol who bear the principal burden for decisions to take into custody ("arrest") and to refer to juvenile court. The typical encounters between young people and the police occur in public places. Moreover, these encounters seldom involve one juvenile and one or two police officers; more often, the police confront several juveniles at once. A judgment by the police must be made under pressure, without as much information as would be desired, and often under the scrutiny of an unsympathetic public.

After the police take a juvenile into custody, there remains the option within the police department of "station adjustment" in lieu of referral to juvenile court. Station adjustment usually entails a warning against future misconduct and a notation in police files of the alleged breach of conduct. In 1997 police departments resolved about one quarter of juvenile cases with station adjustments. Many departments have set down guidelines to channel police judgment regarding station adjustments, and these criteria will almost certainly refer to the severity of the offense alleged, the number of prior police contacts, and the disposition of the victim, if any, to cooperate in filing a complaint. Often the list of criteria includes such personal characteristics as the attitude of the juvenile, the stability of his [or her] home, and his [or her] record of school attendance. The more extensive the list of criteria, the more discretionary the officer's judgments necessarily are, and the less susceptible they are to routinization and review.

The Juvenile Court

A parallel process of screening occurs at the juvenile court, where the intake staff, with the advice of the prosecutor's office, decides whether to release the offender or to prepare a delinquency petition. Again, formal guidelines are commonly used by intake workers; the alleged offender's prior contacts with the juvenile court provide an element to be considered in addition to the criteria of family history, seriousness of the offense, and stability of environment.

Intake workers exercise substantial power. In 1997, for instance, at this stage of the process, over 40 percent of all referrals were handled informally without a filing of a petition requesting an adjudicatory or waiver hearing. Of these cases, close to half were dismissed, and one-third received informal supervision (voluntary probation) for a time. Thus, at the intake screening, the worker acts as a judge in deciding whether a petition should be filed, and may also act as a probation officer in undertaking supervision for a limited period, in the absence of formal adjudicatory and dispositional hearings before a judge. Sometimes, too, cases referred to the juvenile court judge are disposed of by continuance with informal supervision and eventual dismissal, without entry of formal findings.

The intake function of the juvenile court is therefore a judicial mutant in which both legal experts and other trained personnel play an active part. It is a broadly conceived function, in the exercise of which "case screening is an important objective . . . [but] referral to, if not insistence upon, service and imposition of controls are additional goals. Thus the express function of intake is likely to be more ambitious than that of its criminal law counterpart" (President's Commission 1967b, 15). When a formal petition is prepared, the case is set for hearing before a juvenile court judge. Legal counsel, most likely a public defender or assigned counsel, must be provided to the juvenile in all cases in which correctional commitment is possible. In practice, this requirement leads to routine assignment of counsel in delinquency cases.

The juvenile court acts of a few states (for example, California, New York, and Illinois) had already provided for representation by counsel in delinquency cases prior to the *Gault* decision. However, during the midcentury debates over due process in juvenile court, the introduction of counsel in juvenile court was vigorously challenged by some commentators as antithetical to the spirit and goals of the court. The Supreme Court, responding to this concern among others in the *Gault* decision, asserted its belief that "the observance of due process standards, intelligently and not ruthlessly administered, will not compel the States to abandon or displace any of the substantive benefits of the juvenile process." The Supreme Court recognized the oft-asserted claim "that the juvenile obtain benefits from the special procedures applicable to them which more than offset the disadvantages of denial of the substance of normal due process," but it concluded that "while due process requirements will, in some instances, introduce a degree of order and regularity to juvenile court proceedings to determine delinquency, and in contested cases will introduce some elements of the adversary system, nothing will require that the conception of the kindly juvenile judge be replaced by its opposite" (21, 27).

In delinquency cases that reach the point of formal adjudication, the juvenile court judge is required to make determinations of fact under standards that closely resemble those applicable to criminal prosecutions. The judge must observe several constitutionally protected rights, such as the right to counsel noted above, the right to notice of the charge or charges against the juvenile, the privilege against self-incrimination, the right to be heard and cross-examine witnesses, and the right to appeal. The charge of delinquency must be proved "beyond a reasonable doubt," which is the most exacting evidentiary standard of criminal, rather than civil, law.

Once a finding of delinquency has been entered, a dispositional decision (or "sentence") must be considered. Juvenile court legislation in the United States generally requires that a social investigation be prepared and submitted for judicial use in advance of the dispositional hearing. Both the prosecuting and defense attorneys are entitled to be present at this hearing and to present evidence in support of specific dispositional plans. Although the typical juvenile court act is sufficiently flexible to accommodate individualized plans of disposition (or "treatment"), in fact the workload of the court encourages routinization of decisions; it is clear that orders of probation (without additional requirements of either treatment or restitution or community service) and orders of commitment predominate among the array of possible dispositional determinations.

Use of Detention

The practice of referring juveniles for detention reflects some of the deepest tensions inherent in juvenile justice, and it is here that the complex interrelationships of juvenile justice organizations become most apparent. Detention centers are restrictive or secure custodial facilities for holding young people who are, or may become, subjects of juvenile court proceedings. The use of detention can occur prior to the formal petitioning of the young person to the court, during the adjudicatory or dispositional hearings, or after all formal hearings are concluded but prior to transfer to placement or to a correctional facility. Of cases referred to the juvenile courts in 1997, nearly 20 percent were referred to detention at some point. The formal authority to detain may be vested in a judge or a probation officer, depending on state law, but decisions to detain are heavily influenced, if not made, by the police. It should be noted that many more youths are held in detention before trial than are sent to correctional facilities after trial. The ratio of juveniles confined in detention to those confined post-hearing in correctional institutions is much larger than the ratio of adults jailed before trial and sentencing to those sent to prison. This tremendous disparity has led criminologists to describe the juvenile justice system as "uniquely front-loaded." Moreover, a major purpose of juvenile detention is openly acknowledged to be punitive in many instances, whereas in the adult criminal system, with its obeisance to the principle of the presumption of innocence, jail is often a result of inability to post bail. However, both systems, criminal and juvenile, rely more heavily on containment in secure custody prior to adjudication of guilt than after.

In juvenile justice the practice of detention has been justified as necessary to provide the conditions for expert investigation and study of the offender and his background. In practice, however, detention is often used to serve other purposes, most particularly admonitory and corrective purposes, such as a "short, sharp shock" resulting from being locked up. From the standpoint of law enforcement officers, especially where neighborhoods are experiencing unrest or disturbing patterns of offenses, detention offers an opportunity to remove the presumed troublemakers from the scene and gain a breathing spell for community residents as well as police. In some cases, it must be said, the police believe that detention is essential to protect the public against what they see as a vicious pattern of offensive behavior.

Detention referrals are a common focus of friction between the police and the intake workers and judges of juvenile court. The police tend to believe that they are justified in their referrals to detention. They recognize that their decisions are subject to review and reversal by court personnel, but they cannot be expected to appreciate the release of juveniles who, in their eyes, amply deserve a period in detention. Court personnel, on the other hand, approach detention referrals from a different perspective. The intake workers see detention referrals in a broader context than that of the referring police officer. The worker considers detention referrals not only against a spectrum of offensive behaviors, to which the court staff assign their own priorities (not necessarily similar to the police officers'), but also against his [or her] own special knowledge of the population and management conditions of the detention center at any time.

The juvenile court judge, too, brings his own perspective to the case, since he is charged by statute with conforming to criteria for detention. The salient question for the court is whether "probable cause" exists to believe that the juvenile falls under the jurisdiction of the juvenile court. Without a finding that these conditions exist, the court lacks authority to detain a juvenile. Thus, at this juncture, in theory the adequacy of the jurisdictional grounds for proceeding with the case becomes a critical consideration. In practice, however, it is doubtful whether many cases reviewed at the detention hearing are dismissed for jurisdictional reasons. Cases that reach this stage are likely to satisfy a probable cause requirement. Influential issues for the judge are more likely to concern the nature of the alleged offense, the adequacy of possible alternative arrangements for custody, and the presumed efficacy of a short, sharp shock for corrective purposes.

Juvenile Corrections

After an adjudicatory hearing in which a finding of delinquency is made, the judge faces the question of appropriate disposition of the juvenile before him [or her]. In petitioned cases of delinquency, the disposition of choice is probation (55 percent). About 28 percent are placed away from home in public or private agencies, and in about half as many cases (13 percent) the court orders the juvenile to pay restitution, perform community service, or enter a counseling program. In 4 percent, the court releases the juvenile with no additional sanction.

The official names of these institutions are suggestive; many are termed "training schools," and they do seek to retrain their residents in law-abiding ways and to provide for continuation of formal education, usually at the intermediate or high school level. These objectives distinguish juvenile from adult correctional institutions, the latter typically lacking educational or "character-building" programs designed to reach the entire institutional population. The differences also extend to size, length of stay, and control over the decision to release. Juvenile correctional institutions are significantly smaller and more campuslike in layout than adult prisons, and the average length of stay is much briefer for committed juveniles than for adult prisoners. In general, the release decision for juveniles is located within the institution, whereas for adults it is lodged in an autonomous agency, the parole board.

MODERN REFORMS OF JUVENILE JUSTICE

The juvenile court was intended as a significant reform of criminal justice as it was being applied to children and youths. Yet this modern innovation itself has not escaped criticism, which has centered on questions of due process, the scope of state intervention authorized by juvenile court law, and the reliance on institutionalization as a means of treatment. A subsidiary critique concerns the inappropriateness of allocating scarce resources within juvenile justice institutions to minor offenders or to nonoffenders, with resulting diminution of resources available for cases involving serious offenders or children urgently in need of state protection. A more far-reaching position advocates "radical nonintervention," or "leave kids alone whenever possible" (Schur 1973). The several critiques overlap considerably, but the underlying assumptions that animate them differ.

The waves of criticism directed at the juvenile court process directly attack two basic pillars of the court's philosophy. These are the notion that the agencies of the state can properly assume that children who come in contact with the police and the courts are in need of guidance and supervision, and the belief that the process of juvenile justice should be informal and should identify who the child is and how he [or she] has become as he [or she] is, rather than what the child has done. By statute and judicial decision, it is now established that a juvenile delinquent is entitled to many of the major protections of criminal procedure. The state must establish its case and must do so in ways that conform to long-standing criteria of proof and process. Although both courts and legislatures have stopped considerably short of importing into juvenile court proceedings all the procedural elements of a criminal trial, there has been significant impetus to incorporate some of the more essential protections.

The breadth of juvenile court jurisdiction, which gives rise to the charge of official overreaching in state-sanctioned efforts to guide and supervise children, has proved more resistant to reform. Criticism here has focused not so much on delinquency jurisdiction as on the jurisdictional category of incorrigibility or status offenses—that is, acts or behavior proscribed for children but not for adults. The focus on the latter category flows from the belief that state intervention in these cases is often undesirable, even more undesirable than ignoring the behavior or condition, and from the related belief that reducing the court's responsibilities would expand the resources available for intractable youths whose conduct or condition clearly warrants community alarm.

> The major impact of these proposals [to narrow jurisdiction] would be to deemphasize adjudication as the primary method for dealing with difficult children. . . . As a consequence the number of children disposed of through the court's adjudicatory procedures could be expected to be far fewer. . . . [Most] of those who did filter through to adjudication would be youths who already proved resistant to helping services or whose conduct was so repetitive or so clearly dangerous to the community that no other alternatives seemed feasible. For this group, as to whom the condemnatory, deterrent, and incapacitative functions of judicial dispositions would appear to predominate, the use of more structured adjudicatory procedures designed to ensure fairness and reliability of determinations is singularly appropriate. (President's Commission 1967b, 40)

Yet another criticism focuses upon custodial measures as means of reform or protection of children. Detention centers and correctional institutions for committed delinquents both attract critical scrutiny. Critics cite overuse of custodial institutions and the unduly punitive, regimented routines within them. They point to their inadequacy, whether measured by educational, treatment, or general socializing criteria, as appropriate repositories of youth. To the extent that minor offenders or even nonoffenders are commingled with serious offenders, the critics bemoan the opportunities that training schools present for schooling in crime, one of the very reasons claimed by the juvenile court's founders for segregating juveniles from adults in jail and prison. Finally, critics express concern about the impact on a juvenile's development of his removal from home, school, and familiar neighborhoods. This introduces a sharp break with persons significant to the juvenile and impedes his eventual integration into his home community at the point of release, which commonly occurs after a relatively brief span of months.

These threads of criticism, combined, present a powerful argument for deinstitutionalization. Numerous attempts at community treatment have taken place in the United States, but the movement has not proceeded as rapidly as modern reformers had hoped, nor have all results pointed in the intended direction. Deinstitutionalization efforts have been hampered by the resistance of local communities to the presence of young offenders in their midst, a resistance often expressed through opposition to zoning-law changes necessary to run group homes. There is some evidence of a propensity to substitute the use of local secure custodial facilities for the earlier reliance on commitment to state correctional facilities. In addition, although the purpose of deinstitutionalization is to serve all children and youths whose control and resocialization can be met close to home, in actuality the more "desirable" group of delinquents may be selected for community treatment, leaving the less acceptable to commitment in secure state facilities. There is a particular danger here of reinforcing a racial skew toward disproportionate reliance upon commitment for minority-group youths.

A continuing characteristic of juvenile justice, which may limit the effectiveness of efforts at reform, is its age-based jurisdiction. A court for all children has fundamental limits to its capacity for reform. Juvenile court jurisdiction is divided, as already noted, into the major categories of delinquency, status offenses, and neglect; it is unified, however, in a focus on children under a certain age. Thus, a juvenile justice court is potentially a state agency concerned about all juveniles, since few children progress through childhood without becoming vulnerable or antisocial in one or more of the ways in which a literal interpretation of prevailing law would support court action. Fortunately, common sense prevents such expansive application of the law. Nevertheless, there is sufficient breadth and vagueness in the jurisdictional categories to allow the exercise of considerable discretion.

Broad categories generate a huge potential jurisdiction for the juvenile justice system, and the difference between potential jurisdiction and actual intervention is the result of numerous individual judgments—that is, the result of massive exercise of discretion. This fact has worried many observers of juvenile justice because of the opportunity for biased judgments, usually regarded as judgments biased against the poor and minority-group children in the population.

The exercise of discretion is further facilitated by opportunities for reshuffling cases between one jurisdictional category and another. Thus, a child who has run away and has also committed a minor drug offense or a petty larceny may be proceeded against as either a status offender or a delinquent. It is commonly thought that if practices are introduced to restrict and control official conduct in reference to one jurisdictional category, officials will respond to efforts to restrict their discretion by choosing to proceed under another category that equally enables them to accomplish their objective of control or protection. Not very much is known about this "relabeling" phenomenon, but enough is suspected to generate uneasiness.

The labeling problem should not be considered in isolation. Opportunities for reclassification exist as well in criminal justice, mental health, social services, and many other areas of public law that focus on subjects. What generates particular uneasiness among students of juvenile justice is the endorsement of discretion that is traceable to the views of the juvenile court's founders: they assumed that state officials would act benevolently in behalf of the children whom they sought to bring under the mantle of juvenile court jurisdiction, and that consequently the traditional threshold challenges to state intervention were not required to be satisfied. To some extent, the modern insistence on due process in juvenile court serves to assuage this fear, but the special status of children almost inevitably confers upon adults an unspoken aura of authority to intervene with fewer challenges to their actions than would be true of intervening for benevolent motives in the lives of adults.

A further obstacle to reform relates to the multiple jurisdictional character of the juvenile court. Although delinquency cases dominate in the workload of the juvenile courts and the related institutions of juvenile justice, it cannot be assumed that the other facets of juvenile court jurisdiction—neglect and status offense—are unimportant aspects of the court's daily business, or that they have a proportionately modest influence upon the court's ability to handle the crime-violative behavior that delinquency cases present.

First, status offense jurisdiction is often seen as dealing with "predelinquent" behavior. Hence, even though the charge itself alleges acts that would not be criminal if performed by adults (such as curfew violation or truancy), the underlying concern that animates state intervention is often one of correction. This aims either to control young people who are believed to have committed minor criminal acts (in addition to offenses that are the basis for filing a petition), or to exert control over those who seem likely to commit criminal acts because of the wayward nature of their activities. If not in school, where are the children and what are they doing? A hands-off policy by juvenile justice agencies is hard to maintain in the face of community disapproval or concern. Although they are numerically fewer and politically less sensitive than delinquency cases, status offense referrals form a substantial fraction of the juvenile justice system's activity.

Second, both status offense cases and those subsumed under the rubric of neglect (which also encompasses abuse) are difficult cases to try. They require disproportionate amounts of staff and court time, relative to the majority of delinquency petitions in which admissions of guilt are received, so that the exercise of the court's status offense and neglect jurisdiction exacts a higher per-unit investment of resources than the typical delinquency case. In this sense, then, the nondelinquency cases divert valued resources from the processing of delinquents to other types of cases.

In a judicial forum that organizes its activity principally around age (that is, the status of being under a particular age) and only secondarily around specific behaviors or vulnerabilities, the interrelation of act-specific and protectively inspired jurisdictional factors is bound to be intimate and confounding. Thus, the juvenile court can possibly never become a "pure" junior criminal court, if such an outcome is desired, so long as the juvenile court carries jurisdictional responsibility for status offenders and neglected children as well. Similarly, it can be argued that the vexed and politically explosive question of boundaries between the juvenile and adult criminal courts will resist sensible resolution so long as juvenile courts emphasize the status of "juvenility" to the neglect of concentrating on norm-violating conduct that is seen to endanger society, regardless of the age of the offender committing the crime. In short, to require the juvenile court to consider both age and acts creates a tension. Society becomes caught up from time to time in an old argument: whether childhood should confer special regard and protection despite behavior, or whether acts that conform to principles of criminal liability should be punished without regard to the tender age of the perpetrator.

The juvenile justice system responds to this argument ambivalently. Historically, the vast majority of delinquency cases have involved nonviolent offenses. Even though the number of violent offenses increased disproportionately from 1988 through 1997 (these cases of "person offenses" rose from 17 percent to 22 percent in this period), property offenses continued to account for the bulk of the court's work (48 percent in 1997). It also complicates the court's response that a very large number of all offenses are committed in groups. Serious violent crime is largely a problem of late adolescence or early adulthood (Zimring 1981). However, the occasional juvenile delinquency cases involving extremely serious crime, which receive the most publicity, also lead to the most atypical results; they do not contribute to the resolution of the problems inherent in a system that necessarily must accommodate public ambivalence relative to the treatment of children. Children certainly can be alternately vicious and mildly destructive; erratic and calculating; antisocial and merely mistaken or misguided. A jurisprudence based primarily on age must confront the tensions presented by the insertion into the juvenile justice system of children and youths who display the entire range of these contradictory characteristics.

The major focus of legislative activity in the 1990s was handling serious offenses committed by youth still under the maximum jurisdictional age of the juvenile court. The most frequent legislative strategy for such cases was to increase transfer to criminal courts, usually by giving prosecutors rather than judges the authority to make transfer decisions. Almost every state passed some type of transfer enhancement law during the 1990s, but, notwithstanding, no large shifts in caseload from juvenile to criminal courts occurred in the aftermath of the legislation. The operation of transfer systems has been more selective than the rhetoric heard in the political arena (Fagan and Zimring 2000).

Even if juvenile courts have not lost much jurisdictional coverage, the recent politics of punitive response do threaten both the youth service mission and child-protective priorities of the American juvenile court. There is strong political pressure to make the juvenile court more punishment-centered than in early eras and to replace the power of judges and probation staff with greater prosecutor hegemony. This internal threat to the mission of juvenile courts is more significant than most types of transfer enhancement laws.

FUTURE PROSPECTS FOR JUVENILE JUSTICE

The institutions of juvenile justice are by now well established. Judges preside over juvenile courts in every judicial district of the United States. Whether full or part-time, they number in the thousands, and in large cities numerous judges are assigned to the juvenile court. In addition, each court has an auxiliary staff, numbering far in excess of judicial personnel, and there are the staffs of juvenile correctional facilities to reckon with as well. In urban areas, specialized police units focusing on juveniles are commonplace. Added together, all these officials form a substantial group with vested interests in the maintenance of the juvenile justice system. In addition, as mentioned earlier, members of the bar participate increasingly in juvenile court cases, either as prosecutors or as defense counsel, and there is an elaborate network of mutual relationships between the institutions of juvenile justice and those that serve educational, welfare, and health-related interests. Given the entrenchment of these organizations and the extent of demands made daily upon them to control or protect the children for a variety of reasons, it seems unlikely that the organizations of juvenile justice will disappear. Moreover, it is questionable whether they should.

The juvenile court was created principally in response to a demand for better institutional arrangements to enhance child development in urban-industrial America at the turn of the twentieth century. Although the strains and stresses of child rearing are different now, they have not diminished. The need for some set of organizations to concentrate on these tasks seems as great as ever. No doubt there will be new organizations, new procedures, and other changes. Nonetheless, in Francis Allen's words, the juvenile court appears to be "a viable institution and remains one of the most important social inventions of the modern period." Thus, despite a barrage of criticism since the 1960s and the modifications of the 1990s, the institutions of juvenile justice are likely to remain permanent fixtures of modern government.

REFERENCES

Allen, Francis A. 1981. *The Decline of the Rehabilitative Ideal: Penal Policy and Social Purpose.* New Haven, CT: Yale University Press.

American Bar Association—Institute for Judicial Administration, Joint Commission on Juvenile Justice Standards. 1980. *Juvenile Justice Standards Project.* 20 vols. Cambridge, MA: Ballinger.

Fagan, Jeffrey, and Franklin E. Zimring, eds. 2000. *The Changing Borders of Juvenile Justice: The Transfer of Adolescents to Criminal Court.* Chicago: University of Chicago Press.

Feld, Barry C. 1999. *Race and the Transformation of the Juvenile Court.* New York: Oxford University Press.

Lerman, Paul. 1975. *Community Treatment and Social Control: A Critical Analysis of Juvenile Correctional Policy.* Chicago: University of Chicago Press.

Muir, William Ker, Jr. 1977. *Police: Streetcorner Politicians.* Chicago: University of Chicago Press.

President's Commission on Law Enforcement and Administration of Justice. 1967a. *The Challenge of Crime in a Free Society.* Washington, DC: President's Commission.

President's Commission on Law Enforcement and Administration of Justice, Task Force on Juvenile Delinquency and Youth Crime. 1967b. *Task Force Report: Juvenile Delinquency and Youth Crime.* Washington, DC: President's Commission.

Rosenheim, Margaret K., ed. 1976. *Pursuing Justice for the Child.* Chicago: University of Chicago Press.

Schur, Edwin M. 1973. *Radical Nonintervention: Rethinking the Delinquency Problem.* Englewood Cliffs, NJ: Prentice-Hall.

Snyder, Howard N., and Melissa Sickmund. 1999. *Juvenile Offenders and Victims: 1999 National Report.* National Center for Juvenile Justice.

Spergel, Irving A.; Frederic G. Reamer; and James P. Lynch. 1981. "Deinstitutionalization of Status Offenders: Individual Outcome and System Effects." *Journal of Research in Crime and Delinquency* 18, no. 1: 4–33.

Stahl, Anne L.; Melissa Sickmund; Terrence A. Finnegan; Howard N. Snyder; Rowen S. Poole; and Nancy Tierney. 1999. *Juvenile Court Statistics, 1996.* Washington, DC: Office of Juvenile Justice and Delinquency Prevention.

Stapleton, William V., and Lee E. Teitelbaum. 1972. *In Defense of Youth: A Study of the Role of Counsel in American Juvenile Courts.* New York: Russell Sage Foundation.

U.S. National Commission on Law Observance and Enforcement [Wickersham Commission]. *Report of the Child Offender in the Federal System of Justice.* Washington, DC: U.S. National Commission, 1931.

Wheeler, Stanton, ed., with the assistance of Helen M. Hughes. 1967. *Controlling Delinquents.* New York: Wiley.

Wolfgang, Marvin E.; Robert M. Figlio; and Thorsten Sellin. 1972. *Delinquency in a Birth Cohort.* Chicago: University of Chicago Press.

Young, Thomas M., and Donnell M. Pappenfort. 1977. *Secure Detention of Juveniles and Alternatives to Its Use.* National Evaluation Program Phase 1 Report. Washington DC: U.S. Department of Justice, Law Enforcement Assistance Administration, National Institute of Law Enforcement and Criminal Justice.

Zimring, Franklin E. 1978. *Confronting Youth Crime—Report of the Twentieth Century Fund*

Task Force on Sentencing Policy toward Young Offenders: Background Paper. New York: Holmes & Meier.

———. 1981. "Kids, Groups, and Crime: Some Implications of a Well-Known Secret." *Journal of Criminal Law and Criminology* 72: 867–85.

———. 1998. *American Youth Violence.* New York: Oxford University Press.

13 Juvenile Justice in Japan: A Historical and Cross-Cultural Perspective

Akira Morita

Looking back on the path Japanese juvenile law has taken over the past century, we find a continuous cross-cultural dialogue with American law. Twice, American juvenile law has served as a frame of reference. The first time was in 1899, when the Chicago Juvenile Court was founded; the second occurred during the American occupation of Japan after World War II, when the General Headquarters (GHQ)/Supreme Commander of the Allied Powers displayed bold initiative in the legal and political reform of postwar Japan.

American juvenile law between 1899 and 1967 was informed by the doctrine of *parens patriae*—the concept that in dealing with youths who had committed crimes the objective was not punishment but rehabilitation through protective measures guided by parental compassion. During its first encounter with its American counterpart, modern Japanese juvenile law adopted the idea of *parens patriae* on a voluntary and discretionary basis, assimilating it sympathetically, yet critically, to create a system adapted to the needs of Japanese society. But in its second encounter it was directly defined by American ideals imposed under GHQ's direction, and little room was left for discretion.

Despite the different nature of these two sequences, it is undeniable that the rehabilitative ideal espoused by the first American juvenile court greatly influenced both the establishment and the practice of Japanese juvenile law.[1] At the end of the twentieth century, however, we discover strong contrasts between the two systems. The criminalization of juvenile justice—which since the 1970s has progressed, as the rehabilitative ideal has declined—characterizes American juvenile law today. So harshly have the juvenile courts been criticized that their continued existence seems under threat. Legal scholars publishing in major books and journals have advocated the abolition of juvenile courts in the United States.

How, then, have things developed in Japan? According to the Supreme Court's *Annual Report of Judicial Statistics* for 1997, the number of juveniles (excluding traffic offenders) who underwent disposition in family courts nationwide in that year was 164,327. Of these, 4,535 (2.8 percent of the total) were sent to juvenile training school. Family court hearings have adopted the *parens patriae* model, in which a judge and a probation officer preside. An adversarial system, though currently under debate, has yet to be adopted. Only 292 juveniles (0.2 percent of the total) were referred to the public prosecutor for criminal trial "in view of the nature and circumstances of [their] offenses," and a mere 42 were actually convicted and committed to juvenile prison. These numbers, incidentally, need to be weighed against Japan's total population of 120 million.

In Japan it is the juvenile prisons, not the juvenile court system, that seem to be falling into disuse. I am referring not to the physical courts or prisons but to the way perceptions of juvenile justice have moved in opposite directions in the United States and Japan—with emphasis in the former on accountability and punishment, and in the latter on rehabilitation and protection.

The statistics cited above give the impression that the American concept of rehabilitation came into bloom in the post–World War II context and continued to flower. Is Japanese law, then, an enclave in East Asia where American Progressive thinking survives and still exerts a powerful influence on practice? How should we understand the contrasts between these two juvenile justice systems, born of the same parent ideal?

As we seek an answer to these questions by tracing the development of Japanese juvenile law, we make an interesting discovery: the nonpunitiveness displayed by today's juvenile law in Japan is a manifestation of a tradition of maternal protectionism intrinsic to Japanese society,[2] a manifestation exaggerated as a result of Japan's undiluted adoption of American ideals in the postwar period. From such a comparative and historical perspective, I shall discuss in the following pages the establishment and development of the juvenile law of 1922, the Taisho Juvenile Law—the first encounter with *parens patriae;* the enactment of the current juvenile law of 1948 and the ensuing disputes—the second encounter with *parens patriae;* the structure, application, and modifications of the 1948 law; and possibilities for further dialogue between the American and Japanese systems.

THE FIRST ENCOUNTER WITH *PARENS PATRIAE:* THE TAISHO JUVENILE LAW

Sympathy toward *Parens Patriae*

In March 1900, a year after the Chicago Juvenile Court was established, the so-called Reformatory Act was enacted in Japan. It was the first national law for the compulsory housing and correction of children prone to committing misdemeanors. Kosuke Tomeoka, an influential prison official of the day, gave content to this law by creating an American-style cottage system. Tomeoka was a Protestant minister who had journeyed alone to the United States in 1864. Deeply impressed by Enoch C. Wines's *The State of Prisons and of Child-Saving Institutions in the Civilized World* (1880), he was warmly received by American reformers, whose support enabled him to absorb the philosophy of juvenile correction and the zeal with which it was being furthered. Returning home two years later, he launched a movement to establish reformatories in Japan.

In 1907, seven years after enactment of the Reformatory Act, Nobushige Hozumi,[3] the leading Japanese legal scholar of his day, gave a lecture entitled "Children's Courts in America." He had just returned from a trip to observe the juvenile courts then getting under way in Illinois and Colorado. His lecture conveys the paternalistic fervor that characterized those courts.

> The children's court in the United States has only a very brief history. Until 1899, people regarded illegal acts committed by children as constituting crimes. . . . By contrast, the new system that has been established does not consider the child a criminal; it holds that a child, by definition, is incapable of becoming a criminal. . . . In other words, people are beginning to regard the child's behavior not as originating in the child's own free will and autonomy but, rather, as a product of the family and society.
>
> Accordingly, it is believed that children's courts should not be an instrument to punish the child but one that protects and educates.[4]

The "discovery of the child" and the accompanying system that Tomeoka and Hozumi introduced into Japan galvanized legislators and youth workers. Not only in reformatories but even in some prisons for juveniles, children were to be given, and indeed began to receive, "care and education instead of criminal punishment." It was with remarkable speed and compassion that the Japanese reacted to the idealism of the Progressive Era. In 1912, five years after Hozumi's lecture, the Ministry of Justice drew up and began to enact a juvenile law.

The Culture of *Amae* Sensitivity

The Japanese response to the American *parens patriae* doctrine was not simply an ideological appreciation but was underpinned by sociopsychological and cultural commitment. This pattern still persists.

The sensitivity of the Japanese to the human dependency need was brought to the world's attention by the psychiatrist Takeo Doi's *Anatomy of Dependence* (1973).[5] According to Doi, the concept of *amae*—a Japanese word that defies direct translation—bridges both dependence and attachment, which are conceptually distinct in English. Doi finds its psychological archetype in the fundamental desire of an infant for its mother and the infant's attempts to identify with her. This desire is essential to the child's development as well as the source of all protective relationships. The mother, as the recipient of the child's *amae,* experiences joy from her protective emotions toward the child.

In modern Western society the dependency need is generally considered specific to childhood, a passing phenomenon. Yet Doi's analysis of the Japanese experience of *amae* shows that it continues to exist in conscious form, though concealed behind social norms, even into adulthood, when self-determination and accountability are expected. Furthermore, it is considered a valuable feeling that should be held in high regard. For the Japanese, who value interdependence, *amae* is a source of morality, a feeling that should be controlled but not relegated to the subconscious. *Amae* sensitivity detects the dependency need underlying human autonomy. When directed toward the child, it normally expresses itself as the maternal instinct. Though lacking a direct equivalent in European languages, *amae* is a concept and an experience universal to humanity.[6]

The eager response of the Japanese to the *parens patriae* doctrine is best understood in the light of the sensitivity to *amae* that is entrenched in Japanese culture. The discovery of the child posited by the American doctrine was, in a sense, also a discovery of the child's dependency need. In 1913, A. J. Mackelway, a leader in the movement to regulate child labor, published a "Declaration of Dependence by the Children of America." A paragraph in this document resolves "that we declare ourselves to be helpless and dependent; that we are and of right ought to be dependent, and that we hereby present the appeal of our helplessness that we may be protected in the enjoyment of the rights of childhood."[7]

In the writings of those concerned with the juvenile court in its early days, we frequently come across statements like the following: "'The Juvenile Court has discovered that the child is a child. The child should be treated as a child."[8] Progressive reformers in the United States were responding to the child's dependency need with a call for the maternal protective urge—unusual, perhaps, in a land that prizes liberty and independence. Anthony Platt has characterized the juvenile court of that period as "Maternal Justice."[9]

Skepticism toward *Parens Patriae*

The *parens patriae* doctrine was not taken intact as the model for Japan's juvenile law. Japanese legislators in the early twentieth century, while sympathetic toward American protectivism, were sharply critical of its limits. Seeing at first hand how the Reformatory Act was being applied, they harbored doubts about the *exclusive* application of protectivism in the treatment of young offenders. To their eyes, the thinking behind *parens patriae*—that no children younger than eighteen could be held criminally accountable—was just too simplistic.

A year after Hozumi's 1907 lecture, Atsushi Oyama, the chief of the Prison Bureau in the Ministry of Justice, spoke to juvenile prison superintendents from around the country. His words, while critical of the newly introduced, extremely protective treatment of offenders in juvenile prisons, suggest the philosophy of the forthcoming juvenile law in a Japanese context: "It is needless to say that prison officials should have mercy and compassion toward young criminals. However, this mercy and compassion must be, as it were, that of the strict father for his son. It must not be that of the doting mother for her dear child."[10]

The first step taken by the drafters of the new juvenile law was to limit jurisdiction to criminal and semicriminal offenders. The problem of family dissolution faced by American welfare workers at the time was unknown in Japan. To place the protection of neglected and dependent children within the same jurisdiction as the protection and correction of young criminals would cause needless confusion. Sabro Tanida, entrusted with preparing the first draft, examined data from the United States and other countries. Although his model set rehabilitation as the law's prime objective, he did not regard protection and criminal accountability as mutually exclusive; rather, he attempted to combine both within a single, complementary system. In this sense, juvenile law was not juvenile *court* law. This bifocal model provoked a strong backlash from advocates of the Reformatory Act, who argued for exclusively protective treatment of the child. After three years of debate, however, a draft in line with Tanida's model was adopted in 1922. Legislative records from 1912 to 1922 depict efforts to reconcile the ideals of rehabilitation and protection with the conflicting notion of criminal accountability and to bridge the cultural differences between Japan and the United States.[11]

The Bifocal System and the Role of the Prosecutor

The juvenile law of 1922, also known as the Taisho Juvenile Law, was a bifocal system. Juveniles over fourteen years of age were regarded, at least in principle, as criminally accountable. At the same time, the law prescribed that the utmost effort must be made to treat such juveniles with protective measures if circumstances allowed it. Punishment should be placed within the framework of rehabilitation.

At the heart of this system was the Shonen Shimpansho (Juvenile Inquiry and Determination Office), a semijudicial body specializing in protective measures for juveniles aged eighteen and under (figure 13.1). This body was given complete jurisdiction over the investigation, disposition, and subsequent treatment of juveniles referred to it by the police or the prosecutor. It adopted the paternalistic model of the American juvenile court and probation service. Juveniles who had committed misdemeanors, as well as semicriminal offenders in the lower age bracket, were referred by the police directly to the Shonen Shimpansho. More serious offenders and those in the upper age bracket were ex-

Fig. 13.1 Tokyo juvenile inquiry and determination office, 1923.

amined first by the prosecutor, and those actually prosecuted were tried in a special criminal proceeding for juveniles. But the great majority, who did not need to be put on trial and for whom protection was appropriate—in other words, those for whom the dependency need was allowed as relevant and whom society could pardon—were subject to one (or more) of nine measures administered by the Shonen Shimpansho, including placement in a juvenile training school. Whereas the American juvenile court at the turn of the century, concerned strongly with neglected and dependent children, dealt with all offenders under the same informal, welfare style of jurisdiction, Japan's Taisho Juvenile Law provided for offenders to be *selectively* sent for treatment under the Shonen Shimpansho's semijudicial and informal jurisdiction.

The prosecutor's discretion to screen offenders was made the pivot of the legal procedure. On the day that the new law took effect, the Ministry of Justice issued the following guideline: "In view of the spirit of the law, which takes rehabilitation of the juvenile as its primary objective, the prosecutor shall prosecute only those juveniles for whom no prospect of repentance is likely unless punishment is inflicted, and juveniles who must unavoidably be punished as a means of general deterrence. All other cases shall be referred to the Shonen Shimpansho for protective measures."[12] It should be noted that the objective of punishment here is repentance, which is a subjective state. And the prosecutor was responsible not simply for superficial screening but for attempting to elicit repentance in juveniles who confessed.

Repentance, or its absence, was the key to the form and success of the protective measures. At the core of repentance is the emotion of regret, sustained by spontaneous, psychological dependence on the part of the young offender. In order to draw out this emotion, however, the initial, adversarial, prosecutor-versus-suspect relationship had to be changed to an amicable one between protector and ward. Prosecutors of Meiji Japan were trained for this contradictory dual role. What made the role possible was the *amae* sensitivity shared by prosecutors with the rest of Japanese society. The emphasis in *amae* is on dependency rather than autonomy, but this is not a theory of dependency that denies the culpability of the young offender. Here, criminal responsibility and the protection of a juvenile are complementary to each other. The prosecutor's discretion strikes a balance between the two.

According to available statistics, juveniles prosecuted by the prosecutor in 1942 accounted for 2.8 percent of the total number of cases; of the remaining cases, 70.7 percent were referred to the Shonen Shimpansho, and 26.5 percent were dismissed after some kind of informal protective treatment had been ordered and were handed over to parent(s) or guardian(s).[13] Nationwide, fewer than a thousand offenders between fourteen and eighteen years of age were committed to juvenile prisons, which were designed to provide "educational punishment" and rehabilitation. Practitioners in the system at the time characterized its spirit as "the strict-father tender-mother approach." It is fair to say that it achieved its bifocal aim.

THE SECOND ENCOUNTER WITH *PARENS PATRIAE:* THE CURRENT JUVENILE LAW OF 1948

Burdet G. Lewis and the Enactment of the New Law

Japan's defeat at the end of World War II forced it to adopt American *parens patriae* idealism more thoroughly than it had at the time the Taisho law was enacted. Burdet G. Lewis, the GHQ Prison Branch specialist in charge of reforming Japanese juvenile law, did not appreciate the complex structure of the existing system. In particular, he saw the acceptance of criminal accountability and the weighty role assumed by the prosecutor as proof of the backwardness of the Taisho Juvenile Law.[14]

In February 1947, Lewis sent a four-point guideline to Japan's Ministry of Justice, ordering total revision of its juvenile law. A year later he presented the ministry with a twenty-four-article *Suggested Juvenile Court Code of Japan.*[15] The suggested code was, in the main, grounded in *A Standard Juvenile Court Act: Suggested Draft,* prepared in 1943 by the National Probation Association in the United States. The code assigned broad jurisdiction to the juvenile court, including that over neglected and dependent children, and stressed the noncriminal nature of court procedure. A GHQ document from the same period, backing Lewis's proposals, declares, "It is definitely established that the Juvenile Court is a chancery court with jurisdiction based on the doctrine of *parens patriae.* The principle that the Juvenile Court is not a criminal court should be observed in revamping the juvenile court system in Japan."[16] The *parens patriae* doctrine was reaching its culmination in American juvenile courts of the time. No one could have predicted that in twenty years the doctrine would fall from grace.

Although Japan's new juvenile law, enacted in July 1948, deviated somewhat from Lewis's original intentions for the juvenile *court* law, the purpose of transplanting intact the ideal of *parens patriae* was generally achieved, except for the matter of jurisdiction. The law stipulated that all criminal offenders aged twenty and under be referred to the new family court; made protective measures its exclusive objective; disallowed screening by the prosecutor; and allowed—only as an exception—criminal supplementary suits against juveniles aged sixteen and older by the waiver procedure. The paternalistic fervor of the Shonen Shimpansho was inherited, in the form of its informal procedures, by the family court, which now had primary jurisdiction over all criminal offenders.

Fig. 13.2 Tokyo family court.

The Ministry of Justice's Reamendment Proposal

A movement led by the Ministry of Justice to reamend the 1948 law began, not surprisingly, with the end of the Allied occupation of Japan in 1952. As we have noted, the American legal model prescribed by Lewis had already been scrutinized during the years 1912–22 and found inappropriate for Japan. Skepticism toward *parens patriae* reemerged. Critics regarded the 1948 law as having lost a reasonable balance between protection and accountability, in part because of the prosecutor's reduced role. In May 1966, the ministry unveiled its *Proposal for Amendment of the Juvenile Law,*[17] which incorporated the prosecutor's discretion to participation in the hearing procedure. But the proposal, bespeaking as it did an affinity with the Taisho Juvenile Law, was unpopular in the unique atmosphere of post–World War II Japan. The ideological successors of those who, in 1922, had criticized the Taisho law from a protectivist point of view now became zealous defenders of the 1948 law.

The Ministry of Justice took the Japanese public by surprise by drawing up an even more specific *Outline for Amendment of the Juvenile Law.*[18] One of the reasons for this undertaking was a landmark decision by the United States Supreme Court, *In re Gault* (387, US 1, 1967), handed down in May 1967 by Justice Abe Fortas. That decision, critical of the paternalism of American juvenile courts of the time, was based on the rationale that juveniles were entitled, at least in principle, to the same constitutional right of due process as adults: "Neither the Fourteenth Amendment nor the Bill of Rights is for adults alone." The ruling spelled the downfall of *parens patriae*. The *New York Times* ran the entire text of the decision on May 16, 1967.

The impact of *Gault* reached Japan almost immediately. The primary purpose of the Ministry of Justice's *Outline for Amendment*—along with lowering the age for juveniles who fall under family court jurisdiction to eighteen—was to institute a transition from the informal approach of the 1948 law to a framework for "maintaining juvenile procedural rights and bringing the prosecutor to the hearings." As such, it was a catalogue of rights, including (among others) the juvenile's rights to remain silent, to appoint a lawyer, and to examine the evidence. Proposals of this kind were known at the time as "Gaulting the system." As the ministry's commentary on the outline observes, "Quite recently, a United States Supreme Court decision indicated serious reconsideration of the traditional *parens patriae* doctrine held by American law, the mother of our own current juvenile law."[19]

While attempting to ride the tailwind of changes in American juvenile law to restore balance to the Japanese system, the ministry ran into opposition from the Japanese Supreme Court. As noted earlier, the Shonen Shimpansho under the Taisho Juvenile Law was a cultural product that incorporated Japan's traditional protectivism into the framework of a modified American law. After World War II, the family court inherited this spirit after the GHQ's transplantation of American ideology. The legalism of the ministry's *Outline for Amendment* was thus perceived as anachronistic.

We should bear in mind that Japanese ideology in the postwar era was strongly conditioned by American law, the "justice of the times." Both the Ministry of Justice and the Japanese Supreme Court, though on opposite sides of the issue, resorted to the ideology of American law in making their arguments. A 1973 Supreme Court document criticizing the ministry proposal for amendment contends that "the juvenile law adopts a nonadversary, inquiry approach to hearings because this mode is necessary to the application of the educational ideal in juvenile cases. Due process in juvenile hearings must not sacrifice the functioning of educational principles in juvenile cases, but rather should be reconciled with them."[20] The Supreme Court's "educational ideal" reflected an interpretation of the *Gault* decision different from that of the ministry. Motivated by the zeal of the family court practitioners, Supreme Court opposition was powerful, and the two sides remained deadlocked for several years. It was not until 1977 that the ministry finally abandoned its legalistic approach and a compromise was reached—conditional participation by the prosecutor under court discretion. Now, however, the ministry ran up against the Japanese Bar Association, which insisted on a purely protective procedure and, in effect, virtually vetoed the proposal. So the compromise never led to actual amendment.

The juvenile law of 1948, in its unamended state, became entrenched in postwar Japan. The amendment dispute, however, was to reappear in 1996 in a new guise. Before moving on to this new issue, I will outline the structure and application of the still current 1948 system.

THE STRUCTURE AND APPLICATION OF THE CURRENT JAPANESE JUVENILE LAW

Jurisdiction

Lewis's attempt to make Japan's juvenile law fit the mold of the American system, with its focus on neglected and dependent children, was not entirely successful. The jurisdiction of the Japanese family court extends over three categories of delinquent juveniles. The first consists of criminal offenders, fourteen to twenty years of age; article 41 of the penal code stipulates that persons fourteen and older are criminally accountable. (It may be noted that Japan's penal code was established at the end of the nineteenth century on the model of Germany's, which included a fixed age for criminal accountability.) The second category consists of juveniles in danger of committing crimes (*guhan* juveniles), including runaways, incorrigible youths, and others for whom discipline in the home has failed. This category redefines as "in danger of [committing] crimes" a group of juveniles categorized in Lewis's guidelines as "neglected." The third category comprises all juveniles under fourteen who commit an act that would constitute a crime under the penal code for a person fourteen or older.

Juveniles in the first and second categories who are at least fourteen must be referred exclusively to the family court. Youths under that age are initially placed in the custody of a child guidance center provided for by the child welfare law and set up by local governments. Child guidance centers employ casework methods. As a rule, compulsory placement of the child by a center is not allowed without parental consent. The center refers juveniles to the family court only when it concludes that they require protective disposition by the court. The juvenile law and the child welfare law have shared this dual relationship since the Taisho law was enacted in 1922.

According to the *Annual Report of Judicial Statistics* for 1997, of the 164,327 juveniles who underwent disposition by the family court (excluding traffic offenders), 0.87 percent, or 1,426, were *guhan* (second-category) juveniles.[21] Only 222 children were referred to the court by child guidance cen-

Fig. 13.3 Kyoto family court.

ters.[22] Thus, in spite of jolting reform by the GHQ in 1948, the current juvenile law retains the basic structure of the Taisho law: it is constructed around the criminal offender and treats all other problem children with the administrative machinery of the child welfare law. The child guidance centers' requirement that parental consent be obtained for any compulsory measures attests to the fact that dissolution of the family and child abuse in Japan are not yet serious enough to warrant mandatory judicial intervention.[23]

Investigation and Hearing

The family court gives priority to protection and correction in the treatment of all criminal offenders referred to it. The fifteen hundred family court probation officers stationed throughout the country play a substantial role in the treatment of juveniles. From the time a juvenile enters the system until a hearing is conducted, the probation officer makes an in-depth investigation into the child's character, life history, and family background and environment. The officer also contributes—within permissible limits—to adjustment of the child's environment. Since judges appointed to the family court serve for only a few years, the probation officer's report and opinion are paramount to the judge's determination at the hearing. Tentative supervision by a probation officer as ordered by the judge is considered the lifeline of the family court's casework function.

Article 22 of the juvenile law stipulates that "hearings shall be conducted softly and mildly with warm consideration. Hearings shall not be open to the public." Article 14, on examination of witnesses, permits examination "insofar as such application does not run counter to the nature of the case of protection." Only the probation officer, court clerk, parent(s) or guardian(s), and a court-approved lawyer may be present at the hearing. All these persons are expected to assist the judge in their protective roles. Although findings of fact must be established beyond a reasonable doubt, hearings do not employ the rule of evidence stipulated by the Code of Criminal Procedure. In Japan, the processes of adjudication and disposition (in adult as well as juvenile cases) are not separated but are conducted in an integrated fashion.

The greatest impact of the GHQ reform was to expand the hearing into a venue for deciding treatment for all criminal offenders aged twenty or younger, who were made the object of primary protective disposition. Thus, hearings under the existing law are burdened with more "contaminants"—for example, serious offenses, or cases in which the juvenile denies the alleged act—than were hearings under the Taisho law. Nonetheless, and despite criticism by the Ministry of Justice, this procedure has continued to function for more than fifty years, thanks to the extremely low incidence of allegations denied or contested by juveniles.[24] Moreover, violent acts by juveniles diminished noticeably as Japanese society stabilized from around 1965 onward (see fig. 13.4). The success of the system in handling serious cases is also related to the high level of training undergone by judges and probation officers.

Representation

Because the existing law provides for a nonadversarial and inquiry-oriented hearing procedure, it has not adopted a formal system of representation for juveniles. The probation officer normally represents the opinions and wishes of the juvenile. The juvenile or his or her parents may appoint a lawyer or other representative, but there is no public defender system. Until the early 1990s, lawyers were present in fewer than 1 percent of all cases.[25]

Subtle changes, however, have occurred since the 1980s. In a 1983 case, in which a juvenile charged with arson denied the charges, the examination of a witness to establish an alibi became an issue. Supreme Court Justice Shigemitsu Dando, quoting *Gault,* wrote a concurring opinion to the effect that a juvenile's right to due process should be upheld.[26] Justice Dando, who had participated on the Japanese side in postwar GHQ reforms, exerted strong influence in the revision of the Code of Criminal Procedure. Without criticizing the paternalistic philosophy of juvenile law, his opinion gave concrete form to the Supreme Court's view, noted above, that due process in juvenile procedures is permissible only to the degree that it does not sacrifice protection.

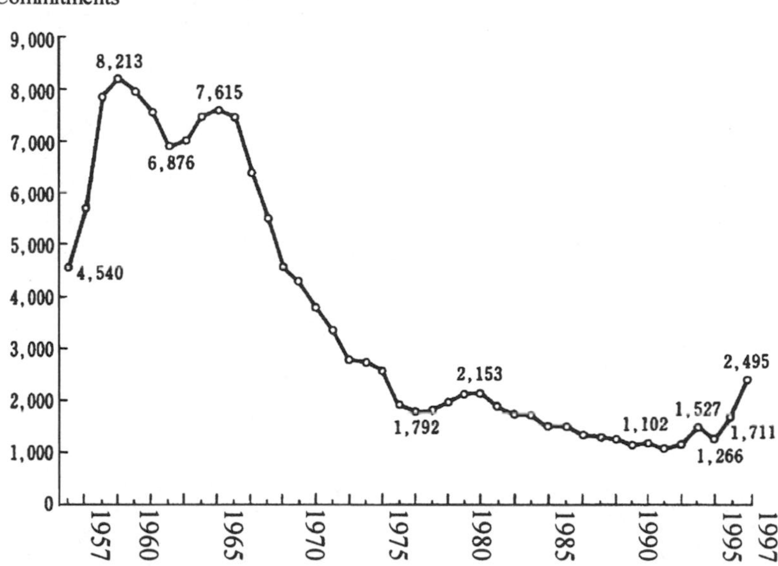

Fig. 13.4 New commitments of violent crimes by youths, 1957–97.

Dando's opinion also aroused the interest of lawyers in private practice, who were becoming responsive to due process and representation in American juvenile law. Those opposed to the Ministry of Justice's stance made the right to due process a byword in their arguments. The paternalistic role of a lawyer at juvenile hearings moved toward that of defense attorney. In 1977, lawyers appeared in fewer than seven hundred cases, but twenty years later this figure had quadrupled.[27]

Disposition

In 1997, family courts ordered formal protective disposition (educative measures), as stipulated in article 24 of the juvenile law, in only 12.1 percent of the total number of cases. Probation, the most frequently employed protective disposition, accounted for 9.1 percent. Probation is carried out by Ministry of Justice probation officers with the assistance of volunteer probation officers, of whom there are now about fifty thousand, appointed within local communities. This community system does much to prevent recidivism. Compulsory commitment to a juvenile training school or educational institution was ordered for 3 percent of the youths. The average length of commitment to a training school is eleven months. (For more statistics covering the years 1993–97, see table 13.1.)

These percentages have remained stable over the last decades of the twentieth century, thanks to the low incidence of violent crime during the period. The male-female ratio for juveniles committed to training schools has

Table 13.1

Annual Comparison of Number of Disposition of General Cases (Traffic Accidents Excluded), by Type of Disposition

Type of Disposition	1993		1994		1995		1996		1997	
	Number	Ratio (%)	Number	Ratio (%)	Number	Ratio (%)	Number	Ratio (%)	Number	Ratio (%)
Educative Measures[a]										
Probationary supervision	11,161	7.2	10,830	7.2	12,256	8.7	13,003	9.0	14,912	9.1
		(73.2)		(73.3)		(76.5)		(76.2)		(75.6)
Commitment to child education and training home, etc.	287	0.2	254	0.2	268	0.2	268	0.2	288	0.2
		(1.9)		(1.7)		(1.7)		(1.6)		(1.5)
Commitment to juvenile training school	3,790	2.5	3,601	2.4	3,493	2.5	3,804	2.6	4,535	2.8
		(24.9)		(24.5)		(21.8)		(22.2)		(22.9)
Totals	15,238	9.9	14,685	9.7	16,017	11.3	17,075	11.8	19,735	12.1
		(100.0)		(100.0)		(100.0)		(100.0)		(100.0)
Dismissal after hearing	21,459	13.9	20,086	13.3	17,130	12.1	15,944	11.0	16,344	9.9
Dismissal without hearing	97,184	62.9	96,961	64.2	90,541	64.0	94,229	65.1	109,455	66.6
Referral to child guidance authority	176	0.1	169	0.1	151	0.1	155	0.1	144	0.1
Referral to public prosecutor for criminal prosecution										
In view of the nature and circumstances of the offense	407	0.3	361	0.2	328	0.2	295	0.2	292	0.2
Upon finding of adulthood	392	0.3	415	0.3	340	0.2	325	0.2	341	0.2
Joinder of cases, transfer to other family court	19,661	12.7	18,347	12.1	16,940	12.0	16,752	11.6	18,016	11.0
Grand Totals	154,517	100.0	151,024	100.0	141,447	100.0	144,775	100.0	164,327	100.0

Source: Supreme Court, *Guide to the Family Court of Japan,* 1999, p. 48.

[a]"Educative measures" are referred to in the text as "protective disposition."

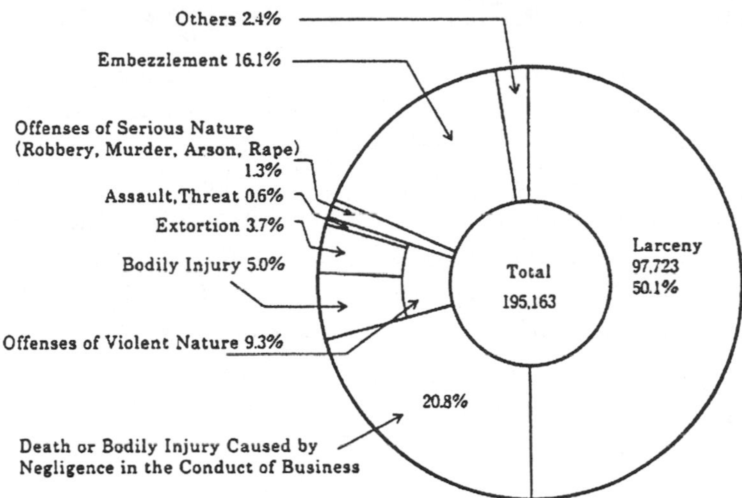

Fig. 13.5 Breakdown of new commitments of criminal offenses by crime.

also remained stable at 10 to 1. In recent years we have seen a rise in violent crimes (mostly robberies), as shown in figure 13.4; it is not clear how this rise will affect commitment. (Figure 13.5 illustrates penal code offenses by percentage for all juveniles.)

Along with the three types of formal protective disposition, family courts can decree a variety of informal treatments when a dismissal determination is made. Tentative probation (already mentioned) is ordered when the judge reserves the final determination; of 16,344 juveniles whose cases were dismissed after the hearing in 1997, for example, 7,750 were placed under this type of supervision.[28] In addition, the family court frequently issues warnings, orders adjustment of a juvenile's environment, or prescribes some other informal protective measure prerequisite to dismissal without a hearing. As shown in table 13.1, 125,799 cases out of a total of 164,327 were dismissed in 1997 after a hearing or without one. Although such rulings may superficially resemble diversion as practiced in European and American law, in Japan they are considered a critical measure for rehabilitation and the prevention of repeat offenses.

There are two conditions for dismissal: (1) the offender must have confessed to the crime and show clear repentance and a commitment not to repeat the offense; and (2) the person appearing in court on the offender's behalf—often a parent or an employer—must express a commitment to working for the offender's rehabilitation. These commitments are legally nonbinding, however. The strategy of seeking maximum effectiveness through informal treatment while minimizing formal, coercive intervention (though the threat of such intervention undergirds the strategy) has become established in Japan since the enactment of the Taisho Juvenile Law and maintains a high degree of stability in the results it achieves.

Referral to the Public Prosecutor and Criminal Disposition

Very few juvenile offenders are referred to the public prosecutor—only 0.2 percent in 1997 (excluding traffic offenders). The prosecutor, having no discretion to dismiss, must prosecute all such cases. The number of juveniles aged twenty and under who were referred to the prosecutor, prosecuted for crimes, found guilty, and committed to a juvenile prison between 1988 and 1997 decreased gradually from ninety-nine to forty-two (see table 13.2). All the others found guilty were granted a reprieve. These figures indicate a radically nonpunitive trend. The major reason for the trend is the reluctance of family court judges and probation officers to refer juveniles to trial. Both protection and punishment are regarded as means of discipline or rehabilitation administered by the state; no clear, qualitative distinction is made between the two.

This protectivism, reinforced by the idealism of the American *parens patriae* doctrine, was balanced by the bifocal approach of the 1922 Taisho Juvenile Law. But removal in 1948 of prior screening by prosecutors—pivotal in the Taisho law—allowed the maternal protectivism intrinsic to Japan's juvenile system to blossom. Reacceptance of *parens patriae* in 1948 resulted in a replay of what had occurred at the beginning of the twentieth century. The 1970 attempt by the Ministry of Justice to counterbalance protectivism with accountability failed because it invoked the increasing legalism of American juvenile justice. *Parens patriae* was embraced in mid-twentieth-century Japan even more strongly than in the United States, its birthplace.

Striking a balance between the conflicting elements of protection and accountability is the task of juvenile justice in any society. Whether the Japanese system should congratulate itself on the smallness of its prison population may require more study.

CONCLUSION

The informal procedures of the 1948 juvenile law have functioned in spite of the law's expanded jurisdiction because few juveniles deny or contest the charges against them. Hearings generally proceed "mildly." The participation of lawyers in juvenile hearings, which began to increase in the 1980s, altered

Table 13.2

Commitments to Juvenile Prison

1988	1989	1990	1991	1992	1993	1994	1995	1996	1997
99	68	63	59	56	50	54	56	41	42

Source: Adapted from the Ministry of Justice, *Annual Report of Statistics on Correction.*

the established pattern. Juveniles who have admitted to certain facts at the police investigative stage will now, occasionally, contest those facts during the court hearing, especially when the physical evidence is weak. Juvenile hearings of this kind, no longer mild, have assumed the one-sided, adversarial nature of criminal trials. In a hearing concerning a 1993 incident of group-inflicted bodily injury resulting in death, the suspects' counsel called testimony that contradicted the police's earlier findings of fact, plunging the court into a state of confusion that would formerly have been unthinkable. In a head-on confrontation between juvenile and judge, as happened in this case, the inquiring, informal model of the existing law was powerless. Certain family court judges urged that a semiadversary procedure in the presence of a prosecutor be adopted for cases of this kind.

These circumstances prompted the Supreme Court, in the spring of 1966, to submit to the Ministry of Justice and the Japanese Bar Association proposals to amend the juvenile hearing procedure. Discussions among the three bodies were carried on fairly smoothly. Driven by public consensus, a proposal was completed in January 1999 and a bill submitted to the legislature.[29] The proposed amendment sets out a double-track system allowing participation by a prosecutor and a lawyer (representing the juvenile), attendant on the judge's discretion, for fact finding in limited cases of serious crime, while maintaining the existing law's nonadversarial format for the majority of juvenile hearings. The prosecutor is given the right to appeal by reason of error in fact finding but is not permitted to set forth an opinion on the judge's disposition of a case. While denial or contestation of facts previously admitted are not the sole criterion of "serious" cases, the Ministry of Justice estimates that fewer than two hundred juveniles a year will be tried under the special procedure.

The prosecutor's essential role here is to assist in fact finding that is directed by the court, not to prosecute the juvenile. The lawyer's role, on the other hand, is not merely to defend the juvenile's right to due process. In deliberating the amendment proposal, the juvenile Law Committee of the Ministry's Legislative Council refused to prescribe the juvenile's right to due process in express terms; in other words, juvenile law escaped getting "Gaulted."

We are now reaching the point at which we can measure how far the American "juvenile court revolution" of 1967 has influenced Japan. The Ministry of Justice's 1970 *Outline for Amendment* was countered by the Supreme Court's support of protectivism. Yet the assertion of juvenile rights since Justice Dando's 1983 opinion seems to be tamed in the double-track system now under consideration. From the perspective of American law, it may seem illogical. From that of Japanese law, however, the double-track system is seen to operate on the discretion of the judge and is thus a variation of the Taisho law, which attempted to secure a balance between protection and accountability via the discretion of the prosecutor. It was the tradition of bifocal thinking, arising from the encounter between *parens patriae* and *amae* sensitivity, that prevented the explicit injection of American-style juvenile law into Japanese juvenile law on two occasions since World War II.

The Taisho law in the first half of the twentieth century exemplified what can be produced from the fusion of two cultures. By contrast, the 1948 law has been engaged in a continuous battle to restore to Japanese law its indigenous identity, weighed down as it is by the influence of American law, yet buffeted by changes in American law since 1967. Japanese juvenile law has yet to enter a period of stable balance.

Has a century of experience given Japanese law anything to offer to American law? With regard to institutional and practical issues the answer is probably no; the social and political conditions sustaining our two juvenile justice systems are simply too divergent. But in terms of the philosophical premises of juvenile law, I would firmly say yes. What Japanese law can offer is the ability to balance opposing forces. American juvenile law has long been characterized by an either-or approach—*parens patriae* or due process, dependence or autonomy, protection or punishment. Excessive idealism has sometimes failed to accept the realities of juvenile experience. Japanese law, on the other hand, has been consistent in its efforts to temper the polarity intrinsic to juvenile law by means of *discretion*. It has managed to reformulate the dichotomous elements of American law into a bifocal structure.

In seeking the source of the Japanese characteristics in balancing disparate elements, we return to *amae* sensitivity. *Amae,* as I have said, recognizes the psychological dependency need that underlies human autonomy. And autonomy, depending on oneself, becomes possible only when one has learned to depend on others. *Amae* sensitivity presupposes human relatedness, thus compensating for weaknesses in the logical, rights-oriented thinking of modern law. This relatedness is bound up with an understanding of human duality.[30] In modern Western society, dependency is viewed as tantamount to subordination or even inferiority, and therefore tends to be suppressed to the subconscious. *Amae* sensitivity, by contrast, though it may obscure individuality, can grasp the elements of dependency and autonomy in human duality. Let me stress that this duality is an essential, universal attribute of human beings and is in no way unique to the Japanese. Yet it is hardly visible in Western society; it is only by virtue of various historical and geopolitical conditions that we can detect it within Japanese culture. I believe that American juvenile justice would benefit from the recognition of duality that informs the Japanese system. In the shifting fashions of American policy toward young offenders, dependency and criminal responsibility are often viewed as mutually exclusive, with no room for consideration of a youth's culpability in the original formulation of *parens patriae* and no room for dependency in recent efforts to treat young offenders as if they were adults.

Japanese juvenile law will no doubt continue to use American juvenile law as its primary frame of reference. I ardently hope that our two countries will find their way to a more genuine dialogue, increasingly constructive for each.[31]

NOTES

1. Akira Morita, "Waga kuni ni okeru shonen hosei no keisei to tenkan—hogo to sekinin" (The formation and development of juvenile law in Japan: protection and responsibility), in *Miseinensha hogo ho to gendai shakai* (Juvenile and children's law and modern society), (Tokyo: Yuhikaku, 1999), 199 ff.

2. For a fine analysis of the characteristics of faith in rehabilitation and the maternal-protection tendencies in Japanese criminal law in general, see Daniel H. Foote, "The Benevolent Paternalism of Japanese Criminal Justice," *California Law Review* 30 (March 1992): 317.

3. Hozumi (1855–1926), the first dean of Tokyo's Imperial University, founded in 1881, left a record of unparalleled achievement in making modern Western law known in Japan.

4. Nobushige Hozumi, "Beikoku ni okeru kodomo saibansho" (Children's courts in the United States), *Hogaku Kyokai Zasshi* 25, no. 9 (1907): 1261–65. Author's abridgment and translation.

5. Takeo Doi, *The Anatomy of Dependence: The Key Analysis of Japanese Behavior* (New York: Kodasha International/U.S.A., through Harper & Row, 1973).

6. Takeo Doi, "On the Concept of *Amae,*" *Infant Mental Health Journal* 13, no. 1 (1992): 348.

7. A. J. Mackelway, "Declaration of Dependence by the Children of America in Mines and Factories and Workshops Asembled," *Child Labor Bulletin* 2 (August 1913): 43.

8. Samuel J. Barrows, *Children's Courts in the United States: Their Origin, Development, and Result,* report prepared for the International Penal and Prison Commission (Washington, DC: Government Printing Office, 1904).

9. Anthony Platt, "The Rise of the Child-saving Movement: A Study in Social Policy and Correctional Reform," *Annals of the American Academy of Political and Social Science* no. 381 (January 1969): 25–28.

10. Morita, "Waga kuni," 203 (Author's translation).

11. Akira Morita, "Taisho shonen ho" (The Taisho juvenile law), in *Nihon rippo shiryo zenshu,* vols. 18–19, pts. 1–2 (Tokyo: Shinzansha Shuppan, 1993).

12. Ministerial notice of January 27, 1923, by the director general of the Criminal Affairs Bureau in the Ministry of Justice (Author's translation).

13. Morita, "Waga kuni," 239.

14. Burdet G. Lewis was a specialist in correctional administration who practiced in New York and New Jersey.

15. GHQ/SCAP Record Sheet No. L-10096, National Diet Library, Tokyo.

16. Donald V. Wilson, *Memorandum for the Record, Juvenile Court Jurisdiction,* August 7, 1947, Public Health and Welfare Section, GHQ/SCAP Record Sheet No. LS-10095, National Diet Library, Tokyo.

17. "Shonen ho kaisei ni kan suru koso setsumeisho" (Commentary on the proposal for amendment of the juvenile law), *Jurist* 348 (1966): 90.

18. "Shonen ho kaisei yoko ni kan suru setsumeisho" (Commentary on the outline for amendment of the juvenile law), *Jurist* 467 (1970): 65.

19. Ibid., 66.

20. Supreme Court General Secretariat, *Shonen ho kaisei yoko ni kan suru iken* (Opinion on the outline for amendment of the juvenile law), 1973 (Author's translation).

21. Supreme Court General Secretariat, *Shiho tokei nenpo 4 shonen hen* (Annual report of judicial statistics, vol. 4, Juvenile cases), 1977, 56.

22. Ibid., 16.

23. Akira Morita, "Family Dissolution and the Concept of Children's Rights: An Observation from Legal and Cross-cultural Perspective," *Comparative Law* (Tokyo) 141 (1997): 35.

24. A 1972 survey by the Supreme Court shows that 98.1 percent of all juveniles confessed to all facts of the accusation against them at the investigation and hearing stages. *Katei Saiban Geppo* (Family Court Monthly) 26, no. 4 (1972): 163.

25. Supreme Court General Secretariat, *Annual Report of Judicial Statistics* for 1983 and 1997.

26. Supreme Court decision of October 26, 1983, *Keishu* 37, no. 8 (1983): 1260.

27. Supreme Court General Secretariat, *Annual Report of Judicial Statistics* for 1977 and 1997.

28. Ibid., 1997, at 94.

29. *Bill for Partial Amendment of the Juvenile Law,* Tokyo, 1999.

30. Takeo Doi, *The Anatomy of Self: The Individual versus Society* (New York: Kodansha International/U.S.A., through Harper & Row, 1986).

31. This article was completed before the day the Japanese Diet passed, in November 2000, the renewed Bill for Amendment of the Juvenile Law, which was to some extent different from the initial proposal of 1999.

14 Child Endangerment and Child Protection in England and Wales

John Eekelaar

The way society responds to the adversities suffered by its most vulnerable members tells us a great deal about that society's image of itself. In the case of its children, we learn not only about its compassion, but also about the way it allows power to be distributed among its adult members. This chapter looks at one particular manifestation of the way one society has responded to the circumstances of large numbers of the children in its midst: the legal structures which were developed to deal with them. It does not, therefore, claim to be a fully rounded account of what all or most people actually thought about children, or even how they actually conducted themselves toward them. The law and its structures have never been a perfect mirror of human thoughts and actions. But it is a social reality, and a powerful one at that, which justifies and restrains, through the use of force, what people often do.

The chapter therefore traces the nature of these legal structures as they developed over time. It will be shown that on the whole, prior to the Age of Enlightenment, these structures tended to treat children primarily as a resource for the adult world. However, especially from around the beginning of the nineteenth century, legal structures began slowly to be modified so that they were more attentive to what the adult world believed to be the interests of the children. The story traced here divides the children who attracted public concern into three categories: those who were thought to be subject to some special vulnerability; those who were perceived to constitute a threat to the adult world; and those who, while appearing to reside within the safety of the home, were in fact threatened by that very environment. While the story might seem to be a happy one, showing the degree of attention being paid to children's welfare gathering apace, destined for a fairy-tale ending, we will see that it is far from simple, and that the last twenty years have produced an unexpected twist in the conclusion, though this conclusion may be a new beginning.

PARENTS AND CHILDREN: A HISTORICAL PERSPECTIVE

During the 1970s, three historians—Shorter (1976); Stone (1977), and de Mause (1976)—shocked many readers by arguing that historical evidence proved that in past centuries parents routinely treated children with indifference and cruelty, and wider society approved or connived at this. They may not have appreciated the irony that they were making their disclosures during a period when the extent of contemporary child abuse was being revealed by pediatricians and others in the United States and Britain, and it is incongruous that the historians' claim that such cruelty was largely a thing of the past coincided with revelations that it was still very much with us. In fact, it is possible that the historians overstated their cases. Pollock (1983), using evidence from private diaries rather than child care manuals, shows many cases during 1500 to 1900 of parents demonstrating love and affection toward their children, and later Shaher (1990) showed that in the Middle Ages, too, parents were not normally indifferent to their children.

These controversies illustrate how difficult it is to form objective judgments about the internal nature of parent-child relationships. Yet even in Pollock's and Shaher's accounts, the dominating concern of parents seems to have been to maintain *authority* over their children, although then, as now, this was not always achieved. In a world which regarded submission to divine will as a prime virtue within a hierarchical society, parents were likely to have had a perception of how they should exercise their authority that *differed* from some contemporary ideas. Love can find expression in a variety of ways, and it cannot be assumed that parents who disciplined their children did not love them or believe they were acting in their interests.

But when we look at the *communal* attitudes to children, as expressed primarily through legal behavior, a more complex picture emerges. The many chilling accounts of criminal penalties, including execution and transportation to the Australian penal settlements, visited on young children in the eighteenth and nineteenth centuries (Pinchbeck and Hewitt 1973, 351–52) may reflect in part the generally harsh and repressive treatment meted out to the poor, but also indicates the degree to which the pervasive belief in the exercise of authority and discipline over children was taken. But the general structure of the law reveals something more interesting. From the earliest times, the basis for legal intervention in family matters was the protection of the interests of parents or other adults in the *value* which the child represented for them. Thus, in medieval law (and up to at least 1660), "Wardship procedures were not designed with the purpose of facilitating judicial intervention into the lives of vulnerable infants" but to benefit the guardian from the ward's land or prospective marriage (Seymour 1994). Similarly, the early action for abduction gave a father a remedy against the defendant on the basis of injury to his pecuniary interest in the child's services. It did not see fit to protect the child's own interest in not being abducted. Common law did nothing about the child's interest in its relationship with its parents, either in ensuring that the father properly discharged his responsibilities under it, or in providing the child with remedies against third parties should they injure that interest.

An appropriate word to describe the public attitude toward children would be "instrumentalist" (seeing them as a resource for others rather than objects of concern). Slavery is the paradigm case, and English law provides an example even of this. A statute of Edward V1 of 1547 allowed those "vagabonds and beggars" who refused work to be branded with a hot iron and enslaved for two years "to woke by beating and cheyninge." Slaves were required to do work "how vyle so ever," and could be rented and sold. The children between five and fourteen of "impotent and lame" beggars could be removed from the parents by "any manner of person" against their will and apprenticed until the child was twenty (girls) or twenty-four (boys): if the apprentice should run away, he or she could be put in chains and be used "as his slave in all points." This enactment was repealed two years later, but these Tudor enactments not only betrayed considerable social anxiety over the threat to stability perceived from the workless poor, but attempted to recruit them to the service of the community. But this attitude permeated poor-law legislation. The formal duty which poor-law authorities had regarding children was to "set" them to work. This was so until 1948.

In none of this can the idea of child *welfare* acquire much purchase. If children are publicly perceived primarily as being destined to serve the interests of others, their own interests will be perceived dimly, if at all. Given this historical background, where does one find the roots of a law which can be said to be directed specifically at child welfare (as distinct from a criminal law which is intended for general protection)? They may be found in three contexts. One is in the special protection gradually afforded to children in circumstances common to others but where children have *special vulnerability.* Apprenticeship and employment are standard cases. But the health of newly born and very young children is another instance, and we also should include children whose vulnerability arises from their family circumstances: the family might be very poor or be unable to cope with looking after them; they may be abandoned or orphaned. Another context is that in which the behavior or conditions of life attract the perception that they constitute a threat. We may refer to these as *deviant* children, but this does not necessarily imply criminal delinquency; the real fear is that they are uncontrolled. Finally, we can examine the willingness of the community to question its assumption that its standard framework for the upbringing of children—the family—always acts in the interests of children. These can be seen as the prime case of child *victims*. Each of these contexts is considered in turn.

ESPECIALLY VULNERABLE CHILDREN

Children in Trades and Other Matters

The early law of child welfare is to be found within the practice of apprenticeship. The Statute of Artificers of 1563 required a seven-year apprenticeship for anyone wishing to take up an industrial craft. This was the basis of a successful system of training for children, but one which was prone to abuse by individuals unless regulated. In fact, regulation and some supervision were provided by the guilds, which were anxious to protect the integrity of their crafts as much as the interests of the apprentices, and justices of the peace had powers to release apprentices from their indentures and punish errant masters. But alongside "normal" industrial apprenticeship there existed "parish apprenticeship," which was also a system for finding homes for the children of the poor. The overseers of the poor were permitted to raise a rate on the parish to cover the costs, and they could also compel individuals to take in such an apprentice. In order to reduce the burden on parish funds, this system was increasingly used to send children beyond the parish. The exploitation to which this system exposed children from the late seventeenth century and through the eighteenth was captured in the poem by George Crabbe of 1810, immortalized in Benjamin Britten's opera *Peter Grimes:*

> Peter had heard there were in London then
> Still have they being! Workhouse clearing men.
> Who, undisturbed by feelings just and kind,
> Would parish-boys to needy tradesmen bind;
> They in their want a trifling sum would take,
> And toiling slaves of piteous orphans make.

Protective legislation gradually accumulated during the nineteenth century: from an Act to Improve Health and Morals of Apprentices and others employed in cotton and other mills of 1802, through the Factory Act of 1833, restricting the working hours of children in textile mills; the Mines Act of 1842, prohibiting the underground employment of children aged under ten, to the prohibition of the use of children as chimney sweeps in 1875 (Heywood 1978,

22–28). The introduction of universal state education in 1870 was a major step in the reduction of child labor. Yet the issue remains a live one to this day, especially in overseas countries, where instrumentalist views of childhood remain strong (Rwezaura 1998). But it is easy to be blind to our own practices. Forcing children through hothouse education systems so they will be useful systems in tomorrow's economy may not reflect a very different perception of children as a resource.

Even in a society where the exploitation of children through employment has been largely eliminated, children's vulnerability attracts legal attention through a host of measures, from protection against sexual exploitation to protection against the sale to children of defective consumer products and of alcohol, cigarettes, and so on. But these measures rest upon certain assumptions about the particular vulnerability of children to harm, and come into conflict with differing perceptions (including those of children themselves) as to when they should be free to exercise their autonomous choices. For example, with regard to the age of consent to sexual conduct, in England a girl may consent to heterosexual intercourse at sixteen, but a boy could not, until very recently, engage in consensual homosexual conduct until eighteen. In *Gillick v. West Norfolk and Wisbech Area Health Authority* (1986), the House of Lords decided that a child of any age can consent to medical procedures without parental consent if in possession of sufficient knowledge and understanding. But that operates in a context in which it is assumed that the medical profession would not carry out a procedure on a child unless it was thought to be in its welfare, and in any case children have not been given a corresponding power to *refuse* treatment that is thought, by their parents or the courts, to be in their interests. It remains unclear whether the *Gillick* principle extends to consent to possibly risky activities—boxing? mountain-climbing? How far are we prepared to allow children to define their own interests?

The Health Care of Very Young Children

Child-protective measures have often been instigated by public scandals. One of the earliest arose in 1870 when Mary Walters was executed for murdering babies, mostly illegitimate children, whose mothers were prevented by ignominy or poverty from caring for them. It was estimated that in 1872 some thirty thousand illegitimate children were dying of neglect every year. The Infant Life Protection Act of 1872 set up a system of registration of people taking in children under one year for more than twenty-four hours for reward, but there was no enforcement mechanism, and another murder trial in 1896 led to the stronger Infant Life Protection Act of 1897, later expanded in the Children Act of 1908 and the Public Health Act of 1936, sec. 206. Various statutory provisions were consolidated in the Children Act of 1989. Essentially these require local-authority social services to inspect the premises of anyone undertaking the "nursing or maintenance" of any child (by 1936, under nine). In the late 1970s some concern was expressed that daily-minded children were emotionally and educationally disadvantaged (Jackson and Jackson 1979), though more recent evidence found some benefits for children receiving out-of-home care, but mostly in center-based day care, which may not be easily available (Acheson Report 1998, pt. 2, sec. 7). Yet government concerns about the quality of day care have persisted, and in August 1999 it was announced that the inspection of childminders, playgroups, and day nurseries was to be switched from local-authority social services departments to OFSTED, the schools inspectorate accountable to the Department of Education, indicating a perception that the physical condition of the relevant children was now no longer a primary concern, and attention should move to the quality of the environment as a learning experience.

It is, however, where the children remain within their homes that control is weakest. Despite cases in the late 1990s in both England and the United States where live-in nannies were convicted of harming children in their care, there is no specific public regulation over the quality of care they provide, or the use made of them by the parents, although there are various guidelines and voluntary codes. But this must be seen within the context of the universal health visiting service. The country had been shocked by the poor health of the population revealed by recruitment for the Boer War, and one reaction was to put health visiting on a statutory basis in part 1 of the Children Act of 1908. It is the responsibility of the service to visit all expectant mothers and children under five, and, although health visitors have no compulsory powers of entry, they are not perceived as being threatening and are always admitted entry. This practice provides a source for advice and assistance, as well as a source of referral. This long-standing involvement of the health services with child welfare and the fact that the Ministry of Health succeeded the Local Government Board as the central authority over the poor law in 1930 gave the Ministry of Health the basis of its claim against the Home Office in the early 1940s to be designated the one central government department with overall responsibility for child welfare. The claim was unsuccessful at the time, but history was on its side, and the Home Office lost its control to the Department of Health when Health and Social Security were amalgamated in 1971.

Despite the realization that child welfare and child health were closely related, it remains true that there are severe inequalities in child health which are related to class and ethnicity. For example, infant mortality (deaths in the first year of life) is 5:1,000 in social classes I and II, and 7:1,000 in social classes IV and V. Babies in the lower social classes have lower birth weight and lower life expectancy (Acheson Report 1998). The government has made a number of proposals designed to address this problem, including targeting the efforts of health visitors toward the more disadvantaged.

Children of Poor and Malfunctioning Families

From the Workhouses to the Curtis Report

From the middle of the seventeenth century, workhouses were seen as a convenient and relatively cheap way of providing for the poor but came to be seen as a source of cheap labor. The eighteenth-century campaigner Jonas Hanway claimed many workhouses had infant mortality rates of over 50 percent. Yet by 1840 there were an estimated 64,570 children in English workhouses. A large number of them would have been born to unmarried mothers. The nineteenth and most of the twentieth centuries saw slow improvement in the provision for these children. The agency through which this was achieved was education, for the poor-law authorities remained primarily responsible for the education of workhouse children until 1929, when their functions were transferred to county councils.

Initially, entrepreneurs in London were allowed to educate children outside the workhouse, in the expectation of benefiting from their eventual labors (figure 14.1). Later, poor-law unions established their own schools, in which the children were also accommodated. These schools were initially large, "barrack" establishments (referred to as "district" or "separate" schools, depending on whether they served one or more poor-law unions), but in 1871 the Nassau Report on the Education of Girls in Pauper Schools recommended to the Local Government Board (which, from 1871, assumed responsibility for the administration of the poor law) that these should be broken down into smaller homes of some 10–20 children, known as "cottage homes," under the supervision of a "housemother." These homes were still grouped together, some having populations exceeding three hundred children, with their education provided centrally, and the Mundella Report on Poor Law Schools (1896) observed that these arrangements failed to integrate the children effectively into the community. Thus a system of ordinary houses "scattered" around the community, accommodating some dozen children who went to the local school with other children of the community, was encouraged. Also, in 1870 the Poor Law Board allowed the boarding out (fostering) of children beyond the boundaries of the poor-law union. This essentially remained the pattern until after the Second World War, although by that time the form of accommodation represented only where the child lived, not its place of education, which was now provided in state schools. The changes that occurred over that period can be seen from the sets of figures in tables 14.1 and 14.2.

Despite the drop in the total number of children maintained by public

Fig. 14.1 Teacher and waifs of North Market Hall School Mission, London, 1850. © Bettmann/CORBIS.

assistance, changes in the distribution among types of accommodation over that period were modest. Although there was a clear move away from workhouses and district and separate schools toward grouped cottage homes and scattered homes, the numbers of children living together in these establishments could still be large. To this must be added the large number of children looked after in voluntary homes without support from public funds. In 1946, these were estimated to amount to 33,500 in homes registered with the Home Office.

How was the well-being of these children assured? The institutional ethos of the poor-law administration was premised on the necessity of "setting the poor to work," supplemented by the policy of less eligibility. So the last consolidating statute of the poor law, the Poor Law Act of 1930, which transferred administration of the poor law from the Local Government Board to the Ministry of Health, acting through local authorities, still required local authorities to "set to work or put out as apprentices all children whose parents are not, in the opinion of the Council, able to keep and maintain their children" (sec. 15). Yet this had for the past sixty years been implemented through the provision of education for the children. Even so, the manner and conditions of the education, and the circumstances in which the children lived, re-

Table 14.1

Places where children were "maintained" under the poor law at 1 January 1907

	Number	Percentage
Infirmaries	5,534	8.0
Workhouses	14,676	21.2
District and separate schools	11,809	17.1
Grouped cottage homes	8,420	12.2
Scattered homes	4,963	7.2
Receiving homes	2,506	3.6
Boarded-out	8,659	12.5
Other[a]	12,511	18.1
Total	69,078	

Source: MacNamara, 1908, 5.

[a]For example, in establishments not maintained by poor-law authorities.

Table 14.2

Children "maintained" by public assistance at 1 May 1946

	Number	Percentage
Sick wards	3,456	10.5
Nurseries	3,044	9.2
Grouped cottage homes	7,024	21.3
Scattered homes	4,662	14.1
Other[a]	5,209	15.8
Voluntary homes (certified or uncertified)	4,598	13.9
Boarded-out	4,892	14.8
Total	32,885	

Source: Curtis Report 1946, para. 32.

[a]Includes unspecified number of children, mostly under three, in workshops with their parents, children in larger "barrack" ("district" and "separate") homes of two hundred or more children and in "single" homes of up to fifty children: cf. Curtis Report, paras. 138 and 158–65. Cretney cites an estimate, taken from a Ministry of Health memorandum, of 1,433 children being in workhouses in 1944, and 10,312 in cottage homes; see *Law, Law Reform, and the Family* (1998), 206.

flected the stern and stigmatizing attitudes of the poor-law administration. It was not that there was official indifference to them. The idea that the Victorian administrators were heartless is refuted by a reading of the Mundella Report of 1896, which must rank as one of the great state papers of the Victorian age, running to hundreds of pages of evidence, and displaying a concern and compassion for the children which would be hard to equal in any epoch. But the circumstances were very difficult. The report observes that, in London alone, there were at that time 74,000 "beds" for poor-law children. Supervision by the Local Government Board was carried out by a general inspector, a medical inspector, an educational inspector, an assistant inspector, an inspector for boarded-out children, and a chief general inspector. Not surprisingly, the committee recommended more and better-trained inspectors. Voluntary-sector schools could be certified to take in poor-law children, but if they did so, they too became subject to inspection. Mundella recommended that this type of inspection should also be improved. Yet when the Curtis Committee, in 1945–46, came to review the circumstances of the (considerably reduced) number of children who were under the responsibility of the poor-law authorities (by then, the Ministry of Health and local authorities), it found much to be desired. The majority of homes "had sent no children to secondary or technical schools," a matter the committee found "extraordinary" and a "serious failure to compensate the child deprived of a normal home life" (Curtis Report 1946, para. 193). Although they found little evidence of "neglect or harsh usage" of children, they found that many who had been placed temporarily in workhouses had been given provision for the barest of physical needs, and although they felt there had been an improvement in the attitudes of society to the treatment of children, "witnesses did however bring home to us the danger, even in an organisation or under an authority with an enlightened policy, that individuals in charge of children may develop harsh or oppressive tendencies or false ideas of discipline" (Curtis Report 1946, para. 417).

Accountability through inspections and occasional reviews by public bodies, such as the Mundella and Curtis committees, was an important element in ensuring some level of protection of the well-being of these children. *But more significant for the children was the general attitude at that time toward the processes of child development and the relationship between children and the adult world.* These can be seen most clearly in the activities of the voluntary societies, which developed rapidly toward the end of the nineteenth century, and were inspired both by passions of pity and horror at the conditions of many children and an evangelical zeal to save them from moral corruption. But what constituted their moral reconstruction, and how was it to be achieved? The former comprised religious instruction, orderly behavior instilled through discipline, and the acquisition of skills, mostly of a practical nature. This was to be achieved by removing the children as completely as possible from their corrupting environment. It was expressed in this way by the most famous English practitioner, Dr. Thomas Barnardo: "If the children of the slums can be removed from their surroundings early enough, and can be kept sufficiently long under training, heredity counts for little, environment counts for everything" (Heywood 1978, 53). Barnardo's is still a significant children's charity in the United Kingdom. If one may employ metaphor, it is as if children were seen as plants, which, if growing in contaminated ground, would be saved by being transplanted into nutritious soil. These features were displayed in their most dramatic form in the policies most strenuously pursued by the voluntary societies from the 1870s until as late as the 1960s of arranging the emigration of children from the U.K. to the then colonies and dominions, especially Canada and Australia. In the public perception, and in the rhetoric of the societies, these children were "orphans," being sent cheerfully to a bright future. In reality, most had been separated from their families against their will, and were compelled to go by means of deception or coercion. Barnardo's alone sent off some thirty thousand children, and the total number of those who emigrated from the 1860s to the 1960s must have been in excess of one hundred thousand (Rose 1989; Eekelaar 1994).

Their certainty of the benefits being conferred on the children blinded the practitioners to the virtual absence of any consideration for the feelings of the children and their parents. One advocate described child emigration as "the chief glory and the most consoling feature of the work of rescue" (Waugh 1911). But even within that ideological context, a responsible child welfare policy must operate a system of control and accountability. For children in poor-law care, this was provided to some degree. As early as 1874, an official investigation was ordered by the Local Government Board into the use made by some poor-law authorities of two independent women who arranged for the migration of the children to Canada. Another state document characterized by its deep humanity, the Doyle Report (1875), sought to discourage the practice, which was seen as being exploitative of the children, and drew attention to weaknesses in the selection of children and their subsequent supervision in Canada. Further criticisms of the circumstances of poor-law children in Canada made by the Mundella report (1896), the MacNamara Report (1908), and the Bondfield Delegation (1924) led to the virtual cessation of emigration to Canada. Furthermore, in the case of poor-law children, legislation required that the child must give his or her consent before a justice of the peace, and each application for emigration must be approved by the Poor Law Board.

Although it is debatable how effective these administrative checks were (one magistrate later commented that "the magistrate always signs"), their very presence stands in stark contrast to the position regarding the voluntary societies. As far as emigration is concerned, the lack of statutory control was remarked upon in the Doyle Report in 1875, in the Curtis Report (1946, para. 515), and in the Ross Report (1956). Yet nothing was ever done. Dr. Barnardo adopted a cavalier attitude to the parents of children whose emigration he arranged and is reported to have appeared in court eighty-eight times on contempt charges (Rose 1989, 577). Yet Barnardo managed to procure a change in the law favorable to him, despite further criticism by the House of Lords for refusing to allow a mother to see her child or to tell her where he was. The Custody of Children Act of 1891 provided that, when a parent had abandoned or deserted a child, or allowed the child to be brought up by another person at that person's expense, for such a length of time and under such circumstances as to satisfy the court that the parent was unmindful of his parental duties, the court should not return the child unless it considered that, having regard to the welfare of the child, the parent was fit to have the child.

Hence a feature of child welfare law at this time was the perceived need to protect children against their parents. This operated for poor-law children as well, and the powers of poor-law authorities to give them this protection were strengthened in 1889 when the Poor Law Amendment Act of that year provided (sec. 1) that "where a child is maintained by guardians of any union and is deserted by its parent" or if the parent was "imprisoned as a result of an offence against the child," the guardians might resolve "that such child be under the control of the guardians until it reaches sixteen (if a boy) or eighteen (if a girl)." The parents had a right of appeal to a magistrate, though no right to be told of this. The scope of these resolutions was extended in 1899 to cover parents who were of "such habits and mode of life as to be unfit to have the care of the child," and they became known as "poor-law adoptions" and were a unique feature of British child welfare law for exactly one hundred years. Although the voluntary associations did not have such powers, the protection given to their operations and relative lack of control over them was extraordinary. They were inspected by the Ministry of Health only if they received poor-law children into their care, and although under the Children and Young Persons Act of 1933 those which received charitable donations needed to be registered with the Home Office, this did not cover those with self-sufficient funding. This leniency can be explained on the basis that those who were engaged in such activities were credited with high moral motives, making criticism difficult to sustain. Yet those homes which were subject to no control whatever came in for scathing criticism from the Curtis Committee (1946, para. 229): "Children may be shut away from any outside contact or advice for the whole of their childhood; they may be in the hands of untrained and narrow-minded staff, with the result that they go out into the world unprepared for adult life."

The Triumph and Subsequent Fall of State Welfarism: From the Children Act of 1948 to the Children Act of 1989

The Children Act of 1948 is generally credited with marking a revolutionary change in policy and attitudes regarding the care of children who lack proper family support. It followed the Curtis Report of 1946, which itself followed the publicity around the death of a poor-law child at the hands of foster parents. Cretney (1998) has shown that reform was already under consideration before that event, instigated by problems created by homeless evacuees in wartime, the prospective break up of the poor law, a campaign by Lady

Allen of Hurtwood, and separate campaigns by magistrates concerned about conditions in remand homes. How far does the claim that the Act was revolutionary hold?

The Curtis Committee itself can be characterized as being concerned primarily with the issue of the *quality* of child care services, rather than overarching policy. It wished to introduce a personal element into the children's care and avoid the stultifying effect of institutions and impersonal bureaucracies. It wanted the children to be better integrated into the whole community. Hence its preference, if a child could not remain at home, for adoption; then fostering; then residential care, though with considerable safeguards. The personal element and reduction of bureaucracy were to be exemplified in the appointment of children's officers in each local authority and the concentration of jurisdiction in matters concerning children in a Children's Committee. All voluntary homes were to be registered and subject to inspection, thus being for the first time fully integrated into the child care field. These reforms were carried out in the Children Act of 1948.

But in themselves these measures were not radical departures. The preference for caring for children in small units, especially families, appeared from the end of the previous century. Adoption, introduced in 1926, had proved a popular way of placing children, and was reinforced by the Adoption of Children (Regulation) Act of 1939, which brought adoption societies and the adoption process under closer supervision. Certainly the emphasis on fostering had important practical effects, and by 1974, 39.9 percent of children in local-authority care were boarded-out, and in 1997, 65 percent of the eighty-nine thousand children "looked after" by local authorities were boarded-out. Nevertheless, as a concept, it had long been advocated. The notorious duty to "set to work" the poor-law child was replaced by a duty "to further his best interests, and to afford him opportunity for the proper development of his character and abilities" (Children Act of 1948, sec. 12). The requirement to seek the optimal benefit for the child was described by Heywood (1978, 158) as being "perhaps unmatched for its humanity in all our legislation." Yet the old poor-law duty had long been abandoned, and both the poor-law authorities and the voluntary society workers would probably have claimed to have been doing something along the lines described by section 12, albeit that their perceptions of children's interests may have been different.

There was no diminution in the scope of public duty toward children; indeed, it was extended insofar as the public authorities' duties to care for children were no longer confined to the destitute, but extended to all children, arising whenever it appeared to the local authority that a child under seventeen "has neither parent nor guardian or has been and remains abandoned by his parents or guardian or is lost," or "that his parents or guardian are, for the time being or permanently, prevented by reason of mental or bodily disease or infirmity or other incapacity or any other circumstances from providing for his proper accommodation, maintenance or upbringing"; and "in either case, that the intervention of the local authority under this section is necessary in the interests of the child" (Children Act 1948, sec. 1[1]). Welfare services were to be more widely available, without stigma.

However, this was subject to the next subsection, which Heywood (1978, 156) describes as being "revolutionary." This imposes on local authorities a duty "in all cases where it appears to them consistent with the welfare of the child to do so to endeavour to secure that the care of the child is taken over either (a) by a parent or guardian of his, or (b) by a relative or friend of his." This does seem to indicate a decisive shift from the earlier attitudes toward parents and the child's environment. The phrasing is cautious: the duty to try to restore the child only arises where this seems to be "consistent with the welfare of the child"; so it was still possible to take a strong view that such restoration, or even contact, was not consistent with the child's welfare, and was therefore not to occur. But it seems that a psychological barrier had been crossed. In 1942, Dorothy Burlingham and Anna Freud had drawn attention to the traumatic effects on children of sudden separation from their families, and the importance of emotional relationships between children and their mothers, something to which scant attention had been given by the child savers. Even more significant would have been the direct evidence given to the Committee by John Bowlby, whose later monograph to the World Health Organization in 1951 was published in 1953 (Bowlby 1953). This coined for the first time the expression, "maternal deprivation," and alleged that severe psychological harm was caused to even very young children by disruption of the maternal tie, a theory greatly elaborated in later works and known as "attachment" theory. The implications of this were clear. It was better to prevent separation of a child from its mother in the first instance. Heywood (1978, 133) goes as far as to describe these events as a "rediscovery of the value of the family."

The consequences were indeed great. The harnessing of psychological theory to social work had assumed increasing importance since the end of the First World War, and this received a strong boost from maternal deprivation theory. The family "caseworker" was now perceived to have the ability, by working with the family, to assist its members in coping with the difficulties in bringing up children. Emphasis was now directed toward preventive work. This was stressed in Circulars from the Home Officer and the Ministry of Health in 1950. The widening of the duty to provide care for children in the 1948 Act had led to an increase in the numbers of children in care from 46,000 in 1946 to 65,309 in 1953. Thereafter, the numbers declined slightly: from 5.6 per 1,000 of the population under eighteen in 1953, to 5.1 in 1959. The preventive role of casework was given statutory recognition in section 1 of the

Children and Young Persons Act of 1963. The proportion of children received into care (as opposed to helped within their homes) thereafter fell (Packman 1975, 69). This encouraged the belief that the proper focus of social casework should be on the family rather than the child and sounded the death-knell of the Curtis system of Children's Officers and Children's Committees. The Seebohm Report (1968) recommended the merger of independent local authority departments into a common social services department, with "generic" social workers trained to assist in all areas of family functioning. The optimistic vision was based on a belief that casework could assist individuals to make their own immediate social units operate more effectively within the larger communal framework. The changes were introduced by the Local Authority Social Services Act of 1970. The prevalent atmosphere is well described by Patron, Thorpe, and Wattam (1997):

> It was assumed that the interests of the social workers and hence the state were similar to, if not the same as, [those of] the people they were trying to *help*. It was essentially a benign, but materialistic, relationship. Interventions in the family were not conceived as a potential source of antagonism between social workers and individual family members—whether parent(s) or child(ren)—who were not seen as having interests or rights distinct from the unitary family itself. When a family required modification, this would be via casework, help and advice, and if an individual did come into state care, this was assumed to be in their interests. Interventions which had therapeutic intentions necessarily had beneficial outcomes, so that social work required and was allowed a large degree of independence and discretion to carry out its work. (22)

The psychological basis of casework represented a perception of the parent-child relationship which received its strongest expression in Goldstein, Freud, and Solnit (1973), who elevated the importance of the *continuity* of the relationship between a child and one parent (the "psychological" parent) to an overriding principle. The belief that ruptured or distorted psychological relationships in the early years caused lasting psychological damage was developed into an explanation for family malfunctioning, which was seen to be "transmitted" between generations, constituting a "cycle of deprivation," which manifested itself in groups of "problem families," where failure appeared to be endemic (Philp 1963). Unlike the child savers, however, social workers did not respond by removing children (which might aggravate the harm) but by attempting to reconstitute the relationships. During the 1970s, a series of empirical studies set up to test these perceptions led the authors to the more balanced, but perhaps not surprising, conclusion that deprivation had both individual and structural causes (Brown and Madge 1982). Yet the psychologically based continuity theory cut both ways, for, while it stressed the dangers of disrupting a child's relationship with its primary psychological parent (the mother), it also stressed the dangers of returning a child to its natural parents if it had established a new relationship with another psychological parent.

There had always been some ambiguity in the "new" emphasis on rehabilitation of the child with its family. Even the Curtis Committee had given adoption as its preferred means of providing for children separated from their parents, and this strong countercurrent coexisted with the policies developed under the Children Act of 1948 and the Seebohm Report. During the 1960s, there was a growing feeling that too much weight was being given to respect for the "blood-tie" both by judges and social workers, which was aggravated by a judicial decision returning a child who had been with prospective adopters for eighteen months to its natural father. The Houghton Report (1972), reflecting the influence of the "permanency planning" movement in the United States, sought to strengthen the position of local authorities when dealing with the parents of children whom they were looking after. It recommended that if the child had been in care for more than a year, the authority should be empowered to require twenty-eight days' notice by the parent before removing the child. It also suggested that "it would be an advantage if . . . local authorities had a discretionary power to assume parental rights in respect of any child who had been in their care for a continuous period of three years" (Houghton Report 1972, para. 156) and made recommendations that courts should be permitted to make orders freeing children for adoption prior to any adoption order actually being made, and that foster parents who had been looking after a child for five years could apply for their adoption. These recommendations were enacted in the Children Act of 1975, which was consolidated with the 1948 Act in the Child Care Act of 1980. The position of local authorities was strengthened still further when the House of Lords confirmed in 1980 that they were under no duty physically to return a child who was in voluntary care simply because a parent asked for it back (though they did cease to be "authorised" to keep it). This meant that, so long as they kept the child, they could pass a resolution depriving the parents of their rights, if the requisite conditions were met. The following year the House held that visits by parents to children in care could be controlled entirely at the discretion of the authorities. We had reached the high-water mark of the state's powers over families in the twentieth century.

But already discontent was growing. The widening of the grounds for passing resolutions led to an increase in the numbers of children subject to such resolutions: from 13,200 in 1975 (26 percent of children in care) to 18,400 in 1979 (40 percent of children in care). By the end of the period 1951–81, children who came into care, either voluntarily or under court order, stayed in care for longer than at the beginning of the period, and a higher proportion of children in care were there under a court order or resolution. But this does not mean that local authorities were intervening more aggressively (Dingwall and Eekelaar 1984); indeed, they operated within an institutional culture biased *against* intervention (Dingwall, Eekelaar, and Murray 1983). It is possible that the changes that did occur (especially the longer time spent by children in care) were a result of a change in the character of the children in care brought about by preventive policies that successfully kept the less problematic cases from coming into care and by the sweeping into care of children convicted of offenses under the Children and Young Persons Act of 1969 (discussed below). But *perceptions* were changing. Radical social work theory was beginning to challenge an approach which accepted existing social frameworks and to criticize social work practice which identified with those structures. Client groups themselves began to question the assumption that their needs could be defined by social workers (Bailey and Brake 1980; Taylor 1993). There could be no objective measure that the state was becoming "too coercive," but the criticisms reflected a growing libertarian ideological perspective (Fox Harding 1991, 24–25; Parton 1991, ch. 2). Furthermore, there was intense controversy over the extent to which local authorities should control contact between children in care and their parents. At the same time, there had been one or more inquiries into social services' role in cases where a child had died in each year since the Maria Colwell case (see below) in 1974. In 1984, therefore, the Parliamentary Select Committee on Social Services (Short Committee) called for the establishment of an Interdepartmental Working Party to review the whole of child care law, and its Consultative Document was published in 1985 (Interdepartmental Report 1985).

Simultaneously, research was beginning to point in new directions. Packman (1986) and Millham et al. (1986) now incorporated interviews with parents into their data, revealing some sharp conflicts between social workers and parents. The idea that social workers should enlist the partnership of informal caregivers in the community gained popularity during the Thatcher years of the 1980s. It was thought to save expenditure and encourage a sense of individual responsibility, fueled by a belief that social workers' alleged "expertise" was no more than ordinary common sense, accessible by everyone. The Griffiths Report (1988) promoted the concept of care in the community, including the notion that children were better off in their own homes, supported by informal caregivers. The role of social workers was to coordinate private and voluntary sector provision (Cochrane 1993). These themes were the background against which the Children Act of 1989 was drawn up.

The Short Report (1984) signaled a significant reorientation of the role of social work in relation to families by attempting to recast the claims made on behalf of parents in terms of "responsibilities." This meant not merely that parents should behave responsibly toward their children, but that it was the responsibility of parents, and not of the state, to care for their children (Eekelaar 1991). The Interdepartmental Report (1985, para. 2.8) made this explicit, proclaiming that "the interests of the children are best served by their remaining with their families, and the interests of their parents are best served by allowing them to undertake their natural and legal responsibility to care for their own children." The difference from the "rediscovery of the family" in 1948 is encapsulated in two expressions: "responsibility" and "partnership." Whereas the Curtis Committee, and the casework approach which followed it, envisioned the role of social services as helping parents care for their children, the new language refers to "allowing" the parents to "undertake" their "natural and legal responsibility" to care for their children. For Curtis, the expression "responsibility" was related to the local authority. In 1985 prominence is given to the "responsibilities" of parents: they are not just there to be helped; they too have a duty to look after their children. Thus the White Paper (1987, para. 5) following the 1985 Interdepartmental Report sets out as the first principle upon which the new law will be built that "the prime responsibility for the upbringing of children rests with parents." The dominant role of the state is to be reduced through the concept of working in "partnership."

Under the Children Act of 1989, therefore, children are not received into care: all the authority does is to provide accommodation for them. The duty to provide accommodation only arises with regard to "children in need," not all children. A child is "in need" only if "he is unlikely to achieve or maintain, or to have the opportunity of achieving or maintaining, a reasonable standard of health or development without the provision for him of services by the local authority . . . ; his health or development is likely to be significantly impaired, or further impaired, without the provision for him of such services; or he is disabled" (sec. 17 [10]). It is not enough for the authority simply to think that taking the child in is "necessary" in the "interests" of its "welfare." It is clear that, by carving out a distinct category of children from the child population at large, the Children Act of 1989 has created a boundary which confines the local authorities' duties and which is policed largely by the authority itself.

The principle of partnership is the other way in which such parental responsibilities have been emphasized. Thus, even where a child is provided with accommodation (on a voluntary basis), the local authority does not acquire parental responsibility over the child. More important, it has lost the powers it acquired in 1975 to require twenty-eight days' notice by a parent wanting to reclaim a child who had been in the authority's care for over six months and, even more significant, the power to acquire parental rights by administrative resolution is now abolished. Instead, the Children Act of 1989 states that "Any person who has parental responsibility for a child may at any time remove the child from accommodation provided for or on behalf of the local authority under this section" (sec. 20 [1]). We now need to consider how these historical developments have affected the position of our final groups of children: "deviant" children and child victims.

DEVIANT CHILDREN: CHILDREN AS THREATS—CRIMINAL AND UNCONTROLLED CHILDREN

The key in considering deviant children is the perception of a breakdown in the control over children which we assume that families provide. The nineteenth-century response was through the criminal law: conviction of traditional criminal offenses or of vagrancy. However, a distinction was drawn between the (traditional) criminal and the vagrant child. Under the Industrial Schools Act of 1866 vagrant children and children under fourteen who were found begging, wandering, or frequenting the company of reputed thieves; children under twelve who were charged with offenses; and children who were beyond the control of their parents were sent to industrial schools. The Report of the Departmental Committee on Reformatory and Industrial Schools (1896) distinguished these from reformatories: "[The] inmates of reformatories are always called youthful offenders, and those of industrial schools always children. It was no doubt to mark this distinction that the two institutions were dealt with in separate Acts and that it was especially forbidden for the same school to be both a reformatory and an industrial school." Thus at that time we can see clearly a child-protective goal in the Industrial Schools legislation. However, as the primary motive for intervention remained "instrumental" (the protection of society's interests), rather than "welfarist" (the protection of the interests of the children), the inspector of industrial schools could remark in 1870 on the similarity of their management to those of reformatories, and in 1927 the Committee for Young Offenders repeated the many calls for their assimilation. Thus the Children and Young Persons Act of 1932 amalgamated the two institutions into "approved schools." The Children and Young Persons Act of 1933 redefined the category of nondelinquent children over whom these powers could be exercised: they were described as children "in need of care and protection."

The assimilation of these children with child offenders was accelerated by the post–World War II emphasis on family context, for failures in the families could lead either to the children offending, being neglected, or becoming beyond control. During the war, the Home Office had argued against the view that "delinquent children form a class apart, who must not be associated with other children" (Cretney 1998, ch. 9), and assimilation was completed by the Ingleby Committee (1960), which included among children in need of "protection or discipline" those under twelve who "were acting in a manner which would render a person over that age liable to be found guilty of an offence," and by a Home Office White Paper of 1965 raising the age to sixteen (Home Office 1965). But in this process, child victims, too, were brought within the same category, as we shall now see.

CHILD VICTIMS WITHIN THE HOME

The Conflation of Child Victims with Uncontrolled Children

As Pollock (1983) demonstrated, the criminal prosecution of parents for offenses against their children was not unknown during the nineteenth century. Yet these were rare events, requiring proof of specific crimes, and conviction of the parents did not necessarily lead to specific protective actions for the children. Society was still reluctant to intervene publicly for the sole purpose of protecting children's interests, and the first efforts in this direction were designed to protect community funds by reinforcing the duties of parents of children who were likely to be a burden on the poor rates to care for them properly. Thus the Poor Law Amendment Act of 1868 allowed the poor-law guardians to prosecute any parent for "wilful neglect to provide adequate food, clothing, medical aid or lodging for his child being in his custody, under the age of fourteen years, whereby the health of the child shall have been or shall be seriously injured." But this overlooked active ill treatment, which was only dealt with in the Prevention of Cruelty to Children Act of 1889 after lobbying by the National Society for the Prevention of Cruelty to Children (Allen and Morton 1961; Parton 1985, ch. 2). On conviction of the adult (usually the parent) of the offenses, the court could commit the child to the charge of a relative or anyone else willing to have the care of the child who would have "like control over the child as if he were its parent and shall be responsible for its maintenance, and the child shall continue under the control of such person, notwithstanding that it is claimed by its parents." This seminal provision was motivated by concern over the well-being of children as an end in itself, but saw the way to achieve this as being through punishing, and, in this way, transforming, the parents. Intervention was conditional on their conviction. In 1904 and 1908, the range of offenses for which parents might be convicted was enlarged (Prevention of Cruelty to Children Act of 1904; Children Act of 1908, sec. 21). The Departmental Committee on Young Offenders (1927), which was required to "inquire into the treatment of young offenders and young people who, owing to bad associations or surroundings, require protection or training," interpreted its remit as extending *also* to "young people who are the victims of cruelty or other offences committed by adults and whose natural guardianship having proved insufficient or unworthy of trust must be replaced." As a result the Children and Young Persons Act of 1933 included as being "in need of care and protection" children who had been victims of certain offenses alongside uncontrolled children. The committee had also called for the assimilation of industrial schools and reformatories, and in 1933 these schools were amalgamated as "approved schools." Child victims would not, however, be placed in approved schools, since the court could commit them into the care of a local authority. But child victims had now, both within official thinking and legal procedures, become intertwined with children with entirely different problems who were regarded as virtually inseparable from juvenile delinquents.

In parallel there occurred a decline in prosecutions of parents. In 1889, the NSPCC prosecuted one case in three; by 1953, it had become one case in forty (Housden 1951, 151). Cruelty to children was now associated with poverty and squalor in the home. Often drunkenness was involved, but even this seemed a sharply declining problem: while 40 percent of the NSPCC's "cases" in 1914–15 involved drunkenness, this was true with regard to only 3.9 percent of its 38,184 cases in 1953. Given this changing perception of child cruelty, and the growing confidence in the ability to transform families by casework, prosecution of the parents was now seldom thought a satisfactory response, and in 1952 prosecution was removed as a condition precedent to intervention. So much had official concerns over parental misbehavior toward their children faded that the Ingleby Committee (1960), which was, among other things, required to make recommendations on the law relating to "the prevention of cruelty to and exposure to moral and physical danger of juveniles," barely considered the issue. The committee stated that this had not raised significant problems over the appropriateness of state intervention because "difficulty has not arisen for several years over the reasonable requirements for nutrition, housing, clothing, and schooling," though there had been some cases (involving unconventional religious sects) where parents had failed to provide their children with proper medical attention. Given this perception, the committee proposed adding the words "and discipline" to the formulation "in need of care and protection," and removing any reference to parental failure among the conditions for intervention. After all, the committee observed, children can perform improper acts without imputed knowledge or failure to the parents (Ingleby Report, Appendix 3). The class of child victims had now totally disappeared from view.

Continued concern over juvenile delinquency dominated official thinking in the 1960s. After two further White Papers, which were wholly devoted to that issue, the Children and Young Persons Act of 1969 recast the law in terms which brought all categories of children within the potential scope of care proceedings: having committed an offense (excluding homicide) would progressively become a reason for bringing care proceedings, not criminal prosecution. Offending children were to be treated the same as nonoffending children who were in need of care and protection. There was no place in this scheme for reference to parental failure, for, as the Home Office Guide observed, such reference "meant that proceedings inevitably appeared to cast blame for the child's situation or behaviour directly on to the parents or those looking after him." So even if the proceedings concerned a child victim, it was the child who was brought before the court, not the parents; there were, therefore, no provisions for their separate representation in such proceedings.

The "Rediscovery" of Child Abuse, the "Cycle of Violence," and the Crisis of the 1970s

At this juncture there occurred what is often referred to as the "rediscovery" of child abuse. The "child savers" who had initiated the late-nineteenth-century protective legislation had certainly been aware of it and treated it as a manifestation of moral degradation, from which the children needed to be permanently separated. As we have seen, this judgmental attitude receded during the early part of the twentieth century. Harms to children began to be seen as primarily the result of poverty; the remedy, therefore, was to lie in improving social conditions of the population. In view of the current prominence given to sexual abuse, it is interesting to observe that the problem was recognized in the 1920s, but it was ascribed largely (though not entirely) to poverty and overcrowding (Departmental Committee on Sexual Offences against Young Persons 1925). Perhaps the optimism caused by the economic boom of the 1950s with its program of slum clearance and manifest improvement in material conditions lulled people into the belief that the abuses associated with poverty and neglect would disappear. Yet already in the United States, pediatric radiologists were suggesting that babies were suffering deliberately inflicted injuries, and in 1961 Dr. C. Henry Kempe, presenting findings to the Children's Bureau, coined the expression, the "battered baby syndrome." The matter remained low-profile, however, during the 1960s, although various doctors were expressing a view that some sort of crusade should be mounted against this "disease." However, after the NSPCC established its Battered Child Research Unit in 1968, the matter attracted more attention through its publication and research (Parton 1985).

In 1974, however, two events occurred which triggered widespread public concern, altering even the language used to the wider and less determinate expression of "nonaccidental injury," and thence to the even more all-embracing term "child abuse." One was the publication by Erin Pizzey (1974) of her account of the first three years of the first women's shelter from domestic violence. The other was the report of the inquiry into the death of Maria Colwell, who had been killed by her stepfather, after having been returned to her natural mother after spending six years with her aunt, despite repeated warnings about the way she had been treated after her return (Field-Fisher Report 1974). But for such incidents to transform perceptions of family relationships and the role of the state, they must relate to current concerns (Dingwall, Eekelaar, and Murray 1984). In the United States, the revelation that the family, too, was a violent place fueled the perception of a violent and fractured society represented by the traumas of the Vietnam war, the Kennedy assassinations, and the civil rights conflicts of the period; it might even be seen as providing a partial explanation for such ills. In the United Kingdom, too, the protest movements of the late 1960s, IRA violence, perceived growing crime rates, and the incidence of divorce and family breakdown of the period could be linked to the perception of failing parental behavior, feminist critiques of the family as a location of male domination, and the inability of the state to deal with such events. In one perception, the state was failing to do enough to breach this cycle of violence, and in another, the state itself was implicated in it.

The initial reaction was to enhance local-authority powers through the Children Act of 1975 and to use them more vigorously. There was an increase in emergency interventions through place of safety orders; more children entered care under compulsory powers; and children remained in care for longer periods (Fox Harding 1991, 67), although the extent of actual committals to care did not change. However, media reports of a succession of instances of child abuse in the 1970s undermined public confidence in social services' abilities to safeguard children. It is perhaps surprising that repeated revelations of parental brutality toward their children should result in questioning the authority of social workers. However, the very authoritarian role they sometimes used when they considered it necessary to protect children was held against them. This was aggravated by the structure of the legislation in which they worked, modeled as it was on child delinquents and uncontrolled children. Initially, the Short Report (1984), the interdepartmental Consultative Document (1985), and the White Paper (1987) responded to the perceived procedural shortcomings of the legal process with respect to the parents, and these matters were addressed in the Children Act of 1989. But the matter was not simply a question of procedural justice. Other events of the 1980s contributed to the construction of a discernibly new configuration of the appropriate relationships between state and families.

The Emergence of the New Vision: The Beckford, Carlile, and Cleveland Cases

Like Maria Colwell, Jasmine Beckford was returned to her mother, only to die at the hands of her stepfather. This time, however, the child continued under the care order under which she had originally been removed, and remained, as the report stated, "a child in trust" (Blom-Cooper Report 1985). The inquiry reiterated the received view about child abuse prominent in the 1970s: that it was akin to disease, detectable by empirical means, and subject to intergenerational transmission. However, the rhetoric of the report sought to pull social workers away from family casework and to concentrate them more directly on their statutory responsibility for children. Where the warning signs of abuse are visible, the properly trained worker will exercise coercive powers in the child's interests and will eschew rehabilitative efforts with the parents. However, such actions would need to be carefully legally monitored. The Kimberley Carlile Report (1987) concerned the death of a child who had not been in care, but of whom the social services had received reports of abuse. Nevertheless, they failed to intervene, largely because of the hostility of the stepfather. This report was more appreciative of the difficulty of evaluating risk, but also felt that greater legal powers could have assisted the social workers in investigating the allegations. Both inquiries, presided over by a prominent lawyer, emphasized the importance of statutory responsibilities and legal processes.

The Cleveland case, however, raised concern about intervention into the family to a new height, partly because the issue was one of sexual abuse, hitherto not a major concern of social work with families. During 1987 two pediatricians claimed that "reflex anal dilatation" constituted a physical sign of abuse and diagnosed 121 children as having been abused, even though in many cases there were no other grounds for suspicion. On their recommendations, many of these children were admitted to hospital, and if the parents objected, place-of-safety orders were issued. While the children were held, access by the parents to them was restricted while the social services attempted to have the child confirm the abuse. The ensuing inquiry (Butler-Sloss Report 1987), presided over by a judge of the Court of Appeal, made no attempt to determine whether the diagnoses were correct. It was confined to the processes and procedures which should be followed. The inquiry saw the assembly of medical information as the acquisition of evidence for social, and particularly legal action. The anal dilatation test would have to come up to forensic scrutiny, and was not in itself to be treated as conclusive of abuse. Furthermore, much more attention was to be paid to the position of the parents, not simply in respect for their rights, but as a proper way of considering the child's interests. The inquiry also advocated greater respect for children's own opinions and a variety of measures to bring social workers' actions under closer legal scrutiny. Subsequent Department of Health Guidance regarding management of child abuse investigations reflected these views.

Perhaps the most powerful consequence of the Cleveland affair was that it moved concerns about sexual abuse into the center of the agenda of child protection work, and this has been a dominant concern during the 1990s. Its immediate aftermath saw social services departments becoming involved in investigations of ritualistic abuse in Rochdale and Nottingham in 1989 and later in the Orkneys. It seems probable that in all these cases the allegations were unfounded, thus enhancing the distrust of social services. Nevertheless, concerns about sexual abuse remained high, though they were now transferred largely to allegations of abuse within public children's homes (discussed later).

The Children Act of 1989: A New Consensus?

The Children Act of 1989 has been seen both nationally and to some extent internationally as one of the most important pieces of twentieth-century legislation concerning children. Much of the political rhetoric around the Act was cast in terms of "finding the right balance" between all the interests involved (Fox Harding 1991; White Paper 1987). But this suggests that "balancing" is a neutral activity and that an optimal equilibrium is attainable. This seems unlikely, and in any case masks the main underlying features of the new attitudes.

Parton (1991) characterizes the new approach as demonstrating two major features: first, a concentration on child protection rather than child welfare and, second, the ascendancy of legalism. The first refers to a movement away from general concern about improving the lives of deprived children (e.g., through preventive work) toward concentrating resources on protecting children thought to be at particular risk from severe harms. This process demands (1) a definition of the degree of risks which justify action and (2) a means of identifying such risks. Both these matters are related to the legalistic or forensic process. The Children Act of 1989 expressly confines intervention to cases where "significant" harm has occurred or is thought "likely." Various routes for intervention on a lower threshold were closed off. But how is this risk to be assessed? Since this area is prone to speculation, extensive attempts have been made to structure risk assessment. Guidance issued shortly before the enactment of the Children Act lists a range of questions to be considered and asks social workers to exercise a "professional judgment" about the weightings to be given to them. Investigations are seen as gathering potential evidence for legally authorized action, and the courts themselves have added to the formalization of the process. In *In re H & R* (1996), the House of Lords held that "likely" did not mean "probable," but "a real possibility, a possibility that cannot sensibly be ignored." The evidence had to show this "real possibility" on the "balance of probabilities." So "likely" does not actually mean (as one might have thought), "more likely to happen than not": just that it could, possibly, happen, and this is not just a theoretical possibility, but a realistic possibility. However, the House of Lords cut away the pro-interventive thrust of this interpretation by saying that the evidence upon which such a conclusion could be reached had to be factual, and not mere rumor or suspicion. The court appears to be saying that prediction must be based on facts "established" about the behavior of the suspect parent (either toward the child in question or other children) rather than unproved allegations about what the suspect may have done. This is fortified by the view expressed that the more serious the anticipated harm, the stronger must be the evidence to establish the likelihood of the harm occurring. Both of these approaches may be questioned. For example, it might be relevant to know who is making the allegations. Similarly, the more risk-averse may require only relatively minor evidence of the risk of catastrophic harm as a basis for taking avoiding action.

Thus we can see that cases demanding active intervention are closely scrutinized. Yet such is the contemporary concern about child abuse, including sexual abuse, that the numbers of cases reported to social services has grown significantly. The result is that significant resources are devoted to processing these cases *out of the system.* The numbers of children on child protection registers have increased from 11,844 in 1978 to 34,900 in 1994 (Parton, Thorpe, and Wattam 1997). Even so, this represents only 15 percent of total referrals: the rest are simply filtered out. Thus, while in the mid-1990s around 160,000 cases were referred to the child protection services each year, 40,000 resulted in no further action at all, and another 80,000 received no further attention after a home visit was made. That left about 40,000 going to a child protection conference. Only about 1,500 resulted in emergency separations. About 3,000 children entered care, and another 3,000 went into voluntary accommodation. About 24,500 were placed on the child protection register. The main concerns about children on child protection registers are physical abuse (37 percent); physical neglect (30 percent); sexual abuse (28 percent); and emotional abuse (13 percent) (Department of Health 1995).

The courts are now also concerned with what happens to a child after intervention has been authorized. There is a presumption of contact unless the court expressly denies it. This has been used by courts effectively to frustrate the local authorities' plans for the child. Even more important, the court must be satisfied that there are not other ways of protecting the child. To answer this question involves detailed consideration of the authority's plans, and possibly the alternatives. The role of the social worker has moved more closely to that of an investigative agent, who, working closely with legal advisers, assembles evidence (or potential evidence) to present to yet another agency—the courts—which will make the decision about what to do. This moves even further away from the casework ideals of the immediate postwar era.

THE CONTEMPORARY SCENE

The most marked feature of contemporary child welfare law has been the emphasis on parental responsibility. This is different both from the late-nineteenth-century attitude to parents and the reemphasis on the family in the early second part of the twentieth. For while the evangelicals certainly ascribed the sufferings they saw being undergone by children to the moral delinquency of their parents, their response was to "rescue" the children from the parents, to "break" their roots from the contaminated soil, and often to deny the parents' very existence. This involved a considerable exercise of power. Such power was legally underwritten in the case of public authorities, while the voluntary associations were given great latitude to exercise unchecked power. The "revolution" of the 1940s brought parents and the family back into the picture. It was now believed that social casework could prop up the families and prevent psychological relationships from fracturing. This new approach involved no diminution of state power; indeed, it led to its increase. It would be wrong to think that the reformers were more deeply imbued with concern for children than those of the late nineteenth century. Their perception of what constituted those interests had changed. The legal structures under which they operated were not, however, significantly different from those of the late nineteenth century.

The change toward the end of the century was a qualitative one, for not only were the child's interests seen as being best served within its family of origin, but it was now claimed that the parents should essentially be left to secure those interests. This was well expressed in a government Consultative Document in 1985:

> The interests of the children are best served by their remaining with their families and the interests of their parents are best served by allowing them to undertake their natural and legal responsibility to care for their own children. Hence the focus of effort should be to enable and assist parents to discharge those responsibilities. (Consultative Document 1985, para. 2.8)

Whereas the Curtis Committee spoke in terms of the responsibility of social services to assist children in their families, the new language talks of "allowing" parents to "undertake" their "natural and legal responsibility" to care for their children. The state's role was to be residual, confined to action only where the risks to the children were thought to be too great. Even then, the intervention should only be on the basis of a partnership with the parents. Any failings are seen to be mainly structural—having to do with economic or social deprivation, or with gender or racial inequality. It is these that must be addressed, not the individual families.

Choice of family form is seen as a parental prerogative. But this does not necessarily mean the state has withdrawn completely. Rather, the authority takes a different form. It is mainly to be exercised through techniques of education and persuasion. The government is proposing to issue advice on marriage and the responsibilities of parenthood and to set up a National Family and Parenting Institute whose tasks, among others, are to "map and disseminate information and good practice; for example, on parenting and relationship support" and to "raise public awareness of the importance of parenting and the needs of children and promote parenting issues in the media" (Home Office 1998). More striking, the government has also stated that

> some parents need support and direction in fulfilling their responsibilities and in helping to prevent a child or young person from turning to crime. To help provide that support and direction, the Crime and Disorder Act 1998 gives courts new powers to impose a parenting order where a child or young person has been convicted of an offence. . . . The order will include a requirement that parents attend counselling and guidance sessions where they will receive help in dealing with their children, for example, to help parents to set and enforce consistent standards of behaviour from the young person. The court may also impose a requirement to exercise control over a child's behaviour where firmer direction to the parents is judged to be necessary and appropriate. For example, the parent could be required to ensure that the child is home between certain hours or ensure that he or she is escorted to and from school by a responsible adult." (Home Office 1998, 43)

While these provisions relate to fears about children as threats, we must remember that such fears gave the earliest impetus to intervention in family life. The modern trend is therefore to proclaim the responsibility of parents to bring up their children, but to proclaim also that this responsibility must be responsibly exercised, and to use institutional pressures to direct parents to do this.

The strategy has, however, been placed under strain by the emerging concerns over sexual abuse. This has drawn the potential for investigation into the most intimate reaches of family life; nor is sexual abuse, like physical abuse or neglect, largely associated with poor or marginalized groups, but potentially can tear apart "normal" families. The push toward intervention triggered by these concerns confronted the countervailing ideology of family autonomy; the two were in direct conflict. The solution to the dilemma has been to develop highly legalized procedures, which would legitimate intervention if correct procedures are followed and rigorous standards of proof are satisfied, and to adopt strategies based on assessment of risk. Thus, if the home circumstances are adjudged low-risk, especially if the mother is reacting supportively and the child is adequately cared for, the matter may be dropped.

Although the NSPCC has continued to campaign vigorously to raise awareness of child abuse among the general public, the excess of reports over action suggests this may have had little impact on the response of public services. Instead, there has been a quite dramatic movement toward submerging the problem of abuse within a general panic over pedophilia. Indeed, it is arguable that this has captured public attention as enthusiasm for intervening within families has waned. Suggestions that over past years many children may have been abused, physically and sexually, in public children's homes, surfaced in the early 1990s with reports of excessive disciplinary and restraint measures in some and sexual abuse in others. In 1996 the government established an independent review under Sir William Utting into "the safeguards introduced in England and Wales by the Children Act 1989 at its implementation in 1991 and the further measures since taken to protect children living away from home, with particular reference to children's residential homes, foster care, and boarding schools." Adopting a somewhat different approach from the alleviation-of-risk strategy used for protecting children within their families, the report stated its belief that "safety is a function of overall effectiveness and that quality protects" (Utting Report 1997, 21). An important element of that was the availability of choice, so that appropriate provision could be made for specific individuals. Characteristically, however, it also stated that "Parents deciding to place a child away from home are . . . responsible for satisfying themselves that arrangements for keeping their children safe exist and are likely to prove effective . . . the decision about placement is ultimately their responsibility. In making it, parents should possess all the information they need about the arrangements for keeping their children safe" (72).

Consistently, the report suggests that "parental responsibilities and rights" should be enshrined in primary legislation or set out in a governmental statement. A further investigation found widespread physical and sexual abuse of children who were resident in local-authority children's homes in North Wales during the 1980s (Waterhouse Report 2000). In October 1999, the government passed the Protection of Children Act of 1999, which requires the minister of health to keep a list of people dismissed from caring for children by child care organizations on the ground of misconduct which harmed, or risked harming, children. Such persons may not be employed by such organizations again. In July 1999 the government had announced prospective legislation which could criminalize employers for employing child abusers in jobs that allow them access to children, thus requiring employers of such people to run checks with the Criminal Records Bureau before engaging people in such positions. This strategy also places the responsibility of ensuring children's safety on members of the public, rather than the public sector. But other concerns were emerging at the same time: for example, over the welfare of thousands of children who visit foreign countries or come to the United Kingdom from those countries on exchange programs, or as live-in domestic servants (such as au pairs), or while at language schools. The elasticity of the concept of abuse seems constantly to open up new areas of "concern for children," which perhaps reflects more on the current preoccupations of the adult word than on those of children themselves.

REFERENCES

Acheson Report. 1998. *Independent Inquiry into Inequalities in Health*. London: The Stationery Office.

Allen, A., and A. Morton. 1961. *This Is Your Child: The Story of the NSPCC*. London: Routledge & Kegan Paul.

Ariès, Philippe. 1960. *L'Enfant et la vie familiale sous l'ancien regime*. Paris: Librairie Plon.

Bailey, Roy, and Mile Brake, eds. 1980. *Radical Social Work and Practice*. London: Edward Arnold.

Blom-Cooper Report. 1985. *A Child in Trust*. London: Borough of Brent.

Bondfield Delegation. 1924. *Report to the Secretary of State for the Colonies, President of the Oversea Settlement Committee: From the Delegation Appointed to Obtain Information regarding the System of Child Migration and Settlement in Canada*. Cmd. 2285. London: HM Stationery Office.

Bowlby, John. 1953. *Child Care and the Growth of Love*. London: Pelican Books.

Brown, Muriel, and Nicola Madge. 1982. *Despite the Welfare State*. London: Heinemann.

Burlingham, Dorothy, and Anna Freud. 1942. *Young Children in Wartime: A Year's Work in a Residential Nursery*. London: George Allen & Unwin.

Butler-Sloss Report. 1987. *Report of the Inquiry into Child Abuse in Cleveland*. C. 412. London: HM Stationery Office.

Cochrane, Allan. 1993. "Challenges from the Centre." In John Clarke, ed., *Crisis in Care? Challenges to Social Work*. London: Sage.

Consultative Document. 1985. *Review of Child Care Law: Report to Ministers of an Interdepartmental Working Party*. London: HM Stationery Office.

Cretney, Stephen. 1998. "The State as Parent: The Children Act 1948 in Retrospect." In *Law, Law Reform, and the Family*. Oxford: Oxford University Press.

Curtis Report. 1946. *Report of the Committee on the Care of Children*. Cmd. 6922. London: HM Stationery Office.

de Mause, Lloyd. 1976. *The History of Childhood*. London: Souvenir Press.

Department of Health. 1995. *Child Protection: Messages from Research*. London: HM Stationery Office.

Departmental Committee on Young Offenders. 1927. Cmnd. 2831. London: HM Stationery Office.

Departmental Committee on Sexual Offences against Young Persons. 1925. Cmd. 2561. London: HM Stationery Office.

Dingwall, R.; J. M. Eekelaar, and T. Murray. 1983. *The Protection of Children: State Intervention and Family Life*. Oxford: Basil Blackwell.

———. 1984. "Childhood as a Social Problem: A Survey of the History of Legal Regulation." *Journal of Law and Society* 11: 207–32.

Dingwall R., and J. M. Eekelaar. 1984. "Re-thinking Child Protection." In M. D. A. Freeman, ed., *State, Law, and the Family: Critical Perspectives*. London: Tavistock, Sweet & Maxwell.

Doyle Report. 1875. *Report to the President of the Local Government Board by Andrew Doyle*. Parliamentary Papers 1875, lxiii. 255.

Eekelaar, John. 1991. "Parental Responsibility: State of Nature or Nature of the State?" *Journal of Social Welfare and Family Law* 37–50.

———. 1994. "The Chief Glory: The Export of Children from the United Kingdom." *Journal of Law and Society* 21: 487–504.

Field-Fisher Report. 1974. *Report of the Committee of Inquiry into the Care and Supervision Provided for Maria Colwell*. London: Department of Health and Social Security.

Fox Harding, Lorraine. 1991. *Perspectives in Child Care Policy*. 2d ed. London: Longman.

Goldstein, J.; A. Freud; and A. J. Solnit. 1973. *Beyond the Best Interests of the Child*. New York: Free Press.

Griffiths Report. 1988. *Community Care: Agenda for Action: A Report to the Secretary of State for Social Services*. London: HM Stationery Office.

Heywood, Jean. 1978. *Children in Care*. 3d ed. London: Routledge.

Home Office. 1965. *The Child, the Family, and the Young Offender*. Cmnd. 2742. London: HM Stationery Office.

———. 1998. *Supporting Families*. London: HM Stationery Office.

Houghton Report. 1972. *Report of the Departmental Committee on the Adoption of Children*. Cmnd. 5107. London: HM Stationery Office.

Housden, L. G. 1951. *The Prevention of Cruelty to Children*. London: Jonathan Cape.

Ingleby Report. 1960. *Report of the Committee on Children and Young Persons*. Cmnd. 1191. London: HM Stationery Office.

Interdepartmental Report. 1985. *Review of Child Care Law: Report to Ministers of an Interdepartmental Working Party*. London: HM Stationery Office.

Jackson, Brian, and Sonia Jackson. 1979. *Childminder*. London: Routledge.

Kimberley Carlile Report. 1987. *A Child in Mind*. London: Borough of Greenwich.

MacNamara Report. 1908. *Children under the Poor Law: A Report to the President of the Local Government Board by T. J. MacNamara*. Cd. 3899. Parliamentary Paper xcii. 455.

Millham, Spencer; Roger Bullock; Kenneth Hosie; and Martin Haak. 1986. *Lost in Care: The Problems of Maintaining Links between Children in Care and Their Families*. London: Gower.

Mundella Report. 1896. *Report of the Mundella Committee on Poor Law Schools*. C. 8027. London: HM Stationery Office.

Packman, Jean. 1975. *The Child's Generation: Child Care Policy from Curtis to Houghton*. Oxford: Basil Blackwell & Martin Robinson.

Packman, Jean, with John Randall and Nicola Jacques. 1986. *Who Needs Care? Social Work Decisions about Children*. Oxford: Basil Blackwell.

Parton, Nigel. 1985. *The Politics of Child Abuse*. London: Macmillan.

———. 1991. *Governing the Family: Child Care, Child Protection, and the State*. London: Macmillan.

Parton, Nigel; David Thorpe; and Corinne Wattam. 1997. *Child Protection: Risk and the Moral Order.* London: Macmillan.

Philp, A. F. 1963. *Family Failure*. London: Faber and Faber.

Pinchbeck, Ivy, and Margaret Hewitt. 1969 and 1973. *Children in English Society.* Vols. 1 and 2. London: Routledge.

Pizzey, Erin. 1974. *Scream Quietly or the Neighbours Will Hear.* Harmondsworth, U.K.: Penguin Books.

Platt, Anthony M. 1969. *The Child Savers: The Invention of Delinquency.* Chicago: University of Chicago Press.

Pollock, Linda. 1983. *Forgotten Children: Parent-Child Relations from 1500 to 1900.* Cambridge: Cambridge University Press.

Rose, June. 1989. *For the Sake of the Children: Inside Barnardo's—110 Years of Caring for Children*. London: Futura.

Ross Report. 1956. *Child Migration to Australia: Report of the Fact-Finding Mission*. Cmd. 9832. London: HM Stationery Office.

Rwezaura, Bart. 1998. "Competing Images of Childhood in Social and Legal Systems of Contemporary Sub-Saharan Africa." *International Journal of Law, Policy, and Family* 12: 253–78.

Seebohm Report. 1968. *Report of the Committee on Local Authority and Allied Social Services*. Cmnd. 3703. London: HM Stationery Office.

Seymour, John. 1994. "*Parens Patriae* and Wardship Powers: Their Nature and Origins." *Oxford Journal of Legal Studies* 14: 159–88.

Shaher, Shulamith. 1990. *Childhood in the Middle Ages*. London: Routledge.

Short Report. 1984. *Children in Care*. Social Services Committee (HC 36). London: HM Stationery Office.

Shorter, Edward. 1976. *The Making of the Modern Family.* London: Collins.

Stone, Lawrence. 1977. *The Family, Sex, and Marriage in England, 1500–1800*. London: Weidenfeld & Nicolson.

Taylor, George. 1993. "Challenges from the Margins." In John Clarke, ed., *A Crisis in Care? Challenges to Social Work*. London: Sage.

Utting Report. 1997. *People Like Us*. London: Department of Health.

Waterhouse Report. 2000. *Lost in Care*. London: The Stationery Office.

Waugh, Rev. N. 1911. *These, My Little Ones: The Origin, Progress, and Development of the Incorporated Society of the Crusade of Rescue Homes for Destitute Catholic Children*. London: n.p.

White Paper. 1987. Department of Health and Social Security, Home Office, Lord Chancellor's Department, Department of Education and Science, Welsh Office, Scottish Office. *The Law on Child Care and Family Services*. Cm. 62. London: HM Stationery Office.

15 The Divergent Development of Juvenile Justice Policy and Practice in England and Scotland

Anthony Bottoms

The nation-state of which I am a citizen is in a number of respects unusual. It has, for example, no written constitution; and its official name (the United Kingdom of Great Britain and Northern Ireland) is so cumbersome that it is hardly ever used except in formal documents, with the result that many ordinary citizens cannot correctly name their own country. These and other oddities all arise from the United Kingdom's complicated constitutional history. That history has also bequeathed to us perhaps the strangest anomaly of all—namely, the fact that, although the United Kingdom is a unitary state with a single sovereign legislature (Parliament), yet it nevertheless contains three almost entirely distinct legal jurisdictions, each with its own *separate* system of policing, courts, judges, prisons, and so on. These three separate jurisdictions are, respectively, England and Wales, Scotland, and Northern Ireland. Parliament, being sovereign, can of course enact legislation for any or all of these jurisdictions, and until very recently it has done so—except in the rather special case of Northern Ireland—without devolution of its powers.[1] In many fields, such as taxation or the economy, the same legislative provisions have generally been applied to all three jurisdictions; but in other matters, such as education, separate arrangements have frequently been enacted. Hence, it is normal practice for a Parliamentary statute to contain a section specifying to which of the three jurisdictions its provisions apply.

Some basic grasp of these constitutional complexities is an essential backdrop to this chapter, the central point of which is to draw attention to the very different juvenile justice systems that have evolved in England[2] and in Scotland during the last thirty years. It is important to emphasize at the outset, however, that significant Anglo-Scottish differences in substantive law and in legal institutions are by no means confined to the sphere of juvenile justice. To take only two examples, Scottish legal principles are (for historical reasons) in some respects closer to French law than to English law, while the Scots had a public prosecutor system long before the English adopted such a system in 1985. All these differences ultimately stem from the circumstances in which Scotland and England became united in 1707.[3]

In the late 1960s, the U.K. Parliament enacted important new legislation in the sphere of juvenile justice, first for Scotland and then for England. Both statutes embraced, to a much greater extent than previously, a "child-welfare-based" approach to juvenile justice, though the detailed arrangements enacted for the two countries differed in important ways. Since the early 1970s, however, the two jurisdictions have experienced radically divergent developments. In Scotland, there has been a very substantial (although not complete) thread of continuity of policy and practice, and the welfare-oriented juvenile justice system that began to operate in 1971 still enjoys generally high esteem. By contrast, in England, the welfare-based Act of 1969 was never fully implemented; and an initial decade of considerable institutional conflict has been succeeded by several—sometimes bewilderingly rapid—changes in official policies. Continuity of policy and practice has rarely been on the agenda.

The primary aim of this chapter is to describe and to analyze these very different developments, occurring as they have within the framework of a single, nonfederal nation-state. In pursuit of this aim, the remainder of the chapter is divided into four principal sections. The first section outlines the legislative reforms of the 1960s in the two countries, against the background of the provisions that preceded them. The next two sections describe in some detail developments in, respectively, England and Scotland in the three decades from 1970. In the concluding section, very recent policy developments in both countries are briefly discussed, some relevant comparative statistics are considered, and an assessment is made of the divergent developments that the chapter has described.

THE WELFARE-ORIENTED REFORMS OF THE 1960s

In order to explain how the legislative reforms of the 1960s came to be enacted, it is necessary first of all to understand the main features of the previous juvenile justice systems in England and Scotland.

Faust and Brantingham (1979, 14–15) have helpfully delineated two very different conceptual models of juvenile justice, as originally created in various jurisdictions early in the twentieth century. Modifying these authors' terminology slightly, the first model may be described as the *socialized juvenile tribunal;* it was this type of system that was created in most American states, beginning with Illinois, and also in the so-called child welfare boards in the Scandinavian countries (see Stang Dahl 1985). In the socialized juvenile tribunal, there is typically a strong emphasis on the welfare of the child, a deliberate move away from formal criminal procedures, and, conceptually, a "dematerialisation of the offense" (Donzelot 1980, 110–11) within the proceedings—or, as an early-twentieth-century American source put it, in such tribunals,

> emphasis is laid, not on the act done by the child, but on the social facts and circumstances that are really the inducing causes of the child's appearance in court. The particular offense which was the immediate and proximate cause of the proceedings is considered only as one of the many other factors surrounding the child. . . . Conservation of the child, as a valuable asset of the community, is the dominant note. (Flexner and Baldwin 1915, 6–7)

The second model of juvenile justice formulated by Faust and Brantingham might be described as the *modified criminal court.* In such a system, the juvenile court is retained as a predominantly criminal court, using for the most part the standard rules of criminal procedure (though sometimes with minor modifications). The court is, nevertheless, by reason of the clientele it deals with, expected to operate with some special understanding of young people. Such a system was created, in the United States, in New York State (see Mack 1909); and in both England and Scotland the juvenile courts in the first half of the twentieth century were emphatically of this type.

For historical reasons, however, the lower criminal courts in England and in Scotland had evolved in different ways. In England, there is only one kind of lower criminal court, called the magistrates' court, which is normally presided over by a group of non–legally qualified members of the community known as magistrates or justices of the peace (the two terms are interchangeable).[4] In Scotland, by contrast, there were historically three different kinds of criminal court that could exercise jurisdiction in less serious (or summary) criminal cases. The first and most prestigious lower court was the sheriff summary court, presided over by a legally qualified judge known as a sheriff, which had (and has) universal jurisdiction over all summary cases. The second kind were the burgh courts, which functioned only in the larger towns and cities; they typically dealt with more minor offenses than the sheriff summary court, and they were presided over by a single "bailie," who was an elected member of the local town council, but here acting in a separate judicial capacity, to which he or she was appointed by the council. Finally, there were justice of the peace courts, presided over by lay magistrates as in England. These latter courts dealt with the same range of more minor cases as the burgh courts, but in the less populous areas; they were therefore "the least in importance and standing of the three forms of summary criminal court" (Cowperthwaite 1988, 6).

In the United Kingdom, the juvenile court was first formally created in the Children Act of 1908, and, unusually in a statute dealing with criminal justice matters, the main legislative provisions were applied identically to both England and Scotland. Essentially, in both countries the existing structure of the lower criminal courts (see above) was retained. However, the Children Act provided that when sitting as a juvenile court, the relevant court must sit in a different place or at a different time than when dealing with adults, and the public were also excluded from the juvenile court. The juvenile courts additionally acquired a limited "care" jurisdiction (analogous to the status offenses of American state juvenile court systems, though in the United Kingdom such jurisdictions typically developed on a much smaller scale).[5]

Limited changes to the provisions of the 1908 Act were made, in both England and Scotland, in the 1930s. Since these changes were, indirectly, to be of vital importance to the 1960s reforms, it is necessary to describe them in more detail than their intrinsic importance might otherwise merit.

An official committee reviewed the English juvenile justice system in the 1920s. The committee carefully considered, but rejected, the possibility of altering the existing system toward a socialized juvenile tribunal model, arguing that "there is some danger in adopting any principle which might lead to ignoring the offence on which the action of the juvenile court in dealing with delinquents must be based" (Home Office 1927, 19). On the other hand, the committee argued for a greater emphasis than heretofore on the child's welfare at the sentencing stage, and this led, in the 1930s, to the enactment of a statutory principle which is still in force in England, namely, "Every court in dealing with a child or young person who is brought before it, either as an offender or otherwise, shall have regard to the welfare of the child or young person and shall in a proper case take steps . . . for securing that proper provision is made for his education and training."[6]

A number of other legislative changes were also made in England in the 1930s. The most important concerned the creation of a so-called juvenile panel in each magistrates' court area. Under the 1908 legislation, any of the local magistrates could sit in the juvenile court, at his or her discretion, and it was apparently not unusual for five or six to be present to hear a single juvenile case (Home Office 1927, 27). The 1930s legislation altered matters in two ways. First, the maximum number of magistrates who could constitute a juvenile court became three (with two as a minimum). Second, it was provided that no magistrate could sit in the juvenile court unless he or she was a member of the juvenile panel of the local magistrates, a new, formally constituted panel that had to be re-chosen every three years, the members being selected as being "specially qualified for dealing with juvenile cases." As a contemporary writer pointed out, there was of course a distinct vagueness about this "specially qualified" formula, and in any event, since the juvenile panel was to be formed only from the existing body of local magistrates, "the degree to which special qualifications are in fact obtainable depends on the extent to which they are to be found among the local justices" (Elkin 1938, 66–67).[7] Nevertheless, from the 1930s onward many magistrates' courts did in practice take both the juvenile panel concept and the statutory welfare principle (see above) very seriously in their juvenile court work (though there was considerable local variation in this respect).[8] These developments in turn helped to create a sense of self-confidence among English juvenile court magistrates, who came to believe that they could combine very effectively the principles and protections of a juridical framework with a real commitment to the welfare of juveniles. These magisterial beliefs were to be of vital significance to developments in England in the 1960s and 1970s, and they were well encapsulated in the following 1976 comment by an English social scientist who was herself a juvenile court magistrate: "[The English] have been leaders in the juvenile court world. Our special contribution has been our adherence to the principle that whilst justice that does not have regard to welfare is no justice, yet also welfare which ignores justice is no justice either" (Cavenagh 1976, 22).

The Scottish 1930s legislation was broadly similar to that for England (though, as is fairly common in United Kingdom legislation, the Scottish reforms were contained in a separate and subsequent Act of Parliament).[9] Thus the Scottish legislation, like the English, provided that the juvenile courts would in future be presided over by a group of "specially qualified" lay justices of the peace. But such provisions were much more complex to implement in Scotland than in England, since in Scotland most of the juvenile courts (and all of the most prestigious juvenile courts) were not justice of the peace courts (see above), and indeed the full implementation of the Act would have removed all juvenile cases from both the sheriff summary courts and the burgh courts. The details of the ensuing story are complex, but, following various forms of local resistance, the eventual net result was that 1930s-style "special" Scottish juvenile courts were set up only in four areas of Scotland, the remainder of the areas retaining the 1908 organizational arrangements (see Cowperthwaite 1988, 9–14 for a detailed account of these developments).[10] This outcome, with part of the country implementing the 1930s reforms but most of it not doing so, was of course obviously administratively anomalous, a fact that in itself was bound to provide some impetus for reform whenever the Scottish system was next reviewed.

Given this background, we can now turn to the main developments in the 1960s in England and Scotland. For both countries, a key initial event was the publication in 1960 of a report by a government-appointed committee (the Ingleby Committee) on juvenile justice and related matters in England (Home Office 1960). In England, influential figures in the Labour Party (the main left-wing political party in the United Kingdom) were dissatisfied with some aspects of the Ingleby Committee's recommendations, and out of their criticisms arose a decade of (sometimes fierce) debate not only about English juvenile justice, but also about the future shape of the personal social services.[11] The details of these debates are complex, but they need not concern us here: it is sufficient simply to note that the eventual outcomes were to be, in the area of juvenile justice, the enactment of the Children and Young Persons Act of 1969 and, in the sphere of personal social services, the creation in 1970 of unified social services departments (SSDs) for each local government area.[12] All of this activity took place within a sociopolitical framework in which both the main political parties (Conservative and Labour) were committed to the basic principles of the so-called welfare state (although, inevitably, the parties brought to this consensus differing points of emphasis and degrees of enthusiasm).[13]

The terms of reference of the Ingleby Committee had been restricted to England. During the period that the committee was gathering evidence, a Scottish Member of Parliament formally asked the Secretary of State for Scotland,[14] in the House of Commons, "why such a committee has not been set up for Scotland" (Cowperthwaite 1988, 17). The Secretary of State's reply committed him, at a minimum, to considering the relevance of Ingleby's eventual recommendations in the Scottish context. Since, however, the principal thrust of the Ingleby Report's recommendations turned out to be simply "a series of detailed proposals for the improvement of the England and Wales arrangements as they stood" (Cowperthwaite 1988, 19), the Scottish Office decided, post-Ingleby, to set up a committee of inquiry of its own, chaired by a senior Scottish judge (Lord Kilbrandon). This, it transpired, was a momentous decision.

Writing about these events a quarter of a century later, David Cowperthwaite, himself formerly a senior government official in Scotland, commented that "the Scottish Office . . . could hardly have expected what they got" from the Kilbrandon Committee (Cowperthwaite 1988, 22). Given the preexisting organizational anomalies in Scottish juvenile justice (see above), some significant proposals for change were inevitable. But what virtually no one had anticipated was that the Kilbrandon Committee would produce a unanimous report (Scottish Office 1964) of a quite radical character, built around "a novel and complex idea" (Cowperthwaite 1988, 77). Moreover, the report quickly found general acceptance in Scotland and constituted the main basis of the subsequent legislation, enacted by Parliament—with little opposition—as the Social Work (Scotland) Act of 1968.[15] Cowperthwaite concludes his illuminating account of the key relevant events by articulating his strong and continuing sense of considerable surprise that Kilbrandon's rather radical approach "should have survived into fruition and general acceptance despite the cumbersome processes (involving Parliament, Ministers, the civil service, local government, and the courts) by which we are governed, particularly in a field traditionally called criminal justice in which so many strong and conflicting ideas are held" (77).

So what was special about Kilbrandon's conceptual framework? To the scholar or policy expert well versed in the literature on juvenile justice, much of the report is in fact reasonably familiar as embodying the kind of thinking that can be expected within the welfare-oriented, socialized juvenile tribunal tradition. Hence, for example, there is a strong emphasis on prevention as a primary goal of the system; in offense cases it is the requirements of prevention, rather than the seriousness of the offense, that are seen as determining the extent of any compulsory intervention in the child's life; and there is said to be no difference in principle between offense-based and other cases, all cases being assessed using the primary criterion of the welfare of the child. However, although this kind of conceptualization was familiar enough to specialists, it must be remembered that the whole of previous British (and especially Scottish) juvenile justice experience was based on the modified criminal court model rather than that of the socialized juvenile tribunal. Hence, in the context of public policy debates on juvenile justice in Britain, there was much that was fresh even in Kilbrandon's basic set of assumptions.

However, the Kilbrandon Report also broke new ground in some respects, even when considered from an international and specialist perspective. Two points were of special importance in this regard: first, a proposed division of functions between the court system and a specialist treatment tribunal, and, second, a proposal that children should be referred to the specialist treatment tribunals "for one reason only, namely, that *prima facie* the child is in need of special measures of education and training" (Scottish Office 1964, para. 138). Each of these ideas requires some elaboration.

The Kilbrandon Report argued that the shortcomings that caused dissatisfaction with the then existing Scottish juvenile courts arose essentially "from the fact that they seek to combine the characteristics of a court of criminal law with those of a specialised agency for the treatment of juvenile offenders, proceeding on a preventive and educational principle" (Scottish Office 1964, para. 71). As one might expect from a committee chaired by a senior judge, there was no hostility in principle to the criminal courts; indeed, the committee considered that courts remained the best forum for the fulfillment of certain functions, such as adjudication on disputed guilt for an alleged offense (or the equivalent of this in "care and protection" cases). Hence, what the Kilbrandon Report eventually proposed can reasonably be described as a *dual system,* in which both courts and treatment tribunals existed side by side but fulfilled different functions. (For the details of these arrangements, see below.)

The second novel Kilbrandon principle was that of the conceptual centrality, within the proposed new system, of the idea of "need for special measures of education and training." The importance of this point can be seen from a volume published in 1998 on juvenile justice systems in nine different European countries (Mehlbye and Walgrave 1998). As one way of helping to highlight differences between the systems in different countries, the editors of this volume requested each national contributor to provide a narrative explaining how their jurisdiction might deal with a fifteen-year-old boy, with two previously proved offenses of burglary, now arrested again for breaking into a private house (acting alone) and stealing a videocassette recorder, some jewelry, and some money, to a total value of about £500. In the chapter on Scotland, the author (Stewart Asquith) imagines that "Hamish, a fifteen-year old Scottish boy" would in these circumstances be referred to the Kilbrandon treatment tribunal (known as a Children's Hearing; see below). However, Asquith is at pains to point out that the fact that Hamish has committed an offense is not enough in itself for him to be referred to a hearing, since the referring official (the reporter) must also be persuaded that Hamish is probably in need of compulsory measures of care, *in the interests of his own welfare,* before a referral may properly be made. Moreover, Asquith points out that when Hamish reaches the Children's Hearing, if the tribunal decides "that [his] parents have control of the situation, and there is evidence that compulsory measures of care are not needed, *then the case, notwithstanding the amount involved in the theft, could be discharged*" (Asquith 1998, 425–26; emphasis added). In other words, in Kilbrandon's conceptual framework, now embodied within the Scottish system, although the commission of an offense is one of the possible so-called grounds that constitute a necessary precondition for compulsory measures of care, *in itself an offense is not a sufficient basis for ordering compulsory measures of care.* This was a very important conceptual innovation, made by the Kilbrandon Committee, which was subsequently to be adopted also within the English 1960s legislation.

The Social Work (Scotland) Act 1968

We are now in a position to understand the broad framework of the Scottish system of juvenile justice, as it was enacted, post-Kilbrandon, in the Social Work (Scotland) Act of 1968, and as it remains today (with only relatively minor modifications).[16] A flowchart of the system is provided in figure 15.1.

It is fundamental to the philosophy of the Scottish system that cases in-

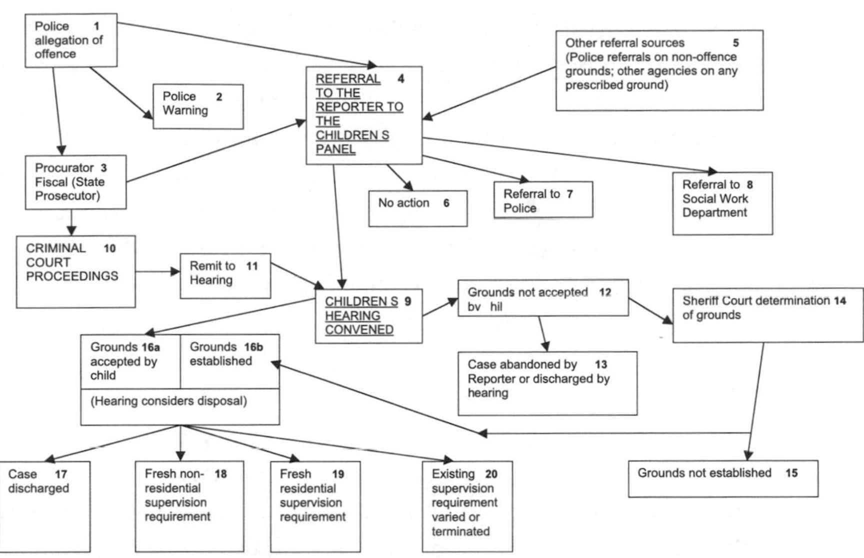

Fig. 15.1 The Scottish juvenile justice system.

volving allegations of offenses are to be treated in a similar manner as other types of cases that might cause the State to decide to take compulsory measures of care in the interests of a child's welfare (such as the child being beyond the control of his or her parents, or the child's health and development being placed at serious risk because of parental neglect). Hence, the system outlined in figure 15.1 applies equally to offense-related and to other cases, but, because the focus of this chapter is upon offense-based cases, I shall here describe the system only as it applies to them.

The vast majority of offense-based cases are initially reported to the police (box 1). If the police decide that an offense has been committed and that a particular child is responsible, they then have three options: they may officially warn the child (box 2), or they may refer the child to an official called the reporter to the Children's Panel (box 4); or, in a restricted range of cases, especially those involving allegations of serious offenses, they may refer the child to the state prosecutor (the procurator fiscal), with a view to possible prosecution (box 3: see further discussion below). The second of these options is by far the most commonly chosen.[17]

The reporter to the Children's Panel occupies a pivotal "gatekeeping" role in the Scottish system, as can be seen from the centrality of box 4 in figure 15.1. On receiving a referral, the reporter is first expected to satisfy himself or herself (seeking additional information if that seems necessary) that there is evidence to support the so-called ground on which the case was referred (e.g., that an offense really has been committed by this child, that he or she really is beyond parental control, etc.). If this test is not satisfied, the reporter takes no action with regard to the referral (box 6).[18] If a ground is believed to exist, then the reporter must further assess (again seeking additional information if necessary) whether the child is potentially in need of compulsory measures of care (as discussed in the case of Hamish, described above); and only if the reporter's answer to this further question is also affirmative may the case be referred on to the Children's Hearing (box 9). If the answer to the second question is negative, the reporter may, but is not obliged to, take no action (box 6); he or she may also refer the case to the local Social Work Department, which may assist the child informally (box 8), or, in offense cases, the reporter may refer the child back to the police with a view to a formal police warning or similar procedure (box 7).

Now let us suppose that the reporter has referred an offense-based case to the Children's Hearing, but the referred child denies involvement in the alleged offense. It is at this point that the dual system element (see above) in the Kilbrandon proposals becomes especially apparent. Asquith explains the procedures, again with reference to the imaginary case of Hamish:

> At the Children's Hearing, Hamish is there with his mother and father. The others present are the Reporter, the panel members, and a Social Worker. There are no police (who do not attend Children's Hearings), and there are also no members of the public. Hamish denies the charge when it is read to him, and the Hearing cannot proceed because it has no jurisdiction over the establishment of the facts of the referral. Hamish has to go to court, the sheriff court, where the facts of the case will be established or not. If they are, then Hamish will go back to the Children's Hearing, where the need for compulsory measures of care will be considered. (1998, 425–26)

These procedures are shown in figure 15.1 at boxes 9, 12, 14, 15, and 16b. They might seem quite cumbersome, but it must be remembered that a division of functions between the courts and the Children's Hearings was central to the thinking of the Kilbrandon Committee. Some procedures of this kind are in fact the necessary consequence of the fact that the Children's Hearing, being solely a treatment tribunal, is structurally precluded from considering any dispute of fact or law pertaining to the alleged grounds of the hearing,[19] while the sheriff court, being a court of law (and therefore in Kilbrandon's thinking an inappropriate tribunal to decide upon treatment issues for a juvenile), is structurally precluded from considering issues of appropriate treatment if the grounds of referral are held to be established.[20]

It should be added that this adjudication/treatment distinction does not exhaust the dual system features of Scottish juvenile justice. We have already seen that the police may, in some cases (especially serious ones), refer a case to the procurator fiscal (box 3), and the fiscal may, at his or her discretion, prosecute the case in the sheriff court (box 10).[21] The two parallel systems (reporter → Children's Hearing; procurator fiscal → sheriff court) are nevertheless linked, in that either the fiscal or the court may refer or remit a case into the Children's Hearing system (boxes 4, 11). However, it is very important to note that while the adjudication/treatment distinction (and the dual system features that flow from it) are integral to Kilbrandon's core philosophy, the fiscal route cases (boxes 3, 10) can only properly be regarded as a quite deliberate *exemption* or *exclusion* of certain cases from the reach of that philosophy, a matter that is further explored in a later section.

Let us now return to the main system, and consider finally the Children's Hearing itself, on the assumption that the ground for the hearing has been accepted by the child, or established by the sheriff court (boxes 16a, 16b). Each local area in Scotland has a so-called Children's Panel, which is made up of lay members of the public who have been appointed by a government minister as being suitable people to officiate at Children's Hearings. When a Children's Hearing is called, arrangements are made to select three members of the Children's Panel to preside over the case (of the three, at least one must be female, and one male). In offense-based cases, it is of course quite common for adolescents to commit crimes as a group; but because the focus of Children's Hearings is not upon the offense but upon the child and his or her needs, in such circumstances if the reporter refers all the children to the Children's Hearing, a separate hearing will be held for each child.

A Children's Hearing is a private occasion, and it must take place in a building other than a court building or a police station. As already indicated in the case of Hamish, the hearing is focused on the child's needs, and in offense-based cases neither the police nor the victim attends. The reporter, however, does attend, and in offense-based cases he or she of course holds all relevant police reports. A social worker from the local authority's Social Work Department also attends (on Social Work Departments, see note 15 above). The intention of the system is that the child, the parent(s), the social worker, and the members of the Children's Panel who are conducting the hearing will have ample opportunity, within an informal atmosphere, of exploring carefully in discussion not only the circumstances that gave rise to the ground for the hearing (e.g., an offense, or persistent truancy), but also all other relevant aspects of the child's social and family situation. The rules for the conduct of Children's Hearings provide that the child and his or her parents may, at their discretion, bring someone to the hearing to speak on their behalf during these discussions (a representative), and this representative may be a lawyer. However, representatives are not permitted to act as agents, in the sense of being permitted to speak *instead* of the party/parties they represent (in other words, even if a representative is present, the hearing may still directly question the child or the parents). Nevertheless, although representatives are thus permitted to attend, there is no provision for publicly funded legal assistance at a Children's Hearing. This is a matter of continuing controversy, to which I shall return in a later section.

At the end of the discussion in the Children's Hearing, the hearing members must decide on the appropriate disposal for the child. In the case of a child attending a hearing for the first time, they have only three choices. First, they may discharge the case, taking no action (box 17); second, they may make a nonresidential supervision requirement, allowing the child to remain in his or her home under the supervision of a social worker (box 18); or third, a residential supervision requirement (box 19) may be made, placing the child in a specified kind of residential establishment, such as a hostel, a local-authority home, or a residential school. In the case of a child already under a supervision requirement who again appears before a hearing on a fresh ground or a review (see below), the hearing has the additional option of varying or terminating the supervision requirement (e.g., a nonresidential supervision requirement might be varied to become a residential supervision requirement [box 20]). Given the Kilbrandon principle of always establishing a welfare-based "need for special measures of education and training" before compulsory action may be taken in a child's case, it will be clear that a supervision requirement—residential or nonresidential—may only be made if the hearing considers that there is such a need (otherwise, it should discharge the case). These principles hold even if a fairly serious offense has been committed, as Asquith's (1998) commentary on the case of Hamish illustrates.[22]

The restricted range of disposals available to the Children's Hearing is worthy of brief comment. Some might be surprised at the absence of measures such as the fine, or the community service order, or compulsory measures of reparation or compensation to victims of offenses. But such omissions are, in the Scottish system, quite deliberate. Since the Children's Hearing system is welfare-based, with no conceptual distinction between offense-based and other cases, it is said to follow, *first,* that all disposals should in principle be equally available in all types of case, and *second,* that measures such as the fine cannot form part of the system, since they are explicitly punitive rather than welfare-based.

Finally, we should note that, in any case where a supervision requirement is made (whether residential or nonresidential), the Children's Hearing has a *continuing jurisdiction* over that case. Supervision requirements remain effective for one year, and must be reviewed by a full Children's Hearing at the end of that period. At any such review, the supervision requirement may only be continued (either in its original or in a varied form) if special compulsory measures of care are still adjudged to be necessary in the interests of the child's welfare. Subject to that important proviso, however, a supervision requirement can in principle be continually renewed (and, if judged appropriate, amended) until the child reaches his or her eighteenth birthday. (Eighteen is the upper limit of the jurisdiction of Children's Hearing in continuation cases, but a case can only be brought before a hearing for the first time if the child has not yet reached his or her sixteenth birthday, an important matter to which we shall return in a later section.) It is important to note that the existence of the continuing jurisdiction in Scotland gives Children's Hearings, in most cases, the *sole right* to determine whether compulsory measures of care remain necessary at all, and also the *sole right* to decide upon, and to vary if necessary, the terms of the supervision requirement (for example, whether the requirement shall be residential, and if so, in what kind of residential accommodation).[23] As we shall see later, in the English welfare-based reforms, different procedures were developed, and they led to some important structural conflicts.

The Children and Young Persons Act 1969

We turn now to the English reform statute of the late 1960s, the Children and Young Persons Act of 1969. As we have previously noted, it is common practice in the United Kingdom for Scottish legislation to be enacted by Parliament a year or so after a similar principle has been enacted into English law. In this instance, however, a number of somewhat accidental factors, essentially revolving around the rather intense English debates on juvenile justice of the 1960s (see above), plus the readiness of the Scottish Office to press ahead with the Kilbrandon-based legislation, led to a reverse temporal order (see Cowperthwaite 1988, 76). Given that the passage of the English legislation through Parliament proved to be very controversial (a point that was to have significant long-term consequences for the English reforms), it is intriguing, though of course ultimately fruitless, to speculate whether the Scottish juvenile justice system would have been very different had the usual "Scotland follows England" temporal sequence been applied in this instance.

In the British academic literature on juvenile justice, the Children and Young Persons Act of 1969 has often been depicted primarily in the light of the preceding decade of policy controversy. Seen through this lens, the Act is normally characterized as something of a compromise measure, because, unlike earlier (1965) legislative proposals, it retained the 1930s-style English juvenile courts, with no change to their basic composition.[24] While such accounts of course contain an important element of truth, in my view the emphasis on compromise tends to deflect attention from the real nature of the enacted 1969 legislation. In this account, I therefore deliberately ignore the decade of controversy before the 1969 Act and concentrate on the Act itself, with particular reference to its similarities and dissimilarities to the Scottish 1968 legislation.

To understand the character of the 1969 Act, it is necessary to appreciate a number of background factors. First, without any question those who developed the details of the legislation were as strongly committed to a welfare approach to juvenile justice as were the members of the Kilbrandon Committee.[25] Second, there is evidence that England directly borrowed from Scotland a central principle of the new legislation, namely, the requirement to establish a "need for special measures of education and training" before compulsory measures of care could be taken in respect of children.[26] Third, however, the English magistrates had been at the heart of the opposition to the 1965 legislative proposals, and their voice was sufficiently self-confident, and carried sufficient political weight, to ensure that the 1930s-style juvenile courts had to be retained in England, at least in outward form (see Bottoms 1974). Fourth, the wider traditions of the English judicial system at that date, and in particular the absence of a state prosecution system, made it effectively impossible to create a key gatekeeping official for the system, who would act as the reporter to the Children's Hearing does in Scotland. Fifth, and finally, arrangements for supporting social work arrangements in the community were to some extent complicated, in England, by the decision (in an Act of 1970) to retain the existing probation service alongside the new local authority Social Services Departments, whereas in Scotland the former probation service was merged into the new Social Work Departments (see notes 12 and 15 above).

Given these background understandings, we can now turn to the details of the 1969 English legislation, focusing (as in the previous description of the Scottish system) especially on offense-based cases. The procedures are most easily understood, in the first instance, in relation to children under fourteen, and they are shown diagramatically in figure 15.2. (For a fuller account of the 1969 Act in its original form, see Bottoms, McClean, and Patchett 1970.)

Perhaps the central feature of the 1969 Act, as it was intended to deal with offense-based cases, was the concept of *care proceedings*. The Act provided that no child under the age of fourteen should be subject to a criminal prosecution, except in cases of homicide. However, the age of criminal responsibility remained technically at age ten.[27] In the age group 10–13, children could, according to the Act, be brought before the courts for having committed an offense, *but only in civil proceedings,* to be known as care proceedings. In such proceedings, in offense-based cases, it would be necessary to prove two separate matters: first, that an offense had indeed been committed; and second, that the child "is in need of care or control which he is unlikely to receive unless the court makes an order."[28] (This was, at the time, sometimes colloquially referred to as the "double-barreled test.") Although formulated in a different way than in the Scottish legislation, these provisions have great conceptual similarity to some of the central ideas underpinning the Scottish system. As in the Scottish system, care proceedings were to be applied in England inter-

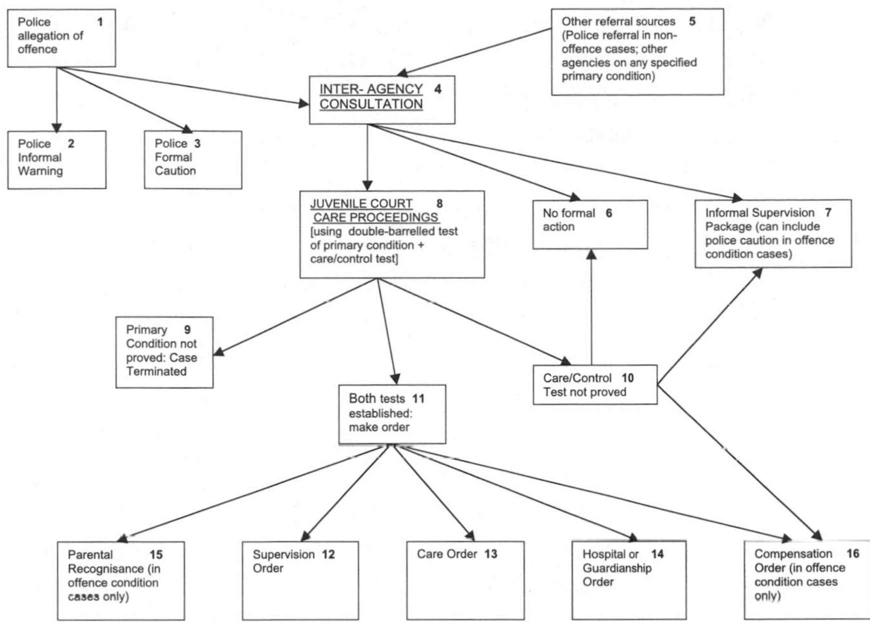

Fig. 15.2 The enacted 1969 English juvenile justice system for children under 14 (excluding homicide cases).

changeably in offense-based and other cases; hence, the first part of the double-barreled test, known in England as the primary condition, could be satisfied *either* by a proved offense *or* by one of the standard "care" conditions (beyond control, parental neglect, truancy, etc.). Also as in the Scottish system, the second part of the English double-barreled test was so worded as to make it, in theory, impossible for the court to make an order against a child offender (however serious the offense) if he or she were receiving good care and control in the home environment.

As already noted, there was no state prosecution system in England in 1969, and this meant that, with some statutory exceptions, the police prosecuted both adult and juvenile criminal cases directly in the courts, at their sole discretion.[29] These structures presented something of a challenge to the framers of the 1969 Act with regard to the new, offense-based, civil care proceedings, since, obviously, while the police in a given case might be able to produce good evidence in relation to the primary condition (the offense), as an agency they were in no position to be able to prove that the child was "in need of care and control which he is unlikely to achieve unless the court makes an order." Government guidance to local areas preparing for the implementation of the 1969 Act was therefore, in offense-based cases, to set up *formal procedures for close consultation* between the police, with their expertise with regard to the offense as the primary condition, and the new, local-authority social services department (SSD; see note 12), with its expertise on matters relating to the care and control of children.[30] (These consultative procedures are shown as box 4 in figure 15.2.) Many police forces, preparing for these changes, set up new "police juvenile liaison bureaux" to facilitate dialogue between themselves and the new social work agency.

To understand the workings of the enacted 1969 English system, let us now imagine that the system has been fully implemented, and that the police have caught two thirteen-year-old boys red-handed while they were stealing goods from a shed. Following the case through figure 15.2, the police then have the choice of an informal warning, a formal caution, or setting up an interagency consultation (boxes 2, 3, 4). Comparing figures 15.1 and 15.2, it will be apparent that the interagency consultation acts as the functional equivalent, in this English legislation, to the reporter as the gatekeeper to the Children's Hearing system in Scotland.

Assume therefore that the case goes to an interagency consultation. Those consulting might decide to take no action; or to set up a voluntary supervision package, perhaps with a police caution as well; or to take the case to the juvenile court in care proceedings (boxes 6, 7, and 8; and note again the similarities to the Scottish system). But as with the reporter's decision in Scotland, those involved in the interagency consultation were not to have an unconstrained choice. In England, the wording of the second part of the double-barreled test for care proceedings *was deliberately phrased to encourage interagency consultation groups to try to develop voluntary supervision packages rather than take cases to court.* The logic was that if adequate voluntary packages could be devised, then it could not be successfully argued that the child was "in need of care and control *which he is unlikely to receive unless the court makes an order*" (emphasis added). These details thus reveal a deliberate policy by the framers of the 1969 Act of maximizing diversion from the juvenile court wherever reasonably possible.

Returning to the case of the two thirteen-year-old boys, let us assume that the interagency consultation considers that voluntary supervision is probably insufficient to secure adequate care and that both boys should therefore be brought before the court in care proceedings. In this particular case, proving the primary condition should be easy, because the boys were caught red-handed. (Were the primary condition not proved, the case would of course have to be terminated: box 9). Establishing the second leg of the test (the care/control part of the test) will be harder, and will, in the juvenile court, require active evidential support by the SSD.

Let us suppose that the magistrates decide that the care/control test is easily satisfied in relation to one boy (John), who comes from difficult home circumstances (box 11). On balance, however, and after careful consideration, they decide that the home and school circumstances of the second boy (Ken) are sufficiently supportive that no compulsory care is necessary for the boy's welfare (box 12). In Ken's case, they may then either take no action or, more likely, establish an informal supervision package (boxes 6, 7).[31] If any of the stolen goods have not been recovered, they may also make a compensation order (box 16), notwithstanding that the care/control test has not been satisfied—an interesting provision for a number of reasons, not least the contrast with the Scottish legislation (see above). John, by contrast, must receive an order of some kind (the care/control test says explicitly that the court must be satisfied the child will not receive adequate care or control *"unless the court makes an order"*). But, as in Scotland, the choice of compulsory orders is a narrow one, and it does not include punitive disposals such as the fine. Rare cases aside, just as in Scotland the real choice of compulsory order effectively lies between the supervision requirement and the residential supervision requirement, so in the English 1969 legislation the main choice lay between the supervision order (nonresidential) and the care order (potentially residential).[32]

A special word is necessary about the care order, since it was to be the subject of much controversy in the 1970s. The care order (under another name) had originally been developed especially to meet the needs of children coming before the juvenile court because of matters such as parental neglect. The effect of the order was to give the local authority (or, in practice, its social workers) the legal powers of a parent over the child in question, so that, even if both natural parents were alive and mentally competent, in law the child's parent was henceforth the local authority. Unless previously discharged, a care order once made would run until the child's eighteenth birthday. Once a child was subject to a care order, he or she could be placed by the local authority wherever it thought fit; the authority had almost complete discretion in the matter. Placements under a care order could, therefore, range widely—from allocation to a residential school to allowing the child to live with his or her natural parents, with some social work oversight. Under the Children and Young Persons Act of 1969, the intention was that the care order should eventually become the only way in which young offenders, and others coming before the juvenile courts, could be placed in residential institutions. With that goal in mind, quite ambitious plans were developed for reshaping, in a more welfare-oriented direction, the content of programs in local-authority residential institutions, to be known as community homes. The plans were especially elaborate in relation to those institutions thought likely to contain a majority population of young offenders (see, generally, Sparks and Hood 1969; Home Office 1970), though in practice they eventually came to mean very little as the use of the care order declined (see below).

The care order was clearly intended to play, within the reshaped English juvenile justice system, the same "end-of-the-line" role as that occupied in Scotland by the residential supervision requirement, but there were some important differences between the two orders. First, as we have noted, in Scotland all supervision requirements last only a year at the time; in England, depending on the age of the defendant, the care order could, without formal review by the court, last for five or even seven years. (This difference arose because the English juvenile courts, unlike the Scottish Children's Hearings, did not hold any continuing jurisdiction over the case.) Second, the decision as to the kind of placement for the child—including the choice of placement across the residential/nonresidential divide—was in England vested in the local authority (in practice the SSD), whereas in Scotland, as we have seen, it was reserved to the Children's Hearing. Third, in the English care order the local authority formally acquired parental powers, but in Scotland the making of a residential supervision requirement did not in itself have any implications for legal parenthood. In short, therefore, the English care order gave substantially greater powers and responsibilities to the local Social Services Department (SSD) than the Scottish residential supervision requirement gave to the area Social Work Department. This was a deliberate choice on the part of the framers of the English Act: it reflected their view that social workers, rather than the courts, were the treatment experts in juvenile justice cases and that they should therefore be given maximum discretion on treatment decisions.[33] It was a view, however, that was to have significant unintended consequences.

If we now stand back and compare the overall shape of the enacted English 1969 legislation for those under fourteen with that of its Scottish counterpart (figures 15.1 and 15.2), we can see that there are considerable similarities in, for example, (1) the initial choices open to the police; (2) the choices available to the reporter or the interagency consultation forum; (3) the restricted range of final disposals; (4) the overarching welfare ethic; and (5) the importance of the question, "Is compulsory care really necessary?" Thus, the similarities between the two enacted systems were great—and certainly far more substantial than one would guess from reading some of the secondary literature. The differences that remained were, nevertheless, very important indeed. These differences included most obviously the retention of the juvenile court in England as a site both for adjudications of fact and of law *and* for treatment decisions, and—the obverse of the first point—a more procedurally elaborate system in Scotland (compare figures 15.1 and 15.2) to take account of the dual system of courts and treatment tribunals that the Kilbrandon Report had insisted upon.

This discussion of the 1969 English Act has so far been restricted to its provisions for those under fourteen. For defendants aged 14–16 in offense-based cases, the situation was to be a little more complex. Care proceedings, using the procedures shown in figure 15.2, were to be available in all cases and were a preferred option. However, in a restricted range of offense-based cases, the possibility of a criminal prosecution was also to be available. Hence, for this older age-group, a hybrid prosecution/care proceedings system was established,[34] with the ancillary statutory provisions giving the government quite extensive powers to restrict the scope of the prosecution route. This feature of the English system at first sight seems much less welfare-oriented than the Scottish system, but in this respect it is instructive to recall the exception to the normal Scottish procedures that is provided by the fiscal → sheriff court route (see figure 15.1, boxes 3 and 10). Once again, therefore, there are in reality some significant similarities between the systems.

Despite these similarities (of substance and ethos) between the 1968 Scottish Act and the 1969 English Act, they were treated very differently by the U.K. Parliament, with much stronger opposition being mounted to the English measure than had been the case for the Scottish.[35] In fact, the Conservative Party, then the main party of opposition, strongly contested some of the proposals of the English Bill, particularly on the grounds that they did not provide for equal justice. One of the main kinds of case highlighted by the Parliamentary opposition was that of offenses committed in a group where (as in the John and Ken example used above) one child might eventually receive compulsory care while another would not, despite their having committed the same offense. It was, in short, a critique founded on the desert-based maxim of "equal state interventions for equal crimes" (on the principle of parity in desert theory, see von Hirsch 1986). Inevitably, however, this critique cut no ice with welfare theorists, who preferred to argue that treating every juvenile offender as an individual, and tailoring the disposal to his or her welfare needs, was of far greater significance in achieving justice than was any mechanical or crude comparison of the extent of intervention in the lives of different children, based on the fact of a joint crime. (Note also the earlier comment that, in the Scottish system, separate Children's Hearings are arranged for children committing offenses in a group, so that their welfare needs can be individually considered.)

This kind of argument, of course, can run and run. What was, however, to prove crucial for subsequent developments in England was that the "equal state interventions for equal crimes" argument had in 1969 been adopted by the Opposition Front Bench in Parliament—and the Conservative opposition were about to win an unexpected election victory in 1970.

Preparing for the Implementation of the 1968 and 1969 Acts

Implementing the juvenile justice provisions of the Social Work (Scotland) Act 1968 was a massive undertaking. There was almost no continuity between the old juvenile courts and the new Children's Hearings, so the latter had to be created from scratch, as did the new reporter system. Given these complexities, there was inevitably quite a long gestation period before the Scottish Act was finally implemented in April 1971. By a delicious irony, it was then brought into force by an Order of a Conservative government, a government whose spokesmen had only two years previously been vigorously opposing the not dissimilar English 1969 Act. (For this "enactment by Order" procedure for U.K. legislation, see note 10 to this chapter.)

In England, full implementation of the 1969 Act would also have been complex. But because, first, the juvenile courts were retained without significant structural change and, second, no major new official such as the reporter was created, it was deemed to be practicable to implement the 1969 Act on a gradual, step-by-step basis. This gradual approach was thought to be particularly appropriate because of some of the anticipated complexities of on-the-ground implementation, especially as regards the supporting service provisions.[36] Accordingly, the Labour government intended, in 1970,

1. to phase in gradually the use of compulsory care proceedings for offense-based cases, beginning with 10–11-year-olds only, and then later adding twelve- and thirteen-year-olds;
2. to transfer various categories of work gradually to the new SSDs from the probation service, as the SSDs grew in strength;
3. to create the care order immediately as an available measure for all kinds of case and for all age-groups; but only gradually—as the new system of community homes became established—to phase out the use of the existing custodial sentences, namely, the detention center and borstal training, as intended by the Children and Young Persons Act 1969.[37]

Hence, powers were included in the English 1969 legislation allowing the government of the day maximum flexibility in the gradual implementation of the various sections of the Act (by the Order procedure; see above). But then the Conservatives, who had strongly opposed many of these legislative provisions, won the election of 1970 at a time when very little of the 1969 Act had been formally implemented. The new Conservative government therefore had to make some rapid decisions concerning the extent and speed of implementation. A Home Office minister quickly announced that,[38] for the foreseeable future,

1. There would be no requirement for the use of compulsory care proceedings in offense-based cases for any age-group. Care proceedings in offense-based cases would be allowed, if the police wished to use them, but criminal prosecutions would also be freely permitted for all age-groups. In practice, after this announcement the police virtually never used care proceedings in offense-based cases, and this type of procedure therefore quickly became a dead letter.[39]

2. Detention centers and borstal training would be retained as custodial sentences for older juveniles, alongside the care order and the new system of community homes.

Thus, at a stroke, the 1969 Act was emasculated. Some of its provisions were implemented, but in a radically different context than that which had been intended by those who had painstakingly constructed the Act.

From the day of the minister's announcement, the trajectories of the juvenile justice systems in England and in Scotland were set on different courses. But what very few could have anticipated in 1970 was that the fledgling Scottish system would quickly prove to be very resilient, while the English system—which in 1970–71 changed much less radically than its Scottish counterpart—would be the subject of constant political and administrative change for the next thirty years. Those contrasting experiences are explored in the next two sections.

ENGLISH JUVENILE JUSTICE 1970–2000: THREE DECADES OF TURBULENCE

The most significant single feature of English juvenile justice policy in the three decades from 1970 is, undoubtedly, its turbulence. This turbulence presents something of a difficulty in presenting this section of the chapter. It would be possible, but hardly fruitful, to offer a great deal of detail about every twist and turn in the changing policy scene. On the other hand, there is a danger that too little context will be provided if one simply picks out a few highlights. To try to resolve this dilemma, tables 15.1 and 15.2 provide some systematic basic information about what has been occurring at each stage of the changing policy process, as a kind of chart of thirty years of change. (As will be seen, these tables focus for each period on five main topics: the national political context; prosecution and diversion policies; the courts; supporting service structures in the community; and residential and custodial institutions.) The text that follows does not attempt to comment on each and every feature mentioned in tables 15.1 and 15.2; rather it develops in particular what I regard as some of the most salient policy themes to have been pursued at various times. Accordingly, readers will probably gain the most accurate overall picture by reading text and tables in close juxtaposition.

The 1970s

For convenience, the first two columns of table 15.1 set out the main features of the pre-1969 English juvenile justice system and of the 1969 Act.

Table 15.1

Key features of English juvenile justice, 1965–1979

	Before the 1969 Act	The 1969 Act (CYPA) as Enacted by Parliament (Labour Majority)	The 1969 Act (CYPA) as Implemented by Conservative Government in 1970	The 1970s
National political context	Philosophy: modified criminal court approach. Administration: practice mainly developed at local level; Home Office (HO) has national oversight.	Philosophy: a more thoroughgoing welfare approach, but JC retained. Administration: Dept. of Health (DoH) to take over from Home Office oversight of most post-court treatments.	Philosophy: CYPA welfare-oriented provisions only selectively implemented. Administration: DoH shares responsibility with HO for oversight of post-court treatments.	No major change from 1970 situation, despite election of Labour government in 1974.
Prosecution and diversion policies	No state prosecution system. Diversion limited and dependent on local police initiatives.	Diversion central to philosophy of CYPA, backed by special wording in Act.	Special wording not implemented, but most police forces had created Juvenile Liaison Bureaux (JLBs) in readiness for implementation of CYPA.	Diversion expanded, largely because of existence of JLB structures.
The courts	Juvenile Courts (JCs) as center-stage. JCs have both criminal and care jurisdictions.	JCs to have much more limited roles and functions. Criminal jurisdiction to be largely subsumed within care jurisdiction.	Criminal jurisdiction of JCs retained in full. Courts' functions larger than intended by CYPA, but restricted by comparison with 1960s.	Deep anxieties among magistrates at restriction of JC powers, esp. re care orders.

Supporting service structures in community	Probation service predominates. Local authority Children's Departments have some functions (esp. re care jurisdiction).	Generic local authority Social Services Departments (SSDs) created (in different Act). SSDs to take over primary juvenile justice responsibilities from probation service in gradual development.	Mixed picture: probation service role retained, but SSDs have greater role than old Children's Depts., and expected to grow.	Use of discretion by social workers in SSDs is very controversial (esp. re care orders). Uncertain beginnings of intermediate treatment (I.T.).
Residential and custodial institutions	1. Local authority and other children's homes 2. Home Office approved schools (HOAS) 3. Detention centers (DCs) 4. Borstal training (BT) [Note: all the above under HO supervision]	Abolish HOAS, DC, BT. Merge HOAS and children's homes in new system of local-authority "community homes" under DcH supervision.	Community homes system created, but DC and BT retained.	Increased use of DC and BT; declining population in community homes.

Table 15.2

Key features of English juvenile justice, 1979–1998

	Thatcher Government policy Initiative, 1979–82	The 1980s	The New Legislative Framework of 1990–92	1993–97	The "New Labour" Policy Framework of 1998
National political context	A "bifurcation" strategy: tough approach with "deep end" offenders, liberal at shallow end.	Main real policy driver is JJM (see row 4), which government does not seriously resist.	Implementation of major review of (non-criminal) child care law. New "punishment in the community" policies.	A more punitive political and public context.	Govt. attempts thorough overhaul of youth justice system. Philosophy: radical rejection of JJM-corrections approach. Administration: national Youth Justice Board (YJB) created.
Prosecution and diversion policies	Cautioning encouraged in government policy document, 1980.	Crown Prosecution Service created. Cautioning grows rapidly, with further government encouragement. Use of informal warnings spreads.	No change.	Government attempts to restrict cautioning, esp. repeat cautioning.	Cautions abolished; replaced by final warning scheme.
The courts	JCs to be given more extensive powers, in deliberate reversal of 1970s situation.	Growth of legal representation. Intended extension of court powers ineffectual. Courts influenced by JJM (see below).	Care jurisdiction removed from JCs. Age limit of JCs raised to 18; JCs renamed Youth Courts (YCs). Formal introduction of desert-based sentencing approach.	Research reveals high use of discharge by courts and multiple court appearances before final disposal.	Fast-tracking. New interventionist orders introduced. Reparation emphasized.

Supporting service structures in community	Govt. encourages use of intermediate treatment (I.T.), esp. as an "alternative to care/custody" in appropriate cases.	Birth of the juvenile justice movement (JJM) and the new orthodoxy, esp. in SSDs. Probation service increasingly marginalized as JJM develops in SSDs.	"Overlapping jurisdiction" concept created: probation service role therefore intended to increase again.	Overlapping jurisdiction does not work as intended.	Introduction of new multiagency Youth Offending Teams (YOTs).
Residential and custodial institutions	"Short sharp shock" DCs to be introduced. Residential care orders to be introduced.	Short sharp shock DCs ineffective; experiment discontinued. Merger of DC/BT into Youth Custody (YCus). Marked decline in use of institutions, largely attributable to influence of JJM.	Abolition of care orders in criminal proceedings. Minimum age for YCus raised.	New Secure Training Centers legislated for, for younger offenders. Increased use of YCus.	New generic legal framework for institutions for young offenders (detention and training order).

The third column then summarizes the hybrid situation that was created by the 1970 Conservative government's selective implementation of the 1969 Act (see above).

From this starting-point, how did English juvenile justice subsequently develop in the 1970s (table 15.1, column 4)? One very significant feature was the growth of formal cautioning by the police for juvenile offenders. A formal caution, in England, is an official warning by the police as to the future behavior of someone who has admitted an offense; it is therefore an action that is taken in lieu of a prosecution. In the case of a juvenile, the caution is usually administered in person: that is, the juvenile must attend a police station with his or her parent(s), and the police then deliver the warning orally. The caution is also officially recorded, and it may in many circumstances be formally cited in court in later criminal proceedings.

We have seen that the wording of the 1969 Act, in its original form, in effect required the police and the SSD *jointly* to consider whether informal action short of formal care proceedings would be sufficient in the particular case, and, in preparation for the expected enactment of this consultation policy, many local police forces had set up Police Juvenile Liaison Bureaus (special organizational units within the police to consider the processing of juvenile offenders). In practice, of course, the compulsory care proceedings element of the Act was not implemented, and so the police were free to continue to prosecute cases as before (see note 39). But most police juvenile liaison bureaus were not dismantled, and this simple organizational change undoubtedly seemed to foster, in the early 1970s, a significant increase in the use of the formal police caution (whether after consultation with the local authority social services department, or, much more frequently, through a police decision taken alone). The very rapid growth of cautioning in the years 1968–1972, according to officially published data, is shown in table 15.3. While there are very good reasons for believing that the trend shown is in part artifactual, there is nevertheless little doubt that the police's use of diversionary measures did expand during this period, despite the fact that the 1969 Act was only partially implemented.[40]

But perhaps the dominant feature of English juvenile justice in the 1970s, certainly in terms of its impact on the national political arena, was a quite intense structural conflict over the care order. In offense-based cases, the main order that the care order replaced was the "approved school order" (abolished by the 1969 Act), whereby the juvenile court could send a young offender (or a child deemed in need of care and protection) to a reform school for an indeterminate period of up to three years. A significant difference between the approved school order and the care order was that, whereas an approved school order made by the court guaranteed an institutional placement, under a care order the local authority (in practice the Social Services Depart-

Table 15.3

Use of the formal caution for young offenders in England and Wales, 1967–1998 (Persons cautioned as a percentage of those found guilty or cautioned for indictable offenses)

	Persons aged 10–13		Persons aged 14–16	
	Males	Females	Males	Females
1967	35	48	17	25
1968	38	52	18	29
1969	45	59	22	36
1970	50	66	24	39
1971	60	80	32	53
1972	63	83	32	58
1973	63	83	33	58
1974	63	83	34	58
1975	63	83	33	57
1976	63	81	32	55
1977	67	85	34	58
1978	64	85	34	57
1979	66	85	35	59
1980	65	85	34	58
1981	68	87	35	60
1982	70	88	38	65
1983	73	90	42	68
1984	75	91	45	71
1985	79	93	51	78
1986	81	94	55	80
1987	86	96	59	82
1988	86	95	60	80
1989	88	95	64	82
1990	90	96	69	86
1991	90	97	70	87
1992	91	97	73	90
			(14–17)	(14–17)
1992*	91	97	63	84
1993*	90	97	63	84
1994*	87	97	60	81
1995*	86	96	58	79
1996*	86	96	54	76
1997*	83	94	52	72
1998*	81	93	50	72

*Data for these years are, in the third and fourth columns, for persons aged 14–17 inclusive, following the raising of the maximum age for inclusion in the youth justice system (effective October 1992). Data for 1992 are given on both bases to aid comparison.

ment of the authority) had full discretion as to the child's placement and hence was not obliged to remove him or her from home to an institution. Hence, after 1970 the locus of decision-making power in this kind of case shifted to a significant extent from the juvenile courts to the social services departments. This shift of power proved extremely unpopular with magistrates—a strong interest group who had already been influential in causing the government to withdraw its original (1965) proposals for juvenile justice reform in England (see note 24). Indeed, during the 1970s allegations were made, in quite influential contexts, that in some cases magistrates would make a care order intending placement in a residential institution, but then the local authority would immediately send the child home (for various possible reasons, including a deliberate treatment decision, and "queuing" for an eventual placement in a suitable residential environment). Although the data that were available on this matter seemed to indicate that cases where the child was sent home by the SSD as a deliberate treatment decision were fairly rare and created little risk of reoffending (see, e.g., Zander 1975), in political terms they were of great importance, and one should not underestimate the depth of feeling on the part of many magistrates about this issue (on this point, see Cowperthwaite 1988, 65–66). In this rather tense atmosphere, it certainly did not help matters that decisions as to a child's placement under the care order were the sole preserve of the Social Services Departments, whereas the probation service had been the traditional providers of social work services to the courts. Many magistrates made it unequivocally clear, at this time, that they greatly preferred the probation service as a supporting community agency, rather than the new social services departments.[41]

The magistrates' dislike of the care order, and their distrust of the Social Services Departments that were responsible for the implementation of those orders, was reflected in the 1970s in a significant decline in the use of care orders in offense-based cases (see table 15.4 for data on 14–16-year-old males). By contrast, the custodial sentences for older juveniles (detention centers and borstals—sentences where an institutional placement was guaranteed) rose in popularity in the eyes of the courts (table 15.4).

Notwithstanding the numerical decline of the care order, research at the end of the 1970s suggested that care orders after criminal proceedings were, in the main, being made on the recommendation of social workers, and that rather than the care order being a remedy of last resort (as had been the approved school order) not a few recommendations for care orders were being made for first offenders (Giller and Morris 1981). These and similar findings then led, at that time, to a substantial critique of the welfare assumptions of the 1969 Act from social scientists who espoused a more justice-oriented (or desert-based) perspective, that is, who believed that court interventions in criminal cases should above all be proportionate to the severity of the offense

Table 15.4

Sentencing of older male juveniles found guilty of indictable offenses, England and Wales, 1970–1997 (percent)

Year	Discharge	Fine	Community Sentences	Care Order	Custody	Other	Total
Age 14–16 Inclusive							
1970	17	38	29	8	6	2	100
1971	17	40	26	8	6	2	100
1972	17	42	24	7	7	2	100
1973	17	40	25	7	8	2	100
1974	18	40	26	6	8	2	100
1975	19	39	25	6	9	2	100
1976	20	38	24	5	10	2	100
1977	19	38	26	5	10	1	100
1978	18	39	25	4	10	1	100
1979	17	37	29	4	10	1	100
1980	17	35	30	4	11	1	100
1981	19	32	33	3	12	1	100
1982	20	31	32	3	12	1	100
1983	21	29	34	2	12	1	100
1984	22	27	37	2	12	1	100
1985	22	25	37	2	12	1	100
1986	24	24	38	2	11	1	100
1987	24	23	39	1	11	1	100
1988	25	22	39	1	11	2	100
1989	29	20	39	1	9	2	100
1990	31	18	41	1	7	3	100
1991	32	14	42	0	8	3	100
1992	34	13	41	—	9	3	100
Age 14–17 Inclusive							
1992*	31	18	39	—	10	2	100
1993*	31	11	44	—	11	2	100
1994*	30	12	44	—	11	2	100
1995*	29	12	44	—	12	2	100
1996*	28	11	44	—	13	2	100
1997*	28	12	43	—	14	2	100

Note: Community sentences include the supervision order and the attendance center order (throughout the period), the community service order (from 1982), the probation order and the combination order (from 1992), and the curfew order with electronic monitoring (in theory from 1995, although in practice there were very few cases in the years shown).

*Data for these years are for persons aged 14–17 inclusive, following the raising of the maximum age for inclusion in the youth justice system (effective October 1992). Data for 1992 are given on both bases to aid comparison. Data for 1998 are not given: they are the latest published data at the time of going to press, but the age-group categories in the national Criminal Statistics have again been changed, this time by restricting this age group to ages 15–17 inclusive.

(see, e.g., Morris et al. 1980; Taylor, Lacey, and Bracken 1979). From these and other sources, the very influential juvenile justice movement of the 1980s was to be born.

The national political context in the 1970s also requires brief attention. The Conservative government that was elected in 1970 lost power in 1974; it might therefore reasonably have been expected that the Labour government of 1974–79 would move to implement in full the Children and Young Persons Act which their predecessors had (with considerable effort) piloted through Parliament in 1969. In fact, however, the new Labour government made no effort to do this. There were probably two main reasons for this: first, a change of policy priorities within the Labour Party itself, and second, the fact that by 1974 the 1969 Act was already the subject of considerable political controversy at the national level. Thus it came about that the next major political initiative in the field of English juvenile justice was postponed until the election of another Conservative government in 1979.

The Thatcher Government's Policy Initiative, 1979–82

Margaret Thatcher became Prime Minister in 1979, at the head of a government elected, in part, on a "law and order" political ticket. The Conservatives were to remain in power for the next eighteen years, but in the criminal policy field these years were by no means entirely dominated by "law and order" approaches. Certainly, in the sphere of juvenile justice, there were to be some surprising developments.

In its early years, the Thatcher government pursued for young offenders a policy of *bifurcation* (on this concept, in the context of other penal thinking of the period, see Bottoms 1980). That is to say, a more restrictive or punitive approach was adopted for more serious or persistent young offenders, while at the same time diversionary policies were developed for those who could reasonably be diverted (diversion here meaning *both* "diversion from court" *and* "diversion from custody"; see Klein 1979 for a contemporaneous discussion of the internationally fashionable diversion policies of the late 1970s and early 1980s).

There were two main planks in the upper end of the Conservatives' early-1980s bifurcation strategy: they were the "short sharp shock experiment," and the introduction of residential care orders. Both initiatives were to prove political failures.

The short sharp shock experiment was highlighted, to rousing cheers, at the Conservative Party conference of 1979. It introduced experimentally, in selected detention centers (short-term, custodial institutions for young offenders), a special regime emphasizing physical education, military-style drill, briskness, and tidiness. This regime was intended to provide an unpleasant experience for those undergoing it, and it was therefore expected to act as an especially effective deterrent sentence. Unfortunately for the government, rigorous research by prison psychologists showed that the new regimes had no better success in reducing recidivism than did the standard detention center regimes (Thornton et al. 1984), and so the experiment was in due course quietly abandoned.

In a policy paper published soon after it was elected (Home Office 1980, 13–14), the government directly addressed the 1970s concerns of juvenile court magistrates about the care order, when applied in offense-based cases (see above). A new residential care order was accordingly proposed and subsequently legislated for in 1982 (although under a different name). This order allowed the juvenile court, under certain circumstances, to insist that a young person who was the subject of a care order must not remain at home. However, the scope of this power was much more restricted than many magistrates had pressed for: it was available only for those who committed a further offense while already the subject of a care order made as a result of an offense, and the maximum length of the compulsory residential element was limited to six months. In view of these restrictions, the residential care order was in practice used by the courts hardly at all. It turned out to be a purely symbolic piece of legislation, with no significant on-the-ground effects.

At the other, more diversionary, end of the bifurcation spectrum, the Thatcher government also relied on two principal initiatives, this time in the areas of cautioning and of so-called intermediate treatment.

The 1980 policy paper encouraged the further growth of formal police cautioning, on the stated grounds that "all the available evidence suggests that juvenile offenders who can be diverted from the criminal justice system at an early stage in their offending are less likely to re-offend than those who become involved in judicial proceedings" (Home Office 1980, 12). (Oddly, however, as Farrington [1984, 92] pointed out at the time, there was virtually no empirical evidence then available to support this claim.) In addition, after some technical modifications to the existing legislation (modifications which reduced social workers' discretion: see note 33 above), the government was happy to encourage so-called intermediate treatment programs in the community, especially as an adjunct to supervision orders for more serious and persistent offenders who might otherwise be given custodial sentences or care orders. In 1983, generous "pump-priming" money (£15 million) was made available by central government to encourage local authorities to develop programs of this kind in conjunction with voluntary agencies. (This cash incentive was widely taken up; see NACRO 1989; Bottoms et al. 1990, 70–75.)

The overall result of these various initiatives was unexpected. Whereas, at the beginning of the 1980s, the dominant political tone had seemed to be a new Conservative "law and order" approach to juvenile justice, by the end of the decade matters appeared in a very different light, although there had been no change of government. The two more restrictive government initiatives had both failed (see above), but the two more diversionary initiatives had flourished. As may be seen from table 15.3, cautioning rates, which had been reasonably stable in the period 1973–80, accelerated upward in the first half of the 1980s, and were then again boosted by a Home Office guidance circular of 1985, offering further encouragement to local police forces to make greater use of the caution. Indeed, cautioning rates for males aged 14–16 actually doubled (from 34 percent to 69 percent) in the course of the decade 1980–90.[42] Intermediate treatment programs for more serious offenders also grew in number and influence during these years, aided by the cash injection of 1983 (see above). By 1988, the government was actually celebrating, in an official policy document, a halving of the number of juvenile offenders in custody during the six-year period 1981–87 (a period during which the use of care orders had also declined significantly). These "achievements," the government document continued, had come about because of "the shared commitment and determination of the social services, the probation service, voluntary organisations and the juvenile courts" (Home Office 1988, para. 2.21).[43]

To understand more fully this marked change of climate, we need now to examine some other developments of the 1980s and how they interacted with government policy.

The 1980s

Any serious account of the 1980s juvenile justice policy in England must give pride of place to a remarkable social movement, colloquially known as the juvenile justice movement, which was to have a massive impact on policy and practice despite the fact that it operated wholly outside the sphere of central government. This movement was mainly the product of a creative partnership between, first, a number of academics working in the juvenile justice field (especially at Lancaster University; see Thorpe et al. 1980), and second, juvenile justice practitioners working in Social Services Departments.

The juvenile justice movement began from the standard critiques of the welfare model of juvenile justice (see, e.g., Morris et al. 1980),[44] and from some alarm at the frequency with which social workers were, in criminal cases, recommending care orders for first offenders on welfare grounds (see above). To these critiques were added a number of further theoretical strands, including: (1) labeling theory, leading to an interest in the possibilities of so-called radical nonintervention (see Schur 1973); (2) a "just deserts" approach to sentencing (see Bottomley 1980 for a review of the growing interest in desert theory in Britain at the start of the 1980s); and (3) a view of adolescent offending as essentially transient (cf. Rutherford 1986).[45] In addition, adherents of the juvenile justice movement developed a marked interest in understanding the juvenile justice system as a system of decision points (see Bottomley 1973), coupled with a desire to intervene effectively, at strategic decision points, in pursuit of their preferred policy objectives. Within a few short years, this mainly practitioner movement had moved from a position of marginality (in the late 1970s) to one of ideological dominance, at least in SSDs; hence it quickly became widely known as "the new orthodoxy" (Jones 1984).

Some of the main tenets of the new orthodoxy have been summarized as follows (Bottoms et al. 1990, 3–4, modifying a characterization originally produced by Pitts 1988, 90–93):

1. The helping professions are sometimes a major source of hindrance to young offenders because they pathologize them, intervene in their lives too readily and too intensively, and may therefore unwittingly encourage courts to use institutional disposals if and when welfare-based community treatments eventually fail.
2. Placing young offenders in residential or custodial institutions is to be avoided whenever possible, because such institutions have an adverse effect on the criminality and social development of these offenders.
3. Placing young offenders in community-based alternatives is clearly to be preferred to institutional sentencing.
4. Minimum intervention is the best approach, if practicable given magistrates' sentencing philosophies and other constraints of the system; hence, among other things, cautioning young offenders is clearly to be preferred to taking them to court.
5. Welfare considerations should not be predominant in criminal proceedings in the juvenile court (e.g., *re* sentencing/remand decisions) or in decisions whether to caution or prosecute.
6. Research and monitoring of local juvenile justice systems is vital in order to discover, for example, what kinds of cases have recently been sent to custody, what recommendations were made by social workers/probation officers in court reports in those cases, etc.; when the information from this monitoring has been absorbed, social workers can target the need for appropriate further action in pursuit of "minimum intervention" goals.

Given these policy preferences, it will be readily apparent that, in local areas, those committed to the new orthodoxy were able to use creatively several features of the government's approach of the early 1980s (see previous subsection)—including especially (1) the official encouragement of cautioning and (2) the boost to intermediate treatment as an alternative to custody and care (including the 1983 injection of finance).[46] However, these features were used by practitioners of the new orthodoxy very much in pursuit of their own diversionary, anticustody agenda, in a process that was described by some of its own advocates as an attempt at "decarceration by stealth" (Tutt and Giller 1987). As previously noted, the 1980s saw a significant reduction in the number of young offenders given custodial sentences and care orders, and all informed commentators agree that the new orthodoxy group played a major role in helping to foster this important change (Allen 1991; Bottoms et al. 1990).

One important, indirect consequence of the growth of the juvenile justice movement concerned the respective roles of SSDs and the probation service as supporting community agencies for the juvenile courts. Empirical research in the 1980s showed clearly that the juvenile justice movement had taken root much more strongly in SSDs than in the probation service (Bottoms et al. 1990), and this fact, coupled with other pressures on the probation service at the time, served increasingly to marginalize the probation service in the juvenile justice system. Even the magistrates, with their strong traditional preference for the probation service (see above), had in most local areas by the end of the 1980s fully accepted the dominance of SSDs; indeed, in many courts, they clearly allowed their sentencing to be influenced by juvenile justice movement policies and strategies developed by local SSD practitioners (Richardson 1987, 1988).

These end-of-the-decade SSDs were, however, radically different in their practice than they had been at the beginning of the 1980s. There was now absolutely no question, in most local areas, of recommending care orders for first offenders on the grounds of the welfare of the child (see the discussion of Giller and Morris's [1981] research, above). Rather, those committed to the juvenile justice movement thought strictly in "tariff-based" terms in offense-based cases, and, within that conceptual framework, they always argued for the minimum possible sentence. To ensure that all workers in SSDs followed these prescriptions, individual social workers' reports to the court were often vetted by team managers before they were presented to the court, and any recommendations that were seen as inappropriately interventionist were altered accordingly. Organizationally, to facilitate the development of the desired philosophy and practices, those within the SSD who worked on offense-based cases were typically gathered together in one specialist team (known informally in many areas as the youth justice team, or YJT). Social workers engaged in the care and protection side of the juvenile courts' work were located elsewhere in the SSD, and they typically worked with a much more welfare-oriented philosophy. Relatively little communication took place between the two groups of workers, notwithstanding that they both formally worked for the same statutory agency and both served the same juvenile courts. This radical organizational and philosophical separation between offense-based and non-offense cases was, of course, completely antithetical to the whole spirit and structure of the Children and Young Persons Act 1969, a statute passed only twenty years beforehand. As we shall see, it is a separation that has, in England, remained as a key organizational feature right up to the present day, in marked contrast to the situation in Scotland.

One final development of the 1980s requires brief mention, although its origins have nothing to do with juvenile justice. In 1980, a Royal Commission on Criminal Procedure (1980) recommended, for the first time in England, the creation of a statutorily based public prosecutor service. This proposal led to the creation, by an Act of 1985, of the Crown Prosecution Service (CPS), an agency that was to deal with juvenile as well as adult criminal cases and which began functioning in 1986. Among other things, the CPS has the power to discontinue a case that the police wish to prosecute, and such discontinuations may take place either immediately (i.e., no prosecution is launched) or subsequently (i.e., after a prosecution has technically begun in court). There is evidence that, for all age groups, discontinuance rates of the second kind rose sharply with the creation of the CPS. Perhaps more unexpectedly, such discontinuations rose particularly sharply in juvenile cases, a matter that was to contribute to a later critique of the English juvenile justice system.[47]

The New Legislative Framework of 1990–92

At the beginning of the 1990s, two new Acts of Parliament came into effect in England. Neither, in origin, was primarily concerned with the English juvenile justice system, but together the two Acts had some important consequences for that system. The first statute was the Children Act 1989, which was brought into effect late in 1991; the second was the Criminal Justice Act 1991, which was brought into effect late in 1992.

The Children Act of 1989 is an extremely comprehensive statute, enacted only after a full and lengthy process of careful consultation with many relevant bodies. It extensively remodels the English law relating to children, in its noncriminal aspects (see, generally, Bainham 1990). It is neither appropriate nor feasible, in the context of the present chapter, to discuss even the main features of the Act (but see chapter 14 by Eekelaar in this volume). However, two of the Act's provisions must be mentioned; both matters relate to previously discussed aspects of the Children and Young Persons Act 1969, namely, care proceedings and the care order.

We have seen that the 1969 Act, in its original formulation, intended to introduce compulsory care proceedings for most offense-based cases. When the Conservative government altered the Act by administrative fiat in 1970, it actually enacted the care proceedings provisions, but made them noncompulsory (and therefore, in practice, nugatory—see note 39 above) in offense-based cases. However, in non-offense-based cases (of parental neglect, truancy, children allegedly out of control, etc.), if the relevant authority wished to take the case to the juvenile court, this had to be done using the care proceedings formula. In the 1989 Act, this whole legal apparatus of care proceedings was swept away and radically reshaped. In consequence, proceedings of this kind were removed from the jurisdiction of the juvenile court, and transferred to a new "family proceedings court." Describing this as a "significant change," a leading commentator on the new Act said, "It is hoped that this will remove the criminal overtones associated with the juvenile court, whose jurisdiction will henceforth be confined to criminal cases" (Bainham 1990, 181–82). In the space of twenty years, official policy had therefore shifted from trying to subsume criminal matters within the framework of care proceedings (in the original intentions of the 1969 Act) to removing care proceedings altogether from the juvenile court, in an attempt to avoid their "criminal" overtones—an interesting reversal! Just as intriguingly, north of the border the original marriage of offense-based and non-offense-based cases in the Children's Hearings continued to flourish, and indeed (as we shall see) non-offense-based cases were, at precisely this period, of rapidly growing numerical importance within the hearings system.

Given the 1989 Children Act's clear structural separation of offense-based and non-offense-based cases, it was logical that the Act should go on to abolish the care order following criminal proceedings, as enacted in the 1969 Act.[48] By 1991, when this abolition was implemented, this was not a change of much numerical significance, since the courts' use of the care order had been in continuous decline since the early 1970s (as a consequence of the structural conflicts of the 1970s, followed by the philosophical preferences of the juvenile justice movement in the 1980s; see table 15.4 for relevant data with regard to 14–16-year-old males). Yet despite this numerical insignificance, the abolition of the care order in criminal proceedings did have one consequence that was to be of considerable political importance. Residential orders were, as we have seen, available to the English juvenile courts, post-1969, *either* through custodial sentences *or* (potentially) via the care order. Henceforth, only the first of these was to be available. But the minimum age of eligibility for most custodial sentences was, at the time of the implementation of the Children Act of 1989, fourteen years, and this was shortly thereafter raised to fifteen.[49] The abolition of the care order in criminal proceedings therefore meant that from October 1992 courts were—save in cases where the alleged offense was one of exceptional seriousness, in which event special provisions applied—precluded from seeking to remove from home any young offender under fifteen. As we shall shortly see, this was a policy that, in the political climate of the mid-1990s, no senior politician was keen to defend.

The Criminal Justice Act 1991 is also a wide-ranging measure. Principally developed with the sentencing of adults in mind (Windlesham 1993), it sought to promote the use of community penalties instead of imprisonment in many cases, using the slogan "punishment in the community." This strategy was linked to the explicit adoption of a desert-based sentencing approach (see Home Office 1990), which was applied equally to juvenile and to adult cases. Although the 1930s "welfare principle" for juvenile cases remained on the statute book, empirical research carried out in youth courts after the Criminal Justice Act 1991 suggested that—consistently with just deserts principles—the seriousness of the offense was the primary factor associated with the sentence actually awarded (O'Mahony and Haines 1996). Once again, however, the really interesting contrast is with the late 1960s. The adoption of desert-based sentencing criteria in offense-based juvenile cases was, of course, completely at odds with the philosophy of the framers of the 1969 Act—and equally at odds with the whole conceptual framework of the Children's Hearing system, still flourishing in another part of the United Kingdom.

One other change in the 1991 Act, more specifically targeted upon young offenders, must also be mentioned. The maximum age for the normal jurisdiction of the juvenile court was raised from the seventeenth birthday (at which it had been fixed in the 1930s legislation) to the eighteenth birthday. The purpose of this change was to bring the upper age of the court's jurisdiction into line with the legal age of majority in the United Kingdom (that is, the age at which one is permitted to vote in public elections, to make contracts that are binding in law, and so on). Given this raised age limit, the Act also renamed the juvenile court as the "youth court." Once again, this change heightened differences between England and Scotland, since in Scotland the maximum age for processing in the Children's Hearing system (except in continuous jurisdiction cases) is the sixteenth birthday.[50]

The Period 1993–97

An extraordinary event that was to have considerable consequences for the English criminal justice system occurred in February 1993. James Bulger, a two-year-old boy, was abducted from a shopping center in Merseyside by two other boys aged respectively ten and eleven, and subsequently murdered. The initial leading away of the toddler was captured on camera by the shopping center's closed-circuit television system, and the frames were played and replayed to a horrified audience on national television. Thus began a period of public furor and massive media coverage on criminal justice issues, followed by an apparent hardening of public opinion in favor of more punitive approaches. Subsequent statistical analyses have revealed that, for defendants in all age groups, the courts' use of custodial sentences underwent a step-change in an upward direction from 1993 onwards (Grove, Godfrey, and Macleod 1999), a trend that can be seen (in a slightly delayed form) for 14–17-year-old males in table 15.4. These events coincided with some significant criticisms by judges and magistrates of the Criminal Justice Act of 1991, which had at that time only recently (October 1992) been brought into force. A particular focus of the judicial criticism concerned the way in which the Act seemed to play down the importance of prior convictions in determining the severity of the sentence.[51]

The Conservative government, still in power (and continuously so since 1979), reacted to this changing public mood by adopting once again a more law-and-order set of policies. For present purposes, two aspects of these policies are of special importance. First, in 1994, new government guidance to police forces was issued on the subject of cautioning. In marked contrast to some of the guidance of the 1980s, a more restrictive use of cautioning was advocated; in particular, the new circular strongly discouraged the (by now quite common) practice of cautioning a young offender on two or more separate occasions for different offenses. This discouragement led to a reduction in the rates of formal cautioning for juveniles (see table 15.3).[52] Second, the government became alarmed by what it saw as the serious depredations of a minority of persistent young offenders and the courts' inability to impose custodial or residential sentences on such offenders if they were under fifteen. (Naturally, little emphasis was placed, by government sources, on the fact that this situation had in part arisen because of recent changes legislated for—by the same government—in the Children Act 1989 and the Criminal Justice Act 1991!) Accordingly, in a 1994 Act, provisions for a new "secure training order" were enacted, whereby repeat offenders aged 12–14 inclusive could in certain circumstances be given a custodial sentence of between six months and two years, for one half of which they would be held in secure detention; and special new centers in which these orders could be served were commissioned.[53]

But the reader will by now have become accustomed to the fact that, in English juvenile justice policy in the period 1970–2000, nothing has stayed the same for very long. Even as these new policies were being put into place, in 1996 a new official report on youth justice was published, this time by a monitoring body known as the Audit Commission (1996).[54] Since this was to be a report from which many of the incoming Labour government's new policies on youth justice were to be developed, some aspects of the Audit Commission's analysis need to be highlighted.

The commission began the final chapter of its report with some uncompromising conclusions. "The current system for dealing with youth crime is inefficient and expensive," it claimed. The system was failing delinquents themselves, the report continued, since they are "not being guided away from offending to constructive activities." It was failing victims. And it was wasteful in a variety of ways, notably in "lost time, as public servants process the same young offenders through the courts time and again" (Audit Commission 1996, 96).

Two issues highlighted in the commission's factual analysis were particularly germane to the above comments. They were, first, the high proportion of cases in which no action was taken against accused young people and, second, the extent of public resources that were devoted simply to processing cases through the system.

The commission pointed out that the vast majority of offenders who were cautioned were simply reprimanded, with little use being made in local areas of the so-called caution-plus schemes, in which a caution was followed up with some positive action with the offender, designed to reduce reoffending (Audit Commission 1996, 23).[55] Later, the commission commented that ("surprisingly," in its view) "little or nothing happens" to half of the young people recommended by the police to the Crown Prosecution Service (CPS) for formal prosecution (35). CPS discontinuations, plus acquittals, were recorded in about a quarter of all cases recommended for prosecution by the police (25; see also note 47 above), and, in another quarter of cases, while the young person was found guilty in court, the magistrates chose to impose an absolute discharge or, more usually, a conditional discharge (35–36). (See table 15.4 on the increasing discharge rates from 1985 among older male offenders found guilty by the courts, with discharges largely replacing fines.)[56] From a technical legal perspective, the Audit Commission's inclusion of CPS discontinuations and acquittals in this "nothing happens" litany is of course problematic. But the commission's report did nevertheless have a significant political effect in drawing forcible attention to the "nothing happens" phenomenon. And even if one disregards discontinuations/acquittals, calculations can readily be made, from available national statistics, that show the high proportion of cases in which, in the English system in 1995, no action other than a reprimand or warning was taken against officially identified young offenders.[57]

There was also the issue of court processing. The commission pointed out that refinements introduced into the English system of criminal justice in the previous twenty years—such as the growth of state-aided legal representation for defendants and advance disclosure of the prosecution case—had slowed down the procedures of the youth court (Audit Commission, 26). Studies suggested that the *average* number of times a prosecuted young person made an appearance in front of the youth court, up to and including the final sentence, was as high as four occasions (29; O'Mahony and Haines 1996). But court appearances, the commission insisted, were expensive, each involving the presence of at least five persons paid from public funds. There should, therefore, the commission argued, be a transfer of public funds devoted to the youth justice system away from processing and toward more effective remedial action with young offenders.

The "New Labour" Policy Framework

The Labour Party gained power in 1997, for the first time in eighteen years. In the run-up to the election, it had deliberately tried to revise its public image in various ways, including describing itself as "New Labour." One "sound bite" that was adopted by the party as part of this process was the claim that it aimed to be "tough on crime, and tough on the causes of crime." By this it meant that crime would be treated as a serious issue, and that those who committed crime would be made to confront the unacceptable nature of their behavior; at the same time, the social roots of offending behavior would, it was claimed, be seriously tackled by the government.

The Labour government deliberately focused on the youth justice system in England as a primary site for the early implementation of this kind of policy. Major changes to the youth justice system were included in the Crime and Disorder Act 1998, and the hyperbolic claim was made by the new government, on its website, that these constituted "the most radical reform of the youth justice system for fifty years." The changes were, however, deliberately not implemented on a national basis in the first instance; rather, they were introduced initially in a small number of pilot areas, so that practical problems with the new system could be identified and, it was hoped, corrected. The new policies of the 1998 Act were then, in the government's parlance, "rolled out nationally" in the spring of 2000.

One of the most interesting elements of the 1998 reforms, which underpins many of the more detailed elements of the legislation, concerns the philosophy of the youth justice system. The government policy paper that preceded the new legislation was, quite deliberately, entitled *No More Excuses* (Home Office 1997). In the preface to this document, Labour's new Home Secretary was blunt in his message:

> An excuse culture has developed within the youth justice system. It excuses itself for its inefficiency, and too often excuses the young offenders before it, implying that they cannot help their behaviour because of their social circumstances. Rarely are they confronted with their behaviour and helped to take more personal responsibility for their actions. The system allows them to go on wrecking their own lives as well as disrupting their families and communities.

This paragraph clearly illustrates the influence of the Audit Commission critique on New Labour's thinking: both the "inefficiency" and the "need for more effective remedial action" elements of the Audit Commission's evaluation are fully endorsed. But the Home Secretary's message goes further. The "minimum intervention" philosophical approach of the juvenile justice movement is now derided as an "excuse culture," which, by taking as little action as possible, "too often excuses the young offenders before it." The government thereby signaled—more clearly than its Conservative predecessors had ever done—an intention to attack and to undermine this philosophy. In pursuit of this aim, the government deliberately enacted—and, in its publicity about the new system, frequently highlighted—a new statutory principal aim for the youth justice system. This aim, which was explicitly correctionalist and constituted a marked contrast to the priorities of the juvenile justice movement, proclaimed that "it shall be the principal aim of the youth justice system to prevent offending by children and young persons."[58] It was additionally statutorily enacted that all persons and bodies carrying out functions within the system had a duty to have regard to this principal aim.[59] In the interim research report on experiences in the pilot areas that have tested the post-1998 system, it is abundantly clear that the culture clash between the respective youth justice philosophies of New Labour and the juvenile justice movement has been a real one, which was, in the pilot areas, being played out very actively at a local level (see Universities of Sheffield and Hull 1999; see also, in a more academic context, some of the papers in the collection edited by Goldson [2000]). How far that will remain the case after the national implementation of the new policies, from 2000 onwards, remains to be seen.

In pursuit of its drive to improve efficiency, to inject a greater element of correctionalism into the system, and to tackle not only crime but also the causes of crime, the new Act introduced a number of fresh initiatives. These can be mentioned here only in outline, but they include the following:

1. *Pre-court procedures.* The previous cautioning system for juvenile offenders was swept away; it was replaced by a new and more tightly restrictive system of reprimands and final warnings. Particular emphasis was placed on the final warning scheme (i.e., the last warning before a youth court appearance), in which a warning to the young offender would normally be accompanied by compulsory participation in a rehabilitation program, colloquially known as a "change package."

2. *Improved efficiency.* Action was taken with a view to speeding up the work of the youth courts and reducing the number of adjournments.

3. *New, interventionist orders for young offenders.* A new "action plan order," designed to produce a short but intensive structural intervention in a young offender's life and seen as particularly appropriate for those making their first or second appearance before the youth court, was introduced. Slightly lower down the tariff, a new reparation order was also established, intended to supplant the conditional discharge.[60] The use of the conditional discharge by the courts was formally discouraged, in an attempt to combat the "nothing happens" phenomenon.

4. *Tackling the causes of crime.* The 1998 Act introduced a so-called par-

enting order, which the youth court may formally impose upon the parent(s) of young offenders. Such an order requires parents to attend counseling or guidance sessions on the subject of good parenting for up to three months. A parent's failure to comply constitutes a criminal offense. This innovation is intended to tackle the well-established link in the criminological research literature between aspects of parenting and the development of criminal careers (Farrington 1997). Another feature of the Act intended to tackle the wider causes of crime is to be seen in the composition of the new, multiagency "youth offending teams" (YOTs), which are being set up in each local area as the new "supporting service in the community" that backs up the 1998 youth justice reforms. Among other innovative features, the YOTs are by statute required to include representatives from the health and education services, in a deliberate attempt to oblige each YOT to tackle not only the acts of individual young offenders but also wider policy issues linked to the genesis of offending behavior. Curiously, however, there has been very little attempt, in these arrangements, to overcome the still quite marked separation between the "youth offending" and the "child protection" elements in the work of the SSD, a separation which was first created at the time of the dominance of the juvenile justice movement in the 1980s, which was in effect encouraged by the provisions of the Children Act 1989 and the Criminal Justice Act 1991, and which has remained prominent in most SSDs throughout the 1990s.[61]

At the time this chapter went to press, the national implementation of these wide-ranging new policies had only recently occurred; hence, it is much too early to judge the success of this fresh initiative. But further changes to the English youth justice system are already envisaged, and I return to these in the concluding section of this chapter.

SCOTTISH JUVENILE JUSTICE, 1971–2000: A WELFARE-ORIENTED SYSTEM IN ACTION WITHIN A DISTINCTIVE SOCIOPOLITICAL CULTURE

Because the Scottish juvenile justice system has, since 1971, proved to be relatively stable, it is not necessary in this section to adopt the chronological approach that is so inescapable when attempting to describe developments in England. Rather, I seek here to identify some main themes that have arisen during thirty years of experience of a welfare-oriented system in Scotland. This is perhaps a topic of importance well beyond the United Kingdom, because, although most early juvenile courts in the United States and elsewhere were developed on the "socialized juvenile tribunal model," many of these jurisdictions have now altered their approach. The Scottish juvenile justice system is therefore a relatively rare surviving example of a full-fledged, welfare-oriented system, and an assessment of its contemporary functioning is of great theoretical interest.

A Developing System

Although the Scottish system has been in many respects remarkably stable, that does not mean that it has been static. Inevitably, new institutions such as the Children's Hearings and the reporter system took some time to develop established patterns of working, and over the years the distributions of types of case, and of certain decisions within the system, have altered significantly. Before turning to statistical detail, however, one fact of great political importance must be emphasized. The Children's Hearings system quickly established itself, in informed circles within Scotland, as a distinctively Scottish system, with many features that were considered specially appropriate for the Scottish context. Asquith's comment is fairly typical in this respect:

> Highlighting the very great differences which exist between how Scotland and England deal with young people who commit offences derives not simply from some sense of nationalism. Rather it derives from the fact that many of the major Scottish institutions are so very different and based on different philosophies from those of our colleagues down south. It also reflects a belief that to understand a juvenile justice system, we have to understand the philosophy on which it is based, and how that philosophy relates to wider issues about the society in which it is located. Scotland has a unique system of juvenile justice which can be best appreciated in reference to the other major social institutions, such as education, which owe more historically to links with Europe, particularly France, than with England. (1998, 426)

In the first sentence of the above comment, Asquith rightly avers that highlighting Scottish-English differences in juvenile justice does not derive simply from nationalism. Significantly, however, he does not deny that an element of Scottish nationalism might be present. In my judgment, there can be no reasonable doubt that, in the years since 1971, those concerned with the Scottish Children's Hearings have developed a very considerable sense of pride in the system, and part of that pride derives from the fact that this is in some respects a juvenile justice system that is unique in the world. The Scots would also be less than human if they did not derive some quiet satisfaction from the fact that their system is distinctive, valued, and stable, whereas the English (the dominant nation within the United Kingdom) have in the last thirty years seemed unable to make up their minds as to what sort of youth justice system they want!

Table 15.5

Alleged grounds in referrals to reporters to Children's Panels in Scotland, 1972–1996

	Care and Protection Referral	Non-offense Behavioral Referral	School Attendance Referral	Alleged Offense Referral	Total
1972	3	3	6	88	100
1973	3	2	7	88	100
1974	4	2	7	87	100
1975	4	2	6	88	100
1976	4	2	10	84	100
1977	4	2	12	82	100
1978	6	2	11	81	100
1979	7	3	10	80	100
1980	9	3	10	79	100
1981	8	3	9	79	100
1982	10	3	9	79	100
1983	9	3	10	78	100
1984	10	4	10	76	100
1985	10	5	10	74	100
1986	13	5	9	72	100
1987	17	4	8	71	100
1988	21	4	8	68	100
1989	25	4	8	63	100
1990	28	5	8	59	100
1991	29	5	8	58	100
1992	30	5	8	57	100
1993	32	5	9	54	100
1994	29	5	8	57	100
1995	29	5	9	57	100
1996*	28	5	9	58	100

Notes: Data given are percentages of all alleged grounds for referral, for males and females together. Where a single referral includes more than one ground, both grounds are counted separately for the purposes of this table; hence, the total of grounds for referral is larger than the total number of referrals.

Care and protection referrals include children alleged to be "suffering by neglect or lack of parental care"; being the victim of an offense, or being a member of a household of a child offended against; being or likely to become a member of a household of a child offender; and "falling into bad associations or exposure to moral danger."

Non-offense behavioral referrals include children allegedly beyond the control of their parents, and (from 1983 onwards) those alleged to have "misused a volatile substance by deliberately inhaling."

*Data for this year are for the period 1 April 1996–31 March 1997. No data for later years had been published at the time of going to press.

A good example of the practical consequences of this Scottish sense of ownership of the hearings system can be seen in a research report by Hallett and Murray (1998), part of the most comprehensive recent assessment of Scottish juvenile justice processes. This study draws attention to a number of weaknesses of the hearings system, both as perceived by various participants and as demonstrated by the research data. Nevertheless, in their concluding chapter the authors emphasize the predominantly positive overall view of the system; and of the principles on which it is based, held by virtually all those who have some official role in, or relating to, the hearings (namely, reporters, members of the Children's Panel, social workers, sheriffs, procurators fiscal, and teachers). One should clearly not underestimate the importance to the functioning of the Children's Hearing system of such widespread support—although the academic analyst should also not allow the fact of such support to divert attention from the tensions and weaknesses in the system.

When we turn to examine the main ways in which the system has evolved over time, the most significant point concerns the relative balance of the different kinds of referrals to the reporter (see table 15.5). In the early 1970s, nearly 90 percent of all referrals related to alleged offenses, but over the years this has steadily declined, to dip below 60 percent in the 1990s. The initial main reason for this trend was a surge in school attendance referrals in the late 1970s, but more recently care and protection referrals have particularly escalated, notably in the short period 1985–1990, when they quickly rose from 10 percent to 28 percent of all referrals. One should note also that, in Scotland as in many other jurisdictions, there is a marked difference by gender in the kinds of case referred to the juvenile justice system; in 1995, for instance, nearly half of referred girls, but only a fifth of the boys, were notified to the system on care and protection grounds.

In offense-based cases (the principal concern of this chapter), reporters have over the years shown an increasing tendency to take no formal action. In 1982, they referred 44 percent of offense-based cases to the Children's Hearing; only ten years later, this figure had reduced by a third, to 29 percent (see table 15.6). This trend mirrors, of course, the growth of cautioning in England. Other trends in the Scottish system were also similar to those in England. For example, there was a declining use of residential supervision requirements, especially those involving placement in residential schools, in the period 1980–1996 (table 15.7). Moreover, while in the late 1970s, "Hearings were generally more reluctant to remove children from home than social workers were to recommend it," a decade later, "it was more likely to be that Hearings were demanding more . . . compulsory intervention" than were social workers (Lockyer and Stone 1998a, 63, 86). This change is very similar to English social workers' willingness to recommend care orders in the late 1970s and their marked reluctance to do so a few years later. In part, the reasons for these trends in the two countries were similar, for the English juvenile justice movement of the 1980s also had a significant influence north of the border—although, as we shall shortly see, that influence was in Scotland never unproblematic, and in one region it would lead to major conflict.

Table 15.6

Initial action by Reporters in Scotland on alleged offense referrals, males and females combined, 1982–1996 (%)

	No Action	Referred to SWD	Referred to Police	Referred to Hearing	Total	*N*
1982	44	4	8	44	100	(22,747)
1983	46	4	9	41	100	(23,291)
1984	49	3	6	42	100	(23,715)
1985	49	4	7	39	100	(25,144)
1986	51	5	6	38	100	(26,222)
1987	55	5	5	35	100	(26,274)
1988	54	5	5	36	100	(25,902)
1989	56	6	5	33	100	(24,210)
1990	56	6	4	33	100	(24,694)
1991	59	6	4	31	100	(25,155)
1992	62	6	3	29	100	(24,589)
1993	61	6	2	31	100	(23,120)
1994	61	6	2	30	100	(25,735)
1995	61	6	3	30	100	(27,606)
1996*	64	6	3	26	100	(28,105)

*Data for this year are for the period 1 April 1996–31 March 1997. No data for later years had been published at the time of going to press.

Challenges to the System

Over the years, the Scottish system has had to face a number of significant challenges. Three of these are of special importance for the purposes of this chapter; they may be described briefly as the law and order challenge, the new orthodoxy challenge, and the rights challenge.

The Law and Order Challenge

When the Thatcher government was elected in 1979 on a "law and order" ticket, it had to decide what to do about the Scottish Children's Hearings system, which of course was based on a completely different philosophy. The government chose to issue a Consultative Memorandum which, while issuing ritual praise of the hearings system, also commented that a number of criticisms had been made to the effect that the hearings did not have sufficient measures of discipline and punishment. Hence, the memorandum sought views from interested parties on questions such as whether the hearings should have the power to impose fines or community service on children, or to require parents to enter into recognizances, or pay "caution money" on behalf of their children. Reaction to the memorandum among those con-

Table 15.7

Children under a current supervision requirement who were originally referred on offense grounds, showing nature of current placement, Scotland, 1908–1996

	Nonresidential Placement	Residential School	Other Residential Placement	Total and *N*
1980	67	20	13	100 (4,634)
1981	69	19	12	100 (4,403)
1982	69	18	13	100 (4,107)
1983	70	17	13	100 (3,718)
1984	70	17	13	100 (3,442)
1985	72	15	12	100 (3,409)
1986	76	13	12	100 (3,616)
1987	75	14	11	100 (3,225)
1988	76	13	12	100 (3,160)
1989	73	15	12	100 (2,910)
1990	75	13	11	100 (2,917)
1991	76	14	11	100 (2,998)
1992	76	14	9	100 (2,810)
1993	75	14	11	100 (2,806)
1994	76	14	11	100 (2,877)
1995	75	14	11	100 (2,926)
1996*	76	14	10	100 (2,810)

Note: Data given are for males and females combined, showing the nature of the current placement on 30 June in the year shown. Figures are in percentages.

*Data for this year are for the period 1 April 1996–31 March 1997. No data for later years had been published at the time of going to press.

cerned with the hearings system was almost uniformly hostile (Lockyer and Stone 1998, 69–71), and shortly afterwards the government quietly withdrew its suggestions. The episode was a powerful demonstration, only a decade after the foundation of the Kilbrandon-based system, of how quickly it had become a valued and distinctive part of Scotland's sociopolitical culture. Interestingly, when the Conservative government again turned to a law and order approach in England in the 1990s, that philosophy was mirrored in the Scottish Office, but ministers were careful not to include the Children's Hearings system in any proposals for change in Scottish criminal justice. The Kilbrandon approach has therefore clearly become sufficiently embedded in Scottish official life that it can relatively easily shake off crude frontal challenges to its philosophy. Whether it is also resilient enough to meet subtler challenges remains an open question. But before we turn to that, one other more direct challenge—that from the "new orthodoxy" juvenile justice movement—must be considered.

The Challenge from the New Orthodoxy

The juvenile justice movement in England was, as we have seen, primarily a practitioner movement in social services departments, linked to academics at Lancaster University. Through practitioner networks, English juvenile justice workers began to influence some Scottish colleagues, and eventually a few fairly prominent members of the juvenile justice movement moved north to middle-management positions in Scottish Social Work Departments. There they sought to introduce "new orthodoxy" thinking into some aspects of Scottish practice. The results were personally painful for many of those concerned, but from a theoretical point of view, they are extremely instructive.

The most celebrated conflict arose in the Fife Region, where the Social Work Department (SWD) was persuaded in 1985 to adopt a child care policy document that relied heavily on juvenile justice movement thinking. Subsequent implementation of this policy led, in time, to a serious loss of confidence in the SWD by the Fife Children's Panel.[62] The eventual outcome was an official inquiry lasting three and one-half years ("the longest-running inquiry into the field of child care in Britain" [Lockyer and Stone 1998a]) and a report running to no less than seven hundred pages (Kearney 1992).

Essentially, the conflict that led to the Fife inquiry can be said to have turned on alternative understandings of the concept of minimum intervention. We have seen that the Kilbrandon philosophy required reporters and hearings not to intervene compulsorily in a child's life unless such compulsory measures of care were really thought to be necessary in the interests of the child's welfare. Such an approach in effect imposes a "minimum necessary conditions for intervention" test, and, over time, reporters have applied such a test more stringently (see table 15.6). But an approach of this kind is, despite the linguistic similarities, significantly different from the "minimum intervention" test adopted by the juvenile justice movement. That test was closer in spirit to Schur's (1973) famous "radical nonintervention" philosophy, and, as we have noted, the juvenile justice movement began from the presupposition that "the helping professions are sometimes a major source of hindrance to young offenders, because they pathologise them, intervene in their lives too readily and too intensively, and may therefore unwittingly encourage courts to use institutional disposals if and when welfare-based community treatments eventually fail" (Bottoms et al. 1990, 3).

Emphatically, such a view was not shared by the Kilbrandon Committee, nor has it ever been held by the great majority of members of Scottish Children's Panels, in Fife or elsewhere. The Scottish juvenile justice system does indeed formally endorse the principle of not intervening compulsorily unless that intervention is perceived to be in the child's best interests; but where a compulsory intervention is made, in Scotland this is generally perceived positively, within the kind of "child-conservationist" perspective that is characteristic of welfare-oriented juvenile justice systems:

> The "welfare model" is associated with . . . protectionist policies. . . . From this perspective, because of their immaturity, children cannot be regarded as rational or self-determining agents, but rather are subject to and are the product of the environment within which they live. Any criminal action on their part can therefore be attributed to dysfunctional elements in that environment. The task of the justice system then, is to identify, treat, and cure the underlying social causes of offending. (Alder and Wundersitz 1994, 3)

By contrast, the Inquiry Report adjudged that in the Fife SWD a "dogma" had been created, advocating diversion from any form of compulsory measure as a matter of principle, and, where such advocacy failed, arguing for "keeping children at home and out of residential care, almost at any cost" (Lockyer and Stone 1998a, 92). The Fife SWD's policy theoretically allowed residential care to be deployed as a last resort, but the inquiry found that the climate of opinion created toward this option was "almost universally negative" (Kearney 1992, 589).

In the end, therefore, and despite superficial agreement about the value of a principle of minimum intervention, the divergences between the Kilbrandon-based system and the juvenile justice movement could not be reconciled. The Inquiry Report ruled against the Fife SWD, commenting in a crucial passage that the region's policy constituted a "simplified approach," applied in a "rigid and dogmatic manner," which "gravely inhibited the discretion of the professional social worker" to make welfare-based recommendations (Kearney 1992, 616).[63] From the point of view of a traditional, welfare-based juvenile justice system, such a judgment was inevitable. The Children's Hearing system was therefore able to shake off a significant frontal challenge from a noninterventionist, left-wing group, just as it had defeated a challenge from the law and order right wing of British politics. But it is interesting that the former challenge had been harder to defeat than had the latter; and, as we shall see later, the juvenile justice movement's challenge has also had some lasting effects on the Scottish system, in a way that the Thatcherite challenge has not. Just as interesting is that the new orthodoxy challenge was successfully resisted in Scotland well *before* the Labour government of 1997 decided to confront head-on the philosophy of the juvenile justice movement in England.

Challenges from a Human Rights Perspective

From an international perspective, the juvenile justice reforms in both England and Scotland in the late 1960s seem in some ways distinctly anomalous. The sixties, after all, was the decade of many demands for freedom from previous restrictions, perhaps most notably encapsulated in the civil rights movement in the United States. In the sphere of juvenile justice, the sixties saw in the United States a serious rebellion against the *parens patriae* approach of the socialized juvenile tribunals established early in the century, and witnessed also the entrenchment of rights and safeguards for child defendants, including the right to counsel as established in the pathbreaking case of *In re Gault.*[64] Though there were indeed reasons for the adoption in the United Kingdom in the 1960s of welfare-based approaches (see concluding section), from an international perspective it was clearly only a matter of time before the Scottish juvenile justice system would become subject to criticism from a rights-based perspective.

I concentrate here only on the most celebrated rights-based challenge that the Scottish system has faced, which concerns the issue of legal representation (or its equivalent).[65] To American readers, it will certainly seem strange that, a third of a century after the *Gault* case, controversy can still rage around the in-principle desirability of a right to publicly assisted legal representation in a juvenile justice tribunal—but in Scotland that is exactly the position at the time of writing.[66]

As noted earlier, parents and children in the Scottish system may ask anyone to come with them to a hearing to speak on their behalf during the discussions, such a person being known as a "representative." Representatives may be (but do not have to be) lawyers, but there is no provision for publicly funded legal representation at Children's Hearings.[67]

Empirical observations of the hearings system have, however, consistently shown, from the 1970s to the 1990s, that at less than 5 percent of hearings are parents/children accompanied by a representative, and interview studies suggest that the vast majority of parents are not aware of their right to ask such a person to attend (see, especially, Martin, Fox, and Murray 1981; Hallett and Murray 1998). Moreover, although families do indeed participate in discussions in hearings to a greater extent than is common in juvenile courts, yet much of that participation can be characterized as *responsive* rather than *interactive* (that is to say, it mostly consists in answering questions put by panel members), and most such responsive remarks are usually quite short (Hallett and Murray 1998). Given this, Hallett and Murray conclude from their research that "the limited contribution of the children and young persons in the . . . observed hearings, and the comments of some of the children and young people interviewed following them . . . are indicative of a need for greater representation within the Children's Hearing system" (100). As these authors point out, however, given that the hearings are, by deliberate design, treatment tribunals only, it does not necessarily follow that such representation should be by professionally qualified lawyers.

Standard objections in Scotland to legal or other representation at hearings are that it would change the atmosphere by making the proceedings more adversarial and that it would significantly discourage children and parents from expressing their own views, so preventing panel members from engaging directly with them. These are reasonable points of concern, but they are not necessarily decisive on the principle of representation, since lawyers and other representatives can fulfill their duties in more than one way, and there are other tribunals in the United Kingdom which allow publicly funded legal representation while also insisting on the need for tribunal members to be able to speak directly with the defendant or plaintiff.[68] Those who argue against publicly funded representation may also fail to note the existence of some situations in Children's Hearings where legal (or similar) representation seems clearly necessary.[69] By its present policy stance on this issue, the Children's Hearings system makes itself look, to many, inescapably paternalist—an image certainly not contradicted by the system's failure, according to the research studies, to communicate to most parents and children the fact that they can, under the existing rules, be accompanied by a representative. Arguably, also, the system is rendering itself unnecessarily vulnerable from an international perspective.[70] The rights-based challenge for effective representation has not yet proved successful, but it seems much more likely to be eventually successful than either the "law and order" or the "new orthodoxy" challenges.[71]

An Overview of a Welfare System in Action in Offense-Based Cases

The information presented in this section is mainly based on empirical research into the Scottish system. The research base is, however, not extensive, and the main studies have been conducted at very different times. To set the context for what follows, a brief initial description of the principal research contributions is therefore appropriate.

A very early project was conducted by Allison Morris and Mary McIsaac (1978), based on fieldwork in two areas in 1972–73. The authors' interpretation of their data has proved to be controversial, but their research has remained as a continual reference point for later studies. A larger and more nationally representative research project was then carried out by Martin, Fox, and Murray (1981), with fieldwork in 1978–79, and until very recently this was universally regarded as the benchmark study of the Scottish system. Two years later Stewart Asquith (1983) published his doctoral dissertation, based on fieldwork conducted in the mid-1970s. This was a small study, but it is of special interest for the present chapter because, uniquely in the published literature, it provides a direct empirical comparison of the English and Scottish systems, based on fieldwork in two local areas, one on each side of the border.

There was then a long hiatus, during which a few papers on particular aspects of the Scottish system were published, but no major research was attempted. This fallow period finally ended when the Scottish Office commissioned two linked research projects that were carried out during the years 1994–97. One of these, based at the University of Stirling, focused on processual aspects of the Children's Hearing system (Hallett and Murray 1998); while the other, based at Edinburgh University, consisted primarily of a thorough statistical description of a representative sample of cases dealt with by reporters and hearings, including some data of a longitudinal character (Waterhouse et al. 2000). Using these sources, several aspects of the Scottish system can be illuminated. We begin by considering the two key decision-making points within the system (see figure 15.1), namely, the work of reporters and of the hearings themselves.

Reporters' Decision Making

The Reporters to Children's Hearings in Scotland hold a special place in this mixed juvenile justice and child care system. Initially employed by local government, since the 1995 Act (see note 16) reporters have been grouped together into a national service. Their numbers, however, are small; in the mid-1990s there were only 140 reporter posts in the whole of Scotland (Kuenssberg and Miller 1998, 173). Their tasks are also challengingly diverse. Some aspects of reporters' functions have an inescapably legal aspect: for example, formally referring a case to a Children's Hearing, citing the appropriate grounds, or, in the event of a remit or reference from the Sheriff Court to the Hearing, explaining to the panel members exactly what are the respective legal powers and duties of the hearing and the court. At other times, however, reporters are required to make judgments that are delicately personal (for example, assessing whether, in the case of a child suffering from parental neglect, the additional guidance that seems needed would, from the perspective of the child's best interests, be optimally provided on a voluntary or a compulsory basis). Given this diversity of tasks, it is not surprising that reporters have been recruited from varied professional backgrounds: in the mid-1990s, one-half were lawyers, one-third from a background in professional social work, and the remainder from other professions, including teaching and nursing (Kuenssberg and Miller 1998, 174). The fifty-four reporters in Hallett and Murray's (1998) broad, nationally representative sample were predominantly female (63 percent) and young (70 percent were under forty-five).

Martin, Fox, and Murray (1981) studied reporters' decision making in offense-based cases, using a multivariate statistical technique. In cases where the child had been referred for the first time on offense grounds, the variables that were significantly associated with reporters' decisions to send the child to a hearing were the number of offenses alleged within the referral; known family problems; poor school attendance; and behavior problems at school. For the "recidivist" sample, all these factors were again significant (though with the "family problems" variable showing a weaker association within this group); additionally, however, the seriousness of the main offense alleged was highly significant. The researchers therefore concluded that reporters seemed to display, in offense-based cases, a "constant attempt to balance . . . the seriousness of the offence or offences committed against an inevitably subjective and indirect estimate of the strengths and weaknesses of the child's home and school situation. Neither set of considerations has an overall dominance" (Martin, Fox, and Murray 1981, 91).

Fifteen years later, in offense-based cases, Hallett and Murray's research similarly showed the influence of a mixture of offense-related and of social factors on reporters' decisions, with school-related issues again prominent (1998, ch. 2). However, these researchers' rather different (more qualitative) methodology highlighted the considerable importance of one factor that had not been included in Martin, Fox, and Murray's statistical analysis, namely, the cooperation or otherwise of families. Cooperation or noncooperation was not of great significance in cases where reporters decided to take no further action, such cases being generally governed by other criteria. However, parental cooperation was a factor of often crucial importance where reporters had to decide between referral to a hearing and referral to the Social Work Department for voluntary advice and guidance: if parents were cooperative, voluntary advice was more likely to be the outcome. Even here, however, there was a complication, in offense-based cases, because "referrals of a serious nature usually led to a hearing [since seriousness] outweighed other considerations," including that of parental cooperation (Hallett and Murray 1998, 38). This last finding, taken together with the other research results summarized above, highlights a pervasive apparent tension within the Scottish Children's Hearing system as it deals with offense-based cases—a tension between the system's official ideology (which strongly prioritizes the child's welfare needs) and the seemingly commonsense requirement of taking some notice of the offenses that have brought the child to official attention. We return to these issues later.

Before leaving reporters' decision making, we should finally note that reporters do not make their decisions in a vacuum. From the outset of the Scottish system, every reporter has had a statutory power to carry out "such initial investigation as he may think necessary," and in practice reporters use this power extensively. In the sample analyzed by Hallett and Murray (1998), reporters formally sought additional information in nearly three-quarters of all cases; where they did not do so, this was usually because there had already been a recent hearing or referral which rendered additional information unnecessary. Requests by reporters for further information are principally directed toward the Social Work Department (who are consulted in almost all cases), the school, and the health authorities. In responding to such requests, social workers from the SWD commonly make a recommendation to the reporter, as well as providing the relevant information, and in Hallett and Murray's (1998, 14) research such recommendations were followed by the reporter in the great majority of cases (86 percent). Reporters, however, are keen to emphasize their professional independence and judgment. They may often follow social work advice, but, as one of them put it, "I like to come to my own view of things in my own way" (Hallett and Murray 1998, 33).

Children's Hearings

The second key decision point in the system is the Children's Hearing itself. Recall that a hearing is always attended by three members of the Children's Panel, the reporter, and a social worker, plus the child and his or her parent(s). Sometimes one or two others attend, but it is rare for a hearing to meet with more than seven non–family members present (Hallett and Murray 1998, 41). In Hallett and Murray's study, the median duration of a hearing was 31–45 minutes. Asquith (1983, 185) reported that, in his study areas, the average hearing took significantly longer than the average case in the English juvenile court.

The Children's Panel members who conduct hearings are lay members of the public. In this regard, the Children's Hearing, although not a court, is continuous with the tradition in Britain whereby the lower criminal courts have so often been presided over by lay people (lay magistrates in England, and to a lesser extent in Scotland; "bailies" in Scotland). The difference, of course, is that Children's Panel members are recruited specifically to deal with children, within an overtly welfare-based system; hence, it is not surprising that, by comparison with the English magistracy, Children's Panels have recruited a higher proportion of members with an occupational background in the spheres of health, education, and welfare (Asquith 1983, 134; and cf. note 8 above on the London magistracy in the early to mid-twentieth century).[72]

Lay tribunals, of course, may from time to time require expert assistance or prompting on points of law or procedure, a function that is fulfilled within the English magistrates courts by an official known as the clerk to the justices. In the Scottish Children's Hearing system, surprisingly, no one formally occupies such a role, though in practice the reporter is quite often, at the beginning of a hearing, referred to by the chair as being "here to keep us right on any legal matters" (Martin, Fox, and Murray 1981, 277). The research evidence is, however, that of all the participants, reporters make the smallest number of oral contributions at hearings themselves (Hallett and Murray 1998, 51). Martin, Fox, and Murray, in their early study, expressed disappointment that reporters were not more proactive in keeping hearings in line with prescribed procedural standards (277). Fifteen years later, hearings' adherence to procedural rules, such as informing parents and children of their rights, had generally improved by comparison with the earlier findings, yet the research data still indicated that there was significant room for improvement (Hallett and Murray 1988, 124). However, "while some Reporters did contribute to Hearings by prompting or correcting panel chairmen about families' rights, there were many instances in which they did not" (Hallett and Murray 1998, 52). Inevitably, findings such as these strengthen the case for Children's Hearings to reconsider the question of legal or other representation.

Over the years, there have been a number of interesting observational studies of Children's Hearings. Martin, Fox, and Murray (1981, ch. 8) attempted to characterize styles of dialogue in 301 observed hearings. They found that, while in over 90 percent of cases there were some passages of dialogue that were "encouraging [and] non-directive," the hearings also contained some exchanges where panel members demonstrated attitudes or behavior such as "shocked [or] indignant, [trying] to elicit guilt [or] shame" (present in 36 percent of cases); "interrogating [or] demanding" (44 percent); "exhorts to shape up [or] threatens with legal consequences" (35 percent); and even "sarcastic [or] contemptuous" (22 percent). A consumer study of 105 children, undertaken as part of the Martin, Fox, and Murray study but published separately, suggested that these dialogue styles were directly related to children's subsequent reactions: for example, those exposed to the "sarcastic/ contemptuous" style were more likely to expect the police subsequently to hold their appearance at a hearing against them, while anticipation of stigma from potential employers was associated with having been on the receiving end of the "exhorting/threatening" approach (Erickson 1982). The author of this study accordingly suggested in her conclusions that "while the potential of Hearings to socialise children in a positive, integrating way to community values was realised to some extent, the capacity to instil or reinforce feelings of rejection or alienation in youthful offenders was also documented" (104).

As Erickson admitted, her study would have been stronger had it contained an element of follow-up; but her explicit reference at one point (1982, 94) to clients' perceptions of legitimacy and fairness anticipates a literature that has richly elaborated such themes in the years since her study was conducted (see especially Tyler 1990; Sparks, Bottoms, and Hay 1996; Paternoster et al. 1997).

Later studies of dialogue in hearings are broadly consistent with the findings of Martin, Fox, and Murray's research. Alison Petch (1988), for example, conducted a consumer study of parents' reactions to 100 Children's Hearings. Before interviewing the parents, she first attended the relevant hearings and classified them according to the "dominant characteristics" of the proceedings. On this basis, 25 were rated as "supportive, encouraging" and 6 as constituting an "open exchange" between panel members and parents/children; but 16 were rated as "formal [or] ritual," 11 as "indecisive [or] amateur"; 11 as "challenging [or] humiliating"; and 9 as "probing." In the most recent research, Hallett and Murray (1998, ch. 3) counted all speech acts in a sample of 60 observed hearings and found that panel members spoke most frequently, followed in descending order by children, mothers, and social workers, with reporters and fathers (often absent) as the least frequent contributors. However, the high ranking of children in this "contribution count" should not be misunderstood, for in no less than three-quarters of all their contributions, children actually spoke one line or less (e.g., a monosyllabic response). Underlying these figures is the important fact, already alluded to, that the typical dialogue in a Children's Hearing is not a naturally flowing discussion between equals; rather, "the contribution of panel members was characterised far more by *questions* (to families and professionals), and the contribution of children and young people (and to a lesser extent, parents) far more by *answers*" (Hallett and Murray 1998, 47; emphasis added).

Some data from Asquith's (1983, ch. 8) research enables us more clearly to understand the character of the dialogue in Children's Hearings by comparison with English juvenile courts. In the Scottish Hearings observed by Asquith, there were (overall) slightly more oral statements made by panel members than by others to panel members (3,118 to 2,815); and—a point of special significance—more than 90 percent of the dialogue in each direction was made among panel members, children, and parents. Taken together with the Hallett/Murray results, this suggests an *inquisitorial, interrogatory* procedure in the Scottish Hearings, with panel members taking a very active role, and the dialogue focused firmly around the panel member/child/parent nexus. By contrast, in the English juvenile court that Asquith studied, the magistrates were much more passive: 915 oral statements were made to them, but only 159 statements were made by them (an imbalance of nearly 6:1). Most of the statements made to magistrates (over three-quarters) were made by those representing the prosecution and (if the defendant was legally represented) the defense; parents and children contributed only one-sixth of these statements. When magistrates did speak, it was predominantly (68 percent) to parents or children, but in general magistrates were neutral receivers of information, not taking a very proactive role. In an *accusatorial, court-based* criminal justice system, none of this is actually very surprising, but the data do point up quite sharply the markedly different character of the dialogue in the Scottish Children's Hearings.

As previously noted, Asquith's data also suggested that the average Scottish Hearing takes longer than the average English court case, a point that is reflected in the markedly different *N*s of the statement counts above.[73] Since parents and children contribute *more often,* within hearings that are *longer,* it is obvious that they participate more in Scottish Hearings than in English court cases, even if much of their participation is very brief. Moreover, we must remember that Hearings do routinely "provide an *opportunity* for families to contribute if they wish to and feel able to" (Hallett and Murray 1998, 47; emphasis in original), an opportunity which a minority of families take up to such an extent that Petch (1988) described the main characteristic of six of her observed Hearings as "parent-dominated."

What might be described as the "staccato participation" of children in the dialogue of hearings is not necessarily seen as a problem by the children themselves. Indeed, in Erickson's (1982) study, the great majority of interviewed children expressed satisfaction with their participation levels, regardless of whether this participation was rated by independent observers as high, medium, or low. In the same research, half the children expressed the view that their input had had some effect on the decision (98), and three-quarters said they had understood everything that had gone on (96), a finding that notably contrasted, to the advantage of the Scottish system, with the few consumer studies of English juvenile courts at that date (e.g., Morris and Giller 1977). Where children did not understand, it was generally because panel members either used "big words," or adopted a style in which "interjections were delivered rapidly, with panel members interrupting the child or each other" (96). From these findings, Erickson (1982, 97) generalized by saying that hearings were best understood when both the *pace* and the *content* of the dialogue was controlled, with proceedings conducted in "a relaxed and orderly fashion . . . with clear and precise vocabulary."

In the more recent commissioned research, both Hallett and Murray (1998, ch. 4) and Waterhouse et al. (2000, ch. 6) carried out consumer studies of parents and children, but in each case with very small samples. The main results are by now familiar: the system was seen as generally fair; the sense of being a participant was valued; both parents and children felt they were listened to; participation was sometimes inhibited by nervousness, or by some panel members seeming to be intimidating or antagonistic; understanding was generally good, but panels' language style could be a problem; and parents and children were not always informed about their legal rights.

What, finally, of the position of social workers in Children's Hearings? Their role is to provide formal written reports on the child's social background, to speak to these reports at the hearing, and thereafter to participate in the dialogue as they consider appropriate, in the child's best interests. Social workers' written reports normally contain formal recommendations about the future treatment of the child, and over the years research has consistently shown that such recommendations are usually accepted by the hearing (Hallett and Murray 1998, 57, citing also earlier research studies). Yet despite this congruence of views on the outcomes of cases, relationships between social workers and panel members are not always good. Indeed, Hallett and Murray (1998) reported that social worker/panel member relationships were, in their research study, more problematic than any other professional relationships within the hearings system (78) and were characterized by "a considerable degree of conflict" (123). There were indications of these tensions in many of the observed hearings, with panel members "holding social workers to account, who were in turn defensive" (123). Using other data from their observational study, Hallett and Murray further reported that "social workers more frequently told Panel members what the families' views were than facilitated families' participation in the Hearings" (51).

Looking back over the research findings reported in this subsection, two points stand out. The first is the issue of *participation,* which is clearly valued by children and parents, even if actual participation levels are not always high. This is a theme that is highly congruent with the research literature on legitimacy and procedural justice: generally speaking, if participants feel they have had an opportunity to have their say, and have been treated with respect in the procedures, they are more likely to regard the whole process as fair, even if the outcome is not wholly to their liking (Tyler 1990). But, secondly, it seems that respect is not in fact always delivered in the Scottish juvenile system, perhaps principally because the interrogatory, inquisitional format of the hearings system can too easily result in panel members' adopting, on occasion, intimidatory styles or inappropriately complex language, and/or neglecting to tell parents and children about their assigned rights within the system. Moreover, since reporters are essentially passive within hearings, social workers are quite often on the defensive vis-à-vis panel members, and legal or other representation is for practical purposes nonexistent, there may be few countervailing forces that can be mobilized to restrain panel members on the minority of occasions when they may seem to exercise their powers or presence too forcefully or weightily.

Deeds in a Needs-Based System

It is time to consider more fully a central conceptual dilemma, previously highlighted, about the way that offenses are considered within the Scottish system. In theory, a criminal offense is simply one of the possible grounds that, if proved or accepted, might bring a child before a hearing; and once a child is before a hearing, the paramount consideration for the members of the panel is his or her welfare need. This approach therefore seems, on the face of it, to place almost no emphasis on the criminal act (of theft, violence, or whatever) in offense-based cases. That is in one sense unsurprising: as was noted in the introduction to this chapter, the welfare-oriented tradition in juvenile justice has always tried to place emphasis "not on the act done by the child, but on the social facts and circumstances that are really the inducing causes of the child's appearance in court" (Flexner and Baldwin 1915, 6). But is such an approach really sustainable in practice?[74]

Morris and McIsaac's (1978) early research caused controversy in Scotland by delivering a robustly negative answer to this question. With the benefit of hindsight, their analysis can be seen to have been partly wrong, and partly right. One claim that these authors made was that "the type of tribunal (juvenile court or welfare tribunal) is largely unimportant. What is crucial is the philosophy underlying that tribunal and the ideology of its practitioners" (Morris and McIsaac 1978, 111). One can see how such a comment might come to be made. Both England and Scotland staff their juvenile justice tribunals with *lay persons,* who adjudicate on a part-time basis and who inevitably bring to their adjudications some aspects of their ordinary, everyday experiences as citizens. It might appear, therefore, not to make a great deal of difference whether these lay people are assembled together as a juvenile court or as a Children's Hearing, especially if they are dealing with offense cases, where some kind of response by the tribunal to the child's delinquent act might seem necessary. Indeed, Allison Morris herself developed such a claim about the Scottish system (in a later publication with other coauthors), arguing that, notwithstanding the Kilbrandon philosophy, in practice the Scottish system had delivered

> the re-emergence of the principle of the offence as the primary criterion of intervention. . . . Although treatment was the *official* goal priority, control of the child's behaviour became the *operational* goal priority. Research suggests that the Hearings, in fact, operate on tariff principles just as in the juvenile courts. . . . What is promoted, therefore, as a welfare jurisdiction is no more than a replication of the practice south of the border. (Morris et al. 1980, 67; emphasis in original)

This line of thinking, at least in this bold form, was convincingly refuted by Asquith's (1983) small comparative study of the English and Scottish systems. As previously noted, the *selection processes* for magistrates and panel members attracted different kinds of applicants in the two countries, particularly because the tasks of Scottish panel members are, while those of English magistrates are not, confined to juvenile cases. Moreover, the *post-selection training and experience* was different, with magistrates' training and experience not only obliging them to consider how to adjudicate on issues of guilt or innocence (an issue reserved, in Scotland's dual system, for the sheriff court, not the hearing), but also placing more emphasis on factors such as how to "think judicially." The net result was that the type of the tribunal was in practice not at all irrelevant for the lay people who presided at the adjudications; indeed, the type of the tribunal actually helped to shape what Morris and McIsaac called "the ideology of its practitioners." Asquith (1983) demonstrated empirically that what he termed the attitudinal "frames of relevance" of Scottish panel members' thinking were substantially more welfare-oriented than were those of English juvenile magistrates, and there was also more internal agreement among the Scottish sample than among the English sample about the importance of welfare factors. In dealing with offense-based cases, Asquith's small empirical study of actual decisions also suggested that issues such as the imputed *intentionality* of the offender and the assessed *seriousness* of the child's delinquent act were of substantially greater direct significance in decision-making thought processes for English magistrates than for Scottish panel members (Asquith 1983, 167). Clearly, therefore, Morris et al.'s claim that the Children's Hearing system is simply "a replication of the practice south of the border" cannot be sustained.

But what about the further claim that the Scottish system *in practice* endorses, in offense-based cases, "the principle of the offence as the primary criterion of intervention" (Morris et al. 1980; see also Morris and McIsaac 1978, 136)? Or, to put the matter another way, has the Scottish system, in offense-based cases, in effect adopted a *tariff principle,* notwithstanding the official ideology of "need, not deed"?

The evidence on this point is both complex and intriguing. Asquith (1983), for example, notwithstanding the sharp attitudinal differences between his English magistrates and Scottish panel members, found that in actual cases, when the type of offense, the number of charges, and the number of previous offenses had been held constant, there were relatively few differences in the way that English magistrates and Scottish panel members operated. Moreover, for the Scottish panel members "social protection and seriousness [of offense] were in fact significantly more important for decision-making in relation to cases with more than one [criminal] charge than for those with only one" (168). Asquith's explanation for these various findings is that offense factors are in practice relevant in both English and Scottish decision making, but in Scotland they are reinterpreted within a welfare-based frame of relevance.

Other researchers have reached broadly similar conclusions. In the most recent research study, Hallett and Murray (1998) comment that "whether [Scottish juvenile justice] has been operating a tariff system" has been a widely discussed issue for twenty-five years. They divide their own discussion of this point between reporters' and hearings' decision making. As to the former, there was clear evidence of the importance of offense-based factors, but there were "many exceptions" to this generalization, and in any event reporters often explained the apparent tariff system by using a "best interests" justification. As one reporter put it, "I know we're not supposed to consider the child's deeds, but it's also in the child's interests to be, to feel, responsible for taking serious actions" (Hallett and Murray 1998, 19).

When it came to the observed hearings in Hallett and Murray's study, in just under a third of all cases (which included care and protection as well as offense-grounds cases), "much of the 'talk' was about issues more readily associated . . . with the criminal justice system," such as the seriousness of the offense, the protection of the public, warnings and tariffs (53). However, the authors comment that when such discourse was in evidence, it was "almost invariably mixed with welfare talk." Hallett and Murray thus endorsed the view of an earlier (and less empirical) researcher: "In offence and truancy cases, there is a constant balancing of the non-punitive and the punitive. Help is offered, advice given, but 'the consequences' of non-co-operation are constantly emphasized" (Adler 1985, 93).

In conclusion, then, it seems clear that deeds are in practice by no means irrelevant within the Scottish welfare-based system of juvenile justice. The principle that the welfare of the child is paramount is wholeheartedly endorsed by most official participants in the system, but in offense-based cases they do not usually ignore the child's offense. Often they will reinterpret offense-related factors into welfarist language;[75] but not infrequently more overt comments about the delinquent act may be made, or the adverse consequences of further offending may be explicitly threatened. There are real tensions here, and they seem to be tensions inherent within the welfare model of juvenile justice itself. The Scottish system has grappled seriously with the tensions, but it has not overcome them.

The Dual System: Hearings and Courts

As we saw earlier in this chapter, a central feature of the Kilbrandon Committee's conceptual framework was the division of labor between the sheriff courts (as adjudicators of disputed matters of fact and law relating to the alleged grounds for intervention) and the Children's Hearings (as treatment tribunals). How have these arrangements been working in practice?

The basic separation of functions seems to have been the subject of no adverse criticism in Scotland. Hallett and Murray (1998, 43–44) do, however, note with regret what they describe as the "inescapable formality" of the proceedings at the beginning of a hearing, when the grounds of referral are being put to families in legal language. They go on to question why Kilbrandon's separation of the adjudication from the disposal was not "followed to its logical conclusion," that is, "for the establishing of the grounds to be removed from the Hearing altogether,"[76] with the hearing only acquiring jurisdiction when grounds have been admitted or established. A revised procedure of this kind seems clearly worth considering: among other things, it would also avoid the administrative cumbersomeness of the present system, where a child denying a ground of referral first appears at a hearing, then goes to the sheriff court for the adjudication, then (if the ground is established) returns to the hearing for a discussion of treatment (see figure 15.1, and note also the case of Hamish, discussed earlier in this chapter).[77]

The so-called dual system creates some additional dilemmas as regards appeals against the decisions of hearings. In the 1968 Act, to protect a child's rights, an appeal to the sheriff court against the treatment decision of a Children's Hearing was permitted. However, if the appeal was considered to have merit, the sheriff's courses of action were restricted to (1) discharging the child or (2) remitting the case back to the hearing for reconsideration of the decision. This was to preserve the Kilbrandon principle that a court was not a good forum for making treatment decisions about disturbed or delinquent children. In the 1995 Act (see note 16) an additional power was given to the sheriff court, namely, that on successful appeal the sheriff may substitute for the actual decision of the Children's Hearing any decision that the hearing could lawfully have made when first determining the case. This new provision has been strongly criticized in Scotland; for example, Lockyer and Stone (1998a, 117) argue that it is bad in principle because it violates "the entire rationale for the Hearings system." In one sense, the issue is of little importance, because only a few cases will be affected by the change in the law;[78] but the theoretical and symbolic significance of the new provision should not be underestimated. In this context, it is also worth noting that the then government promoted the new power simply in order to avoid falling foul of the European Convention on Human Rights (and a member of the government which proposed the change actually argued that "sheriffs should think carefully" before using the newly enacted provision!) (quoted in Lockyer and Stone 1998a, 118). The real point illustrated by this episode is therefore the continuing tension, on a number of points, between the welfare-based hearings system and contemporary, rights-based conceptual frameworks.

We noted earlier that, as well as their role in adjudications and in appeals, the courts may be brought into play in one other way for those under sixteen in Scotland: in dealing with a prosecution brought by the procurator fiscal in a minority of (mostly serious) juvenile cases (see boxes 3 and 10 in figure 15.1). We also observed that this provision was a quite deliberately created exception to the Kilbrandon principle that the courts were not an appropriate forum in which to consider or decide issues relating to the treatment or disposal of a juvenile offender. An obvious danger, of course, with an alternative route of this kind is that it will become frequently used, but in practice this seems not to have happened. Indeed, in 1989 government guidance was issued to procurators fiscal to use their power to prosecute juveniles more restrictively (see note 21), and since that date the number of cases per annum in which children under sixteen have been successfully prosecuted has, in the whole of Scotland, never exceeded 200. In 1997, the most recent year for which full data is available, there were 148 successful prosecutions of those under sixteen, following which the courts remitted over a third of these cases (57) to the Children's Hearing for disposal (Scottish Office 1999, table 12).[79] But to end on a more somber note, the recent statistical research of Waterhouse et al. indicates that the small number of Scottish children who are, in the jargon, "jointly reported" (that is, referred simultaneously to the reporter and to the procurator fiscal; see figure 15.1) are in many ways a particularly difficult group:

> Most had experienced major social adversity, had a long history in the Children's Hearing system, and had been subject to supervision at some time in their lives. . . . [This administrative] category may prove an effective mechanism for identifying young people who are amongst the most "vulnerable" in terms of their social characteristics and offending behaviour. (Waterhouse et al. 2000, 96)

Dealing with such young offenders, the authors go on to state, raises "many dilemmas at the interface of the children's and adult systems" (96). This topic is indeed a central one for the Scottish welfare-based system, as the final subsection on Scotland shows.

Outcomes and Careers

Welfare-based juvenile justice systems have, historically, been the subject of criticism because of their *paternalistic interventionism,* leading to high levels of placement in restrictive environments on welfare grounds. Wheeler et al. (1968) found, for example, in a 1960s study of juvenile court judges in Boston, Massachusetts, that juvenile court judges with more liberal social and political attitudes, and a "humanistic, social welfare ideology" (55), actually ordered a greater degree of intervention in the lives of those adjudged delinquent than did more socially conservative judges—and they did so because they thought that they were acting in the interests of the young offenders. In its early days, the Scottish system was the subject of some adverse comments of this kind. The more recent operation of the system, however, provides little evidence to sustain such a criticism.

One key issue is the use of residential supervision. Unfortunately, the routinely published annual data on the decisions of Children's Hearings distinguish only between offense-based cases where the hearing discharges the child (box 17 in figure 15.1) and those where it makes a supervision requirement (boxes 18 *and* 19); but of course from the child's point of view "the more important distinction is whether [he or she] is permitted to remain at home" (Lockyer and Stone 1998a, 37). Data are, however, available on the nature of the current placement of all children subject to a supervision requirement whose original referral was on offense grounds (see table 15.7), and over the years these data show, first, a decline in the total *numbers* of such cases currently under supervision (notwithstanding—as is shown in the concluding section—an increase in referrals to reporters during the period in question); and, second, a declining *proportion* of residential placements (from 33 percent to 24 percent) among those who are currently subject to supervision. Thus, the actual *numbers in residential supervision* have declined substantially.

We saw earlier that the frontal challenge to the Scottish system from some "radical nonintervention" social work staff had been defeated, but it is clear nevertheless—from these data and from various accounts of the system—that aspects of their philosophical approach have had an aggregate effect on decision making within the system. Among other things, this has certainly prevented the contemporary Scottish system from sliding into what was described above as "paternalistic interventionism."

Lockyer and Stone have summarized the present situation on residential care as one which has seen

> over two and a half decades [a] growing preference for children to remain in family homes, with one or both parents or with substitute families rather than in institutional settings. . . . The almost doctrinal opposition to the use of residential care which developed in social work circles in the 1980s (never endorsed by Panel members) has dissolved to a point where good-quality residential care is seen as a "positive choice" for a limited number of children. . . . We believe that at present there are no great ideological differences between those [in Social Work Departments] who provide resources and propose their use and the Panel members who make disposals. (1998b, 264)

What, however, is left unsaid in this comment is that the influences have not all been in one direction. Extreme radical noninterventionism might indeed have been dissolved in response to (among other things) the opposition of panel members, but panel members have clearly themselves been influenced by the antiresidential stance of the post-1980 social workers. Thus, there has been no sign, in Scotland, that the system is willing to move toward any general stance of increased interventionism or punitiveness, as has been evidenced in England since 1993 (although some legitimate concerns have been expressed on the issue of secure accommodation within the Children's Hearings system; see Whyte 1998, 208–9). Indeed, there is even evidence that "no action" disposals are running at perhaps surprisingly high levels in Scotland; and north of the border there has never been any formal critique of the "no action" approach, akin to that mounted by the Audit Commission in England in 1996.[80]

An important part of the most recent Scottish Office–financed research into the Children's Hearings system focused on questions concerning the characteristics of children dealt with by the system and their contacts with various official agencies at different time periods. Within this research, some special attention was paid to children who are referred to the Children's Hearings system for their offending behavior (Waterhouse et al. 2000, ch. 5). Many of the results of this research will surprise no one who is familiar with the literature on longitudinal studies of criminal careers and on youth offending more generally (for a summary, see Farrington 1997). For example, the Scottish study found that the social characteristics of the children referred for offending reasons were "broadly similar" to the research cohort as a whole; and the social background of the child offenders was frequently evidenced by "family poverty, disruption, and difficulty," with many also having "experience of public care and poor educational experience." Many of the children were considered to have "broader and major care needs, in addition to offending" (95), and it was clear from the research data that many of the children eventually referred to the system—perhaps in their teens—for offending behavior had initially been referred at a younger age for reasons other than offending. Findings such as these do, of course, tend to provide empirical support for policy systems such as that in Scotland which offer close integration between the mechanisms for dealing with offenders and those for dealing with children in social need. By contrast—and this is now one of the strongest points of comparison between the two countries—in England since the 1980s offenders and children in need have been perceived as two very separate categories in policy terms, with only very limited links between those operating the two systems, even after the creation of Youth Offending Teams in the 1998 Crime and Disorder Act.

Consistently with much other criminological research, Waterhouse et al. (2000, 83) also found that a smallish group of offenders in the Scottish system is responsible for a disproportionate percentage of all the offenses known to have been committed by the cohort. Disturbingly, however, in the concurrent research by Hallett and Murray (1998), many professionals involved in the Children's Hearing system (reporters, panel members, and police officers), while very supportive of the hearings system in general, expressed little confidence in the system's capacity to deal well with those older juveniles who are persistent offenders. There seemed to be several reasons for this low confidence level, including a lack of appropriate resources to deal with this group;[81] "a reluctance on the part of some Panel members directly to address in Hearings the offences which constituted the grounds of referral" (93); and a feeling by some that the system is not philosophically well geared to dealing with persistent offenders, because there is too much stress on voluntary participation and cooperation, and not enough on discipline and punishment where that seems needed.

We have previously noted (though the point was not much emphasized) that the upper age limit for the initial jurisdiction of the Children's Hearing system is the child's sixteenth birthday (whereas, in England, the upper limit of the youth court's jurisdiction is now the eighteenth birthday). The difficulties reported in the previous paragraph suggest that any higher upper age limit for the Children's Hearing system might be difficult to sustain. Yet there has also for some time been widespread anxiety among relevant professionals in Scotland about the present arrangements whereby young persons aged sixteen and over are routinely dealt with in the adult criminal justice system,[82] and anxiety has also been expressed about the apparently high rates of custodial sentencing for young adults—including those aged sixteen and seventeen. These concerns are given weight by some findings in the recent research of Lorraine Waterhouse and her colleagues (2000). As part of this study, a representative sample of children referred to reporters in 1995 (for any reason, offense-based or otherwise) was followed up statistically for a period of two years. Of those aged sixteen or over by 1997, and for whom matching identifiers could be provided, over half had a conviction in an adult criminal court by 1997; and, of those acquiring one or more such convictions, no fewer than 28 percent had received a custodial sentence.[83] The evidence seems to suggest, therefore, that while the very close interrelation of the mechanisms for dealing with offense-based and other referrals at younger ages is a major strength of a welfare-based system such as that in Scotland, by the time the child/young person reaches older adolescence, a straightforwardly welfare-based system for dealing with offenders carries less confidence among professionals in the system and can perhaps (although this point is not yet definitively established) lead to especially severe interventions in the adult system for those who are seen to have "failed" in the juvenile system.

CONCLUSION

This short concluding section is divided into three parts. The first outlines briefly some very recent developments in the two countries, while the second presents some intriguing statistical comparisons. Finally, an overall assessment is made as to what can be learned from the comparative analysis that has been developed in this chapter.

Recent Developments

All of the more recent developments previously outlined in this chapter had been fully implemented when this volume went to press. That is not the case for the matters now to be mentioned, but to give a rounded picture it is important to briefly describe these further matters.

The package of youth justice changes contained in the Crime and Disorder Act of 1998 did not exhaust the energy of the new Labour government in trying to drive forward its reform of the English youth justice system. A further Act (the Youth Justice and Criminal Evidence Act 1999) was quickly introduced, enacting an additional reform which had been tentatively flagged in the 1997 policy paper *No More Excuses*. Like the 1998 reforms, this new measure will be piloted in a small number of local areas before it is "rolled out nationally"; hence, national implementation will not occur before 2002. Very briefly, the 1999 Act envisages that, except in the case of crimes considered by the court to merit a custodial sentence, when a young offender appears for the first time in the youth court *and pleads guilty* (a very important proviso), he or she will normally receive a sentence known as a referral order (and this will be a mandatory sentence if the defendant pleads guilty to all charges). If a referral order is made, there is then a referral of the young offender to a meeting of a so-called youth offender panel, consisting of two lay persons and one member of the local Youth Offending Team. As in Scotland, the child and his or her parents may take with them to such a meeting a representative, but no provision for publicly assisted legal representation is to be made. Unlike Scotland, but like the Family Group Conferences in New Zealand (see Maxwell and Morris 1993), any victim of the offense(s) will also be encouraged, but not required, to attend. Unlike the Scottish Children's Hearings, the youth offender panels will, at least in strict theory, have no power to make any orders. Rather, the purpose of the meeting of the panel is to seek to reach a contractual agreement with the offender for a "programme of behaviour the . . . principal aim of which is the prevention of reoffending by the offender" (sec. 8(1) of the 1999 Act). If such an agreement is reached, the panel then has a "continuing jurisdiction" to monitor the offender's performance of his or her obligations under the contract. If no agreement can be reached, the case then returns to the youth court for the young offender to be sentenced. It is anticipated, in government guidance, that reparation will loom large in the programs likely to be agreed upon between the youth offender panels and offenders.

Looked at in one way, these provisions may seem to be merely a further manifestation of the apparently never-ending process of continuous change that has characterized the English juvenile justice system for the last quarter-century. But in another sense, they mark a very new departure, with the arrival in the United Kingdom for the first time—at least in a national youth justice context[84]—of a policy based in significant part on the principles of restorative justice (for a full discussion of restorative justice, see Braithwaite 1999). The restorative justice movement in U.K. juvenile justice has also been given further impetus by a very recent development in Northern Ireland. The official Criminal Justice Review Group in that jurisdiction has recommended that restorative justice principles should underpin the new juvenile justice system that is proposed there as a part of the comprehensive political settlement after the Troubles of the last thirty years (Northern Ireland Office 2000, chs. 9 and 10).

Assuming that these various planned changes are implemented as intended, Scotland will then be the only jurisdiction in the United Kingdom with no significant restorative justice element in its juvenile justice system. As previously indicated (see note 1), under the new arrangements for devolved government in Scotland, day-to-day responsibility for the Scottish juvenile justice system passed to the new Scottish Executive in 1999. The Executive quickly established an Advisory Group on Youth Crime, which reported in 2000 (Scottish Executive 2000). In its quite short report, the Advisory Group proposed no fundamental changes to the Children's Hearing system, but it did highlight two matters of particular policy concern, both of which had been clearly identified by previous research. The first of these was the need for an improved handling of *persistent young offenders,* which the Advisory Group hoped could be achieved by an expansion of "the range and availability of effective, quality assessed, community-based interventions and programmes" (3), requiring substantial extra resources. Second, the Advisory Group noted that there were "widespread criticisms" of the existing procedures across the transition from the Children's Hearing system to the adult criminal justice system, a transition which the report characterized as "too abrupt." In particular, the Advisory Group commented,

> - The criminal justice system is described as too focused on adults and unable to deal with the particular aspects of youth offending.
> - The Children's Hearings system is described as too focused on welfare issues and unable to address the particular aspects of youth offending. (Scottish Executive 2000, 4)

To attempt to deal with this dual problem, the Advisory Group recommended, "for early implementation," a detailed feasibility study of a possible "bridging pilot scheme which would refer as many 16–17-year-olds as pos-

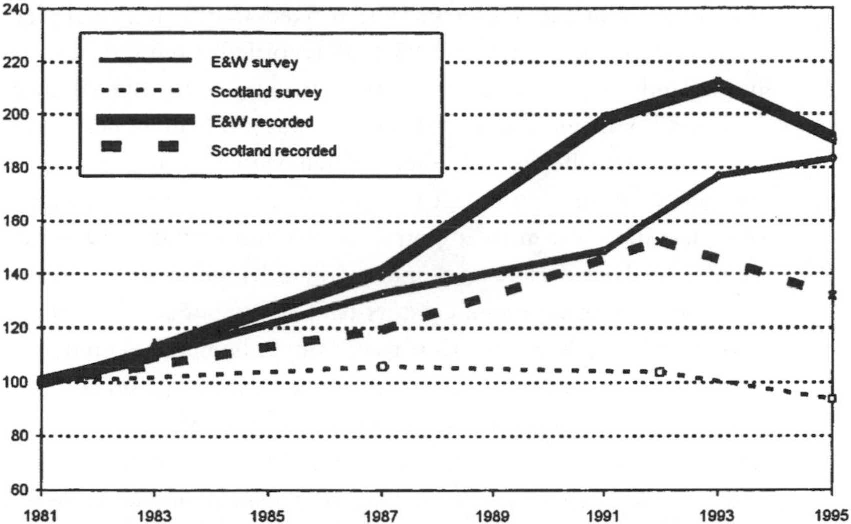

Fig. 15.3 Trends in survey and police-recorded crime: Scotland compared with England and Wales, 1981–95 (indexed, 1981 = 100). Taken from *Criminal Justice in Scotland,* ed. Peter Duff and Neil Hutton (Aldershot: Dartmouth, 1999), p. 33.

sible to the Hearings system" (3). This, and indeed all the recommendations of the Advisory Group, were immediately accepted by the Scottish Executive.

The next few years therefore seem likely to be full of interest for observers of U.K. youth justice. The Scottish system will attempt seriously to tackle two of its admitted problems: those of dealing with persistent young offenders and of the transition between the juvenile and adult systems. Meanwhile, English youth justice will introduce a version of restorative justice at a key strategic point in the system, namely, a child or young person's first appearance in the youth court; and, with the introduction of a restorative philosophy as the mainstay of juvenile justice in Northern Ireland, there may also be pressure on the Scottish system to begin to adopt a more victim-focused approach. Only time will tell.

Some Intriguing Statistical Comparisons

No mention has so far been made of crime trends in England and Scotland in the period under discussion, but these too have shown an interesting divergence since the early 1980s. For technical reasons, it is extremely difficult to compare crime rates in England and Scotland before 1981, but, in the light of some special research analyses, we can reasonably conclude that crime rates were broadly similar in the two countries in that year.[85] Since 1981, however, England has experienced a much sharper growth in crime. Figure 15.3, which is derived from a paper by Smith and Young (1999), shows this clearly by "indexing" all the data, that is, standardizing each of the data sources so that the rate for that data source in 1981 is fixed at 100, and then plotting comparative trends thereafter. In 1995, both recorded crime and survey crime rates in England had risen by over 80 percent from their 1981 levels; by contrast, in Scotland the increase in recorded crime was less than 40 percent, and survey crime rates actually showed a slight overall decrease from 1981 to 1995. These differences are much too large to be dismissed as statistically insignificant, and of course they raise many important problems of explanation for those interested in analyzing crime rates in the United Kingdom.

Some Scottish commentators have suggested as a hypothesis that one reason for these divergent crime trends might lie in the existence of the Scottish Children's Hearing system. This hypothesis, in its broad form, raises so many research questions that it would be extraordinarily difficult to test. There is, however, one issue that is related to the hypothesis, and for which data are readily obtainable from standard statistical sources. I have collated relevant data on this issue, as shown in table 15.8.

The data in question use the best statistics that we have on *juveniles formally processed for offense-related reasons* in the two jurisdictions since 1981. For England, these data include *persons found guilty* and *persons who have received a formal caution,* added together as an aggregate figure. For Scotland, the data cover simply *all persons referred to reporters for offense-based reasons*. Because the two countries' juvenile justice systems have different age cutoff points, and because they group some of their age categories differently in official statistics, it has been necessary to restrict the comparisons to young persons aged 12–15 inclusive, using disaggregated data for single ages.

The results shown in table 15.8 are surprising. In England, although the crime rate has risen quite sharply over this period, rates of official processing of 12–15-year-olds have dropped (sharply for males, marginally for females). This pattern is first discernible in the late 1980s (1986 onwards), at which date it is known to be largely attributable to certain special factors operating at that time, which were noted earlier in this chapter (i.e., the growth of informal police warnings and of CPS discontinuations; see notes 42 and 47 above). However, the decline in the rate of official processing has continued in England in the 1990s, for reasons that are much less obvious. By contrast, in Scotland referrals to reporters of 12–15-year-olds for offense-related reasons have *increased* during the same period, for both males and females, despite the fact that crime rates have risen much less quickly than in England. Obviously, the data in table 15.8 and in figure 15.3 show markedly different trends.

The comments above refer only to the *trends over time* shown in table 15.8. But it is also possible to compare directly the actual rates shown for the two countries, since both sets of data are expressed in the form "rates per 1,000 young persons in the age-group." Looking at the data in this way, they show reasonably similar rates for the two countries in the early 1980s; by the mid-

Table 15.8

Selected indices of offense-based formal processing of young persons per 1,000 population in the age group, England and Scotland, 1980–1998

	England: Males				Scotland: Males				England: Females				Scotland: Females			
	Age 12	Age 13	Age 14	Age 15	Age 12	Age 13	Age 14	Age 15	Age 12	Age 13	Age 14	Age 15	Age 12	Age 13	Age 14	Age 15
A 1980–82	34	48	67	82	31	48	73	82	11	16	18	17	5	10	16	17
B 1983–85	34	51	70	85	35	56	82	91	11	17	20	19	5	10	16	18
C 1986–88	27	42	61	76	36	59	94	110	8	12	17	18	6	13	21	23
D 1989–91	23	36	53	68	36	57	91	115	6	11	16	17	6	13	22	24
E 1992–93	22	33	49	64	34	57	85	103	8	15	21	20	8	16	23	28
F 1994–96	18	30	45	60	38	59	87	103	8	15	19	17	10	19	28	30
G 1997–98	16	26	40	55	*	*	*	*	5	10	15	17	*	*	*	*
(Rate change A–F)	(–16)	(–18)	(–22)	(–22)	(+7)	(+11)	(+14)	(+21)	(–3)	(–1)	(+1)	(–)	(+5)	(+9)	(+12)	(+13)
(Percent change A–F)	(–47)	(–38)	(–33)	(–27)	(+23)	(+23)	(+19)	(+26)	(–27)	(–6)	(+6)	(–)	(+100)	(+47)	(+75)	(+77)

Note: The chosen indices of offense-based processing follow:

England: Annual average of persons found guilty or formally cautioned for indictable offenses per 1,000 population in the age group.

Scotland: Annual average of persons referred to a reporter on offense grounds per 1,000 population in the age group.

*Scottish data for the years 1997 and 1998 had not been published at the time of going to press.

1990s, however, the Scottish processing rates for males were substantially higher than those for England (though the differences for females were small).

It is theoretically possible that the data shown in table 15.8 and figure 15.3 are causally connected. Important cross-national research work on crime trends by Farrington, Langan, and Wikström (1994), covering the United States, Sweden, and England, showed that the strongest negative correlation in the analysis "was between changes in the survey crime rate and changes in the probability of an offender being convicted" (127). This strong correlation does not, of course, in itself point to the existence of any causal link, but the authors' data are consistent with a hypothesis that crime rates are inversely related to the probability of sanctioning, for reasons of deterrence. (For a fuller discussion of this research, and of the many pitfalls in seeking to establish valid inferences of deterrent effects in criminological analysis, see von Hirsch et al. 1999.)

The data in table 15.8 and figure 15.3 are consistent with this line of reasoning, in that rates of crime (committed, of course, by persons of all ages) are inversely correlated with the rates of official processing of adolescents for criminal activities. One could therefore perhaps develop a complex hypothesis to the effect that (1) the existence in Scotland of a welfare-based system of juvenile justice, which is widely supported by influential voices in Scottish communities, has encouraged the official processing of juveniles through that welfare-based system; (2) this relatively high rate of official processing has had a deterrent effect on potential offenders; and (3) similar social processes have not occurred in England.[86]

The very simple data in figure 15.3 and table 15.8 do not begin to substantiate such a hypothesis. But they can, I believe, reasonably be said to raise the hypothesis. And in my view, they certainly justify the title of this subsection: the data are indeed both intriguing and thought-provoking.

A Concluding Assessment

In bringing this chapter to a close, I offer a general comment; some thoughts on the problem of explanation; and an assessment of some key points of difference between the English and Scottish systems that have been highlighted by the preceding analysis.

General Comment

This essay must end where it began. On any rational assessment, it is simply astonishing that two jurisdictions within a single, nonfederal nation-state can have had such different experiences in the field of juvenile justice as those described in this chapter. The differences, moreover, arise not simply because the two systems differ significantly in character, but also because one system has been remarkably stable over time, while the other has been subject to constant change.

What is, in some ways, equally surprising is the relative lack of comparative analysis of the two systems by British scholars. Asquith's (1983) small study stands out like a beacon as the only serious empirical comparison of English and Scottish juvenile justice—but the fieldwork for that research was conducted a quarter of a century ago. The present chapter is also unusual, in the sense that most reviews of juvenile justice by British researchers confine themselves to one or other of the two main jurisdictions. I hope that this analysis will stimulate further cross-border comparisons and debate.

The Problem of Explanation

Faced with surprising or unusual social phenomena, social historians and social scientists inevitably look for explanations. *Why* was English juvenile justice in the 1990s so different from that in Scotland? And *why* has the English system been so much more subject to change? A detailed answer to these questions would require another paper. But some broad-brush comments can be made here. And these comments reflect what one finds so often in historical explanations of social phenomena, namely, a mixture of some broad movements of thought, coupled with very particular events and decisions at particular moments.

An initial problem for explanation lies in the adoption, in both England and Scotland in the 1960s, of welfare-based systems of juvenile justice, just at the time when several other jurisdictions were turning away from aspects of their welfarist systems, toward more rights-based approaches. The kernel of the explanation of this problem lies, I believe, in two factors: first, the strength of welfarist modes of thought in postwar Britain, linked to the United Kingdom's adoption of a rather strong version of the welfare state; and, second, the fact that the early juvenile justice systems in both England and Scotland were firmly based on the "modified criminal court" model, rather than that of the "socialized juvenile tribunal." The *combination* of these two factors produced its own dynamic: key figures, committed to welfarist modes of thought, wished to see these applied more fully to juvenile justice than had been the case in the past.

Ironically, though, these key figures were more often to be found in England than in Scotland, and the Scottish reforms of 1968 can thus be attributed, with unusual precision, to the very thorough work of a particular official committee (the Kilbrandon Committee). Even then, there were special "accidents of timing" (Cowperthwaite 1988, 76) which enabled the Kilbrandon Report to be implemented in full, when it otherwise might not have been.

Post-1970, looked at in one way, the English system never recovered from the structural conflicts of the 1970s, themselves resulting from the deliberately emasculated implementation of the 1969 Act. Looked at in another—and broader—way, English juvenile justice policy post-1970 underwent continual processes of change because this was a society bewildered with itself—experiencing the social transformations of "late modernity" (Giddens 1990), including escalating crime rates, but very unsure how to deal with them. On this view, it was no accident that the Conservative Party in 1979 and New Labour in 1997 both gave juvenile crime policy a key place in their respective electoral manifestoes: juvenile crime was serving as a metaphor for wider social anxieties.

By contrast, in Scotland the much more stable Children's Hearing system has become "an established part of Scottish government, even a matter of Scottish pride" (Cowperthwaite 1988, 76). Somehow, this system, whose birth took place only because of the discussions within a particular official committee in the 1960s, struck a wider chord, and enabled many in Scotland to feel a sense of ownership of a particular social institution. Such achievements are very hard to orchestrate, but of great social importance when they occur. An in-depth research analysis of this wider achievement of the Scottish Children's Hearing system would be of considerable interest.

Some Key Points of Difference

What, finally, are the key points of difference between the two systems, as revealed in the detailed analyses of this chapter? Many matters could be raised, but I shall highlight just five—and I would suggest that these are five issues which any juvenile justice system should consider with care.

The first issue is *participation in the key tribunal* by the child, developed, it would seem, to a greater extent by the Scottish system, though by no means fully achieved in every hearing. This matter links up with the emerging research literature on *procedural justice* (Tyler 1990; Paternoster et al. 1997), a topic rarely considered in traditional writings on juvenile justice but now beginning to receive attention as part of the new emphasis on restorative juvenile justice in many jurisdictions.

Second, there is the *rights* issue, with which the more legally focused English system seems significantly more comfortable than does the Scottish. As the U.K. Parliament has recently implemented a Human Rights Act, which incorporates the European Convention on Human Rights into U.K. law, there are likely to be a significant number of rights-based challenges to both the English and the Scottish systems in the years immediately ahead.

Third, there is the question of *links between child care systems and juvenile justice systems,* especially in a context where criminological research has revealed that young offenders share many of the same characteristics as—and, indeed, are often the same people as—those who are dealt with as children in need. Here, Scotland's close links seem clearly preferable to the English 1990s policy of attempted rigid separation between the supporting social services for these two systems.

Fourth, there is the difficult question of how *offenses are to be conceptualized* within a juvenile justice system. We have seen that the Scottish system's intended downplaying of offenses has not been entirely sustainable and has created some unresolved tensions. Those tensions, in that form, have not developed in England, but there may sometimes be a reverse danger that the child's offenses (particularly in a conceptual climate of "no more excuses") are seen too much in isolation from their social context. Getting the balance right is not easy.

Fifth, there is the problem of the *transition from the juvenile to the adult system*. This is an area where the Scots have had more difficulty, precisely because their juvenile system is more obviously different from the adult courts. But the transition to the adult system is one which creates some difficulties for many juvenile justice systems.

Participation and procedural justice; the rights of children; links between the juvenile justice and child care systems; how offenses are to be conceptualized; and how one manages the institutional transitions from a juvenile to an adult system—this is, by any standard, an important list of topics to leave readers to consider as they reflect upon the very divergent juvenile justice systems of England and Scotland in the last third of the twentieth century.

NOTES

1. A new Scottish Parliament was established in Edinburgh in July 1999, and devolved Assemblies have also recently been created for Wales and for Northern Ireland. The powers of these various devolved bodies differ. The Welsh Assembly is of little significance for the purposes of this chapter. Responsibility for the Scottish juvenile justice system has, however, now been transferred to the Scottish Parliament, and an early decision of the new Scottish Executive was to commission a Review of Youth Crime, which is discussed in the final section of this chapter. None of these devolutionary developments affects the principle of the sovereignty of the U.K. Parliament, since Parliament has retained the power to abolish or suspend the various devolved bodies that have been created. (On the same principle, the devolved Parliament for Northern Ireland that had been set up in 1920 was suspended in 1972, and subsequently abolished.)

2. For simplicity, and following the usual convention, hereafter I shall normally speak of England rather than the more technically correct England and Wales.

3. Both the Scottish Parliament and the English Parliament passed Acts of Union in 1707, abolishing themselves and creating henceforth the United Kingdom of Great Britain, with a single U.K. Parliament. However, although the legislatures of the two countries

were thus united, by the terms of the Acts of Union Scotland was to retain its own substantive law, its own historic system of courts, and its non-episcopalian established church. A Scottish historian has commented that the union "made two countries one and yet, by deliberately preserving the Church, the Law, the Judicial System, and some of the characteristics of the smaller kingdom, it ensured that Scotland should preserve the definite nationality which she had won for herself and had preserved so long" (Mackie 1978, 263).

4. In an exception to this general pattern, in some large urban areas (particularly, in the first half of the twentieth century, Inner London) magistrates' courts are presided over by a legally qualified judicial officer known until recently as a "stipendiary magistrate" (now a "district judge"). Such judicial officers deal with most cases sitting alone. On the consequences of the stipendiary magistrate system for juvenile courts in Inner London, see note 8 below.

5. For example, in 1967 the juvenile court covering the Chicago area dealt with 21,409 cases, of which only 54 percent related to allegations of criminal behavior, the remainder consisting of "runaways, truants, ungovernables . . . dependency, neglect," and so on (Morris and Hawkins 1970, 160). By contrast, in England and Wales in the same year, 28,202 young persons under seventeen were found guilty of an offense (excluding motoring offenses) in the juvenile or magistrates' courts, while 6,408 young people were placed under supervision (residential or nonresidential) for non-offense reasons (Home Office 1968, 98, 205–6). Thus, 81 percent of juveniles who were made the subject of orders by the lower courts in England in that year were dealt with for criminal offenses.

6. Children and Young Persons Act 1933, sec. 44(1); as amended in minor particulars by the Children and Young Persons Act 1969.

7. This selection procedure had the consequence that magistrates selected for the juvenile panel were already experienced in presiding over the adult magistrates' court. Most of those appointed to the juvenile panel continued sometimes to sit in the adult court.

8. Special arrangements applied in Inner London. Magistrates' courts for adults in Inner London were all presided over by stipendiary magistrates (see note 4 above), and it was considered that these officials (at least when sitting alone) were not necessarily the most appropriate for dealing with juvenile cases. Special legislative provisions were therefore enacted whereby, from 1920 onwards, juvenile courts in the capital were mostly staffed by lay magistrates who did not sit in the adult magistrates' courts, and who were therefore initially selected for their special qualities in dealing with juvenile cases. As Winifred Cavenagh (1976, 7) has noted, "The difference in method of selection and of judicial experience has obvious implications," and in consequence the Inner London juvenile courts developed a reputation as being more welfare-oriented than those in most other areas.

9. As Cowperthwaite (1988, 76), a Scottish author, explains, "It is common practice, where reforming legislation is contemplated on the internal legislation of both England and Scotland, for the English legislation to come first and for the Scottish legislation to follow in the next Session of Parliament. The practice is not unreasonable having regard to the relative areas and populations of the two law districts, and it gives a degree of latitude to the Scottish legislation which might not exist if Parliament considered both measures, and the controversies raised during their passage, simultaneously."

10. The formal legal mechanism lying behind this situation was that the 1932 Scottish Act contained a section stating that the new arrangements would come into force for a given geographical area only when the Secretary of State for Scotland made an Order applying them to that area. This kind of procedure, which might be described as "piecemeal

legislative implementation by Executive Order," is normal in U.K. statutes where significant administrative preparations are necessary before a statute can be fully implemented. (On the office of Secretary of State for Scotland, see note 14 below.)

11. *Personal social services* is a phrase used in the United Kingdom to refer to a wide range of publicly financed services that deliver direct personal care or assistance to or oversight of individual citizens—from home help for elderly persons to services designed to prevent the physical or sexual abuse of children. Probation orders, and other community-based work with offenders—especially juvenile offenders—were in the 1960s normally understood as forming part of the personal social services.

12. For various accounts of the juvenile justice controversies of the 1960s in England and related issues, see, for example, Bottoms (1974), Clarke (1980), Packman (1975), Nellis (1990), and Gelsthorpe and Morris (1994). The pressure for reform of the personal social services in England arose from the fact that there were in the 1960s various different state social services dealing with a number of specific functions (e.g., the child care service, medical social workers, etc.), but quite a few families in poorer areas had multiple needs that required them to become clients of several different organizations. Hence, a unified personal social service was advocated by many and was finally achieved by an Act of 1970, which required each local government area to set up such a service (see, generally, Hall 1976). It was a matter of active debate whether the English probation service should be integrated within these new unified social services departments (SSDs), but in the end the probation service remained separate.

13. In the mid-twentieth century, "a growth of government expenditure on welfare, both in total and in relation to national product," occurred in many industrialized countries (Sleeman 1973, 156). However, the United Kingdom's provision was in some respects more comprehensive than that of most other countries (e.g., it created a National Health Service where medical treatment was free at the point of delivery). In the United Kingdom, the personal social services were seen in the 1960s and 1970s as just one element of welfare-state provision, alongside unemployment and social security benefits, health care, housing policies, and so on; see, for example, Marshall 1975.

14. The Secretary of State for Scotland is the senior U.K. government minister with responsibility for Scottish affairs. He or she is a member of the Cabinet, and therefore a member of the political party able to command a majority in the U.K. Parliament. Throughout almost all of the period under discussion in this chapter, the Secretary of State was in charge of the Scottish Office, a U.K. government department based in Edinburgh with a range of subdepartments such as health, education, home affairs, and agriculture. (By contrast, in England and Wales these various responsibilities are each handled by a separate government minister.) Since the creation of the devolved Scottish Parliament in 1999 (see note 1 above) these administrative arrangements have altered significantly, with most of the functions formerly exercised by the Scottish Office having been devolved to the new Scottish Executive, which is responsible to the Scottish Parliament. However, the office of Secretary of State for Scotland still exists, with altered powers and functions.

15. There were a number of reasons for the four-year delay in moving from the Kilbrandon Report (Scottish Office 1964) to the 1968 Act. The most important of these was the need for consultations about the future shape of the personal social services in Scotland, a topic seen by the government as vital if the Kilbrandon reforms were to be implemented successfully. (On personal social services in the United Kingdom, see note 11 above.) The Social Work (Scotland) Act of 1968, as its name implies, contained provisions for the reorganization of the personal social services as well as for juvenile justice. This reorgan-

ization, like that subsequently enacted in England (see note 12) involved the creation of a unified social work organization for each local government area, known in Scotland as the Social Work Departments (SWDs). In Scotland, in contrast to England, the probation service was abolished, and its work was incorporated into that of the new Social Work Departments.

16. The Scottish system is now based upon Part Two of the Children (Scotland) Act 1995. That Act, and other changes to the Scottish system in the 1990s, have made a number of important administrative and technical adjustments, but the basic philosophy and procedures of the originally enacted system remain essentially intact. For an account of the historical evolution of the 1995 Act, see Lockyer and Stone (1998a); for a comprehensive legal analysis of the Scottish system after the Act, see Norrie (1997). For present purposes, it is necessary to note only (1) that the 1995 Act reformulates the welfare principle in different language, requiring it to be the "paramount consideration" in decisions within the system (s. 16(i)); but (2) for the first time, an explicit derogation from the paramountcy of welfare is permitted "for the purpose of protecting members of the public from serious harm (whether or not physical harm)" (s. 16(5)). The derogation provision is of course of considerable theoretical interest and importance, but it will probably have only a limited impact in practice, since it is restricted to protection from *serious* harm, and (see subsequent discussion) serious offenses have since 1971 always been able to be prosecuted in the sheriff court, as an exception to the normal system of decision making.

17. The last year for which we have full figures for this stage of the process is 1989. In that year, there were 26,300 cases in which the police took some formal steps in relation to acknowledged or alleged offenses by children under sixteen. Of these cases, 76 percent were referred to the reporter, 11 percent were given a police warning, and 13 percent were reported to the procurator fiscal (Scottish Office 1991, 5).

18. In 1995, 6 percent of all referrals were not proceeded with by reporters for reasons of evidential insufficiency. The proportion was higher for care and protection referrals than for offense referrals, where the rate was 4 percent (Scottish Office 1997, 13).

19. However, if, for example, a child is alleged to have committed two offenses but admits only one, then the Children's Hearing has full jurisdiction to deal with the child (of course on a welfare-oriented basis) in the light of the one admitted offense. There may then be little point in pursuing the disputed ground to the sheriff court, and that ground might well be abandoned by the reporter or discharged by the hearing (box 13).

20. This division of functions has created some difficulties with regard to appeals against the treatment decisions of the Children's Hearing. This issue is considered in a later section of this chapter.

21. The Lord Advocate (the senior law officer for Scotland in the U.K. government) may and does issue guidelines to procurators fiscal on how to approach cases of this kind. Since 1987, when the Lord Advocate's guidelines were made more restrictive, the main categories where prosecution is recommended are (1) certain serious crimes, and (2) offenses alleged to have been committed by children aged fifteen or over where, following a conviction, disqualification from driving is a likely outcome (Scottish Office 1991, 4).

22. The "need for special measures of education and training" approach is, in the 1995 Act (see note 16 above), framed as the principle that no requirement or order shall be made unless it would be better for the child than making no order (s. 16(1)). The comment in the text about the case of Hamish assumes that the "serious harm derogation" (see note 16) does not apply to property offenses of moderate gravity.

23. An important exception to this principle, which concerns the small number of cases involving placement in secure accommodation, has been in force in Scotland since 1983. Children's Hearings must always *authorize* the potential use of secure accommodation (using statutory criteria, on which see Norrie 1997, 120–22). However, the director of the local Social Work Department has the final discretion as to whether the secure provision will actually be used, a provision on which there are mixed opinions (see Lockyer and Stone 1998a, 38, 74–76).

24. A Labour government policy paper of 1965 (Home Office 1965) had proposed the abolition of the juvenile courts in England. It advocated, as an alternative mechanism, the creation of family councils (composed of social workers and others experienced in dealing with children). These councils would try to reach voluntary agreements with the child and his or her parents about the child's proposed treatment, in his or her best interests. As a backup to the family councils, a new family court was proposed. This court would have jurisdiction if, for example, voluntary agreement in the family council was not forthcoming, and a compulsory treatment order was thought necessary, or if the child disputed the grounds of the referral (i.e., by claiming that he or she had not committed the alleged offense, was not beyond parental control, etc.).

25. Of particular importance in this regard were two civil servants who developed many of the conceptual foundations of what became the 1969 Act: Derek Morrell (formerly of the Ministry of Education) and Joan Cooper (chief inspector in the Home Office Children's Department). A good indication of Morrell's (somewhat visionary) philosophical approach can be found in a short paper on the residential treatment of delinquents that he contributed to the collection edited by Sparks and Hood (1969).

26. Cowperthwaite (1988, 29–30) reports that, in cross-departmental policy analyses carried out in 1964 by government officials in the Home Office and the Scottish Office, this "special measures" requirement was noted as being present in the Kilbrandon Report, but not in an English report on crime policy that had been prepared in the same year by the Labour Party (then the opposition in Parliament). The eventual appearance of the "special measures" requirement in the Labour government's Children and Young Persons Act of 1969 can therefore be read as constituting a direct English acceptance of this Kilbrandon principle.

27. That is to say, only a child aged ten or over could appear in care proceedings where an *offense* was alleged as the primary condition (on the concept of the primary condition, see further below). If a child under ten were, say, to shoplift, he or she could, however, still be brought before the court in care proceedings with a non-offense-based alleged primary condition, such as being beyond the control of his or her parents. Similar arrangements apply in Scotland, where the age of criminal responsibility is eight.

28. Children and Young Persons Act 1969, sec. 1(2)(b). Note also that proceedings before Children's Hearings in Scotland have been described in a leading case as "civil proceedings *sui generis*": see Kearney 1998, 160.

29. That is to say, the local police were, in law, the party initiating the prosecution. It did not necessarily follow that a police officer would actually conduct the case in court, because the local police service might appoint a lawyer to represent them; but in practice, in many juvenile courts the police did at this time conduct prosecutions themselves (see, e.g., the description by Asquith [1983, ch. 8] of an English juvenile court in the 1970s).

30. In preparation for the implementation of the 1969 Act, the Home Office issued guidelines about how these consultative procedures might be carried out; see Home Office (1970, part 3).

31. There is a small but quite important difference here between the English and the Scottish legislation. In the English Act, the intention was that courts should themselves "investigate whether satisfactory arrangements could be made without a court order" (Bottoms, McClean, and Patchett 1970, 371). By contrast, in Scotland, a Children's Hearing cannot make a decision as to voluntary supervision; it can only "discharge the case and suggest or assume or hope that there is *subsequent* voluntary contact between the family and the Social Work Department" (Hallett and Murray 1998, 56; emphasis added).

32. As the bottom row of figure 15.2 shows, there were three other orders available for those under fourteen in the English 1969 legislation. However, for various technical reasons, none of these orders challenged the effective supremacy of the supervision order and the care order.

33. That view was also apparent in some of the other provisions of the 1969 Act in its original form (e.g., the original version of the provisions for "supervision order with intermediate treatment"); for details, see Bottoms, McClean, and Patchett 1970, 381.

34. There were some important continuities in these arrangements with some of the thinking of the Ingleby Committee (Home Office 1960), whose conceptual model of offending I once described as being one of "social pathology for the younger child, but more classical assumptions about choice of evil for the older child"—a model that was reflected in Ingleby's proposals for "civil proceedings for the younger child and criminal for the older" (Bottoms 1974, 324).

35. An important reason for this stark difference arose from the U.K. Parliamentary custom whereby, if the text of a given Bill restricts its application solely to Scotland, then normally only Members of Parliament who represent Scottish constituencies will speak in the debates on that Bill.

36. In the English reforms, unlike the Scottish, the probation service was retained as a separate service when the personal social services were reorganized (see notes 12 and 15 above). It was intended that the new SSDs would eventually take over from the probation service the lead role as a supporting social service agency for the juvenile court, especially for younger children; and they would also take the lead role in the development of the new system of community homes. However, the on-the-ground reality in 1970 was that the new SSDs were far from ready to assume such responsibilities, so gradual implementation seemed politically sensible.

37. "Detention center" was a short-term custodial sentence normally of less than six months; while "borstal training" was a medium-term custodial sentence for a minimum of six months and a maximum of two years. Like all other so-called custodial sentences in England, both were administered by the (national) English Prison Service. In this respect they differed from the new community homes system, which was predominantly the responsibility of the local authorities. Unlike detention centers and borstals, the community homes system contained very little secure (i.e., locked and barred) accommodation, a point that was to cause controversy later in the 1970s. As indicated in the main text, the ultimate intention of the framers of the 1969 Act was to eliminate completely detention centers and borstal training as sentences available to the juvenile court, even for older juvenile offenders. Offenders previously sentenced to borstal training would, it was envisaged, normally be given a care order and sent to a community home; those previously sentenced to detention centers would normally receive a supervision order with intermediate treatment.

38. The Home Office is a department of the U.K. government. It has a miscellaneous range of areas of responsibilities, among the most important of which are crime pre-

vention policy and criminal justice policy (for England and Wales), and immigration (for the whole of the United Kingdom). The senior minister in the Home Office is known as the Secretary of State for Home Affairs (or, more colloquially, the Home Secretary). Like the Secretary of State for Scotland (see note 14 above), the Home Secretary is always a member of the U.K. Cabinet.

39. It is very easy to understand why the police adopted this approach: following the Conservative government's decision, all police services had an *unconstrained* choice between (1) a prosecution, in which they would need to prove only that an offense had been committed; or (2) offense-based care proceedings, in which they would need to prove *both* the offense *and* (after appropriate detailed consultation) that the child "is in need of care or control which he is unlikely to receive unless the court makes an order."

40. Farrington and Bennett (1981), in an empirical study of police cautioning in London, showed that there were strong reasons for inferring that in the capital much of the apparent growth in cautioning in the early 1970s was artifactual (i.e., it resulted from a switch from informal warnings [unrecorded] to formal cautions [recorded]). However, these authors also found evidence of genuinely increased diversion for those aged 10–13 (but not those aged 14–16). For data on other areas in England and Wales during the same period, see Ditchfield 1976.

41. Indeed, magistrates even lobbied central government in the mid-1970s to reinstate the probation service as the dominant service provider in the juvenile court. Social services departments and their staff were seen by courts at this time as "nascent (or naive) and . . . untutored in the demands and the expectations of the magistrates" (Morris and Giller 1987, 166).

42. In fact, the data in table 15.3 almost certainly understate the rapid increase in the rate of diversion from prosecution in the late 1980s. The 1985 Home Office guidance circular explicitly raised the issue whether an "informal warning" might sometimes be more appropriate than a formal caution, the main difference between the two being that only the caution could be officially recorded and placed on an offender's record. Data on informal warnings are not nationally available. However, research into the effects of the 1985 circular showed that police services varied greatly in their take-up of the suggestion about informal warnings (Evans and Wilkinson 1990), with one English county in particular enthusiastically embracing the informal warning approach (Farrington and Burrows 1993, 67). By definition, the data in table 15.3 do not include the apparent increase in informal warnings after 1985.

43. This decline in custodial sentencing during the 1980s is not immediately apparent from the data in table 15.4. However, the baseline for those data is "persons found guilty of indictable offences." Because there was a large rise in the cautioning rate for older males in the 1980s (see table 15.3), the number of persons found guilty declined. Hence, the basically static rate of custodial sentences *as a proportion of those found guilty* (table 15.4) masks an actual numerical decline in such sentences. For a fuller discussion, with additional data, see Bottoms et al. 1990, 4–6, 98–100.

44. The welfare model of juvenile justice was closely aligned with the so-called rehabilitative ideal in penology more generally. For a contemporaneous account of how such movements of thought were seen in Britain in the late 1970s, see Bottoms 1980; for a wider treatment, see Francis Allen 1964 and 1981.

45. Andrew Rutherford (1986, 13) advocated the "developmental approach," which emphasizes the transience of adolescent offending, and "regards crime and other

misbehaviours by young people as . . . [an] integral part of the process of growing up." In policy terms, the implications were that "sooner rather than later matters will be worked out," so that "instead of exclusion, the approach seeks absorption and fortifies the developmental role of home and school." Rutherford was aware (23–23) of the findings from longitudinal studies (for a review, see Farrington 1997) that persistent offenders do not fit this "transience" pattern, tending to begin their criminal careers early and to be significantly socially deviant on a range of indicators in their mid-twenties. This important occasional/persister distinction was, however, rarely mentioned when advocates of the juvenile justice movement emphasized the transience of adolescent offending.

46. Many new orthodoxy practitioners in local areas also sought to make creative use of some new statutory "criteria for custody" that were inserted (by backbench amendment) into the Criminal Justice Act 1982, creating formal restrictions on the circumstances in which courts could sentence young offenders to custody. Initial indications were that the enactment of these criteria had had little practical effect (see Burney 1985), but later in the 1980s some took a more positive view of their impact.

47. An unpublished paper entitled "Statistics on Juvenile Offenders" was prepared by the Home Office Research and Statistics Department in 1993. This contains a table showing the percentage of cases where proceedings were discontinued or withdrawn after having been formally commenced. For indictable offenses, overall the rate rose from 7 percent in 1985 to 22 percent in 1991. For juvenile defendants, the rates of increase for indictable cases in the same years were greater: for males, from 6 percent to 28 percent for 10–13-year-olds and from 7 percent to 27 percent for 14–16-year-olds; for females, from 6 percent to 31 percent for 10–13-year-olds and from 7 percent to 25 percent for 14–16-year-olds.

48. The essential raison d'être of the care order was that a child should be placed in the legal care of the local authority, in the interests of his or her own welfare, if (and only if) the child's home environment was considered to be deficient in some important respect. In the context of the welfare-oriented philosophy underpinning the Children and Young Persons Act of 1969, it was considered very appropriate that the care order should become the major order through which the residential treatment of delinquents was delivered, even in cases coming before the court through a prosecution, rather than through offense-based care proceedings. In the very different philosophical climate of 1989 in England, it made no sense to attempt to subsume orders that followed a criminal prosecution within the framework of a welfare-oriented system of child care law.

49. This was done in the Criminal Justice Act 1991, for male offenders. The minimum age for females was already fifteen.

50. There were also some additional reforms in the 1991 Act, but these proved to be of only short-term significance. One was an attempt, in cases involving children of compulsory school age (up to sixteen), to strengthen parental responsibility for the child's behavior through the use of the recognizance (binding over a parent, so that he or she would potentially forfeit a fixed financial sum if the child reoffended). Another was a complex attempt to create a so-called overlapping jurisdiction of noncustodial penalties for sixteen- and 17-year-olds, whereby the youth courts would have available to them not only community orders normally reserved for juvenile cases, but also some orders previously available only in the adult court. The rationale behind this latter change was said to be the very different maturity levels sometimes found in adolescents of similar chronological age. Had the reform worked as intended, one of its consequences would have been again to increase significantly the role of the probation service in the youth court. But neither reform

worked as intended by the legislation: for further details, see Bottoms, Haines, and O'Mahony 1998, 177–79.

51. Judicial criticism of the Act came to a peak in an extraordinarily outspoken address made during a visit to Scotland by the then Lord Chief Justice of England. "Congratulating the Scottish judiciary on the fact that the Act did not apply to Scotland, Lord Taylor CJ said that parts of the Act defied common sense and hoped that it would be reviewed and that sanity would be restored" (Thomas 1995, 145).

52. Research on the government's revised cautioning guidelines was carried out by Evans and Ellis (1997). They showed that there was an overall decrease in the cautioning of juveniles from 1994 onwards, but not of those aged eighteen and over. This difference they attributed to the fact that, before 1994, repeat cautions had been much more commonly used for juveniles than for adults.

53. Also, and as an innovation in English penal practice for juveniles, the management of these new centers was to be contracted out to private-sector companies, although operating within a framework of Home Office control.

54. The Audit Commission is a statutory body which oversees the external audit of local government authorities, and some other bodies, in England and Wales. As part of this function, from time to time it undertakes studies "to enable it to make recommendations for improving the economy, efficiency, and effectiveness of services provided by these bodies" (Audit Commission 1996, 3).

55. Evans and Ellis (1997) found that, in 1995, twenty-four out of forty-two police forces in England and Wales claimed to be running some kind of caution-plus scheme, but the Audit Commission's evidence suggested that these typically involved very small numbers. In law, caution-plus was voluntary treatment, with no sanction available if the young person failed to appear for the scheduled program of activity.

56. A conditional discharge allows the offender to go free but specifies that if he or she commits a further offense within a named period, he or she may be sentenced for the original offense as well as for the fresh offense.

57. In that year, the total of "known young offenders" (i.e., persons under eighteen found guilty of or cautioned for an indictable offense) was 132,800. Of these, 14,000 were discharged by the youth courts, and one can estimate that perhaps 87,000 were cautioned with no caution-plus component. Hence, the proportion of known young offenders to whom "nothing happened" was approximately 75 percent.

58. Crime and Disorder Act 1998, sec. 37 (1). On the contrast with the priorities of the juvenile justice movement, compare the following comment from a research report on late-1980s intermediate treatment programs designed as alternatives to custody: "[Project workers] had a much stronger commitment to the aim of 'providing an alternative to custody' . . . than they did to the explicit goal of 'reducing reoffending.' Accordingly, relatively little hard thought was given to precise mechanisms by which the reduction of reoffending might be achieved" (Bottoms 1995, 31).

59. The new "principal aim" is potentially in conflict with the desert-based emphasis of the sentencing provisions of the 1991 Criminal Justice Act, which are still on the statute book. Official guidance on this point has been that the 1991 provisions should be adhered to, but subject to that, regard should be had to the best option for preventing reoffending. There is, however, little doubt that the government is, in substance, much more committed to the new principal aim than it is to the desert-based principles underpinning the 1991 Act.

60. The interim research report on the pilot areas makes it clear that several types of intervention were being developed under the umbrella of the reparation order. Disappointingly, the most common was "indirect reparation" (a kind of community service for juveniles), which "provides no direct benefit to the victim of the offence and is likely to be less powerful in bringing home to offenders the consequences of their behaviour" (Universities of Sheffield and Hull 1999, 38). The research further reported that attempts to establish victim-offender mediation dialogues were being hampered by the government's emphasis on the speedy resolution of youth court cases: the "fast-tracking" requirement ran directly counter to the delicate process of setting up mediation dialogues in individual cases.

61. From the perspective of national government, there has probably seemed little reason to promote dialogue between youth offending teams and the child protection services of the SSD. This is because SSDs necessarily always provide some key members of the YOT, and it has therefore been assumed that links will automatically be established with other relevant workers in the SSD. So far, however, this has not usually proved to be the case in practice.

62. As previously explained, in Scotland lay members of the public are appointed as members of the Children's Panel for a geographical area. A Children's Hearing is a tribunal that deals with a particular case; it is presided over by three panel members. The Children's Panel as a whole meets collectively from time to time to discuss issues of policy and practice in the area. At a national level, the chairmen of the various area Children's Panels meet informally in a Children's Panel Chairmen's Group.

63. The Inquiry Report was here focusing on social workers' formal reports to hearings. Recall that a standard procedure in many English SSDs in the 1980s was for the recommendations from individual social workers in court reports to be "vetted" by SSD team managers, with recommendations that were considered inappropriately interventionist being altered accordingly. A similar approach had been adopted in the Fife SWD.

64. The *Gault* case was decided by the U.S. Supreme Court in 1967 (387 U.S. 1); key parts of the judgments are reprinted in Faust and Brantingham (1979, 283–333).

65. There have been other rights-based challenges: for example, the case of *McMichael v. United Kingdom* (1995) 20 EHRR 205 was taken as far as the European Court of Human Rights (ECHR) in Strasbourg. The European Convention on Human Rights provides (in Article 6) that "in the determination of his civil rights and obligations or of any criminal charge against him," every citizen is entitled to a "fair and public hearing." The ECHR held that, in McMichael's case, this Article was contravened by the parents not having been given sight of written reports which had informed the decision of the Children's Hearing.

66. For differing views on this topic by leading Scottish writers, see Norrie (1997, 4), who regards the present position as "entirely unjustifiable"; and Lockyer and Stone (1998b, 256), who take the view that "it is not essential to have anyone specifically designated as a 'representative,'" since all persons present at a Children's Hearing "have a responsibility to represent the interests of the child."

67. Publicly assisted legal representation is, however, available for appearances of juveniles before the sheriff court, including cases where the ground of the referral has been contested by the child (see figure 15.1, boxes 12 and 14).

68. The so-called discretionary lifer panels of the Parole Board for England and Wales are an example. These panels meet in prisons, under the chairmanship of a judge, to decide whether or not to recommend the release of certain prisoners serving sentences of

life imprisonment. Research on the functioning of discretionary lifer panels has recently been completed by Padfield and Liebling (2000).

69. For an admittedly extreme instance, see the case described by Erickson (1982, 103–4), where a boy was sent to a residential school on the occasion of his first appearance at a Children's Hearing (on grounds of truancy and theft). The residential placement was ordered because of additional police allegations that were introduced to the hearing by the chairman, but which were never put to the child (who was waiting outside when the chairman introduced this information), nor otherwise tested or challenged. The child remained completely unaware of the real reason for the decision.

70. For example, in 1990 the international community promulgated the United Nations Convention on the Rights of the Child. In ratifying the Convention in 1991, the U.K. government entered a number of formal reservations, largely relating to the Children's Hearing system in Scotland. For a very useful volume on the U.N. Convention, viewed from both an international and a Scottish perspective, see Asquith and Hill 1994.

71. Since 1985, it has been possible for a hearing to appoint a "safeguarder" to safeguard the interests of the child in the proceedings. Originally, this power could be exercised only where the chairman considered that there is or may be a conflict of interest between the child and his or her parent(s), and safeguarders were therefore appointed much more frequently in care and protection cases than in offense-based cases. Since the 1995 Act (see note 16), the "conflict of interest" requirement has been removed, but safeguarders are still appointed primarily in care and protection cares. If a solicitor is appointed as a safeguarder, he or she is not entitled to legal aid from public funds.

72. The characteristics of panel members have changed from the 1970s to the 1990s; in particular, there is now a majority of female members and a significantly greater representation of those not in professional and managerial socioeconomic groups (Reid 1998, 185–87). How far these changes might have affected the finding quoted in the text is not clear.

73. Especially as Asquith (1983, 157) observed slightly more English court cases (35) than Scottish Children's Hearings (30).

74. Note that the problem of the relationship between the act that has precipitated the referral to the hearing, and the subsequent decision taken by the hearing in the interests of the child's welfare, is not confined to offense-based cases. Indeed, one of the most important legal cases on the Children's Hearing system was a care and protection case which raised precisely such issues: see *O v. Rae* 1992 SCLR 318, discussed in Norrie (1997, ch. 8) and Kearney (1998).

75. Such an approach has been supported by the Scottish courts, for example in *Humphries v. S* 1986 SLT 683, where "it was held to be in the child's own interests to grant a warrant for his detention in order to prevent him from making his position worse by continuing to offend" (Kearney 1998, 169).

76. Hallett and Murray (1998) suggest that this could be achieved by assigning to the reporter the preliminary task of putting grounds to parents and children and establishing whether or not they are accepted. There are, however, some possible technical objections to granting such a role to the reporter.

77. Over the years, there has been a significant increase in the proportion of all cases referred to hearings that first go to the sheriff court because of the denial of a ground. This increase has occurred principally because non-offense-based referrals have been increasing, proportionately, within the system as a whole (see table 15.5), and denial of grounds is

much more common in non-offense-based cases. (In 1996–97, 48 percent of non-offense-based referred grounds were denied, as against 14 percent of offense-based referred grounds.) However, the percentage of offense-based referrals that are denied is also higher now than it was in the early days of the Scottish system.

78. In 1995, there were only 145 appeals to sheriff courts against the treatment decisions of Children's Hearings, and it is unlikely that the new power is being used in more than a small percentage of appeal cases.

79. Anxiety was expressed in some quarters in the mid-1990s that, given the new provision in the 1995 Act for a derogation from the paramountcy of welfare (see note 16 above), "unless Panel members are seen to take sufficient account of the public interest, more offending children may be removed from the Hearings system and directed to courts" (Reid 1998, 196). There is so far no evidence of this; indeed, prosecutions of those under sixteen are running at a slightly lower level than they were in the early 1990s.

80. On the proportion of offense-based cases where reporters take no action, see table 15.6 (though it must be noted that in some of these cases the child is already under supervision, and in a welfare-based system the only justification for a reference to the hearing would then be if it were thought that a variation in the supervision requirements would be in the child's interest). National statistics give data on the proportion of children *not already under supervision* whose cases are referred to the Children's Hearing and discharged by the hearing: this figure has remained steady at around 45 percent for the last decade.

81. In Hallett and Murray's (1998) research, professionals concerned with the hearings system, especially panel members and chairmen of the area Children's Panels, identified a lack of resources as one of the hearings system's greatest weaknesses (89). Hallett and Murray themselves note the existence of a structural problem, namely, that the ethos of the system places great emphasis on exploring the problems and needs of young people, with a view to ameliorating them, yet "the powers of Reporters and Panel members to command resources are limited, in contrast to some others, such as sheriffs in the criminal justice system" (89).

82. As previously noted, Children's Hearings have a *continuing jurisdiction* over young persons who are the subject of supervision requirements made by hearings. That continuing jurisdiction extends up to the age of eighteen, and a child under supervision who commits an offense at age sixteen may therefore be dealt with either in the adult criminal court or by the hearings system. In practice, most such cases are currently prosecuted in the adult courts.

83. However, because of the technical problems of matching identifiers experienced by the researchers, it is not clear whether this figure is based on a wholly representative sample of cases.

84. A few local police forces had previously experimented—one in a major way—with policies of "restorative cautioning," i.e., a "caution-plus" intervention focused on restorative justice principles.

85. Radically different legal categories greatly complicate comparisons of recorded crime rates in England and Scotland. A special analysis conducted on police-recorded data for 1981 suggested, however, that Scotland had the higher rate in five out of the six offense categories examined (Smith 1983). The first nationwide crime surveys of the British population were also carried out in 1981, and, in contrast to the police-recorded data, these suggested that (at least for crimes against individuals and against households, which is all that crime surveys of residential populations cover) the crime rates for the two countries were

similar in 1981 for eleven of the thirteen offenses examined, with England having the higher rate in the other two. An important reason for the difference in the results between the recorded crime data and the survey data was that in Scotland proportionately more people reported their victimizations to the police (Mayhew and Smith 1985).

86. Smith and Young (1999, 27–28) have an alternative hypothesis relating to the contrast in crime rates between the two countries, and the existence of the Children's Hearing system is mentioned in their reasoning. They were not, however, aware of the differences in the rates of official processing of juveniles as between England and Scotland, as shown in table 15.8, and these data would seem to present some difficulties for their suggestions.

REFERENCES

Adler, R. M. 1985. *Taking Juvenile Justice Seriously.* Edinburgh: Scottish Academic Press.

Alder, C., and J. Wundersitz, eds. 1994. *Family Conferencing and Juvenile Justice: The Way Forward or Misplaced Optimism?* Canberra: Australian Institute of Criminology.

Allen, F. 1964. *The Borderland of Criminal Justice.* Chicago: University of Chicago Press.

———. 1981. *The Decline of the Rehabilitative Ideal: Penal Policy and Social Purpose.* New Haven, CT: Yale University Press.

Allen, R. 1991. "Out of Jail: The Reduction in the Use of Penal Custody for Male Juveniles 1981–88." *Howard Journal of Criminal Justice* 30: 30–52.

Asquith, S. 1983. *Children and Justice: Decision-Making in Children's Hearings and Juvenile Courts.* Edinburgh: Edinburgh University Press.

———. 1998. "Scotland." In J. Mehlbye and L. Walgrave, eds., *Confronting Youth in Europe: Juvenile Crime and Juvenile Justice.* Copenhagen: AKF Forlaget.

Asquith, S., and M. Hill, eds. 1994. *Justice for Children.* Dordrecht: Martinus Nijhoff.

Audit Commission. 1996. *Misspent Youth: Young People and Crime.* London: Audit Commission.

Bainham, A. 1990. *Children—The New Law: The Children Act 1989.* Bristol: Jordan and Sons.

Bottomley, A. K. 1973. *Decisions in the Penal Process.* London: Martin Robertson.

———. 1980. "The 'Justice Model' in America and Britain: Development and Analysis." In A. E. Bottoms and R. H. Preston, eds., *The Coming Penal Crisis.* Edinburgh: Scottish Academic Press.

Bottoms, A. E. 1974. "On the Decriminalisation of English Juvenile Courts." In R. Hood, ed., *Crime, Criminology, and Public Policy: Essays in Honour of Sir Leon Radzinowicz.* London: Heinemann.

———. 1980. "An Introduction to 'The Coming Crisis.'" In A. E. Bottoms and R. H. Preston, eds., *The Coming Penal Crisis.* Edinburgh: Scottish Academic Press.

———. 1995. *Intensive Community Supervision for Young Offenders: Outcomes, Process, and Cost.* Cambridge: University of Cambridge Institute of Criminology.

Bottoms, A. E.; P. Brown; B. McWilliams; W. McWilliams; and M. Nellis. 1990. *Intermediate Treatment and Juvenile Justice.* London: HMSO.

Bottoms, A. E.; K. Haines; and D. O'Mahony. 1998. "England and Wales." In J. Mehlbye and L. Walgrave, eds., *Confronting Youth in Europe: Juvenile Crime and Juvenile Justice*. Copenhagen: AKF Forlaget.

Bottoms, A. E.; J. D. McClean; and K. Patchett. 1970. "Children, Young Persons and the Courts—A Survey of the New Law." *Criminal Law Review* 368–95.

Braithwaite, J. 1999. "Restorative Justice: Assessing Optimistic and Pessimistic Accounts," *Crime and Justice: A Review of Research* 25: 1–127.

Burney, E. 1985. *Sentencing Young People: What Went Wrong with the Criminal Justice Act 1982*. Aldershot: Gower.

Cavenagh, W. E. 1976. *The Changing Face of Juvenile Justice* (Eleanor Rathbone Memorial Lecture). Birmingham: University of Birmingham.

Clarke, J. 1980. "Social Democratic Delinquents and Fabian Families: A Background to the 1969 Children and Young Persons Act." In National Deviancy Conference, *Permissiveness and Control: The Fate of the Sixties Legislation*. London: Macmillan.

Cowperthwaite, D. J. 1988. *The Emergence of the Scottish Children's Hearings System*. Southampton: Institute of Criminal Justice, University of Southampton.

Ditchfield, J. 1976. *Police Cautioning in England and Wales*. Home Office Research Study no. 37. London: HMSO.

Donzelot, J. 1980. *The Policing of Families*. London: Hutchinson.

Elkin, W. 1938. *English Juvenile Courts*. London: Kegan Paul.

Erickson, P. 1982. "The Client's Perspective." In F. M. Martin and K. Murray, eds., *The Scottish Juvenile Justice System*. Edinburgh: Scottish Academic Press.

Evans, R., and R. Ellis. 1997. *Police Cautioning in the 1990s*. Home Office Research Findings no. 52. London: Home Office.

Evans, R., and C. Wilkinson. 1990. "Variations in Police Cautioning Policy and Practice in England and Wales." *Howard Journal of Criminal Justice* 29: 155–76.

Farrington, D. P. 1984. "England and Wales." In M. W. Klein, ed., *Western Systems of Juvenile Justice*. Beverly Hills, CA: Sage.

———. 1997. "Human Development and Criminal Careers." In M. Maguire, R. Morgan, and R. Reiner, eds., *The Oxford Handbook of Criminology*. 2nd ed. Oxford: Clarendon Press.

Farrington, D. P., and T. H. Bennett. 1981. "Police Cautioning of Juveniles in London." *British Journal of Criminology* 21: 123–35.

Farrington, D. P., and J. N. Burrows. 1993. "Did Shoplifting Really Decrease?" *British Journal of Criminology* 33: 57–69.

Farrington, D. P.; P. A. Langan; and P-O. H. Wikström. 1994. "Changes in Crime and Punishment in America, England, and Sweden in the 1980s and 1990s." *Studies in Crime and Crime Prevention* 3: 104–31.

Faust, F. L., and P. J. Brantingham. eds., 1979. *Juvenile Justice Philosophy*. 2nd ed. St. Paul, MN: West Publishing.

Flexner, B., and R. N. Baldwin. 1915. *Juvenile Courts and Probation*. London: Grant Richards. (Copyright 1914, U.S.A.: Century Co.)

Gelsthorpe, L. R., and A. M. Morris. 1994. "Juvenile Justice, 1945–1992." In M. Maguire, R. Morgan, and R. Reiner, eds., *The Oxford Handbook of Criminology*. Oxford: Clarendon Press.

Giddens, A. 1990. *The Consequences of Modernity*. Cambridge: Polity Press.

Giller, H., and A. M. Morris. 1981. *Care and Discretion: Social Workers' Decisions with Delinquents*. London: Burnett Books.

Goldson, B., ed. 2000. *The New Youth Justice*. Lyme Regis, Dorset: Russell House.

Grove, P. G.; D. A. Godfrey; and J. F. Macleod. 1999. *Long-Term Prison Population Projection: Operational Research Unit Model*. London: Home Office Research, Development, and Statistics Directorate.

Hall, P. 1976. *Reforming the Welfare: The Politics of Change in the Personal Social Services*. London: Heinemann.

Hallett, C., and C. Murray. 1998. *The Evaluation of Children's Hearings in Scotland*. Vol. 1. *Deciding in Children's Interests*. Edinburgh: Scottish Office Central Research Unit.

Home Office. 1927. *Report of the Departmental Committee on the Treatment of Young Offenders*. Cmd. 2831. London: HMSO.

———. 1960. *Report of the Committee on Children and Young Persons*. Cmnd. 1191 (Ingleby Report). London: HMSO.

———. 1965. *The Child, the Family, and the Young Offender*. Cmnd. 3601. London: HMSO.

———. 1968. *Criminal Statistics, England and Wales 1967*. London: HMSO.

———. 1970. *Part 1 of the Children and Young Persons Act, 1969: A Guide for Courts and Practitioners*. London: HMSO.

———. 1970. *Care and Treatment in a Planned Environment: A Report on the Community Homes Project*. London: HMSO.

———. 1980. *Young Offenders*. Cmnd. 8045. London: HMSO.

———. 1988. *Punishment, Custody, and the Community*. Cm. 424. London: HMSO.

———. 1990. *Crime, Justice, and Protecting the Public*. Cm. 965. London: HMSO.

———. 1997. *No More Excuses: A New Approach to Tackling Youth Crime in England and Wales*. Cm. 3809. London: Stationery Office.

Jones, R. 1984. "Questioning the New Orthodoxy." *Community Care*, 11 October, 26–29.

Kearney, B. 1992. *The Report of the Inquiry into Child Care Policies in Fife*. Edinburgh: HMSO.

———. 1998. "The Relationship between Courts and Hearings." In A. Lockyer and F. H. Stone, eds., *Juvenile Justice in Scotland: Twenty-Five Years of the Welfare Approach*. Edinburgh: T. & T. Clark.

Klein, M. 1979. "Deinstitutionalization and Diversion of Juvenile Offenders: A Litany of Impediments." *Crime and Justice: A Review of Research* 1: 145–201.

Kuenssberg, S., and A. Miller. 1998. "Towards a National Reporter Service." In A. Lockyer and F. H. Stone, eds., *Juvenile Justice in Scotland: Twenty-Five Years of the Welfare Approach*. Edinburgh: T. & T. Clark.

Lockyer, A., and F. H. Stone. 1998a. "Foundations and Development." In A. Lockyer and F. H. Stone, eds., *Juvenile Justice in Scotland: Twenty-Five Years of the Welfare Approach*. Edinburgh: T. & T. Clark.

———. 1998b. "Prospects." In A. Lockyer and F. H. Stone, eds., *Juvenile Justice in Scotland: Twenty-Five Years of the Welfare Approach*. Edinburgh: T. & T. Clark.

Mack, J. W. 1909. "The Juvenile Court." *Harvard Law Review* 23: 104.

Mackie, J. D. 1978. *A History of Scotland*. 2nd ed. Harmondsworth: Penguin Books.

Marshall, T. H. 1975. *Social Policy.* 4th ed. London: Hutchinson University Library.

Martin, F. M.; S. Fox; and K. Murray. 1981. *Children Out of Court.* Edinburgh: Scottish Academic Press.

Maxwell, G., and A. M. Morris. 1993. *Family, Victims, and Culture: Youth Justice in New Zealand.* Wellington: Social Policy Agency and Victoria University of Wellington.

Mayhew, P., and L. J. F. Smith. 1985. "Crime in England and Wales and Scotland: A British Crime Survey Comparison." *British Journal of Criminology* 25: 148–59.

Mehlbye, J., and L. Walgrave, eds. 1998. *Confronting Youth in Europe: Juvenile Crime and Juvenile Justice.* Copenhagen: AKF Forlaget.

Morris, A. M., and H. Giller. 1977. "The Juvenile Court—The Client's Perspective." *Criminal Law Review,* 198–205.

———. 1987. *Understanding Juvenile Justice.* London: Croom Helm.

Morris, A. M.; H. Giller; M. Szwed; and H. Geach. 1980. *Justice for Children.* London: Macmillan.

Morris, A. M., and M. McIsaac. 1978. *Juvenile Justice?* London: Heinemann Educational Books.

Morris, N., and G. Hawkins. 1970. *The Honest Politician's Guide to Crime Control.* Chicago: University of Chicago Press.

NACRO. 1989. *Replacing Custody.* London: National Association for the Care and Resettlement of Offenders.

Nellis, M. 1990. "Intermediate Treatment and Juvenile Justice in England and Wales, 1960–1985." Unpublished Ph.D. diss. University of Cambridge.

Norrie, K. 1997. *Children's Hearings in Scotland.* Edinburgh: W. Green/Sweet and Maxwell.

Northern Ireland Office. 2000. *Review of the Criminal Justice System in Northern Ireland.* Belfast: Stationery Office.

O'Mahony, D., and K. Haines. 1996. *An Evaluation of the Introduction and Operation of the Youth Court.* Home Office Research Study no. 152. London: Home Office.

Packman, J. 1975. *The Child's Generation: Child Care Policy from Curtis to Houghton.* Oxford: Basil Blackwell.

Padfield, N., and A. Liebling. 2000. *An Exploration of Decision-Making at Discretionary Lifer Panels.* Home Office Research Study no. 213. London: Home Office.

Paternoster, R.; R. Brame; R. Bachman; and L. W. Sherman. 1997. "Do Fair Procedures Matter? The Effect of Procedural Justice on Spouse Assault." *Law and Society Review* 31: 163–204.

Petch, A. 1988. "Answering Back: Parental Perspectives on the Children's Hearing System." *British Journal of Social Work* 18: 1–24.

Pitts, J. 1988. *The Politics of Juvenile Crime.* London: Sage.

Reid, B. 1998. "Panels and Hearings." In A. Lockyer and F. H. Stone, eds., *Juvenile Justice in Scotland: Twenty-Five Years of the Welfare Approach.* Edinburgh: T. & T. Clark.

Richardson, N. 1987. *Justice by Geography?* Manchester: Social Information Systems.

———. 1988. *Justice by Geography II.* Manchester: Social Information Systems.

Royal Commission on Criminal Procedure. 1980. *Report.* Cmnd. 8092. London: HMSO.

Rutherford, A. 1986. *Growing Out of Crime,* Harmondsworth: Penguin.

Schur, E. M. 1973. *Radical Nonintervention: Rethinking the Delinquency Problem.* Englewood Cliffs, NJ: Prentice-Hall.

Scottish Executive. 2000. *It's a Criminal Waste: Stop Youth Crime Now.* Report of the Advisory Group on Youth Crime. Edinburgh: Scottish Executive.

Scottish Office. 1964. *Report of the Committee on Children and Young Persons (Scotland).* Cmnd. 2306 (Kilbrandon Report). Edinburgh: HMSO.

———. 1991. *Children and Crime, Scotland, 1989.* Edinburgh: Scottish Office Statistical Bulletin (Criminal Justice Series).

———. 1997. *Referrals of Children to Reporters and Children's Hearings, 1995–96.* Edinburgh: Scottish Office Statistical Bulletin (Social Work Series).

———. 1999. *Criminal Proceedings in Scottish Courts, 1997.* Edinburgh: Scottish Office Statistical Bulletin (Criminal Justice Series).

Sleeman, J. F. 1973. *The Welfare State.* London: George Allen and Unwin.

Smith, D. J., and P. Young. 1999. "Crime Trends in Scotland since 1950." In P. Duff and N. Hulton, eds., *Criminal Justice in Scotland.* Aldershot: Ashgate/Dartmouth.

Smith, L. J. F. 1983. *Criminal Justice Comparisons: The Case of Scotland and England and Wales.* Research and Planning Unit Paper no. 17. London: Home Office.

Sparks, J. R.; A. E. Bottoms; and W. Hay. 1996. *Prisons and the Problem of Order.* Oxford: Clarendon Press.

Sparks, R. F., and R. G. Hood, eds. 1969. *The Residential Treatment of Disturbed and Delinquent Boys.* Cambridge: University of Cambridge Institute of Criminology.

Stang Dahl T. 1985. *Child Welfare and Social Defence.* Oslo: Norwegian University Press.

Taylor L.; R. Lacey; and D. Bracken. 1979. *In Whose Best Interests? The Unjust Treatment of Children in Courts and Institutions.* London: Cobden Trust/Mind.

Thomas, D. A. 1995. "Sentencing Reform: England and Wales." In C. Clarkson and R. Morgan, eds., *The Politics of Sentencing Reform.* Oxford: Clarendon Press.

Thornton, D.; L. Curran; D. Grayson; and V. Holloway. 1984. *Tougher Regimes in Detention Centres: Report of an Evaluation by the Young Offender Psychology Unit.* London: HMSO.

Thorpe, D.; D. Smith; C. Green; and J. Paley. 1980. *Out of Care: The Community Support of Juvenile Offenders.* London: George Allen and Unwin.

Tutt, N., and H. Giller. 1987. "'Manifesto for Management': The Elimination of Custody." *Justice of the Peace* 151: 200–202.

Tyler, T. R. 1990. *Why People Obey the Law.* New Haven, CT: Yale University Press.

Universities of Sheffield and Hull. 1999. *Youth Justice Pilots Evaluation: Second Interim Report—Youth Offending Teams after One Year.* Sheffield: University of Sheffield Department of Law.

von Hirsch, A. 1986. *Past or Future Crimes.* Manchester: Manchester University Press.

von Hirsch, A.; A. E. Bottoms; E. Burney; and P-O. H. Wikström. 1999. *Criminal Deterrence and Sentencing Severity.* Oxford: Hart Publishing.

Waterhouse, L.; J. McGhee; B. Whyte; N. Loucks; H. Kay; and R. Stewart. 2000. *The Evaluation of Children's Hearings in Scotland.* Vol. 3. *Children in Focus.* Edinburgh: Scottish Executive.

Wheeler, S.; E. Bonacich; M. R. Cramer; and I. K. Zola. 1968. "Agents of Delinquency Control." In S. Wheeler, ed., *Controlling Delinquency.* New York: John Wiley.

Whyte, B. 1998. "Rediscovering Juvenile Delinquency." In A. Lockyer and F. H. Stone, eds., *Juvenile Justice in Scotland: Twenty-Five Years of the Welfare Approach*. Edinburgh: T. & T. Clark.

Windlesham, Lord. 1993. *Responses to Crime*. Vol. 2. *Penal Policy in the Making*. Oxford: Clarendon Press.

Zander, M. 1975. "What Happens to Young Offenders in Care." *New Society*, 24 July, 185–87.

16 Modern Juvenile Justice in Europe

Jaap E. Doek

On February 12, 1993, two ten-year-old British boys, playing truant, abducted a two-year-old boy from a shopping mall, battered him to death two miles away, and threw his body onto a railroad track to be run over by the next train. They were arrested within a month, thanks to video surveillance of the mall. Their trial by jury, accompanied by massive national and international publicity, took place in November 1993. The trial was conducted with the formality of an adult criminal court; judge and counsel wore wigs and gowns. The boys were seated in a specially raised dock, with their parents, social workers, and lawyers seated nearby. A hostile crowd greeted the boys' daily arrival at court. The boys were convicted of murder and sentenced to detention "during Her Majesty's pleasure"—that is, indefinitely. "Not only must they be fully rehabilitated and no longer a danger to others," the judge observed, "but there is a very real risk of revenge attacks upon them by others." He considered eight years' detention necessary "to meet the requirement of retribution and general deterrence for the murder, taking into account its appalling circumstances and the age of the defendants when it was committed." Later, after widespread public demands for a life sentence, the boys were informed they would serve for fifteen years.[1]

Both boys filed complaints with the European Court on Human Rights, alleging violation of article 3 (concerning inhumane punishment); article 5, paragraphs 1 and 4 (concerning deprivation of liberty); and article 6, paragraph 1 (concerning privacy and the exclusion of the public from juvenile hearings). On December 16, 1999, the court concluded that no such violation had occurred in either trial or sentencing procedures.[2]

On January 13, 2000, barely a month after the European Court's decision, a Michigan judge pronounced sentence on a thirteen-year-old boy convicted of second-degree murder for shooting another boy to death at the age of eleven. Rejecting the option of sentencing the defendant as an adult, the judge ordered that the boy be placed in training school until the age of twenty-one, with a twice-yearly review of his progress. "I urge the legislation to lean toward improving the resources and programs within the juvenile justice system," he said, "rather than diverting more youth into an already failed adult system."[3]

These two cases, though far from typical, highlight certain issues the juvenile justice system is struggling with on both sides of the Atlantic: the increasing rate of juvenile violent crime; the minimum age for criminal responsibility; the principle of fair trial, including respect for privacy and the right to counsel; the role and quality of the juvenile judge and court; and the tension between punishment (or revenge) and rehabilitation (or treatment) as the objective in sentencing.

The variety of legal traditions in Europe precludes a unified approach to juvenile justice. This chapter merely attempts to identify the similarities as well as the differences among the systems in three Scandinavian and four western European countries, and to offer some recommendations. For lack of sufficient documentation, the former Soviet Union and eastern Europe are not covered here. Nonetheless, all European states, both east and west, are parties to the United Nations Convention on the Rights of the Child, and most are parties to the Convention for the Protection of Human Rights and Fundamental Freedoms, a Council of Europe treaty, compliance with which is ensured by the European Human Rights Commission. It should be noted at the outset that the general principles of criminal justice apply equally to juvenile and to adult offenders.

SCANDINAVIA

Denmark

The minimum age for criminal responsibility in Denmark is fifteen years. Those below that age can be questioned by the police after the local welfare authority has been informed, but they cannot be arrested. Only persons aged fifteen, sixteen, or seventeen at the time of a crime in which they are involved are referred to as juvenile offenders. They can be arrested, interrogated by the police (also with the approval of the local welfare authority), prosecuted, and held in pretrial detention. In the rare event that detention is imposed, a social welfare officer normally ensures that the juvenile is placed in an institution capable of dealing with serious juvenile offenders.

Juveniles have the right to legal counsel (usually appointed and paid by the state). If a juvenile is convicted, a social welfare officer develops a plan of action, sometimes with the involvement of the parents. The public prosecutor may then ask for suspension of the sentence or even drop the charge. Sentence may be suspended on condition that the juvenile perform up to 240 hours of community service, or a custodial sentence—simple detention for a period of seven days to six months—may also be imposed. Some juveniles are subject to modest fines, payable in installments. The maximum penalty that can be imposed is eight years' imprisonment, in separate quarters from adult prisoners.

Finland

As in Denmark, the minimum age for criminal responsibility in Finland is fifteen years. A younger child may be questioned in connection with a crime but only in the presence of a parent or other custodian. Those at least fifteen years old but younger than twenty are classified as "young offenders." No suspect below age eighteen is to be interrogated without a witness. The presence of a representative of the municipal social welfare board is required; parents are given the opportunity to be present. These rules may be waived, however, if immediate action is warranted. For a crime that carries a custodial sentence, a report on the personal background of the suspect must be furnished to the court.

As in Denmark, young offenders have the right to legal counsel, the state to cover the costs if necessary. The court—not a specialized juvenile court—can order that the trial take place behind closed doors. Few young offenders under the age of eighteen are sent to prison, and most of these are in pretrial detention. Settlement between offender and victim through work or in money is the goal; trained volunteers facilitate this conciliation—most successfully in municipalities where social welfare authorities and police cooperate closely. Mandatory conciliation is being considered.

Sweden

In Sweden, too, fifteen is the minimum age for criminal responsibility. Since 1985, however, the police, in close cooperation with the social welfare authorities, can investigate crimes committed by children at least twelve years old but younger than fifteen. These authorities, however, can ask for suspension of such an investigation. In order to address the individual or social causes of a child's delinquency, they may propose therapy or economic support for the family. Such measures are usually noncoercive and require the cooperation of both the offender and his or her family. Where twelve- to fourteen-year-olds exhibit extremely asocial behavior or are involved in drug abuse, stricter measures may be taken—placement in a foster home or an institution, for example. Such measures are approved by a county administrative court, which is quite separate from criminal courts.

Social welfare authorities play (or are supposed to play) an important role with offenders aged fifteen, sixteen, and seventeen, known as "juveniles." (Eighteen-, nineteen-, and twenty-year-olds, "young adults," are dealt with more like adult criminals; since they are no longer minors, they are omitted from this survey.) Crimes allegedly committed by juveniles are usually investigated by police officers in special youth units working closely with social welfare officers. The results of an investigation are sent to the public prosecutor, who has various options:

- The prosecutor may stop the investigation if the act does not constitute a crime or there is insufficient evidence.
- If the offender has confessed to the crime he or she is charged with, a waiver of prosecution may be issued, meaning the defendant will not be subjected to any further acts of prosecution. (This occurs in 40–45 percent of juvenile cases.)
- Again, after a suspect has confessed, the prosecutor may issue an order of summary punishment, the size of the sanction being agreed to by the juvenile.
- The offender may be tried in a regular court. (This occurs in only about 15 percent of all juvenile cases. Juvenile courts do not exist in Sweden.) Sanctions are limited and welfare-oriented. They include fines; probation; transfer of the juvenile to the care of a social welfare board, which determines an appropriate measure; a conditional sentence, which may be suspended under certain conditions; and, for very serious crimes, a prison sentence.

WESTERN EUROPE

France

In France, the juvenile justice system is governed by the *ordonnance* of February 2, 1945, amended in 1951, 1993, and 1994. The 1994 amendment required the introduction of a special code for juvenile defendants; this code, however, is still under discussion, and no bill has yet been submitted to parliament. Since 1945, the minimum age for criminal responsibility has been thirteen years. Offenders below the age of eighteen, however, can receive a criminal sentence only if the crime is extremely serious and the sanction is likely to deter the offender from further crimes. The French system is thus still based on a welfare approach: minors are to receive, "according to the case, measures of protection, assistance, supervision, and education that seem appropriate." Even eighteen- to twenty-year-olds may benefit from the mitigating criteria applicable to younger defendants.

The police, though supposed to report to the public prosecutor's office all alleged crimes known to them, may merely caution a young offender if the offense is not serious. If further investigation is warranted, a young offender may be subject to police custody *(garde à vue)*. This measure, which requires the permission of the prosecutor's office and of a judge, may be imposed even on children between ten and thirteen, but only if the crime would normally carry a penalty of at least seven years' imprisonment. For such children, police custody is limited to ten hours; for thirteen- to seventeen-year-olds, twenty-four hours. Any prolongation requires the approval of a judge. For offenders under sixteen, a medical examination is mandatory before custody can begin; sixteen- to seventeen-year-olds need not submit to such an examination, although they or their parents can demand it. In all cases of police custody, parents must be informed immediately. A lawyer is appointed to assist any juvenile below the age of sixteen.

The prosecutor's office has wide discretionary power based on the "principle of opportunity." If evidence is lacking, or if prosecution does not serve the public interest—for example, if the offense was not violent and the victim has received compensation from the offender—a case can be dismissed, either conditionally or unconditionally. Some cases get brought to court without further investigation. If more investigation is needed, a juvenile thirteen years or older may receive pretrial detention. For thirteen- to fifteen-year-olds the normal maximum is six months; for older offenders, twelve months.

In October 1991, the French minister of justice confirmed that a prosecutor responsible for cases involving minors should be a specialist. Some large jurisdictions have a special juvenile unit in the prosecutor's office. A 1912 law (no doubt inspired by the establishment of the first juvenile court in Chicago in 1899) created a special court, the *tribunal pour enfants,* for juvenile offenders aged thirteen and above. The judge in that court is responsible for cases involving not only crime but also child abuse or neglect, truancy, runaways, and other child-related matters.

The prosecutor refers most juvenile cases to the juvenile judge *(juge des enfants)* in his capacity as examinating or investigating judge *(juge d'instruction)*. Thus the juvenile judge is already involved in the case in the pretrial stage and can take provisional measures such as observation of the juvenile in his or her regular environment, placement in an institution, or detention. During this stage, the judge will interview the child and the parent(s) in an informal setting—often the judge's office. A court social worker is usually involved as an adviser. After trial, the results of the provisional measures may influence the sentence. The judge may even declare the juvenile guilty but impose no penal sanction.

More serious cases, which could carry the sanction of imprisonment, are referred to the *tribunal pour enfants,* a panel of three judges. The juvenile judge, who presides over this court, is assisted by two lay judges *(assesseurs).* The latter, appointed by the minister of justice, must be at least thirty years of age and have a clear interest in children's affairs.

The most serious offenses *(les crimes)* are dealt with by the *cour d'assises des mineurs.* This court is composed of a presiding judge, two juvenile judges, and a jury of nine. Only about a hundred cases a year, fewer than 0.2 percent of all juvenile offense cases, are referred to this court. Sentences passed by the judges may be appealed; a special, three-judge chamber in the appeal court has been established for this purpose.

For juveniles tried in court, various educational measures can be imposed, including supervised liberty *(la liberté surveillée);* placement in a foster home (with whatever support is needed); compensation to the victim; or community service. Juveniles sixteen years or older may opt for community service—with a maximum of 240 hours of work—as an alternative to a custodial sentence. When traditional sanctions (fines or imprisonment) are imposed, the maximum amount or length is usually one-half of what would be imposed on an adult for the same offense.

Germany

In Germany, the minimum age for criminal responsibility is fourteen years. Juvenile justice rules apply to those under eighteen *(die Jugendlichen)* at the time the offense is committed, though eighteen- to twenty-year-olds *(die Heranwachsenden)* can also be tried in juvenile court. A clear distinction is made between the handling of juvenile offenses on the one hand and procedures for child protection on the other. The former are dealt with in juvenile court *(Jugendgericht)* and the latter in family court.

Once investigated by the police, a case must be referred to the prosecutor's office; the police have no power to drop a case at this stage. Police custody is permitted for up to forty-eight hours; for a longer period, a judge's consent is required. The juvenile has the right to call a lawyer, but the lawyer does not automatically have the right to be present when the police interrogate the juvenile.

Prosecutors dealing with juvenile offenses must have experience in juvenile education—indeed, larger prosecutor's offices often have a separate unit for juveniles. Exercising considerable discretionary power, the prosecutor can formally charge the juvenile and submit the case to the juvenile court, conduct further investigation, or simply dismiss a case. Some cases are dismissed for such technical reasons as insufficient evidence. Other dismissals may involve, for example, a first offender who has committed a minor crime, or an offender who has already been subjected to a disciplinary measure by the director of the institution in which he or she resides. Dismissals may be conditional: the prosecutor may dismiss a case after the offender has completed a mediation process with the victim, has repaired the damage resulting from the offense, has performed community service, or has paid a specific amount of money to a charitable organization.

Pretrial detention can be imposed on fourteen- to fifteen-year-olds only if they have no permanent place to stay or have tried to escape. Those sixteen or older can be placed in detention only if there is no educational or other option. Six months is the maximum length, but few pretrial detentions last more than a couple of months.

An important arm of the juvenile court consists of a body of social workers who investigate the personal background of young offenders and provide the prosecutor, the judge, and other participants in the process with relevant information. These social workers can make recommendations to the court concerning the kinds of measures or sanctions that might be imposed. They also supervise disciplinary orders and stay in touch with juveniles in prison so as to help them reintegrate into the community on their release.

Juvenile courts were first established in Germany in 1908, influenced in part by the Chicago model. A single juvenile judge has jurisdiction in cases for which the prosecutor recommends educational or quasi-punitive measures. The judge is assisted by two laypersons experienced in youth education (similar to the French *assesseurs;* see above). More serious cases are submitted to a panel of three professional judges. Capital cases and other offenses that may carry more than three years' imprisonment are referred to the juvenile chamber of the regional court, composed of three professional judges and two lay judges. This chamber, reduced to one professional and two lay judges, can also serve as a court of appeal, though the defendant has the option of appealing to the high court of appeal.

A wide variety of nonpunitive measures is available to the court. Offenders may be referred to an educational institution or a foster home; they may be required to participate in a social-skills training course or a victim-offender mediation program or to undergo alcohol- or drug-abuse treatment. For such measures, parental consent is required for offenders up to the age of seventeen; above that age, the offender must give consent. Quasi-punitive and disciplinary measures include (among others) a formal reprimand; an order to repair the damage inflicted by the offender; to apologize personally to the victim; to take a job; to perform community service; or to pay a fixed amount to a charitable organization; and detention of no more than four weeks, to be served all at once or during different weekends. As noted above, a number of these nonpunitive measures may be used by the prosecutor as conditions for dismissing cases.

The harshest penalty that can be imposed—when a juvenile evinces very negative tendencies or when the crime appears to warrant it—is imprisonment of six months to five years (or more, occasionally, in the case of extremely serious crime).

Italy

In Italy, as in Germany, the minimal age for criminal responsibility is fourteen years, and the upper limit for treating an offender as a juvenile is eighteen (at the time a crime is committed). An offender below the age of fourteen, if considered dangerous, can be placed in the care of the social services or in a reformatory. In principle, prosecution of juveniles is mandatory if a crime has been committed and the evidence is sufficient. In practice, however, juveniles are often diverted from trial in court by means similar to those used in the Scandinavian and western European countries outlined above. A presidential decree of 1988 emphasized prevention and the social rehabilitation of juvenile offenders. The approach is nonpunitive, seeking reparation of damage done to the victim and reconciliation between offender and victim.

Police officers arresting a juvenile are supposed to take the offender's age and personality and the nature of the offense into consideration. They may detain a juvenile for up to ten hours. When a juvenile is taken into police custody, the prosecutor's office orders immediate transfer to a special reception center. If longer custody is needed, a preliminary social investigation must be carried out within ninety-six hours and reported to the juvenile judge.

As in Germany, juvenile cases are handled by prosecutors with specialized knowledge, and the juvenile court is composed of professional judges assisted by lay judges, who are informed about the defendant's personal, family, and social circumstances. For crimes that carry a penalty of twelve years or more, pretrial detention may be imposed, not to exceed six months. The judge may also issue an order for the juvenile to remain at home or be placed in an institution.

The Netherlands

Twelve years is the minimum age for criminal responsibility in the Netherlands. The upper limit for the juvenile justice system is eighteen, as

Fig. 16.1 Illustration of Dutch juvenile court, 1930. Source: unknown.

elsewhere. Children under twelve can be interviewed by the police and detained in the police station for up to six hours. Offenders of sixteen or seventeen, though tried in juvenile court, occasionally receive an adult penalty, and eighteen- to twenty-year-olds, appearing in adult court, can receive sentences usually reserved for juveniles.

Cases reported to the police can be handled in different ways. The police have no formal power to dismiss a case; that power rests with the public prosecutor. But the prosecutor's guidelines for juvenile cases delegate some discretionary power to the police. First, these guidelines provide the police with criteria for referring—or not referring—a case to the prosecutor. Second, when dealing with a first offender who has committed and confessed to a minor crime (specified in the guidelines), the police may refer the offender to the so-called Halt (or Stop) service. This service, in consultation with the offender and his or her parents or guardians, and with their joint consent if the offender is below sixteen, arranges for appropriate action—up to twenty hours' community service, reparation of the damage inflicted, or some similar action. About 35 percent of cases known to the police are dealt with in this manner.[4]

The police refer about 60 percent of the juvenile cases known to them to the public prosecutor. The prosecutor has wide discretionary power in handling these cases, including dismissal for lack of evidence. If further investigation and trial seem inappropriate, a case may be dismissed (as in Germany; see above) on condition that the offender has made reparations, apologized to the victim, paid a fine, done up to forty hours' community service, or performed some similar action. An offender who agrees to such a condition but fails to meet it will go to trial. Occasionally, a prosecutor who decides against disciplinary measures will file for child protection. Only about 30 percent of all cases reported to the prosecutor end up in court; thus, the juvenile court deals with only 15–20 percent of all juvenile offenders known to the police.

Since 1922, juvenile judges in the Netherlands have been considered specialists within the judiciary for cases of child protection as well as for delinquency. The system, originally based on the 1899 Chicago model, has evolved in various respects. A juvenile judge now hears and decides most civil law cases involving minors—ranging from paternity or custody disputes to child protection. Other such cases are referred to a chamber of three judges, one of whom is the juvenile judge. Most delinquency cases fall within the juvenile judge's jurisdiction. Exceptions are minor infractions that are tried in county court or, more commonly, settled out of court; and more serious cases, likely to receive heavy sanctions, that are heard before a three-judge panel, again with the juvenile judge as a member.

The juvenile judge's approval is required for police custody (to a maximum of 3 days and 15 hours), for its prolongation (another 3 days), and for pretrial detention (up to 10 days). Since 1995, a continuation of pretrial detention (up to 30 days, renewable twice to a total of 106 days) must be approved by a three-judge panel. If the prosecutor has failed to bring formal charges and to present the case to the juvenile court before the end of the permissible detention time, the juvenile must be released.

Although changes in the system introduced in 1995 have limited the juvenile judge's role in delinquency cases, this judge is still heavily involved in decision making. He or she also serves as trial judge, except in cases in which the prosecutor seeks detention of more than six months or placement in a treatment facility for more than two years. A single juvenile judge may handle all cases in smaller district courts, but is assisted by deputies in large ones.

In sentencing, the juvenile judge or the three-chamber panel may impose such sanctions as a fine, payable in installments; detention up to twelve months for those below sixteen and twenty-four months for sixteen- and seventeen-year-olds; placement for up to two years (or, sometimes, longer) in a treatment center if the offenders are not considered legally responsible for their crimes; or "alternative sanctions," including community service up to two hundred hours, participation in social-skills training or a course designed for juvenile sex offenders, or a combination of work and training. The judge or judges may also make a sentence conditional. If certain conditions are met, usually within a probation period of two years and with the support of youth probation services, the sentence will not be executed.

SOME GENERAL OBSERVATIONS

The introduction of juvenile courts in Europe was clearly connected to developments in the United States. The French system seems to have remained closest to an integrated, welfare-based concept of children in trouble, an approach that makes no clear distinction between delinquent juveniles and children in need of care and protection. That distinction is most clearly drawn in Germany and less so in Italy and the Netherlands.

The differences in the minimum age for criminal responsibility seem arbitrary. The upper age limit for applying juvenile law, however, is uniformly (and logically) eighteen, the age of majority. Yet there seems to be a desire, especially in Germany and the Netherlands, to let eighteen- to twenty-year-olds benefit from the juvenile justice system. As to dealing with juvenile offenders, an immediate, limited, and clearly pedagogical approach is considered appropriate in all the countries surveyed. We may question how far an anonymous or impersonal sanction—one imposed by an institution rather than a person—can be effective.

I believe more attention should be paid to the role of the police in the dynamics of the juvenile justice system. The police can "divert" cases with the unspoken permission of the prosecutor. "Diverting" is rare in Italy but more common in France and Germany and most frequent in the Netherlands. While in line with a welfare approach, such activity can disrupt the lives of juveniles and their families. Children should not be pressured to confess to an alleged offense or to agree too readily to a condition (which may not survive the scrutiny of a juvenile court). Similar observations apply to the discretionary power of public prosecutors.

Police custody and pretrial detention are important instruments in the justice system—for adults as well as for juveniles. But changes in the role of the juvenile judge, resulting in part from interpretation of the due process principles of the European Court on Human Rights (art. 6), diminish the welfare aspects of those instruments and orient them more toward protecting public order and safety. Since the beginning of the 1990s, all kinds of "alternative sanctioning" have been developed at the police level, in the prosecutor's office, and in court. As a result, formal reactions to juvenile offenses have expanded, but only a limited number of cases actually get tried. As to procedural aspects, the rules for adult criminal procedures generally apply. Specific rules for the juvenile system include the presence of parents or other representatives at interrogations; trial behind closed doors; and the assignment of a lawyer. Since a juvenile's right to legal counsel is rather limited in some European countries, the Council of Europe should issue guidelines so as to bring that right into more consistent practice.

In imposing sanctions or other measures, some countries (France and Italy) have what might be called a "reduced-fee" system for juveniles. Fines or prison sentences are usually only about 50 percent of the amount that would be imposed on adults in similar circumstances. Other countries (Germany and the Netherlands) have sanctions specially designed for juveniles. While the difference may be important conceptually, what really counts is how these measures are executed—especially the deprivation of liberty, under whatever label it is ordered. All the countries surveyed espouse the principle of separating juveniles from adults in prison; practical considerations, however, often prevent its implementation.

A CLOSER LOOK AT SOME EUROPEAN TRENDS

Is Juvenile Crime Increasing and Growing More Violent?

There is a perception that juvenile crime has increased and has become more violent in the 1990s. This perception—or is it more than a perception?—has led politicians and others to urge tougher policies and sanctions (Bitscheidt and Lindenberg 1998). Reliable statistical comparison among different time periods is hampered by a number of factors: the level of political attention to juvenile crime as a social problem; the level of activity on the part of the police and prosecutors, sometimes depending on available resources; the willingness of the public and of concerned professionals to report juvenile crime to the police; and different definitions and classifications of criminal behavior—what is meant by *serious, less serious, violent, nonviolent,* and so forth (see Coleman and Moynihan 1996). Furthermore, most official statistics are based on cases reported to the police. Only a few countries (Denmark, Sweden, and the Netherlands, for example) complement the official crime statistics by self-report studies, victim surveys, and other data.

In an assessment of the quantitive developments in juvenile crime over the last three decades of the twentieth century, based on statistical data from various European countries, Felipe Estrada (1999) identifies the following major trends:

- In England, Finland, and Germany, juvenile crime increased steadily.
- In Denmark, the Netherlands, Norway, Scotland, and Sweden, juvenile crime rose rather sharply from the mid-1970s to the early 1980s and then leveled off, becoming stable by the early 1990s.
- In the 1990s, registered cases of juvenile crime increased significantly in France (from about 92,200 in 1993 to 154,500 in 1997; Aubusson de Cavarley 1998) and the Netherlands (from 40,000 in 1993 to 52,000 in 1996; Laan et al. 1998).
- The official statistics indicate an increase in violent juvenile crime from the end of the 1980s to the beginning of the 1990s in Denmark, Germany, the Netherlands, Norway, and Sweden. In the Netherlands, the number of juveniles suspected of violence against persons increased from 1,500 in 1990 to 3,700 in 1996; these cases, however, represented less than 10 percent of all reported juvenile crimes. In France, cases of violence committed by minors against property and persons increased from 11 percent of all reported juvenile cases in 1974 to 23.8 percent in 1996.
- Juveniles from ethnic minorities (North Africans, especially Algerians, in France; Turks in Germany; Moroccans, Surinamese, and Turks in the Netherlands) appear to be overrepresented in registered crime. The problem is no doubt connected with poverty and social exclusion, among other factors.

After a thorough review of police records, victim surveys, and self-report data, Junger-Tas (1996) concluded merely that "there has probably been a moderate increase in less serious violent crimes." Violence leading to the death of a victim has not increased. Junger-Tas noted that inconsistency between crime statistics and other reports makes it difficult to quantify the increase in violent crime.

The Minimum Age for Criminal Responsibility

For a number of reasons, the appropriate minimum age for criminal responsibility requires greater attention than it has received so far. First, the minimum age is extremely low in certain countries—seven years in Ireland and Cyprus; ten years in the United Kingdom. Second, the perception, only slightly corroborated by empirical data (Traulson 1997), that crimes are being committed by younger and younger children has led some politicians (in the Netherlands, for example) to call for a lower minimum age for criminal responsibility. Third, as a result of that perception, children below the age of criminal responsibility are increasingly dealt with in a manner closer to punishment than to care (Bol 1999).

Some European countries, because they take a welfare approach to juvenile offenders, either prescribe no minimum age (Belgium, Denmark, and Scotland) or have a rather high one (in Sweden, fifteen years). Others, depending on the seriousness of a crime, refer juvenile offenders to an adult criminal court or allow adult sanctions at a specific age (in Scotland, eight years). In its review of the British case mentioned at the beginning of this chapter, the European Human Rights Commission concluded that there was no common standard among member states of the Council of Europe concerning minimum age, and that the low minimum age in England (ten years) did not of itself lead to inhuman or degrading treatment.

Article 40 of the Convention on the Rights of the Child requires that a minimum age for criminal responsibility be set but does not prescribe the age.[5] Reports on crimes committed by very young children seem to generate downward pressure on the minimum age. For example, members of the Dutch parliament in 1998 proposed lowering the age from twelve to ten—a proposal that the minister of justice firmly rejected. The rare cases of violent crime committed by children younger than twelve years do not justify a general lowering of the minimum. Nor is prosecution of ten- or eleven-year-olds an appropriate response to crimes they may have committed. Yet the minister of justice, feeling the need for some response to the problem, supported the Halt program mentioned earlier, whereby sanctions of a sort could be imposed on juveniles younger than twelve years. The child, with the consent of the parent(s), might write a short essay about what happened, offer an apology to the victim, be temporarily deprived of pocket money, help repair (by work or a financial contribution) the damage done, or perform some similar task. This approach raises questions about the legitimacy of a state intervention that is not clearly based on the law. The argument that the child's and the parents' cooperation is voluntary is unconvincing, since one can hardly speak of voluntariness in such situations. The formal guidelines for the Halt program, though emphasizing the preventive and educational nature of its responses, cannot conceal their punitive aspect.

The establishment of a minimum age for criminal responsibility, therefore, does not preclude quasi-penal intervention into the lives of the very young who infringe the penal law. Nor does such intervention make a fixed minimum age superfluous. A more common European approach is clearly needed.

Juvenile Justice and Fair Trial

Article 6 of the European Commission on Human Rights is a bible of fair trial, for juveniles as well as for adults. It spells out principles such as *nullum crimen sine lege* (no criminal charges for acts that at the time of commission were not punishable under the criminal law); *nulla poena sine lege* (no penalties not foreseen in the criminal law); the presumption of innocence; the right to be informed of the charges; and the rights to counsel, to an impartial judge or tribunal, and to a fair hearing without undue delay. For the most part, these principles seem to be followed, though there are, of course, violations. In the British case mentioned earlier, an expert witness testified that one of the boys had been shocked at seeing the public in the courtroom and felt terror at being looked at as he sat in the raised dock. Although the boys' appeal was rejected by the European Court on Human Rights, the trial proceedings (in my opinion, as in that of the dissenting judges) were a clear violation of a child's right to have his or her privacy respected.

A French law of 1993 strengthened the right to legal counsel by ruling that a minor defendant should have a lawyer appointed, if necessary, by the juvenile judge or the pretrial, investigative judge. Similar provisions exist in Dutch criminal law. But in both countries a minor can be interviewed by the police without having a lawyer present.

Article 12 of the Commission on Human Rights not only gives minors the right to voice their views but also requires that due weight be given to those views, in accordance with the age and maturity of the child concerned, in any judicial proceedings. A German study (Ludwig-Mayerhofer 1997) has shown that judges often disregard minors' objections to the charges brought against them. As a juvenile court judge myself, I have rarely experienced lively communication between judge and juvenile defendants. Not only have many juveniles already confessed to the charges, but they tend—understandably, in view of the rather intimidating environment of a court hearing—to display a submissive attitude. It is up to the juvenile judge to create a positive atmosphere that will allow a juvenile to participate effectively in the proceedings. Sentencing should reflect the fact that the defendant's views have been taken into account or, if they have not, why they have been rejected.

Noting the diminishing gap between adult and juvenile criminals, some have urged that juveniles be accorded the same procedural rights as adults. It is also argued that more rights for minors imply responsibility and therefore justify heavier penalties, a less tolerant approach to juvenile crime, or both. A 1997 white paper published in the United Kingdom was titled "No More Excuses: A New Approach to Tackling Youth Crime in England and Wales" (Hakkert 1998).

The Juvenile Court: An Endangered Species?

In most European countries, juvenile courts or judges have played—and are still playing at the beginning of the twenty-first century—an important role. The juvenile judge was introduced in Germany (1908), Belgium and

France (1912), and the Netherlands (1922) as a specialist within the judiciary who was to deal not only with the protection of abused or neglected children (civil law cases) but also with juvenile offenders (criminal law cases). In Belgium, a legal continuum was established between the child victim of bad parents, the misbehaving child, and the juvenile offender. This welfare model allowed juveniles of all three kinds to be brought before the same juvenile judge (Christiaens 1999). In France and the Netherlands, children in danger, and hence in need of protection, were distinguished from delinquent children—that is, children who were themselves dangerous. Germany has two kinds of juvenile judges: one competent in child protection and the other competent in juvenile crime. But whether one judge acts in two capacities or responsibility is divided between two judges, the goal is basically the same—to harmonize interventions and to increase the effectiveness of measures taken in either area (protection or punishment). It is assumed that there is no fundamental difference between the child in danger and the dangerous child; both need protection in terms of reeducation and treatment.

In France and the Netherlands, the role of the juvenile judge (or judges) encompasses the pretrial stage as well as trial and sentencing. This combined role has put the impartiality of the judge in question. An appeals court in Reims, in 1992, concluded that a juvenile judge who has been actively involved in the pretrial investigative stage of a case should not act as the trial judge in the same case. It has been argued that such a conclusion undermines the principle of a specialized judge in the juvenile justice system. Yet we should be able to reconcile the principle of specialization and that of impartiality; for example, stronger procedural guarantees for juveniles and expert legal representation could help counteract any potential partiality (Blatier and Bourquin 1995). In 1993, the European Court ruled that the fact that a juvenile judge has also made pretrial decisions, including decisions on detention, does not of itself preclude the judge's impartiality.[6] What matters is the scope of the pretrial decisions. Clearly, a judge heavily involved in gathering evidence against a suspect should not participate in that suspect's trial. Dutch juvenile judges can no longer participate in the decision whether to prosecute and, as mentioned above, cannot order pretrial detention for more than ten days without the approval of a three-judge panel.

To ensure that juvenile judges and courts meet expected standards, the Committee of Ministers of the Council of Europe has recommended that all those involved with the procedural levels of the juvenile justice system—police, lawyers, prosecutors, judges—should receive specialized training. It is generally agreed that the juvenile judge, in addition to expertise in children's rights and juvenile law, should have special knowledge of child development, child psychology, and child psychiatry and should be fully informed of existing institutions and programs designed for young offenders. The judge also needs empathy and communication skills in dealing successfully not only with young offenders but also with other professionals (police, social workers, and so on).

In the countries surveyed, however, little training is offered. Many judges simply lack the time for such preparation. In the Netherlands during the decades under review, barely more than 50 percent of juvenile judges enrolled in a one-week basic course; fewer than 50 percent took a course on juvenile law or children's rights, and only about 30 percent on child psychology or psychiatry. Many took such courses only after becoming juvenile judges. The majority learn on the job, but too few juvenile judges remain long enough in the position to gain the necessary skills. Two to four years seems to be the norm, in part because they are not held in high regard by other judges, nor do they have adequate opportunities for promotion.

Nonetheless, as I have argued elsewhere (Doek 1994), juvenile judges in Europe are unlikely to become extinct. There is no call for abolition of the juvenile court. The prevailing opinion is that it works and should be maintained and improved. We should bear in mind, however, that the judge is only one element of the juvenile justice system; many juvenile offenders known to and questioned by the police never meet a judge. In the 1990s, only about 15–20 percent of young offenders in the Netherlands were actually tried before a judge; in France, about 40 percent; in Austria, about 30 percent. The reduction in Austria from nearly 50 percent in the late 1970s may be attributed in part to the introduction in the 1988 juvenile penal code of a "conflict-regulation model" *(Konfliktsregelungsmodell),* which allows the prosecutor to refrain from prosecution even in quite serious cases. A similar trend is apparent in Germany. Furthermore, when cases do come to court, the outcome has been largely predetermined by evidence prepared by the prosecutor. As Schüler-Springorum (1999) has observed, the function of the judge seems to have been reduced, and that of the prosecutor widened, in juvenile as well as in adult courts.

THE MISSION OF JUVENILE JUSTICE: PUNISHMENT OR SOMETHING ELSE?

In a 1987 report, the Committee of Ministers of the Council of Europe noted a gradual return over the previous twenty years to a "just deserts" approach to juvenile crime.[7] Offenders should get what they deserve, not what they need. Involved in this trend was more frequent use of detention or other measures for incapacitating offenders. In being held accountable for their criminal acts, juveniles were expected to compensate victims (or society in general) for damage. On the other hand, a blurring of the distinction between criminal justice for minors and that for adults had led to stronger legal safeguards for minors. This conceptual change in the juvenile justice system stems from a changing concept of childhood itself, reflected in and promoted by the Convention on the Rights of the Child: children are regarded not only as vulnerable and developing individuals but also—and equally—as individuals who are developing the capacity for rational choice, more independent decision making, and, hence, a growing moral and legal responsibility. Minors, in other words, are increasingly recognized as competent persons, accountable for their behavior.

Toward a More Punitive Juvenile Justice?

There is some evidence of a more punitive trend in Europe during the 1990s. In the Netherlands in 1995, the maximum length of detention was increased from six to twelve months for those under sixteen at the time of a crime, and to twenty-four months for sixteen- and seventeen-year-old offenders. In Germany, the city of Hamburg developed a zero tolerance approach in 1997 (Bitscheidt and Lindenberg 1998). The welfare approach and the idea of reeducation as an instrument of control came under attack (Herz 1993). The 1997 British government white paper "No More Excuses" (mentioned above) emphasized early and efficient interventions.

A perceived increase in violent crime seems not to be correlated with harsher punishment. In France, for example, aggravated theft, drug-related offenses, and voluntary acts of violence increased significantly between 1990 and 1994. But during this period the juvenile courts sentenced only 3.4 percent of the offenders to prison, and only 2.1 percent of those sentences exceeded one year. In 35.2 percent of the cases, a simple warning was given. Other sentences included assigning the juvenile to the care of a special person (13.3 percent), educational measures (12.6 percent), compensating the victim (7.9 percent), and fines (5.5 percent); about 12 percent received a suspended sentence (Blatier 1999). In the Netherlands, statistical data indicate that the increased length of detention permitted under law was not matched by actual detention imposed (a discrepancy that does not disturb me). The only notable increase was in the number of juveniles placed for treatment in closed institutions.

My preliminary conclusion is that concern about growing and more violent juvenile crime has resulted in the call for tougher and more punitive juvenile justice but not in its implementation. Has the call, then, had no impact on the practice of juvenile justice?

Less Punitive Measures

Even with the "just deserts" approach, most European juvenile justice systems include other measures: a warning or a reprimand; supervision or probation, often as a condition of suspended sentence; a fine; detention or other custodial measures; placement for treatment in an institution (usually closed, sometimes open). These sanctions can be imposed by the juvenile judge (or judges), whose discretionary powers vary from country to country. Also, as we have seen, more than half of all cases of juvenile crime are dealt with out of court.

Among nonpunitive programs that have been developed are the "community service order," first introduced in the United Kingdom in the 1970s as an alternative to probation or a fine; and the Halt program and "alternative sanctions" in the Netherlands. The authors of a 1996 study concluded, among other things, that "juveniles sentenced to an alternative sanction today are younger; there are more girls among them and more juveniles of non-Dutch descent, more juveniles who committed violence involving property, but also more first offenders or offenders with only one previous offense. The average seriousness of the offenses does not appear to have altered" (Blees and Brouwers 1996). As many as 87 percent of the offenders given alternative sanctions—activities, courses, or whatever was proposed—completed them. In Germany, the 1990 act that reformed existing juvenile law has provided a legal basis for expanding "ambulant" measures such as social training, victim-offender mediation, and community service (Böttcher 1990).

A "restorative" response to juvenile crime emphasizes repair of the damage caused by the offender to victim and society rather than deterrence or treatment of the offender (Bazemore and Walgrave 1999). The content of community service should be symbolic of the harm done, and its duration should depend on the seriousness of the harm. Its appropriateness (or painfulness) for the offender is secondary. Community service should be evaluated on the basis of its success in achieving peace in the community. So far, however, community service programs have rarely been based on restorative criteria and seem unlikely to take their place in the already busy field of out-of-court measures.

This admittedly incomplete picture hardly indicates a more punitive approach to juvenile crime. On the contrary, emphasis in most places is on the rehabilitation of the offender in a manner appropriate to his or her treatment needs, along with increasing attention to the victim and to society. This development satisfies article 40 of the Convention on the Rights of the Child, which urges that treatment of a juvenile offender should take into account a child's age, reinforce the child's respect for the rights of others, and promote the child's assumption of a constructive role in society.

Do Children's Rights Have an Impact on Juvenile Justice?

Thus far, emphasis on children's rights has been limited to certain procedural changes. Since 1995 in the Netherlands, for example, juvenile offenders have the right to object to inadequately founded charges. The fact that pretrial detention beyond ten days must be approved by a panel of three judges is also supposed to protect a juvenile's rights. A 1995 law in France mandates that the name of a judge be mentioned, a lawyer be appointed, and the parents be notified when a child is charged with a crime. These and similar adjustments are generally in conformity with the standards established by the Convention for the Protection of Human Rights and Fundamental Freedoms and the Convention on the Rights of the Child. Whether they really give a child confidence that he or she is being listened to is unclear.

SOME OBSERVATIONS AND RECOMMENDATIONS

A major problem that has only been touched on here is delinquency attributed to ethnic minorities. Juveniles from ethnic communities in Europe are strongly overrepresented in the statistics. In the Netherlands, for example, non-Dutch juveniles compose more than 50 percent of the population of closed institutions. Policymakers are aware that the issue must be dealt with constructively: root causes such as poverty, lack of education, and social exclusion must be tackled; traditional western European approaches may be inappropriate for some young offenders from ethnic minorities. The statistics—though they contain many truths—should not scare us, but they should be analyzed in a historical and international context if we are to make a balanced assessment of the situation.

I believe the minimum age for criminal responsibility should be increased to at least twelve years of age in those countries with a low minimum. With a higher minimum age in England, for example, the conviction of a ten-year-old (as discussed at the beginning of this chapter) would not have been possible, and rightly so. The justice system would be compelled to find creative ways of dealing with criminal behavior in the very young. Raising the minimum age in just a few countries would help set an international standard for the more than forty countries in eastern and western Europe.

As to fair trial, which seems to provoke little debate in Europe, more attention should be paid to criminal records regarding juvenile offenders, for such records can be very damaging for an offender's reintegration into his or her community. The Council of Europe should try to establish international standards for the type of sentences that are to be recorded, the length of time a record should be kept (a maximum of three to five years since the most recent offense), access to records for nonjudicial authorities, and the right of juveniles to examine records and to propose correction where appropriate. Another aspect of fair trial is the right to be heard and to have one's views given due weight. Essential to this right is good communication—between the juvenile and the judge, and between the juvenile and the lawyer.

A Council of Europe treaty of January 25, 1996, which focused on procedural rights, unfortunately ignored the position of juveniles in criminal proceedings. To correct this omission, the council could issue a recommendation on the administration of juvenile justice that not only would reaffirm existing international standards—such as Article 40 of the Convention on the Rights of the Child, and the U.N. Standard Minimum Rules for the Administration of Juvenile Justice ("Beijing Rules")—but also would give content to those standards. Topics might include the right of legal assistance, the conditions for other appropriate assistance, the minimum age for criminal responsibility, and the guarantee of privacy. Such standards are needed in part because of the increasing use of out-of-court, often informal settlements of juvenile cases. Concerns about the quality of juvenile courts and judges might be addressed by the Council of Europe's setting of minimum standards—not only for judges but also for other players (including the police) in the juvenile justice system. Systematic attention to selection and training is needed.

I doubt that we should spend more time on the debate about welfare, punishment, or other models of juvenile justice. We shall continue to see cases in which the public need for revenge sweeps away any arguments based on common sense or sound research. Yet such instances should not be equated with a trend toward a more punitive system. Professionals working with juvenile offenders, while not ruling out punishment that fits the crime, continue to emphasize rehabilitation, reeducation, and reintegration into society.

Greater attention to preventing juvenile crime has been called for (Heinz 1998), and some prevention policies have been formulated (Lazerges and Balduyck 1998) or implemented (Hakkert 1999). Actual results, however, are far from clear (Mehlbye and Walgrave 1998). Prevention efforts driven by concerns about more violent and ever younger juvenile offenders do not contribute to constructive solutions. Given the crucial role of parents, various prevention projects are focusing not only on parents but also on families and are struggling with such questions as how far intervention in family life should go: Is persuasion enough? Which carrot is effective, and which stick permissible? Can force be used, and on what grounds? Many forces, including schools, community, and improvement in the socioeconomic condition of low-income families should be mobilized to prevent juvenile crime.

If juvenile crime is a disease, we should certainly try to cure it. We know that prevention is better and less costly than treatment. But we also know that the disease sometimes goes into remission without strong medicine. As with the common cold, an aspirin or a spoonful of cough syrup is often enough.

NOTES

1. *T. v. United Kingdom* (24724/94), December 16, 1999. European Court of Human Rights; published on website: www.echr.coe.int/Eng.

2. Ibid.

3. Judge Eugene Arthur Moore, in *Michigan v. Abraham,* 6th Circuit Court for the County of Oakland Family Division, January 13, 2000.

4. There are more than sixty Halt offices in the Netherlands. A ministerial decree of January 1995 lists the type of crimes that may be referred to Halt. In May 1995 the national prosecutor's office issued guidelines concerning the conditions and procedures for a Halt referral.

5. Although the text of article 40 is not conclusive, it does indicate that children cannot be prosecuted or given criminal sentences for crimes they commit before reaching a specified age. I consider the inevitable arbitrariness of any minimum age less problematic than leaving a judge to decide whether a juvenile may be prosecuted. Discretionary power of that kind can lead to all kinds of inequality and discrimination.

6. *Nortier v. The Netherlands,* European Court of Human Rights, August 24, 1993, series A, vol. 267.

7. Final Activity Report, Strasbourg, August 10, 1987. Addendum 3 to CM (87) 167; adopted by the Committee on Crime Problems at its thirty-sixth plenary session, June 22–26, 1987.

REFERENCES

Aubusson de Cavarley, Bruno. 1998. Annex 4 to *Réponses à la délinquance des mineurs: Rapport au Premier Ministre: Mission interministérielle sur la prévention et le traitement de la délinquance des mineurs.* April. Paris: Government of France.

Bazemore, Gordon, and Lode Walgrave, eds. 1999. *Restorative Juvenile Justice: Repairing the Harm of Youth Crime.* Monsey, NY: Criminal Justice Press. (See especially the contributions by Walgrave, 129–54; Daniel W. van Ness, 265–82; and Mara F. Schiff, 327–56.)

Bitscheidt, Dorothee, and Michael Lindenberg. 1998. "Zero Tolerance in Umgang mit Jugendelinquenz." *Neue Kriminalpolitik* no. 3.

Blatier, Catherine. 1999. "Juvenile Justice in France: The Evolution of Sentencing for Children and Minor Delinquents." *British Journal of Criminology* 39, no. 2: 240–52.

Blatier, Catherine, and J. Bourquin. 1995. *Écriture et secret: Rapport du groupe de travail.* Vaucresson: Ministère de la Justice.

Blees, L. W., and M. Brouwers. 1996. *Taakstraffen voor minderjarigen.* Arnhem: Gouda Quint, and The Hague: WODC (Scientific Documentation and Research Center, Ministry of Justice).

Bol, Menke. 1991. *Leeftijdsgrenzen in het strafrecht bezien vanuit de ontwikkelingspsychologie.* Arnhem: Gouda Quint.

———. 1999. Dr. M. W. "Doorgaan met Stop? Voorwaarden voor een geslaagde aanpak van zeer jeugdige delictplegers." *Justitiële Verkenningen* 25, no. 6: 56–67.

Böttcher, Reinhard. 1990. "Erstes Gesetz zur Änderung des Jugendgerichtsgesetzes." *Neue Zeitschrift für Strafrecht* 10, no. 12: 561–66.

Christiaens, Jenneke. 1999. "A History of Belgium's Child Protection Act of 1912: The Redefinition of the Juvenile Offender and His Punishment." *European Journal of Crime, Criminal Law, and Criminal Justice* 7, no. 1: 5–21.

Coleman, C., and J. Moynihan. 1996. *Understanding Crime Data: Haunted by the Dark Figure.* Buckingham, U.K.: Open University Press.

Doek, Jaap E. 1994. "The Juvenile Court: An Endangered Species?" *European Journal on Criminal Policy and Research* 2: 42–56.

Doek, Jaap E., and P. Vlaardingerbroek. 1998. *Jeugdrecht en Jeugdhulpverleningsrecht: Derde herziene druk.* The Hague: Elseviers bedrijfsinformatie.

Estrada, Felipe. 1999. "Juvenile Crime Trends in Post-war Europe." *European Journal on Criminal Policy and Research* 7: 23–42.

Hakkert, Alfred. 1998. "No More Excuses: A New Approach to Youth Crime in England and Wales; A Summary." *European Journal on Criminal Policy and Research* 6, no. 2: 279–91.

———. 1999. *Ouders en reacties op jeugdcriminaliteit.* The Hague: Ministerie van Justitie.

Heinz, Wolfgang. 1998. "Reformbedarf des Jugendstrafrechts?" *Monatschrift für Kriminologie* 81, no. 6: 399–435.

Herz, Ruth G. 1993. "Eine Jugend in Deutschland? Anmerkungen zum Diskurs über den Erziehungsgedanken im Jugendstrafrecht." In *Festschrift für Horst Schüler-Springorum zum 65. Geburtstag,* 291–306. Cologne: Heijmanns Verlag.

Junger-Tas, Josine. 1996. "Youth and Violence in Europe." *Studies on Crime and Crime Prevention* 5: 31–58.

Laan, Peter H. van der, et al. 1998. *Ontwikkeling van de jeugdcriminalitet: Periode 1980–1996.* Onderzoeksnotitie WODC.

Lazerges, Christine, and Jean-Pierre Balduyck. 1998. *Réponses à la délinquance des mineurs: Mission interministérielle sur la prévention et le traitement de la délinquance des mineurs.* Rapport au Premier Ministre. April. Paris: Government of France.

Ludwig-Mayerhofer, Wolfgang. 1997. "Kommunikation in jugendstrafrechtlichen Hauptverhandlungen: Von den Grenzen rechtlicher und soziologischer Modelle." *Zeitschrift für Rechtssoziologie* 18, no. 2: 180–204.

Mehlbye, Jill, and Lode Walgrave, eds. 1998. *Confronting Youth in Europe: Juvenile Crime and Juvenile Justice.* Copenhagen: AKF Forlaget.

Schüler-Springorum, Horst. 1999. "Juvenile Justice and the 'Shift to the Left.'" *European Journal on Criminal Policy and Research* 7: 353–62.

Traulson, Monika. 1997. "Werden die Täter immer junger? Zur Altersstruktur der Tatverdächtigen." *Monatschrift für Kriminologie* 80, no. 6: 430.

Contributors

Anthony Bottoms has been Wolfson Professor of Criminology at the University of Cambridge, England, since 1984, and he is also a visiting professor of criminology at the University of Sheffield. He is a Fellow of the British Academy. In 1996, he was the recipient of the Sellin-Glueck Award of the American Society of Criminology, for international contributions to the study of criminology.

Jaap E. Doek is professor of private law, in particular family and juvenile law, at the Vrije Universiteit (since 1985) and extraordinary professor of juvenile law at the University of Leiden (since 1998). He has been a juvenile court judge (1978–1985) and is still a deputy judge in the district court of the Hague. He has been visiting scholar at the Law School of the Georgetown University (Washington, DC, 1993) and the Law School of the University of Michigan (Ann Arbor, 1993). He was a visiting professor at the Northwestern University School of Law (Chicago, 1999). Since March 1999 he has been a member (Rapporteur) of the UN Committee on the Rights of the Child, which monitors the implementation of the Convention on the Rights of the Child. Prof. Doek publishes on matters of family law and juvenile law (including juvenile justice and international children's rights issues)

Bernardine Dohrn is director of the Children and Family Justice Center and clinical professor at Northwestern University School of Law, Legal Clinic. The center is a multifaceted children's law center, an interdisciplinary policy and training center for the justice needs of adolescents and their families, providing critical knowledge about youth law and practice, matters associated with the administration of justice, and the preparation of professionals and scholars who advocate for children. Dohrn is the coeditor of *Zero Tolerance: A Handbook for Parents, Teachers, and Community,* to be published in 2001, and author of "'Look Out Kid, It's Something You Did': The Criminalization of Youth," in Valerie Polakow, *The Public Assault on America's Children: Poverty, Violence, and Juvenile Justice* (2000). She teaches and lectures on children in trouble with the law, child welfare, justice within schools, family violence, and human rights.

PETER EDELMAN is a professor of law at Georgetown University Law Center. He served in the U.S. Department of Health and Human Services during the Clinton Administration, first as counselor to the secretary and then as assistant secretary for planning and evaluation. He was director of the New York State Division for Youth in the late seventies, was a legislative assistant to Senator Robert F. Kennedy, and was a law clerk to Justice Arthur J. Goldberg on the Supreme Court of the United States. His book, *Searching for America's Heart: RFK and the Renewal of Hope,* was published by Houghton Mifflin in 2001, and his article in the *Atlantic Monthly,* "The Worst Thing Bill Clinton Has Done," was honored with the Harry Chapin Media Award. He is the author of numerous articles on poverty, youth, and juvenile justice, and serves on many nonprofit boards. He is a graduate of Harvard College and Harvard Law School.

JOHN EEKELAAR is a reader in family law at the University of Oxford and Fellow of Pembroke College. He has written on, and conducted research into, family law over many years. Major publications include *Family Law and Social Policy* (1978 and 1984); *The Protection of Children: State Intervention and Family Life* (with Robert Dingwall and Topsy Murray, 1983 and 1995); *Maintenance after Divorce* (with Mavis Maclean, 1986); *Regulating Divorce* (1991); *Parental Obligation: A Study of Parenthood across Households* (with Mavis Maclean, 1997); *Family Lawyers: The Divorce Work of Solicitors* (with Mavis Maclean, 2000); and *Cross Currents: Family Law in the United States and England* (ed. with Sanford N. Katz and Mavis Maclean, 2000).

DAVID FARRINGTON is professor of psychological criminology at the Institute of Criminology, Cambridge University. He is a Fellow of the British Academy and of the Academy of Medical Sciences. He is co-chair of the OJJDP Study Group on Very Young Offenders, and Chair of the Campbell Collaboration Crime and Justice Steering Group. He has been president of the American Society of Criminology, president of the European Association of Psychology and Law, and president of the British Society of Criminology. He has received the Sellin-Glueck Award of the American Society of Criminology for international contributions to criminology.

FRANK F. FURSTENBERG JR. is the Zellerbach Family Professor of Sociology and research associate in the Population Studies Center at the University of Pennsylvania. His interest in the American family began at Columbia University, where he received his Ph.D. in 1967. His recent books include *Managing to Make It: Urban Families in High-Risk Neighborhoods,* with Thomas Cook, Jacquelynne Eccles, Glen Elder, and Arnold Sameroff (1999); *Adolescent Mothers in Later Life,* with J. Brooks-Gunn and S. Philip Morgan (1987); and *Divided Families,* with Andrew J. Cherlin (1991). He has published numerous articles on teenage sexuality, pregnancy, and childbearing, as well as on divorce, remarriage, and stepparenting. His current research projects focus on the family in the context of disadvantaged urban neighborhoods, adolescent sexual behavior, cross-national research on children's well-being, urban education, and the transition from adolescence to adulthood.

MICHAEL GROSSBERG is professor of history and law at Indiana University and editor of the American Historical Review. His research and teaching focus on United States legal and social history. He has written a number of books and articles on these subjects, including *Governing the Hearth: Law and the Family in Nineteenth-Century America* (1985) and *A Judgment for Solomon: The d'Hauteville Case and Legal Change in Antebellum America* (1996). He is currently working on a study of child protection in the United States and coediting *The Cambridge History of Law in the United States*.

JOHN H. LAUB is a professor in the Department of Criminology and Criminal Justice at the University of Maryland, College Park. He is also an affiliated scholar at the Henry A. Murray Center, the Radcliffe Institute for Advanced Study, Harvard University. His areas of research include crime and deviance over the life course, juvenile delinquency and juvenile justice, and the history of criminology. He has published widely, his works including *Crime in the Making: Pathways and Turning Points through Life,* with Robert Sampson, Harvard University Press. With Robert Sampson, he is writing a book on the natural history of crime using data from a long-term follow-up study of a sample of juvenile delinquents at age seventy.

PAUL LERMAN retired as a distinguished professor of social work and sociology from Rutgers University in 1994. He has authored books and articles on deinstitutionalization, community treatment, and youth policy. Since retirement from teaching, he has worked as the co-principal investigator of the Developmental Disabilities Planning Institute, located at the New Jersey Institute of Technology. Recent research efforts have evaluated the impact of institutional closures on the quality of life of individuals, as well as assessing the problems faced by families caring for disabled persons in their own homes. He also advises the State of New Jersey on evaluating new community-based services.

ROLF LOEBER, Ph.D., is professor of psychiatry, psychology, and epidemiology at the Western Psychiatric Institute and Clinic, School of Medicine, University of Pittsburgh, Pittsburgh, PA, and professor of developmental psychotherapy, Free University, Amsterdam, Netherlands. He is co-director of the Life History Program and is principal investigator of three longitudinal studies, the Pittsburgh Youth Study, the Developmental Trends Study, and the Pittsburgh Girls Study. He has published widely in the fields of juvenile antisocial behavior and delinquency, substance use, and mental health problems (more than one hundred peer-reviewed papers and more than seventy book chapters and other papers). His latest books are *Serious and Violent Juvenile Offenders: Risk Factors and Successful Interventions* (1998), coedited with David P. Farrington; *Antisocial Behavior and Mental Problems: Explanatory Factors in Childhood and Adolescence* (1998), coauthored with David P. Farrington, Magda Stouthamer-Loeber, and Welmoet B. Van Kammen; and *Child Delinquents: Development, Interventions, and Service Needs* (in press), coauthored with David P. Farrington.

AKIRA MORITA is director of the Institute of Comparative Law, Tokyo University, where he has also been professor of juvenile and children's law and constitutional law since 1992. Born in 1943, he started his teaching career upon joining the staff of the Law Department at Tokyo University, his alma mater, in 1969. He has also taught at Ochanomizu University and done research at the University of Cologne, Germany, and has served as a volunteer probation officer since 1985. Authored works include *Juvenile and Children's Law in Modern Society—Between Protection and Autonomy* (Yuhikaku, 1999; in Japanese).

MARGARET K. ROSENHEIM is the Helen Ross Professor Emerita in the School of Social Service Administration at the University of Chicago and was the dean of the school from 1978 to 1983. She participated in the Juvenile Justice Standards Project, cosponsored by the Institute of Judicial Administration and the American Bar Association, and was a consultant to the President's Commission on Law Enforcement and the Administration of Justice. She has been a trustee of Children's Home and Aid Society of Illinois since 1981 and served as chairman of the board from 1996 to 1998. She is editor of *Justice for the Child* (Free Press of Glencoe, 1962; reprint, Midway, 1977); *Pursuing Justice for the Child* (University of Chicago Press, 1976); and, with Mark F. Testa, *Early Parenthood and Coming of Age in the 1990s* (Rutgers University Press, 1992).

ELIZABETH SCOTT is University Professor at the University of Virginia School of Law, where she has been on the faculty since 1988. She has written extensively on marriage, divorce, child custody, adolescent decision making, and juvenile delinquency. Much of her research is interdisciplinary, applying behavioral economics, social science research, and developmental theory to legal policy issues involving children and families. Scott is a coauthor of widely used casebooks on family law and children in the legal system. She is currently a member of the John D. and Catherine T. MacArthur Foundation Research Network on Adolescent Development and Juvenile Justice. She is also founder and co-director of the Center for Children, Family, and the Law at the University of Virginia, an interdisciplinary center that promotes research and informs policymakers and practitioners on issues relating to children and families.

DAVID S. TANENHAUS is an assistant professor of history and law at the University of Nevada, Las Vegas. He is a graduate of Grinnell College and received his Ph.D. in American History from the University of Chicago. During 2000–2001, he was a Mellon Postdoctoral Research Fellow at the Newberry Library. He is the author of "The Evolution of Transfer out of the Juvenile Court," in Jeffrey Fagan and Franklin E. Zimring's *The Changing Borders of Juvenile Justice: Transfer of Adolescents to the Criminal Court* (University of Chicago Press, 2000).

LEE TEITELBAUM is the Allan R. Tessler Dean and professor of law at Cornell University Law School. Dean Teitelbaum became the law school's fourteenth dean in July, 1999. Prior to that, he was dean of the University of Utah College of Law from 1990 to 1998 and had been a tenured member of the faculty there for fourteen years. A prolific scholar, he has written five books and many articles on family law and related topics. His most recent book, a collection of works on family law, was published in July 1999.

MARK TESTA is an associate professor in the School of Social Work at the University of Illinois at Urbana-Champaign. Since 1994, he has held a joint appointment as the research director for the Illinois Department of Children and Family Services (IDCFS). He was a member of the Kinship Care Advisory Panel to the United States Department of Health and Human Services and received the Adoption 2002 Excellence Award for Applied Scholarship and Research for his work on kinship care and permanency. His most recent articles include "The Gift of Kinship: Foster Care" in *Children and Youth Services Review* (2002); "Kinship Care and Permanency," in the *Journal of Social Service Research* (2002); and "The Risk of Subsequent Maltreatment Allegations in Families with Substance-Exposed Infants," in *Child Abuse and Neglect: The International Journal* (2002).

Franklin E. Zimring is the William G. Simon Professor of Law and Director of the Earl Warren Legal Institute at the University of California at Berkeley. He has authored or coauthored twenty books, most recently *American Youth Violence* (1998), and (with Gordon Hawkins) *Crime Is Not the Problem: Lethal Violence in America* (1997), along with a series of empirical studies on violence, on legal change, and on adolescent development. Professor Zimring served on the National Academy of Sciences panel on juvenile justice. He is the former director of the Center for Studies in Criminal Justice at the University of Chicago, where he served as the Karl N. Llewellyn Professor of Jurisprudence. Zimring is a fellow of the American Society of Criminology and a member of the American Academy of Arts and Sciences.

Index